AMERICAN LAW IN A GLOBAL CONTEXT

AMERICAN LAW
in a Global Context
THE BASICS

George P. Fletcher
and Steve Sheppard

OXFORD
UNIVERSITY PRESS

2005

OXFORD
UNIVERSITY PRESS

Oxford   New York
Auckland   Bangkok   Buenos Aires   Cape Town   Chennai
Dar es Salaam   Delhi   Hong Kong   Istanbul   Karachi   Kolkata
Kuala Lumpur   Madrid   Melbourne   Mexico City   Mumbai   Nairobi
São Paulo   Shanghai   Taipei   Tokyo   Toronto

Copyright © 2005 by George P. Fletcher and Steve Sheppard

Published by Oxford University Press, Inc.
198 Madison Avenue, New York, New York 10016

www.oup.com

Oxford is a registered trademark of Oxford University Press

Library of Congress Cataloging-in-Publication Data
Fletcher, George P.
American law in a global context : the basics / by George P. Fletcher and Steve Sheppard.
    p. cm.
Includes index.
ISBN-13 978-0-19-516722-1; 978-0-19-516723-8 (pbk.)
ISBN 0-19-516722-8; 0-19-516723-6 (pbk.)
1. Law—United States.   2. Lawyers, Foreign—United States—Handbooks, manuals, etc.
I. Sheppard, Steve, 1963–   II. Title.
KF380.F59 2004
349.73—dc22   2003028123

9 8 7 6 5 4

Printed in the United States of America
on acid-free paper

For Khamla and Christine and

for the next generation:

Deborah, Gabriel, Katie,

Maggie, Rebecca, and William

PREFACE

The study of law is one of the great intellectual adventures of our time. True, there are many who mire it in the rote, the mundane, and the simple-minded. Yet for those who look past the shallows, the depths of law offer excitement and wisdom. Those who learn these nuances gain a particular authority in modern culture. They become effective citizens in the modern state.

This contrast between simplicity and intellectual adventure is especially clear in the legal education of the United States. Those who seek no more than a quick entrance to a profession equate the whole of American law to an inventory of rules. True, a lawyer must know enough rules to answer basic questions asked by clients and examiners. On the other hand, those who seek to know the law fully must probe the ideas from which the rules gain their contours and authority. Knowing the law of the United States requires not only mastery of the detailed doctrines derived from cases, legislation, and scholarship but also a feeling of ease in negotiating the broad planes and narrow corners of the law.

One early tradition of legal thought—evident in the writings of John Adams, James Kent, Joseph Story, and other teachers of the nineteenth century—required a solid commitment to comparative analysis of legal doctrines, to explore every doctrine in the light of its own history and of the manner in which competing legal systems regulated similar subjects. This comparative tradition grew less popular in the twentieth century, but a growing awareness of the interdependence of American interests with those of other nations has led to a renewed understanding of the significance of the relationship between the U.S. and the other legal traditions of the globe.

By analysis and comparison, students can see not only the transient and coincidental symmetries of the law but also its more enduring character, including its contradictions, its limits, its ambiguities, and its changes. Lawyers trained in this knowledge learn to manage uncertainty and thus become better lawyers, more capable of practicing, adjudicating, and reforming the laws.

In time, American lawyers, professors, and students will more readily perceive the necessity of understanding U.S. law in its relationship to the other legal systems of the globe. This understanding is already pervasive among foreign students, whose natural approach is to integrate newly acquired tools of American law into their existing understanding of the law of their native legal systems. The reciprocal process is equally important—that American students reach out and begin to the think of the word "law" as referring not simply to the practices of their own country rather to the basic doctrines that govern the world community.

This book is an introduction to this fuller study of U.S. law. A short work cannot, of course, be the study as a whole. In these pages, though, the whole required curriculum of an American law school is introduced. In these pages, that curriculum is explored both for the big ideas it holds and for the edges and counters to those ideas that one might find in other legal systems. At times, we discuss these ideas in the same vein that most law classes discuss them, so that a diligent reader will acquire rules that can be redacted from the various materials, while also perceiving some of the ambience of the class. At other times, we will stretch those materials with the tension of history, or theory, or comparative alternatives. In both times, we hope that you will be skeptical, questioning, bringing your own experience and understanding to bear in your own quest to understand the law. With luck, this is your entrance to the grand adventure of American law, and we wish you well.

ACKNOWLEDGMENTS

These materials grew out of three years' experience teaching cases to the incoming class of LLM students at Columbia University. There were at least 160 students from 40 different countries in each class, each a trained lawyer in his or her home legal system. The class met for two hours a day in the course of thirteen consecutive days, excluding weekends. In addition, the students had smaller sections one hour per day with an associate in the class. The associates were chosen for their academic excellence and their understanding of comparative legal methods, coupled with their commitment to further work in the field.

The students and associates provided an invaluable stimulus to the evolution of these materials into the form of a book that can serve as a teaching tool, a reference book, and an introduction to law for the curious general reader. Though too numerous to mention, the students knew of my respect for them and of my appreciation for their classroom contributions to the course. The associates with whom I have served include Joshua Fairfield, Chris Gosnell, Malcolm Thorburn, Chris Gulinello, Kyle Duncan, Hoi Kong, William Merkel, and Ryan Rabinovitch. Wonderful scholars and teachers, all.

Two people deserve special mention. Without the faithful editorial assistance and advice of Lenge Hong, I doubt that we could have finished the book, or at least its final form would not have much to recommend it. Lenge is one of those gifted people who enables projects to come to realization. I am deeply indebted.

Steve Sheppard has added important historical and jurisprudential perspectives to my comparative materials. We hope that the book will be easily grasped by undergraduates, and if it is, the credit will be Steve's. I am grateful to have had him with me, on this and many projects, as a colleague and critic.

GPF

Working on this book has been a great adventure for me. Fundamentally, it has been a privilege to work with such an inventive and keen mind as that of George Fletcher, from whom I have learned so much, and about much more than law. George's commitment to a robust understanding of the law and his respect for others have been an example to me for many years, and it has been a real treat to collaborate on a project that manifests these values so obviously.

I am grateful to the University of Arkansas summer research stipend, which supported much of my work on this book, as well as to the dean's fund that paid my skullduggerous assistants, Blake Rutherford and Marc Zelnick, to unearth many of my more surprising research requests. Many passages in this book are vastly clearer thanks both to Christine Sheppard and Lenge Hong. Last but not least, I am very grateful to Dedi Felman at OUP, whose patience and guidance were essential not just to our completing this project but truly to the decisions that led to many of its most useful bits.

SS

CONTENTS

INTRODUCTION   3

PART I   **Common Law and Civil Law**

ONE   The Common Law   15
TWO   The Civil Law   29
THREE   The Language of Law: Common
                and Civil   54
FOUR   Legal Reasoning   75

PART II   **Constitutional Identity**

FIVE   The Constitution as Code   111
SIX   Judicial Review   132
SEVEN   Federalism   150
EIGHT   The Alternative Constitution   172
NINE   Equality Prevails   201
TEN   Freedom Fights Back   224
ELEVEN   The Jury   243
TWELVE   Due Process Ascendant   259
THIRTEEN   Coordinating the States   276
FOURTEEN   Multiple Common Laws?   302

PART III The Theory of the Common Law:
Liberalism and Its Alternatives

FIFTEEN Feudalism in Land Law 319
SIXTEEN The Triumph of Equity 338
SEVENTEEN Contemporary Property 358
EIGHTEEN The Frontiers of Property 376
NINETEEN Contract as Law 395
TWENTY Contract as Justice 413
TWENTY-ONE Contractual Harm 426
TWENTY-TWO Foundations of Tort Law 440
TWENTY-THREE Economic Efficiency 452
TWENTY-FOUR From Contributory to Comparative
Fault 472
TWENTY-FIVE Disputed Boundaries: Punitive Damages 488
TWENTY-SIX The American Civil Trial in Outline 502

PART IV Criminal Law:
The Adversary System and Its Alternatives

TWENTY-SEVEN Where Would You Rather Be Tried? 531
TWENTY-EIGHT The Fate of Bernhard Goetz 549
TWENTY-NINE Self-Defense: Domestic and
International 568

SUMMARY The Right and the Reasonable 591

Appendices

APPENDIX ONE How to Read (and Brief) a Case 615
APPENDIX TWO Common Law Method; or, How to Do
Things with Cases 625
APPENDIX THREE The Interpretation of Statutes 642

INDEX 649

AMERICAN LAW IN A GLOBAL CONTEXT

Introduction

Welcome to the study of American law.

Perhaps you are a college or graduate student in the United States, and you want a taste of what law school might be like (at its best). Or perhaps you believe that learning the rudiments of legal culture is necessary for a proper education in economics, history, or philosophy.

Perhaps you are reading for a law degree in Europe, Asia, Africa, the Americas, or elsewhere, or you are already a lawyer trained in a foreign legal system, and you want to learn American law. You might have come to the United States to study, most probably for an LL.M. degree. You might be studying American law in a special course offered abroad. Or perhaps you are following a course offered on the Internet or studying on your own.

Whatever your background, if you seek an understanding of the legal system of the United States, this is the book for you.

If you have already been trained in one legal system, you probably have had experience with reading a statute, working with cases, analyzing the facts of a legal problem, and then applying the law to the problem. These are universal legal skills. If you already possess these skills in, say, German law or Korean law, you can learn American law efficiently without repeating all the basic tasks that first-year law students must learn in order to "think like a lawyer." You already know how to think like a lawyer in your home country. You know English well enough to read this book and participate in class discussion. You need only learn how American lawyers think.

Of course, it is quite possible that you have come to this book without prior legal training. Because this book is a summation of the law and lawyering tools taught mainly in the *first* year in most U.S. law schools, we have intended it to be understandable to the literate reader with no legal training. If you are such a reader, we hope that we will at least start you on the road toward understanding the basic ideas of law—both common law and civil law—as well as the way lawyers are trained in better U.S. law schools. You will also have the benefit of overhearing, as it were, our dialogue with lawyers trained in foreign legal systems, whose references we will use from time to time to help them better understand U.S. law.

Most people assume that there are two great families of legal systems in the world. Whether this classification is an oversimplification or not, the labels are useful—at least for the time being. The common law applies in all the countries that speak English. The civil law applies just about everyplace else, with a few important exceptions, areas governed by tribal law, Islamic law, or the Chinese legal system. For the most part, however, those readers with prior legal training are likely to have had it in a common law or civilian system, and this book will be particularly easy for such readers to understand.

For now, the civil law reader should assume that American law is just like his or her system at home. Despite the many variations, there are no great differences based on statutory law or case law. There is no overwhelming difference due to language, history, legal method, federalism, or ideology. The starting assumption should be that you are at home.

But for the civilian reader, you are not exactly at home. Our job is to alert you to the curious things you will encounter in American law. Some of them may surprise the undergraduate as well. Looking at American law from a global point of view highlights new issues and problems.

We shall pinpoint the ways in which common law and, in particular, American law differ from what you can safely assume about legal systems in general. We will not repeat the many similarities. We seek the specific differences, and we emphasize those aspects of the required courses of a

U.S. law school that we believe are the most essential in understanding common law and the culture of American legal education. If you master the chapters in this book, you should be prepared to enter law school with greater sophistication. If you are already trained in a foreign legal system, you should be able to pursue elective law courses on a par with American students who have completed the first year of law school.

Most important, you are now in the company of authors who insist on bringing a global perspective to American law. This is not the only legal culture in the world. It has advantages and disadvantages. These become clear by contrast with other legal systems. Our explanations of American law will be grounded in familiarity with the legal cultures not just of England and America but of Continental Europe, Latin America, and the Far East.

We hope that future editions of this book will also be capable of offering explanations designed for students and lawyers from countries with legal systems based primarily on Islamic, Chinese, and tribal jurisprudence. But our ambitions here are limited. If we can contribute to bridging the gap between the civil law and the common law, this book will serve its purpose.

To begin thinking about the law of the United States, consider ten introductory facts, ten "simple" ideas that will help you distinguish American law from civilian and even other common law legal systems. You should learn these immediately and consider them as underpinnings to all of the later chapters. Keep in mind that these statements are broad generalizations and that, as this course proceeds, you will learn the exceptions and qualifications:

TEN "SIMPLE" FACTS ABOUT AMERICAN LAW

1. *American law is basically state law.* Federal law—that is, national law—is reserved for certain well-defined areas. The private law of torts, contracts, and property, as well as family law, commercial law, corporation law, criminal law—these are all grounded in state codes and interpretative decisions. There are fifty-one jurisdictions among the states and the District of Columbia, and each one is different—not to mention Puerto Rico, the Virgin Islands, and other ambiguous appendages of the United States. Among these fifty-one jurisdictions, the statutes are different, and the cases are different. Federal law, on the other hand, controls certain

limited areas—for example, internal revenue, immigration, patents and copyright, and the marketing of corporate securities—in a uniform, national set of laws.

2. *The first-year curriculum is almost entirely state law.* The exception is that courses on civil procedure examine the Federal Rules of Civil Procedure. If there are fifty-one jurisdictions, how do we teach law in a "national" law school? The answer is that we teach the basic principles that are reflected in diverse statutes and cases across the variety of jurisdictions and usually (but not always) emphasize the principles accepted in the majority of them. This is the core of the material tested on the bar examinations in the particular states, although there is a preparatory course in each state on the idiosyncrasies of its laws. In comparison with the civilian's detailed study of code provisions, American legal education— particularly in the first year—is abstract, theoretical, and controverted. How could it be otherwise if the purpose is to teach the common core of fifty-one different jurisdictions?

3. *The jury system shapes the law that is taught in American law schools.* The importance of the jury is a hallmark of U.S. law, distinguishing American common law not only from civilian law but even from English common law. The jury is like a black box: The judge gives a group of up to twelve laypeople instructions about the law, and a definitive decision comes out. No one knows precisely how the decision is reached. Americans tend to believe that juries do their job conscientiously. Europeans are more skeptical. For our purposes, the important points are that juries—unlike civil law judges—do not write opinions, and the difficulty that lawyers have in predicting their decisions is an important factor in counseling clients not only in preparing for trial but also in assessing potential liability.

4. *In the typical American state, there are two tiers of appellate decisions.* In California, for example, the appeal runs from the superior court (the trial court) of the county (usually containing several cities) to the court of appeal of the particular judicial district (encompassing several counties) and then to the supreme court of the state. It might help to know that the names of state courts differ from state to state. Most confusing is the nomenclature in New York, where the trial court is called the supreme court, the first appellate court is called the appellate division of the supreme court, and the highest court is called the court of appeals.

The federal system has a parallel structure. Appeals run from the federal district court to the circuit court of appeals for one of the twelve regional circuits (e.g., New York is in the Second Circuit) and then to the Supreme Court. These are two parallel systems: state courts for state law and federal courts for federal law. State courts represent the last word on matters of state law, including the state constitution. For a federal court to intervene in a case initiated in a state court is to raise a federal question (an issue under a federal statute, treaty, or the U.S. Constitution) or to consider a dispute between citizens of different states. The latter dispute, a case with "diversity of citizenship," may be held in a federal district court and be subject to federal appeal, but all of the federal courts apply state law. We will discuss this further in Chapter Fourteen.

5. *Civilian-trained lawyers will be surprised to find that there is only a single unified system of courts in every jurisdiction, state or federal.* A single court, with the same judge, hears and decides private law disputes, both regular and commercial, criminal cases, administrative complaints, and constitutional issues. This stands in contrast to the civilian system of specialized courts—for example, civil, criminal, and administrative. American judges are generalists; civilian judges specialize.

Admittedly, there are some specialized courts in the United States, such as state family courts and probate courts (for the administration of estates at death) and federal courts for bankruptcy and taxes. Yet there is nothing in the United States like the *Conseil d'État* for administrative issues or the constitutional courts that have taken hold in Europe since the Second World War. Essentially, in comparison with the civilian tradition, Americans have one court for everything, one size that fits all. The same is usually true about the appellate courts—one court hears all disputes.[1]

6. *In American jury trials, trial judges have no duty to summarize or determine the facts of the dispute.* This is the responsibility of the lawyers who present evidence and of the jury members who decide between the competing views presented. The judge's role is ordinarily limited to supervising the selection of the jury, managing the trial, ruling on questions of evidence, formulating instructions to the jury, and deciding whether to send the case to the jury.

---

[1] There is, though, an increasing trend toward courts of criminal appeals, illustrated in *Rogers v. Tennessee* in Chapter Four.

7. *The American legal system is decentralized and relies on coordinate bodies of equal authority.* This is true among the state supreme courts and among the twelve circuit courts of appeal in the federal system. It is also true among the district attorneys who prosecute criminal cases on the state level. Every county (e.g., Kings County, New York) has its own district attorney, who is not subject to the administrative authority of any higher official. The federal system of prosecution is hierarchically organized under the Attorney General of the United States, whose role is equivalent not to a European minister of justice but rather to a chief prosecutor. But the state system consists of prosecutors of coordinate authority, who are not subject to central control in the state capital.

8. *Appeals are nearly always about questions of law, not of fact.* But the notion of law includes important issues that are not found in any great measure in civil law jurisdictions. These are:

A. the law of jury instructions, which specifies exactly what the judge should tell the jury about a particular body of law before submitting the case to the jury for resolution,

B. the law of evidence, which specifies in detail the kinds of evidence that the jury should be allowed to hear, and

C. the practices concerning the amount of evidence necessary to require the judge to send the case to the jury.

A word about each of these areas of law:

A. Jury instructions are found in books of standard jury instructions, composed by committees of various semi-official groups of lawyers in every state, and drafted ad hoc by judges and lawyers for each trial. This vast repository of law and lore—critical in practice—is generally ignored in law school and in legal research.

B. The law of evidence is an important upper-level course (second- and third-year, graduate). The subject is generally ignored in first-year courses.

C. The standards for sending cases to the jury are extremely vague. If there are "reasonable grounds" to support the plaintiff's or the prosecution's case, the case should go to the jury. But, if, after a party has fully argued its civil case, the judge decides there is no legally sufficient evidentiary basis for a reasonable jury to find for that party, that judge can give judgment as a matter of law, or "dismiss the complaint" or "direct a verdict" for the defendant. In a criminal case, if the judge decides the evidence "is insufficient to sustain a conviction," the judge may enter an acquittal of the defendant and not send the case to the jury. If the judge decides that there is insufficient evidence for the jury, he or she can "dismiss the complaint or indictment" or "direct a verdict" for the defendant. In an unusual private law dispute, where the evidence so clearly favors the plaintiff that "no reasonable jury could disagree," the judge may direct a verdict against the defendant. This is not possible in criminal cases.

D. You should know that the side that loses at trial can appeal on the facts, questioning whether there was sufficient evidence to sustain a jury verdict or a judge's bench ruling, but these appeals are subject to a very high "standard of review" and will not be reversed unless the evidence is so weak to support the verdict that no rational trier of fact could have reached it. It is quite unusual for one of these appeals to succeed.

9. *Appellate opinions are the primary materials used for teaching law in the United States.* This is less true in Great Britain and in Canada, where textbooks play a greater role in classroom instruction. The hegemony of appellate opinions in American instruction is best explained as a matter of history. There was once something called the "case method" for discovering the law buried in the cases. One result of the case method is the continuing prevalence of casebooks—collections of appellate opinions and a few notes—as the primary teaching tool for each American law school course. Because of the ubiquity of casebooks in U.S. law schools, of the rarity of casebooks in other legal systems, and the great difficulty that all students have in using casebooks properly, this book incorporates many case opinions.

Today one of the primary purposes in the use of cases is that it suits the American preference for argumentative discourse in the classroom. There are at least three levels on which the cases assigned in class are subject to discussion and disagreement: (1) Does the reasoning of the opinion support the court's conclusion? (2) Is the case consistent with other cases studied in the course? (3) Is the result in the case right as a matter of policy, economic efficiency, or moral principle? These questions generate a vast field for potential disagreement and debate in first-year courses based on the reading of appellate opinions.

10. *The emphasis on discussion and argument in first-year courses high-lights the distinctive purpose of American legal education, which is to train lawyers who negotiate points of law and argue cases.* It is often said that civilian legal education is designed to train judges rather than lawyers. American students generally do not learn how to write legal opinions as though they were judges. They learn to write office memoranda defending one side in a dispute or a brief for arguing an appeal. Keep this critical difference in mind when you wonder why there is no clear answer to questions discussed in class and why you are expected to argue both sides of any given question. Moreover, the purpose of the discussion and argument is to explore not just legal rules, which change frequently, vary among jurisdictions, and often lack the necessary specificity to resolve a narrow question. Instead, the discussion focuses on the process of legal reasoning and the nature of the legal system and how it evolves. This is to see the law not as black and white but as various shades of gray. Experience has shown us that the lawyer who can see the subtleties, the gaps, and the unexpected in the law will be of much better service to clients than the lawyer who merely parrots old cases and statutes.

Of all of these ten points, we suspect that the most difficult, especially for civilian students, is the last one, particularly as it is why there is not necessarily a right answer to every question posed in class. Not having a right answer to write down in your notes can be extremely frustrating. First-year American law students have the same complaint. They, too, want certainty. They learn that they cannot have it. The better the law school, the less certainty, and the more students have to think for themselves.

This book is a small step in the movement from "national" to "international" legal education. There will come a time, we believe, when it will be assumed that all lawyers will be "at home" in the civil law as well as the common law, and perhaps religious law as well as secular law. When we speak of "the law," we do not mean American law or Japanese law but "the law" as it applies to all peoples who accept the rule of law. As national legal education seeks a synthesis among the various jurisdictions of the United States, international legal education will seek a synthesis among the great legal cultures of the world.

Whether you are a student reading your first case or a lawyer already trained in Asia or Latin America, you are part of that process of seeking a new synthesis. When you think about law, when you speak in class, and when you write papers and examinations, you should think of yourselves as working at the cutting edge of legal thought in the twenty-first century.

We need your contribution and your ideas. Feel free to write us to share your comments and criticism at Amlawglobal@aol.com.

Further Reading

The global point of view we take, which requires us to explore one legal system by comparison and contrast with other systems, is broadly that of "comparative law." There are not many books in the field of comparative law. The best contemporary book in English is H. Patrick Glenn, *Legal Traditions of the World* (New York: Oxford University Press, 2000). The leading text for many years has been René David, *Les grands systems de droit comparé*, published in English, coauthored with John Brierly, as *Major Legal Systems in the World Today: An Introduction to the Comparative Study of Law* (New York: Free Press, 1978). Two German scholars, Konrad Zweigert and Heinz Kötz, produced a more thorough book, published in English with Tony Weir as *Introduction to Comparative Law* (Oxford: Clarendon Press, 1998). Rodolfo Sacco has made the definitive Italian contribution, *L'Apporto della Comparazione alla Scienza Guiridica* (Milano: A. Giuffrè, 1980), and *Trattato di diritto comparato* (Sacco ed., 1992). Older classics in English worth mentioning are Sir Henry Maine's *Ancient Law* (1861, reprinted New Brunswick, NJ: Transaction Publishers, 2002) and John H. Wigmore, *Panorama of the World's Legal Systems* (St. Paul, MN: West Pub. Co., 1928). See also George P. Fletcher, "Comparative Law as a Subversive Discipline," 46 *Am. J. of Comp. L.* 683 (1998); Vivian Curran, "Romantic Common Law, Enlightened Civil Law," 7 *Colum. J. of Euro. L.* 63 (2001).

The books recommended in the previous paragraph are usually described as "comparative law" in the United States. In Europe, many scholars consider them to be "horizontal comparative law," that is, the study of the differences and similarities among different states. Our approach, as you will see in Chapter Fifteen and elsewhere, also respects "vertical comparative law," which studies the significance of the law among many states as derived from a common past. Several books are quite useful in this study, emphasizing the influence of Roman law upon canon law and, ultimately, the constitutional law of states. See Manlio Bellomo, *The Common Legal Past of Europe: 1000–1800* (Lydia G. Cochrane, trans.) (Washington, D.C.: Catholic University of America Press, 1995); Kenneth Pennington, *The Prince and the Law, 1200–1600: Sovereignty and Rights in the Western Legal Tradition* (Berkeley: University of California Press, 1993); Harold J. Berman, *Law and Revolution: The Formation of the Western Legal Tradition* (Cambridge, MA: Harvard University Press, 1985) and *Law and Revolution: The Impact of the Protestant Reformations on the Western Legal Tradition*, vol. 2 (Cambridge, MA: Harvard University Press, 2003).

I

Common Law
and Civil Law

ONE

The Common Law

If the "common law" and the "civil law" lie at the center of our attention, we should begin by focusing on what these terms mean. What is
the common law? Some people say that the common law is a method—a
technique for deriving the law from precedent. There is no doubt that
some courts engage in deriving rules by reading precedent and seeking
the thread that ties them together, but this purely methodological view
of the common law is a modern invention. It ignores the complexity of
history and, in particular, the way in which the great text writers fashioned the common law of England.

Without the treatises of Sir Edward Coke (pronounced "Cook") in
the seventeenth century and Sir William Blackstone in the eighteenth
century, we would not have the body of principles we now call the
English Common Law. Both Coke and Blackstone believed that the common law was the law of reason. *Lex est ratio summa.* They believed, as do
most Continental European lawyers today, that case law is merely evidence of the law—not the law itself. The beliefs that the common law
is to be found primarily in precedents and that the law can be inferred
just from the cases are ideas that did not take hold until quite late in the
nineteenth century.

Many lawyers outside the United States—civilian lawyers and others—believe today that the common law is essentially case law. This view is false, for many reasons that you will come to understand in the course of this and ensuing chapters. At the outset, however, we should explore some of the ways that English and American lawyers explained the idea of the common law to themselves. In other words, what is the self-understanding of the common law? Here are some views that have figured prominently in Anglo-American legal history:

1. *The common law expresses reason.* One of the great exponents of this view was Sir Edward Coke as both treatise writer and judge. In *Dr. Bonham's Case* (1610), while sitting as Chief Justice of Common Pleas, Coke declared a law passed by Parliament void, as a violation of "common right and reason." Parliament had enacted a law giving the College of Physicians in London the power to assess, judge, and collect fines against physicians who violated their rules. Coke wrote that this law violated a basic principle of justice: "No person should be a judge in his own case."[1] In other words, if an act of Parliament violates a basic principle of justice, of "common right and reason," it cannot be considered a valid modification of the common law. The common law claims its authority not just from custom and the authority of the courts but from basic principles of reason and justice.

Coke wrote later in the first part of his *Institutes of the Laws of England: Lex est ratio summa, quae jubet quae sunt utilia et necessaria, et contraria prohibet* ("Law is the perfection of reason, which commands what is useful and necessary and prohibits the contrary"). The question is, Whose reason did he have in mind? It was not the reason of the man in the street; indeed Coke convinced even the king that the reason of the law is artificial, made by the lawyers, and not easily comprehended without long study of the law and the sources of its reason.[2] This understanding of reason is sometimes called the *lex non scripta*, the unwritten law.[3] We will

---

[1] We discuss the influence of Coke's opinion on the relationship between courts and legislatures in the discussion of *Marbury v. Madison*, Chapter Six.

[2] Sir Edward Coke, Prohibitions del Roy, 12 *Reports* 63 (collected in Steve Sheppard, *Selected Writings of Sir Edward Coke* [3 vols.] [Indianapolis: Liberty Fund, 2004]). See also the criticism in Thomas Hobbes, *A Dialogue Between a Philosopher and a Student of the Common Laws of England* 54–57 (Thomas Cropsey ed.) (Chicago: University of Chicago Press, 1971).

[3] Sir Edward Coke, *First Part of the Institutes of the Laws of England* 319b (Section 579; see also §§ 96, 103, 184, 194, 273, his *Second Part of the Institutes* 689, his fourth volume of *Reports* at 38b, and his seventh volume of *Reports* at 7). Coke's first *Institute* was a

return to this question again in Chapter Sixteen, when we encounter Coke's role in the struggle for supremacy between the common law and equity in the early seventeenth century. We can learn an important point from this debate about the institutional conflicts underlying the common law. The great lawyers of English history were at the forefront in working out the boundaries of the institutions of government—the king, Parliament, and the courts.

The claim that the common law expresses reason does not distinguish the common law from the French *Code civil*, whose advocates also claim that it is the perfect embodiment of reason.

2. *The common law is linked to language.* The English language and the common law stand in a close, almost mystical relationship. All the English-speaking countries of the world have adopted the common law, and there is no common law country that has succeeded in translating the common law into another language. Of course, it is possible to translate the common law word for word, as some law schools in Canada have done, into French, but the English template always remains the foundation of legal discourse. That is, when French-speaking lawyers make arguments based on the common law, they rely upon an artificial set of translations of key words like *fairness*, *due process*, *estoppel*, and *probable cause*. We devote the entirety of Chapter Three to the particularities of language in the common law and civil law.

This remarkable one-to-one correspondence between the common law and the English language stands in contrast to the pattern in the so-called civil law countries of the world. The French, Germans, and Italians have exported their codes and their doctrinal teachings all over the world. Their concepts are expressed in dozens of languages, ranging from Spanish to Turkish to Chinese. When one of these receiving languages lacked a necessary term, it was simply made up and used to translate the Continental civilian sources. In the Continental civil law, then, there is no connection between the law and a particular language. (To avoid confusion, note that the terms *civil law* and *Continental law* are used interchangeably, and *civil law* in this sense should not be confused with civil codes, which are found in every state of the United States.)

---

commentary on *Tenures*, a medieval treatise on land law by Judge Thomas de Littleton, and so Coke's work is also known as *Coke on Littleton*.

3. *The common law is based on history.* The roots of the common law lie in the Middle Ages. In many areas of law, we rely upon principles that scholars and courts developed before anybody had an inkling of democracy or human rights or many other values that we now take for granted. This is particularly true in the law of property, contract, and some aspects of procedure. The law of torts is relatively modern, but its basic concepts of trespass and negligence take us back to the distant past. The jury system is thought to be democratic, but, in fact, it is far older than European democracy.

The common law has seen no rupture in its historical development comparable to the revolutions and movements toward codification that occurred in the civil law world. The codifications of private law in France (1804), Germany (1900), and other Continental countries represent broad and sudden substantive changes, particularly a nationalizing decentralization of the common heritage derived from Roman and canon (church) law. The great significance of codification is not that the language of the code decides concrete cases (more about that later) but that the legislative intervention broke with the feudal past. The codes represent a new beginning. In the common law, there is no "new beginning." The common law always builds on the past, frequently reinterpreting the past in order to solve modern problems. As Coke was fond of saying, "out of old fields must spring and grow the new corn."[4]

4. *The common law is the king's law.* The common law stood in contrast to the law of the local courts, but the English progressively asserted the central jurisdiction of the king's court and of Parliament. This is not to say that the king could decree the law but that the common law was the national law, common to all the king's subjects and embodying principles applicable to all. According to this view, the common law—the law of the whole realm—consists not only of cases and precedents but also of legislative interventions by Parliament. This, as we shall see later, was particularly significant in the field of land law; the system of estates in land was a function of legislation as well as case law development. The same is true of many areas of criminal law, where early statutory intervention helped shape the common law definitions of offenses. Remember, the idea that "common law" is synonymous with precedent and case law is a modern idea—probably of no greater vintage than dis-

---

[4] See Sheppard, *Selected Writings of Sir Edward Coke*, at p. 6.

cussions about the importance of precedent and *stare decisis*[5] in the late nineteenth century.

5. *The common law merges substance and procedure.* One bias of civil law training is the view that substance and procedure represent two entirely different realms of law. This is a consequence of the civilian educational system, which follows the structure of the codes. Most Continental professors specialize in particular bodies of law, such as the law of obligations or family law. Their professional horizons are defined by the code provisions that define their area. Criminal and civil procedures are regulated in entirely separate codes, and the entire field is therefore considered basically irrelevant to the study of substantive law. German students can spend four years studying law and take their first bar exam without learning anything about procedure (though things are changing). This way of thinking is foreign to the common law frame of mind; from the very first day of law school, common law students must read cases that are incomprehensible without a minimal understanding of procedure.

The study of cases in the common law tradition seeks always to locate the case in a procedural context. Of course, common lawyers understand the difference between substance and procedure, and in some legal contexts the distinction is critical. The *Erie* doctrine, which we take up in Chapter Fourteen, is based on the distinction between substance and procedure. Yet in legal education and scholarship, the two realms flow into each other. For example, the doctrine *res ipsa loquitur* ("the thing speaks for itself": if a chair falls out the window and hits you on the head, someone was probably negligent) has a major influence in tort law, yet it is impossible to classify neatly the doctrine as a matter of substance or a matter of procedure. In learning the art of reading cases, common law students must learn to pay attention to the "procedural posture" of the case. We do not read cases just to extract a rule of law. We want to know precisely how the question was posed to the judges, how the matter got to court, and what the judges had to decide.

Some cases, as we shall see, are dramatic events. This is particularly true of the landmark cases in American constitutional law, discussed in Chapters Five through Fourteen. Other cases become cornerstones of

[5] On the meaning of *stare decisis*, see Chapter Four.

legal education, even if they are not widely cited in the courts. A good example is *Vincent v. Lake Erie Transportation Company*, the focal point of Chapter Twenty-Two.

The close unity of substance and procedure found expression in the words of the nineteenth-century English legal historian and anthropologist Sir Henry Maine: "[S]ubstantive law has at first the look . . . of being secreted in the interstices of procedure."[6] What he meant was that procedure dominates the common law, and in the cracks and joints of the procedural machine we can find rules of substantive law.

This way of thinking is just the opposite of that preached under the great codes of the civilian tradition. The first question for the civilian is, What is the rule? and the second question is, How do we enforce it? The common lawyer wants to know first how the procedure works and then what the rules may be that influence the outcome.

6. *The (early) common law relied on the writ system.* The writ system exemplifies the interweaving of substance and procedure. The way you sued somebody in the English common law of the Middle Ages was to go to the chancellor and request a writ that would enable you to invoke the assistance of a court for a particular purpose. The writs had different names—trespass, trespass on the case, trover, assumpsit, debt, ejectment, and the like—and each writ covered a body of private law that we now associate with tort, contract, or property.

The plaintiff had the responsibility, with the assistance of a lawyer, of analyzing the facts of his claim and requesting the correct writ. If the plaintiff chose the wrong writ—or a judge said it was the wrong writ— the defendant could move to dismiss the action for this procedural mistake. The writ was like a license to sue, and you had to have the right license to get into court. New York abolished the forms of action in 1848 when it adopted the Field Code of Civil Procedure, which authorized one complaint for all civil actions. England adopted a similar reform in a series of statutes from 1832 to 1873. Similar codes have been adopted by the federal courts and the rest of the states.

Yet we have never managed to escape the historical foundations of the common law. As the English legal historian Frederic W. Maitland

---

[6] Sir Henry Maine, *On Early Law and Custom* 389 (New York: Henry Holt and Company, 1883).

famously wrote: These "forms of action we have buried, but they still rule us from their graves."

Most important, even though the pleading for most writs has evolved into the modern, single pleading called the "complaint," the courts still rely on the plaintiff's selection of a proper remedy, and that selection is determined by a different aspect of the early common law, namely, the radical division between law (and the writ system), on the one hand, and equity (which functioned outside the writ system), on the other. The requirement that the plaintiff choose the right remedy—damages or specific performance—stands as a reminder of the strict rules of pleading that prevailed under the ancient system of writs.

The following case raises the question whether the plaintiff chose the correct writ in suing the defendant. Read it carefully with a view to the question, Is this case about substance or about procedure?

One word of advice before you begin: We noted in the Introduction that U.S. law schools teach through the reading and discussion of cases. This is your first case opinion in this book. As you read, begin training yourself to be aware of the choices the judges are making, not only what the answers to the questions of law might be but also what facts are the most important and how to phrase the questions of law in dispute. As this is the first opinion we have presented to you to read, you might also consult Appendix One (at the end of this book), where we discuss writing a brief, which is the customary manner in which law students take notes on cases they study, and where we give you a sample brief of this case.

Scott v. Shepherd

Court of King's Bench
2 Blackstone's Reports 892, 96 Eng. Rep. 525 (1773)

Trespass and assault for throwing, casting, and tossing a lighted squib at and against the plaintiff, and striking him therewith on the face, and so burning one of his eyes, that he lost the sight of it, whereby, &c. On Not Guilty pleaded, the cause came on to be tried before Nares, J., last

Summer Assizes,[7] at Bridgwater, when the jury found a verdict for the plaintiff with £100 damages, subject to the opinion of the Court on this case:—On the evening of the fair-day at Milborne Port, 28th October, 1770, the defendant threw a lighted squib, made of gun powder &c. from the Street into the market-house, which is a covered building, supported by arches, and enclosed at one end, but open at the other and both the sides, where a large concourse of people were assembled; which lighted squib, so thrown by the defendant, fell upon the standing of one Yates, who sold gingerbread, &c. That one Willis instantly, and to prevent injury to himself and the said wares of the said Yates, took up the said lighted squib from off the said standing, and then threw it across the said market-house, when it fell upon another standing there of one Ryal, who sold the same sort of wares, who instantly, and to save his own goods from being injured, took up the said lighted squib from off the said standing, and then threw it to another part of the said market-house, and, in so throwing it, struck the plaintiff then in the said market-house in the face therewith, and the combustible matter then bursting, put out one of the plaintiff's eyes.

Query. If this action be maintainable? . . .

Nares, J.,[8] was of opinion, that trespass would well lie[9] in the present case. That the natural and probable consequence of the act done by the defendant was injury to somebody, and therefore the act was illegal at common law. And the throwing of squibs has by statute W.3,[10] been since made a nuisance. Being therefore unlawful, the defendant was liable to answer for the consequences, be the injury mediate or immediate. 21 Hen. 7, 28,[11] is express that *malus animus*[12] is not necessary to constitute a trespass. . . .

---

[7] The Assizes were circuit courts with a jury, held in the counties of England by judges of the royal courts, who would otherwise hear cases in the permanent courts at Westminster.

[8] *J.* means Justice; *C.J.* means Chief Justice. The abbreviations sometimes mean "Judge" or "Chief Judge."

[9] When a judge says an action "will lie" or "will well lie," the judge means that the action is meritorious because the facts justify the relief the plaintiff seeks and that the plaintiff should win.

[10] This is a statute made during the reign of William III (1694–1702).

[11] This is a citation to a judge's statement, reported in the Year Book for 21 Hen. 7, or 1505, on page 28, in a case of trespass.

[12] Literally, "bad will," but better understood as "malicious intent." An intent to do harm would have been necessary to bring a criminal indictment.

Blackstone, J., was of opinion, that an action of trespass did not lie for Scott against Shepherd upon this case. He took the settled distinction to be, that where the injury is *immediate,* an action of trespass will lie; where it is only *consequential,* it must be an action on the case: Reynolds and Clarke, Lord Raym. 1401, Stra. 634; . . . The lawfulness or unlawfulness of the original act is not the criterion; though something of that sort is put into Lord Raymond's mouth in Stra. 635,[13] . . . [L]awful or unlawful is quite out of the case; the solid distinction is between direct or immediate injuries on the one hand, and mediate or consequential on the other. And trespass never lay for the latter. If this be so, the only question will be, whether the injury which the plaintiff suffered was immediate, or consequential only; and I hold it to be the latter. The original act was, as against Yates, a trespass; not as against Ryal, or Scott. The tortious act was complete when the squib lay at rest upon Yates's stall. He, or any bystander, had, I allow, a right to protect themselves by removing the squib, but should have taken care to do it in such a manner as not to endanger others. But Shepherd, I think, is not answerable in an action of trespass and assault for the mischief done by the squib in the new motion impressed upon it, and the new direction given it, by either Willis or Ryal; who both were free agents, and acted upon their own judgment. This differs it from the cases put of turning loose a wild beast or a madman. They are only instruments in the hand of the first agent. Nor is it like diverting the course of an enraged ox, or of a stone thrown, or an arrow glancing against a tree; because there the original motion, the *vis impressa,*[14] is continued, though diverted. Here the instrument of mischief was at rest, till a new impetus and a new direction are given it, not once only, but by two successive rational agents. But it is said that the act is not complete, nor the squib at rest, till after it is spent or exploded. It certainly has a power of doing fresh mischief, and so has a stone that has been thrown against my windows, and now lies still. Yet if any

---

[13] These are cites to a case between Reynolds and Clark, published by Sir John Strange in 1781, in a collection of earlier cases. Note that Blackstone lacks confidence that Strange's report is accurate. Blackstone suggests that someone has put words in Lord Robert Raymond's mouth. He says this in part because the phrase from the opinion Strange collected is not in Lord Raymond's own report of the same case, which Blackstone also cites.

[14] Literally, "The force that strikes."

person gives that stone a new motion, and does farther mischief with it, trespass will not lie for that against the original thrower. No doubt but Yates may maintain trespass against Shepherd. And, according to the doctrine contended for, so may Ryal and Scott Three actions for one single act! nay, it may be extended in infinitum. If a man tosses a football into the street, and, after being kicked about by one hundred people, it at last breaks a tradesman's windows; shall he have trespass against the man who first produced it? Surely only against the man who gave it that mischievous direction. But it is said, if Scott has no action against Shepherd, against whom must he seek his remedy? I give no opinion whether case would lie against Shepherd for the consequential damage; though, as at present advised, I think, upon the circumstances, it would. But I think, in strictness of law, trespass would lie against Ryal, the immediate actor in this unhappy business. Both he and Willis have exceeded the bounds of self-defense, and not used sufficient circumspection in removing the danger from themselves. The throwing it across the market-house, instead of brushing it down, or throwing [it] out of the open sides into the street, (if it was not meant to continue the sport, as it is called), was at least an unnecessary and incautious act. Not even menaces from others are sufficient to justify a trespass against a third person; much less a fear of danger to either his goods or his person—nothing but inevitable necessity; Weaver and Ward, Gilbert and Stone, Al. 35, Styl. 72. . . . And I admit that the defendant is answerable in trespass for all the direct and inevitable effects caused by his own immediate act. . . . But what is his own immediate act? The throwing the squib to Yates's stall. Had Yates's goods been burnt, or his person injured, Shepherd must have been responsible in trespass. But he is not responsible for the acts of other men. The subsequent throwing across the market-house by Willis, is neither the act of Shepherd, nor the inevitable effect of it; much less the subsequent throwing by Ryal. . . . It is said by Lord Raymond, and very justly, in Reynolds and Clarke, "We must keep up the boundaries of actions, otherwise we shall introduce the utmost confusion." As I therefore think no immediate injury passed from the defendant to the plaintiff (and without such immediate injury no action of trespass can be maintained), I am of opinion, that in this action judgment ought to be for the defendant.

De Grey, C.J.: This case is one of those wherein the line drawn by the law between actions on the case and actions of trespass is very nice and delicate. Trespass is an injury accompanied with force, for which an action of trespass *vi et armis*[15] lies against the person from whom it is received. The question here is, whether the injury received by the plaintiff arises from the force of the original act of the defendant, or from a new force by a third person. I agree with my Brother Blackstone as to the principles he has laid down, but not in his application of those principles to the present case. . . . The true question is, whether the injury is the direct and immediate act of the defendant; and I am of opinion, that in this case it is. The throwing the squib was an act unlawful and tending to affright the bystanders. So far, mischief was originally intended; not any particular mischief, but mischief indiscriminate and wanton. Whatever mischief therefore follows, he is the author of it;—*Egreditur personam*,[16] as the phrase is in criminal cases. And though criminal cases are no rule for civil ones, yet in trespass I think there is an analogy. Every one who does an unlawful act is considered as the doer of all that follows; if done with a deliberate intent, the consequence may amount to murder; if incautiously, to manslaughter; Fost. 261. So too, in 1 Ventr. 295. a person breaking a horse in Lincoln's Inn Fields hurt a man; held, that trespass lay: and, 2 Lev. 172, that it need not be laid *scienter*.[17] I look upon all that was done subsequent to the original throwing as a continuation of the first force and first act, which will continue till the squib was spent by bursting. And I think that any innocent person removing the danger from himself to another is justifiable; the blame lights upon the first thrower. The new direction and new force flow out of the first force, and are not a new trespass. . . . It has been urged, that the intervention of a free agent will make a difference: but I do not consider Willis and Ryal as free agents in the present case, but acting under a compulsive necessity for their own safety and self-preservation. On these reasons I concur with Brothers Gould and Nares, that the present action is maintainable.

---

[15] "Trespass with force and arms," from the Law French, in which *vi* was pronounced "vay." The form of trespass for damages caused by the defendant by any force or violence against either the plaintiff or the plaintiff's property.

[16] This means: "It goes out from that person." In other words, that person caused it.

[17] "Done with knowledge of the danger."

QUESTIONS AND COMMENTS

1. Notice that the beginning of the opinion reads like a criminal opinion, even though it is a civil, or private, suit. "Trespass" could be a criminal charge, then and now. The defendant pleads "not guilty," which has the effect of requiring the plaintiff to prove all his factual allegations.

2. The court sets forth a series of facts. These do not recount the findings of the jury, but they are rather the court's inferences from the pleadings. Read these facts carefully with a view to making the following distinctions: (1) facts relevant to the legal issue in dispute; (2) facts irrelevant to the dispute but added simply to give us some local color and background information; (3) simple facts, brute facts, concealing no value judgments or legal evaluation; and (4) factual statements that have built into them legally relevant conclusions. For example, how do you classify the statement, "That one Willis instantly, and to prevent injury to himself . . . ?"

3. How would you summarize the legal position of Nares, J.?

4. Blackstone, J., is Sir William Blackstone, author of the famous Blackstone's *Commentaries*, who is also the reporter of this case. He develops a contrary argument based on analogical reasoning. He offers an example of activity that differs from the case before the court (also known as the case "at hand," the case "at bar," or the "instant" case), as well as an example that is like the case at hand. What is the example of throwing a football into a marketplace? You can find more information on analogy as a basis for common law reasoning in Appendix Two, at the end of this book.

5. Blackstone, J., offers a rule for deciding the case. What is it? Is this rule more or less helpful than the guidance gained by situating the case at hand between two hypothetical cases, one for the plaintiff, one for the defendant?

6. Note that Chief Justice De Grey brings in an entirely different perspective. His view might be described as the perspective of criminal law, whereas Blackstone has an orientation based on private law. Can you explain this difference in the context of the opinion?

7. Who prevailed in this case? The plaintiff or the defendant?

8. Did you notice that Blackstone refers to the other judges as "brother"? Judges used to refer to each other as brothers. We have

yet to see a case in which a judge referred to a female colleague as "sister." The neutral term *colleague* would be preferred today. But note the traditional terminology in Bob Woodward and Scott Armstrong's best seller, *The Brethren: Inside the Supreme Court* (New York: Simon and Schuster, 1979).

9. On a more general note, you may have noticed the relationships between the common law on the one hand and the civil (or Roman) law and the canon (or church) law on the other. Students pursuing a master of laws, or LL.M., degree should know that the origins of this degree lie in the study of the civil law and the canon law, both of which were taught in the English universities long before the common law was studied there. The doubling of a letter is a method in Latin for connoting a plural, hence the LL. designates these two ancient forms of law. Even though the study for the LL.M. rarely now embraces only canon and civil law, universities have adopted the old degree designation as a means of respect for this tradition.

■

Further Reading

A thorough and modern study of the common law approach to the resolution of dispute and the creation and application of rules is in Patrick S. Atiyah and Robert S. Summers, *Form and Substance in Anglo-American Law: A Comparative Study of Legal Reasoning, Legal Theory, and Legal Institutions* (Oxford: Clarendon Press, 1981). The best one-volume introduction to English legal history is John H. Baker, *An Introduction to English Legal History* (London: Butterworths, 1990). Professor Baker is overseeing a new multivolume edition of English legal history, until which time the reigning authority remains William W. Holdsworth's *History of English Law* (Boston: Little Brown, 1937) (16 vols.). The best selection of cases and materials on English legal history as it affected the development of American law is Daniel R. Coquillette, *The Anglo-American Legal Heritage: Introductory Materials* (Durham, NC: Carolina Academic Press, 1999). On the codification of Continental private law and its nationalizing effects, the leading book is Alan Watson, *The Making of the Civil Law* (Cambridge, MA: Harvard University Press, 1981). On the continuing influence of Roman Law in the late common law, see M. H. Hoeflich, *Roman and Civil Law and the Development of Anglo-American Jurisprudence in the Nineteenth Century* (Athens: University of Georgia Press, 1997).

The two judges and authors discussed previously are Coke and Blackstone.

Sir Edward Coke, Chief Justice of Common Pleas and, later, of the King's Bench under James I, was the author of a very influential series of case reports and law treatises, as well as a powerful influence on the development of the common law in England and the United States. See Steve Sheppard, *The Selected Writings of Sir Edward Coke* (3 vols.) (Indianapolis: Liberty Fund, 2004). The most useful introduction to William Blackstone remains the study of his four elegantly written volumes, *Commentaries on the Laws of England*, which went through numerous editions, especially in the United States. Many of these editions were given new notes by their editors, updating and criticizing the original text. The most comprehensive of these is William Draper Lewis's edition of 1897. A wonderful discussion of it is in Daniel J. Boorstin, *The Mysterious Science of the Law: An Essay on Blackstone's Commentaries Showing How Blackstone, Employing Eighteenth Century Ideas of Science, Religion, History, Aesthetics, and Philosophy, Made of the Law at Once a Conservative and a Mysterious Science* (Chicago: University of Chicago Press, 1996).

As to placing all of this in the perspective of American law, there are many excellent overviews of modern U.S. law. Two careful but brief introductions are E. Allen Farnsworth, *An Introduction to the Legal System of the United States* (New York: Oceana, 1983), and Lawrence Friedman, *American Law: An Introduction* (New York: Norton, 1984); the most recent is Jay Feinman's popular *Law 101: Everything You Need to Know about the American Legal System* (New York: Oxford University Press, 2000).

TWO

The Civil Law

Before we go further in developing an understanding of the common law, it will be useful to contrast its methods with those of the civil law.

The identity of "civilian lawyers" is born when they go abroad. It is a little like being an "African." Only when the Kenyan or Nigerian (or, the Kikuyu or Yoruba) comes to another continent does she begin to think of herself as an African. The same thing is true of lawyers in Italy, Spain, France, Germany, Korea, and Japan. The sense that they all belong to the same "legal family" is acquired when they leave their homeland and confront the other family, the common law. The Francophones of Québec think of themselves as adherents of the "civil law" only because they are confronted on a daily basis with the "other"—the Anglophone common lawyers. But the Germans and French and Spaniards read few contemporary books about the "civil law" and do not use a term in their respective languages to refer to themselves as "civil lawyers." Their common identity is geographical, not legal. They think of themselves most likely as Germans, French, or Spaniards or, increasingly, as "Europeans"— perhaps as "Continental Europeans" to distinguish themselves from the English, Scots, and Irish.

The numerous Eastern European, Latin American, and Asian coun-

tries that rely on Western European legal sources are more likely to identify themselves as descendants of a particular system: French, German,
Spanish, or Italian. Do they share any characteristics that make them different from the English-speaking, common law countries? Many observers
think that the civil law is codified and the common law depends entirely
on case law analysis. Upon examination, this generalization begins to fall
apart.

It is true that the French adopted a civil code in 1804, Germany in
1900, and Italy in 1865. But California adopted a civil code in 1872 and
New York in 1848 and 1881. These days everybody has a civil code.
There are as many statutes that call themselves "codes" in the United
States as in any country of Europe (e.g., the Internal Revenue Code, the
Model Penal Code, the Uniform Commercial Code), and there are many
bodies of codelike rules, particularly in fields like procedure and ethics
(e.g., the Federal Rules of Civil Procedure, the Federal Rules of Criminal
Procedure, and the Rules of Professional Responsibility). But civilian
codes are supposedly different. Well, perhaps they are, but understanding
how they are different will take time and reflection.

Civilian codes are sometimes said to determine the outcome of all
disputes in advance, before they arise, but this claim is made only by the
naive. The language of the codes consists of propositions of great generality and abstraction, which implies that they require additional commentary or case law for their application. The French *Code civil* tries to
regulate the entire body of tort law (*responsabilité civile*) in five brief provisions. The primary provision is Article 1382: "*Tout fait quelconque de
l'homme, qui cause à autrui un dommage, oblige celui par la faute duquel il est
arrivé, à le reparer*" ("Every action of a person that causes damage to another imposes an obligation of repair on the person whose fault the action
is").

Obviously, the breadth of this provision's application requires judicial
interpretation in concrete cases. No one could solve a legal problem—
say, liability for infecting another person with the AIDS virus—just on
the basis of this language. Some elaboration of the code is necessary. The
basic reference tool for French lawyers, the Dalloz edition of the *Code
civil*, contained (as of 2001) fourteen pages of fine print on the meaning
of these five provisions, including several paragraphs on whether the loss
of an opportunity or the imposition of a risk of AIDS constitutes "damage" within the meaning of Article 1382. This commentary consists of

ninety-nine distinct paragraphs, and each paragraph relies on a judicial decision or a scholarly article.

It is important to distinguish two variations of the proposition that the civilian codes determine all cases in advance. One view is that the code actually dictates the result of particular cases, like algorithms determine the electronic responses of a computer. This naive conception of the statutory law is expressed in the metaphor coined by Montesquieu that the judge is merely *la bouche de la loi* ("the mouthpiece of the law").[1] No one who has actually tried to solve a problem of tort liability under the few words devoted to torts in the *Code civil* could possibly hold this view.

The more sophisticated version of the argument that a code in the Continental tradition determines the outcome of all disputes is that the code prescribes the concepts and the terminology for thinking about all legal disputes. This is also not true. Consider the problem of the plaintiff's negligence in tort cases. This is called contributory or comparative negligence, and we take up the issue in Chapter Twenty-Four. The French Civil Code of 1804 says nothing about this problem—either about the rule or the terminology for discussing the problem. The courts invented the phrase *faute commune* (shared fault or, more literally, communal fault) for assaying the matter, but this term in itself does not inform us whether the guiding rule should be comparative or contributory negligence. One might expect a modernized version of the 1804 French Civil Code to address this problem. But even in the 1994 revision of the Québec Civil Code (said to be faithful to "civil law" tradition), the code addresses apportionment, in section 1478, but does not specifically mention the plaintiff's negligence.

The German Civil Code of 1900 (abbreviated BGB) is no more successful than the French code of 1804 in addressing and resolving all problems that might arise in private law litigation. Shortly after the BGB came into force, a scholar noticed that the provisions of the code had no answer for the case of negligent contractual breach that result in physical damage to the other party.[2] Quite recently, the German Parliament amended the

---

[1] Charles de Secondat, Baron de Montesquieu, *The Spirit of Laws*, Book 11, Chapter 6 (1748) (reprinted Cambridge: Cambridge University Press, 1989): "The national judges are no more than the mouth that pronounces the words of the law, mere passive beings, incapable of moderating either its force or rigor."

[2] Hermann Staub, *Die positiven Vertragsverletzungen und ihre Rechtsfolgen*, in *Festschrift für den XXVI Deutschen Juristentag in Beiträgen* (Berlin: T. Guttentag, 1902).

code to incorporate the new doctrine, though it had been recognized by the courts for a hundred years, in BGB § 280 (2002). A good example would be medical malpractice or a defective product resulting in harm. These problems could be handled as torts under the BGB, but there were good reasons for approaching them as problems of contract rather than tort. The primary reasons for this approach were the advantages of holding principals liable for the actions of their agents. Contract law recognizes the principle of vicarious liability—see BGB § 278 (2002)—but tort liability requires that the principal be negligent in the selection or supervision of the agent who unlawfully causes harm (BGB § 831 (2002)).

To extend the scope of contractual liability to cover these cases, the scholars invented the term "positive breach of contract," and since then, the concept has been absorbed into German law as a standard category of contractual liability.

Admittedly, there is an important difference between statutes and a code. Americans have many statutes but comparatively few codes. A code has structure. It reveals considerable thought in its choices of language and its internal organization. A statute states one provision after another. You need not master the whole of the statutes book in order to understand the parts. A code, by contrast, hangs together as an organic whole. Individual provisions are read against the background of the entire code. Also, though the language of a code does not exhaust the vocabulary of the legal culture, the words of the code enjoy an honored place, an almost liturgical quality. The French *Code civil* is a cultural monument—both for its content and for its style. According to legend, the great novelist Henri Stendhal reportedly revered the French code so much, he read ten provisions of the *Code civil* every night before retiring.[3] When the Québecois argue that they have a distinctive culture, one of the primary supports for their sense of identity is their version of the *Code civil*.

As we shall see in Chapter Five, the leading code in the American experience is the Constitution of 1787, even though Americans very rarely think of it in these terms. But in the twentieth century, other codes have made a more acknowledged mark in the United States—the Model

---

[3] James Huneker, *Egoists: A Book of Supermen: Stendhal, Baudelaire, Flaubert, Anatole France, Huysmans, Barraes, Nietzsche, Blake, Ibsen, Stirner, and Ernest Hello* (New York: Charles Scribner, 1909). Stendhal was, of course, one of the pen names of Marie-Henri Beyle.

Penal Code, the Uniform Commercial Code, and other uniform codes on a range of topics of private law. The word *code* is used often to describe federal statutes, such as the Internal Revenue Code, the Federal Codes of Criminal and Civil Procedure, and the Federal Criminal Code. Deciding whether these federal codes are really just complicated statutes and not codes at all must await further reflection on the nature of codification.

One thing is certainly true about the code culture in Continental Europe. When lawyers begin their research on a legal problem, they turn first to the relevant code and the commentaries on the code that lead them to the case law and to the other scholarly commentaries. Recall the discussion about the Dalloz edition of the *Code civil*, a primary research tool. They do not go directly, as American lawyers do, to a database on their computers (like Lexis-Nexis) and search for cases based on similar facts. This means that the codes, their language, and their structure play a more important part in the process of thinking like a Continental lawyer. The code may not provide the answer, but at least it supplies the structure for thinking about the problem.

Three Types of Legal Culture

Let us take a step back and consider a more systematic approach to the problem of understanding and classifying diverse legal cultures. Sources of law play a critical part in the consciousness of lawyers trying to solve legal problems. "Sources of law" refers to the places where lawyers look for solutions to problems and to the materials they cite as authority in arguments with other lawyers and judges. For these purposes, it is useful to think of legal cultures as having either one, two, or three sources of law, thus labeling them *monistic*, *diadic*, and *triadic* systems. A system that relied solely either on statutory law or on judicial-created case law would be monistic. To be sure, there have been legal systems that have presented themselves as statutorily monistic. Jewish law purports to be based entirely on the words that, according to the Bible, were revealed to Moses on Mount Sinai.[4] Some people believe the "civil law" is monistic as codified

---

[4] Menachem Elon, *Jewish Law: History, Sources, Principles* (4 vols.) (Bernard Auerbach and Melvin J. Sykes trans.) (Philadelphia: Jewish Publication Society, 1994).

law, but we have tried to show earlier that this assumption is false because civilian codes require supplementary elaboration either by case law or in scholarly commentary.

Likewise, some people believe that, early on, the common law was a monistic case law system. But as we shall see throughout this book, this assumption is false. Parliament intervened in the criminal law and in the law of property as early as the thirteenth century. Although it might be theoretically possible to have a monistic system, it is difficult to find actual examples—particularly among modern legal systems. Moreover, there is a risk identified as long ago as Aristotle that attaches to a monistic system, or any system with only one source of laws, in that such systems are prone to abuse. It is this abuse that Lord Acton had in mind in saying that "absolute power corrupts absolutely."[5]

If the claim is that legislation—either human or divine—is the sole source of law, then that proposition invariably collapses in the face of necessary interpretation and adaptation of the legislated sources. No matter how detailed the rules might be, there is no way, *ex ante*,[6] to regulate all the problems that might arise in the course of social life. Unexpected situations inevitably arise, and they must be solved on the basis of authoritative words received from the past.

As soon as the process of interpretation and adaptation begins, a class of recognized interpreters gains influence in the legal culture.[7] Those who expound the law might be scholars, as they were in the Talmudic culture or in the Italian universities of the thirteenth and fourteenth centuries. Or they might be judges, as in the common law and in Western European legal systems.

When courts provide the interpretations the system needs to function, their output is called "case law," *Rechtssprechung* ("the Law speaking"), or, in the intriguing phrase used in Romance languages, *jurisprudence* ("wisdom of the law"). (In English, *jurisprudence* carries a different connota-

---

[5] John Emerich Edward Dalberg-Acton, *Essays on Freedom and Power* 364 (Boston: Beacon Press, 1948).

[6] In American legal discourse today, theorists frequently use the terms *ex ante* (before the fact) and *ex post* (after the fact).

[7] The fear of interpreters is expressed in Thomas Hobbes, *Leviathan* 205 (Michael Oakeshott ed.) (orig. published 1651) (New York: Collier Books, 1962): "[B]y the craft of an interpreter, the law may be made to bear a sense, contrary to that of the sovereign; by which means the interpreter becomes the legislator."

tion—referring to wisdom *about* the law, or legal philosophy.) To avoid misleading or charged associations, we will use the terms *theory* to refer to the doctrinal teachings of scholars and *case law* to refer to the interpretations of the law found in written legal opinion.

If the primary source of law is a statute, therefore, the system will produce a second source of law in the form of a gloss or interpretation of the authoritative legislative words, written by either scholars, the courts, or, occasionally, officials in the bureaucracy. The designedly monistic systems invariably become diadic. Interpretation makes this process inescapable.

Note that at this stage of the argument, we make no distinction between two different kinds of interpreters—judges and scholars. Both have the capacity to interpret the statutory law and thus convert a monistic system into a diadic—and potentially triadic—one. A system is diadic if it recognizes one interpreter of the law and triadic if it recognizes both courts and scholars as interpreters of the authoritative words of the statute. The key to understanding the difference between the common law and the civil law is to grasp the role of these two interpreters of legislation.

Case Law

In the eighteenth century, common lawyers regarded cases as "evidence of the law"; that is, the opinions of the judges as interpreters of the law were considered as evidence of what the common law really was. This was the view expressed by Coke and followed by Blackstone, that "judgments should be according laws not precedents."[8] Sometime in the late nineteenth century, however, lawyers in England and the rest of common law world began to pay less attention to the theories of law professors and more attention to the courts. The view took hold—among scholars and courts—that precedents were not merely evidence of the law but the law itself. This is the principle of *stare decisis* ("let the decision stand") that will concern us in Chapter Four.

Paradoxically, at the time *stare decisis* was introduced in the common law, the English legal system was becoming more dependent on legisla-

---

[8] Proem to the Third *Institute*, in Sheppard, *Selected Writings of Sir Edward Coke*, at 950.

tion. Thus two authoritative lawgivers—the courts and the legislators—started competing for supremacy. Even in *Scott v. Shepherd* (1773), there is a dispute about determining that throwing a squib is "unlawful." Judge Nares cites a statutory source—from the time of William III (1689–1702)—and a case from the twenty-first year of the reign of Henry VII (1506). Significantly, the other judges ignore these references, thereby testifying to the disputed status of statutory and case law sources. The conflict between the courts and legislative authority eventually became the preoccupation of common law courts, thus demoting the relevance of scholarly authority. It is doubtful that the rule of the common law would have ever crystallized without the influence of great writers and systematizers like Edward Coke and William Blackstone. Though their influence was greater than that of any court, their position as "oracles of the law" eventually declined to the point that they came to be labeled "secondary" authorities, as opposed to the "primary authority" of courts and legislatures.

In the Continental tradition, the relationship of scholars to courts took a different turn. For one, the attitude toward precedent remains similar to Blackstone's view that cases are merely evidence of the law. Continental lawyers are fond of saying that they need a string of precedents—*jurisprudence constante, ständige Rechtsprechung* ("the settled practice of the courts")—to derive a rule of law from the cases. That is, they claim that the interpretation is entitled to respect as law only if different judges converge on a single interpretation over time. At the same time they have more room within the legal culture for scholarly authority as a source of law. Scholars in the civilian tradition never suffered a demotion of status to secondary authority. They remain as much a source of law as does the *jurisprudence* of the courts. Our task is to understand, then, how this struggle for influence is played out in the "civil law" systems.

Scholarly Authority

The idea that scholars shape the law is well known in religious legal cultures. The learned ones—whether the rabbis, the bishops, the Ulama in Islam, or the Brahmans—instruct the people on the meaning of the law revealed by God. It is no accident that the words *dogma* and *doctrines* are used today to explain the teachings of scholars in secular law. These words are also characteristic of the Catholic Church's teachings on theology. The intellectual ties of law and theology were obvious in medieval universities. They are less obvious today because of the modern emphasis on law as a social science. So far as we think of law as a process of interpreting authoritative texts, however, we are more likely to appreciate the overlap of law with the other important textual study of the Middle Ages—namely, theology.

In Continental Europe, the study of law was first and foremost a university activity. The tradition dates back to Bologna in the thirteenth century, when scholars rediscovered Roman legal texts and began to write commentaries on them. By contrast, the training of English lawyers and the refinement of the law were not located in the universities but in the Inns of Court, organized in the fourteenth century. The first university lectures on English law in English were not established until 1756 by the lawyer Charles Viner to inject such instruction into the university, allowing William Blackstone to begin his lectures at Oxford in 1758.[9]

The role of scholars in German legal developments of the nineteenth century enables us to understand the enormous difference in depth and organization between the French Civil Code of 1804 and the German Civil Code of 1900. The French Civil Code was drafted quickly, under pressure from Napoleon, and designed to be read by laypeople. The German Civil Code represents the culmination of a century of academic reflection on the foundations of private law and the elaboration of basic concepts of liability.

The great intellectual achievement of the German Code (BGB) is the General Part, which states the concepts and principles that govern the entire code. The key to the General Part is the idea that all private legal transactions have something in common. They represent the declaration of a will to be legally bound (*Willenserklärung*).[10] This idea cuts across the law of contract, torts, property, family law, and inheritance. The BGB united the entire field of private law. The French *Code civil* has no general part.

The doctrines of the common law hold that scholarly writing con-

---

[9] Harold Greville Hanbury, *The Vinerian Chair and Legal Education* (Oxford: Blackwell, 1958).

[10] BGB §§ 116–144. Interestingly, the code does not mention the term *Willenserklärung*, but its invisible presence overwhelms the reader of the code.

stitutes merely a secondary authority relative to the primary authority of statutes and precedents. This is, at least, the official view. In practice, the differences between the common law and civil law are subtler. American courts often cite the work of scholars, but many European courts do not (Spain, Italy, France). Of course, it is possible that American courts cite more scholarship but that European courts rely on it as much or more without attribution. Nonetheless, the work of scholars in the common law has long had an enormous influence on the shape of the law.[11] This is notably true in the constitutional law of the United States and in the economic analysis of law. In Canada, the Supreme Court takes particular note of current scholarly trends in criminal law.

It is not easy to make generalizations about the relative influence of scholars in North America and on the Continent. Yet it *is* true that law students in common law countries primarily read cases and pay less attention to scholarly work. Students in civilian law countries learn the law primarily from textbooks written by scholars.

The different attitudes toward scholarship on the Continent and in the United States are expressed in a contrasting set of social customs. When a professor in Germany goes to court to argue a case, the judges address him or her as "Professor." This would never happen in the United States, nor would the professor want it to happen. In contrast, when a professor becomes a judge in the United States, the former academic colleagues will call him or her "Judge." For example, the most widely cited legal scholar in the United States is Richard Posner. He has been a professor for many years and one of the founders of the law and economics movement. Then he was "elevated" to the federal Court of Appeals. Now the practice in the law reviews is to refer to him as "Judge Posner." These subtleties of speech reveal fundamental differences in attitude toward legal scholarship as a source of law.

To oversimplify the differences between the common law and civil law cultures, we could say that the civil law is an outgrowth of the authoritarian intellectual structures bequeathed to the West by Judaism and the Catholic Church and that the common law expressed the intellectual decentralization and democratic spirit later connected to and reinforced

---

[11] See Michael Höflich and Steve Sheppard, "Judicial Scholarship in the United States," forthcoming in *Zeitschrift für neue Rechtsgeschichte* (2004).

by the Protestant Reformation.[12] The difference is expressed clearly in attitudes toward the word *dogma*, which comes from the Greek *dokein* ("to seem or to appear") and has become associated with the tenets of faith in the Catholic Church. In German today, it is perfectly acceptable to use the terms *dogma* or *Dogmatik* to describe principles and theories of law developed in the scholarly literature. Few scholars in a Protestant country would claim that his or her teachings constituted "dogmas." To use the term in English is laughable. Why is this? In our view, the difference lies in the cultural attitudes toward intellectual authority. In Catholic countries, the leading minds are entitled to prescribe the principles that the legal culture should follow. This idea is regarded as offensive in the self-consciously democratic countries of the Protestant world.

And yet in countries relying on English or any of the Romance languages, we have a term very much like *Dogmatik*. The term *doctrine* deriving from the Latin *docere* ("to teach") communicates the same idea of the "teachings of the best minds." This is clear in French (*la doctrine*), Spanish (*la doctrina*), and Italian (*la dottrina*). In English, the term *doctrine* simply refers to the recognized rule or principle, whether it derives from the case law or from scholarly writings.

Another example of intellectual authority in the Continental system, particularly in the German legal culture, is the idea of "prevailing teachings or theory" (*herrschende Lehre*). The "prevailing theory" is the view endorsed by the inner group of most prestigious law professors.

Similar ideas shape American law. It would be impossible to teach law without relying on "prevailing theories." The very idea that scholarly commentary constitutes secondary authority is itself a "prevailing theory." No constitution ever prescribed that case law constitutes primary authority and scholarly commentary is merely secondary authority. And yet it is assumed to be true. It is a "prevailing theory." Less polite phrases for "prevailing teaching or theory" are "orthodoxy" and "hegemonic theory."

The remarkable fact about doctrine (*Dogmatik*) in the Continental

---

[12] This point is made with great authority and clarity, but much subtlety, in Harold Berman's recent comparison of German and English legal responses to the Reformation. See Harold J. Berman, *Law and Revolution II: The Impact of the Protest Reformations on the Western Legal Traditions* (Cambridge, MA: Harvard University Press, 2003).

tradition is that it has a life of its own. This should not surprise us; a young country may more easily adopt a single code than create or adopt a whole legal culture. Germany developed doctrines of private law in the nineteenth century that are readily exported to countries that have codes other than the German Civil Code. There are many countries in Latin America and in Asia that have a version of the French *Code civil* but use German doctrines as their grid of interpretation. The same is true in criminal law. The German doctrines of criminal law have had an enormous influence throughout the world, but no country, so far as we know, has adopted even a close facsimile of the German criminal code of 1975. Take Spain, for example. All the *Tratados de derecho penal*—all the treatises of criminal law—follow the German line of analysis, but the new Spanish criminal code of 1995 does not, on the surface at least, look very much like the German code.

One example of this dissonance between doctrine and codification is the use of the concepts of justification and excuse. These concepts are fundamental in the German doctrinal system, and they shape several provisions in the criminal code of the 1975, but then, even in countries that follow German doctrines, the criminal codes are drafted without incorporating this structural principle.

The centerpiece of the German doctrinal system is what one of us elsewhere labeled "comprehensive rules" of criminal liability.[13] Americans would say that self-defense and insanity are "defenses" against liability. But the German response in the early-twentieth-century literature was that they are not defenses. They are denials of affirmative dimensions of criminal liability. This distinction needs a word of application.

To use an analogy from American football (a common trait of American culture), a defense is an end-around run. "You say I killed him. Well, I don't deny I killed, but I did it in self-defense." A denial is a run right up though the middle of the opposing line: "Your charge is that I killed him wrongfully. Well, if it was self-defense, it was not wrongful." Notice that on the model of defense, the defense does not negate any allegation by the prosecution. On the German model, the claim of self-defense negates the wrongfulness of the killing.

---

[13] On this and many other points raised in this discussion of German theory, see generally George P. Fletcher, "Two Kinds of Legal Rules: A Comparative Study of Burden-of-Persuasion Practices in Criminal Cases," 77 *Yale L.J.* 880, 892 (1968).

In order to deny the role of defenses as end-around runs, the German system had to develop a more robust line of concepts setting forth the prosecution's case. The system that crystallized early in the twentieth century consisted of the three basic concepts encompassing all the issues that bear on the guilt or innocence of the suspect. They are:

1. The Definition, or Paradigm, of the Offense[14]
2. Wrongfulness or Unlawfulness[15]
3. Culpability or Responsibility[16]

The key to this structure lies in its lexical ordering. Step 1 comes before 2, and 2 before 3. If Step 1 is not satisfied, you never get to 2; if Step 2 is not satisfied, you never get to 3. In other words, if the conduct is not wrongful (or unlawful), you need not consider whether it is culpable. Insanity provides a good example. Suppose an insane person sits in somebody else's car without permission. If sitting in another person's car without permission is not criminally wrongful conduct, there is no need to consider the excuse of insanity.

All the issues that common lawyers call "defenses" are incorporated within this *tripartite* structure—they negate one of the three dimensions. Claims of justification negate the dimension of wrongfulness; that is, if the conduct is justified, it is not wrongful or unlawful. Excuses negate the dimension of culpability. For example, a claim that the victim was already dead when shot negates the definition of homicide, which requires the killing of a living person. Self-defense negates the wrongfulness or unlawfulness of the killing. And insanity negates the personal responsibility or the culpability of the unlawful actor.

As German law stood in the early 1920s, the codes—criminal and civil taken together—contained a very limited set of grounds for justification. There was, of course, a well-entrenched principle of self-defense, including the defense of others and the defense of property and other basic interests against unlawful attacks. The civil code contained several provisions on the justification of necessity, at least as applied to property interests threatening superior interests in property or higher ranking val-

---

[14] German: *Tatbestand*; Spanish: *tipo*; Italian: *fattispecie*.
[15] German: *Rechtswidrigkeit*; Spanish: *Antijuridicidad*; Italian: *Antigiuridicità*.
[16] German: *Schuld*; Spanish: *culpabilidad*; Italian: *colpevolezza*.

ues, such as human life.[17] There were also excuses applicable to cases of invading interests other than property, but there was no available claim of justification for invading basic rights such as the right to life, or the potential right of the foetus to develop to term. Because there was no justification for invading these rights, physicians had no effective way to argue in court that an abortion was justified to save the life of the pregnant woman.

This lacuna in the law led to the following dramatic decision:

A Problematic Case of Abortion

Decided by the German Supreme Court, March 11, 1927.
61 Entscheidungen des Reichsgerichts in Strafsachen 242
[Decisions of the Supreme Court in Criminal Cases]

The unmarried co-defendant, Rosa S., had an affair with a traveler and became pregnant. At this time, she was in the care of a nerve specialist, Dr. S. because of her nervous condition. When she first heard mention of pregnancy and when Dr. S. told her the affirmative results of a pregnancy examination, she displayed emotional outbursts, followed by profound depressions, and she expressed suicidal tendencies. Dr. S. diagnosed Rosa S.'s condition as being one of "reactive depression" caused by her pregnancy and concluded that she suffered an imminent risk of self–induced miscarriage; accordingly Dr. S. induced Dr. W. to terminate the pregnancy in order to obviate the risk of suicide. Dr. W., who is not a specialist in the field of psychiatry, relied upon Dr. S.'s opinion and terminated the pregnancy by removing the foetus.

On the basis of these facts, complaints were filed against Dr. W., against Dr. S., and against Rosa S. for the felony of abortion in violation of secs. 218(1) and 219 of the Criminal Code.[18] According to the complaints, there was no serious risk of suicide, and even if there had been

---

[17] BGB §§ 227 (*Notwehr*), 228 (*Aggressiv-Notstand*), 229 (*Selbsthilfe*), and 904 (*Defensiv-Notstand*).

[18] StGB §218 (*Abtreibung*):

> *Eine Schwangere, welche ihre Frucht vorsätzlich abtreibt oder im Mutterleibe tötet, wird mit Zuchthaus bis zu fünf Jahren bestraft.* ("A pregnant woman who intentionally aborts her foetus or kills it in utero is punished by five years of hard labor.")

or if the doctors thought that such a risk existed, the termination of the pregnancy would not have been permissible. The trial court [*Landgericht*] dismissed the charges against the three defendants. It assumed that a serious risk of suicide existed and that both doctors could have regarded the termination of the pregnancy as permissible according to the grounds stipulated in a decree of the Bavarian Ministry of the Interior dated September 11, 1917. The trial court concluded accordingly that the doctors had not acted wrongfully [*rechtswidrig*]. The court also concluded that Rosa S. was convinced of the necessity of the abortion on the basis of the doctors' advice, and that therefore she was in a situation of necessity according to § 54 of the Criminal Code.[19]

By virtue of the prosecutor's appeal, the Intermediate Appellate Court [*Oberlandesgericht*] held Dr. S. to answer on charges of violating § 218(III) of the Criminal Code and Rosa S. to answer on charges of violating § 218(I) of the Criminal Code. The rest of the prosecutor's appeal was dismissed. The Intermediate Appellate Court agreed with the trial court that an essential condition for the punishability of both doctors was the wrongfulness [= unlawfulness, or *Rechtswidrigkeit*][20] of their conduct, as well as their consciousness of wrongdoing. The Intermediate Appellate Court concluded, however, that the abortion was not appropriate and found that the charges against Dr. S. and Rosa S.

Sind mildernde Umstände vorhanden, so tritt Gefängnisstrafe nicht unter 6 Monaten ein. ("If there are mitigating circumstances, the punishment is to be not less than six months in prison.")

Dieselben Strafvorschriften finden auf denjenigen Anwendung, welcher mit Einwilligung der Schwangeren die Mittel zu der Abtreibung oder Tötung bei ihr angewendet oder ihr beigebracht hat. ("The same provisions apply to those who with the consent of the pregnant mother apply or supply the means for procuring the abortion.")

[19] StGB §54 (*Notstand*):

Eine strafbare Handlung ist nicht vorhanden, wenn die Handlung außer dem Falle der Notwehr in einem unverschuldeten, auf andere Weise nicht zu beseitigendem Notstande zur Rettung aus einer gegenwärtigen Gefahr für Leib oder Leben des Täters oder eines Angehörigen begangen worden ist. ("The act is not punishable if in cases other than self-defense the act is performed in order to save the life or limb of the actor or a relative from a situation of otherwise unavoidable emergency that it is not attributable to the fault of the actor.")

[20] The problem of translating the German term *Rechtswidrigkeit* is explored in Chapter Three.

were supported by probable cause. Dr. W. was viewed as the innocent agent of Dr. S.; the latter was regarded, therefore, as the true actor in the case.

Thereafter, the trial court once again found Dr. S. and Rosa S. innocent. It cited the following considerations in support of its judgment: (1) that invasions of legally protected interests are not wrongful if they represent the appropriate means to achievement of an officially recognized state policy, (2) that the state regards and promotes the preservation of health as an official policy goal, (3) that the preservation of the mother's life meant that an abortion could not be wrongful, and (4) that a doctor who, after conscientious examination, regarded an abortion for this purpose as necessary and who committed an abortion for this purpose could not thereafter be prosecuted if his diagnosis subsequently turned out to be false. Factually, the trier-of-fact assumed that the diagnosis of "reactive depression" was mistaken and that it was more likely that Rosa S. suffered from "hysteria"; that, however, hysterical people also suffer from a risk of self–induced abortion; and that therefore Dr. S. might conscientiously have concluded that such a risk existed. The trier-of-fact also concluded that Rosa S. found herself in a situation of necessity according to § 54 of the Code or that in any event she believed in the factual preconditions of necessity.

The prosecutor appealed from this judgment insofar as Dr. S. was acquitted. He argued that according to case law of the Supreme Court consciousness of wrongdoing is not essential in proving intent and further, according to that case law, that all medical abortions are wrongful or unlawful and can be excused only within the boundaries of § 54 of the Code.

This court cannot but approve the prosecutor's appeal even if it does not agree with the reasons advanced.

I. . . . Abortion operations, particularly the sort in question here, represent not only an invasion of the body of the mother in danger, but also an invasion of the foetus which, according to contemporary conditions and particularly in the view embodied in the law [Recht], is not only a part of the uterus of the pregnant woman, but is an incipient independent legal interest. This latter invasion falls unquestionably under the concept of "killing the foetus" and therefore fulfills the external requirements of § 218 of the Criminal Code. From the prohibitions of the Code alone, one cannot infer the condition under which killing the foetus for the purpose of saving the mother is permissible. The rule would read exactly the same in a legal system that followed the decisions of the Roman Curate that every direct killing of the foetus is forbidden. . . . The concept of an offense requires both that the alleged conduct conform to the Definition (or Paradigm) of the offense and that it be wrongful. This is true even if the contours of wrongfulness are not expressly mentioned in the Code.

The facts in this case require us to examine the question whether the requirement of wrongfulness is satisfied when a doctor commits an abortion in order to save the mother from a medically-substantiated risk to her life or health.

If an act satisfies the requirements of the Definition, the question arises whether it is wrongful. That question must be resolved not only by reference to the criminal law, but by reference to the entire Legal Order. § 20 of the pending draft criminal code reads: "No act is criminal if the element of wrongfulness is negated by public or private law." This provision is already operative law [*Recht*]. The principles for determining when conduct is wrongful (namely the principles of justification) may be derived from both statutory and non-statutory law. These principles can, in particular, be derived by interpreting written norms with a view to the purpose and context of these norms.

According to a law submitted to the Parliament by the medical profession in 1918, abortions would be permissible if they represent the only means to avoid a medically-substantiated serious risk to the life or health of the mother. This proposal rejected abortion for social or eugenic reasons. These provisions have found widespread approval, particularly in the ministries of Prussia, Baden and Württenberg. It is obvious that this proposal encompasses the case of necessity, namely a case in which there is an imminent danger to the legally protected interests of life and health which cannot be overcome except by invading the interests of the foetus, and thereby fulfilling the Definition of abortion. It is significant that the case involves a necessitated invasion against the particular legal interest that is the source of the danger. Nonetheless, this is not a case of necessity within the meaning of existing statutory provisions on the subject.

Before the current Criminal Code came into force [in 1871], most German writers took the case of medical abortion to be one of justifiable necessity. After the introduction of the Criminal Code, however, it appeared that no provision in the Criminal Code covered the case; the excuse regulated in § 54 does not apply because the mother is not a dependent of the doctor. Accordingly, theorists have considered the following theories of justification in an effort to resolve the case:

(1) It is a hotly disputed question whether § 54 represents a defense of justification or merely grounds for professional exemption. The Supreme Court has regularly taken the position that § 54 is not merely a case of personal exemption. The question is still unresolved whether § 54 provides an excuse or whether it represents a justification that would negate the wrongfulness of the act. . . . If the principle of protecting the greater interest or the more important right had found expression in § 54, that section could be viewed as a justification. But the principle of protecting the more important interest relative to the less important interest is not to be found in the Code. Someone who acts to save his own life is not punishable according to the Code, even if he thereby sacrifices a greater interest. This provision is comprehensible only on the premise that in such a case of necessity the pressures of the instinct for survival strongly influence the actor's capacity for choice, though these pressures may not totally remove the actor's capacity for choice; on this view of the matter, necessity provides an excuse for ostensibly criminal conduct. In the absence of an express declaration by the legislature, it cannot be assumed that § 54 implies that the destruction of a higher valued good for the sake of a lower valued good is not to be viewed as wrongful [rechtswidrig]. It is only from this point of view that one can understand why coming to the assistance of others is protected by § 54 (in contrast with rules of self-defense) only when the others thereby protected are dependents. If the legislature had regarded necessity as a case of justification negating wrongfulness in the conduct, it would not have introduced this limitation. . . .

(2) § 54 of the Criminal Code provides an excuse for a limited number of actors. It does not follow from this provision, however, that no case of necessity negates the wrongfulness of the conduct. According to written and unwritten principles of law [Recht], this line of reasoning is not at all foreign to the Supreme Court, which recognizes in a decision in Vol. 23 that cases of necessity sometimes appear as wrongful acts and sometimes as acts that are not wrongful. The court has thus

recognized that self-defense is sometimes permissible against necessitated conduct and sometimes impermissible.[21]

(3) There are no written norms that apply to this case. The relevant norms of necessity in the Civil Code apply only to necessitated attacks upon property interests.

The theoretical literature has attempted to solve this problem by introducing a justification of medical privilege. This effort has been abandoned and indeed in Vol. 25 the Supreme Court rejects the concept of professional privilege.

The concept of consent, which was used as a justification for a medical operation in a case printed in Vol. 25 of the reports, does not suffice to solve the problem of abortion. Abortion is more than an invasion of the body of the pregnant woman, but also an invasion of the foetus's interest; and the mother is not in a position to waive the foetus's interest as she is in a position to waive her own bodily security. In particular, one should reject the analysis that if the pregnant mother could kill the foetus and be excused under § 54, she should be able to delegate someone else to perform the operation for her. § 54 provides only an excuse and not a justification. Therefore the mother's act of aborting the foetus remains wrongful, and having someone else perform the operation for the mother does not remove the wrongfulness of the conduct. Therefore one must search for a ground of decision which would apply to the case of the mother's aborting the foetus and render that act not only excusable but justifiable. It is only when her act would be justifiable that she would be in a position to delegate her rights to a third party. This matter remains to be discussed.

The principle adopted by the trial court, namely that invasions of legally protected interests are not wrongful when they represent the appropriate means of an officially recognized policy (the policy–theory), has found widespread approval and is no doubt an underlying principle of many rules of law. Yet it should be noted that this principle is far from universally accepted, and the loose formulation of the principle would lead to questionable results in practice which could hardly be regarded as compatible with higher principles of Law [Recht].

In contrast, another more narrowly formulated principle has found

---

[21] See question 8 in Questions and Comments, following this opinion.

almost universal acceptance; if conduct conforming to the Definition of an offense in the Code is the only means to protect a legally recognized interest or to fulfill a duty prescribed by law, the question whether the act is wrongful and therefore prohibited should be determined by balancing the interests or duties in conflict (balancing-theory).

In a case in which duties come into conflict, the Supreme Court has already reportedly recognized that the more important duty is to be fulfilled and that the non-fulfillment of the less important duty is not wrongful [citations omitted].

Also in the case of a conflict of interests the Supreme Court has already recognized that if there is no alternative solution possible, destroying the less important interest for the sake of the more important interest is not wrongful.

(4) The principle of balancing interests leads to a satisfactory solution of the question: if and under which circumstances is a medically indicated abortion legally permissible.

The general requirement is that there must be a threat to a legally protected interest. There must be an imminent danger to the pregnant mother that cannot be eliminated by other means. The examination of this requirement requires particular sensitivity to medical science, which a layman would presumably not possess. The concept of imminent danger is to be understood as a condition which, according to common experience, would certainly lead to harm if preventive action is not taken. In balancing interests one should conform to the values expressed in the norms of the Criminal Code. Comparing secs. 211, 224, 225, and 218 of the Criminal Code, one readily concludes that as a general matter death and serious bodily harm are more serious evils than the loss of the life of a foetus.[22] In a particular case, of course, a different decision might be required. . . .

Therefore, medical abortions, whether performed by the mother

---

[22] This conclusion is based on the relative penalties threatened for assault and homicide, on the one hand, and abortion, on the other. Homicide carries a minimum penalty of five years at hard labor (§ 212); assault (§ 223), not more than three years; and aggravated assault (§ 223a), not less than two months. Abortion (§ 218) was punished by a maximum of five years at hard labor. The court interprets this disparity to prove that the legal culture values born human beings more than it values the unborn foetus.

herself or by a doctor with the actual or presumed consent of the mother, are not wrongful if the abortion is the only means to protect the pregnant mother from an imminent risk of death or serious bodily injury. . . . On the basis of the view put forward here, the abortion in the instant case is to be regarded as not wrongful and therefore exempt from punishment if it is medically substantiated that Rosa S. suffered an imminent risk of suicide and that this risk was not to be avoided by any means other than the abortion. To satisfy the Definition § 218 it is necessary that the actor have the intent merely to kill the foetus. Consciousness of wrongdoing is not an element of the required intention; therefore it is immaterial if the actor should assume, mistakenly, that his conduct is justified by a non-existent defense such as the alleged professional privileges of physicians. A mistake of this sort is immaterial in assessing liability. On the other hand, if he is mistaken about the applicability of a recognized justification, even if that justification is not expressed in the Criminal Code, or, if he makes a mistake of fact which leads him to think that the conduct is justified under a recognized defense, then § 59 of the Code requires us to conclude that his act was not intentional.[23] This is also true in the event that his mistake is his own fault. . . . If the judgment challenged in this case is examined from the point of view of the foregoing considerations, it follows that only one justificatory element has been established, namely the serious risk of suicide. It has not been established whether this risk could have been avoided by other means. It is only when this question is resolved that we can turn to the problem whether the accused was of the opinion, perhaps mistakenly, that the conditions of justification were satisfied. The judgment therefore cannot stand. The case is remanded for a new trial. The trier-of-fact is not bound in any way by prior determinations of fact.

---

[23] StGB § 59 (Culpability and mistake)

> If in the commission of a criminal act the actor was not aware of circumstances that constitute the offence or that raise the level of punishment, he or she is not accountable for these circumstances. If the offence is one that can be committed negligently, this rule applies only so far as the actor is not negligently culpable for his or her ignorance.

QUESTIONS AND COMMENTS

1. As in most judicial opinions written in continental legal systems, the publication of the case conceals the identity of the parties. There is no *Scott*, no *Shepherd*, no *Marbury*, and no *Madison* to help law students and lawyers remember the case as an event in the lives of particular people. Why should this be so? Do you think it is a matter of protecting the privacy of the litigants? It is doubtful that privacy is generally regarded as a greater value in civil law than in common law countries, so why should this situation be selected as one in which the names of the affected individuals are systematically concealed? Perhaps the names are concealed to lend to the case a greater sense of abstraction, to confer upon it a message that transcends the particular resolution of the case, which is simply to remand the case for further proceedings about whether Dr. S. should be punished for having committed an abortion.

2. The basic structure of this decision can be outlined as follows:

   A. The statutory definition of a crime prescribes the Definition or Paradigm of the offense, which in this case is constituted by the act of killing a foetus.

   B. For the act prescribed by the code to be punishable, it must satisfy two additional dimensions of liability: wrongfulness and culpability.

   C. Conduct that is justified is not wrongful.

   D. The statutory law—in this case, the civil and criminal codes—prescribes some but not all possible cases of justification.

   E. The courts may recognize additional grounds of justification.

   F. In this case the court recognizes an additional extrastatutory justification of necessity based on balancing the conflicting interests, namely, the value of the foetus and the risk to the mother's life.

3. As a result of this case, the justification of "extrastatutory necessity" (*übergesetzlicher Notstand*) became entrenched in German law, and that precise phrase became a well-recognized category in the scholarly literature and the case law covering the period from 1927 to 1975, when the Federal Republic of Germany enacted a new criminal code and recognized "extrastatutory necessity" in Article 34 as a statutory justification.

4. The phrase "extrastatutory justification" also entered the literature of other legal systems that draw heavily on German scholarship. (See, e.g., the discussion in Luis Jimenez de Asua, *4 Tratado de Derecho Penal* 343 (Buenos Aires: Editorial Losada, 1952).

5. Compare Article 34 of the new German Criminal Code with § 3.02 of the Model Penal Code (MPC) in the United States (the model of legislation in at least thirty-five states of the United States). Article 34 reads:

> § 34. State of emergency as justification.
> Whoever commits an act in a present and otherwise unavoidable danger to life, body, liberty, honor, property or another law good to avert the danger from himself or another, acts not unlawfully if in weighing the conflicting interests, particularly the affected law goods and the degree of the danger threatening them, the protected interest substantially outweighs the impaired one. However, this is applicable only insofar as the act is an appropriate means to avert the danger.

MPC § 3.02(1) provides:

> JUSTIFICATION GENERALLY: Choice of Evils.
>
> (1) Conduct which the actor believes to be necessary to avoid a harm or evil to himself or to another is justifiable, provided that:
>
> (A) the harm or evil sought to be avoided by such conduct is greater than that sought to be prevented by the law defining the offense charged; and
>
> (B) neither the Code nor other law defining the offense provides exceptions or defenses dealing with the specific situation involved; and
>
> (C) a legislative purpose to exclude the justification claimed does not otherwise plainly appear.

Note that the MPC is also premised on the principle that justified or justifiable conduct is exempt from criminal punishment, but if you look closely you will notice ways in which the MPC differs from the German statute. Consider the following:

1. *The relevance of the actor's beliefs.* § 34 says nothing about the actor's intention or beliefs. Do you think that this "subjective

factor" is irrelevant? What can you learn from the 1927 case
about the relevance of the actor's beliefs?

2. *The connection between wrongfulness or unlawfulness and the concept of
the justification.* MPC does not use the language of wrongfulness
or unlawfulness in connection with the theory of justification.
MPC § 3.01 prescribes that "justification is an affirmative defense" but fails to make the move that the German court makes
to locate claims of justification within a general theory of criminal conduct.

3. *The relevance of "legislative purpose."* Why does the MPC provide
an exception in (c) for cases in which a legislative purpose appears to exclude the justification? Does that mean that the idea
of necessity as justification is implicitly endorsed by the legislature enacting the criminal code? Is that the logic underlying the
1927 abortion case?

6. One sign of the scholarly or academic influence in the abortion case
is the reference to numerous theories or doctrines identified by specific names, such as the "policy" theory and the "balancing" theory.
These theories took shape and acquired their names in the scholarly
literature. They are referred to by their specific names, much in the
same way that case holdings in the common law acquire shorthand
labels, such as the *Palsgraf* doctrine of proximate cause or the *Marbury*
principle of judicial review.

There are important doctrines that figure in the case but are denominated by their usual names. For example, the conflicting views
about whether a mistake about wrongdoing negates the required intention for an intentional offense are known by their shorthand labels—
the "intention" theory and the "guilt" theory. The former holds that
a mistake about wrongdoing would negate the intention required for
abortion; the latter, that mistakes should be relevant only if they are
reasonable or free from fault.

7. The important impression to be retained from this case is that the
court established a new justification for abortion and did so on the
basis of a conceptual restructuring of the criminal law that left room
for judicial innovation in the field of justifications. The twin principles that "no crime is punishable unless it is wrongful" and "no
crime is wrongful unless the court says it is" liberated the courts from
legislative control over the criminal law. The case bears many rhetori-

cal similarities to *Marbury v. Madison*, which we take up in Chapter Six.

8. The permissibility of self-defense depends on whether it is used against an imminent "wrongful attack." Therefore, there is no self-defense against justifiable force, but self-defense is permissible against unjustified but excused uses of force. This is why the penal code, the *Strafgasetzbuch* (StGB), comprises two different kinds of necessity: the excusing in § 35 and the justifying in § 34. See StGB § 32.

■

THREE

The Language of Law

Common and Civil

The exact differences between law in the English-speaking world and law originating in the countries on the European continent remain disputed, but we may continue to work with the labels classifying legal systems as "common law" and "civil law." We have probed the matter sufficiently to know that language plays a major role in generating the distinctive personality of each family of legal systems. Discussing law in English differs in fundamental respects from parallel conversations in French, German, and other Continental languages. The purpose of this chapter is to alert students to the particularities of English as a legal language.

Law

The particularities of English begin with the word *law*. Continental legal systems typically use two terms for "law"—one that stresses the written law enacted by the legislature (*Gesetz, loi, legge, zakon, törvény*)[1] and a

---

[1] For those mystified by the final terms in these ordered pairs, they are Hungarian. The influence of Hungarian on American culture is the subject of many gags. In the 1950s, there were so many Hungarians (from Miklós Rozsa to Zsa Zsa Gabor) in the Holly-

second that emphasizes that the law is a body of principles based on various sources (*Recht, droit, diritto, pravo, jog*). This distinction is best expressed as the difference between the law as statutory law (the law laid down by the legislature) and the Law as a set of principles that appeal to us by their intrinsic merit.[2] *Gesetz* is statutory law; *Recht* is Law as principle.

To grasp this distinction, think of the difference between the text of the Constitution of the United States and constitutional law. The Constitution is the set of authoritative rules and principles written down within the four corners of a specific document. It is a finite set of words. Constitutional law is the body of principles that has evolved and continues to evolve from the written text. It obviously includes principles that go beyond the finite words of the document and the cases that have interpreted it. When a lawyer argues in a case of first impression, "The Constitution requires that we recognize this right," the appeal runs in fact not to the text but to the principles that constitute the body of constitutional law.

Criminal law must be understood in the same way. It contains some authoritative words—words written down in codes and statutes and often in leading cases. Yet no one in the Continental tradition would say that the criminal law can be reduced to the criminal code. That would be to confuse *Strafrecht* (the whole of the criminal law) with the *Strafgesetz* (a particular criminal law or statute). Similarly, it would not make sense to say that criminal law in the common law tradition is exhaustively defined by the statutes and the cases. Although our word *law* sometimes refers to *Gesetze* (statutory laws) and sometimes to *Recht* (the Law as principle), the term *criminal law* is always used, it seems, in the broader, more inclusive sense.

The ambiguity of the word *law* in English accounts for the difficulty of understanding the term that played a central role in the 1927 abortion case, namely, *wrongfulness* or *unlawfulness*. The term *Rechtswidrigkeit* in German (*antijuridicidad* in Spanish, *antigiuridicità* in Italian) is constructed of the following three parts: (*Recht*, or Law) + (anti) + (ness). The temp-

---

wood film business that a billboard appeared on Sunset Boulevard: "It is not enough to be Hungarian. You also need talent."

[2] For more on this distinction, see George P. Fletcher, *Basic Concepts of Legal Thought* 11–12 (New York: Oxford University Press, 1996).

tation is to translate this term as anti-law-ness, or "unlawfulness"; the problem, of course, is the difficulty of translating *Recht* as "law." Something is lost in this translation if we forget that the term *Recht* includes the higher sense of law as morally binding principles. For this reason, we have usually used the term *wrongfulness* to capture the evaluative connotations of the German term. Wrong is the opposite of right, and therefore acting contrary to the Law (in the sense of right) is best described as "wrongfulness" or "wrongdoing."

The danger of translating *Rechtswidrigkeit* or *antijuridicidad* as "unlawfulness" is that common lawyers often understand the law in a narrowly positive sense of the law laid down by the legislature (or the courts). Using this narrow definition would make it impossible to grasp the point of the 1927 abortion case, which is that "acting contrary to law" must be understood as acting contrary to the *basic principles* of law. The task of courts, relying upon the theories developed by scholars, is regularly to reinterpret the requirements of legal principle and the meaning of "acting contrary to law."

The difference between the two senses of *law* raises questions about the proper translation of "common law" and "civil law" into Continental legal languages. The question is whether the common law should be understood as customary law enacted by the courts or as a set of evolving principles regularly reinterpreted by courts and scholars. If understood as the former, the common law would correspond to law in the positive (statutory) sense (*Gesetz, loi, legge, zakon*); if understood in the latter sense, the proper translation would be the term for the Law as principle (*Recht, droit, diritto, pravo*).

One way that this problem of translation gets formulated in countries that use Romance languages is whether the "common law," when used in their respective languages, should be understood as masculine or feminine. That is, is the correct article in French "*le common law*" (masculine) or "*la common law*" (feminine)? They must choose one way or the other, and the choice is shaped by whether one associated the concept of "law" with *loi* or *droit*. *Loi* is feminine; *droit*, masculine. Therefore, the elementary grammatical dispute about the proper article for the noun raises deep jurisprudential questions about the nature of the common law. Our preference would be to think of the common law as "*le common law*," by association with the concept of *droit* as a set of principles transcending the positive sources of law.[3] The dominant view seems to be, however, that both the common law and civil law are understood as forms of *loi*, the common law embodied in the case law, as well as the civil law fully expressed in the codes adopted on the Continent. Thus the standard syntax seems to be "la common law." But you can experiment with this matter on your own. Go to the Web search engine Google, type in, using quotation marks, "la common law" and then "le common law," and see how many hits you get.

In the seventeenth century, the discourse of lawyers included a term *right* that corresponded to the higher concepts of *Recht, droit, diritto*, and *pravo*. We see traces of this concept in some translations of works by Kant and Hegel on the concept of Law (Kant's *Rechtslehre* as "Doctrine of Right" and Hegel's *Rechtsphilosophie* as "Philosophy of Right"). But generally, the notion of Law as synonymous with Right has almost disappeared except in esoteric English usage. In its place have come a variety of terms to express the idea that law consists not only in the law laid down by lawgivers but also in higher principles that motivate the entire legal culture and demand constant reinterpretation in keeping with the needs of the time.

A survival of the distinction between Right and Statute is sometimes noted in the distinction between law (Right) and laws (Statutes). For example, the Fourteenth Amendment to the U.S. Constitution holds that "no state shall . . . deprive any person of life, liberty, or property without due process of law nor deny to any person . . . the equal protection of the laws." Note that the due process is associated with law in the singular and equal protection with laws in the plural. The more you study these particular provisions, the more you will see that in fact this subtle grammatical difference conveys a jurisprudential point very similar to the civilian difference between the two concepts of law.

---

[3] Legrand comes near to this argument but does not make it there expressly. See Pierre Legrand Jr., "Pour le Common law," 44 *Revue Internationale de Droit Comparé* 941 (1992). An argument that certain core expressions of common law cannot be translated is in Pierre Legrand, "Le droit de Blackstone et la langue de Moliere: une valse a mille temps," in Pierre Legrand ed., *Common law d'un siecle a l'autre* (Québec: Cowansville, 1992) entry VII at p. XII.

Policy

If the English language formally lacks the distinction between *Gesetz* and *Recht* (*loi* and *droit*), it compensates for this deficiency in part with a subtle concept of "policy" difficult to express in Continental languages. The concept of policy is a spin-off from the notion of politics (both deriving from the same Greek root—*polis*). The difference is that "policy" and "policies" are neutral and clean. "Politics" is partisan and dirty. There are entire institutions in the United States devoted to the study of "public policy" on the apparent assumption that this subject is an objective body of knowledge. This refinement of meaning and connotation is a remarkable feature of current English legal usage. To say the law pursues policies is considered up-to-date and sophisticated. But to say that law is *political* is supposedly to undermine the neutrality and autonomy of the legal culture.

This is amusing because in many Continental languages there is no clear distinction between policies and politics. German marks the distinction between *politisch* ("political") and *rechtspolitisch* ("policy") by combining the word *Recht* with the idea of politics. The distinction is harder to note in French, which relies on *politique* to express both ideas.

The legal philosopher Ronald Dworkin puts great weight on the distinction between principles and policies.[4] His claim is that policies represent instrumental goals, that is, social interests that the law might aim to maximize. These interests would include deterrence of crime, promoting security of expectations, distributing risks, and promoting democratic institutions. By contrast, principles state the requirements of justice. They are of the form: No person should profit from his own wrong. No person should be a judge in his own case. No innocent person should suffer at the hands of the state. These principles are formulated as absolute demands. They apply regardless of contingent circumstances. They are treated as imperatives of justice.

The distinction between policies and principles captures the ongoing debate in legal philosophy about the basic nature of the law. Does the law serve Kantian principles, sometimes called the deontological demands of justice, focusing on protecting rights and compelling the performance of duties? Or does the law promote the utilitarian goals of efficiency,

---

[4] Ronald Dworkin, *Taking Rights Seriously* 82–84, 90 (London: Duckworth, 1977).

promoting the social good with less attention to individual rights and duties?

Even though Dworkin's distinction between policy and principle is not universally followed, it underscores an important difference between two different kinds of values that influence the law.

Due Process

An alternative way to express the idea of Right (*Recht, droit, diritto, pravo*) has emerged in the American constitutional concept of due process. The original use of this phrase in the Fifth Amendment (ratified in 1791) said simply that "no person shall be deprived of life, liberty, or property without due process of law." This was understood at the time to restrict only the actions of the federal government. The Fourteenth Amendment (1868) applied the same principle to the states: "no state shall deprive any person of life, liberty, or property without due process of law." As originally used, the notion of "due process" carries procedural overtones. It seems to refer to the procedure that is fair and necessary to protect life, liberty, and property. But over time the concept has acquired a substantive content reflecting basic principles of human rights. For example, the leading case of *Roe v. Wade* (410 U.S. 113) held in 1973 that state laws prohibiting abortion in the first trimester of pregnancy violated the due process clause of the Fourteenth Amendment. The problem was not the procedure for forbidding abortions but the more basic question whether pregnant women had a right to abort in particular cases. At stake was "the right to privacy," a right not mentioned in the text of the Constitution but now understood to be a principle implicit in the idea of due process.

Unfortunately, no one knows which principles are included within the notion of substantive due process and which are not. Justice Benjamin Cardozo defined substantive due process as the "principles of ordered liberty."[5] Those additional words did not help much by way of definition except to remind us that liberty lies at the foundation of due

---

[5] *Palko v. Connecticut*, 302 U.S. 319, 325–326 (1937). Cardozo, J. for the majority, based his analysis of the meaning of due process to include immunities and rights "implicit in the concept of ordered liberty."

process, precisely as Immanuel Kant wrote that liberty—or freedom—is the central value protected by the concept of Right and the rule of law.

The problem is defining the boundaries of liberty. For example, a decades-long dispute over whether the due process right to privacy should include the right of homosexuals to engage in sexual relations was decided only in 2003. In 1986, in *Bowers v. Hardwick* (478 U.S. 186), the majority of the Court upheld the power of the state to prohibit homosexual sodomy. The Court defined the issue narrowly not as a problem of liberty or of privacy but as a question whether an individual has a right to gay sex. That, they said, was not foreseen by the Constitution. In the succeeding years, *Bowers* met with nearly universal condemnation by legal theorists and commentators. The academic community in the United States was obviously not prepared to give the last word on the details of due process to the courts. The scholarly writers properly claimed for themselves the authority to interpret the demands of due process, precisely as scholars in the Continental tradition interpret the demands of Right for their time.

Eventually, in the summer of 2003, the Court reexamined the question under the broader question whether prosecuting gay men for private consensual sodomy violated the protection of liberty under the due process clause. The majority held that it did, in *Lawrence v. Texas*, 539 U.S. 588 (2003). One of the striking features of Justice Kennedy's opinion for the majority is that he cites a parallel decision by the European Court of Human Rights, thus signaling a global perspective in interpreting the concept of due process.

Fairness

Let us return to the original conception of due process as a standard of procedure. The term that naturally comes to mind to English-speakers when they seek to describe due process is "fair trial." Though the U.S. Constitution does not use the terms *fair* or *fairness*, the requirement of a fair trial has become a standard element of due process under the Fourteenth Amendment. Americans have exported the term abroad, and it has acquired international currency, despite the difficulties of translation. Article 6 of the European Convention of Human Rights provides that, in all cases, "Everyone is entitled to a fair and public hearing." The Canadian Charter of Rights and Freedoms recognizes in Article 11(d) that everyone charged with a crime is presumed innocent until proven guilty "in a fair and public hearing." The standard translations of these provisions fail to capture the associations that English-speaking cultures invest in the notion of fair trial and, more broadly, in the idea of fair play.

The most dramatic example of reliance on fairness in international treaties comes to the fore in the Rome Statute establishing the International Criminal Court (ICC),[6] which uses the term *fair* more than fifteen times in a dozen different expressions—including "fair trial" (ICC § 8(2)(a)(vi)), "the requirements of fairness" (ICC § 55(1)(c)), and even, unexpectedly, the "fair representation of male and female judges" (ICC § 36(8)(a)(iii)).

It is a war crime "wilfully to deprive a prisoner of war or other protected person of the rights of a fair and regular trial" (ICC § 8(2)(a)(vi)). The effort to translate this provision into Spanish, French, Russian, Arabic, and Chinese—the other five official languages of the ICC—has revealed the uniqueness of English as the natural habitat of fair play and the language of fairness. The Spanish text originally rendered the key phrase as "*juicio justo e imparcial*," which brought back into English would be "just and impartial trial."[7] But then, in the current version of the statute, the phrase reads "*a ser juzgado legítima e imparcialmente*" ("to be tried legitimately and impartially"). This conforms to the French translation, which also defines the war crime as "*le fait de priver intentionnellement . . . de son droit d'être jugé régulièrement et impartialment*."[8] Remarkably, these translations drop the concept of fairness altogether.

The Russian version uses the term *spravedlivoe* as equivalent to "fairness." The term actually means "just," but there is no better term in Russian. The "regularity" of the trial is captured by the popular Russian word *normalnoe* or "normal" trial. Arabic and Chinese also rely on rough approximations of the concept of a "fair and regular trial." It is "fair" to

---

[6] U.N. Doc. A/CONF.183/9* (July 17, 1998) (entered into force July 1, 2002).

[7] This translation is on the Web. See http://www.un.org/law/icc/statute//spanish/rome_statute(s).pdf, p. 39, § 68 (1)(3), and (5).

[8] This translation highlights another problem in the English text, namely, the concept of "wilful deprivation." There is nothing like this loaded term in any of the other languages of the Rome Statute.

generalize and conclude that none of the five other languages of the Rome Statute grasp the associations of English-speaking lawyers when they speak of a right to a fair trial.

The basic problem is that Romance and Slavic languages make no distinction between "justice" and "fairness." A fair trial does not necessarily reach a just result, which presumably would require that the innocent are acquitted, and the guilty are convicted. Fair trials often result in injustice, in particular, the risk that the guilty go free. The "presumption of innocence" is often justified by saying that it is better to let ten guilty defendants go free than to convict one innocent. If justice requires the punishment of the guilty, then this concept of fairness, skewed as it is to the interests of the defendant, permits some injustice to occur.[9]

The difference between justice and fairness is evident in the alignment of these terms with different parties in the criminal process. Victims demand justice. Defendants want fairness. Recall the chant: "No justice, no peace." This was a demand not for a fair procedure but for a "just" outcome. This confusion of justice and fairness plagues efforts to translate the philosopher John Rawls's key phrase, "justice as fairness," into European languages. This phrase is the cornerstone of Rawls's influential work, *A Theory of Justice*, the thesis of which is that the principles of justice should be grounded in fair procedures of negotiations. Because the Romance languages recognize a term for "justice" but do not distinguish between justice and fairness, translators sometimes adopt the word "fairness" to avoid the collapse of thesis into "justice is justice."[10]

Sometimes translators seek to recapture the distinction in English by treating fairness as an equivalent to "equity" (French *équité*; Spanish *equidad*). Thus "fair trial" becomes *process équitable*. But "equity" is clearly

---

[9] In the common law system, this balance is sometimes claimed to turn on the burden of proof—how well must the state prove a defendant has committed a crime to ensure a fair system and also a just result. In the Rawlsian system, these are cases of imperfect procedural justice. Following the rules does not preclude injustice. His methodology for choosing principles of justice, however, is based on pure procedural justice, which implies that if fair procedural rules are followed, the outcome will automatically be just.

[10] See John Rawls, *A Theory of Justice* (Cambridge: Harvard University Press, 1971). Rawls's theory of justice as fairness is further developed in John Rawls, *Justice as Fairness: A Restatement* (Erin Kelly ed.) (Cambridge: Harvard University Press, 2001). The difficulty of distinguishing Rawls's concepts of justice and fairness is illustrated in the German translation of his collection of articles, *Gerechtigkeit als Fairness* (Joachim Schulte trans.) (Freiburg: Alber, 1977).

a different idea. In its origins in English law, equity represented the nuanced judgment of the chancellor, an officer of the king, which served to mitigate the rigors of the common law. Equity lacks the special feature of procedural justice that is implicit in fairness.

The particular attachment of Anglo-American legal culture to the concept of "fairness" derives from the emphasis in the common law on procedural regularity as a value in itself, a value worth respecting apart from justice in the individual case. Our notions of fairness and fair play draw heavily on analogies from competitive sports and games, which pervade idiomatic English. Fair procedures are those in which both sides have an equal chance of winning. The playing field is level. Neither side hides the ball. No one draws from the bottom of the deck. Regardless of the sport or game, no one seeks an "unfair" advantage—by "hitting below the belt," "stacking the deck," or "loading the dice."

It seems that only English—among the languages of the West—relies so heavily on these metaphors of fair play. English-speaking children are reared on the maxim: "It is not whether you win or lose, but how you play the game." Because the notion of fair play is so basic in American culture, the requirements of a fair trial understandably lie at the foundations of the American legal culture.

Relying on a sporting ethic to design the contours of criminal trials would strike lawyers from other parts of the world as misplaced enthusiasm for games and competition.[11] And yet the language of fairness has entered the international discourse of criminal law, and with the word comes the Anglo-American ethic that seems to downplay justice and emphasize "playing the game" fairly.

Reasonableness

The notion of reasonableness plays a critical role in defining the contemporary Anglo-American legal mind. English-speaking lawyers refer rou-

---

[11] Some observers believe that the ethic of playing the game has also influenced the making of legislation, as parliamentarians and legislators vote not for or against a bill owing to its policies but according to whether their team supports it. See C. Northcote Parkinson, *Parkinson's Law and Other Studies in Administration* 14–23 (Boston, MA: Houghton Mifflin, 1957). On the centrality of games in our institutional and cultural life, see the argument in Johan Huizinga, *Homo Ludens* (Boston: Beacon Press, 1971) (in English).

tinely to reasonable time, reasonable care, reasonable mistake, reasonable risk, reasonable doubt, and reasonable force. Every time the term is used, the implicit reference is to the behavior of a "reasonable person under the circumstances."[12] This hypothetical character summons us to recognize and apply a community standard for judging individual behavior. Those who fail to meet the standard of the reasonable person are at fault and deserve to be blamed for their "unreasonableness" of belief or behavior.

There is no technical problem in translating "reasonableness" into Western languages that draw on the Hellenistic understanding of reason as a source of truth. French vocabulary includes *raisonnable*, Germans understand what it means to be *vernünftig*, and Russians have no trouble with *razumnyj*. The problem is that although lawyers could use this term in legal argument and in drafting statutory provisions, they traditionally have not. The French Civil Code uses *raisonnable* just once, and the German Civil Code never couches a rule in the analogous demands of *Vernunft* ("reason"). These legal cultures have a proper translation for *reasonable* at their disposal, but until recently they have preferred not to use it.

For languages outside the sphere of Hellenistic influence, however, the problem comes close to the difficulty of adopting the term *fairness*. When the concept of "reason" is not in common usage, it is difficult to find a cognate for *reasonable*. In modern Hebrew, for example, the lawyers had considerable difficulty translating the phrases employing reasonableness that appeared in the English statutes that they adopted as their own, in particular, James Fitzjames Stephen's draft criminal code, which became standard in many of the former English colonies. Finally, sometime after the founding of the state of Israel, a group of experts convened at the Department of Justice in Jerusalem and decided to introduce the word *savir* as the designated equivalent of *reasonableness*.[13] Consequently, the term not only became common in legal usage but also soon spread to the

---

[12] The meaning of this usage has, however, changed over time, at least in the context of the criminal burden of proof, and perhaps more widely. See Steve Sheppard, "The Metamorphoses of Reasonable Doubt: How Changes in the Burden of Proof Have Weakened the Presumption of Innocence," 78 *Notre Dame L. Rev.* 1165 (2003).

[13] This story is reminiscent of the legend about the way the Japanese introduced the word *kenri* to mean "rights" after the Meiji Restoration in 1869. Just as the Israelis thought they had to conform to the vocabulary of the common law, the Japanese thought that to trade with the West they had to have a legal vocabulary that included the idea of individual rights.

language as a whole, to the point that native speakers today are unaware of the calculated way the word was coined.[14] We can expect a similar development to occur, eventually, in Arabic, Chinese, and other languages in which the concept of reason has weaker cultural roots than it does in the European languages.

It is interesting to observe, however, that different legal cultures respond at different rates to the challenge of integrating the concept of reasonableness into their legal vocabulary. The Rome Statute uses the term *reasonable* more than twenty times, and the French and Spanish translators have no trouble adapting their cognate (*raisonnable* and *razonable*) and using it as the equivalent of the American word. In their unofficial translation of the Rome Statute, however, the Germans appear to be more closed to the process of linguistic amalgamation. They could use the German word *vernünftig* whenever the English draft says "reasonable," but they do not. They find about seven or eight different phrases for translating the concept of reasonableness as it appears in different contexts. The only place they use the term *vernünftig* is to capture the famous common law phrase "proof beyond a reasonable doubt."[15]

Eventually, however, the English pattern of usage—relying heavily on "fairness" and "reasonableness"—will creep into all cultures engaged in international commerce and legal relations. International negotiation in English will demand that lawyers start thinking in the idiom of reasonableness.

Another example of linguistic transmission is the growing influence of a familiar figure of common law rhetoric, the "reasonable person." French lawyers have never traditionally spoken of the "reasonable person"—they prefer the quainter and politically incorrect expression *bon père de famille*, which we discuss in greater detail in Chapter Twenty-One. Under the influence of the common law, however, French-speaking Québecois lawyers now routinely speak of *la personne raisonnable*.

The movement toward linguistic convergence in this area should not becloud the strong cultural forces that issued in the initial divergence—between the common law's attachment to reasonableness and the Continental preference not to use the term. There is in fact a profound point

---

[14] My source for this story is the late Professor Shalev Ginossar—GPF.

[15] Rome Statute of the International Criminal Court (U.N. Doc. A/CONF.183/9*), entered into force July 1, 2002.

about legal method implicit in these two patterns of discourse.[16] The reliance on the concept of reasonableness reveals a holistic style of legal thought. The opposing civil law methodology relies on structured or layered principles to achieve the same result. These terms *holistic* and *structured* required some clarification.

Holistic legal thought is based on the use of a single rule to resolve a complex legal problem, such as the use of force in self-defense. The word *reasonable* facilitates this way of thinking because the rule can be simply formulated: "Any who *reasonably* believes that he is about to be attacked may use *reasonable* force to repel the attack." This rule works as a summary of the law of self-defense because the variable "reasonable" is sufficiently protean to address various legal questions.

By comparison, think of the rule of self-defense formulated in Article 32 of the German Criminal Code: "A defensive use of force is legitimate when necessary to avert an imminent unlawful attack to oneself or others." This formulation leaves unmentioned both the problem of mistaken but reasonable belief about the imminence of the attack and the problem of proportionality or reasonableness of the degree of force used. Both of these issues are addressed in distinct dimensions of analysis. The problem of reasonable belief is filtered off into the separate dimension of excusing conditions. If the actor's belief is mistaken and he falsely believes that the attack is about to occur, the mistaken perception might be excused—typically on the grounds of reasonable belief. The conditions are not stated in Article 32, and yet every lawyer knows that this provision of the code is embedded in a structure that permits an excuse in certain cases of mistaken belief.

Similarly, the problem of proportionality is formulated in a doctrine unique to the civil law tradition, namely, *abus de droit*, or abuse of rights. A structured legal theory is able, at the first level of analysis, to stipulate an absolute right—say, to use all force necessary under the circumstances—and at the second level, to qualify the right by proviso: If you use too much force relative to the interests protected, then you abuse your right and your action is no longer lawful.

Though the term *abus de droit* is mentioned in neither the French nor the German civil codes, it is fundamental to civilian legal thought.[17] It is

---

[16] See George P. Fletcher, "The Right and the Reasonable," 98 *Harv. L. Rev.* 949 (1985).

[17] The German code contains a provision that comes close to *abus de droit*. See BGB § 226

important to know in order not to be misled by the seemingly absolute statements of the Continental codes. For example, if a defender uses deadly force to prevent the escape of an apple thief or to prevent being tickled by a child, the use of force might be necessary and thus meet the formal definition of Article 32. Yet the subsidiary doctrine of "abuse of rights" would presumably apply and lead to the conclusion that the force was disproportionate and therefore unlawful.

Thus, the structured approach to self-defense enables the legislator to state a simple rule, with difficult questions of accessibility and proportionality reserved for secondary levels of argument. In the common law tradition, these distinct levels tend to be absorbed into a single holistic rule based on the concept of reasonableness.

It would be a mistake to think that using or not using the open-ended standard of reasonableness renders the rule either more or less precise. Article 32 of the German code appears to be more strictly defined than the common law rule, but this appearance depends on the lower visibility of the secondary levels of analysis. Neither one nor the other is more precise; both require judgments about the relevant factors that make a belief or the use of force reasonable under the circumstances. In the end—to use Karl Llewellyn's[18] classic phrase—the "reasons that do the singing" are the same.[19] Only the form in which they are presented differs.

Apart from these issues of form—holistic as opposed to structured

---

(*Schikaneverbot*) ("It is impermissible to exercise a right if the exercise can only have the purpose of causing harm to another"). More relevant in German practice, however, is § 242, which requires general good faith and fair dealing in contractual relationships; compare *Code civil du Québec* (C.C.Q.) Art. 317: *La personnalité juridique d'une personne morale ne peut être invoquée à l'encontre d'une personne de bonne foi, dès lors qu'on invoque cette personnalité pour masquer la fraude, l'abus de droit ou une contravention à une règle intéressant l'ordre public* ("In no case may a legal person set up a juridical personality against a person in good faith if it is set up to dissemble fraud, abuse of right (law) or contravention of a rule of public order").

[18] Karl Llewellyn was leading figure in the American Realist movement that began in the late 1930s. After having served in the German Army in the First World War, and having written about the common law system of precedent in German, he returned to the United States to study law at Yale. As a professor of law at Columbia University, he spent a year at the University of Leipzig, where he taught common law and the system of precedent and wrote an introduction to American law in German. See Karl Llewellyn, *Präjudizienrecht und Rechtsprechung in Amerika* (Leipzig: J. Weicher, 1933).

[19] Karl Llewellyn, *The Common Law Tradition: Deciding Appeals* 183 (Boston: Little, Brown, 1960).

analysis—the reliance on reasonableness in the common law carries moral and political significance. In the suggestive phrase of English-speaking lawyers, a decision by a governmental official or a private individual might be "reasonable but wrong." That is, the ambit of reasonable decision making encompasses many possible positions, some right, some wrong, and some not easily classified. The pervasiveness of reasonableness in legal culture serves as an invitation to tolerance, to the recognition of many acceptable answers.[20]

This characteristic of common law thinking derives, in part, from the jury system. The basic rule guiding the competence of the jury is that laypeople should decide those questions on which reasonable people might differ. If reasonable jurors would not disagree, then the judge should direct a verdict.[21] Thus reasonableness becomes the standard for demarcating the realm where expertise and official power come to an end. When reasonable people disagree, then the people—constituted by a jury of ordinary citizens—should deliberate and resolve the issue.

This dimension of tolerance in reasonableness stands in contrast to the mentality of structured legal analysis, where the emphasis is on finding the single right answer that applies in the particular case. Law in the Continental tradition is synonymous with the Right (*Recht, droit*). There might be many scholarly opinions, and many professors might have their schools of followers, but the assumption underlying the debate is that one school is right and should triumph in the debate.[22] The idea that many "right" answers may coexist in the legal culture has yet to take hold in the Continental legal culture, but with the growing influence of American legal terminology and thought, this day may yet come.

The appeal of tolerance and pluralism might make us enthusiastic about the gradual diffusion of these English concepts—fairness and rea-

---

[20] This dimension of reasonableness is inconsistent with the idea of reasonable care as a test for negligence—at least in the way the concept is analyzed by economists. Cost-benefit analysis should produce a single right answer, not a range of acceptable answers. This should follow from the concept of efficiency, which we take up later in Chapter Twenty-One.

[21] In criminal cases, the judge may direct in favor of acquittal but not in favor of guilt. In private law case, the option runs both ways.

[22] Robert Cover stressed the phenomena of jurisgenerative movements within every legal culture and the power of the courts to kill off or at least to suppress deviant schools of thought. These decisions are called "jurispathic." See Robert M. Cover, "The Supreme Court, 1982 Term: Foreword: Nomos and Narrative," 97 *Harv. L. Rev.* 4 (1983).

sonableness—in the Rome Statute and other international treaties. Yes
... and no. It would be desirable for Right-oriented legal cultures to
develop a deeper appreciation for the potential of pluralistic thought in
the law. But the imperial flavor of Anglo-American legal influence should
be a cause for concern. The fact that international negotiations are conducted primarily in English gives Anglo-American lawyers a natural advantage in the marketplace of ideas and terminology. It would be better
if American jurists developed more respect for the languages and legal
cultures of the rest of the world so that these exchanges became reciprocal
and mutually enriching.

Deference

One of the characteristic features of American law is its decentralization—
the rejection of an ordered hierarchy in favor of legal entities with un-
defined powers relative to each other. This principle is expressed in the
Constitutional principle of separation of powers among the legislative,
executive, and judicial branches of government. The three branches of
government are of equal power. There is no rule of law for resolving
conflicts among them.

Similarly, judges, lawyers, and jurors have overlapping powers in a
common law trial. They are not exactly of equal power, but it is not
clear, as it is in a Continental civilian trial, that the judge is in charge.
The lawyers are responsible for producing evidence, but the judge can
also introduce evidence, as they say, *sua sponte* ("on his or her own motion"), although this is rarely done. In the routine case, the jury determines the facts of the case, but the judge can take the case away from
the jury, at least in private disputes, if the judge finds that no reasonable
jury could disagree. The judge can preempt the authority of the jury by
directing a verdict for the plaintiff or the defendant. In a criminal case,
the judge can dismiss the charges, but unless the defendant waives his or
her right to a jury, only the jury may pronounce the defendant guilty.

To regulate disputes among the branches of government and to work
out the relative roles of judge, jury, and lawyers, we need rules of deference. A rule of deference is not a precise statement about who should
do what; rather, it is a description of an attitude or disposition. The
Supreme Court sometimes defers to Congress about the constitutionality

of legislation. In some cases—such as declaring war—Congress now defers to the power of the president. If there is a dispute between the Court and the president—say, about whether the president must turn over a tape recording of private conversations in the Oval Office—the president defers to the power of the Court. The key feature of deference is that you have to qualify all of these preceding sentences with the phrase "but not always." There is no precise rule for determining the limits of deference.

There are also rules of deference in working out the practical authority of judges, jurors, and lawyers. Judges defer to juries to determine the facts—but not always. Juries defer to judges when the judges define the law applicable to the case—but not always. (Juries defy judges when they engage in "jury nullification" by deciding contrary to the instructions.) Appellate judges apply rules known as "standards of review" to defer in varying degrees to the decisions of trial judges on evidentiary and procedural decisions—but not always. As in deference among the three branches of government, there is no precise rule for determining who should defer to whom and when.

If there is no precise rule, then how does the system work? The answer is that lawyers and citizens are socialized into a legal culture that informs their judgments about appropriate deference. They learn what it means to "go too far" or to not "go far enough." These rules cannot be taught through texts or rules. They are learned by acquiring experience in a new legal culture.

It is not easy to translate *deference* into Continental legal languages. The idea bears some similarity to the principle of complementarity as it is recognized in the Rome Statute. According to the latter, the International Criminal Court should defer to national courts unless the latter "are unwilling or unable" to decide the case (Rome Statute § 17(1)(a)). How much deference is implied by this standard remains an open question. The international community will have to generate a culture in which the participants have an intuitive sense about how far the ICC should go in taking cases away from local officials.

Discretion

We end this survey of discourse in the common law with another term that has acquired great significance in American legal thinking. Like *deference*,

the term *discretion* is often used today to imply imprecision and the breakdown of strict legal control under teachable rules. But this was not always
the case. *Discretion* has its origins in administrative law and in the administrative decisions made by judges in the course of a trial. The appropriate
translation in German is *Ermessen* and in French, *pouvoir discretionnaire*.

All administrators—whether they are running governmental agencies,
schools, or private firms—make decisions to maximize the goals of their
enterprise. This is the sense of *discretion* used to describe administrative
decisions to allocate funds to build highways, to order books for the
library, or to send troops into battle. The test for making a sound decision
of this sort is not whether the decision maker respects the rights of the
parties or does justice, but whether the decision efficiently promotes
agreed goals. The logic is instrumental: how best to adapt the possible
means to the relevant end.

The traditional approach to adjudication under law was different. For
Coke or Blackstone, legal decision making was not about promoting policy objectives but about protecting and enforcing the rights of the parties.
Under the influence of the American Realists of the 1920s and 1930s, the
meaning of the term *discretion* gradually changed so that it became plausible and commonplace to describe judges as exercising discretion in this
administrative sense when they decided cases under the law. This shift
was furthered by the continuing expansion of the nineteenth-century
utilitarian influence in American legal thought under the slogan that the
purpose of the law is to promote the social good. The combination of
the two strains of thought is expressed in this formula: Judges exercise
discretion when they make decisions, and they should make decisions by
promoting the basic policies of the law.

As the term is used today, *discretion* has two radically opposed meanings or homonyms. One of the opposing ideas is that the rules of law
determine the outcome of particular cases. This is the view naively attributed to the civilian codes, as in Montesquieu's tag that the judge is
but *la bouche* or mouthpiece of the law. No one seriously holds this view
today about the rules of the common law. Justice Oliver Wendell Holmes
Jr. disposed of the naive view when he wrote in 1905 in the dissenting
opinion of *Lochner v. New York* (198 U.S. 34, at 76): "General propositions
do not decide concrete cases." If the norms of the law do not determine
the outcome, then it must follow that judges exercise choice or discretion
when they decide cases.

But there is also another logical opposite of discretion, which requires that we first understand the views of the Realists who prevailed in American legal thought from the 1930s to the 1960s and, some would say, continue to reign today. According to their view, judges always exercise discretion when they decide cases. In this respect the use of *discretion* clearly differs from European usage. It would be unusual for a German to claim that all legal decisions reflect *Ermessensfreiheit* ("freedom of discretionary decision"). The Realist understanding of discretion implies that judges pursue policies in the same way administrators do. The opposite of *discretion*, then, would be a commitment to decide on the basis of principles rather than policies, to focus on the rights and duties of the party, and to reach a decision that is the right answer under the law.[23] This is the line that Ronald Dworkin took in his classic article arguing against the Realist philosophy of pervasive judicial discretion.[24]

Because the concept of discretion agilely shifts between two meanings—(1) the inevitability of judicial choice in applying the law and (2) a preference for pursuing policies over principles—the advocates of pervasive judicial discretion have gradually gained ground in American legal thought. Today they are often called "pragmatists." One of their leading advocates is Judge Richard Posner.

The recognition of discretion in decision making seems to be compatible in the American legal mind with the idea that judges are bound by the law. The problem is what it means to be "bound." There are two views, each corresponding to one of the two senses of discretion. As a physical metaphor, the judge's being bound suggests that the rule of law determines his or her decision. There is no choice in the decision. The rule is something like a whip beating the judge into marching in a particular direction. The other sense of being "bound" emphasizes the obligations of judging. To be bound by the law in this alternative sense means to be required to focus solely on legal criteria when making a decision. The personalities and wealth of the parties, their prior histories, their nationalities, their popularity and influence—these are all irrelevant. The first sense of being bound is external—something like being bound

---

[23] On the difference between principles and policies, see pp. 58–59.
[24] See Ronald Dworkin, "The Model of Rules," 35 *U. Chi. L. Rev.* 14, reprinted in Ronald Dworkin, *Taking Rights Seriously* (Cambridge: Harvard University Press, 1977).

in chains. The second sense is to bear a duty to think and act in a particular way.

One apparent compromise between these senses is to consider the discretion within a boundary, or role, set by rules, such a limit of jurisdiction or, more important, a discretion to select only among several outcomes that are justified by rules.[25] To exercise discretion in this sense is to have freedom to act within the boundary but to have no freedom to act outside that boundary. Even that compromise, however, fails to recognize that one form of discretion is the freedom to alter the boundary.

These ambiguities about discretion and being bound by law are by no means unique to American law. The German Basic Law (Constitution) contains two clauses that illustrate the difference between the physical metaphor of being bound and the alternative sense of obligation to think in a particular way. Article 97 of the Basic Law informs us that judges are subject only to *Gesetz*, the statutory law: *Der Richter ist nur dem Gesetz unterworfen* ("The judge is subject only to the statutory law"). The verb *unterworfen* literally means "thrown under." The image conveyed is that the judge is saddled and bound by a strict master called the statutory law.

Yet Article 20(3) tells us more broadly that the judges are bound by both principles of higher law and the statutory law: *Die Rechtsprechung ist am Recht und Gesetz gebunden* ("Case law is bound by both right and law"). This second sense of being bound emphasizes the duty of judges to think about higher principles at the same time that they are "subject" only to the statutory law.

This tension is readily understood by analogy to the problem of understanding discretion and its opposites. The first provision stresses the physical metaphor—being thrown under the yoke of law. The second, and historically the more recent provision, shifts the focus from physical control to the obligation of the judge to be guided by higher values of principle as well as by the letter of the law.

To sum up, then, discretion has at least these meanings: (1) being free to choose, (2) being free to choose within boundaries set by rules, and (3) functioning like an administrator required to maximize the future wel-

---

[25] This discretion is based on the rejection of the two criticisms of positivism that come from claims of formalism and skepticism in H. L. A. Hart, *The Concept of Law* 121–150 (2d ed) (Oxford: Oxford University Press, 1995).

fare of society. The opposites of discretion are (1) being subject to control by rules of law, (2) being constrained from altering the boundaries set by rules, and (3) being bound to focus on the rights and duties of the particular parties before the court and to ignore the general interests of society. The reliance on the concept of discretion, with all its subtle ambiguities, is a unique feature of the common law and, in particular, of American legal thought in the late twentieth and early twenty-first centuries.

Further Reading

In addition to the books noted, an excellent introduction to the culture of American law is Karl Llewellyn's classic, *The Bramble Bush* (New York: Oceana, 1951). For a useful introduction to the modern idea of the *lex non scripta*, see the recent reissue of Roscoe Pound's *The Ideal Element in Law* (Indianapolis: Liberty Fund, 2002). For the idea of the common law's relationship to liberty, see Frederic Pollock's *The Genius of the Common Law* (New York: Columbia University Press, 1912). For a recent examination of many of the issues raised in this chapter, see George P. Fletcher, *Basic Concepts of Legal Thought* (New York: Oxford University Press, 1996).

For more on the dispute over the regulation of sodomy, see Steve Sheppard, "Arkansas 1, Texas 0: Sodomy Laws Reformed at Last," 2003 *Arkansas Law Notes* 87. On the incoherence of *Bowers*, see Steve Sheppard, "The State Interest in the Good Citizen: Constitutional Balance Between the Citizen and the Perfectionist State," 45 *Hastings L.J.* 969 (1994). On the homophobic culture of the *Bowers* court, see Kendall Thomas, "Beyond the Privacy Principle," 92 *Colum. L. Rev.* 1431 (1992). For a prophetic illustration of a catalytic role for the court in ending such a culture among the populace, see Cass R. Sunstein, "Homosexuality and the Constitution," 70 *Ind. L.J.* 1 (1994).

FOUR

Legal Reasoning

When we talk about "reasoning," we are never entirely clear about whether we mean to refer to internal mental processes or to public argument and justification. Lawyers argue conflicting points of view. Judges decide disputes and write opinions justifying their decisions in light of the prevailing legal sources (statutes, cases, scholarly commentary). Both engage in internal ratiocination, as well as interactive efforts to persuade others. Both lawyers and judges engage in mental and verbal efforts properly called "legal reasoning."

Arguing for a client is a particular form of reasoning—but it is partial and subjective and sometimes excessively passionate. The way a judge decides a case—the process of looking at the statute and prior cases and commentary—and comes up with a decision is also called legal reasoning. This process is supposedly neutral and objective and dispassionate. The form of legal reasoning must be accessible to study and review by other judges, lawyers, and scholars. Most relevant to legal studies is the written opinion, in which the judge explains and justifies the decision in the light of the relevant sources of law.

The puzzle is understanding the relationship between the psychological process of reasoning to decide the case and the "reasoning" written down in the opinion. Is the latter a mirror of the former? Hardly. It is at best a reconstruction of how an ideal judge would reason in search of a decision.

The concept of motivation enters into both of these spheres of "reasoning." The motive or motivations of the decision would be the factors that actually drive it, psychologically. In most European languages, the "motivation" includes the written opinion explaining and justifying the decision. The English equivalent of this Continental term would be the "rationale" of the decision.

Where judges have motives not recorded in the opinion—in particular, political motives—their decisions tend to lack legitimacy. Some people levy this criticism against *Bush v. Gore* (531 U.S. 98), decided in 2000 to resolve the electoral impasse in Florida. The five judges voting to make George Bush president were widely thought to have partisan and political motives. Their opinions were, in fact, "well reasoned," but most observers think that the five-person majority and perhaps also the four dissenters had other "motives."

The fact is that there is no way of knowing the mind of any particular judge or juror—whether they were motivated by politics, by prejudice, or by self-interest. They think and then decide, sometimes better, sometimes worse. The only proper focus of legal reasoning is the motivation, or rationale, offered by the judge in the opinion. We can analyze these opinions as faithful or unfaithful to the sources of law, as convincing or unconvincing, as reaching the "right" result or the "wrong" result. The reasoning of judges on paper—their written opinions—are a necessary subject of study, not only in the common law but also in all national and international legal systems. Lawyers must read these opinions, which are their only source of knowledge for predicting how the court will decide in the next case. Also, when lawyers argue in the future, they cannot make a convincing argument by referring to the supposed political motives of the judges. They must limit their arguments to an analysis of the relevant statutes, judicial opinions, and legal commentary. Judges in inferior courts must read these opinions in order to know both how to decide their cases and how to write their opinions to avoid reversal on appeal.

Legal reasoning is bound by a set of conventions, and these conventions are different in every legal culture. These conventions prescribe the materials that judges may cite in their opinions and that lawyers may invoke in their legal arguments. At one time in English history, it was perfectly appropriate for lawyers, scholars, and judges to invoke the Bible as a source of legal authority. This is now taboo.[1] Economic arguments used to be irrelevant in common law cases. In recent years, they have become influential—whether the economic principles are properly understood or not.

In this chapter we review two of these conventions. One is the use of deduction and analogy, and the other is that set of conventions about how to read a case as precedent.

Deduction and Analogy

If we look back at the two opinions considered in Chapters One and Two, we notice the use of different techniques of legal reasoning. The 1927 German abortion case is an exemplar of deductive reasoning:

1. There is no criminal liability without a finding of wrongfulness.
2. The conduct is not wrongful if, in a conflict of duties, the actor acts according to the higher duty.
3. There is no criminal liability if, in a conflict of duties, the actor acts according to the higher duty.

This is but one of the many deductions that motivate the 1927 decision. By contrast, in Blackstone's opinion in *Scott v. Shepherd*, it is much more difficult to isolate a deduction that structures the opinion. True, Nares offers a deduction: If it is unlawful, then it is trespass. Unlawfulness is determined by Parliament, there is a statute of Parliament on the point, and therefore it is unlawful and trespass lies. Blackstone rejects this deductive reasoning in a phrase: "The lawfulness or unlawfulness of the original act is not the criterion" and at the same time concedes that for some other judges this might not be true. But what does Blackstone offer in place of "the criterion" offered by Nares? He tells us that the harm must be immediate, and immediacy depends on whether the squib was picked up and thrown by a "free agent." There would be a syllogism based on this phrase:

---

[1] In *Bowers v. Hardwick*, 478 U.S. 186 (1986), Justice Burger invoked "Judeo-Christian moral and ethical standards" to justify a state's prohibition of homosexual sodomy. This reference triggered nearly universal disapproval from the commentators.

1. Throwing a thing that causes harm constitutes an immediate injury unless a "free agent" intervenes.
2. In this case, a free agent intervened.
3. Therefore, this was not an immediate injury.

This deduction is not very helpful, as Blackstone concedes, because the term *free agent* requires further elaboration. The analogical method becomes evident in the way Blackstone proceeds to expound the pivotal idea of free agency. He gives us examples of the two extremes: At one pole there is no intervention by a free agent, and at the other, there is clear intervention by an obviously free agent. This is the way the examples line up:

1. No intervention by a free agent (trespass will lie)
   A. turning loose a wild beast or a madman
   B. diverting the course of an enraged ox
   C. diverting a stone thrown
   D. an arrow glancing against a tree
2. Intervention by a free agent
   A. a stone that has been thrown against my windows, and then falls still. It is then picked up and thrown.
   B. a man tosses a football into the street, and, after being kicked about by one hundred people, it at last breaks a tradesman's windows

Blackstone concludes that the second pair of examples is more compelling. This case, in his view, is like them, and they should be treated in the same way. Note that Blackstone has no authority for the way the latter two cases—stone lying still and football kicked about—should be treated. He just assumes that these two are intuitively clear. They are consequential injuries. It is also clear to Blackstone, without prior cases, that the first set of examples would justify a finding of immediate injury.

Lining up the examples in this way, you always need two poles. It is not enough to argue that A is like B and therefore ought to be treated in the same way. You need a matrix of alternatives. For example: At one pole B is treated as X; at the other pole C is treated as Y. If the problem is whether A should receive X or Y treatment, then the case should be resolved by asking whether A is more like B or like C.

The critical point here is that analogical reasoning always requires a proposition of the form *more like* B than C. *More like* is a matter of degree. A is like C in some respects. Indeed, A is like everything in the world in some respect (e.g., existing, having mass, taking up space). Throwing the squib is like turning loose a wild beast in some respects. The critical point is whether the flying squib is *more like* the wild beast turned loose or *more like* the football being kicked about by a hundred children.

Relationships of "more like-ness" are not a matter of strict logic. Reasonable people might disagree whether an airplane is more like a bird than an automobile or vice versa, or whether abortion is more like infanticide than like birth control. Analogies are typically subject to dispute. They are the stuff of disagreement—and dissenting opinions.

De Grey, J., agrees with the way Blackstone lays out the problem, but he disagrees about the proper analogy to throwing the squib. He concludes that the injury is immediate. This is more like turning loose a wild beast to run in the marketplace.

Note that Blackstone and De Grey do not let the argument rest with a simple claim of analogy. Blackstone contends that the deeper issue in the case is that no one should be "responsible [in trespass] for the acts of other men." De Grey agrees that this is the issue but again disagrees at the level of application. He distinguishes Blackstone's examples of consequential injury by characterizing the squib throwing as intending mischief (not just kicking about a football in the street). Further, this was "not any particular mischief, but mischief indiscriminate and wanton. Whatever mischief therefore follows, [the defendant] is the author of it." Blackstone might have made the subtler argument, but together Nares and de Grey carry the day.

Contrasting the opinion in *Scott v. Shepherd* with the 1927 abortion case reveals different modes of legal argumentation and reasoning. The former emphasizes analogical reasoning; the latter, deductive reasoning. The important point is that the mode of argument used in a judicial opinion depends on local conventions and attitudes. As a general matter, the common law tradition prefers analogical arguments, and the Continental tradition favors deductive reasoning. But this generalization is easily overstated.

Both deductive and analogical reasoning are indispensable forms of reasoning and justification. Their mutually reinforcing use can be seen in the Book of Exodus, which relies on both methods in setting forth God's law. In Exodus 20, the Ten Commandments invite deductive reasoning from the Commandments such as "Thou shalt not kill." Activity X is killing, and therefore activity X is prohibited. By contrast, most of the surrounding passage emphasizes specific factual situations that invite analogical extension to related cases. Thus, Exodus 21:28 requires that, If an ox gores a man and kills him, the ox shall be put to death. What about other animals who kill? Or is this a rule just for oxen? Analogical reasoning allows this rule to be applied more broadly to cover dangerous domestic animals. These analytical concepts of deduction and analogy in law are discussed in greater detail, and an exercise in their use is provided, in Appendix Two, at the end of this book.

Reading Cases

Legal cultures differ in the way their participants read and argue from prior cases. German lawyers are accustomed to looking for the *Rechtsatz*— that is, the succinct statement of law that can be cited as though it were a statutory rule. Common lawyers have cultivated a more refined way of citing precedents. This refinement brings to bear customary rules on which cases constitute precedents and how the case should be stated as precedent. Understanding these rules requires that we understand the doctrines of *stare decisis* (letting prior cases stand as binding precedents), *ratio decidendi* (the holding or reason for the decision), and *obiter dicta* (peripheral argument that is not strictly binding).

Here are some technical points about the doctrine of *stare decisis*. This principle of binding precedent applies both to a single court and to all of the courts that are within the appellate jurisdiction of that court. Thus, a decision concerning a federal question rendered by the Supreme Court of the United States is binding not only upon the Supreme Court but also upon all of the state and federal courts in the United States, because a case in any of those courts could be appealed to that court. Similarly, a decision by the British House of Lords binds all of the courts of England and Wales, Scotland, and Northern Ireland. Conversely, *stare decisis* does not bind courts that are not subject to appeal to a given court to follow that court's opinions. Thus, *stare decisis* does not bind a court in the United States to apply a decision of the House of Lords or a court in England to apply a decision of the U.S. Supreme Court.

In situations in which *stare decisis* does not apply, the precedents of other common law courts remain "persuasive" as authority. As we have seen in the *Lawrence* case by the Supreme Court (2003), decisions by the European Court of Human Rights can also become "persuasive" in American opinions. While not bound to follow a foreign precedent, both the House of Lords and the U.S. Supreme Court have taken note of the decisions of the other foreign courts in reaching their own opinions to decide cases before them.

There are considerable variations in the degree to which *stare decisis* is observed in the various national systems of the common law. For instance, the U.S. Supreme Court has displayed considerable willingness to overturn precedent, not only in the mid-twentieth century, when the Court was often described as liberal or activist, but also in recent decades in which it is described as conservative or restrained. In contrast, the House of Lords is much more likely to adhere to precedent, even unpopular precedent, and await a change in the law to be initiated through legislation.

The doctrine of *stare decisis* is limited in two ways by the interpretation of the language of a precedent. The first is that a later court is bound to apply only the most essential portions of a precedent opinion, not all of the language in it.

The most important language in a legal opinion is the consideration of the narrowest questions of law that are logically necessary to resolve the dispute before the court. This language is sometimes called the *ratio decidendi* or the "reason for the decision."

Language or reasoning in an opinion that is thought not to have been necessary, owing either to the claims presented or to the logical evaluation of those claims, is often described as *obiter dicta*, or "incidental statements." A *dictum* is not subject to *stare decisis*, although it may be persuasive.

It is no small matter to sort out the statements and ideas in a single opinion, even a carefully written and accurately transcribed opinion, between those that are the *ratio* and those that are *dicta*. For example, how do we decide the *ratio* of *Scott v. Shepherd*? The first problem is whether we should rely on the opinion by Nares or the opinion by De Grey. Let's take the latter because it is more fully argued. Now, choose the narrowest question of law presented in the case: (1) whether the writ of trespass will lie, (2) whether the injury is immediate or consequential, or (3) whether the intervening third parties who threw the squid further were acting as "free agents." You can see right away that finding the narrowest question in the opinion is not so simple. It is subject to dispute, much in the same way that claims of analogy are subject to differing interpretations.

There is a second manner in which *stare decisis* is limited by the interpretation of precedent. The delimitation of language in a precedential opinion into *dicta* and *ratio* is nearly always a matter for later judges and not for the judge who initially issued the precedent. It is excessively rare for a judge writing or speaking an opinion to identify the statements made as one or another, and in any event, such an identification would not be binding on a later judge. Thus the actual holding—the *ratio*—of *Scott v. Shepherd* would be decided by later judges who found it useful to cite the case as authority for their decisions.

The necessity that a later judge must interpret the opinion of an earlier judge to determine which part of the opinion is binding upon the later case thus gives the later judge some leeway in disregarding or "interpreting away" portions of some precedents without violating the doctrine of *stare decisis*.

Reasoning from Statutes

Working with statutes is not a prominent part of the first-year curriculum in most law schools, and we will therefore content ourselves with pointing out some of the peculiarities of working with statutes in the common law tradition. In addition to these illustrations, a more comprehensive discussion is presented in Appendix Three.

A maxim long in force held that statutes in derogation of the common law had to be strictly construed. This maxim reflected a certain uneasiness about legislative intervention changing the common law. The practice was to require a statute that displaced a common law rule to do so in clear language that makes certain the intent of the legislature that the common law rule be abandoned or replaced. Most statutes that alter the common law are, at least in the years immediately following their passage, narrowly construed, or interpreted to include the fewest possible cases within the new rule.[2]

This narrow rule of interpretation seems to be on the wane. In crim-

---

[2] For a good example, see the history of comparative negligence discussed in Chapter Twenty-Two.

inal cases, where statutory notice of the crime is generally required (*nullum crimen sine lege*—there is no crime not made by statutory law), the modern trend, as exemplified in the Model Penal Code,[3] is to interpret legislation according to the "fair import" of its terms in order to fulfill the general purposes of the statute (see MPC Art. 1, § 1.02(3)).

Despite this trend toward the greater acceptance of legislative purposes as a guide to interpretation, American courts and scholars emphasize the original legislative intention as the controlling perspective in interpreting both the Constitution and particular statutes. This is called "historical interpretation" in Continental legal thinking and counts as one approach to the interpretation of code provisions. Yet it would be odd in France or in Germany to argue that "historical interpretation" of the *Code civil* or of the BGB was the only legitimate reading of the codes.

Virtually all of these arguments about reading precedent and interpreting statutes come into play in a recent remarkable decision by the U.S. Supreme Court: *Rogers v. Tennessee*, 532 U.S. 451 (2001). The question in this case was relatively simple. The State of Tennessee prosecuted one Wilbert Rogers for a murder on the basis of a stabbing committed in May 1994, with the victim's death occurring in August 1995. There would be nothing controversial about that except that the common law supposedly had a rule holding that an actor could be guilty of murder only if the victim died within a year and a day of the homicidal act. The best evidence that this was the common law was that Blackstone said so.[4]

This rule was once widely accepted in common law jurisdictions. The California Criminal Code, adopted in 1872, contained this provision as a black-letter rule because it assumed that it was part of the common law and the purpose of the code was to state the common law in legislative form. According to California Penal Code § 194:

> To make the killing either murder or manslaughter, it is requisite that the party die within a year and a day after the stroke received or the cause of death administered.

---

[3] The Model Penal Code was proposed in the 1960s by the American Law Institute, a private organization of lawyers, judges, and scholars, led then by Herbert Wechsler, a professor of criminal law at the Columbia Law School. The MPC has stimulated criminal law reform and the enactment of new criminal codes in more than thirty-five states.

[4] See 4 W. Blackstone, *Commentaries on the Laws of England* 197–198 (1769).

In the current period of legislative reform of the criminal law, beginning with the Model Penal Code (MPC) in the 1960s, everybody has
tried to extricate the law of homicide from this rule of the common law.
California amended its code in 1969 to make the requisite period three
years and a day. The MPC simply ignored this heavy-handed rule of
causation altogether, provided the jury finds that the defendant's act
caused the victim's death.

In Tennessee, the legislature reformed the law of homicide in line
with the MPC in 1989 and defined homicide and murder without mentioning the "year and a day" rule or anything like it. The only question
would be whether the defendant's act caused the victim's death. The 1989
statute also abolished all common law criminal defenses without itemizing
them. The defendant appealed on the ground that the year and a day rule
was part of Tennessee law, the 1989 statute had not abolished it, and
therefore the defendant was not guilty. The first court of appeals in Tennessee—called the Court of Criminal Appeals—affirmed the conviction
on the ground that the 1989 statute had abolished the rule. The Tennessee
Supreme Court affirmed the conviction but rather surprisingly held that
the rule had survived the 1989 statute but that they were abolishing it.
The defendant appealed[5] to the U.S. Supreme Court on the ground that
if the year and a day rule was part of the law of Tennessee, the Tennessee
Supreme Court's abolishing the rule and applying the abolition in his case
was equivalent to retroactive legislation and therefore a violation of the
Ex Post Facto Clause in the Constitution.[6]

At the level of the Supreme Court, the issue was surprisingly divisive.
The justices were divided on fundamental questions concerning the
meaning of the common law, the interpretation of legislation, and when
a judicial decision can be regarded as equivalent to legislation. These are
the basic issues at play in this chapter.

---

[5] Technically, the defendant did not appeal. He applied for a writ of certiorari, which the
Court grants as a matter of discretion. It takes four of the nine possible votes to grant
the writ. See 529 U.S. 1129 (2000).

[6] U.S. Constitution, Article I, Sec. 10, Cl. 1. No State shall enter into any treaty, alliance,
or confederation; grant letters of marque and reprisal; coin money; emit bills of credit;
make anything but gold and silver coin a tender in payment of debts; pass any bill of
attainder, ex post facto law, or law impairing the obligation of contracts, or grant any
title of nobility.

To find for Rogers, the U.S. Supreme Court would have to answer each of the following three questions in the affirmative:

1. Was "the year and a day" rule [hereafter called the "rule"] part of the common law of Tennessee?
2. Did the rule survive the 1989 statute, which abolished all common law defenses?
3. Was the decision by the Tennessee Supreme Court to affirm Rogers's conviction equivalent to a legislative act and therefore prohibited by the Ex Post Facto Clause?

For the sake of clarity on the issues that concern us in this chapter, we have organized the justices' view according to the three questions:

Question 1: Was the rule part of the common law of Tennessee?

Justice Sandra Day O'Connor wrote the "opinion of the Court," a majority of five justices:

> Finally, and perhaps most importantly, at the time of petitioner's crime the year and a day rule had only the most tenuous foothold as part of the criminal law of the State of Tennessee. The rule did not exist as part of Tennessee's statutory criminal code. And while the Supreme Court of Tennessee concluded that the rule persisted at common law, it also pointedly observed that the rule had never once served as a ground of decision in any prosecution for murder in the State. *Indeed, in all the reported Tennessee cases, the rule has been mentioned only three times, and each time in dicta.* [Emphasis added.]
>
> The first mention of the rule in Tennessee, and the only mention of it by the Supreme Court of that State, was in 1907 in *Percer v. State*, 118 Tenn. 765, 103 S.W. 780. In *Percer*, the court reversed the defendant's conviction for second-degree murder because the defendant was not present in court when the verdict was announced and because the proof failed to show that the murder occurred prior to the finding of the indictment. In discussing the latter ground for its decision, the court quoted the rule that "it is . . . for the State to show that the crime was committed before the indictment was found, and, where it fails to do

so, a conviction will be reversed." *Id.* at 777, 103 S.W. at 783 (quoting 12 *Cyclopedia of Law and Procedure* 382 (1904)). The court then also quoted the rule that "in murder, the death must be proven to have taken place within a year and a day from the date of the injury received." 118 Tenn. at 777, 103 S.W. at 783 (quoting F. Wharton, *Law of Homicide* § 18 (3d ed. 1907)).

While petitioner relies on this case for the proposition that the year and a day rule was firmly entrenched in the common law of Tennessee, we agree with the Supreme Court of Tennessee that the case cannot establish nearly so much. After reciting the rules just mentioned, the court in *Percer* went on to point out that the indictment was found on July 6, 1906; that it charged that the murder was committed sometime in May 1906; and that the only evidence of when the victim died was testimony from a witness stating that he thought the death occurred sometime in July, but specifying neither a date nor a year. From this, the court concluded that it did "not affirmatively appear" from the evidence "whether the death occurred before or after the finding of the indictment." 118 Tenn. at 777, 103 S.W. at 783. The court made no mention of the year and a day rule anywhere in its legal analysis or, for that matter, anywhere else in its opinion. Thus, whatever the import of the court's earlier quoting of the rule, it is clear that the rule did not serve as the basis for the *Percer* court's decision.

The next two references to the rule both were by the Tennessee Court of Criminal Appeals in cases in which the date of the victim's death was not even in issue. Sixty-seven years after *Percer*, the court in *Cole v. State*, 512 S.W.2d 598 (Tenn. Crim. App. 1974), noted the existence of the rule in rejecting the defendants' contentions that insufficient evidence existed to support the jury's conclusion that they had caused the victim's death in a drag-racing crash. *Id.* at 601. Twenty-one years after that, in State v. Ruane, 912 S.W.2d 766 (Tenn. Crim. App. 1995), a defendant referred to the rule in arguing that the operative cause of his victim's death was removal of life support rather than a gunshot wound at the defendant's hand. The victim had died within 10 days of receiving the wound. The Court of Criminal Appeals rejected the defendant's argument, concluding, as it had in this case, that the year and a day rule had been abolished by the 1989 Act. It went on to hold that the evidence of causation was sufficient to support the conviction. *Id.* at 773–777. Ruane, of course, was decided after peti-

tioner committed his crime, and it concluded that the year and a day
rule no longer existed in Tennessee for a reason that the high court of
that State ultimately rejected. But we note the case nonetheless to complete our account of the few appearances of the common law rule in
the decisions of the Tennessee courts.

[A]s Justice Scalia correctly points out, the court viewed the year
and a day rule as a "substantive principle" of the common law of Tennessee. . . . As such, however, it was a principle in name only, having
never once been enforced in the State. The Supreme Court of Tennessee also emphasized this fact in its opinion, see 992 S.W.2d at 402,
and rightly so, for it is surely relevant to whether the court's abolition
of the rule in petitioner's case violated due process limitations on retroactive judicial decision making. And while we readily agree with
Justice Scalia that fundamental due process prohibits the punishment of
conduct that cannot fairly be said to have been criminal at the time the
conduct occurred, nothing suggests that is what took place here. . . .
Far from a marked and unpredictable departure from prior precedent,
the court's decision was a routine exercise of common law decision
making in which the court brought the law into conformity with
reason and common sense. It did so by laying to rest an archaic
and outdated rule that had never been relied upon as a ground of
decision in any reported Tennessee case. (532 U.S. 451, 466–467 (2001)
(O'Connor, J.))

Justice Scalia wrote for the four justices in dissent:

Though the Court spends some time questioning whether
the year-and-a-day rule was ever truly established in Tennessee, see
ante, at 12–15, the Supreme Court of Tennessee said it was, see 992
S.W.2d at 396, 400, and this reasonable reading of state law by the State's
highest court is binding upon us. (532 U.S. at 468–469 (Scalia, J., dissenting)

Question 2: Did the rule survive the 1989 Statute, which abolished all common law defenses?

Both the majority and the dissent seem to follow the Tennessee Supreme Court on this point, however implausible that decision had been. The Court of Criminal Appeals had the better argument, namely, that the 1989 legislative reform abolished the rule, but their opinion did not survive under the rulings of the higher courts.

Question 3: Was the decision by the Tennessee Supreme Court to affirm the Rogers conviction equivalent to a legislative act and therefore prohibited by the Ex Post Facto Clause?

The answer to this question must be divided into two parts. The first is the general understanding from history of when a judicial decision could repeal a rule of the common law, and the second is whether a particular Supreme Court precedent, the *Bouie* case, offers sufficient instruction for resolving the question.

PART A: HISTORY

Justice Scalia, dissenting (with three other justices joining him), said to this point:

> The Court today approves the conviction of a man for a murder that was not murder (but only manslaughter) when the offense was committed. It thus violates a principle—encapsulated in the maxim nulla poena sine lege—which "dates from the ancient Greeks" and has been described as one of the most "widely held value-judgments in the entire history of human thought." J. Hall, *General Principles of Criminal Law* 59 (2d ed. 1960). Today's opinion produces, moreover, a curious constitution that only a judge could love. One in which (by virtue of the Ex Post Facto Clause) the elected representatives of all the people cannot retroactively make murder what was not murder when the act was committed; but in which unelected judges can do precisely that. One in which the predictability of parliamentary lawmaking cannot validate the retroactive creation of crimes, but the predictability of ju-

dicial lawmaking can do so. I do not believe this is the system that the Framers envisioned—or, for that matter, that any reasonable person would imagine.

To begin with, let us be clear that the law here was altered after the fact. Petitioner, whatever else he was guilty of, was innocent of murder under the law as it stood at the time of the stabbing, because the victim did not die until after a year and a day had passed. The requisite condition subsequent of the murder victim's death within a year and a day is no different from the requisite condition subsequent of the rape victim's raising a "hue and cry" which we held could not retroactively be eliminated in *Carmell v. Texas*, 529 U.S. 513, 146 L. Ed. 2d 577, 120 S. Ct. 1620 (2000). Here, as there, it operates to bar conviction. Indeed, if the present condition differs at all from the one involved in *Carmell* it is in the fact that it does not merely pertain to the "quantum of evidence" necessary to corroborate a charge, *id.* at 530, but is an actual element of the crime—a "substantive principle of law," 992 S.W.2d 393, 399 (Tenn. 1999), the failure to establish which "entirely precludes a murder prosecution," *id.* at 400. (532 U.S. at 467–468 (Scalia, J., dissenting))

Justice Stevens (though part of the Scalia dissent) added this separate comment:

I must add this brief caveat. The perception that common-law judges had no power to change the law was unquestionably an important aspect of our judicial heritage in the 17th century but, as he has explained, that perception has played a role of diminishing importance in later years. Whether the most significant changes in that perception occurred before the end of the 18th century or early in the 19th century is, in my judgment, a tangential question that need not be resolved in order to decide this case correctly. For me, far more important than the historical issue is the fact that the majority has undervalued the threat to liberty that is posed whenever the criminal law is changed retroactively. (532 U.S. at 467 (Stevens, J., dissenting)).

Note that up to this point the dispute is about the lawmaking by common law courts. The majority seems to think that the Tennessee Supreme Court's modifying the common law of homicide was simply a "routine exercise of common law decision-making in which the court brought the law into conformity with reason and common sense." For the four justices in dissent, this was not acceptable. Giving so much power to unelected judges "is [not] the system that the Framers envisioned—or, for that matter, [one] that any reasonable person would imagine." The principle *nulla poena sine lege* should, in the mind of the dissenters, be more compelling than that.

PART B. PRECEDENT

Both the majority and dissenters are troubled by one case in which the Supreme Court held that judicial interpretation of a crime can run afoul of the Constitution. The case, *Bouie v. City of Columbia*, 378 U.S. 347 (1964), arose in the heat of the civil rights sit-in campaign in the South. The general practice was for black youths to march into drug stores, get seated at the soda fountain (where they were not allowed in the all-white store), and wait until they were served. In *Bouie*, the state of South Carolina prosecuted them for criminal trespass. This is the way the majority of *Rogers* Court describes and distinguishes the case:

> We have observed, however, that limitations on ex post facto judicial decision making are inherent in the notion of due process. In *Bouie v. City of Columbia*, we considered the South Carolina Supreme Court's retroactive application of its construction of the State's criminal trespass statute to the petitioners in that case. The statute prohibited "entry upon the lands of another . . . after notice from the owner or tenant prohibiting such entry. . . ." 378 U.S. at 349, n. 1 (citation and internal quotation marks omitted). The South Carolina court construed the statute to extend to patrons of a drug store who had received no notice prohibiting their entry into the store, but had refused to leave the store when asked. Prior to the court's decision, South Carolina cases construing the statute had uniformly held that conviction under the statute required proof of notice before entry. None of those cases, moreover, had given the "slightest indication that that requirement

could be satisfied by proof of the different act of remaining on the land after being told to leave." *Id.* at 357.

We held that the South Carolina court's retroactive application of its construction to the store patrons violated due process. Reviewing decisions in which we had held criminal statutes "void for vagueness" under the Due Process Clause, we noted that this Court has often recognized the "basic principle that a criminal statute must give fair warning of the conduct that it makes a crime." . . . For that reason, we concluded that "if a judicial construction of a criminal statute is 'unexpected and indefensible by reference to the law which had been expressed prior to the conduct in issue,' [the construction] must not be given retroactive effect." *Id.* at 354 (quoting J. Hall, *General Principles of Criminal Law* 61 (2d ed. 1960)). We found that the South Carolina court's construction of the statute violated this principle because it was so clearly at odds with the statute's plain language and had no support in prior South Carolina decisions. 378 U.S. at 356.

Relying largely upon *Bouie*, petitioner argues that the Tennessee court erred in rejecting his claim that the retroactive application of its decision to his case violates due process. Petitioner contends that the Ex Post Facto Clause would prohibit the retroactive application of a decision abolishing the year and a day rule if accomplished by the Tennessee Legislature. He claims that the purposes behind the Clause are so fundamental that due process should prevent the Supreme Court of Tennessee from accomplishing the same result by judicial decree. Brief for Petitioner 8–18. In support of this claim, petitioner takes *Bouie* to stand for the proposition that "in evaluating whether the retroactive application of a judicial decree violates Due Process, a critical question is whether the Constitution would prohibit the same result attained by the exercise of the state's legislative power." Brief for Petitioner 12.

[P]etitioner misreads *Bouie*. To be sure, our opinion in *Bouie* does contain some expansive language that is suggestive of the broad interpretation for which petitioner argues. Most prominent is our statement that "if a state legislature is barred by the Ex Post Facto Clause from passing . . . a law, it must follow that a State Supreme Court is barred by the Due Process Clause from achieving precisely the same result by judicial construction." 378 U.S. at 353–354; see also *id.* at 353 ("An

unforeseeable judicial enlargement of a criminal statute, applied retroactively, operates precisely like an ex post facto law"); *id*. at 362 ("The
Due Process Clause compels the same result" as would the constitutional proscription against ex post facto laws "where the State has
sought to achieve precisely the same [impermissible] effect by judicial
construction of the statute"). *This language, however, was dicta.* [Emphasis
added.] Our decision in *Bouie* was rooted firmly in well established
notions of due process. See supra, at 5. Its rationale rested on core due
process concepts of notice, foreseeability, and, in particular, the right to
fair warning as those concepts bear on the constitutionality of attaching
criminal penalties to what previously had been innocent conduct. See,
e.g., 378 U.S. at 351, 352, 354, 354–355. And we couched its holding
squarely in terms of that established due process right, and not in terms
of the ex post facto–related dicta to which petitioner points. *Id*. at 355
(concluding that "the South Carolina Code did not give [the petition-
ers] fair warning, at the time of their conduct . . . , that the act for
which they now stand convicted was rendered criminal by the statute").
Contrary to petitioner's suggestion, nowhere in the opinion did we go
so far as to incorporate jot–for–jot the specific categories of *Calder* into
due process limitations on the retroactive application of judicial decisions. Nor have any of our subsequent decisions addressing *Bouie*–type
claims interpreted *Bouie* as extending so far. Those decisions instead
have uniformly viewed *Bouie* as restricted to its traditional due process
roots. In doing so, they have applied *Bouie's* check on retroactive judicial decision making not by reference to the ex post facto categories
set out in *Calder*, but, rather, in accordance with the more basic and
general principle of fair warning that *Bouie* so clearly articulated. See,
e.g., *United States v. Lanier*, 520 U.S. 259, 266, 137 L. Ed. 2d 432, 117
S. Ct. 1219 (1997) ("Due process bars courts from applying a novel
construction of a criminal statute to conduct that neither the statute
nor any prior judicial decision has fairly disclosed to be within its
scope"); *Marks v. United States*, 430 U.S. at 191–192 (Due process protects against judicial infringement of the "right to fair warning" that
certain conduct will give rise to criminal penalties); *Rose v. Locke*, 423
U.S. 48, 53, 46 L. Ed. 2d 185, 96 S. Ct. 243 (1975) (per curiam)
(upholding defendant's conviction under statute prohibiting "crimes
against nature" because, unlike in *Bouie*, the defendant "[could] make
no claim that [the statute] afforded no notice that his conduct might

be within its scope"); *Douglas v. Buder*, 412 U.S. 430, 432, 37 L. Ed. 2d 52, 93 S. Ct. 2199 (1973) (per curiam) (trial court's construction of the term "arrest" as including a traffic citation, and application of that construction to defendant to revoke his probation, was unforeseeable and thus violated due process); *Rabe v. Washington*, 405 U.S. 313, 316, 31 L. Ed. 2d 258, 92 S. Ct. 993 (1972) (per curiam) (reversing conviction under state obscenity law because it did "not give fair notice" that the location of the allegedly obscene exhibition was a vital element of the offense).

Petitioner observes that the Due Process and Ex Post Facto Clauses safeguard common interests—in particular, the interests in fundamental fairness (through notice and fair warning) and the prevention of the arbitrary and vindictive use of the laws. Brief for Petitioner 12–18. While this is undoubtedly correct, see, e.g., *Lynce v. Mathis*, 519 U.S. 433, 439–440, 137 L. Ed. 2d 63, 117 S. Ct. 891, and n. 12 (1997), petitioner is mistaken to suggest that these considerations compel extending the strictures of the Ex Post Facto Clause to the context of common law judging. The Ex Post Facto Clause, by its own terms, does not apply to courts. Extending the Clause to courts through the rubric of due process thus would circumvent the clear constitutional text. It also would evince too little regard for the important institutional and contextual differences between legislating, on the one hand, and common law decision making, on the other.

Petitioner contends that state courts acting in their common law capacity act much like legislatures in the exercise of their lawmaking function, and indeed may in some cases even be subject to the same kinds of political influences and pressures that justify ex post facto limitations upon legislatures. Brief for Petitioner 12–18; Reply Brief for Petitioner 15. A court's "opportunity for discrimination," however, "is more limited than [a] legislature's, in that [it] can only act in construing existing law in actual litigation." *James v. United States*, 366 U.S. 213, 247, n. 3, 6 L. Ed. 2d 246, 81 S. Ct. 1052 (1961) (Harlan, J., concurring in part and dissenting in part). . . .

That is particularly so where, as here, the allegedly impermissible judicial application of a rule of law involves not the interpretation of a statute but an act of common law judging. In the context of common law doctrines (such as the year and a day rule), there often arises a need to clarify or even to reevaluate prior opinions as new circumstances and fact patterns present themselves. Such judicial acts, whether they be characterized as "making" or "finding" the law, are a necessary part of the judicial business in States in which the criminal law retains some of its common law elements. Strict application of ex post facto principles in that context would unduly impair the incremental and reasoned development of precedent that is the foundation of the common law system. The common law, in short, presupposes a measure of evolution that is incompatible with stringent application of ex post facto principles. It was on account of concerns such as these that *Bouie* restricted due process limitations on the retroactive application of judicial interpretations of criminal statutes to those that are "unexpected and indefensible by reference to the law which had been expressed prior to the conduct in issue." *Bouie v. City of Columbia*, 378 U.S. at 354 (internal quotation marks omitted).

We believe this limitation adequately serves the common law context as well. It accords common law courts the substantial leeway they must enjoy as they engage in the daily task of formulating and passing upon criminal defenses and interpreting such doctrines as causation and intent, reevaluating and refining them as may be necessary to bring the common law into conformity with logic and common sense. It also adequately respects the due process concern with fundamental fairness and protects against vindictive or arbitrary judicial lawmaking by safeguarding defendants against unjustified and unpredictable breaks with prior law. Accordingly, we conclude that a judicial alteration of a common law doctrine of criminal law violates the principle of fair warning, and hence must not be given retroactive effect, only where it is "unexpected and indefensible by reference to the law which has been expressed prior to the conduct in issue." . . .

Justice Scalia makes much of the fact that, at the time of the framing of the Constitution, it was widely accepted that courts could not "change" the law, see post, at 5–7, 11–12 (dissenting opinion), and that (according to Justice Scalia) there is no doubt that the Ex Post Facto Clause would have prohibited a legislative decision identical to the Tennessee court's decision here, see post, at 3–4, 12. This latter argument seeks at bottom merely to reopen what has long been settled by the constitutional text and our own decisions: that the Ex Post Facto Clause does not apply to judicial decision making. The former argu-

ment is beside the point. Common law courts at the time of the framing undoubtedly believed that they were finding rather than making
law. But, however one characterizes their actions, the fact of the matter
is that common law courts then, as now, were deciding cases, and in
doing so were fashioning and refining the law as it then existed in light
of reason and experience. Due process clearly did not prohibit this
process of judicial evolution at the time of the framing, and it does not
do so today.

The majority holds firm, therefore, to the idea that the ex post
facto clause does not apply to judicial law-making. Any suggestion
to the contrary in *Bouie* was just dicta. (532 U.S., at 462–469)
(O'Connor, J.)

Here is the response of the dissent and its own characterization of
what happened in *Bouie*:

We concluded that, "[if] a state legislature is barred by the Ex Post
Facto Clause from passing such a law, it must follow that a State Supreme Court is barred by the Due Process Clause from achieving precisely the same result by judicial construction." *Id.* at 353–354. *The
Court seeks to avoid the obvious import of this language by characterizing it as
mere dicta.* [Emphasis added.] See ante, at 7. Only a concept of dictum
that includes the very reasoning of the opinion could support this characterization. *The ratio decidendi of Bouie was that the principle applied to the
legislature though the Ex Post Facto Clause was contained in the Due Process
Clause insofar as judicial action is concerned.* [Emphasis added.] I cannot
understand why the Court derives such comfort from the fact that later
opinions applying *Bouie* have referred to the Due Process Clause rather
than the Ex Post Facto Clause, see ante, at 7–8; that is entirely in accord
with the rationale of the case, which I follow and which the Court
discards.

The Court attempts to cabin *Bouie* by reading it to prohibit only
"unexpected and indefensible" judicial law revision, and to permit retroactive judicial changes so long as the defendant has had "fair warning"
that the changes might occur. Ante, at 10. This reading seems plausible

because *Bouie* does indeed use those quoted terms; but they have been wrenched entirely out of context. The "fair warning" to which *Bouie* and subsequent cases referred was not "fair warning that the law might be changed," but fair warning of what constituted the crime at the time of the offense. And *Bouie* did not express disapproval of "unexpected and indefensible changes in the law" (and thus implicitly approve "expected or defensible changes"). It expressed disapproval of "judicial construction of a criminal statute" that is "unexpected and indefensible by reference to the law which had been expressed prior to the conduct in issue." 378 U.S. at 354 [emphasis added; internal quotation marks omitted]. It thus implicitly approved only a judicial construction that was an expected or defensible application of prior cases interpreting the statute. Extending this principle from statutory crimes to common–law crimes would result in the approval of retroactive holdings that accord with prior cases expounding the common law, and the disapproval of retroactive holdings that clearly depart from prior cases expounding the common law. According to *Bouie*, not just "unexpected and indefensible" retroactive changes in the common law of crimes are bad, but all retroactive changes.

Bouie rested squarely upon "the fundamental principle that 'the required criminal law must have existed when the conduct in issue occurred,'" *ibid*. (Nulla poena sine lege.) Proceeding from that principle, *Bouie* said that "a State Supreme Court is barred by the Due Process Clause from achieving precisely the same result [prohibited by the Ex Post Facto Clause] by judicial construction." *Id*. at 353–354. There is no doubt that "fair warning" of the legislature's intent to change the law does not insulate retroactive legislative criminalization. Such a statute violates the Ex Post Facto Clause, no matter that, at the time the offense was committed, the bill enacting the change was pending and assured of passage—or indeed, had already been passed but not yet signed by the President whose administration had proposed it. It follows from the analysis of *Bouie* that "fair warning" of impending change cannot insulate retroactive judicial criminalization either.

Nor is there any reason in the nature of things why it should. According to the Court, the exception is necessary because prohibiting retroactive judicial criminalization would "place an unworkable and unacceptable restraint on normal judicial processes," would be "incompatible with the resolution of uncertainty that marks any evolving legal system," and would "unduly impair the incremental and reasoned development of precedent that is the foundation of the common law system." Ante, at 9. That assessment ignores the crucial difference between simply applying a law to a new set of circumstances and changing the law that has previously been applied to the very circumstances before the court. Many criminal cases present some factual nuance that arguably distinguishes them from cases that have come before; a court applying the penal statute to the new fact pattern does not purport to change the law. That, however, is not the action before us here, but rather, a square, head–on overruling of prior law—or, more accurately, something even more extreme than that: a judicial opinion acknowledging that under prior law, for reasons that used to be valid, the accused could not be convicted, but decreeing that, because of changed circumstances, "we hereby abolish the common law rule," 922 S. W. 2d, at 401, and upholding the conviction by applying the new rule to conduct that occurred before the change in law was announced. Even in civil cases, and even in modern times, such retroactive revision of a concededly valid legal rule is extremely rare. With regard to criminal cases, I have no hesitation in affirming that it was unheard–of at the time the original Due Process Clause was adopted. As I discuss in detail in the following section, proceeding in that fashion would have been regarded as contrary to the judicial traditions embraced within the concept of due process of law. (532 U.S., at 469–471)

The dispute here is about the correct reading of *Bouie*, about what was *ratio* and what was *dicta*. This proves that the process of finding *ratio* and *dicta* is not an automatic task that could be assigned to a computer. It requires judgment and argument. You need not worry much at this point about the specific clauses of the Constitution invoked by the Court—namely, whether *Bouie* is really about the Due Process Clause (majority) or about the Ex Post Facto Clause (dissent). This will become clear in the ensuing chapters. There is still a matter of principle to be discussed, namely, whether the Tennessee Supreme Court's abolition of the "year and a day" rule was so "unexpected and indefensible" as to

violate the general requirement of "fair warning" as an agreed-upon principle of due process. This is the majority's argument:

Turning to the particular facts of the instant case, the Tennessee
court's abolition of the year and a day rule was not unexpected and
indefensible. The year and a day rule is widely viewed as an outdated
relic of the common law. Petitioner does not even so much as hint that
good reasons exist for retaining the rule, and so we need not delve too
deeply into the rule and its history here. Suffice it to say that the rule
is generally believed to date back to the 13th century, when it served
as a statute of limitations governing the time in which an individual
might initiate a private action for murder known as an "appeal of
death"; that by the 18th century the rule had been extended to the
law governing public prosecutions for murder; that the primary and
most frequently cited justification for the rule is that 13th century medical science was incapable of establishing causation beyond a reasonable
doubt when a great deal of time had elapsed between the injury to the
victim and his death; and that, as practically every court recently to
have considered the rule has noted, advances in medical and related
science have so undermined the usefulness of the rule as to render it
without question obsolete. See, e.g., *People v. Carrillo*, 164 Ill. 2d 144,
150, 646 N.E.2d 582, 585, 207 Ill. Dec. 16 (1995); *Commonwealth v.
Lewis*, 381 Mass. 411, 414–415, 409 N.E.2d 771, 772–773 (1980); *People
v. Stevenson*, 416 Mich. 383, 391–392; 331 N.W.2d 143, 146 (1982);
State v. Hefler, 310 N.C. 135, 138–140, 310 S.E.2d 310, 313 (1984); see
generally Comment, 59 *U. Chi. L. Rev.* 1337 (1992) (tracing the history
of the rule).

For this reason, the year and a day rule has been legislatively or
judicially abolished in the vast majority of jurisdictions recently to have
addressed the issue. See 992 S.W.2d at 397, n. 4 (reviewing cases and
statutes). Citing *Bouie*, petitioner contends that the judicial abolition of
the rule in other jurisdictions is irrelevant to whether he had fair warning that the rule in Tennessee might similarly be abolished and, hence,
to whether the Tennessee court's decision was unexpected and indefensible as applied to him. Brief for Petitioner 28–30. In discussing the
apparent meaning of the South Carolina statute in *Bouie*, we noted that
"it would be a rare situation in which the meaning of a statute of

another State sufficed to afford a person 'fair warning' that his own State's statute meant something quite different from what its words said." 378 U.S. at 359–360. This case, however, involves not the precise meaning of the words of a particular statute, but rather the continuing viability of a common law rule. Common law courts frequently look to the decisions of other jurisdictions in determining whether to alter or modify a common law rule in light of changed circumstances, increased knowledge, and general logic and experience. Due process, of course, does not require a person to apprise himself of the common law of all 50 States in order to guarantee that his actions will not subject him to punishment in light of a developing trend in the law that has not yet made its way to his State. At the same time, however, the fact that a vast number of jurisdictions have abolished a rule that has so clearly outlived its purpose is surely relevant to whether the abolition of the rule in a particular case can be said to be unexpected and indefensible by reference to the law as it then existed.

Finally, and perhaps most importantly, at the time of petitioner's crime the year and a day rule had only the most tenuous foothold as part of the criminal law of the State of Tennessee. The rule did not exist as part of Tennessee's statutory criminal code. And while the Supreme Court of Tennessee concluded that the rule persisted at common law, it also pointedly observed that the rule had never once served as a ground of decision in any prosecution for murder in the State. *Indeed, in all the reported Tennessee cases, the rule has been mentioned only three times, and each time in dicta.* [Emphasis added.] (532 U.S. at 462–465) (O'Connor, J.)

That is, because the rule was so tenuous to begin with and the rule was universally disapproved, the abolition of the rule could not be considered "unexpected and indefensible." But this set of moves does not satisfy the defense. All four dissenters join this portion of Scalia's opinion:

Even if I agreed with the Court that the Due Process Clause is violated only when there is lack of "fair warning" of the impending retroactive change, I would not find such fair warning here. It is not clear to me, in fact, what the Court believes the fair warning consisted of. Was it the mere fact that "the year and a day rule is widely viewed as an outdated relic of the common law"? Ante, at 11. So are many of the elements of common–law crimes, such as "breaking the close" as an element of burglary, or "asportation" as an element of larceny. See W. LaFave & A. Scott, *Criminal Law* 631–633, 708–710 (1972). Are all of these "outdated relics" subject to retroactive judicial rescission? Or perhaps the fair warning consisted of the fact that "the year and a day rule has been legislatively or judicially abolished in the vast majority of jurisdictions recently to have addressed the issue." Ante, at 11. But why not count in petitioner's favor (as giving him no reason to expect a change in law) those even more numerous jurisdictions that have chosen not "recently to have addressed the issue"? And why not also count in petitioner's favor (rather than against him) those jurisdictions that have abolished the rule legislatively, and those jurisdictions that have abolished it through prospective rather than retroactive judicial rulings (together, a large majority of the abolitions, see 922 S. W. 2d, at 397, n. 4, 402 (listing statutes and cases))? That is to say, even if it was predictable that the rule would be changed, it was not predictable that it would be changed retroactively, rather than in the prospective manner to which legislatures are restricted by the Ex Post Facto Clause, or in the prospective manner that most other courts have employed.

In any event, as the Court itself acknowledges, "due process . . . does not require a person to apprise himself of the common law of all 50 States in order to guarantee that his actions will not subject him to punishment in light of a developing trend in the law that has not yet made its way to his State." Ante, at 12. The Court tries to counter this self–evident point with the statement that "at the same time, however, the fact that a vast number of jurisdictions have abolished a rule that has so clearly outlived its purpose is surely relevant to whether the abolition of the rule in a particular case can be said to be unexpected and indefensible by reference to the law as it then existed," *ibid*. This retort rests upon the fallacy that I discussed earlier: that "expected or defensible" "abolition" of prior law was approved by *Bouie*. It was not—and according such conclusive effect to the "defensibility" (by which I presume the Court means the "reasonableness") of the change in law will validate the retroactive creation of many new crimes.

Finally, the Court seeks to establish fair warning by discussing at great length, ante, at 12–15, how unclear it was that the year-and-a-day rule was ever the law in Tennessee. As I have already observed, the Supreme Court of Tennessee is the authoritative expositor of Tennessee law, and has said categorically that the year-and-a-day rule was the law. Does the Court mean to establish the principle that fair warning of impending change exists—or perhaps fair warning can be dispensed with—when the prior law is not crystal clear? Yet another boon for retroactively created crimes.

I reiterate that the only "fair warning" discussed in our precedents, and the only "fair warning" relevant to the issue before us here, is fair warning of what the law is. That warning, unlike the new one that today's opinion invents, goes well beyond merely "safeguarding defendants against unjustified and unpredictable breaks with prior law," ante, at 10 (emphasis added). It safeguards them against changes in the law after the fact. But even accepting the Court's novel substitute, the opinion's conclusion that this watered–down standard has been met seems to me to proceed on the principle that a large number of almost–valid arguments makes a solid case. As far as I can tell, petitioner had nothing that could fairly be called a "warning" that the Supreme Court of Tennessee would retroactively eliminate one of the elements of the crime of murder.

To decide this case, we need only conclude that due process prevents a court from (1) acknowledging the validity, when they were rendered, of prior decisions establishing a particular element of a crime; (2) changing the prior law so as to eliminate that element; and (3) applying that change to conduct that occurred under the prior regime. A court would remain free to apply common–law criminal rules to new fact patterns, see ante, at 9–10, so long as that application is consistent with a fair reading of prior cases. It would remain free to conclude that a prior decision or series of decisions establishing a particular element of a crime was in error, and to apply that conclusion retroactively (so long as the "fair notice" requirement of *Bouie* is satisfied). It would even remain free, insofar as the ex post facto element of the Due Process Clause is concerned, to "reevaluate and refine" the elements of common-law crimes to its heart's content, so long as it does so prospectively. (The majority of state courts that have abolished the year-and-a-day rule have done so in this fashion.) And, of course (as Blackstone and the Framers envisioned), legislatures would be free to eliminate outmoded elements of common-law crimes for the future by law. But what a court cannot do, consistent with due process, is what the Tennessee Supreme Court did here: avowedly change (to the defendant's disadvantage) the criminal law governing past acts. (532 U.S. at 478–82. (Scalia, J., dissenting)).

There is no doubt that Justice Scalia mounts a powerful dissent against the decision of the Court. It is significant that he is joined by two liberal justices, Stevens and Breyer, as well as a conservative justice, Clarence Thomas.

In this case we not only encounter deep disagreement about the jurisprudential nature of the common law but also get a glimpse of the difficulty that the Supreme Court encounters in resolving rather elementary constitutional issues. The spirit of American law is divided, and the Supreme Court is at the center of that conflict.

To make headway in understanding American law, then, over the next nine chapters we turn more systematically to the Constitution and to the conflicts and disputes that it has both resolved and engendered.

Further Reading

Appendices Two and Three of this book present more material on common law reasoning. Appendix Two has material on the tools of informal logic and the manner in which common law analysis employs them in case discussion. Appendix Three considers the special problems that arise in the use of statutes.

There is a rich literature on common law reasoning, as well as its analysis of cases and statutes. A modern and comprehensive survey that is easy to read is Steven Burton's *An Introduction to Law and Legal Reasoning* (New York: Aspen Law and Business, 1995). A short and clear approach to case-based and analogical reasoning is in Edward H. Levy's *A Introduction to Legal Reasoning* (Chicago: University of Chicago Press, 1948). The determination of the rationale of a case is considered in many articles, and an unusually clear exposition is Neil MacCormack's "Why Cases Have Rationales and What These Are," in the useful collection *Precedent in Law* (Laurence Goldstein ed.) (Oxford: Clarendon Press,

1987). The problem of precedent itself is wonderfully explored in the classic article by Lon L. Fuller, "Reason and Fiat in Case Law," 59 *Harv. L. Rev.* 376. The nature of statutory application in the common law is very usefully developed in Kent Greenawalt's *Legislation: Statutory Interpretation: 20 Questions* (New York: Foundation Press, 1999).

II

Constitutional Identity

There might be something that all English-speaking, common law legal systems have in common, but that common core is constantly diminishing. The reason is that each legal culture now has its own constitutional foundation and, in many cases, a transnational set of principles that shape the development of domestic law. Canadian law, both common law and civil law, is governed by the Charter of Rights and Freedoms, adopted in 1982. English law is subject to both the European Convention on Human Rights and the jurisprudence of the European Court in Strasbourg. In addition, the United Kingdom is embedded in the regulations and the jurisprudence of the European Union, which generate a common denominator with Continental legal systems. Similarly, in the field of criminal law, Canada, the United Kingdom, and Australia all support the International Criminal Court. The United States does not. It is clear that in many significant areas of law the United States has departed from the basic assumptions shared by other common law countries.

Many of the distinctive features of American law are attributable to its constitutional history—dating back to the Declaration of Independence in 1776 and the Constitution Convention in 1787. The country was founded in a (relatively) unified revolt against the English monarchy.

The war against the British in 1775–1783 was not only a war of independence against a colonial power but also a revolution against the principle of monarchial rule. Yet there was no intent to break with the English legal tradition. For some purposes, the revolt was well within the English traditions of common law resistance to monarchical concentrations of power and of popular, armed resistance to the king, traditions manifest from Wat Tyler's Peasant Revolt in 1381 to the English Civil War and to the Wilkesite riots of the eighteenth century. For other purposes it was an internal revolution establishing a new form of government, enshrining in it a project of the enlightenment that incorporated the rule of law and a new, democratic ideal.

If you are in New York and you want to get a feel for the war, go up to Washington Heights in northern Manhattan to a little park called Fort Washington at the corner of Fort Washington and 181st Street. There you find a plaque indicating that the American army valiantly defended the area against British troops in November 1776, but the Heights soon fell to British military occupation. The American army

did not return until 1783. These battles occurred within a few miles of
the present campus of Columbia University. The bulk of Americans today have lost a direct knowledge of such battles, yet our general sense
of identity as Americans is still broadly rooted in a notion of a nation
peopled with individuals who left undemocratic states to forge in conflict an exceptional state, based on the respect of rights and equality.

The belief in an American "exceptionalism," including a willingness to go to war with their mother country for their rights and equality within their nation, distinguishes Americans from their Canadian
neighbors, who only won independence and the "repatriation" of their
constitution after two hundred years of participating in the Commonwealth. The basic spirit of American law, therefore, reflects a desire to
guard its independence and to cultivate its own constitutional principles. Though the American commitment to international organizations
waxes and wanes, today the attitude seems to be one of suspicion toward restraints on national freedom of action. This is evident in the
suspicious attitude toward the International Criminal Court and the debates of early 2003 about going to war in Iraq.

The Constitution came into force in 1788 after ratification by nine
of the thirteen states. This date marks a point of America's departure
from full membership in the family of common law legal systems.
Though American lawyers studied Blackstone as their Bible, they came
under the influence of new constitutional ideas centering on three principles: freedom (not equality), the voluntary association of states and
citizens (not organic nationhood), and republican self-government (not
popular democracy).[1]

The particular doctrines of the 1787 Constitution, as it has been interpreted by the Courts, intensify the gap between American and European legal thought. Americans are committed to certain applications of
their basic postulates; the rest of world—including Canada—finds these
doctrines puzzling. Among these doctrines are a very strong commitment to freedom of speech and the press, the entrenchment of jury trials in both criminal and civil cases, and an ongoing recognition that a
unified country consists of fifty separate states, each with its own au-

---

[1] For further exploration of these foundational ideas and how they were transformed after
the Civil War (1861–1865), see George P. Fletcher, *Our Secret Constitution: How Lincoln
Redefined American Democracy* (New York: Oxford University Press, 2001).

tonomy and legal competence, and in some of which there is a judicial tolerance for the death penalty. It is not surprising that these doctrines would be difficult for civilian and other common lawyers to understand and endorse. The purpose of these chapters is to make some of these basic ideas comprehensible to Americans beginning their study of law as well as to lawyers trained in jurisdictions that do not share the same premises.

At the same time, at the level of legal method, the study of American constitutional law provides a bridge to legal traditions based on codification. The claim is that the United States Constitution is a code in much the same sense that the French *Code civil* and the German Civil Code (BGB) are foundational codes in their respective legal cultures. To draw this parallel is to emphasize a number of significant features about these European codes and the Constitution. Here are some characteristics in common:

1. *All three documents take their language very seriously.* Lawyers learn the wording by heart. The wording acquires an almost liturgical quality. The provisions are recited as a way of invoking the "rule of law." Recall that the novelist Stendhal read the French code each night before retiring. Americans are so committed to the language of their "constitutional code" that they reprint the language even after it is repealed. (See the infamous "three-fifths" provision below in Article I, Section 2, Clause 3, which still appears in every currently published text of the Constitution.)

2. *The reverence for the document as a whole leads to the interpretation of each provision in the context of the entire document.* The provisions are constantly compared with each other in order to discuss the internal structure of values and ideas that bind the discrete provisions together. You can read an ordinary statutory provision as a self-standing rule, but this is not true in a code. Think of houses and neighborhoods. You can look at each house standing alone, or you look at each in the context of all the other houses in the area. To understand a code, you have to appreciate each house as an expression of its neighborhood. This sense of the organic whole shapes the reading of the civil codes of Europe as well as the Constitution.

3. *The historical significance of the Constitution resembles that of the* Code civil *or the BGB.* The latter are symbols of national unity. They have survived numerous constitutional regimes, dictatorships, democ-

racy, fascism, and then democracy again. Every regime tries to leave its mark on the civil code, but the code somehow shakes off these political influences and lives on at the center of the legal culture. The same is true of the U.S. Constitution. The Constitution was born in slavery, survived a civil war, and experienced precedents that many factions despised, but it has continued to live at the center of the American legal culture.

Think of the Constitution, therefore, as the American national code. It is the most important document for understanding the spirit of American law.

FIVE

The Constitution as Code

The words of the Constitution are treated as nearly sacred. Read this abridged version very carefully, and then answer the questions posed at the end of the chapter.

United States Constitution

(drafted in Philadelphia in 1787; ratified by nine states in 1788; effective 1789)

Preamble

We the people of the United States, in order to form a more perfect Union, establish justice, insure domestic Tranquility, provide for the common defense, promote the general Welfare, and secure the Blessings of Liberty to ourselves and our Posterity, do ordain and establish this Constitution for the United States of America.

Article I. The Legislative Power

ARTICLE I, SECTION I. Legislative powers vested in Congress.

All legislative Powers herein granted shall be vested in a Congress of the United States, which shall consist of a Senate and House of Representatives.

ARTICLE I, SECTION 2, CLAUSE I.
House of Representatives: Composition, Electors.

The House of Representatives shall be composed of Members chosen every second Year by the People of the several States, and the Electors in each State shall have the Qualifications requisite for Electors of the most numerous Branch of the State Legislature.

ARTICLE I, SECTION 2, CLAUSE 2.
Qualifications of Representatives.

No person shall be a Representative who shall not have attained to the Age of twenty five Years, and been seven Years a Citizen of the United States, and who shall not, when elected, be an Inhabitant of that State in which he shall be chosen.

ARTICLE I, SECTION 2, CLAUSE 3.
Apportionment of Representatives and direct taxes.

[Representatives and direct Taxes shall be apportioned among the several States which may be included within this Union, according to their respective Numbers, which shall be determined by adding to the whole Number of free Persons, including those bound to Service for a Term of Years, and excluding Indians not taxed, three-fifths of all other Persons.] The actual Enumeration shall be made within three Years after the first Meeting of the Congress of the United States, and within every subsequent Term of ten Years in such Manner as they shall by Law direct. The Number of Representatives shall not exceed one for every thirty Thousand, but each State shall have at Least one Representative; and until such enumeration shall be made, the State of New Hampshire shall be entitled to chuse three, Massachusetts eight, Rhode Island and Providence Plantations one, Connecticut five, New York six, New Jersey four, Pennsylvania eight, Delaware one, Maryland six, Virginia ten, North Carolina five, South Carolina five, and Georgia three.

ARTICLE I, SECTION 2, CLAUSE 4. Vacancies.

When vacancies happen in the Representation from any State, the Executive Authority thereof shall issue Writs of Election to fill such Vacancies.

ARTICLE I, SECTION 2, CLAUSE 5. Officers and impeachment.

The House of Representatives shall chuse their Speaker and other Officers; and shall have the sole Power of Impeachment.

ARTICLE I, SECTION 3, CLAUSE 1. Senate–Composition.

The Senate of the United States shall be composed of two Senators from each State, [chosen by the Legislature thereof,][1] for six Years; and each Senator shall have one Vote.

ARTICLE I, SECTION 3, CLAUSE 2. Classification of Senators.

Immediately after they shall be assembled in Consequence of the first Election, they shall be divided as equally as may be into three Classes. The Seats of the Senators of the first Class shall be vacated at the Expiration of the second Year, of the second Class at the Expiration of the fourth Year, and of the third Class at the Expiration of the sixth Year, so that one third may be chosen every second Year; [and if Vacancies happen by Resignation, or otherwise, during the Recess of the Legislature of any State, the Executive thereof may make temporary Appointments until the next Meeting of the Legislature, which shall then fill such Vacancies].

ARTICLE I, SECTION 3, CLAUSE 3. Qualifications of Senators.

No person shall be a Senator who shall not have attained to the Age of thirty years, and been nine Years a Citizen of the United States, and who shall not, when elected, be an Inhabitant of that State for which he shall be chosen.

ARTICLE I, SECTION 3, CLAUSE 4. President of the Senate.

The Vice President of the United States shall be President of the Senate, but shall have no Vote, unless they be equally divided.

---

[1] Bracketed text void under the Seventeenth Amendment (1913).

ARTICLE I, SECTION 3, CLAUSE 5. Officers of the Senate.

The Senate shall chuse their other Officers, and also a President pro tempore, in the Absence of the Vice President, or when he shall exercise the Office of President of the United States.

ARTICLE I, SECTION 3, CLAUSE 6. Trial of impeachments.

The Senate shall have the sole Power to try all Impeachments. When sitting for that Purpose, they shall be on Oath or Affirmation. When the President of the United States is tried, the Chief Justice shall preside: and no Person shall be convicted without the Concurrence of two thirds of the Members present.

ARTICLE I, SECTION 3, CLAUSE 7.
Judgment in cases of impeachment.

Judgment in Cases of Impeachment shall not extend further than to removal from Office, and disqualification to hold and enjoy any Office of honor, Trust or Profit under the United States: but the Party convicted shall nevertheless be liable and subject to Indictment, Trial, Judgment and Punishment, according to Law.

ARTICLE I, SECTION 4, CLAUSE 1. Elections.

The Times, Places and Manner of holding Elections for Senators and Representatives, shall be prescribed in each State by the Legislature thereof; but the Congress may at any time by Law make or alter such Regulations, except as to the Places of chusing Senators.

ARTICLE I, SECTION 4, CLAUSE 2. Meetings.

The Congress shall assemble at least once in every Year, and such Meeting shall be on the [first Monday in December], unless they shall by Law appoint a different Day.

ARTICLE I, SECTION 5, CLAUSE 1. Organization of Congress.

Each House shall be the Judge of the Elections, Returns and Qualifications of its own Members, and a Majority of each shall constitute a Quorum to do Business; but a smaller Number may adjourn from day to day, and may be authorized to compel the Attendance of absent Members, in such Manner, and under such Penalties as each House may provide.

ARTICLE I, SECTION 5, CLAUSE 2.
Rules of proceedings: Punishment of members.

Each House may determine the Rules of its Proceedings, punish its Members for disorderly Behavior, and, with the Concurrence of two thirds, expel a Member.

ARTICLE I, SECTION 5, CLAUSE 3. Journal of proceedings.

Each House shall keep a Journal of its Proceedings, and from time to time publish the same, excepting such Parts as may in their Judgment require Secrecy; and the Yeas and Nays of the Members of either House on any question shall, at the Desire of one fifth of those present, be entered on the Journal.

ARTICLE I, SECTION 5, CLAUSE 4. Adjournment.

Neither House, during the Session of Congress, shall, without the Consent of the other, adjourn for more than three days, nor to any other Place than that in which the two Houses shall be sitting.

ARTICLE I, SECTION 6, CLAUSE 1.
Compensation and privileges of members.

The Senators and Representatives shall receive a Compensation for their Services, to be ascertained by Law, and paid out of the Treasury of the United States. They shall in all Cases, except Treason, Felony and Breach of the Peace, be privileged from Arrest during their Attendance at the Session of their Respective Houses, and in going to and from the same; and for any Speech or Debate in either House, they shall not be questioned in any other Place.

ARTICLE I, SECTION 6, CLAUSE 2. Holding other offices.

No Senator or Representative shall, during the Time for which he was elected, be appointed to any civil Office under the Authority of the United States, which shall have been created, or the Emoluments whereof shall have been encreased during such time; and no Person holding any Office under the United States, shall be a Member of either House during his Continuance in Office.

ARTICLE I, SECTION 7, CLAUSE 1.
Bills and Resolutions: Revenue bills.

All Bills for raising Revenue shall originate in the House of Representatives; but the Senate may propose or concur with Amendments as on other Bills.

ARTICLE I, SECTION 7, CLAUSE 2.
Approval or veto of bills: Passage over veto.

Every Bill which shall have passed the House of Representatives and the Senate, shall, before it become a Law, be presented to the President of the United States; If he approve he shall sign it, but if not he shall return it, with his Objections to that House in which it shall have originated, who shall enter the Objections at large on their Journal, and proceed to reconsider it. If after such Reconsideration two thirds of that House shall agree to pass the Bill, it shall be sent, together with the Objections, to the other House, by which it shall likewise be reconsidered, and if approved by two thirds of that House, it shall become a Law. But in all such Cases the Votes of both Houses shall be determined by yeas and Nays, and the Names of the Persons voting for and against the Bill shall be entered on the Journal of each House respectively.

If any Bill shall not be returned by the President within ten Days (Sundays excepted) after it shall have been presented to him, the Same shall be a Law, in like Manner as if he had signed it, unless the Congress by their Adjournment prevent its Return, in which Case it shall not be a Law.

ARTICLE I, SECTION 7, CLAUSE 3.
Approval or veto of Resolutions, orders, or votes—Passage over veto.

Every Order, Resolution, or Vote to which the Concurrence of the Senate and House of Representatives may be necessary (except on a question of adjournment) shall be presented to the President of the United States; and before the Same shall take Effect, shall be approved by him, or being disapproved by him, shall be repassed by two thirds of the Senate and House of Representatives, according to the Rules and Limitations prescribed in the Case of a Bill.

ARTICLE I, SECTION 8, CLAUSE 1.
Powers of Congress: Taxation.

The Congress shall have Power To lay and collect Taxes, Duties, Imposts and Excises, to pay the Debts and provide for the Common Defence and general Welfare of the United States; but all Duties, Imposts and Excises shall be uniform throughout the United States.

ARTICLE I, SECTION 8, CLAUSE 2.
Power of Congress to borrow money.

To borrow money on the credit of the United States.

ARTICLE I, SECTION 8, CLAUSE 3.
Power of Congress to regulate commerce.

To regulate commerce with foreign nations, and among the several States, and with the Indian tribes.

ARTICLE I, SECTION 8, CLAUSE 4. Naturalization: Bankruptcy.

To establish an uniform Rule of Naturalization, and uniform Laws on the subject of Bankruptcies throughout the United States.

ARTICLE I, SECTION 8, CLAUSE 5.
Coinage, weights and measures.

To coin Money, regulate the Value thereof, and of foreign Coin, and fix the Standard of Weights and Measures.

ARTICLE I, SECTION 8, CLAUSE 6. Counterfeiting.

To provide for the Punishment of counterfeiting the Securities and current Coin of the United States.

ARTICLE I, SECTION 8, CLAUSE 7. Post offices and post roads.

To establish Post Offices and post Roads.

ARTICLE I, SECTION 8, CLAUSE 8. Patents and copyrights.

To promote the Progress of Science and useful Arts, by securing for limited Times to Authors and Inventors the exclusive Right to their respective Writings and Discoveries.

ARTICLE I, SECTION 8, CLAUSE 9. Inferior tribunals.

To constitute tribunals inferior to the supreme Court.

ARTICLE I, SECTION 8, CLAUSE 10. Offenses.

To define and punish Piracies and Felonies committed on the High Seas, and Offenses against the Law of Nations.

ARTICLE I, SECTION 8, CLAUSE 11. Declare War.

To declare War, grant Letters of Marque and Reprisal, and make Rules concerning Captures on Land and Water.

ARTICLE I, SECTION 8, CLAUSE 12. Raise and support armies.

To raise and support Armies, but no Appropriation of Money to that Use shall be for a longer Term than two Years.

ARTICLE I, SECTION 8, CLAUSE 13. Navy.

To provide and maintain a Navy.

ARTICLE I, SECTION 8, CLAUSE 14.
Government and regulation of land and naval forces.

To make Rules for the Government and Regulation of the land and naval Forces.

ARTICLE I, SECTION 8, CLAUSE 15. Calling forth militia.

To provide for calling forth the Militia to execute the Laws of the Union, suppress Insurrections and repel Invasions.

ARTICLE I, SECTION 8, CLAUSE 16. Organizing militia.

To provide for organizing, arming, and disciplining, the Militia, and for governing such Part of them as may be employed in the Service of the United States, reserving to the States respectively, the Appointment of the Officers, and the Authority of training the Militia according to the discipline prescribed by Congress.

ARTICLE I, SECTION 8, CLAUSE 17.
Authority over places purchased or ceded.

To exercise exclusive Legislation in all Cases whatsoever, over such District (not exceeding ten Miles square) as may, by Cession of particular States, and the Acceptance of Congress, become the Seat of the Government of the United States, and to exercise like Authority over all Places purchased by the Consent of the Legislature of the State in which the Same shall be, for the Erection of Forts, Magazines, Arsenals, dock-Yards, and other needful Buildings.

ARTICLE I, SECTION 8, CLAUSE 18.
All necessary and proper laws.

To make all Laws which shall be necessary and proper for carrying into Execution the foregoing Powers, and all other Powers vested by this Constitution in the Government of the United States, or in any Department or Officer thereof.

ARTICLE I, SECTION 9, CLAUSE 1.
Prohibited powers: Migration or importation of persons.

The Migration or Importation of such Persons as any of the States now existing shall think proper to admit, shall not be prohibited by the Congress prior to the Year one thousand eight hundred and eight, but a Tax or duty may be imposed on such Importation, not exceeding ten dollars for each Person.

ARTICLE I, SECTION 9, CLAUSE 2. Habeas corpus.

The privilege of the writ of habeas corpus shall not be suspended, unless when in cases of rebellion or invasion the public safety may require it.

ARTICLE I, SECTION 9, CLAUSE 3.
Bill of attainder, Ex post facto laws.

No Bill of Attainder or ex post facto Law shall be passed.

ARTICLE I, SECTION 9, CLAUSE 4. Capitation or direct taxes.

No Capitation, or other direct, Tax shall be laid, unless in Proportion to the Census or Enumeration herein before directed to be taken.

ARTICLE I, SECTION 9, CLAUSE 5. Tax on exports from state.

No Tax or Duty shall be laid on Articles exported from any State.

ARTICLE I, SECTION 9, CLAUSE 6. Preference of ports.

No Preference shall be given by any Regulation of Commerce or Revenue to the Ports of one State over those of another: nor shall Vessels bound to, or from, one State, be obliged to enter, clear, or pay Duties in another.

ARTICLE I, SECTION 9, CLAUSE 7.
Expenditures of public money.

No Money shall be drawn from the Treasury, but in Consequence of Appropriations made by Law; and a regular Statement and Account of the Receipts and Expenditures of all public Money shall be published from time to time.

ARTICLE I, SECTION 9, CLAUSE 8.
Titles of nobility, Presents from foreign state.

No Title of Nobility shall be granted by the United States: and no Person holding any Office of Profit or Trust under them, shall, without the Consent of the Congress, accept of any present, emolument, Office, or Title of any kind whatever from any King, Prince, or foreign State.

ARTICLE I, SECTION 10, CLAUSE 1.
Powers denied states: Treaties, Money, Ex post facto laws,
Obligation of contracts.

No State shall enter into any treaty, alliance, or confederation; grant letters of marque and reprisal; coin money; emit bills of credit; make anything but gold and silver coin a tender in payment of debts; pass any bill of attainder, ex post facto law, or law impairing the obligation of contracts, or grant any title of nobility.

ARTICLE I, SECTION 10, CLAUSE 2. Imposts or duties.

No State shall, without the Consent of the Congress, lay any Imposts or Duties on Imports or Exports, except what may be absolutely necessary for executing its inspection Laws: and the net Produce of all Duties and Imposts, laid by any State on Imports or Exports, shall be for the Use of the Treasury of the United States; and all such Laws shall be subject to the Revision and Control of the Congress.

ARTICLE I, SECTION 10, CLAUSE 3.
Tonnage, State compacts, War.

No State shall, without the Consent of Congress, lay any Duty of Tonnage, keep Troops, or Ships of War in time of Peace, enter into any Agreement or Compact with another State, or with a foreign Power, or engage in War, unless actually invaded, or in such imminent Danger as will not admit of delay.

Article II. The Executive Power

ARTICLE II, SECTION 1, CLAUSE 1. President: Tenure.

The executive Power shall be vested in a President of the United States of America. He shall hold his Office during the Term of four Years, and, together with the Vice President, chosen for the same Term, be elected, as follows:

ARTICLE II, SECTION 1, CLAUSE 2. Presidential electors.

Each State shall appoint, in such Manner as the Legislature thereof may direct, a Number of Electors, equal to the whole Number of Senators and Representatives to which the State may be entitled in the Congress: but no Senator or Representative, or Person holding an Office of Trust or Profit under the United States, shall be appointed an Elector.

ARTICLE II, SECTION 1, CLAUSE 3. Election day.

The Congress may determine the Time of chusing the Electors, and the Day on which they shall give their Votes; which Day shall be the same throughout the United States.

ARTICLE II, SECTION 1, CLAUSE 4.
Eligibility for office of president.

No Person except a natural born Citizen, or a Citizen of the United States, at the time of the Adoption of this Constitution, shall be eligible to the Office of President; neither shall any Person be eligible to that Office who shall not have attained to the Age of thirty five Years, and been fourteen Years a Resident within the United States.

ARTICLE II, SECTION I, CLAUSE 5.
Succession to office of president.

In Case of the Removal of the President from Office, or of his Death, Resignation, or Inability to discharge the Powers and Duties of the said Office, the Same shall devolve on the Vice President, and the Congress may by Law provide for the Case of Removal, Death, Resignation, or Inability, both of the President and Vice President, declaring what Officer shall then act as President, and such Officer shall act accordingly, until the Disability be removed, or a President shall be elected.

ARTICLE II, SECTION I, CLAUSE 6. Compensation of president.

The President shall, at stated Times, receive for his Services, a Compensation, which shall neither be increased nor diminished during the Period for which he shall have been elected, and he shall not receive within that Period any other Emolument from the United States, or any of them.

ARTICLE II, SECTION I, CLAUSE 7. Oath of office.

Before he enter on the Execution of His Office, he shall take the following Oath or Affirmation: "I do solemnly swear (or affirm) that I will faithfully execute the Office of President of the United States, and will to the best of my Ability, preserve, protect and defend the Constitution of the United States."

ARTICLE II, SECTION 2, CLAUSE I.
Commander in Chief, Opinions of department heads, Reprieves and pardons.

The President shall be Commander in Chief of the Army and Navy of the United States, and of the Militia of the several States, when called into the actual Service of the United States; he may require the Opinion, in writing, of the principal Officer in each of the executive Departments, upon any Subject relating to the Duties of their respective Offices, and he shall have Power to grant Reprieves and Pardons for Offenses against the United States, except in Cases of Impeachment.

ARTICLE II, SECTION 2, CLAUSE 2.

Treaties, Appointment of officers.

He shall have Power, by and with the Advice and Consent of the Senate, to make Treaties, provided two thirds of the Senators present concur; and he shall nominate, and by and with the Advice and Consent of the Senate, shall appoint Ambassadors, other public Ministers and Consuls, Judges of the Supreme Court, and all other Officers of the United States, whose Appointments are not herein otherwise provided for, and which shall be established by Law: but the Congress may by Law vest the Appointment of such inferior Officers, as they think proper, in the President alone, in the Courts of Law, or in the Heads of Departments.

ARTICLE II, SECTION 2, CLAUSE 3.

Appointments during recess of Senate.

The President shall have Power to fill up all Vacancies that may happen during the Recess of the Senate, by granting Commissions which shall expire at the End of their next Session.

ARTICLE II, SECTION 3.

Recommendations to Congress—Convene and adjourn Congress—Receive ambassadors—Execute laws—Commission officers.

He shall from time to time give to the Congress Information of the State of the Union, and recommend to their Consideration such Measures as he shall judge necessary and expedient; he may, on extraordinary Occasions, convene both Houses, or either of them, and in Case of Disagreement between them, with Respect to the Time of Adjournment, he may adjourn them to such Time as he shall think proper; he shall receive Ambassadors and other public Ministers; he shall take Care that the Laws be faithfully executed, and shall Commission all the Officers of the United States.

ARTICLE II, SECTION 4. Removal from office.

The President, Vice President and all civil Officers of the United States, shall be removed from Office on Impeachment for, and Conviction of, Treason, Bribery, or other high Crimes and Misdemeanors.

Article III. The Judicial Power

ARTICLE III, SECTION 1.

Supreme Court and inferior courts: Judges and compensation.

The judicial Power of the United States, shall be vested in one supreme Court, and in such inferior Courts as the Congress may from time to time ordain and establish. The Judges, both of the supreme and inferior Courts, shall hold their Offices during good Behavior, and shall, at stated Times, receive for their Services, a Compensation, which shall not be diminished during their Continuance in Office.

ARTICLE III, SECTION 2, CLAUSE 1. Subjects of jurisdiction.

The judicial Power shall extend to all Cases, in Law and Equity, arising under this Constitution, the Laws of the United States, and Treaties made, or which shall be made, under their Authority,—to all Cases affecting Ambassadors, other public Ministers and Consuls;—to all Cases of admiralty and maritime Jurisdiction;—to Controversies to which the United States shall be a Party;—to Controversies between two or more States;—between a State and Citizens of another State;—between citizens of different States,—between citizens of the same State claiming Lands under Grants of different States, and between a State, or the Citizens thereof, and foreign States, Citizens or Subjects.

ARTICLE III, SECTION 2, CLAUSE 2.

Jurisdiction of Supreme Court.

In all Cases affecting Ambassadors, other public Ministers and Consuls, and those in which a State shall be Party, the supreme Court shall have original Jurisdiction. In all the other Cases before mentioned, the supreme Court shall have appellate Jurisdiction, both as to Law and Fact, with such Exceptions, and under such Regulations as the Congress shall make.

ARTICLE III, SECTION 2, CLAUSE 3. Trial by jury.

The Trial of all Crimes, except in Cases of Impeachment, shall be by Jury; and such Trial shall be held in the State where the said Crimes shall have been committed; but when not committed within any State, the Trial shall be at such Place or Places as the Congress may by Law have directed.

ARTICLE III, SECTION 3, CLAUSE 1. Treason.

Treason against the United States, shall consist only in levying War against them, or in adhering to their Enemies, giving them Aid and Comfort. No Person shall be convicted of Treason unless on the Testimony of two Witnesses to the same overt Act, or on Confession in open Court.

ARTICLE III, SECTION 3, CLAUSE 2. Punishment of Treason.

The Congress shall have Power to declare the Punishment of Treason, but no Attainder of Treason shall work Corruption of Blood, or Forfeiture except during the Life of the Person attainted.

Article IV. Guarantees to States.

ARTICLE IV, SECTION 1. Full Faith and Credit.

Full Faith and Credit shall be given in each State to the public Acts, Records, and judicial Proceedings of every other State. And the Congress may by general Laws prescribe the Manner in which such Acts, Records and Proceedings shall be proved, and the Effect thereof.

ARTICLE IV, SECTION 2, CLAUSE 1.
Privileges and immunities of citizens.

The Citizens of each State shall be entitled to all Privileges and Immunities of Citizens in the several States.

ARTICLE IV, SECTION 2, CLAUSE 2. Delivery of fugitives.

A Person charged in any State with Treason, Felony, or other Crime, who shall flee from Justice, and be found in another State, shall on Demand of the executive Authority of the State from which he fled, be delivered up to be removed to the State having Jurisdiction of the Crime.

ARTICLE IV, SECTION 2, CLAUSE 3. Runaway slaves.

[No Person held to Service or Labour in one State, under the Laws thereof, escaping into another, shall, in Consequence of any Law or Regulation therein, be discharged from such Service or Labour, but shall be delivered upon Claim of the Party to whom such Service or Labour may be due.][2]

ARTICLE IV, SECTION 3, CLAUSE 1. Admission of new states.

New States may be admitted by the Congress into this Union; but no new State shall be formed or erected within the Jurisdiction of any other State; nor any State be formed by the Junction of two or more States, or Parts of States, without the Consent of the Legislatures of the States concerned as well as of the Congress.

ARTICLE IV, SECTION 3, CLAUSE 2.
Territory or property of United States.

The Congress shall have Power to dispose of and make all needful Rules and Regulations respecting the Territory or other Property belonging to the United States; and nothing in this Constitution shall be so construed as to Prejudice any Claims of the United States, or of any particular State.

ARTICLE IV, SECTION 4. Form of State governments: Protection.

The United States shall guarantee to every State in this Union a Republican Form of Government, and shall protect each of them against Invasion; and on Application of the Legislature, or of the Executive (when the Legislature cannot be convened) against domestic Violence.

Article V. Amendment.

The Congress, whenever two thirds of both Houses shall deem it necessary, shall propose Amendments to this Constitution, or, on the Application of the Legislatures of two thirds of the several States, shall call a Convention for proposing Amendments, which, in either Case, shall be valid to all Intents and Purposes, as Part of this Constitution, when ratified by the Legislatures of three fourths of the several States, or by Convention in three fourths thereof, as the one or the other Mode of Ratification may be proposed by the Congress; Provided that no Amendment which may be made prior to the Year One thousand eight hundred and eight shall in any Manner affect the first and fourth Clauses

---

[2] Bracketed text void under the Thirteenth Amendment (1865).

in the Ninth Section of the first Article; and that no State, without its Consent, shall be deprived of its equal Suffrage in the Senate.

Article VI. Miscellaneous Provisions.

CLAUSE 1. Prior debts valid under Constitution.

All Debts contracted and Engagements entered into, before the Adoption of this Constitution, shall be as valid against the United States under this Constitution, as under the Confederation.

CLAUSE 2. Supreme law.

This Constitution, and the Laws of the United States which shall be made in Pursuance thereof; and all Treaties made, or which shall be made, under the Authority of the United States, shall be the supreme Law of the Land; and the Judges in every State shall be bound thereby, any Thing in the Constitution or Laws of any State to the Contrary notwithstanding.

CLAUSE 3. Oath of office.

The Senators and Representatives before mentioned, and the Members of the several State Legislatures, and all executive and judicial Officers, both of the United States and of the several States, shall be bound by Oath or Affirmation, to support this Constitution; but no religious Test shall ever be required as a Qualification to any Office or public Trust under the United States.

Article VII. Ratification

The Ratification of the Conventions of nine States, shall be sufficient for the Establishment of this Constitution between the States so ratifying the Same.

Bill of Rights [ratified as the first ten amendments to the Constitution in 1791]

First Amendment

Congress shall make no law respecting an establishment of religion, or prohibiting the free exercise thereof; or abridging the freedom of speech, or of the press; or the right of the people peaceably to assemble, and to petition the Government for a redress of grievances.

Second Amendment

A well regulated Militia, being necessary to the security of a free State, the right of the people to keep and bear Arms, shall not be infringed.

Third Amendment

No Soldier shall, in time of peace be quartered in any house, without the consent of the Owner, nor in time of war, but in a manner to be prescribed by law.

Fourth Amendment

The right of the people to be secure in their persons, houses, papers, and effects, against unreasonable searches and seizures, shall not be violated, and no Warrants shall issue, but upon probable cause, supported by Oath or affirmation, and particularly describing the place to be searched, and the persons or things to be seized.

Fifth Amendment

No person shall be held to answer for a capital, or otherwise infamous crime, unless on a presentment or indictment of a Grand Jury, except in cases arising in the land or naval forces, or in the Militia, when in actual service in time of War or public danger; nor shall any person be subject for the same offence to be twice put in jeopardy of life or limb; nor shall be compelled in any criminal case to be a witness against himself, nor be deprived of life, liberty, or property, without due process of law; nor shall private property be taken for public use, without just compensation.

Sixth Amendment

In all criminal prosecutions, the accused shall enjoy the right to a speedy and public trial, by an impartial jury of the State and district wherein the crime shall have been committed, which district shall have been previously ascertained by law, and to be informed of the nature and cause of the accusation; to be confronted with the witnesses against him; to have compulsory process for obtaining witnesses in his favor, and to have the Assistance of Counsel for his defense.

Seventh Amendment

In Suits at common law, where the value in controversy shall exceed twenty dollars, the right of trial by jury shall be preserved, and no fact tried by a jury shall be otherwise re-examined in any Court of the United States, than according to the rules of the common law.

Eighth Amendment

Excessive bail shall not be required, nor excessive fines imposed, nor cruel and unusual punishments inflicted.

Ninth Amendment

The enumeration in the Constitution, of certain rights, shall not be construed to deny or disparage others retained by the people.

Tenth Amendment

The powers not delegated to the United States by the Constitution, nor prohibited by it to the States, are reserved to the States respectively, or to the people.

QUESTIONS AND COMMENTS

1. Does the Constitution reveal a sense of history prior to its enactment? Does it refer to the Articles of Confederation that preceded it as the constitution of the colonies united in rebellion and of the early republic? Does it refer to God or any higher power? To force of arms? What is the ultimate source of legitimacy of the Constitution? Why should we take it seriously? Why should the president, Congress, federal judges, or state officials take it seriously?
2. The German Basic Law (constitution) begins by claiming that it binds *alle staatliche Gewalt* ("all state power"). Does this document bind all state power in the United States? Whom or what does it bind? When the Constitution refers to the United States, what does it mean? Who can "obey" a constitution?
3. How many branches of government are there? What are they called? How is the Supreme Court different from a constitutional court on the European continent? What does the word *case* mean in Art. III, Section 2, Clause 1? How is it different from *controversy* in the next clause?
4. Suppose that Congress enacted a dress code for schools on the

ground that a dress code for children would promote the general welfare of the United States. Would the national dress code be constitutional under Article I?

5. Does the president of the United States have any duties? What can't the president do?

6. How could the president go to war in Iraq without a declaration of war by Congress? Would it have been possible for the president to commit American troops without any authorization by Congress?

7. Does either the Congress or the president have the capacity either to establish or to abolish the Supreme Court? Or determine its jurisdiction? How about the lower federal courts? The state courts? How are the state courts established?

8. What is the supreme law of the United States? Does the Constitution make the decisions of the Supreme Court binding on the state courts? Can a treaty violate the Constitution?

9. Which provisions reveal the historical context of this document? Is there a provision on equality? Why not? Is there anything that works toward the equality of all citizens?

10. Is there a "right" of free speech in the Bill of Rights? Does everyone have the right to publish in the *New York Times*? If this is not a right, what is it?

11. Notice that there are two provisions on religion, the "free exercise" clause and the "establishment" clause. Are these two consistent? If a group is given the right not to work on governmental jobs on Friday because Friday is their Sabbath, would that recognition of a special privilege be an "establishment" of religion?

12. Some people have argued that the principle of privacy is implicit in several provisions in the Bill of Rights. Where in the text can you locate such a principle? Is it mentioned by name anywhere?

13. Notice that there are two clauses in the Fourth Amendment: the warrant clause and the "reasonableness" clause. What is the relevance of the warrant requirement if the question always is whether the search is reasonable under the circumstances?

14. Can you find any language in the Constitution that grants the Supreme Court the power to declare an act of Congress unconstitutional? Is it easier to justify using the text to support a decision declaring an act by a state legislature unconstitutional?

Note on Later Amendments

The Constitution has been amended sixteen times since 1791. The Eleventh Amendment (ratified in 1798) barred most lawsuits against the states from federal courts. The Twelfth (1804) redefined the procedure for electing the president. The Thirteenth (1865) abolished slavery. The Fourteenth (1868), quoted in part on page 180, established a national definition for citizenship and federal guarantees of due process of law and equal protection of the laws. It also repealed the infamous three-fifths clause, reduced congressional representation from any state that abridged rights to vote, barred most former Confederates from political office, and denied federal liability for Confederate debts. The Fifteenth (1870) forbade denying or abridging the right to vote "on account of race, color, or previous condition of servitude." The Sixteenth (1913) enabled a national personal income tax. The Seventeenth (also 1913) established the direct popular election of U.S. senators. The Eighteenth (1919) banned "intoxicating liquors" but was repealed by the Twenty-first (1933). The Nineteenth (1920) ended discrimination against women in voting. The Twentieth (1933) advanced the inauguration of the president, vice president, and members of Congress from March to January and authorized Congress to determine the order of presidential succession. The Twenty-second (1951) limits presidents to no more than two terms of four years. The Twenty-third (1961) extended the franchise in presidential elections to the District of Columbia. The Twenty-fourth (1964) outlawed the poll tax, which had been used to bar the poor and nonwhites from voting. The Twenty-fifth (1967) clarifies the succession in the event of death or incapacity of the president. The Twenty-sixth (1971) forbids discrimination in voting on the basis of age for persons over the age of eighteen. The Twenty-seventh Amendment, proposed in 1789 but not ratified until 1992, prevents Congress from raising its members' salary to take effect before another congressional election.

Further Reading

There are any number of books on the framing of the Constitution. Recent books of particular interest include an encyclopedia of constitutional sources and Jack Rakove's careful study of the original intent: *The Founders' Constitution* (Philip Kurland et al. eds.) (Chicago: University of Chicago and Indianapolis: Liberty Fund, 2000); Jack M. Rakove, *Original Meanings: Politics and Ideas in the Making of the Constitution* (New York: Knopf, 1997). A fascinating study of Americans' reverence for the Constitution is in Sanford Levinson, *Constitutional Faith* (Princeton, NJ: Princeton University Press, 1988).

SIX

Judicial Review

In the early nineteenth century, no facet of U.S. law distinguished American law more from civilian legal systems—indeed, from many common law systems—than did the institution of judicial review, the idea that courts have the authority to review the acts of legislatures or officials and to declare void statutes and orders that conflict with the Constitution. Our sense of this institution is rooted in the famous case of *Marbury v. Madison*, and therefore we shall refer to it as judicial review in the *Marbury* sense or judicial review over legislation. The same power of review is held by the various state courts, which measure state laws and official actions under both the federal and state constitutions. Judicial review over legislation is distinct from the power of courts to review and overrule administrative decisions. This is also called "judicial review" in Great Britain, where the courts are not thought to have the power of judicial review over acts of Parliament.

Since the Second World War, judicial review over legislation has become commonplace in Western democracies. The German *Bundesverfassungsgericht* or Federal Constitutional Court (FCC) was established in 1951 on the American model to test legislation for conformity with the German Basic Law. There are many differences between the *Marbury* and

FCC models, and one of the most salient is whether the court is regarded as a component of the judicial branch of government. Under the American Constitution, the Supreme Court is obviously part of the judiciary. This means that it is a coequal branch of government. If it is, how does it acquire the power to invalidate the solemn acts of another branch of government?

The idea that courts could nullify statutes has its roots in Chief Justice Coke's 1610 opinion in *Dr. Bonham's Case*.[1] That decision tested the enforceability of a statute of Parliament that enabled the London College of Physicians to levy fines and collect them against those who were allegedly violating their rules. The college accused Dr. Bonham of practice without a license and levied a fine on him according to the statute. Coke, however, found that their statutory authority violated "common right or reason." Coke concluded that the statute violated the principle that "no person should be a judge in his own case." While the idea that courts could declare statutes invalid waxed and then waned in seventeenth-century England,[2] the practice was well known in the American colonies and in the bars of young states. The doctrine was specifically enshrined in some state constitutions, and it had been employed in both state courts[3] and federal courts[4] in actions dealing with state statutes. Still, the text of the U.S. Constitution, Article III, to hear all cases "arising under this constitution" does not clearly confer this authority, and the interpretation of Article III to include it was made conclusively in Chief Justice Marshall's monumental 1803 opinion in *Marbury v. Madison* (1 Cranch (5 U.S.) 137 (1803)).

The dispute arose after Thomas Jefferson won the presidency in 1800 and the Federalist Party, which had ruled since the nation's founding, had

---

[1] 8 Co. Rep. 107a. For more on Sir Edward Coke, see Steve Sheppard, *The Selected Writings of Sir Edward Coke* (3 vols.) (Indianapolis: Liberty Fund, 2004).

[2] See John H. Baker, *An Introduction to English Legal History* 208–212 (4th ed.) (London: Butterworth's, 2002).

[3] See *Whittington v. Polk*, 1 H. & J. 236 (Md.Gen. 1802) (Samuel Chase, J.); *State v. Parkhurst*, 9 N.J.L. 427 (N.J. 1802); *Republica v. Duquet Shippen*, 2 Yeates 493 (Pa. 1799); *Williams Lindsay v. East Bay Street Com'rs*, 2 Bay (S.C.L.) 38 (S.C.Const.App. 1796) (Thomas Waties, J.).

[4] See *Ware v. Hylton*, 3 Dallas (3 U.S.) 199 (1796); *Calder v. Bull*, 3 Dallas (3 U.S.) 386 (1798); *Cooper v. Telfair*, 4 Dallas (4 U.S.) 14 (1800); *Vanhorne's Lessee v. Dorrance*, 28 F. Cas. 1012, 2 Dallas (2 U.S.) 304; 1 L. Ed. 391; C. Pa. 1795).

to surrender authority to a new administration. In the last days of the outgoing administration, the lame-duck[5] president John Adams conferred commissions as federal judges of the peace on William Marbury, Dennis Ramsay, Robert Townsend Hooe, and William Harper. James Madison—the same person who was a primary architect of the Constitution in 1787—became secretary of state under Jefferson. Madison refused to deliver the commissions. The would-be judges sued in the U.S. Supreme Court, seeking a writ of mandamus[6] to order James Madison, the new secretary of state, to deliver their commissions. The key feature of this suit is that it was "in the original jurisdiction" of the Supreme Court, that is, not treating the Court as an appellate body but as a trial court. The question is whether Marbury had the right to do that.

This dispute came before the new chief justice, John Marshall, himself a last-minute Adams appointee and, indeed, the former secretary of state who had left the commissions with his clerk for delivery just before Madison assumed office. As you read the following opinion, look carefully for the word *unconstitutional* and the way it comes into play in the argument.

Marbury v. Madison

The Supreme Court of the United States
1 Cranch (5 U.S.) 137 (1803)

MARSHALL, C.J.

At the last term . . . [the Court granted an order or rule] requiring the secretary of state[7] to show cause why a mandamus should not issue, directing him to deliver to William Marbury his commission as a justice of the peace for the county of Washington, in the district of Columbia.

---

[5] This expression is used to refer to an elected official who continues to serve in the period between a democratic election ousting the official and the successor's being sworn into office.

[6] See Blackstone's definition of *mandamus* as "a command issuing in the king's name from the court of king's bench, and directed to any person, corporation, or inferior court of judicature within the king's dominions, requiring them to do some particular thing therein specified which appertains to their office and duty, and which the court of king's bench has previously determined, or at least supposes, to be consonant to right and justice."

[7] James Madison. The secretary of state at the time of the appointment was John Marshall.

[In other words, unless the secretary could prove that it should not, the Court would issue the writ of mandamus.]

. . . [T]he present motion is for a mandamus. The peculiar delicacy of this case, the novelty of some of its circumstances, and the real difficulty attending the points which occur in it, require a complete exposition of the principles on which the opinion to be given by the court is founded.

. . . .

In the order in which the court has viewed this subject, the following questions have been considered and decided.

1. Has the applicant a right to the commission he demands?
2. If he has a right, and that right has been violated, do the laws of his country afford him a remedy?
3. If they do afford him a remedy, is it a mandamus issuing from this court?

The first object of inquiry is,

1. Has the applicant a right to the commission he demands?

His right originates in an act of congress passed in February 1801, concerning the district of Columbia. . . . [I]n compliance with this law, a commission for William Marbury as a justice of peace for the county of Washington was signed by John Adams, then president of the United States; after which the seal of the United States was affixed to it; but the commission has never reached the person for whom it was made out.

In order to determine whether he is entitled to this commission, it becomes necessary to inquire whether he has been appointed to the office. For if he has been appointed, the law continues him in office for five years, and he is entitled to the possession of those evidences of office, which, being completed, became his property.

The second section of the second article of the constitution declares, "the president shall nominate, and, by and with the advice and consent of the senate, shall appoint ambassadors, other public ministers and consuls, and all other officers of the United States, whose appointments are not otherwise provided for."

The third section [of Article II] declares, that "he shall commission all the officers of the United States."

An act of congress directs the secretary of state to keep the seal of the United States, "to make out and record, and affix the said seal to all civil commissions to officers of the United States to be appointed by the president, by and with the consent of the senate, or by the president alone; provided that the said seal shall not be affixed to any commission before the same shall have been signed by the president of the United States."

These are the clauses of the constitution and laws of the United States, which affect this part of the case. They seem to contemplate three distinct operations:

1. The nomination. This is the sole act of the president, and is completely voluntary.
2. The appointment. This is also the act of the president, and is also a voluntary act, though it can only be performed by and with the advice and consent of the senate.
3. The commission. To grant a commission to a person appointed, might perhaps be deemed a duty enjoined by the constitution. "He shall," says that instrument, "commission all the officers of the United States."[8]

The acts of appointing to office, and commissioning the person appointed, can scarcely be considered as one and the same; since the power to perform them is given in two separate and distinct sections of the constitution. . . .

This is an appointment made by the president, by and with the advice and consent of the senate, and is evidenced by no act but the commission itself. In such a case therefore the commission and the appointment seem inseparable; it being almost impossible to show an appointment otherwise than by proving the existence of a commission: still the commission is not necessarily the appointment; though conclusive evidence of it.[9]

It is therefore decidedly the opinion of the court, that when a commission has been signed by the president, the appointment is made;

---

[8] It is not clear what either the Constitution or the Court means by "commission." Is it the job or a document proving that someone has the job? And does it make a difference whether the word is used as verb, as in the Constitution, or as a noun in the opinion?

[9] The Court's detailed analysis of the moment when an appointment is complete is omitted.

and that the commission is complete when the seal of the United States has been affixed to it by the secretary of state. . . .

Mr. Marbury, then, since his commission was signed by the president and sealed by the secretary of state, was appointed; and as the law creating the office gave the officer a right to hold for five years independent of the executive, the appointment was not revocable; but vested in the officer legal rights which are protected by the laws of his country.

To withhold the commission, therefore, is an act deemed by the court not warranted by law, but violative of a vested legal right.

This brings us to the second inquiry; which is,

2. If he has a right, and that right has been violated, do the laws of his country afford him a remedy?

The very essence of civil liberty certainly consists in the right of every individual to claim the protection of the laws, whenever he receives an injury. One of the first duties of government is to afford that protection. In Great Britain the king himself is sued in the respectful form of a petition, and he never fails to comply with the judgment of his court. . . .

The government of the United States has been emphatically termed a government of laws, and not of men. It will certainly cease to deserve this high appellation, if the laws furnish no remedy for the violation of a vested legal right.

If this obloquy is to be cast on the jurisprudence of our country, it must arise from the peculiar character of the case.

It behooves us then to inquire whether there be in its composition any ingredient which shall exempt from legal investigation, or exclude the injured party from legal redress. In pursuing this inquiry the first question which presents itself, is, whether this can be arranged with that class of cases which come under the description of *damnum absque injuria*—a loss without an injury [i.e., damage without a legally cognizable wrong]. . . .

It is then the opinion of the court,

1. That by signing the commission of Mr. Marbury, the president of the United States appointed him a justice of peace for the county of Washington in the district of Columbia; and that the seal of the

United States, affixed thereto by the secretary of state, is conclusive testimony of the verity of the signature, and of the completion of the appointment; and that the appointment conferred on him a legal right to the office for the space of five years.

2. That, having this legal title to the office, he has a consequent right to the commission; a refusal to deliver which is a plain violation of that right, for which the laws of his country afford him a remedy.[10]

It remains to be inquired whether,

3. He is entitled to the remedy for which he applies.

This depends on, 1. The nature of the writ applied for. And, 2. The power of this court.

1. The nature of the writ.

Blackstone[11] defines a mandamus to be, [other authorities on the nature of mandamus omitted].

This, then, is a plain case of a mandamus, either to deliver the commission, or a copy of it from the record; and it only remains to be inquired,

2. Whether it can issue from this court.

The act to establish the judicial courts of the United States [the Judiciary Act of 1789, an important statute still in force] authorizes the supreme court "to issue writs of mandamus, in cases warranted by the principles and usages of law, to any courts appointed, or persons holding office, under the authority of the United States."[12]

The secretary of state, being a person, holding an office under the authority of the United States, is precisely within the letter of the description; and if this court is not authorized to issue a writ of mandamus to such an officer, it must be because the law is unconstitutional, and

---

[10] Is point two consistent with point one? If he had the appointment, why did he need the piece of paper?

[11] Sir William Blackstone, 3 *Commentaries on the Laws of England* 110 (1768) [cited originally by Chief Justice Marshall, in the text].

[12] Chief Justice Marshall is here quoting the Judiciary Act, Sess. 1, ch. 20 § 13 (Sept. 24, 1789), 1 Stat. 80.

therefore absolutely incapable of conferring the authority, and assigning the duties which its words purport to confer and assign.

The constitution vests the whole judicial power of the United States in one supreme court, and such inferior courts as congress shall, from time to time, ordain and establish. This power is expressly extended to all cases arising under the laws of the United States; and consequently, in some form, may be exercised over the present case; because the right claimed is given by a law of the United States.

In the distribution of this power it is declared that "the supreme court shall have original jurisdiction in all cases affecting ambassadors, other public ministers and consuls, and those in which a state shall be a party. In all other cases, the supreme court shall have appellate jurisdiction."[13]

It has been insisted at the bar, that as the original grant of jurisdiction to the supreme and inferior courts is general, and the clause, assigning original jurisdiction to the supreme court, contains no negative or restrictive words; the power remains to the legislature to assign original jurisdiction to that court in other cases than those specified in the article which has been recited; provided those cases belong to the judicial power of the United States. If it had been intended to leave it in the discretion of the legislature to apportion the judicial power be-

---

[13] Section thirteen of the Judiciary Act of 1789 provided, in full:

> *And be it further enacted,* That the Supreme Court shall have exclusive jurisdiction of all controversies of a civil nature, where a state is a party, except between a state and its citizens; and except also between a state and citizens of other states, or aliens, in which latter case it shall have original but not exclusive jurisdiction. And shall have exclusively all such jurisdiction of suits or proceedings against ministers, ambassadors, or other public ministers, or their domestics, or domestic servants, as a court of law can have or exercise consistently with the law of nations; and original, but not exclusive jurisdiction of all suits brought by ambassadors, or other public ministers, or in which a consul or vice consul, shall be a party. And the trial of issues of fact in the Supreme Court, in all actions at law against citizens of the United States, shall be by jury. The Supreme Court shall also have appellate jurisdiction from the circuit courts and courts of the several states in the cases herein after specially provided for and shall have power to issue writs of prohibition to the district courts, when proceeding as courts of admiralty and maritime jurisdiction, and writs of mandamus in cases warranted by the principles and usages of law, to any courts appointed, or persons holding office, under the authority of the United States.

1 Stat. 80–81, First Congress, Session I, Chapter 20 (1789).

tween the supreme and inferior courts according to the will of that body, it would certainly have been useless to have proceeded further than to have defined the judicial power, and the tribunals in which it should be vested. The subsequent part of the section is mere surplusage, is entirely without meaning, if such is to be the construction. If congress remains at liberty to give this court appellate jurisdiction, where the constitution has declared their jurisdiction shall be original; and original jurisdiction where the constitution has declared it shall be appellate; the distribution of jurisdiction made in the constitution, is form without substance.

Affirmative words are often, in their operation, negative of other objects than those affirmed; and in this case, a negative or exclusive sense must be given to them or they have no operation at all.

It cannot be presumed that any clause in the constitution is intended to be without effect; and therefore such construction is inadmissible, unless the words require it.

If the solicitude of the convention, respecting our peace with foreign powers, induced a provision that the supreme court should take original jurisdiction in cases which might be supposed to affect them; yet the clause would have proceeded no further than to provide for such cases, if no further restriction on the powers of congress had been intended. That they should have appellate jurisdiction in all other cases, with such exceptions as congress might make, is no restriction; unless the words be deemed exclusive of original jurisdiction.

When an instrument organizing fundamentally a judicial system, divides it into one supreme, and so many inferior courts as the legislature may ordain and establish; then enumerates its powers, and proceeds so far to distribute them, as to define the jurisdiction of the supreme court by declaring the cases in which it shall take original jurisdiction, and that in others it shall take appellate jurisdiction, the plain import of the words seems to be, that in one class of cases its jurisdiction is original, and not appellate; in the other it is appellate, and not original. If any other construction would render the clause inoperative, that is an additional reason for rejecting such other construction, and for adhering to the obvious meaning.

To enable this court then to issue a mandamus, it must be shown to be an exercise of appellate jurisdiction, or to be necessary to enable them to exercise appellate jurisdiction.

It has been stated at the bar that the appellate jurisdiction may be exercised in a variety of forms, and that if it be the will of the legislature that a mandamus should be used for that purpose, that will must be obeyed. This is true; yet the jurisdiction must be appellate, not original.

It is the essential criterion of appellate jurisdiction, that it revises and corrects the proceedings in a cause already instituted, and does not create that case. Although, therefore, a mandamus may be directed to courts, yet to issue such a writ to an officer for the delivery of a paper, is in effect the same as to sustain an original action for that paper, and therefore seems not to belong to appellate, but to original jurisdiction. Neither is it necessary in such a case as this, to enable the court to exercise its appellate jurisdiction.

The authority, therefore, given to the supreme court, by the act establishing the judicial courts of the United States, to issue writs of mandamus to public officers, appears not to be warranted by the constitution; and it becomes necessary to inquire whether a jurisdiction, so conferred, can be exercised.

The question, whether an act, repugnant to the constitution, can become the law of the land, is a question deeply interesting to the United States; but, happily, not of an intricacy proportioned to its interest. It seems only necessary to recognize certain principles, supposed to have been long and well established, to decide it.

That the people have an original right to establish, for their future government, such principles as, in their opinion, shall most conduce to their own happiness, is the basis on which the whole American fabric has been erected. The exercise of this original right is a very great exertion; nor can it nor ought it to be frequently repeated. The principles, therefore, so established are deemed fundamental. And as the authority, from which they proceed, is supreme, and can seldom act, they are designed to be permanent.

This original and supreme will organizes the government, and assigns to different departments their respective powers. It may either stop here; or establish certain limits not to be transcended by those departments.

The government of the United States is of the latter description. The powers of the legislature are defined and limited; and that those limits may not be mistaken or forgotten, the constitution is written. To what purpose are powers limited, and to what purpose is that limitation committed to writing; if these limits may, at any time, be passed by those intended to be restrained? The distinction between a government with limited and unlimited powers is abolished, if those limits do not confine the persons on whom they are imposed, and if acts prohibited and acts allowed are of equal obligation. It is a proposition too plain to be contested, that the constitution controls any legislative act repugnant to it; or, that the legislature may alter the constitution by an ordinary act.

Between these alternatives there is no middle ground. The constitution is either a superior, paramount law, unchangeable by ordinary means, or it is on a level with ordinary legislative acts, and like other acts, is alterable when the legislature shall please to alter it.

If the former part of the alternative be true, then a legislative act contrary to the constitution is not law: if the latter part be true, then written constitutions are absurd attempts, on the part of the people, to limit a power in its own nature illimitable.

Certainly all those who have framed written constitutions contemplate them as forming the fundamental and paramount law of the nation, and consequently the theory of every such government must be, that an act of the legislature repugnant to the constitution is void.

This theory is essentially attached to a written constitution, and is consequently to be considered by this court as one of the fundamental principles of our society. It is not therefore to be lost sight of in the further consideration of this subject.

If an act of the legislature, repugnant to the constitution, is void, does it, notwithstanding its invalidity, bind the courts and oblige them to give it effect? Or, in other words, though it be not law, does it constitute a rule as operative as if it was a law? This would be to overthrow in fact what was established in theory; and would seem, at first view, an absurdity too gross to be insisted on. It shall, however, receive a more attentive consideration.

It is emphatically the province and duty of the judicial department to say what the law is. Those who apply the rule to particular cases, must of necessity expound and interpret that rule. If two laws conflict with each other, the courts must decide on the operation of each.

So if a law be in opposition to the constitution: if both the law and the constitution apply to a particular case, so that the court must either decide that case conformably to the law, disregarding the constitution; or conformably to the constitution, disregarding the law: the court must determine which of these conflicting rules governs the case. This is of the very essence of judicial duty.

If then the courts are to regard the constitution; and the constitution is superior to any ordinary act of the legislature; the constitution, and not such ordinary act, must govern the case to which they both apply.

Those then who controvert the principle that the constitution is to be considered, in court, as a paramount law, are reduced to the necessity of maintaining that courts must close their eyes on the constitution, and see only the law.

This doctrine would subvert the very foundation of all written constitutions. It would declare that an act, which, according to the principles and theory of our government, is entirely void, is yet, in practice, completely obligatory. It would declare, that if the legislature shall do what is expressly forbidden, such act, notwithstanding the express prohibition, is in reality effectual. It would be giving to the legislature a practical and real omnipotence with the same breath which professes to restrict their powers within narrow limits. It is prescribing limits, and declaring that those limits may be passed at pleasure.

That it thus reduces to nothing what we have deemed the greatest improvement on political institutions—a written constitution, would of itself be sufficient, in America where written constitutions have been viewed with so much reverence, for rejecting the construction. But the peculiar expressions of the constitution of the United States furnish additional arguments in favour of its rejection.

The judicial power of the United States is extended to all cases arising under the constitution.

Could it be the intention of those who gave this power, to say that, in using it, the constitution should not be looked into? That a case arising under the constitution should be decided without examining the instrument under which it arises?

This is too extravagant to be maintained.

In some cases then, the constitution must be looked into by the judges. And if they can open it at all, what part of it are they forbidden to read, or to obey?

There are many other parts of the constitution which serve to illustrate this subject.

It is declared that "no tax or duty shall be laid on articles exported from any state." Suppose a duty on the export of cotton, of tobacco, or of flour; and a suit instituted to recover it. Ought judgment to be rendered in such a case? ought the judges to close their eyes on the constitution, and only see the law.

The constitution declares that "no bill of attainder or ex post facto law shall be passed."

If, however, such a bill should be passed and a person should be prosecuted under it, must the court condemn to death those victims whom the constitution endeavours to preserve?

"No person," says the constitution, "shall be convicted of treason unless on the testimony of two witnesses to the same overt act, or on confession in open court."

Here the language of the constitution is addressed especially to the courts. It prescribes, directly for them, a rule of evidence not to be departed from. If the legislature should change that rule, and declare one witness, or a confession out of court, sufficient for conviction, must the constitutional principle yield to the legislative act?

From these and many other selections which might be made, it is apparent, that the framers of the constitution contemplated that instrument as a rule for the government of courts, as well as of the legislature.

Why otherwise does it direct the judges to take an oath to support it? This oath certainly applies, in an especial manner, to their conduct in their official character. How immoral to impose it on them, if they were to be used as the instruments, and the knowing instruments, for violating what they swear to support!

The oath of office, too, imposed by the legislature, is completely demonstrative of the legislative opinion on this subject. It is in these words: "I do solemnly swear that I will administer justice without respect to persons, and do equal right to the poor and to the rich; and that I will faithfully and impartially discharge all the duties incumbent on me as according to the best of my abilities and understanding, agreeably to the constitution and laws of the United States."

Why does a judge swear to discharge his duties agreeably to the constitution of the United States, if that constitution forms no rule for his government? if it is closed upon him and cannot be inspected by him.

If such be the real state of things, this is worse than solemn mockery. To prescribe, or to take this oath, becomes equally a crime.

It is also not entirely unworthy of observation, that in declaring what shall be the supreme law of the land, the constitution itself is first mentioned; and not the laws of the United States generally, but those only which shall be made in pursuance of the constitution, have that rank.

Thus, the particular phraseology of the constitution of the United States confirms and strengthens the principle, supposed to be essential to all written constitutions, that a law repugnant to the constitution is void, and that courts, as well as other departments, are bound by that instrument.

The rule must be discharged [i.e., there is no further burden on the secretary of state and the writ will not issue].

∎

QUESTIONS AND COMMENTS

1. Note the similarity between this momentous opinion establishing the principle of judicial review and Blackstone's opinion in *Scott v. Shepherd*. Blackstone thought that Scott should be able to recover for his injuries but that he had chosen the wrong writ. He should have sued in trespass on the case rather than in trespass. Here, in this case, Chief Justice Marshall thought that Marbury and the other disappointed judges should get their commissions, but that they had chosen the wrong court. They could get a writ of mandamus from the district court but not from the Supreme Court.

2. A strong commitment to the rule of law generally means that judges defer to the legislative branch of government. The supremacy of the written law means that judges should not legislate or supersede the power of the legislature. In this context, the rule of law has the opposite political effect. A strong commitment to the written Constitution enhances the power of the judiciary relative to the legislature. Would it have been possible for Marshall to reason in a way that would have enhanced the power of Congress, for example: "Congress takes the Constitution just as seriously as we do in the Supreme Court and they, in their collective wisdom, decided that Congress had the authority to enact the provision of the Judiciary Act of 1789

that gave original jurisdiction to this court to issue the writ of mandamus. Why should we, the judges, second-guess the Congress?"
The unarticulated premise of Marshall's opinion is that the rule of
law requires judges to be the final word in reading and interpreting
the language of the Constitution.

3. The long-range effect of this decision was to increase the authority
and political power of judges. *Marbury* inspired the post–Second
World War constitutional courts of Europe, which have the specific
function of passing on the constitutionality of legislation. Their
power is even greater than that claimed by Marshall in *Marbury* because they can engage in the "abstract review" of legislation without
a specific controversy coming before the court. This is not possible
under the U.S. Constitution, Article III, Section 2, Clause 1, which
says that the courts shall have jurisdiction over "all Cases, in Law and
Equity, arising under this Constitution, the Laws of the United States,
and Treaties. . . ." The key word is *case*, which is interpreted to mean
a "case or controversy," an actual dispute between parties who have a
stake in the outcome. The Supreme Court could render an opinion
about the applicability of the Judiciary Act of 1789 in a specific dispute but not its constitutionality in the abstract.

4. Despite the influence of *Marbury* on the jurisprudence of the world,
the principle of judicial review remains controversial. Since the days
of Sir Edward Coke, lawyers and politicians have debated whether
the courts should have the authority to defy the will of Parliament.
In a democratic system, the claim that the courts have the last word
raises what is sometimes called the "countermajoritarian difficulty."
See Alexander M. Bickel, *The Least Dangerous Branch: The Supreme
Court at the Bar of Politics* 16–17 (New York: Bobbs-Merrill, 1962).
The idea that the legislature ought to have the last word is based on
the notion that most legitimate laws are those that best represent the
will of the people who are governed by them, and the legislature is
more representative than any other aspect of government. See Jeremy
Waldron, *The Dignity of Legislation* (New York: Oxford University
Press, 2001).

5. Could you respond to the argument in point four by invoking the
principle of *Dr. Bonham's Case*, namely: No one should be a judge in
his own case? That means that Congress cannot impartially decide
whether its own statutes are constitutional. Is there a better solution

than vesting this authority in the Supreme Court, a coequal branch of government? Would it make a difference if there were a special court whose task was just to assess the constitutionality of legislation?

6. When the decision was announced in 1803, it provoked outrage from President Thomas Jefferson and his party, not for the assertion of judicial review but for the presumptions that the plaintiffs had been harmed and that the Court might have granted the mandamus. This is thought by many scholars to be a great tactical decision by Chief Justice Marshall, forgoing a preferred outcome under the law while laying the groundwork for later decisions by the Court. Judges, however, must be aware that their decisions are vulnerable to being ignored by the other departments of the government; the rule of law succeeds only so long as the decisions are respected (or at least usually obeyed) by the losers, especially when the losers are those parts of the government that control the military. Can you imagine circumstances in which Marshall's approach would have failed?

7. The Judiciary Act of 1789 was the statute that Marshall declared "repugnant" to the Constitution, because it gave original jurisdiction to the Supreme Court for a matter that Article III gave only appellate jurisdiction. Section 13 of the Act provided:

> Section 13. *And be it further enacted*, That the Supreme Court shall have exclusive jurisdiction of all controversies of a civil nature, where a state is a party, except between a state and its citizens; and except also between a state and citizens of other states, or aliens, in which latter case it shall have original but not exclusive jurisdiction. And shall have exclusively all such jurisdiction in suits or proceedings against ambassadors, or other public ministers, or their domestics, or domestic servants, as a court of law can have or exercise consistently with the law or nations; and original, but not exclusive jurisdiction of all suits brought by ambassadors, or other public ministers, or in which a consul or vice consul shall be a party. And the trial of issues in fact in the Supreme Court, in all actions at law against citizens of the United States, shall be by jury. The Supreme Court shall also have appellate jurisdiction from the circuit courts and courts of the several states, in the cases herein after specially provided for; and shall have power to issue writs or prohibition to the

district courts, when proceeding as courts of admiralty and maritime jurisdiction, and writs of mandamus in cases warranted by the principles and usages of law, to any courts appointed, or persons holding office, under the authority of the United States.

Compare this provision with the constitutional provision defining the authority of the Supreme Court, Article III, Section 2, Clause 1 [see page 124]. Looking back at Chief Justice Marshall's opinion, you should see many reasons for the manner in which he excerpts from these provisions. In part it is to remove irrelevant language. In part, though, does the quote not give a different impression from the full sections? Some commentators have suggested that Marshall's reading was strained to find a constitutional violation in the act. Do you think so? Could you have seen a manner in which the requirements of the judiciary act were not completely inconsistent with the constitutional provision? By long practice, if the Court has been given two readings of a statute, in which one is constitutional and one is unconstitutional, the Court will adopt the constitutional reading. If the statute was read in a constitutional light, the Court could have said it allowed mandamus only in cases against officials properly in its appellate or original jurisdiction. If the statute is read that way, then Marbury had no claim under the statute to mandamus, and would still have lost, but the act would not have been unconstitutional. Would that have been a fair reading of the act?

8. Although it is similar to judicial review in other states and regions, the concept of judicial review in the United States is both wider and narrower than in many countries that have adopted the model of the German Constitutional Court. All federal courts may review nearly any federal statute, executive action, or administrative decision to determine whether it accords with the federal constitution, whether or not the statute, action, or decision directly affects an individual right. The nature of the federal structure, in which national laws are supreme over state laws, requires judicial review by the federal courts over not only state laws but also state constitutions. You should review the supremacy clause, Article VI, clause 2 [see page 127].

9. John Marshall was almost certainly present at a well-known treason trial in Virginia, decided in 1782 by his teacher, George Wythe, in Marshall's first year of practice and first year of membership in the

state assembly. Wythe, chancellor of Virginia and the first law professor in the United States, was one of the Virginia's most respected
judges. The issue in the trial was whether a pardon issued by the
state assembly, the lower house, but not concurred in by the state
senate was enforceable. In his opinion, Wythe noted first that judges'
oaths required that they address the validity of the pardon whether
they liked the question or not. He considered first, whether the
court had jurisdiction, and second, whether the pardon was valid. His
answers to both questions strongly presaged the outline of much of
Marshall's *Marbury* opinion. See *Commonwealth v. Caton*, 8 Va. (4 Call)
5 (1782). Scholars frequently write of Marshall's *Marbury* opinion as if
he acted deliberately to create law beyond the existing precedents in
order to pursue a political agenda, although it is rare for them to
consider the influence of *Caton* or even of *Dr. Bonham's Case* on
Marshall's reasoning or his beliefs about what he should do.

10. We should refer to Chief Justice Marshall's approach to the Constitution in *Marbury* as "strict construction" of the document. That is, he
argued that words mean what they purport to mean. *Appellate* means
"appellate," and *original* means "original." The Constitution defines
and establishes the federal government. As Marshall argued, this is
what it means to have a rule of law, not of men. According to "strict
construction," with its new champion Justice Scalia,[14] the text of the
Constitution is everything. Congress may legislate if and only if the
language of the Constitution so defines its authority. In the next
chapter, we shall see, in a case decided sixteen years later, that there
is another way of reading the Constitution. For every thesis in
American law, there is also an antithesis.

■

Further Reading

Two recent and recommended works on *Marbury* and its influence are William
E. Nelson, *Marbury v. Madison: The Origins and Legacy of Judicial Review* (Lawrence,
KS: University Press of Kansas, 2000), and R. Kent Newmyer, *John Marshall and
the Heroic Age of the Supreme Court* (Baton Rouge: Louisiana State University Press,
2001).

[14] See Justice Scalia's analysis in *Rogers v. Tennessee*, discussed in Chapter Four.

SEVEN

Federalism

There is a major difference between the Supreme Court's reviewing the constitutionality of an act of Congress and the Court's reviewing the states' interpretations of federal law. Under the supremacy clause, there is little doubt that federal law trumps inconsistent state law. The Court's power to review state court decisions about federal law was settled in 1816 in *Martin v. Hunters Lessee* (14 U.S. 304). In that case, the Court interpreted and applied a treaty of 1783 that protected Lord Fairfax's claim to certain pieces of land in Virginia.

Three years later, in *McCulloch v. Maryland*, the Court faced the dual challenge of assessing national legislation under the standard of *Marbury* and of declaring conflicting state legislation unconstitutional. Congress had established a national bank, and the State of Maryland sought to impose a tax on all banks, including the federal bank. There is nothing in the Constitution about the federal government establishing banks. Indeed, the question whether the federal government should, as a matter of politics and policy, establish a bank was one of the most hotly disputed questions of the time. The bank represented a commitment to industrialization and commerce, a conception of the United States strongly resisted by the agrarian populists.

The appeal of this case lies not only in the questions of law presented but also in the radically different approach suggested for interpreting the Constitution. Recall the "strict constructionist" approach that Chief Justice Marshall advocated in *Marbury*. Under that approach, the Court would have invalidated the bank, but this time the Court took a different approach toward interpretation. Think about what you would call this alternative style of interpretation.

McCulloch v. The State of Maryland et al.

Supreme Court of the United States
17 U.S. 316 (1819)

This was in action of debt[1] brought by the defendant in error, John James, who sued as well for himself as for the State of Maryland, in the County Court of Baltimore County, in the said State, against the plaintiff in error,[2] McCulloch, to recover certain penalties under the act of the legislature of Maryland, hereafter mentioned. Judgment being rendered against the plaintiff in error, upon the following statement of facts, agreed and submitted to the Court by the parties, was affirmed by the Court of Appeals of the State of Maryland, the highest Court of law of said State, and the cause was brought, by writ of error, to this Court.

It is admitted by the parties in this cause, by their counsel, that there was passed on the 10th day of April, 1816, by the Congress of the United States, an act, entitled, "an act to incorporate the subscribers to the Bank of the United States;" and that there was passed, on the 11th day of February, 1818, by the General Assembly of Maryland, an act, entitled, "an act to impose a tax on all Banks, or branches thereof, in the State of Maryland, not chartered by the legislature." . . .

The question submitted to the Court for their decision in this case, is as to the validity of the said act of the General Assembly of Maryland, on the ground of its being repugnant to the constitution of the United States, and the act of Congress aforesaid, or to one of them. Upon the foregoing statement of facts . . . if the Court should be of opinion that

---

[1] Note the reference to the common law writ of debt.
[2] The plaintiff in error is the party who commenced the appeal.

the plaintiffs are entitled to recover, then judgment it is agreed shall be entered for the plaintiffs for twenty-five hundred dollars, and costs of suit. But if the Court should be of opinion that the plaintiffs are not entitled to recover upon the statement and pleadings aforesaid, then judgment of non pros shall be entered, with costs to the defendant.

[James sued McCulloch in state court to collect the tax imposed against "foreign banks," which included the Bank of the United States, established by Congress in 1816. It was foreign in the sense that it was not incorporated in Maryland.]

MARSHALL, C.J.:

In the case now to be determined, the defendant, a sovereign State, denies the obligation of a law enacted by the legislature of the Union, and the plaintiff, on his part, contests the validity of an act which has been passed by the legislature of that State. The constitution of our country, in its most interesting and vital parts, is to be considered; the conflicting powers of the government of the Union and of its members, as marked in that constitution, are to be discussed; and an opinion given, which may essentially influence the great operations of the government. No tribunal can approach such a question without a deep sense of its importance, and of the awful responsibility involved in its decision. But it must be decided peacefully, or remain a source of hostile legislation, perhaps of hostility of a still more serious nature; and if it is to be so decided, by this tribunal alone can the decision be made. On the Supreme Court of the United States has the constitution of our country devolved this important duty.

The first question made in the cause is, has Congress power to incorporate a bank?

It has been truly said, that this can scarcely be considered as an open question, entirely unprejudiced by the former proceedings of the nation respecting it. The principle now contested was introduced at a very early period of our history, has been recognized by many successive legislatures, and has been acted upon by the judicial department, in cases of peculiar delicacy, as a law of undoubted obligation. . . .

The power now contested was exercised by the first Congress elected under the present constitution. The bill for incorporating the bank of the United States did not steal upon an unsuspecting legislature, and pass unobserved. Its principle was completely understood, and was opposed with equal zeal and ability. . . .

In discussing this question, the counsel for the State of Maryland have deemed it of some importance, in the construction of the constitution, to consider that instrument not as emanating from the people, but as the act of sovereign and independent States. The powers of the general government, it has been said, are delegated by the States, who alone are truly sovereign; and must be exercised in subordination to the States, who alone possess supreme dominion.

It would be difficult to sustain this proposition. The Convention which framed the constitution was indeed elected by the State legislatures. But the instrument, when it came from their hands, was a mere proposal, without obligation, or pretensions to it. It was reported to the then existing Congress of the United States, with a request that it might "be submitted to a Convention of Delegates, chosen in each State by the people thereof, under the recommendation of its Legislature, for their assent and ratification." This mode of proceeding was adopted; and by the Convention, by Congress, and by the State Legislatures, the instrument was submitted to the people. They acted upon it in the only manner in which they can act safely, effectively, and wisely, on such a subject, by assembling in Convention.[3] It is true, they assembled in their several States—and where else should they have assembled? No political dreamer was ever wild enough to think of breaking down the lines which separate the States, and of compounding the American people into one common mass. Of consequence, when they act, they act in their States. But the measures they adopt do not, on that account, cease to be the measures of the people themselves, or become the measures of the State governments.

From these Conventions the constitution derives its whole authority. The government proceeds directly from the people; is "ordained and established" in the name of the people; and is declared to be ordained, "in order to form a more perfect union, establish justice, ensure domestic tranquillity, and secure the blessings of liberty to them-

---

[3] Note that Article VII of the Constitution prescribes: "The Ratification of the Conventions of nine States, shall be sufficient for the Establishment of this Constitution between the States so ratifying the Same."

selves and to their posterity." The assent of the States, in their sovereign capacity, is implied in calling a Convention, and thus submitting that instrument to the people. But the people were at perfect liberty to accept or reject it; and their act was final. It required not the affirmance, and could not be negatived, by the State governments. The constitution, when thus adopted, was of complete obligation, and bound the State sovereignties.

It has been said, that the people had already surrendered all their powers to the State sovereignties, and had nothing more to give. But, surely, the question whether they may resume and modify the powers granted to government does not remain to be settled in this country. . . .

The government of the Union, then, (whatever may be the influence of this fact on the case,) is, emphatically, and truly, a government of the people. In form and in substance it emanates from them. Its powers are granted by them, and are to be exercised directly on them, and for their benefit.

This government is acknowledged by all to be one of enumerated powers. The principle, that it can exercise only the powers granted to it, would seem too apparent to have required to be enforced by all those arguments which its enlightened friends, while it was depending before the people, found it necessary to urge. That principle is now universally admitted. But the question respecting the extent of the powers actually granted, is perpetually arising, and will probably continue to arise, as long as our system shall exist. . . .

If any one proposition could command the universal assent of mankind, we might expect it would be this—that the government of the Union, though limited in its powers, is supreme within its sphere of action. This would seem to result necessarily from its nature. It is the government of all; its powers are delegated by all; it represents all, and acts for all. Though any one State may be willing to control its operations, no State is willing to allow others to control them. The nation, on those subjects on which it can act, must necessarily bind its component parts. But this question is not left to mere reason: the people have, in express terms, decided it, by saying, "this constitution, and the laws of the United States, which shall be made in pursuance thereof," "shall be the supreme law of the land," and by requiring that the members of the State legislatures, and the officers of the executive and judicial departments of the States, shall take the oath of fidelity to it.

The government of the United States, then, though limited in its powers, is supreme; and its laws, when made in pursuance of the constitution, form the supreme law of the land, "any thing in the constitution or laws of any State to the contrary notwithstanding."

Among the enumerated powers, we do not find that of establishing a bank or creating a corporation. But there is no phrase in the instrument which, like the articles of confederation,[4] excludes incidental or implied powers; and which requires that every thing granted shall be expressly and minutely described. Even the 10th amendment, which was framed for the purpose of quieting the excessive jealousies which had been excited, omits the word "expressly," and declares only that the powers "not delegated to the United States, nor prohibited to the States, are reserved to the States or to the people;" thus leaving the question, whether the particular power which may become the subject of contest has been delegated to the one government, or prohibited to the other, to depend on a fair construction of the whole instrument. The men who drew and adopted this amendment had experienced the embarrassments resulting from the insertion of this word in the articles of confederation, and probably omitted it to avoid those embarrassments. A constitution, to contain an accurate detail of all the subdivisions of which its great powers will admit, and of all the means by which they may be carried into execution, would partake of the prolixity of a legal code, and could scarcely be embraced by the human mind. It would probably never be understood by the public. Its nature, therefore, requires, that only its great outlines should be marked, its important objects designated, and the minor ingredients which compose those objects be deduced from the nature of the objects themselves. That this idea was entertained by the framers of the American constitution, is not only to be inferred from the nature of the instrument, but from the language. Why else were some of the limitations, found in the ninth section of the 1st article, introduced?[5] It is also, in

---

[4] This is a reference to the Articles of Confederation, which established the first government of the independent colonies.

[5] What is the point that Marshall is making here? Article I, section 9, refers to specific powers that Congress does not have. For example, this section prohibits ex facto laws. What follows from these specific prohibitions?

some degree, warranted by their having omitted to use any restrictive term which might prevent its receiving a fair and just interpretation. In considering this question, then, *we must never forget, that it is a constitution we are expounding.*[6] [Emphasis added.]

Although, among the enumerated powers of government, we do not find the word "bank" or "incorporation," we find the great powers to lay and collect taxes; to borrow money; to regulate commerce; to declare and conduct a war; and to raise and support armies and navies. The sword and the purse, all the external relations, and no inconsiderable portion of the industry of the nation, are entrusted to its government. It can never be pretended that these vast powers draw after them others of inferior importance, merely because they are inferior. Such an idea can never be advanced. But it may with great reason be contended, that a government, entrusted with such ample powers, on the due execution of which the happiness and prosperity of the nation so vitally depends, must also be entrusted with ample means for their execution. The power being given, it is the interest of the nation to facilitate its execution. It can never be their interest, and cannot be presumed to have been their intention, to clog and embarrass its execution by withholding the most appropriate means. Throughout this vast republic, from the St. Croix to the Gulf of Mexico, from the Atlantic to the Pacific, revenue is to be collected and expended, armies are to be marched and supported. The exigencies of the nation may require that the treasure raised in the north should be transported to the south, that raised in the east conveyed to the west, or that this order should be reversed. Is that construction of the constitution to be preferred which would render these operations difficult, hazardous, and expensive? Can we adopt that construction, (unless the words imperiously require it,) which would impute to the framers of that instrument, when granting these powers for the public good, the intention of impeding their exercise by withholding a choice of means? If, indeed, such be the mandate of the constitution, we have only to obey; but that instrument does not profess to enumerate the means by which the powers it confers may be executed; nor does it prohibit the creation of a corporation, if the existence of such a being be essential to the

---

[6] This is a famous line. What does it imply about the theory and method of interpreting the Constitution?

beneficial exercise of those powers. It is, then, the subject of fair inquiry, how far such means may be employed.

It is not denied, that the powers given to the government imply the ordinary means of execution. That, for example, of raising revenue, and applying it to national purposes, is admitted to imply the power of conveying money from place to place, as the exigencies of the nation may require, and of employing the usual means of conveyance. But it is denied that the government has its choice of means; or, that it may employ the most convenient means, if, to employ them, it be necessary to erect a corporation.

On what foundation does this argument rest? On this alone: The power of creating a corporation, is one appertaining to sovereignty, and is not expressly conferred on Congress. This is true. But all legislative powers appertain to sovereignty. The original power of giving the law on any subject whatever, is a sovereign power; and if the government of the Union is restrained from creating a corporation, as a means for performing its functions, on the single reason that the creation of a corporation is an act of sovereignty; if the sufficiency of this reason be acknowledged, there would be some difficulty in sustaining the authority of Congress to pass other laws for the accomplishment of the same objects.

The government which has a right to do an act, and has imposed on it the duty of performing that act, must, according to the dictates of reason, be allowed to select the means; and those who contend that it may not select any appropriate means, that one particular mode of effecting the object is excepted, take upon themselves the burden of establishing that exception.

The creation of a corporation, it is said, appertains to sovereignty. This is admitted. But to what portion of sovereignty does it appertain? Does it belong to one more than to another? In America, the powers of sovereignty are divided between the government of the Union, and those of the States. They are each sovereign, with respect to the objects committed to it, and neither sovereign with respect to the objects committed to the other. We cannot comprehend that train of reasoning which would maintain, that the extent of power granted by the people is to be ascertained, not by the nature and terms of the grant, but by its date. Some State constitutions were formed before, some since that of the United States. We cannot believe that their relation to each other is in any degree dependent upon this circumstance. . . . But the constitution of the United States has not left the right of Congress to employ the necessary means, for the execution of the powers conferred on the government, to general reasoning. To its enumeration of powers is added that of making "all laws which shall be necessary and proper, for carrying into execution the foregoing powers, and all other powers vested by this constitution, in the government of the United States, or in any department thereof." . . .

But the argument on which most reliance is placed, is drawn from the peculiar language of this clause. Congress is not empowered by it to make all laws, which may have relation to the powers conferred on the government, but such only as may be "necessary and proper" for carrying them into execution. The word "necessary," is considered as controlling the whole sentence, and as limiting the right to pass laws for the execution of the granted powers, to such as are indispensable, and without which the power would be nugatory. That it excludes the choice of means, and leaves to Congress, in each case, that only which is most direct and simple. Is it true, that this is the sense in which the word "necessary" is always used? Does it always import an absolute physical necessity, so strong, that one thing, to which another may be termed necessary, cannot exist without that other? We think it does not. If reference be had to its use, in the common affairs of the world, or in approved authors, we find that it frequently imports no more than that one thing is convenient, or useful, or essential to another. To employ the means necessary to an end, is generally understood as employing any means calculated to produce the end, and not as being confined to those single means, without which the end would be entirely unattainable. Such is the character of human language, that no word conveys to the mind, in all situations, one single definite idea; and nothing is more common than to use words in a figurative sense. Almost all compositions contain words, which, taken in their rigorous sense, would convey a meaning different from that which is obviously intended. It is essential to just construction, that many words which import something excessive, should be understood in a more mitigated sense—in that sense which common usage justifies. The word "necessary" is of this description. . . .

It must have been the intention of those who gave these powers, to insure, as far as human prudence could insure, their beneficial execution. This could not be done by confiding the choice of means to such narrow limits as not to leave it in the power of Congress to adopt any which might be appropriate, and which were conducive to the end. This provision is made in a constitution intended to endure for ages to come, and, consequently, to be adapted to the various crises of human affairs. To have prescribed the means by which government should, in all future time, execute its powers, would have been to change, entirely, the character of the instrument, and give it the properties of a legal code.[7] It would have been an unwise attempt to provide, by immutable rules, for exigencies which, if foreseen at all, must have been seen dimly, and which can be best provided for as they occur. . . .

So, with respect to the whole penal code of the United States: whence arises the power to punish in cases not prescribed by the constitution? All admit that the government may, legitimately, punish any violation of its laws; and yet, this is not among the enumerated powers of Congress. The right to enforce the observance of law, by punishing its infraction, might be denied with the more plausibility, because it is expressly given in some cases. Congress is empowered "to provide for the punishment of counterfeiting the securities and current coin of the United States," and "to define and punish piracies and felonies committed on the high seas, and offences against the law of nations." The several powers of Congress may exist, in a very imperfect state to be sure, but they may exist and be carried into execution, although no punishment should be inflicted in cases where the right to punish is not expressly given. . . .

In ascertaining the sense in which the word "necessary" is used in this clause of the constitution, we may derive some aid from that with which it is associated. Congress shall have power "to make all laws which shall be necessary and proper to carry into execution" the powers of the government. If the word "necessary" was used in that strict and rigorous sense for which the counsel for the State of Maryland contend, it would be an extraordinary departure from the usual course of the human mind, as exhibited in composition, to add a word, the only possible effect of which is to qualify that strict and rigorous mean-

---

[7] It is not clear which code the chief justice is thinking about, but this comment reveals a typical American bias about codes in the civil law tradition.

ing; to present to the mind the idea of some choice of means of legislation not straitened and compressed within the narrow limits for which gentlemen contend.

But the argument which most conclusively demonstrates the error of the construction contended for by the counsel for the State of Maryland, is founded on the intention of the Convention, as manifested in the whole clause. To waste time and argument in proving that, without it, Congress might carry its powers into execution, would be not much less idle than to hold a lighted taper to the sun. As little can it be required to prove, that in the absence of this clause, Congress would have some choice of means. That it might employ those which, in its judgment, would most advantageously effect the object to be accomplished. That any means adapted to the end, any means which tended directly to the execution of the constitutional powers of the government, were in themselves constitutional. This clause, as construed by the State of Maryland, would abridge, and almost annihilate this useful and necessary right of the legislature to select its means. . . .

The result of the most careful and attentive consideration bestowed upon this clause is, that if it does not enlarge, it cannot be construed to restrain the powers of Congress, or to impair the right of the legislature to exercise its best judgment in the selection of measures to carry into execution the constitutional powers of the government. . . .

We admit, as all must admit, that the powers of the government are limited, and that its limits are not to be transcended. But we think the sound construction of the constitution must allow to the national legislature that discretion,[8] with respect to the means by which the powers it confers are to be carried into execution, which will enable that body to perform the high duties assigned to it, in the manner most beneficial to the people. Let the end be legitimate, let it be within the scope of the constitution, and all means which are appropriate, which are plainly adapted to that end, which are not prohibited, but consistent with the letter and spirit of the constitution, are constitutional. . . .[9]

[8] What does the Court mean by discretion in this context? See the analysis of discretion in Chapter Three.

[9] The invocation of the "spirit" of the Constitution is the last of several very clever moves by the chief justice to counteract the theory of "strict construction" advocated in *Marbury*. What are some of the other rhetorical moves made in the opinion?

After this declaration, it can scarcely be necessary to say, that the existence of State banks can have no possible influence on the question. No trace is to be found in the constitution of an intention to create a dependence of the government of the Union on those of the States, for the execution of the great powers assigned to it. Its means are adequate to its ends; and on those means alone was it expected to rely for the accomplishment of its ends. To impose on it the necessity of resorting to means which it cannot control, which another government may furnish or withhold, would render its course precarious, the result of its measures uncertain, and create a dependence on other governments, which might disappoint its most important design, and is incompatible with the language of the constitution. But were it otherwise, the choice of means implies a right to choose a national bank in preference to State banks, and Congress alone can make the election.

After the most deliberate consideration, it is the unanimous and decided opinion of this Court, that the act to incorporate the Bank of the United States is a law made in pursuance of the constitution, and is a part of the supreme law of the land. . . .

It being the opinion of the Court, that the act incorporating the bank is constitutional; and that the power of establishing a branch in the State of Maryland might be properly exercised by the bank itself, we proceed to inquire—

2. Whether the State of Maryland may, without violating the constitution, tax that branch?

That the power of taxation is one of vital importance; that it is retained by the States; that it is not abridged by the grant of a similar power to the government of the Union; that it is to be concurrently exercised by the two governments: are truths which have never been denied. But, such is the paramount character of the constitution, that its capacity to withdraw any subject from the action of even this power, is admitted. The States are expressly forbidden to lay any duties on imports or exports, except what may be absolutely necessary for executing their inspection laws. If the obligation of this prohibition must be conceded—if it may restrain a State from the exercise of its taxing power on imports and exports; the same paramount character would seem to restrain, as it certainly may restrain, a State from such other exercise of this power, as is in its nature incompatible with, and repugnant to, the constitutional laws of the Union. A law, absolutely repugnant to another, as entirely repeals that other as if express terms of repeal were used.

On this ground the counsel for the bank place its claim to be exempted from the power of a State to tax its operations. There is no express provision for the case, but the claim has been sustained on a principle which so entirely pervades the constitution, is so intermixed with the materials which compose it, so interwoven with its web, so blended with its texture, as to be incapable of being separated from it, without rending it into shreds.

This great principle is, that the constitution and the laws made in pursuance thereof are supreme; that they control the constitution and laws of the respective States, and cannot be controlled by them. From this, which may be almost termed an axiom, other propositions are deduced as corollaries, on the truth or error of which, and on their application to this case, the cause has been supposed to depend. These are, 1st. that a power to create implies a power to preserve. 2nd. That a power to destroy, if wielded by a different hand, is hostile to, and incompatible with these powers to create and to preserve. 3d. That where this repugnancy exists, that authority which is supreme must control, not yield to that over which it is supreme.

These propositions, as abstract truths, would, perhaps, never be controverted. Their application to this case, however, has been denied; and, both in maintaining the affirmative and the negative, a splendor of eloquence, and strength of argument, seldom, if ever, surpassed, have been displayed.

The power of Congress to create, and of course to continue, the bank, was the subject of the preceding part of this opinion; and is no longer to be considered as questionable.

That the power of taxing it by the States may be exercised so as to destroy it, is too obvious to be denied. But taxation is said to be an absolute power, which acknowledges no other limits than those expressly prescribed in the constitution, and like sovereign power of every other description, is trusted to the discretion of those who use it. But the very terms of this argument admit that the sovereignty of the State, in the article of taxation itself, is subordinate to, and may be controlled by the constitution of the United States. How far it has been controlled by that instrument must be a question of construction. In making this construction, no principle not declared, can be admissible, which would defeat the legitimate operations of a supreme government. It is of the very essence of supremacy to remove all obstacles to its action within its own sphere, and so to modify every power vested in subordinate governments, as to exempt its own operations from their own influence. This effect need not be stated in terms. It is so involved in the declaration of supremacy, so necessarily implied in it, that the expression of it could not make it more certain. We must, therefore, keep it in view while construing the constitution.

The argument on the part of the State of Maryland, is, not that the States may directly resist a law of Congress, but that they may exercise their acknowledged powers upon it, and that the constitution leaves them this right in the confidence that they will not abuse it.

Before we proceed to examine this argument, and to subject it to the test of the constitution, we must be permitted to bestow a few considerations on the nature and extent of this original right of taxation, which is acknowledged to remain with the States. It is admitted that the power of taxing the people and their property is essential to the very existence of government, and may be legitimately exercised on the objects to which it is applicable, to the utmost extent to which the government may chuse to carry it. The only security against the abuse of this power, is found in the structure of the government itself. In imposing a tax the legislature acts upon its constituents. This is in general a sufficient security against erroneous and oppressive taxation.

The people of a State, therefore, give to their government a right of taxing themselves and their property, and as the exigencies of government cannot be limited, they prescribe no limits to the exercise of this right, resting confidently on the interest of the legislator, and on the influence of the constituents over their representative, to guard then against its abuse. But the means employed by the government of the Union have no such security, nor is the right of a State to tax them sustained by the same theory. Those means are not given by the people of a particular State, not given by the constituents of the legislature, which claim the right to tax them, but by the people of all the States. They are given by all, for the benefit of all—and upon theory, should be subjected to that government only which belongs to all.

It may be objected to this definition, that the power of taxation is not confined to the people and property of a State. It may be exercised upon every object brought within its jurisdiction.

This is true. But to what source do we trace this right? It is obvious, that it is an incident of sovereignty, and is co-extensive with that to which it is an incident. All subjects over which the sovereign power of a State extends, are objects of taxation; but those over which it does not extend, are, upon the soundest principles, exempt from taxation. This proposition may almost be pronounced self-evident.

The sovereignty of a State extends to every thing which exists by its own authority, or is introduced by its permission; but does it extend to those means which are employed by Congress to carry into execution powers conferred on that body by the people of the United States? We think it demonstrable that it does not. Those powers are not given by the people of a single State. They are given by the people of the United States, to a government whose laws, made in pursuance of the constitution, are declared to be supreme. . . . *That the power to tax involves the power to destroy*;[10] [emphasis added] that the power to destroy may defeat and render useless the power to create; that there is a plain repugnance, in conferring on one government a power to control the constitutional measures of another, which other, with respect to those very measures, is declared to be supreme over that which exerts the control, are propositions not to be denied. But all inconsistencies are to be reconciled by the magic of the word CONFIDENCE. Taxation, it is said, does not necessarily and unavoidably destroy. To carry it to the excess of destruction would be an abuse, to presume which, would banish that confidence which is essential to all government.

But is this a case of confidence? Would the people of any one State trust those of another with a power to control the most insignificant operations of their State government? We know they would not. Why, then, should we suppose that the people of any one State should be willing to trust those of another with a power to control the operations of a government to which they have confided their most important and most valuable interests? In the legislature of the Union alone, are all represented. The legislature of the Union alone, therefore, can be trusted by the people with the power of controlling measures which

---

[10] This is the second unforgettable line in this opinion.

concern all, in the confidence that it will not be abused. This, then, is not a case of confidence, and we must consider it as it really is. . . .

If the States may tax one instrument, employed by the government in the execution of its powers, they may tax any and every other instrument. They may tax the mail; they may tax the mint; they may tax patent rights; they may tax the papers of the custom-house; they may tax judicial process; they may tax all the means employed by the government, to an excess which would defeat all the ends of government. This was not intended by the American people. They did not design to make their government dependent on the States. . . .

In the course of the argument, the Federalist has been quoted; and the opinions expressed by the authors of that work have been justly supposed to be entitled to great respect in expounding the constitution. No tribute can be paid to them which exceeds their merit; but in applying their opinions to the cases which may arise in the progress of our government, a right to judge of their correctness must be retained; and, to understand the argument, we must examine the proposition it maintains, and the objections against which it is directed. The subject of those numbers, from which passages have been cited, is the unlimited power of taxation which is vested in the general government. The objection to this unlimited power, which the argument seeks to remove, is stated with fullness and clearness. It is, "that an indefinite power of taxation in the latter (the government of the Union) might, and probably would, in time, deprive the former (the government of the States) of the means of providing for their own necessities; and would subject them entirely to the mercy of the national legislature. As the laws of the Union are to become the supreme law of the land; as it is to have power to pass all laws that may be necessary for carrying into execution the authorities with which it is proposed to vest it; the national government might at any time abolish the taxes imposed for State objects, upon the pretense of an interference with its own. It might allege a necessity for doing this, in order to give efficacy to the national revenues; and thus all the resources of taxation might, by degrees, become the subjects of federal monopoly, to the entire exclusion and destruction of the State governments." . . .

It has also been insisted, that, as the power of taxation in the general and State governments is acknowledged to be concurrent, every argument which would sustain the right of the general government to tax banks chartered by the States, will equally sustain the right of the States to tax banks chartered by the general government.

But the two cases are not on the same reason. The people of all the States have created the general government, and have conferred upon it the general power of taxation. The people of all the States, and the States themselves, are represented in Congress, and, by their representatives, exercise this power. When they tax the chartered institutions of the States, they tax their constituents; and these taxes must be uniform. But, when a State taxes the operations of the government of the United States, it acts upon institutions created, not by their own constituents, but by people over whom they claim no control. It acts upon the measures of a government created by others as well as themselves, for the benefit of others in common with themselves. The difference is that which always exists, and always must exist, between the action of the whole on a part, and the action of a part on the whole—between the laws of a government declared to be supreme, and those of a government which, when in opposition to those laws, is not supreme. . . .

We are unanimously of opinion, that the law passed by the legislature of Maryland, imposing a tax on the Bank of the United States, is unconstitutional and void.

This opinion does not deprive the States of any resources which they originally possessed. It does not extend to a tax paid by the real property of the bank, in common with the other real property within the State, nor to a tax imposed on the interest which the citizens of Maryland may hold in this institution, in common with other property of the same description throughout the State. But this is a tax on the operations of the bank, and is, consequently, a tax on the operation of an instrument employed by the government of the Union to carry its powers into execution. Such a tax must be unconstitutional . . . it is further Adjudged and Ordered, that the judgment of the said Baltimore County Court be reversed and annulled, and that judgment be entered in the said Baltimore County Court for the said James W. McCulloch.

■

QUESTIONS AND COMMENTS

1. Chief Justice Marshall urges the construction of the Constitution as a whole with an emphasis on the spirit as well as the letter of the na-

tional charter. The creation of the bank is legitimate as a necessary means to achieve the implied purposes of the Constitution. True, the Constitution does authorize Congress "To make all Laws which shall be necessary and proper for carrying into Execution" the other "enumerated going Powers, and all other Powers vested by this Constitution in the Government of the United States" (Article I, Section 8, Clause 18). But could not this approach have justified Congress's grant of original jurisdiction to the Supreme Court to issue writs of mandamus? Was that grant of jurisdiction not "necessary and proper" as means of executing the president's power to appoint judges according to Article II, Section 2, Clause 2 of the same Constitution?

2. The mode of interpretation explicated in *McCulloch* has various names. It could be called "pragmatic," "purposive," or "teleological." The term *pragmatic* would probably be the most commonly used today. The conflict between the philosophies of strict and pragmatic interpretation continues to this day. The difference is captured nicely by the terms *letter* and *spirit* of the Constitution or by the emphasis on particular words such as *appellate* and *original* as opposed to Marshall's argument here that the decision should turn on "a fair construction of the whole instrument."

3. The second half of the *McCulloch* opinion raises an issue that remains as troubling as the proper mode of interpreting the Constitution. And that question is, What is the nature of the states in the American federation? Are they independently sovereign entities? Are these merely administrative units—something like the *départments* in France? Notice that the chief justice begins his opinion by describing Maryland as "a sovereign state." But later he says that the attributes of sovereignty are divided between the federal government and the states. Does this language matter? The language of sovereignty was popular in the nineteenth century but may be less so today. The proposed Constitution for Europe, the first part of which was published in June 2003, seems to disregard the word altogether. There is no discussion about whether the member states retain sovereignty or sovereignty is vested in the union.[11]

4. The language aside, the problem remains whether the American Union draws its authority from the states or from some other source.

[11] We are relying here on the French text as published in *Le Monde*, June 18, 2003.

For Chief Justice Marshall, the critical word in the Constitution is *people*, as in the first words of the preamble: "We the *People* of the United States." The use of the singular as opposed to the plural *peoples* suggests a unity of the people that transcends the power of the states.[12] Compare the Preamble to the proposed Constitution for Europe, which explicitly refers repeatedly to the "peoples of Europe," recognizing that each people seeks to retain its "national identity."

5. On the other hand, the procedure for ratifying the Constitution, Article VII, refers only to the states: "The Ratification of the Conventions of nine States, shall be sufficient for the Establishment of this Constitution between the States so ratifying the Same." It seems that this language recognizes that just as the European Union shall be constituted by its member states, the American federal government was as well. If the states gave birth to the federal government, they arguably enjoy greater powers than they would if the federal government had created them. But even if it is true that the states created the federal government, it would not necessarily follow that Maryland had the authority to tax the bank. Yet the argument based on the sources of authority carries some weight.

6. Chief Justice Marshall was fully aware of this textual argument in the ratification clause and he was ready with a response: "It is true, they [the people] assembled in their several States—and where else should they have assembled?" In other words, the fact that the people met and voted state by state did not mean that the states were ratifying the Constitution. The states just happened to be where the people were meeting—as irrelevant to the nature of the Constitution as the fact that it was drafted in Philadelphia. Yet this interpretation does not square with the procedure for amending the Constitution, which in Article V requires ratification by three-fourths of the states, either as expressed by the state legislature or "in Convention." If the states have the power both to initiate and to block amendments to the Constitution,[13] then are they not the final repository of authority in the constitutional system?

---

[12] The singular term is used seven times in the Constitution. The plural is never used.

[13] The Article V power to initiate a convention requires a petition to Congress by the legislatures of two-thirds of the states. Congress is then supposed to call a convention

7. To be fair, we have to concede that the Constitution is simply ambiguous about whether the ultimate source of constitutional authority
is "the people" or the "states." The ambiguity is captured in the
Tenth Amendment, which provides: "The powers not delegated to
the United States by the Constitution, nor prohibited by it to the
States, are reserved to the States respectively, or to the people." The
undelegated powers are retained either by the states or the people,
but we do not know which one.

8. In the thirty-two years that followed the *McCulloch* decision, the
problem of defining the status of the states became ever more acute,
and for reasons that generated much more passion than the problem
of a state's taxing a federal bank. The great problem of the time was
slavery. In several passages the Constitution recognized the "peculiar
institution" of property rights over the lives of other human beings.
The Northern colonies and states had progressively abolished slavery,
in line with the general trend in Europe and Latin America. The
Southern states retained the practice, largely because the invention of
the cotton gin in 1793 encouraged an agricultural economy and plan-
tation culture based on slave labor. By the 1830s, Northern abolitionists were becoming so influential in opposition to slavery that, with
the rapid expansion of the United States and the addition of ever
more states, the Southern slave states feared that a three-fourths majority of the states would eventually amend the Constitution to abolish slavery in the entire country. There were many signs that this
would eventually happen.

9. The second great event of 1803, even more important for the history
of the United States than the *Marbury* decision, was Jefferson's purchase of the Louisiana Territory from Napoleon's France. This territory, stretching from New Orleans to the present-day states of Montana, Wyoming, and Colorado, doubled the size of the United States.
The big question was whether slavery would be allowed in the new
states that would be carved out of the new territory. Missouri was
one of these proposed states, and its legal system had permitted slavery. The question was whether it could enter the Union as a "slave"
state. At that point the slave and free states were at parity. Neither

to adopt the proposed amendment, which in turn is submitted to the states for ratification.

side wanted to see the other camp gain in numbers. Under the compromise of 1820, Missouri was admitted as a slave state and Maine as
a free state, but more significantly, slavery was thereafter prohibited in
the vast northern portion of the Louisiana Purchase. With the expansion toward the West (California was admitted in 1850), the number
of "free" states would be constantly increasing.

10. It is unimaginable today that slavery could withstand constitutional
scrutiny in a modern democratic society. Why is that? The simple
explanation is that every modern written constitution adopted since
the Second World War recognizes the principle of equality under the
law. There is much more to say later about the theory and practice
of equality, but for now we need to underscore the great scar on the
Constitution of 1789. There was no mention of equality among human beings as a constitutional principle. That thought is worth repeating a dozen times. The Bill of Rights recognized all sorts of
rights and freedoms but remains studiously silent on the subject of
equality.

11. But the issue of the times was not simply equality among persons.
The dispute about slavery was never clearly separated from the basic
issue in *McCulloch*; namely, what was the authority of each state (its
sovereignty, if you will) to determine its own path on the great moral
issue of slavery? There were many who believed that slavery was a
moral evil but still held fast to the idea that each state should decide
the matter for itself.

12. In 1857, in *Dred Scott v. Sanford*, 60 U.S. 393, the Supreme Court
held the Missouri Compromise unconstitutional—in particular, the
clauses preventing the spread of slavery into the northern territories.
We turn to that American watershed in the next chapter, but to grasp
the full significance of what happened in 1857, we have to explore a
contrary constitutional tradition in the United States.

■

Further Reading

The development of federalism up to the time of *McCulloch* is well depicted in
Stanley M. Elkins and Eric L. McKitrick, *The Age of Federalism: The Early American
Republic, 1788–1800* (Oxford: Oxford University Press, 1994). The effects of fed-

eralism and the westward expansion on one another is detailed in Jon Kukla, *A Wilderness So Immense: The Louisiana Purchase and the Destiny of America* (New York: Knopf, 2003). As to what remains to the states in the federal system, see *The Tenth Amendment and State Sovereignty: Constitutional History and Contemporary Issues* (Mark R. Killenbeck, ed.) (Lanham, MD: Rowman & Littlefield, 2002).

EIGHT

The Alternative Constitution

This chapter is more complicated than most, and therefore we present you with an outline of the materials in advance:

A. The idea of an alternative Constitution
B. The Bill of Rights
C. The Gettysburg Address
D. The Reconstruction Amendments
E. A case upholding the new amendments: *Strauder*
F. A case defeating the new amendments: Civil rights cases

All of these themes revolve around the central question of whether there is an alternative Constitution, what it means, what its sources are, and whether it has ultimately triumphed in American law. First we need to explain the concept of an alternative Constitution.

Lawyers like to pretend that the law is a single unified and consistent whole. But in fact there are always countervoices within the tradition. A countervoice is an expression of law that was once dominant but is no longer so or a legal principle that seeks to establish itself but is not yet fully recognized. The civil law tradition, based on codification and the dominant doctrine (*herrschende Lehre*), may appear to suppress countervoices. Yet these countervoices do survive in the scholarly literature of the civilian tradition.

The common law cherishes its dissenters. They are kept alive in dissenting opinions and as "minority" rules that survive in a portion of the many jurisdictions that make up the common law. The U.S. Supreme Court can rule one way, but the state supreme courts can rule another way under their state constitutions (and these decisions are not subject to appeal). The countervoices are also found in the academic literature and in the "nonjusticiable" decisions of the executive and legislative branches. For example, the Supreme Court has never decided (yet) whether the wars in Vietnam and Iraq were legal or illegal, but there has been a lively debate about those questions in the academic literature and popular press. On many questions of American law, there are two or more answers: the dominant view of the case law or scholarly opinion and many dissenting views.

The chapter introduces you to an idea that began as a dissenting view and eventually became the dominant view of the Constitution. The place to begin is with the recognition that the Constitution was but the third in a series of basic documents establishing the United States: (1) the Declaration of Independence (1776), (2) the Articles of Confederation (signed 1777; final ratification, 1781), and finally (3) the Constitution, drafted in 1787. It is generally agreed that the Constitution replaced the Articles of Confederation, but neither the 1777 nor the 1787 charters nullified, in any way, the Declaration of Independence. It was always and is still the source of national inspiration. No one celebrates and few know the date the Constitution was ratified or entered in force, but every American recognizes July 4, 1776, as beginning the American experience of self-government (although a little-known fact is that the Declaration was only adopted by the Continental Congress on that day and was not signed by the delegates until August 2, 1776).

The problem is, What is the relationship between the Declaration and the Constitution? There are some important differences between the two documents. See if you can identify them by reading through this excerpt:

IN CONGRESS, July 4, 1776.

The unanimous Declaration of the thirteen united States of America,

When in the Course of human events, it becomes necessary for one people to dissolve the political bands which have connected them with another, and to assume among the powers of the earth, the separate and equal station to which the Laws of Nature and of Nature's God entitle them, a decent respect to the opinions of mankind requires that they should declare the causes which impel them to the separation.

We hold these truths to be self-evident, that all men are created equal, that they are endowed by their Creator with certain unalienable Rights, that among these are Life, Liberty, and the pursuit of Happiness—That to secure these rights, Governments are instituted among Men, deriving their just powers from the consent of the governed, that whenever any Form of Government becomes destructive of these ends, it is the Right of the People to alter or to abolish it, and to institute new Government, laying its foundation on such principles, and organizing its powers in such form, as to them shall seem most likely to effect their Safety and Happiness. Prudence, indeed, will dictate that Governments long established should not be changed for light and transient causes; and accordingly all experience hath shewn, that mankind are more disposed to suffer, while evils are sufferable, than to right themselves by abolishing the forms to which they are accustomed. But when a long train of abuses and usurpations, pursuing invariably the same Object, evinces a design to reduce them under absolute Despotism, it is their right, it is their duty, to throw off such Government, and to provide new Guards for their future security. Such has been the patient sufferance of these Colonies; and such is now the necessity which constrains them to alter their former Systems of Government. The history of the present King of Great-Britain is a history of repeated injuries and usurpations, all having in direct object the establishment of an absolute Tyranny over these States. To prove this, let Facts be submitted to a candid world.

[A list of complaints against George III follows, which is omitted here.]

And for the support of this Declaration, with a firm reliance on the protection of divine Providence, we mutually pledge to each other our Lives, our Fortunes, and our sacred Honor.

QUESTIONS AND COMMENTS

1. Notice that this document has religious overtones that are entirely absent in the Constitution drafted eleven years later. There are frequent references to "Nature's God" and "divine Providence." Why did these religious references disappear from the Constitution? In early 2003, many Europeans were concerned that the concepts of God and Providence failed to gain inclusion in the proposed draft Constitution of Europe. In this respect, the European and the American constitutions share a common emphasis on human will as the motivating force for establishing the union. But the Declaration was different. It was drafted after the war of independence against Great Britain had already begun. Its signers feared that they might be arrested and tried for treason against the Crown.

2. In terms of the debate that would soon ensue about slavery, the most significant and famous line in the Declaration provided a benchmark for the abolitionist case: "All men are created equal." In light of the total silence of the Constitution on the issue of equality, this proposition provides a moral guidepost in morally confused times. Affirming the moral equality of all "men" was a remarkable statement. Its sources and its proper interpretation are open to debate. Jefferson drafted the document, but how he came to the idea is not clear. The world had never seen anything quite like it. Immanuel Kant had not written about the necessity of equality under the rule of law; the French had yet to coin their revolutionary slogan *liberté, égalité, fraternité* ("liberty, equality, fraternity"); John Locke had written about equality—among human beings, although also among all God's creatures and not necessarily just among human beings.[1]

3. The famous maxim "All men are created equal" lends itself to four different interpretations, each of which is plausible:

[1] See Jeremy Waldron, *God, Locke, and Equality: Christian Foundations in Locke's Political Thought* (Cambridge: Cambridge University Press, 2002).

1. *All peoples [all nations] are created equal.* That is, the Americans are equal to the English, and therefore the Americans are entitled to decide for themselves what kind of government they wish to have. This idea expresses the notion rooted in the common law since Sir Edward Coke's opinion in *Calvin's Case*[2] that all subjects of the same king are equal in their rights.

2. *The people are equal in stature to King George III.* The people can decide for themselves whether to submit to the authority of a king. In other words, there is no "divine right of kings," because no human is created to rule, nor is any created subservient.

3. *All men (meaning males) are equal.* Could this really have been the intent? Would it have made any sense to make a radical affirmation of human equality and leave women out of the picture?

4. *All individuals are equal in the sight of God.* This idea, known as *imago dei*, was very important to John Locke.[3] It not only reflects the creation text of Genesis but also respects the idea of God as an infinite, in comparison to which all people would be the same.

Any of these interpretations is possible. If the fourth interpretation of universal human equality was the correct one at the time, it is clear that it did not survive the drafting of the clauses in the Constitution recognizing the existence of slavery. Yet the Declaration of Independence lived on as a countervoice of the American constitutional tradition. It inspired the abolitionists of the 1830s and 1840s to fight for the equal legal status of black Americans. Yet lawyers were fully aware of the contradiction between the Declaration, interpreted as an affirmation of human equality, and the Constitution.

4. The fight between the dominant voice and the countervoice came to a head in the notorious case of *Dred Scott v. Sanford* (60 U.S. 393 (1857)), in which the Supreme Court reached many controversial and provocative conclusions. This was the decision that held the Missouri Compromise of 1820 unconstitutional because it interfered with the right to own property—namely, slaves in the northern territories.

---

[2] *7 Coke Reports* 1 (1608). Coke appears also to have been responsible for drafting the principle that colonists would have the rights of Englishmen into the early charters for the Massachusetts colonies.

[3] See Waldron, *supra* note 1, at 22–43, discussing the problem of Adam, Eve, the image of God, and equality between the sexes.

With Chief Justice Taney writing the opinion, the Court also held
that black slaves could never become citizens of the United States. As
part of his argument, Taney sought to resolve the contradiction between the Declaration of Independence and the Constitution:

> But it is too clear for dispute, that the enslaved African race
> were not intended to be included [in the affirmation "all
> men are created equal"], and formed no part of the people
> who framed and adopted this declaration; for if the language,
> as understood in that day, would embrace them, the conduct
> of the distinguished men who framed the Declaration of In-
> dependence would have been utterly and flagrantly inconsis-
> tent with the principles they asserted, [namely, all men are
> created equal]; and instead of the sympathy of mankind, to
> which they so confidently appealed, they would have de-
> served and received universal rebuke and reprobation. (*Scott
> v. Sanford*, 60 U.S. 393, 702-03 (1856))

■

The *Dred Scott* decision is widely regarded as one of the worst ever
rendered by the U.S. Supreme Court. Abraham Lincoln lost so much
respect for the chief justice that he later asserted his rejection of this
opinion when he refused to obey a writ of habeas corpus to release prisoners held in Baltimore. This was a rare moment in history when an
American president refused to obey an order issued by the Supreme Court
or a justice of the court.

After the *Dred Scott* decision and Lincoln's election in November
1860, civil war was inevitable. Lincoln and Congress sought to assure the
Southern states that they preferred the "Union" to the abolition of slavery.
But it did not matter. At dawn on April 12, 1861, the military force of
South Carolina started shelling a federal fortress in the middle of Charles-
ton harbor. The bloodiest war in American history was under way. More
than 620,000 men died, on both sides, before General Robert E. Lee
handed Ulysses S. Grant his sword at Appomattox Courthouse, Virginia,
on April 9, 1865.[4] More Americans died in the Civil War than in all other
wars fought by the United States—*put together.*

---

[4] Americans familiar with the Civil War would know that the effective end of large-scale
combat came with Lee's surrender, although a large army under Joseph Johnston did

The war tested two questions. The original question motivating the fighting and dying was whether the United States would remain one Union or split into two. The Confederacy of eleven states claimed the right to secede from the Union, precisely as the thirteen colonies had seceded from Great Britain in 1776. In his famous Second Inaugural Address in 1865, Lincoln wisely commented that both sides in the Civil War "read the same Bible and prayed to the same God." They also both claimed authority for their actions in the Declaration of Independence. Secession, then, was one question. But as became clear to Lincoln and the Northern forces by January 1863, the real question was whether the United States that survived the war would be a Union that tolerated slavery in those states that wanted it or whether it would be a country based on freedom and equality for all.

In the middle of the war, on November 19, 1863, Lincoln traveled to Gettysburg, Pennsylvania, to dedicate a burial ground for the Union troops who died there in a bloody but critical battle fought in the early days of July 1863. The "address" that Lincoln gave at Gettysburg has turned out to be the most important speech ever given in American history. Read it carefully:

> Four score and seven years ago our fathers brought forth on this continent a new nation, conceived in liberty and dedicated to the proposition that all men are created equal. Now we are engaged in a great Civil War, testing whether that nation or any nation so conceived and so dedicated can long endure. We are met on a great battle-field of that war. We have come to dedicate a portion of that field as a final resting place for those who here gave their lives that that nation might live. It is altogether fitting and proper that we should do this. But in a larger sense, we cannot dedicate— we cannot consecrate—we cannot hallow this ground. The brave men, living and dead, who struggled here have consecrated it far

not surrender until April 26, 1865, and Confederate units in the Western states did not disband or surrender until even later. An important regional difference among Americans is that Southerners often consider the war to include the military occupation of the southern states, which did not end until 1877. See Eric Foner, *Reconstruction: America's Unfinished Revolution, 1863–1877* (illustrated ed.) (New York: HarperCollins, 1988; Saint Helens, OR: Perennial Press, 2002).

above our poor power to add or detract. The world will little note nor long remember what we say here, but it can never forget what they did here. It is for us the living, rather, to be dedicated here to the unfinished work which they who fought here have thus far so nobly advanced. It is rather for us to be here dedicated to the great task remaining before us—that from these honored dead we take increased devotion to that cause for which they gave the last full measure of devotion—that we here highly resolve that these dead shall not have died in vain, that this nation, under God, shall have a new birth of freedom, and that government of the people, by the people, for the people shall not perish from the earth.

This is all there is to the most famous speech in U.S. history. It took Lincoln two minutes to deliver it. Notice the unintended irony of his statement: "The world will little note nor long remember what we say here." Perhaps in all modesty Lincoln thought this was true, but history has decided otherwise.

Note the following features of this 268-word address:

1. "Four score and seven years ago." A score is twenty. Lincoln was referring to something that happened eighty-seven years prior to 1863. What was that? The adoption of the Constitution?
2. "All men are created equal." Where does this phrase come from? What does it mean in this context?
3. "A new nation." Notice that the constitutional text relies on the word *people* and never refers to Americans as a nation. In 1863 the Americans are no longer a people but a nation. Does this shift in usage have any significance? Does it provide an argument against secession by the eleven states in the South? What is the argument?
4. Note that the nation is now a "nation under God." Is this way of speaking more consistent with the Constitution or with the Declaration of Independence?
5. The word *people* returns in the explanation of the commitment to democracy in the last line of the address: "Government of the people, by the people, for the people." Review the Constitution and its attitude toward democracy. Is there anything like this phrase in the document of 1789?

It was clear that when the guns fell silent in April 1865 a new constitutional order would have to be created. The new order is found in the Reconstruction amendments, adopted respectively in 1865, 1868, and 1870: All of these amendments include provisions that authorize Congress to enforce the amendment "by appropriate legislation."

Thirteenth Amendment (1865)

SECTION 1. Slavery prohibited.

Neither slavery nor involuntary servitude, except as a punishment for crime thereof the party shall have been duly convicted, shall exist within the United States, or any place subject to their jurisdiction.

Fourteenth Amendment (1868)

SECTION 1. Citizens of the United States.

All persons born or naturalized in the United States, and subject to the jurisdiction thereof, are citizens of the United States and of the State wherein they reside. No State shall make or enforce any law which shall abridge the privileges or immunities of citizens of the United States; nor shall any State deprive any person of life, liberty, or Property, without due Process of law; nor deny to any person within its jurisdiction the equal Protection of the laws.

[Sections 2, 3, 4 are omitted here.]

Fifteenth Amendment (1870).

SECTION 1.
Right of citizens to vote; Race or color not to disqualify.

The right of citizens of the United States to vote shall not be denied or abridged by the United States or by any State on account of race, color, or previous condition of servitude.

Note that all three of these amendments contain a supplementary provision, written in more or less identical language, which holds: "Congress shall have power to enforce this article by appropriate legislation."

The significance of this language will become apparent later, when we take up the civil rights cases.

QUESTIONS AND COMMENTS

1. Recall that the *Dred Scott* decision had held that blacks could not become citizens of the United States. Which provision in these three amendments overrides that holding?

2. Note the difference in structure between the Thirteenth and Fourteenth Amendments. The Thirteenth is written without reference to the states: "Neither slavery nor involuntary servitude . . . shall exist. . . ." The Fourteenth is written with the states as subject: "No state shall make or enforce any law. . . ." What is the difference?

3. Does the Fifteenth Amendment grant the right to vote to former slaves? If not, what does it do? Subsequent extensions of the franchise have been made on the basis of the same formula that is used in the Fifteenth Amendment, "The right . . . to vote shall not be denied or abridged . . . [on the basis of race, etc.]. The prohibited grounds for denying the right to vote are extended to include sex (Nineteenth Amendment), failure to pay a poll tax (Twenty-Fourth Amendment), and age for those over eighteen (Twenty-Sixth Amendment).

4. Recall the phrase used in the Declaration of Independence: "[All men] are endowed by their Creator with certain unalienable Rights, that among these are Life, Liberty and the pursuit of Happiness." What is the analogous phrase adopted in the Fourteenth Amendment?

5. The inclusion in the Reconstruction Amendments of the language "Congress shall have the authority to enforce this article by appropriate legislation" was a sign of a new beginning, the commitment to a new legal order based on the principles of the Declaration of Independence and the Gettysburg Address. The major question after the war was whether this new legal order would triumph in the courts.

6. There was little doubt that the courts would protect former slaves from the worst forms of depersonalization and degradation that had prevailed under the ancien régime. But the problem was the extent the Court and Congress would go to eliminate the social implications of slavery and racial discrimination.

7. For an excellent study of the momentous events in April 1865 (including both Lee's surrender and the assassination of Abraham Lin-

coln), see Jay Winik, *April 1865: The Month That Saved America* (New York: HarperCollins, 2001). The Confederate generals surrendered honorably, but the spirit of the South was hardly defeated. Slavery was gone, but the idea of states' rights and autonomy survived. If you look at the subsequent history of the United States, there is some truth in the paradoxical statement that the Confederacy was born when Lee handed Grant his sword.

8. The new battlefield was the courts. The fight between those who believe in a single nation governed by Washington and those who believe in the autonomy of the states continues to this day. The following two cases signaled the combat lines that took hold in the decades immediately after the Civil War.

Strauder v. West Virginia

Supreme Court of the United States
100 U.S. 303 (1879)

STRONG, J.:

The plaintiff in error, a colored man, was indicted for murder in the Circuit Court of Ohio County, in West Virginia, on the 20th of October, 1874, and upon trial was convicted and sentenced. The record was then removed to the Supreme Court of the State, and there the judgment of the Circuit Court was affirmed. The present case is a writ of error to that court, and it is now, in substance, averred that at the trial in the State court the defendant (now plaintiff in error) was denied rights to which he was entitled under the Constitution and laws of the United States.

In the Circuit Court of the State . . . the defendant [complained] that "by virtue of the laws of the State of West Virginia no colored man was eligible to be a member of the grand jury or to serve on a petit jury in the State[5]; that white men are so eligible, and that by

---

[5] The "grand jury" decides whether there is probable cause to indict a potential defendant for a crime, after which the defendant is prosecuted in a trial before the "petit jury," which determines whether the defendant is guilty of that crime. Historically, the grand jury had more jurors assigned to it, hence the names of both.

reason of his being a colored man and having been a slave, he had reason to believe, and did believe, he could not have the full and equal benefit of all laws and proceedings in the State of West Virginia for the security of his person as is enjoyed by white citizens. . . ." This petition was denied by the State court, and the cause was forced to trial. . . .

The law of the State to which reference was made in the petition for removal and in the several motions was enacted on the 12th of March, 1873 (Acts of 1872–73, p. 102), and it is as follows: "All white male persons who are twenty-one years of age and who are citizens of this State shall be liable to serve as jurors, except as herein provided." The persons excepted are State officials.

In this court, several errors have been assigned, and the controlling questions underlying them all are, first, whether, by the Constitution and laws of the United States, every citizen of the United States has a right to a trial of an indictment against him by a jury selected and impaneled without discrimination against his race or color, because of race or color. . . .

It is to be observed that [this] question is not whether a colored man, when an indictment has been preferred against him, has a right to a grand or a petit jury composed in whole or in part of persons of his own race or color, but it is whether, in the composition or selection of jurors by whom he is to be indicted or tried, all persons of his race or color may be excluded by law, solely because of their race or color, so that by no possibility can any colored man sit upon the jury.

The questions are important, for they demand a construction of the recent amendments of the Constitution. If the defendant has a right to have a jury selected for the trial of his case without discrimination against all persons of his race or color, because of their race or color, the right, if not created, is protected by those amendments, and the legislation of Congress under them. . . .

[The Fourteenth Amendment] is one of a series of constitutional provisions having a common purpose; namely, securing to a race recently emancipated, a race that through many generations had been held in slavery, all the civil rights that the superior race enjoy. The true spirit and meaning of the amendments, as we said in the Slaughter-House Cases (16 Wall. 36), cannot be understood without keeping in view the history of the times when they were adopted, and the general objects they plainly sought to accomplish. At the time when they were incorporated into the Constitution, it required little knowledge of human nature to anticipate that those who had long been regarded as an inferior and subject race would, when suddenly raised to the rank of citizenship, be looked upon with jealousy and positive dislike, and that State laws might be enacted or enforced to perpetuate the distinctions that had before existed. Discriminations against them had been habitual. It was well known that in some States laws making such discriminations then existed, and others might well be expected. The colored race, as a race, was abject and ignorant, and in that condition was unfitted to command the respect of those who had superior intelligence. Their training had left them mere children, and as such they needed the protection which a wise government extends to those who are unable to protect themselves. They especially needed protection against unfriendly action in the States where they were resident. It was in view of these considerations the Fourteenth Amendment was framed and adopted. It was designed to assure to the colored race the enjoyment of all the civil rights that under the law are enjoyed by white persons, and to give to that race the protection of the general government, in that enjoyment, whenever it should be denied by the States. It not only gave citizenship and the privileges of citizenship to persons of color, but it denied to any State the power to withhold from them the equal protection of the laws, and authorized Congress to enforce its provisions by appropriate legislation. . . .

If this is the spirit and meaning of the amendment, whether it means more or not, it is to be construed liberally, to carry out the purposes of its framers. . . . It ordains that no State shall deprive any person of life, liberty, or property, without due process of law, or deny to any person within its jurisdiction the equal protection of the laws. What is this but declaring that the law in the States shall be the same for the black as for the white; that all persons, whether colored or white, shall stand equal before the laws of the States, and, in regard to the colored race, for whose protection the amendment was primarily designed, that no discrimination shall be made against them by law because of their color? The words of the amendment, it is true, are prohibitory, but they contain a necessary implication of a positive immunity, or right, most valuable to the colored race—the right to exemption from unfriendly legislation against them distinctively as colored—exemption from legal discriminations, implying inferiority in civil society, lessening the security of their enjoyment of the rights which others enjoy, and discriminations which are steps towards reducing them to the condition of a subject race.

That the West Virginia statute respecting juries—the statute that controlled the selection of the grand and petit jury in the case of the plaintiff in error—is such a discrimination ought not to be doubted. Nor would it be if the persons excluded by it were white men. If in those States where the colored people constitute a majority of the entire population a law should be enacted excluding all white men from jury service, thus denying to them the privilege of participating equally with the blacks in the administration of justice, we apprehend no one would be heard to claim that it would not be a denial to white men of the equal protection of the laws. . . .

The right to a trial by jury is guaranteed to every citizen of West Virginia by the Constitution of that State, and the constitution of juries is a very essential part of the protection such a mode of trial is intended to secure. The very idea of a jury is a body of men composed of the peers or equals of the person whose rights it is selected or summoned to determine; that is, of his neighbors, fellows, associates, persons having the same legal status in society as that which he holds. Blackstone, in his Commentaries, says, "The right of trial by jury, or the country, is a trial by the peers of every Englishman, and is the grand bulwark of his liberties, and is secured to him by the Great Charter."[6] . . .

We do not say that within the limits from which it is not excluded by the amendment a State may not prescribe the qualifications of its jurors, and in so doing make discriminations. It may confine the selection to males, to freeholders, to citizens, to persons within certain ages, or to persons having educational qualifications. We do not believe the Fourteenth Amendment was ever intended to prohibit this. Looking at its history, it is clear it had no such purpose. Its aim was against discrimination because of race or color. As we have said more than once, its design was to protect an emancipated race, and to strike

---

[6] Notice that this language about "trial by one's peers" does not appear in the U.S. Constitution. It comes from the Magna Carta, Chapter Thirty-Nine.

down all possible legal discriminations against those who belong to it. . . .

There was error, therefore, in proceeding to the trial of the indictment against him after his petition was filed, as also in overruling his challenge to the array of the jury, and in refusing to quash the panel.

The judgment of the Supreme Court of West Virginia will be reversed, and the case remitted with instructions to reverse the judgment of the Circuit Court of Ohio county; and it is

So ordered.

FIELD, J.:

I dissent from the judgment of the court in this case, on the grounds stated in my opinion in Ex parte Virginia (infra, p. 349), and Justice Clifford concurs with me.[7]

In reading the next case, keep in mind that the Reconstruction Amendments (Thirteenth, Fourteenth, and Fifteenth) explicitly expanded the power of Congress to include the authority "to enact appropriate legislation" to enforce the new amendments.

Civil Rights Cases

Supreme Court of the United States
109 U.S. 3 (1883)

These cases were all founded on the first and second sections of the Act of Congress, known as the Civil Rights Act, passed March 1, 1875, entitled

---

[7] Ex parte Virginia, 100 U.S. 339 (1879), in which Justice Field's dissent raised a different problem: whether a judge could be imprisoned for having failed to select blacks to sit on a jury in a state case. Justice Field ends his long dissent with general skepticism about the trend of the Court in interpreting and applying the equal protection clause:

> The legislation of Congress is founded, and is sustained by this court, as it seems to me, upon a theory as to what constitutes the equal protection of the laws, which is purely speculative, not warranted by any experience of the country, and not in accordance with the understanding of the people as to the meaning of those terms since the organization of the government. 100 U.S. at 370.

"An Act to protect all citizens in their civil and legal rights" (18 Stat. 335).
Two of the cases, those against Stanley and Nichols, were indictments for de-
nying to persons of color the accommodations and privileges of an inn or hotel;
two of them, those against Ryan and Singleton, were, one on information,
the other an indictment, for denying to individuals the privileges and accom-
modations of a theatre, the information against Ryan being for refusing a col-
ored person a seat in the dress circle of Maguire's theatre in San Francisco;
and the indictment against Singleton was for denying to another person,
whose color was not stated, the full enjoyment of the accommodations of the
theatre known as the Grand Opera House in New York, "said denial not
being made for any reasons by law applicable to citizens of every race and
color, and regardless of any previous condition of servitude." . . .

BRADLEY, J.:

[After stating the facts, he continued:]
It is obvious that the primary and important question in all the cases is
the constitutionality of the law: for if the law is unconstitutional none
of the prosecutions can stand.

The sections of the law referred to provide as follows:

SECTION 1. That all persons within the jurisdiction of the
United States shall be entitled to the full and equal enjoyment
of the accommodations, advantages, facilities, and privileges of
inns, public conveyances on land or water, theatres, and other
places of public amusement; subject only to the conditions and
limitations established by law, and applicable alike to citizens
of every race and color, regardless of any previous condition
of servitude.

SECTION 2. That any person who shall violate the foregoing
section by denying to any citizen, except for reasons by law
applicable to citizens of every race and color, and regardless of
any previous condition of servitude, the full enjoyment of any
of the accommodations . . . [shall pay a fine of $500.00].

Are these sections constitutional? . . .

The essence of the law is, not to declare broadly that all persons
shall be entitled to the full and equal enjoyment of the accommodations, advantages, facilities, and privileges of inns, public conveyances,

and theatres; but that such enjoyment shall not be subject to any conditions applicable only to citizens of a particular race or color, or who had been in a previous condition of servitude. . . . The second section makes it a penal offence in any person to deny to any citizen of any race or color, regardless of previous servitude, any of the accommodations or privileges mentioned in the first section.

Has Congress constitutional power to make such a law? Of course, no one will contend that the power to pass it was contained in the Constitution before the adoption of the last three amendments.[8] . . . But the responsibility of an independent judgment is now thrown upon this court; and we are bound to exercise it according to the best lights we have. . . .

It is State action of a particular character that is prohibited. Individual invasion of individual rights is not the subject-matter of the [Fourteenth] amendment. It has a deeper and broader scope. It nullifies and makes void all State legislation, and State action of every kind, which impairs the privileges and immunities of citizens of the United States, or which injures them in life, liberty or property without due process of law, or which denies to any of them the equal protection of the laws. It not only does this, but, in order that the national will, thus declared, may not be a mere brutum fulmen, the last section of the amendment invests Congress with power to enforce it by appropriate legislation. To enforce what? To enforce the prohibition. To adopt appropriate legislation for correcting the effects of such prohibited State laws and State acts, and thus to render them effectually null, void, and innocuous. This is the legislative power conferred upon Congress, and this is the whole of it. It does not invest Congress with power to legislate upon subjects which are within the domain of State legislation; but to provide modes of relief against State legislation, or State action, of the kind referred to. It does not authorize Congress to create a code of municipal law for the regulation of private rights; but to provide modes of redress against the operation of State laws, and the action of State officers executive or judicial, when these are subversive of the fundamental rights specified in the amendment. Positive rights and

---

[8] Is this point so obvious? Is there absolutely no basis in the Constitution for legislation prohibiting discrimination in access to public facilities?

privileges are undoubtedly secured by the Fourteenth Amendment; but they are secured by way of prohibition against State laws and State proceedings affecting those rights and privileges, and by power given to Congress to legislate for the purpose of carrying such prohibition into effect: and such legislation must necessarily be predicated upon such supposed State laws or State proceedings, and be directed to the correction of their operation and effect. . . . In fine, the legislation which Congress is authorized to adopt in this behalf is not general legislation upon the rights of the citizen, but *corrective* legislation, that is, such as may be necessary and proper for counteracting such laws as the States may adopt or enforce, and which, by the amendment, they are prohibited from making or enforcing, or such acts and proceedings as the States may commit or take, and which, by the amendment, they are prohibited from committing or taking. It is not necessary for us to state, if we could, what legislation would be proper for Congress to adopt. It is sufficient for us to examine whether the law in question is of that character.

An inspection of the law shows that it makes no reference whatever to any supposed or apprehended violation of the Fourteenth Amendment on the part of the States. It is not predicated on any such view. It proceeds ex directo to declare that certain acts committed by individuals shall be deemed offences, and shall be prosecuted and punished by proceedings in the courts of the United States. . . .

If this legislation is appropriate for enforcing the prohibitions of the amendment, it is difficult to see where it is to stop. Why may not Congress with equal show of authority enact a code of laws for the enforcement and vindication of all rights of life, liberty, and property? If it is supposable that the States may deprive persons of life, liberty, and property without due process of law (and the amendment itself does suppose this), why should not Congress proceed at once to pre- scribe due process of law for the protection of every one of these fundamental rights, in every possible case, as well as to prescribe equal privileges in inns, public conveyances, and theatres? . . . The assump- tion is certainly unsound. It is repugnant to the Tenth Amendment of the Constitution, which declares that powers not delegated to the United States by the Constitution, nor prohibited by it to the States, are reserved to the States respectively or to the people. . . .

In this connection it is proper to state that civil rights, such as are guaranteed by the Constitution against State aggression, cannot be impaired by the wrongful acts of individuals, unsupported by State authority in the shape of laws, customs, or judicial or executive proceedings. *The wrongful act of an individual, unsupported by any such authority, is simply a private wrong,*[9] [emphasis added] or a crime of that individual; an invasion of the rights of the injured party, it is true, whether they affect his person, his property, or his reputation; but if not sanctioned in some way by the State, or not done under State authority, his rights remain in full force, and may presumably be vindicated by resort to the laws of the State for redress. . . .

Conceding the major proposition to be true, that Congress has a right to enact all necessary and proper laws for the obliteration and prevention of slavery with all its badges and incidents, is the minor proposition also true, that the denial to any person of admission to the accommodations and privileges of an inn, a public conveyance, or a theatre, does subject that person to any form of servitude, or tend to fasten upon him any badge of slavery? If it does not, then power to pass the law is not found in the Thirteenth Amendment.

In a very able and learned presentation of the cognate question as to the extent of the rights, privileges and immunities of citizens which cannot rightfully be abridged by state laws under the Fourteenth Amendment, made in a former case, a long list of burdens and disabilities of a servile character, incident to feudal vassalage in France, and which were abolished by the decrees of the National Assembly, was presented for the purpose of showing that all inequalities and observances exacted by one man from another were servitudes, or badges of slavery, which a great nation, in its effort to establish universal liberty, made haste to wipe out and destroy. But these were servitudes imposed by the old law, or by long custom, which had the force of law, and exacted by one man from another without the latter's consent. Should any such servitudes be imposed by a state law, there can be no doubt that the law would be repugnant to the Fourteenth, no less than to the

---

[9] Note the parallel between this conception of private wrong versus national wrong and the problem of distinguishing in the international arena today between national crime and international war crime.

Thirteenth Amendment; nor any greater doubt that Congress has adequate power to forbid any such servitude from being exacted. . . .

It may be that by the Black Code (as it was called), in the times when slavery prevailed, the proprietors of inns and public conveyances were forbidden to receive persons of the African race, because it might assist slaves to escape from the control of their masters. This was merely a means of preventing such escapes, and was no part of the servitude itself. A law of that kind could not have any such object now, however justly it might be deemed an invasion of the party's legal right as a citizen, and amenable to the prohibitions of the Fourteenth Amendment. . . .

We must not forget that the province and scope of the Thirteenth and Fourteenth amendments are different; the former simply abolished slavery: the latter prohibited the States from abridging the privileges or immunities of citizens of the United States; from depriving them of life, liberty, or property without due process of law, and from denying to any the equal protection of the laws. The amendments are different, and the powers of Congress under them are different. What Congress has power to do under one, it may not have power to do under the other. Under the Thirteenth Amendment, it has only to do with slavery and its incidents. Under the Fourteenth Amendment, it has power to counteract and render nugatory all State laws and proceedings which have the effect to abridge any of the privileges or immunities of citizens of the United States, or to deprive them of life, liberty or property without due process of law, or to deny to any of them the equal protection of the laws. . . .

After giving to these questions all the consideration which their importance demands, we are forced to the conclusion that such an act of refusal has nothing to do with slavery or involuntary servitude, and that if it is violative of any right of the party, his redress is to be sought under the laws of the State; or if those laws are adverse to his rights and do not protect him, his remedy will be found in the corrective legislation which Congress has adopted, or may adopt, for counteracting the effect of State laws, or State action, prohibited by the Fourteenth Amendment. It would be running the slavery argument into the ground to make it apply to every act of discrimination which a person may see fit to make as to the guests he will entertain, or as to the people he will take into his coach or cab or car, or admit to his concert or theatre, or deal with in other matters of intercourse or business. Innkeepers and public carriers, by the laws of all the States, so far as we are aware, are bound, to the extent of their facilities, to furnish proper accommodation to all unobjectionable persons who in good faith apply for them. If the laws themselves make any unjust discrimination, amenable to the prohibitions of the Fourteenth Amendment, Congress has full power to afford a remedy under that amendment and in accordance with it.

When a man has emerged from slavery, and by the aid of beneficent legislation has shaken off the inseparable concomitants of that state, there must be some stage in the progress of his elevation when he takes the rank of a mere citizen, and ceases to be the special favorite of the laws, and when his rights as a citizen, or a man, are to be protected in the ordinary modes by which other men's rights are protected. There were thousands of free colored people in this country before the abolition of slavery, enjoying all the essential rights of life, liberty and property the same as white citizens; yet no one, at that time, thought that it was any invasion of his personal status as a freeman because he was not admitted to all the privileges enjoyed by white citizens, or because he was subjected to discriminations in the enjoyment of accommodations in inns, public conveyances and places of amusement. Mere discriminations on account of race or color were not regarded as badges of slavery. If, since that time, the enjoyment of equal rights in all these respects has become established by constitutional enactment, it is not by force of the Thirteenth Amendment (which merely abolishes slavery), but by force of the [Fourteenth] and Fifteenth Amendments. . . .

On the whole we are of opinion, that no countenance of authority for the passage of the law in question can be found in either the Thirteenth or Fourteenth Amendment of the Constitution; and no other ground of authority for its passage being suggested, it must necessarily be declared void, at least so far as its operation in the several States is concerned.

And it is so ordered.

HARLAN, J., DISSENTING:

The opinion in these cases proceeds, it seems to me, upon grounds entirely too narrow and artificial. I cannot resist the conclusion that the substance and spirit of the recent amendments of the Constitution have been sacrificed by a subtle and ingenious verbal criticism. "It is not the words of the law but the internal sense of it that makes the law: the letter of the law is the body; the sense and reason of the law is the soul."[10] Constitutional provisions, adopted in the interest of liberty, and for the purpose of securing, through national legislation, if need be, rights inhering in a state of freedom, and belonging to American citizenship, have been so construed as to defeat the ends the people desired to accomplish, which they attempted to accomplish, and which they supposed they had accomplished by changes in their fundamental law. By this I do not mean that the determination of these cases should have been materially controlled by considerations of mere expediency or policy. I mean only, in this form, to express an earnest conviction that the court has departed from the familiar rule requiring, in the interpretation of constitutional provisions, that full effect be given to the intent with which they were adopted.

The purpose of the first section of the act of Congress of March 1, 1875, was to prevent race discrimination in respect of the accommodations and facilities of inns, public conveyances, and places of public amusement. . . .

The court adjudges, I think erroneously, that Congress is without power, under either the Thirteenth or Fourteenth Amendment, to establish such regulations, and that the first and second sections of the statute are, in all their parts, unconstitutional and void. . . .

The terms of the Thirteenth Amendment are absolute and universal. They embrace every race which then was, or might thereafter be, within the United States. No race, as such, can be excluded from the benefits or rights thereby conferred. Yet, it is historically true that that amendment was suggested by the condition, in this country, of that race which had been declared, by this court, to have had—according to the opinion entertained by the most civilized portion of the white race, at the time of the adoption of the Constitution—"no rights

---

[10] Is this dissenting opinion a repeat of the conflict in interpretation between *Marbury* and *McCulloch*?

which the white man was bound to respect," none of the privileges or immunities secured by that instrument to citizens of the United States. . . . This court has uniformly held that the national government has the power, whether expressly given or not, to secure and protect rights conferred or guaranteed by the Constitution. *United States v. Reese*, 92 U.S. 214; *Strauder v. West Virginia*, 100 U.S. 303. That doctrine ought not now to be abandoned when the inquiry is not as to an implied power to protect the master's rights, but what may Congress, under powers expressly granted, do for the protection of freedom and the rights necessarily inhering in a state of freedom.

The Thirteenth Amendment, it is conceded, did something more than to prohibit slavery as an institution, resting upon distinctions of race, and upheld by positive law. My brethren admit that it established and decreed universal civil freedom throughout the United States. But did the freedom thus established involve nothing more than exemption from actual slavery? Was nothing more intended than to forbid one man from owning another as property? Was it the purpose of the nation simply to destroy the institution, and then remit the race, theretofore held in bondage, to the several States for such protection, in their civil rights, necessarily growing out of freedom, as those States, in their discretion, might choose to provide? Were the States against whose protest the institution was destroyed, to be left free, so far as national interference was concerned, to make or allow discriminations against that race, as such, in the enjoyment of those fundamental rights which by universal concession, inhere in a state of freedom? . . .

Before the adoption of the recent amendments, it had become, as we have seen, the established doctrine of this court that Negroes, whose ancestors had been imported and sold as slaves, could not become citizens of a State, or even of the United States, with the rights and privileges guaranteed to citizens by the national Constitution; further, that one might have all the rights and privileges of a citizen of a State without being a citizen in the sense in which that word was used in the national Constitution, and without being entitled to the privileges and immunities of citizens of the several States. . . .[11]

The assumption that this amendment consists wholly of prohibitions upon State laws and State proceedings in hostility to its provisions,

---

[11] This is a reference to the *Dred Scott* decision discussed earlier.

is unauthorized by its language. The first clause of the first section—
"All persons born or naturalized in the United States, and subject to
the jurisdiction thereof, are citizens of the United States, and of the
State wherein they reside"—is of a distinctly affirmative character. In
its application to the colored race, previously liberated, it created and
granted, as well citizenship of the United States, as citizenship of the
State in which they respectively resided. It introduced all of that race,
whose ancestors had been imported and sold as slaves, at once, into the
political community known as the "People of the United States." They
became, instantly, citizens of the United States, and of their respective
States. Further, they were brought, by this supreme act of the nation,
within the direct operation of that provision of the Constitution which
declares that "the citizens of each State shall be entitled to all privileges
and immunities of citizens in the several States." Art. 4, § 2.

The citizenship thus acquired, by that race, in virtue of an affirmative grant from the nation, may be protected, not alone by the judicial branch of the government, but by congressional legislation of a
primary direct character; this, because the power of Congress is not
restricted to the enforcement of prohibitions upon State laws or State
action. It is, in terms distinct and positive, to enforce "the provisions
of this article" of amendment; not simply those of a prohibitive character, but the provisions—all of the provisions—affirmative and prohibitive, of the amendment. It is, therefore, a grave misconception to
suppose that the fifth section of the amendment has reference exclusively to express prohibitions upon State laws or State action. . . . If,
then, exemption from discrimination, in respect of civil rights, is a new
constitutional right, secured by the grant of State citizenship to colored
citizens of the United States—and I do not see how this can now be
questioned—why may not the nation, by means of its own legislation
of a primary direct character, guard, protect and enforce that right? It
is a right and privilege which the nation conferred. . . .[12]

This court has always given a broad and liberal construction to the
Constitution, so as to enable Congress, by legislation, to enforce rights

---

[12] What is the significance of Justice Harlan's relying here on the notion of the nation
acting to protect "colored citizens"? Is the significance of the "nation" here the same
as that of the "people" in Chief Justice Marshall's argument in *McCulloch* for ground
for the authority of the federal government relative to the states?

secured by that instrument. . . . "The sound construction of the Constitution," said Chief Justice Marshall, "must allow to the national legislature that discretion, with respect to the means by which the powers it confers are to be carried into execution, which will enable that body to perform the high duties assigned to it in the manner most beneficial to the people. Let the end be legitimate, let it be within the scope of the Constitution, and all means which are appropriate, which are plainly adapted to that end, which are not prohibited, but consist with the letter and spirit of the Constitution, are constitutional." *McCulloch v. Maryland*, 4 Wh. 421. . . .

But the court says that Congress did not, in the act of 1866 [or 1875], assume, under the authority given by the Thirteenth Amendment, to adjust what may be called the social rights of men and races in the community. I agree that government has nothing to do with social, as distinguished from technically legal, rights of individuals. No government ever has brought, or ever can bring, its people into social intercourse against their wishes. Whether one person will permit or maintain social relations with another is a matter with which government has no concern. I agree that if one citizen chooses not to hold social intercourse with another, he is not and cannot be made amenable to the law for his conduct in that regard; for even upon grounds of race, no legal right of a citizen is violated by the refusal of others to maintain merely social relations with him. What I affirm is that no State, nor the officers of any State, nor any corporation or individual wielding power under State authority for the public benefit or the public convenience, can, consistently either with the freedom established by the fundamental law, or with that equality of civil rights which now belongs to every citizen, discriminate against freemen or citizens, in those rights, because of their race, or because they once labored under the disabilities of slavery imposed upon them as a race. The rights which Congress, by the act of 1875, endeavored to secure and protect are legal, not social rights. . . . For the reasons stated I feel constrained to withhold my assent to the opinion of the court.

■

QUESTIONS AND COMMENTS

1. After the Civil War, the victorious Union Congress and armies sought to guarantee equal rights for blacks in the former Confeder-

acy. The pro-civil rights Reconstruction governments were, in effect, propped up by federal troops. The presidential election dispute of 1876 between Samuel Tilden and Rutherford B. Hayes (which was very similar to the contest between Bush and Gore in 2000) was part of the political compromise under which the federal government agreed to withdraw its troops from the South. The judicial analogue to this political decision was the extraordinary defeat for civil rights in the civil rights cases. That defeat was further entrenched when the Supreme Court announced seven years later that, as a general principle, states were entirely immune from suits in federal courts. (See *Hans v. Louisiana*, 134 U.S. 1 (1890).)

2. The strict limitation of the postbellum amendments to state action expresses the view called "states' rights"—the very position that the South fought for in the Civil War, which had ostensibly been repudiated not only by the war but also by the Thirteenth, Fourteenth, and Fifteenth Amendments, as well as the civil rights acts of 1866 and of 1875. According to the civil rights cases, the states have the exclusive right and the power to regulate the social relations between the races. The federal government may intervene only if the state abuses its authority by entrenching upon principles of due process or violating the equal protection of the laws. An important corollary of the civil rights cases—though it was made explicit only recently—is that the state does not violate individual rights by omissions, that is, by the failure to intervene to protect people against private or "social" discrimination. (See *DeShaney v. Winnebago County Department of Social Security*, 489 U.S. 189, 195–197 (1989).)

3. In German constitutional terms, the civil rights cases should be seen as a struggle between the view that the Constitution has third-party effects (*Drittwirkung*) and the view that it does not. (See BVerfGE 15.1.1958 (7, 198): Lüth-Urteil (*Drittwirkung*).) The third-party effect would be to render private acts of discrimination unconstitutional. Interestingly, the Thirteenth Amendment has a third-party effect because it is written in the impersonal form: "Neither slavery nor involuntary servitude . . . shall exist within the United States." The prohibition is violated by private as well as state action. By contrast, the Fourteenth and Fifteenth Amendments are directed exclusively to action by the states. Thus the controversy about the third-party effect reduces to the question whether the Thirteenth or Fourteenth

Amendment should be basis for upholding the legislation of 1875.
The majority favors the Fourteenth Amendment; Justice Harlan, the
Thirteenth.

4. The question of when the state acts or does not act remains controversial, but it certainly extends beyond merely state employees. Many
federal cases have considered how closely related an otherwise private
actor must be to the state to be within the "state actor" definition,
which includes private parties acting "under color of state law" under
the Civil Rights Act at 42 U.S.C. § 1983. "Color of state law" is the
"misuse of power, possessed by virtue of state law and made possible
only because the wrongdoer is clothed with the authority of state
law" (*United States v. Classic*, 313 U.S. 299, 326 (1941)). (State political party election primaries were acts "under color of state law" and
subject to federal protection from deprivation on the basis of race.)
For a recent illustration, see *Brentwood Acad. v. Tenn. Secondary Sch.
Ath. Ass'n* (531 U.S. 288 (2001)), in which a private association of
public high school sports teams is considered a state actor. You can
ponder the problem by thinking about whether the actions of a so-
called private university, which receives a substantial portion of its
budget from the state and federal governments, constitute state action. Then consider the results in *Hack v. President & Fellows of Yale
College* (237 F.3d 81 (2d Cir. 2000)), in which a private university was
not a state actor, and the court did not decide if it was required to
give its religious students an alternative to co-educational housing,
and *Rendell–Baker v. Kohn* (457 U.S. 830, 840 (1982)), in which government contracts did not turn a private school into a government
actor.

5. The Supreme Court continues to debate the scope of Congress's enforcement powers under Section Five of the Fourteenth Amendment.
In *Alden v. Maine* (527 U.S. 706 (1999)), the Court emphasized the
amendment's fundamental alteration of the balance of state and federal
power struck by the Constitution, by the explicit limits on the powers of the states and grant to Congress of the power to enforce those
limits, but the Court still found no basis to limit the Eleventh
Amendment immunity of states from suits to enforce a federal wage-
and-hour law. The *Alden* court applied the test in *City of Boerne v.
Flores* (521 U.S. 507 (1997)), that statutes under the section must be

remedial and not substantive, requiring congruence and proportionality between the already unconstitutional injury to be prevented or
remedied and the means adopted to that end. Thus, Congress could
not limit a state's Eleventh Amendment immunity against employment discrimination without finding a history of state discrimination
against the disabled (*Bd. of Trs. of the Univ. of Ala. v. Garrett*, 531
U.S. 356 (2001)). On the other hand, the Court found that Congress did find such a history and so was acting validly under Section
Five when barring discrimination based on gender when applying
the Family Medical Leave Act to the states and allowing suits
against them (*Nev. Dep't of Human Res. v. Hibbs*, 123 S. Ct. 1972
(2003)).

6. If the Reconstruction Amendments represented a new beginning, a
new constitution as argued in Fletcher, *Our Secret Constitution*, then it
became a constitution in hiding. It was suppressed in the late nineteenth century. It became the countervoice, destined to reemerge in
the twentieth century. The Declaration of Independence and the
Gettysburg Address became the foundation for the great social movements of the 1960s. See Charles Black, *A New Birth of Freedom* (New
York: Grosset/Putnam, 1997). Lincoln's vision became the foundation
for the great speech by perhaps the greatest orator in American history, Martin Luther King Jr., on August 28, 1963:

> I have a dream that one day this nation will rise up and live
> out the true meaning of its creed: "We hold these truths to
> be self-evident: that all men are created equal." I have a
> dream that one day on the red hills of Georgia the sons of
> former slaves and the sons of former slave owners will be
> able to sit down together at a table of brotherhood. I have a
> dream that one day even the state of Mississippi, a desert
> state, sweltering with the heat of injustice and oppression,
> will be transformed into an oasis of freedom and justice. I
> have a dream that my four children will one day live in a
> nation where they will not be judged by the color of their
> skin but by the content of their character. I have a dream
> today.

■

Further Reading

For additional reflections on the themes of this chapter, see Bruce Ackerman, *We the People: Foundations* (Cambridge, MA: Belknap Press of Harvard University, 1991); George P. Fletcher, *Our Secret Constitution: How Lincoln Redefined American Democracy* (Oxford: Oxford University Press, 2001). Materials on framing and signing of the Declaration of Independence are available online from the National Archives at http://www.archives.gov/. For materials on the years following the Civil War, see Eric Foner, *Reconstruction: America's Unfinished Revolution, 1863–1877* (illustrated ed.) (New York: HarperCollins, 1988) (Saint Helens, OR: Perennial Press, 2002).

NINE

Equality Prevails

The civil rights cases led to eighty years of de facto apartheid in the United States. The legitimation of racial discrimination came in 1898, when the Supreme Court, in *Plessy v. Ferguson*, 163 U.S. 537 (1896), upheld racially segregated railroad cars as "separate but equal" and therefore consistent with the Fourteenth Amendment. Only after World War II, after blacks and whites fought again side by side (though in separate units), did the country undertake a systematic effort to realize the aims that Justice Harlan thought were imperative in the 1880s. The first major step came in 1954, when a unanimous court, under the leadership of Chief Justice Earl Warren, held, in *Brown v. Board of Education*, 347 U.S. 483 (1954); 349 U.S. 294 (1955), that segregated schools were inherently unequal. The effort to translate this decision of the Supreme Court into actual practice lasted many more years, and in the end it would be difficult to say that we have achieved the goal of school integration that the Court then thought was desirable.

The final overruling of the *Civil Rights Cases* occurred not in the Supreme Court but in Congress, which, under the urging of President Lyndon Johnson, passed the Civil Rights Act of 1964. The country finally prohibited racial discrimination in public facilities. The foundation of the legislation was not section 5 of the Fourteenth Amendment but rather the Interstate Commerce Clause, Article I, section 8, clause 2, which authorizes Congress "to regulate commerce with foreign nations, and among the several States, and with the Indian tribes." The Commerce Clause was available to the Court in 1883, but it would not then have seemed plausible.

The Commerce Clause came into its own as a ground for congressional action in the late 1930s, when the Supreme Court groped for some basis to justify President Franklin Roosevelt's New Deal legislation designed to manage and stimulate the economy, as well as regulate working conditions and protect the welfare of workers. For a long period, the Commerce Clause appeared to be infinitely elastic. It would support any form of congressional action. In recent years, however, a more conservative Supreme Court has taken a renewed interest in states' rights and has held several statutes unconstitutional because they have exceeded Congress's authority under the Commerce Clause.[1]

The use of the Fourteenth Amendment has, however, expanded dramatically. The Due Process Clause has become the repository of a vast jurisprudence for regulating state criminal justice. This process began in the 1930s, largely in response to Southern courts' suppression of the rights of blacks. We shall turn in due course to some aspects of this "due process" revolution.

For over a century, the primary question under the Equal Protection Clause was the protection of racial minorities, primarily but not exclusively the descendants of former slaves. It was not until the 1970s that the Supreme Court expanded the jurisprudence of equality to include the protection of women, children born out of wedlock, the mentally ill, and noncitizens. The last category is probably the most difficult to domesticate under the theory of equal treatment under the law. The following case illustrates the problem.

---

[1] See *U.S. v. Morrison*, 529 U.S. 598, 120 S. Ct. 1740, 146 L. Ed. 2d 658 (2000) (providing a federal civil remedy for the victims of gender-motivated violence beyond the commerce clause and the Fourteenth Amendment, § 5), and *U.S. v. Lopez*, 514 U.S. 549, 115 S. Ct. 1624, 131 L. Ed. 2d 626 (1995) (enactment of the Gun-Free School Zone Act of 1990 beyond the power of Congress under the commerce clause).

In Re Griffiths

Supreme Court of the United States
413 U.S. 717; 93 S. Ct. 2851 (1973)

POWELL, J.:

This case presents a novel question as to the constraints imposed by the Equal Protection Clause of the Fourteenth Amendment on the qualifications which a State may require for admission to the bar. Appellant, Fre Le Poole Griffiths, is a citizen of the Netherlands who came to the United States in 1965, originally as a visitor. In 1967 she married a citizen of the United States and became a resident of Connecticut. After her graduation from law school, she applied in 1970 for permission to take the Connecticut bar examination. The County Bar Association found her qualified in all respects save that she was not a citizen of the United States as required by Rule 8 (1) of the Connecticut Practice Book (1963), and on that account refused to allow her to take the examination. She then sought judicial relief, asserting that the regulation was unconstitutional but her claim was rejected, first by the Superior Court and ultimately by the Connecticut Supreme Court. 162 Conn. 249, 294 A. 2d 281 (1972). We noted probable jurisdiction, 406 U.S. 966 (1972), and now hold that the rule unconstitutionally discriminates against resident aliens.

I.

We begin by sketching the background against which the State Bar Examining Committee attempts to justify the total exclusion of aliens from the practice of law. From its inception, our Nation welcomed and drew strength from the immigration of aliens. Their contributions to the social and economic life of the country were self-evident, especially during the periods when the demand for human resources greatly exceeded the native supply. This demand was by no means limited to the unskilled or the uneducated. In 1873, this Court noted that admission to the practice of law in the courts of a State "in no sense depends on citizenship of the United States. It has not, as far as we know, ever been made in any State, or in any case, to depend on citizenship at all. Certainly many prominent and distinguished lawyers have been admitted to practice, both in the State and Federal courts, who were not citizens of the United States or of any State." *Bradwell v. State*, 16 Wall. 130, 139.[2]

But shortly thereafter, in 1879, Connecticut established the predecessor to its present rule totally excluding aliens from the practice of law. 162 Conn., at 253, 294 A. 2d, at 283. In subsequent decades, wide-ranging restrictions for the first time began to impair significantly the efforts of aliens to earn a livelihood in their chosen occupations.[3] In the face of this trend, the Court nonetheless held in 1886 that a lawfully admitted resident alien is a "person" within the meaning of the Fourteenth Amendment's directive that a State must not "deny to any person within its jurisdiction the equal protection of the laws." *Yick Wo v. Hopkins*, 118 U.S. 356, 369. The decision in *Yick Wo* invalidated a municipal ordinance regulating the operation of laundries on the ground that the ordinance was discriminatorily enforced against Chinese operators. . . .

To be sure, the course of decisions protecting the employment rights of resident aliens has not been an unswerving one. In *Clarke v. Deckebach*, 274 U.S. 392 (1927), the Court was faced with a challenge to a city ordinance prohibiting the issuance to aliens of licenses to operate pool and billiard rooms. Characterizing the business as one having "harmful and vicious tendencies," the Court found no constitutional infirmity in the ordinance:

> It was competent for the city to make such a choice, not shown to be irrational, by excluding from the conduct of a dubious business an entire class rather than its objectionable members selected by more empirical methods. *Id.*, at 397

This easily expandable proposition supported discrimination against resident aliens in a wide range of occupations.

But the doctrinal foundations of Clarke were undermined in *Takahashi v. Fish & Game Comm'n*, 334 U.S. 410 (1948), where, in ruling

---

[2] This case held that states may, consistently with the Constitution, refuse admission to the bar to women.

[3] See John Higham, *Strangers in the Land: Patterns of American Nativism* 46, 161, 183 (Westport, CT: Greenwood Press, 1963). The full scale of restrictions imposed on the work opportunities of aliens in 1946 is shown by M. Konvitz, *The Alien and the Asiatic in American Law* 190–211 (Ithaca, NY: Cornell University Press, 1946). [In original.]

unconstitutional a California statute barring issuance of fishing licenses to persons "ineligible to citizenship," the Court stated that "the power of a state to apply its laws exclusively to its alien inhabitants as a class is confined within narrow limits." *Id.*, at 420. Indeed, with the issue squarely before it in *Graham v. Richardson*, 403 U.S. 365 (1971), the Court concluded:

> Classifications based on alienage, like those based on nationality or race, are inherently suspect and subject to close judicial scrutiny. Aliens as a class are a prime example of a "discrete and insular" minority. . . .

The Court has consistently emphasized that a State which adopts a suspect classification "bears a heavy burden of justification," *McLaughlin v. Florida*, 379 U.S. 184, 196 (1964), a burden which, though variously formulated, requires the State to meet certain standards of proof. In order to justify the use of a suspect classification, a State must show that its purpose or interest is both constitutionally permissible and substantial, and that its use of the classification is "necessary . . . to the accomplishment" of its purpose or the safeguarding of its interest.

Resident aliens, like citizens, pay taxes, support the economy, serve in the Armed Forces, and contribute in myriad other ways to our society. It is appropriate that a State bear a heavy burden when it deprives them of employment opportunities.

We hold that the Committee, acting on behalf of the State, has not carried its burden. The State's ultimate interest here implicated is to assure the requisite qualifications of persons licensed to practice law. It is undisputed that a State has a constitutionally permissible and substantial interest in determining whether an applicant possesses " 'the character and general fitness requisite for an attorney and counselor-at-law.' " [citations omitted] But no question is raised in this case as to appellant's character or general fitness. Rather, the sole basis for disqualification is her status as a resident alien.

The Committee defends Rule 8 (1)'s requirement that applicants for admission to the bar be citizens of the United States on the ground that the special role of the lawyer justifies excluding aliens from the practice of law. In Connecticut, the Committee points out, the maxim that a lawyer is an "officer of the court" is given concrete meaning by a statute which makes every lawyer a "commissioner of the Superior

Court." As such, a lawyer has authority to "sign writs and subpoenas, take recognizances, administer oaths and take depositions and acknowledgements of deeds." Conn. Gen. Stat. Rev. § 51–85. In the exercise of this authority, a Connecticut lawyer may command the assistance of a county sheriff or a town constable. Conn. Gen. Stat. Rev. § 52–90. Because of these and other powers, the Connecticut Supreme Court commented that

> the courts not only demand [lawyers'] loyalty, confidence and respect but also require them to function in a manner which will foster public confidence in the profession and, consequently, the judicial system. 162 Conn., at 262–263, 294 A. 2d, at 287

In order to establish a link between citizenship and the powers and responsibilities of the lawyer in Connecticut, the Committee contrasts a citizen's undivided allegiance to this country with a resident alien's possible conflict of loyalties. From this, the Committee concludes that a resident alien lawyer might in the exercise of his functions ignore his responsibilities to the courts or even his clients in favor of the interest of a foreign power.

We find these arguments unconvincing. It in no way denigrates a lawyer's high responsibilities to observe that the powers "to sign writs and subpoenas, take recognizances, [and] administer oaths" hardly involve matters of state policy or acts of such unique responsibility as to entrust them only to citizens. Nor do we think that the practice of law offers meaningful opportunities adversely to affect the interest of the United States. Certainly the Committee has failed to show the relevance of citizenship to any likelihood that a lawyer will fail to protect faithfully the interest of his clients.[4]

---

[4] Lawyers frequently represent foreign countries and the nationals of such countries in litigation in the courts of the United States, as well as in other matters in this country. In such representation, the duty of the lawyer as an "officer of the court" is to further the interests of his clients by all lawful means, even when those interests are in conflict with the interests of the United States or of a state. But this representation involves no conflict of interest in the invidious sense. Rather, it casts the lawyer in his honored and traditional role as an authorized but independent agent acting to vindicate the legal rights of a client, whoever it may be. It is conceivable that an alien licensed to practice law in this country could find himself in a position in which he might be called upon to represent his country of citizenship against the United States in circumstances in

Nor would the possibility that some resident aliens are unsuited to the practice of law be a justification for a wholesale ban. . . .

This constitutional warning is especially salient where, as here, a State's bar admission standards make explicit use of a suspect classification. Although, as we have acknowledged, a State does have a substantial interest in the qualifications of those admitted to the practice of law, the arguments advanced by the Committee fall short of showing that the classification established by Rule 8 (1) of the Connecticut Practice Book (1963) is necessary to the promoting or safeguarding of this interest.

Connecticut has wide freedom to gauge on a case-by-case basis the fitness of an applicant to practice law. Connecticut can, and does, require appropriate training and familiarity with Connecticut law. Apart from such tests of competence, it requires a new lawyer to take both an "attorney's oath" to perform his functions faithfully and honestly[5] and a "commissioner's oath" to "support the constitution of the United States, and the constitution of the state of Connecticut." Appellant has indicated her willingness and ability to subscribe to the substance of both oaths,[6] and Connecticut may quite properly conduct a character investigation to insure in any given case "that an applicant is not one who 'swears to an oath pro forma while declaring or manifesting his

which there may be a conflict between his obligations to the two countries. In such rare situations, an honorable person, whether an alien or not, would decline the representation. [This and the remaining notes were in the original opinion.]

[5] The text of the attorney's oath is as follows:

> You solemnly swear that you will do no falsehood, nor consent to any to be done in court, and, if you know of any to be done, you will give information thereof to the judges, or one of them, that it may be reformed; you will not wittingly, or willingly promote, sue or cause to be sued, any false or unlawful suit, or give aid, or consent, to the same; you will delay no man for lucre or malice; but will exercise the office of attorney, within the court wherein you may practice, according to the best of your learning and discretion, and with fidelity, as well to the court as to your client, so help you God." *Jurisdictional Statement* 44

[6] Because the commissioner's oath is an oath to "support the constitution of the United States, and the constitution of the State of Connecticut, so long as you continue a citizen thereof," *Conn. Gen. Stat. Rev.* § 1-25 (emphasis added), appellant could not of course take the oath as prescribed. To the extent that the oath reiterates Rule 8 (1)'s citizenship requirement, it shares the same constitutional defects when required of prospective members of the bar.

disagreement with or indifference to the oath.' " [citations omitted].[7] Moreover, once admitted to the bar, lawyers are subject to continuing scrutiny by the organized bar and the courts. In addition to discipline for unprofessional conduct, the range of post-admission sanctions extends from judgments for contempt to criminal prosecutions and disbarment. In sum, the Committee simply has not established that it must exclude all aliens from the practice of law in order to vindicate its undoubted interest in high professional standards.

III.

In its brief, the Examining Committee makes another, somewhat different argument in support of Rule 8 (1). Its thrust is not that resident aliens lack the attributes necessary to maintain high standards in the legal profession, but rather that lawyers must be citizens almost as a matter of definition. The implication of this analysis is that exclusion of aliens from the legal profession is not subject to any scrutiny under the Equal Protection Clause. The argument builds upon the exclusion of aliens from the franchise in all 50 States and their disqualification under the Constitution from holding office as President, Art. 2, § 1, Clause 5, or as a member of the House of Representatives, Art. 1, § 2, Clause 2, or of the Senate, Art. 1, § 3, Clause 3. These and numerous other federal and statutory and constitutional provisions reflect, the Committee contends, a pervasive recognition that "participation in the government structure as voters and office holders" is inescapably an aspect of citizenship. Brief for Appellee 11. Offered in support of the

---

[7] We find no merit in the contention that only citizens can in good conscience take an oath to support the Constitution. We note that all persons inducted into the Armed Services, including resident aliens, are required by 10 U. S. C. § 502 to take the following oath:

> I, _____, do solemnly swear (or affirm) that I will support and defend the Constitution of the United States against all enemies, foreign and domestic; that I will bear true faith and allegiance to the same; and that I will obey the orders of the President of the United States and the orders of the officers appointed over me, according to regulations and the Uniform Code of Military Justice. So help me God.

If aliens can take this oath when the Nation is making use of their services in the national defense, resident alien applicants for admission to the bar surely cannot be precluded, as a class, from taking an oath to support the Constitution on the theory that they are unable to take the oath in good faith.

claim that the lawyer is an "office holder" in this sense is an enhanced version of the proposition, discussed above, that he is an "officer of the court." Specifically, the Committee states that the lawyer "is an officer of the Court who acts by and with the authority of the State" and is entrusted with the "exercise of actual government power." *Id.*, at 5.

Lawyers do indeed occupy professional positions of responsibility and influence that impose on them duties correlative with their vital right of access to the courts. Moreover, by virtue of their professional aptitudes and natural interests, lawyers have been leaders in government throughout the history of our country. Yet, they are not officials of government by virtue of being lawyers. Nor does the status of holding a license to practice law place one so close to the core of the political process as to make him a formulator of government policy.

We hold that § 8 (1) violates the Equal Protection Clause. The judgment of the Connecticut Supreme Court is reversed, and the case is remanded for further proceedings not inconsistent with this opinion.

It is so ordered.

REHNQUIST, J., DISSENTING.

The Court in these two cases holds that an alien is not really different from a citizen, and that any legislative classification on the basis of alienage is "inherently suspect." The Fourteenth Amendment, the Equal Protection Clause of which the Court interprets as invalidating the state legislation here involved, contains no language concerning "inherently suspect classifications," or, for that matter, merely "suspect classifications." The principal purpose of those who drafted and adopted the Amendment was to prohibit the States from invidiously discriminating by reason of race, Slaughter-House Cases, 16 Wall. 36 (1873), and, because of this plainly manifested intent, classifications based on race have rightly been held "suspect" under the Amendment. But there is no language used in the Amendment, or any historical evidence as to the intent of the Framers, which would suggest to the slightest degree that it was intended to render alienage a "suspect" classification, that it was designed in any way to protect "discrete and insular minorities" other than racial minorities, or that it would in any way justify the result reached by the Court in these two cases.

Two factual considerations deserve more emphasis than accorded by the Court's opinions. First, the records . . . contain no indication that the aliens suffered any disability that precluded them, either as a group or individually, from applying for and being granted the status of naturalized citizens. . . . In [*Griffiths*], appellant was eligible for naturalization but "elected to remain a citizen of the Netherlands," 162 Conn. 249, 250, 294 A. 2d 281, 282, and deliberately chose not to file a declaration of intent under 8 U. S. C. §§ 1427 (f), 1430 (a). The "status" of these individuals was not, therefore, one with which they were forever encumbered; they could take steps to alter it when and if they chose. . . .

The Court, by holding in these cases and in *Graham v. Richardson*, 403 U.S. 365 (1971), that a citizen-alien classification is "suspect" in the eyes of our Constitution, fails to mention, let alone rationalize, the fact that the Constitution itself recognizes a basic difference between citizens and aliens. That distinction is constitutionally important in no less than 11 instances in a political document noted for its brevity. Representatives, U.S. Const. Art. I, § 2, Clause 2, and Senators, Art. I, § 3, Clause 3, must be citizens. Congress has the authority "to establish an uniform Rule of Naturalization" by which aliens can become citizen members of our society, Art. I, § 8, Clause 4; the judicial authority of the federal courts extends to suits involving citizens of the United States "and foreign States, Citizens or Subjects," Art. III, § 2, Clause 1, because somehow the parties are "different," a distinction further made by the Eleventh Amendment; the Fifteenth, Nineteenth, Twenty-Fourth, and Twenty-Sixth Amendments are relevant only to "citizens." The President must not only be a citizen but "a natural born Citizen," Art. II, § 1, Clause 5. One might speculate what meaning Art. IV, § 2, Clause 1, has today.

Not only do the numerous classifications on the basis of citizenship that are set forth in the Constitution cut against both the analysis used and the results reached by the Court in these cases; the very Amendment which the Court reads to prohibit classifications based on citizenship establishes the very distinction which the Court now condemns as "suspect." The first sentence of the Fourteenth Amendment provides:

> All persons born or naturalized in the United States and subject to the jurisdiction thereof, are citizens of the United States and of the State wherein they reside.

In constitutionally defining who is a citizen of the United States, Congress obviously thought it was doing something, and something important. Citizenship meant something, a status in and relationship with a society which is continuing and more basic than mere presence or residence. The language of that Amendment carefully distinguishes between "persons" who, whether by birth or naturalization, had achieved a certain status, and "persons" in general. That a "citizen" was considered by Congress to be a rationally distinct subclass of all "persons" is obvious from the language of the Amendment.

It is unnecessary to venture into a detailed discussion of what Congress intended by the Citizenship Clause of the Fourteenth Amendment. The paramount reason was to amend the Constitution so as to overrule explicitly the Dred Scott decision. *Scott v. Sanford*, 19 How. 393 (1857) [holding that African Americans could never become citizens]. . . .

This Court explicitly held that it was not a violation of the Equal Protection Clause for a State by statute to limit employment on public projects to citizens. *Him v. McCall*, 239 U.S. 175 (1915); *Crane v. New York*, 239 U.S. 195 (1915). Even if the Court now considers that the justifications for those enactments are "not controlling," those decisions clearly hold that the rational-basis test applies. . . . [Note the rational basis test requires a less compelling justification than the majority's premise that alienage was a "suspect classification."]

The only other apparent rationale for the invocation of the "suspect classification" approach in these cases is that alienage is a "status," and the Court does not feel it "appropriate" to classify on that basis. . . . But there is a marked difference between a status or condition such as illegitimacy, national origin, or race, which cannot be altered by an individual and the "status" of the appellant. . . . There is nothing in the record indicating that their status as aliens cannot be changed by their affirmative acts.

In my view, the proper judicial inquiry is whether any rational justification exists for prohibiting aliens from employment in the competitive civil service and from admission to a state bar. . . .

These statutes do not classify on the basis of country of origin; the distinctions are not between native Americans and "foreigners," but between citizens and aliens. The process of naturalization was specifically designed by Congress to require a foreign national to demonstrate that he or she is familiar with the history, traditions, and institutions of our society in a way that a native-born citizen would learn from formal education and basic social contact. Congress specifically provided that an alien seeking citizenship status must demonstrate "an understanding of the English language" and "a knowledge and understanding of the fundamentals of the history, and of the principles and form of government, of the United States." 8 U. S. C. § 1423. The purpose was to make the alien establish that he or she understood, and could be integrated into, our social system. . . .

See also 8 U. S. C. § 1424, which precludes aliens who manifest certain opposition to our society or form of government from being naturalized. An alien must demonstrate "good moral character," 8 U. S. C. § 1427 (a)(3), which was intended by Congress to mean a broad "attach[ment] to the principles of the Constitution of the United States, and [disposition] to the good order and happiness of the United States." H. R. Rep. No. 1365, supra, at 80. See also 8 CFR § 332b (1973), detailing the cooperation between the Immigration and Naturalization Service and local schools conducting citizenship education for applicants for naturalization. The above is sufficient to demonstrate, I believe, that Congress provided that aliens seeking citizenship status prove what citizens by birth are, as a class, presumed to understand: a basic familiarity with our social and political mores and institutions. The naturalized citizen has demonstrated both the willingness and ability to integrate into our social system as a whole, not just into our "political community," as the Court apparently uses the term. He proved that he has become "like" a native-born citizen in ways that aliens, as a class, could be presumed not to be. The Court simply ignores the purpose of the process of assimilation into and dedication to our society that Congress prescribed to make aliens "like" citizens. In [*Griffiths*] the answer is not clear cut. The States traditionally have had great latitude in prescribing rules and regulations concerning technical competence and character fitness, governing those who seek to be admitted to practice law. See, e.g., *Konigsberg v. State Bar of California*, 366 U.S. 36 (1961). The importance of lawyers and the judiciary in our system of government and justice needs no extended comment. An attorney is an "officer of the court" in Connecticut, a status this Court has also recognized. See, e.g., *Powell v. Alabama*, 287 U.S. 45, 73 (1932); Ex parte Garland, 4 Wall. 333, 370 (1867). He represents his client, but also, in Connecticut, may "sign writs and subpoenas, take recognizances, [and] administer oaths." Conn. Gen. Stat. Rev. § 51–85.

More important than these emoluments of their position, though, is the tremendous responsibility and trust that our society places in the hands of lawyers. The liberty and property of the client may depend upon the competence and fidelity of the representation afforded by the lawyer in any number of particular lawsuits. But by virtue of their office lawyers are also given, and have increasingly undertaken to exercise, authority to seek to alter some of the social relationships and institutions of our society by use of the judicial process. No doubt an alien even under today's decision may be required to be learned in the law and familiar with the language spoken in the courts of the particular State involved. But Connecticut's requirement of citizenship reflects its judgment that something more than technical skills are needed to be a lawyer under our system. I do not believe it is irrational for a State that makes that judgment to require that lawyers have an understanding of the American political and social experience, whether gained from growing up in this country, as in the case of a native-born citizen, or from the naturalization process, as in the case of a foreign-born citizen. I suppose the Connecticut Bar Examining Committee could itself administer tests in American history, government, and sociology, but the State did not choose to go this route. Instead, it chose to operate on the assumption that citizens as a class might reasonably be thought to have a significantly greater degree of understanding of our experience than would aliens. Particularly in the case of one such as appellant, who candidly admits that she wants to live and work in the United States but does not want to sever her fundamental social and political relationship with the country of her birth, I do not believe the State's judgment is irrational.

BURGER, C.J., WITH WHOM
REHNQUIST, J. JOINS, DISSENTING.

I agree generally with Justice Rehnquist's dissent and add a few observations.

In the rapidly shrinking "one world" we live in there are numerous reasons why the States might appropriately consider relaxing some of the restraints on the practice of professions by aliens. The fundamental factor, however, is that the States reserved, among other powers, that of regulating the practice of professions within their own borders. If that concept has less validity now than in the 18th century when it was made part of the "bargain" to create a federal union, it is nonetheless part of that compact.

A large number of American nationals are admitted to the practice of law in more than a dozen countries; this will expand as world trade enlarges. But the question for the Court is not what is enlightened or sound policy but rather what the Constitution and its Amendments provide; I am unable to accord to the Fourteenth Amendment the expansive reading the Court gives it.

In recent years the Court, in a rather casual way, has articulated the code phrase "suspect classification" as though it embraced a reasoned constitutional concept. Admittedly, it simplifies judicial work as do "per se" rules, but it tends to stop analysis while appearing to suggest an analytical process.

Much as I agree with some aspects of the policy implicit in the Court's holding, I am bound—if I apply the Constitution as its words and intent speak to me—to reject the good policy the Court now adopts.

I am unwilling to accept what seems to me a denigration of the posture and role of a lawyer as an "officer of the court." It is that role that a State is entitled to rely on as a basis for excluding aliens from the practice of law. By virtue of his admission a lawyer is granted what can fairly be called a monopoly of sorts; he is granted a license to appear and try cases; he can cause witnesses to drop their private affairs and be called for depositions and other pretrial processes that, while subject to the ultimate control of the court, are conducted by lawyers outside courtrooms; the enormous power of cross-examination of witnesses is granted exclusively to lawyers. Inherent in these large powers is the ability to compel answers subject, of course, to such limiting restraints as the Fifth Amendment and rules of evidence. In most States a lawyer is authorized to issue subpoenas commanding the presence of persons and even the production of documents under certain circumstances. The broad monopoly granted to lawyers is the authority to practice a profession and by virtue of that to do things other citizens may not lawfully do. In the common law tradition the lawyer becomes the attorney—the agent—for client only by virtue of his having been first invested with power by the State, usually by a court. The lawyer's obligations as an officer of the court permit the court to call on the lawyer to perform duties which no court could order citizens generally to do, including the obligation to observe codes of ethical conduct not binding on the public generally. . . .

The role of a lawyer as an officer of the court predates the Constitution; it was carried over from the English system and became firmly embedded in our tradition. It included the obligation of first duty to client. But that duty never was and is not today an absolute or unqualified duty. It is a first loyalty to serve the client's interest but always within—never outside—the law, thus placing a heavy personal and individual responsibility on the lawyer. That this is often unenforceable, that departures from it remain undetected, and that judges and bar associations have been singularly tolerant of misdeeds of their brethren, renders it no less important to a profession that is increasingly crucial to our way of life. The very independence of the lawyer from the government on the one hand and client on the other is what makes law a profession, something apart from trades and vocations in which obligations of duty and conscience play a lesser part. It is as crucial to our system of justice as the independence of judges themselves.

The history of the legal profession is filled with accounts of lawyers who risked careers by asserting their independent status in opposition to popular and governmental attitudes, as John Adams did in Boston to defend the soldiers accused in what we know in our folklore as the "Boston Massacre." To that could be added the lawyers who defended John Peter Zenger and down to lawyers in modern times in cases such as *Johnson v. Zerbst*, 304 U.S. 458 (1938). The crucial factor in all these cases is that the advocates performed their dual role—officer of the court and advocate for a client—strictly within and never in derogation of high ethical standards. There is thus a reasonable, rational basis for a State to conclude that persons owing first loyalty to this country will grasp these traditions and apply our concepts more than those who seek the benefits of American citizenship while declining to accept the burdens of citizenship in this country.

At the very least we ought not stretch the Fourteenth Amendment to force the States to accept any national of any country simply because of a recital of the required oath and passing of the bar examination. . . .

About Lawyers, Their Roles,
and Their Ethics: A Comment

As can be seen in the *Griffiths* case, the manner in which lawyers carry out their obligations is a question of great significance to a variety of people. Other lawyers, judges, and citizens, both locally and nationally, all have an interest in the ethics of an attorney. Few lawyers practice for long without being confronted by important choices between the narrow interests or demands of their clients and the good of the public or the state as a whole.

These questions of ethics rarely provoke rich debates among lawyers over the morality of the situation, nor do they give rise to thoughtful guides to the deep ethical dilemmas lawyers face. The term *ethics* has come to refer to a canon of rules governing practice. Where lawyers might be expected to pursue a moral or conscientious answer, they are instead given a few formulae by which to keep from being disbarred.

Befitting the decentralized nature of the law in the United States, American lawyers have no national, centralized regulation. There is no national law society or general, federal system of examinations. Instead, the regulation of attorneys is highly fragmented, with each state setting different standards for entrance into the field and regulation of its participants.

The regulation of lawyers is subdivided among the system of state courts as a whole, the statewide association of lawyers, and the various individual courts. State legislatures are occasionally the source of standards that govern some portion of attorney conduct, although the courts more often select codes of lawyers' professional responsibility. The federal courts add yet another layer of independent authority, as each court remains independent of the others, at least in some degree, in their licensing and discipline.

Beyond the multiplicity of sources of authority, there are multiple forms of professional standards. Most U.S. lawyers are governed simultaneously by at least five sources of professional regulation: (1) standards adopted by courts and legislatures, particularly the canons of legal ethics or the code of professional responsibility; (2) the oaths of practice taken at the time of acceptance into the bar; (3) the particular rules governing practice, such as Rule 11 of the Federal Rules of Civil Procedure;[8]

---

[8] Rule 11 of the Federal Rules imposes sanctions on lawyers who make "frivolous" legal arguments or make allegations that have no evidentiary support.

(4) the precedents of disciplinary boards; and (5) the inherent power of the courts over their own bars.

Despite this manifold jurisdiction and multilayered regulation, the standards of proper attorney conduct are very similar. Effectively, they amount to rules forbidding the unauthorized practice of law, rules governing admission to the bar, and standards of "professional responsibility," those minimal ethics necessary to avoid sanction for misconduct.

Standards of professional responsibility include duties to the client, to the courts, and to third parties. Duties toward the client broadly include duties of loyalty, including an obligation to give each client that independent counsel and service that is in the best interest of that client and none other, as well as an obligation, generally, not to represent two clients whose needs are in conflict. They include fundamental duties of professional competence and the obligation not to take representation beyond the attorney's knowledge or ability, as well as the duty of diligence, the obligation to accept only such representation as can be reasonably performed and to do all that is necessary to perform it. Further, a lawyer has an obligation to guard a client's confidences and to protect the client's money and property in the attorney's care. Most famously, the attorney has an obligation to zealously advocate the client's claims to the extent of the merits of those claims.

Duties toward third parties include obligations to other attorneys, to whom professional courtesy and fairness are required. Duties toward third parties, particularly opponents, include obligations of truthfulness and of communicating either through counsel for those represented or with care for the rights of the third party when that party is unrepresented.

Last, duties toward the court require candor and fairness, as well as the obligation to promote the fairness and impartiality of the court. The duty to maintain an appropriate decorum might be seen as an obligation to the court and to the profession as a whole.

Each of these three broad areas of duty is elaborated in each state's code. Beyond these three forms of duty, special rules and codes establish further standards for prosecutors and for judges. All of these rules and codes are usually promulgated and enforced in each state by the bar, an organization that is, in effect, that state's guild of lawyers.

The disciplinary rules occupy most of the attention of the bar, and they are the focus of most legal education in professional responsibility.

Even so, they do not exhaust the formal bases for either identifying or enforcing legal ethical obligations.

Beyond the specific obligations stated in the state codes of professional responsibility, each court has broad powers of discipline over the lawyers who practice before it. Some of these powers are within the inherent powers of the court, arising both from the authority of the court and from the oath each lawyer takes prior to appearing before it. Some are within the discretion given to judges by rules governing particular situations of procedure, most prominently the power to sanction an attorney for misstatements of law or fact under Rule 11 of the Federal Rules of Civil Procedure. Last, the courts may determine that a lawyer has violated the oath that was required to be admitted to practice before the court. See, for instance, *Maryland State Bar Assoc., Inc. v. Agnew*, 271 Md. 543 (1973) (the disbarment of former Vice President Spiro Agnew).

None of these rules, though, not even the oaths, can take the place of an attorney's good-faith judgment about the right thing to do. The attorney is more than the agent of the client; the attorney always retains moral and professional independence. The clients' interests do not prevail over questions of the right, the good, the lawful, and the just. If this is true—and the rules do not completely define the role of lawyers—should we consider the relevance of national identity on the likelihood of sound moral judgment in the American tradition? Does this put the problem of the *Griffiths* case in a new light?

About Equal Protection of the Laws: Questions and Comments

1. The discussion about whether being an alien or a noncitizen is a suspect classification brings to bear a complex body of doctrine developed by the Supreme Court to distinguish between two types of "equal protection" cases. This doctrine distinguishes between two questions:
   A. The first question is, What kind of distinction is at play? Is the distinction a run-of-the-mill classification in a regulatory statute, for example, the distinction between opticians and ophthalmologists or between eighteen-year-olds and sixteen-year-olds? Or

is the distinction one that, on its face, looks suspicious? These are called "suspect classifications." They include race, national origin, and (at least as to state statutes) alienage. Gender is considered an almost suspect classification. These are the categories that raise associations with past discriminatory practices. Several cases uphold the relevance of sex or gender in state laws defining statutory rape (i.e., intercourse with a "female" who is under age) or federal laws on registration for a possible military draft (applicable to men only).

B. The second question is, How powerful is the state or federal government's reason for making this distinction? This is sometimes asked as how "compelling" the rationale for the legislation is. The basic principle is that the more "suspect" the classification, the more compelling the state's reasons must be. In *Griffiths*, the Court decided that the classification was inherently suspect and that the state's reasons were not strong enough. If the classification had been less controversial (say, the question whether convicted felons could be admitted to the bar), the state's reasons could be less persuasive. This is called the "level of scrutiny." In this case, the Court applied strict scrutiny.

In *Strauder*, it was clear that keeping blacks off the jury was invidious discrimination. Although the Court did not then use the doctrine of compelling state interest, it could invalidate the legislation as a per se violation of equal protection. In the *Bradwell* case, preventing women from joining the bar was also invidious discrimination, or at least that is the way we would look at it today. The problem in *Griffiths* is whether preventing foreigners from joining the bar carries the same discriminatory sting. Obviously, the dissenters did not think so.

2. Let us consider how Mrs. Griffiths would have fared under other contemporary provisions that ensure equality under the law. The German Basic Law, Article 3 (1949) provides:

   (1) All human beings are equal before the law.

   (2) Men and women have equal rights. The state will further the practical realization of this equality of rights between men and women and will take measures to eliminate ongoing disadvantages [for women].

   (3) No one may be advantaged or disadvantaged on the basis of sex,

ancestry, race, language, homeland and provenance, faith, religious or political commitments. No one may be disadvantaged on the basis of a [physical] handicap.

The Basic Law says nothing about the impermissibility of relying on citizenship as a factor justifying restrictions on admission to the bar. The list of prohibited criteria mentions "ancestry" and "homeland and provenance," but denying the relevance of these factors is compatible with distinguishing citizens and noncitizens.

3. The Canadian Constitution Article 15 (1982):

   (1) Every individual is equal before and under the law and has the right to the equal protection and equal benefit of the law without discrimination and, in particular, without discrimination based on race, national or ethnic origin, color, religion, sex, age or mental or physical capacity.

   (2) Subsection (1) does not preclude any law, program or activity that has as its object the amelioration of conditions of disadvantaged individuals or groups including those that are disadvantaged because of race, national or ethnic origin, color, religion, sex, age or mental or physical capacity. [Other provisions make it clear that this provision applies only to actions of government.]

Note that the Article 15(1) uses the phrase "in particular," which opens the way to judicial expansion of the impermissible grounds of discrimination. The Canadian Supreme Court has in fact reached a decision similar to *Griffiths*. See *Andrews v. Law Society of British Columbia* [1989] 1 S.C.R. 143.

4. The European Convention on Human Rights Article 14 (1950):

The enjoyment of the rights and freedoms set forth in this Convention shall be secured without discrimination on any ground such as sex, race, color, language, religion, political or other opinion, national or social origin, association with a national minority, property, birth or other status.

The inclusion of the phrases "such as" and "other status" at least carries the possibility of an expanded jurisprudence similar to the result in *Griffiths* and *Andrews*.

5. The proposed Constitution for Europe, as the latest in the field of egalitarian jurisprudence, has some intriguing provisions.[9] Article II-

---

[9] The text of the treaty is online at http://european-convention.eu.int.

21 is structured much like the European Convention on Human
Rights, with a general prohibition of discrimination based on the
following categories: "sex, race, colour, ethnic or social origin, genetic features, language, religion or belief, political or any other opinion, membership of a national minority, property, birth, disability, age,
or sexual orientation." This is a wonderful and very progressive statement of the egalitarian principle. The only problem is that it is hard
to believe that the drafters are serious about the principled irrelevance
of wealth, age, language, and other factors. Not all of these categories
can be considered as per se prohibitions, or even "suspect classifications" as the *Griffiths* opinion uses that term. Some discrimination
based on wealth is obviously permissible. So far as we know, all European societies impose compulsory retirement on professors (unlike
the United States). Is this not discrimination based on age? And all
European states have a national language or languages. Is this not a
form of discrimination against minorities who want the public schools
to teach in their language? Significantly, the extensive list of prohibited factors fails to mention citizenship.

6. The second part of Article II-21, of the Constitution for Europe,
contains a provision that might speak to the *Griffiths* issue:

> *Dans ce domaine d'application de la Constitution* [Within its sphere
> of application] *et sans préjudice de ses dispositions particulières,* [and
> without prejudice to particular provisions] *toute discrimination
> fondée sur la nationalité est interdite.*

This is very unclear. The first half of the provision already prohibited
discrimination based on "membership in a national minority." The
drafters must have a different sense of nationality in mind in this half
of the provision, namely, the various nationalities that constitute the
European Union. The point of the provision, it seems, is to prohibit
discrimination among nationalities within the sphere of the constitution's application. The implication is that different, less favorable
rules might apply to "nationals" from outside the union.

7. Do not ignore the fact that *Griffiths* is an appeal from a state law, not
a federal law. The Supreme Court held in a later case that Congress
has plenary authority to impose whatever restrictions it desires on the
entrance of "aliens" to the United States. See *Mathews v. Diaz*, 426
U.S. 67 (1976) (upholding a residency requirement applicable only to

aliens seeking to qualify for certain Medicare benefits). This is the only area of the egalitarian jurisprudence where the federal government enjoys radically different authority from state governments. If admission to the bar were a matter of federal rather than state law, would Congress be able to limit membership to citizens? Should the holding of this case extend to judges? To members of the jury? To voting rights in state and federal elections?

8. Despite the qualifications and limitations, *Griffiths* must be considered a very liberal decision. Our review of other provisions protecting equality under law leaves a great deal of doubt about whether American lawyers abroad would be treated as well. The liberal open-mindedness of the Supreme Court in 1973 should not make us blind to the enormous failures of the Court in other areas of discrimination. As of this writing, the Court has not intervened against states that deprive convicted felons of the right to vote.[10] Also the Court has actually tolerated a system of public school financing that gives pupils from wealthier homes a better education than that received by students from poorer families.[11]

9. The biggest challenge to the jurisprudence of equality is whether it is justified to engage in affirmative action in order to generate a society that offers greater advantage to previously excluded groups. Notice that the German, Canadian, and European constitutions all recognize affirmative action of one sort or another. The Canadian provision is the broadest. The proposed European provision is limited to provisions in favor of a *"sexe sous-représenté"* ("underrepresented sex"). In light of the particular history of the United States, the most serious question is whether race should function in the same way Europeans want to consider gender. The U.S. Supreme Court has taken a more nuanced approach. In *University of California v. Bakke*, 438 U.S. 265 (1975), the Court allowed race to be a factor in state university admissions, but barred racial quotas under the Equal Protection Clause. In its latest pronouncements, *Gratz v. Bollinger*, 539 U.S. 244 (2003), and *Grutter v. Bollinger*, 539 U.S. 306 (2003), the

---

[10] In *Richardson v. Ramirez*, 418 U.S. 24 (1974), the Court upheld this form of discrimination.

[11] In re Rodriguez, 14 Cal. 3d 639, 537 P.2d 384, 122 Cal. Rptr. 552 (1975) (wealth discrimination not a basis for invalidating a system of school financing).

Court struck down a college admissions program that applied an across-the-board preference to promote racial diversity. A similar law school program in law school admissions was upheld for minority candidates who were likely to contribute to a "critical mass" of that group. These subtle distinctions have provoked both confusion and disagreement and will undoubtedly be litigated again soon.

Further Reading

On the history of equal protection, see William E. Nelson, *The Fourteenth Amendment: From Political Principle to Judicial Doctrine* (Cambridge, MA: Harvard University Press, 1995). The common law origins of the constitutional doctrine are considered in Charles Monroe Haar and Daniel Fessler, *The Wrong Side of the Tracks: A Revolutionary Rediscovery of the Common Law Tradition of Fairness in the Struggle Against Inequality* (New York: Simon and Schuster, 1986).

The literature on equality is daunting. Questions abound of whether equality is of opportunity to compete or of access to resources; whether equality is to be measured between groups or between individuals; whether compensation for handicaps or past ill-treatment is required; whether a moment of equilibrium, once satisfied, can justify later inequalities that arise from bargaining, luck, or choice; whether equality can be understood only within a single nation or if it must be understood throughout humanity; and how any mechanism to achieve equality can be realized. A few samples are all that will be offered here.

An overview of equality, focusing on its implementation by law, is in George P. Fletcher, "Equality" in *Basic Concepts of Legal Thought* 121–135 (New York: Oxford University Press, 1996). A recent scholarly exercise in the philosophy of equality, summarizing two decades of Dworkin's theory, is in Ronald Dworkin, *Sovereign Virtue: The Theory and Practice of Equality* (Cambridge, MA: Harvard University Press, 2000). Much of contemporary thinking about egalitarian social justice stems from John Rawls's classic work, *A Theory of Justice* (Cambridge, MA: Harvard University Press, 1971). See also Bruce Ackerman, *Social Justice and the Liberal State* (New Haven, CT: Yale University Press, 1980). We take up the general theory of liberalism later, in the chapters devoted to private law. At the level of public and constitutional law, the most influential criticism of Rawls came from Nozick on the right—see Robert Nozick, *Anarchy, State and Utopia* (New York: Basic Books, 1977)—and from Sandel on the communitarian left: see Michael J. Sandel, *Liberalism and the Limits of Justice* (Cambridge, MA: Harvard University Press: 1982).

TEN

Freedom Fights Back

Constitutional history, at least in the United States, could be written as a struggle between the commitment to freedom and the commitment to equality. The more freedom people have, the less they are equal. The more equality they enjoy, the less freedom they are allowed to exercise. The more equality, the less freedom. This was the view—if slightly perverse—of the Supreme Court in the *Dred Scott* decision, which held that the Missouri Compromise violated the freedom to take one's property (i.e., slaves) wherever one went. The conflict also applies to the accumulation of wealth. The freedom to own property and to earn money in a free market stands in opposition to the equal distribution of wealth. The American Supreme Court has consistently rejected the relevance of wealth in applying the principle of equality under law.[1]

Prior to the Civil War, the dominant theme of American law was freedom from interference by the federal government. Review the first eight amendments in the Bill of Rights to see how strong the emphasis was on freedom in the late eighteenth century. The Civil War brought

---

[1] See *San Antonio School District v. Rodriguez*, 411 U.S. 1 (1973) (holding that some school districts in Texas could permissibly spend significantly more per pupil than others).

equality front and center, and we saw in the last chapter that in the period between 1954 and 1974 the Supreme Court expanded the American commitment to the "equal protection of the laws" under the Fourteenth Amendment. But the commitment to freedom remains robust and vigorous.

The most significant assertion of freedom in the United States is the faith in freedom of speech and of the press. As the First Amendment provided, as of 1791: "Congress shall make no law . . . abridging the freedom of speech or of the press." It has not always been the case, however, that free speech in the United States was as highly cherished as these words suggest. The courts' cultivation of free speech as a fundamental value of the American democracy began after the First World War. If the principle of equality under the law generates common ground with other social democracies in the industrialized world, then the doctrine of nearly absolute freedom of speech reveals that Americans are different after all. The following case, won by Herbert Wechsler, a famous professor at the Columbia Law School, reveals how distinctive American legal thinking can be and how it departs from the prevailing principles of law both in the common law and in the civil law world. Keep in mind that this case came to the Supreme Court one year after Martin Luther King Jr. delivered his famous speech "I Have a Dream."

New York Times Co. v. Sullivan

Supreme Court of the United States
376 U.S. 254; 84 S. Ct. 710 (1964)

BRENNAN, J.:

We are required in this case to determine for the first time the extent to which the constitutional protections for speech and press limit a State's power to award damages in a libel action brought by a public official against critics of his official conduct.

Respondent L. B. Sullivan is one of the three elected Commissioners of the City of Montgomery, Alabama. He testified that he was "Commissioner of Public Affairs and the duties are supervision of the Police Department, Fire Department, Department of Cemetery and Department of Scales." He brought this civil libel action against the four individual petitioners, who are Negroes and Alabama clergymen, and against petitioner the New York Times Company, a New York corporation which publishes the New York Times, a daily newspaper. A jury in the Circuit Court of Montgomery County awarded him damages of $500,000, the full amount claimed, against all the petitioners, and the Supreme Court of Alabama affirmed. 273 Ala. 656, 144 So. 2d 25.

Respondent's complaint alleged that he had been libeled by statements in a full-page advertisement that was carried in the New York Times on March 29, 1960. Entitled "Heed Their Rising Voices," the advertisement began by stating that "As the whole world knows by now, thousands of Southern Negro students are engaged in widespread non-violent demonstrations in positive affirmation of the right to live in human dignity as guaranteed by the U.S. Constitution and the Bill of Rights." It went on to charge that "in their efforts to uphold these guarantees, they are being met by an unprecedented wave of terror by those who would deny and negate that document which the whole world looks upon as setting the pattern for modern freedom. . . ." Succeeding paragraphs purported to illustrate the "wave of terror" by describing certain alleged events. The text concluded with an appeal for funds for three purposes: support of the student movement, "the struggle for the right-to-vote," and the legal defense of Dr. Martin Luther King, Jr., leader of the movement, against a perjury indictment then pending in Montgomery.

The text appeared over the names of 64 persons, many widely known for their activities in public affairs, religion, trade unions, and the performing arts. Below these names, and under a line reading "We in the south who are struggling daily for dignity and freedom warmly endorse this appeal," appeared the names of the four individual petitioners and of 16 other persons, all but two of whom were identified as clergymen in various Southern cities. The advertisement was signed at the bottom of the page by the "Committee to Defend Martin Luther King and the Struggle for Freedom in the South," and the officers of the Committee were listed.

Of the 10 paragraphs of text in the advertisement, the third and a portion of the sixth were the basis of respondent's claim of libel. They read as follows:

Third paragraph:

> In Montgomery, Alabama, after students sang "My Country, 'Tis of Thee" on the State Capitol steps, their leaders were expelled from school, and truckloads of police armed with shotguns and tear-gas ringed the Alabama State College Campus. When the entire student body protested to state authorities by refusing to re-register, their dining hall was padlocked in an attempt to starve them into submission.

Sixth paragraph:

> Again and again the Southern violators have answered Dr. King's peaceful protests with intimidation and violence. They have bombed his home almost killing his wife and child. They have assaulted his person. They have arrested him seven times—for "speeding," "loitering" and similar "offenses." And now they have charged him with "perjury"—a felony under which they could imprison him for ten years . . .

Although neither of these statements mentions respondent by name, he contended that the word "police" in the third paragraph referred to him as the Montgomery Commissioner who supervised the Police Department, so that he was being accused of "ringing" the campus with police. He further claimed that the paragraph would be read as imputing to the police, and hence to him, the padlocking of the dining hall in order to starve the students into submission. As to the sixth paragraph, he contended that since arrests are ordinarily made by the police, the statement "They have arrested [Dr. King] seven times" would be read as referring to him; he further contended that the "They" who did the arresting would be equated with the "They" who committed the other described acts and with the "Southern violators." Thus, he argued, the paragraph would be read as accusing the Montgomery police, and hence him, of answering Dr. King's protests with "intimidation and violence," bombing his home, assaulting his person, and charging him with perjury. Respondent and six other Montgomery residents testified that they read some or all of the statements as referring to him in his capacity as Commissioner.

It is uncontroverted that some of the statements contained in the two paragraphs were not accurate descriptions of events which occurred in Montgomery. Although Negro students staged a demonstration on the State Capitol steps, they sang the National Anthem and not "My Country, 'Tis of Thee." Although nine students were expelled by the State Board of Education, this was not for leading the demonstration at the Capitol, but for demanding service at a lunch counter in the Montgomery County Courthouse on another day. Not the entire student body, but most of it, had protested the expulsion, not by refusing to register, but by boycotting classes on a single day; virtually all the students did register for the ensuing semester. The campus dining hall was not padlocked on any occasion, and the only students who may have been barred from eating there were the few who had neither signed a preregistration application nor requested temporary meal tickets. Although the police were deployed near the campus in large numbers on three occasions, they did not at any time "ring" the campus, and they were not called to the campus in connection with the demonstration on the State Capitol steps, as the third paragraph implied. Dr. King had not been arrested seven times, but only four; and although he claimed to have been assaulted some years earlier in connection with his arrest for loitering outside a courtroom, one of the officers who made the arrest denied that there was such an assault.

On the premise that the charges in the sixth paragraph could be read as referring to him, respondent was allowed to prove that he had not participated in the events described. Although Dr. King's home had in fact been bombed twice when his wife and child were there, both of these occasions antedated respondent's tenure as Commissioner, and the police were not only not implicated in the bombings, but had made every effort to apprehend those who were. Three of Dr. King's four arrests took place before respondent became Commissioner. Although Dr. King had in fact been indicted (he was subsequently acquitted) on two counts of perjury, each of which carried a possible five-year sentence, respondent had nothing to do with procuring the indictment.

Respondent made no effort to prove that he suffered actual pecuniary loss as a result of the alleged libel. One of his witnesses, a former employer, testified that if he had believed the statements, he doubted whether he "would want to be associated with anybody who would be a party to such things that are stated in that ad," and that he would not re-employ respondent if he believed "that he allowed the Police

Department to do the things that the paper say he did." But neither this witness nor any of the others testified that he had actually believed the statements in their supposed reference to respondent. . . .

The trial judge submitted the case to the jury under instructions that the statements in the advertisement were "libelous *per se*" and were not privileged,[2] so that petitioners might be held liable if the jury found that they had published the advertisement and that the statements were made "of and concerning" respondent. The jury was instructed that, because the statements were libelous *per se*, "the law . . . implies legal injury from the bare fact of publication itself," "falsity and malice are presumed," "general damages need not be alleged or proved but are presumed," and "punitive damages may be awarded by the jury even though the amount of actual damages is neither found nor shown." An award of punitive damages—as distinguished from "general" damages, which are compensatory in nature—apparently requires proof of actual malice under Alabama law, and the judge charged that "mere negligence or carelessness is not evidence of actual malice or malice in fact, and does not justify an award of exemplary or punitive damages." He refused to charge, however, that the jury must be "convinced" of malice, in the sense of "actual intent" to harm or "gross negligence and recklessness," to make such an award, and he also refused to require that a verdict for respondent differentiate between compensatory and punitive damages. The judge rejected petitioners' contention that his rulings abridged the freedoms of speech and of the press that are guaranteed by the First and Fourteenth Amendments.

In affirming the judgment, the Supreme Court of Alabama sustained the trial judge's rulings and instructions in all respects. . . .

Because of the importance of the constitutional issues involved, we granted the separate petitions for certiorari of the individual petitioners

---

[2] Libel is a common law tort. It refers to defamation in print as opposed to slander, which addresses aural defamation. Libel *per se* means "libel in itself" as opposed to libel *per quod*, which is established by proving some additional facts known to the audience of people affected. The elements of libel per se are:

(1) A false written statement
(2) "Of an concerning the plaintiff,"
(3) Which in itself holds the plaintiff up to contempt or ridicule or damages his or her reputation, and
(4) Is published, that is, made known to a person other than the person defamed.

and of the Times. We reverse the judgment. We hold that the rule of law applied by the Alabama courts is constitutionally deficient for failure to provide the safeguards for freedom of speech and of the press that are required by the First and Fourteenth Amendments in a libel action brought by a public official against critics of his official conduct. We further hold that under the proper safeguards the evidence presented in this case is constitutionally insufficient to support the judgment for respondent.

I.

We may dispose at the outset of two grounds asserted to insulate the judgment of the Alabama courts from constitutional scrutiny. The first is the proposition relied on by the State Supreme Court—that "The Fourteenth Amendment is directed against State action and not private action." That proposition has no application to this case. Although this is a civil lawsuit between private parties, the Alabama courts have applied a state rule of law which petitioners claim imposes invalid restrictions on their constitutional freedoms of speech and press. It matters not that that law has been applied in a civil action and that it is common law only, though supplemented by statute. . . .

The second contention is that the constitutional guarantees of freedom of speech and of the press are inapplicable here, at least so far as the Times is concerned, because the allegedly libelous statements were published as part of a paid, "commercial" advertisement . . .

The publication here was not a "commercial" advertisement in the sense in which the word was used in [prior cases]. It communicated information, expressed opinion, recited grievances, protested claimed abuses, and sought financial support on behalf of a movement whose existence and objectives are matters of the highest public interest and concern. See *N.A.A.C.P. v. Button*, 371 U.S. 415, 435. That the Times was paid for publishing the advertisement is as immaterial in this connection as is the fact that newspapers and books are sold. *Smith v. California*, 361 U.S. 147, 150; cf. *Bantam Books, Inc., v. Sullivan*, 372 U.S. 58, 64, n. 6. Any other conclusion would discourage newspapers from carrying "editorial advertisements" of this type, and so might shut off an important outlet for the promulgation of information and ideas by persons who do not themselves have access to publishing facilities—

who wish to exercise their freedom of speech even though they are not members of the press. Cf. *Lovell v. Griffin*, 303 U.S. 444, 452; *Schneider v. State*, 308 U.S. 147, 164. The effect would be to shackle the First Amendment in its attempt to secure "the widest possible dissemination of information from diverse and antagonistic sources." . . .

II.

Under Alabama law as applied in this case, a publication is "libelous per se" if the words "tend to injure a person . . . in his reputation" or to "bring [him] into public contempt"; the trial court stated that the standard was met if the words are such as to "injure him in his public office, or impute misconduct to him in his office, or want of official integrity, or want of fidelity to a public trust. . . ." The jury must find that the words were published "of and concerning" the plaintiff, but where the plaintiff is a public official his place in the governmental hierarchy is sufficient evidence to support a finding that his reputation has been affected by statements that reflect upon the agency of which he is in charge. Once "libel per se" has been established, the defendant has no defense as to stated facts unless he can persuade the jury that they were true in all their particulars. . . .

The question before us is whether this rule of liability, as applied to an action brought by a public official against critics of his official conduct, abridges the freedom of speech and of the press that is guaranteed by the First and Fourteenth Amendments. . . .

The general proposition that freedom of expression upon public questions is secured by the First Amendment has long been settled by our decisions. . . . Thus we consider this case against the background of a profound national commitment to the principle that debate on public issues should be uninhibited, robust, and wide-open, and that it may well include vehement, caustic, and sometimes unpleasantly sharp attacks on government and public officials. . . . The constitutional protection does not turn upon "the truth, popularity, or social utility of the ideas and beliefs which are offered." *N.A.A.C.P. v. Button*, 371 U.S. 415, 445. As Madison said, "Some degree of abuse is inseparable from the proper use of every thing; and in no instance is this more true than in that of the press." 4 Elliot's Debates on the Federal Constitution (1876), p. 571. . . . That erroneous statement is inevitable in free debate, and that it must be protected if the freedoms of expression are to have the "breathing space" that they "need . . . to survive," *N.A.A.C.P. v. Button*, 371 U.S. 415, 433.

Injury to official reputation affords no more warrant for repressing speech that would otherwise be free than does factual error. Where judicial officers are involved, this Court has held that concern for the dignity and reputation of the courts does not justify the punishment as criminal contempt of criticism of the judge or his decision . . . surely the same must be true of other government officials, such as elected city commissioners. Criticism of their official conduct does not lose its constitutional protection merely because it is effective criticism and hence diminishes their official reputations.

If neither factual error nor defamatory content suffices to remove the constitutional shield from criticism of official conduct, the combination of the two elements is no less inadequate. This is the lesson to be drawn from the great controversy over the Sedition Act of 1798, 1 Stat. 596, which first crystallized a national awareness of the central meaning of the First Amendment. See Levy, Legacy of Suppression (1960), at 258 et seq.; Smith, Freedom's Fetters (1956), at 426, 431, and passim. That statute made it a crime, punishable by a $5,000 fine and five years in prison, "if any person shall write, print, utter or publish . . . any false, scandalous and malicious writing or writings against the government of the United States, or either house of the Congress . . . , or the President . . . , with intent to defame . . . or to bring them, or either of them, into contempt or disrepute; or to excite against them, or either or any of them, the hatred of the good people of the United States." The Act allowed the defendant the defense of truth, and provided that the jury were to be judges both of the law and the facts. Despite these qualifications, the Act was vigorously condemned as unconstitutional in an attack joined in by Jefferson and Madison. In the famous Virginia Resolutions of 1798, the General Assembly of Virginia resolved that it

> doth particularly protest against the palpable and alarming infractions of the Constitution, in the two late cases of the "Alien and Sedition Acts," passed at the last session of Congress. . . . [The Sedition Act] exercises . . . a power not delegated by the Constitution, but, on the contrary, expressly and

positively forbidden by one of the amendments thereto—a power which, more than any other, ought to produce universal alarm, because it is leveled against the right of freely examining public characters and measures, and of free communication among the people thereon, which has ever been justly deemed the only effectual guardian of every other right. 4 Elliot's Debates, supra, pp. 553–554

Madison prepared the Report in support of the protest. His premise was that the Constitution created a form of government under which "The people, not the government, possess the absolute sovereignty." The structure of the government dispersed power in reflection of the people's distrust of concentrated power, and of power itself at all levels. This form of government was "altogether different" from the British form, under which the Crown was sovereign and the people were subjects. "Is it not natural and necessary, under such different circumstances," he asked, "that a different degree of freedom in the use of the press should be contemplated?" *Id.*, pp. 569–570. Earlier, in a debate in the House of Representatives, Madison had said: "If we advert to the nature of Republican Government, we shall find that the censorial power is in the people over the Government, and not in the Government over the people." 4 Annals of Congress, p. 934 (1794). Of the exercise of that power by the press, his Report said:

> In every state, probably, in the Union, the press has exerted a freedom in canvassing the merits and measures of public men, of every description, which has not been confined to the strict limits of the common law. On this footing the freedom of the press has stood; on this foundation it yet stands. . . . 4 Elliot's Debates, supra, p. 570

The right of free public discussion of the stewardship of public officials was thus, in Madison's view, a fundamental principle of the American form of government.

Although the Sedition Act was never tested in this Court [the act expired by its own terms in 1801], the attack upon its validity has carried the day in the court of history.[3] Fines levied in its prosecution

---

[3] Note this very important argument that the Constitution is not dependent on judicial

were repaid by Act of Congress on the ground that it was unconstitutional. See, e.g., Act of July 4, 1840, c. 45, 6 Stat. 802, accompanied by H. R. Rep. No. 86, 26th Cong., 1st Sess. (1840). Calhoun, reporting to the Senate on February 4, 1836, assumed that its invalidity was a matter "which no one now doubts." Report with Senate bill No. 122, 24th Cong., 1st Sess., p. 3. Jefferson, as President, pardoned those who had been convicted and sentenced under the Act and remitted their fines, stating: "I discharged every person under punishment or prosecution under the sedition law, because I considered, and now consider, that law to be a nullity, as absolute and as palpable as if Congress had ordered us to fall down and worship a golden image." Letter to Mrs. Adams, July 22, 1804, 4 Jefferson's Works (Washington ed.), pp. 555, 556. The invalidity of the Act has also been assumed by Justices of this Court. . . . These views reflect a broad consensus that the Act, because of the restraint it imposed upon criticism of government and public officials, was inconsistent with the First Amendment.

There is no force in respondent's argument that the constitutional limitations implicit in the history of the Sedition Act apply only to Congress and not to the States. It is true that the First Amendment was originally addressed only to action by the Federal Government, and that Jefferson, for one, while denying the power of Congress "to controul the freedom of the press," recognized such a power in the States. See the 1804 Letter to Abigail Adams quoted in *Dennis v. United States*, 341 U.S. 494, 522, n. 4 (concurring opinion). But this distinction was eliminated with the adoption of the Fourteenth Amendment and the application to the States of the First Amendment's restrictions. . . .

What a State may not constitutionally bring about by means of a criminal statute is likewise beyond the reach of its civil law of libel. The fear of damage awards under a rule such as that invoked by the Alabama courts here may be markedly more inhibiting than the fear of prosecution under a criminal statute. . . .[4]

A rule compelling the critic of official conduct to guarantee the truth of all his factual assertions—and to do so on pain of libel judg-

interpretation. "The court of history" includes many voices, some political, some academic, and some popular.

[4] Does this remind you of the principle in *McCulloch* that "the power to tax is the power to destroy"?

ments virtually unlimited in amount—leads to a comparable "self-censorship." Allowance of the defense of truth, with the burden of proving it on the defendant, does not mean that only false speech will be deterred.[5] . . .

The constitutional guarantees require, we think, a federal rule that prohibits a public official from recovering damages for a defamatory falsehood relating to his official conduct unless he proves that the statement was made with "actual malice"—that is, with knowledge that it was false or with reckless disregard of whether it was false or not. An oft-cited statement of a like rule, which has been adopted by a number of state courts, is found in the Kansas case of *Coleman v. MacLennan*, 78 Kan. 711, 98 P. 281 (1908). . . .[6]

We conclude that such a privilege is required by the First and Fourteenth Amendments.

III.

We hold today that the Constitution delimits a State's power to award damages for libel in actions brought by public officials against critics of their official conduct. Since this is such an action, the rule requiring proof of actual malice is applicable. While Alabama law apparently requires proof of actual malice for an award of punitive damages, where general damages are concerned malice is "presumed." Such a presumption is inconsistent with the federal rule. . . .

Applying these standards, we consider that the proof presented to

---

[5] The Court's citations on this point are significant: Even a false statement may be deemed to make a valuable contribution to public debate, since it brings about "the clearer perception and livelier impression of truth, produced by its collision with error." John Stuart Mill, *On Liberty* (Oxford: Blackwell, 1947), at 15; see also John Milton, *Areopagitica*, in *Prose Works* (Yale, 1959), Vol. II, at 561 (and see the new edition, John Milton, *Areopagitica and Other Political Writings* (Indianapolis, IN: Liberty Fund, 1999).

[6] Note the following authority cited for the Court's proposed rule: The consensus of scholarly opinion apparently favors the rule that is here adopted. E.g., 1 Harper and James, *Torts*, § 5.26, at 449–450 (1956); Noel, "Defamation of Public Officers and Candidates," 49 *Col. L. Rev.* 875, 891–895, 897, 903 (1949); Hallen, "Fair Comment," 8 *Tex. L. Rev.* 41, 61 (1929); Smith, "Charges Against Candidates," 18 *Mich. L. Rev.* 1, 115 (1919); Chase, "Criticism of Public Officers and Candidates for Office," 23 *Am. L. Rev.* 346, 367–371 (1889); Cooley, *Constitutional Limitations* (7th ed., Lane, 1903), at 604, 616–628. But see, e.g., American Law Institute, *Restatement of Torts*, § 598, Comment a (1938) (reversing the position taken in Tentative Draft 13, § 1041 (2) (1936)); Veeder, "Freedom of Public Discussion," 23 *Harv. L. Rev.* 413, 419 (1910).

show actual malice lacks the convincing clarity which the constitutional standard demands, and hence that it would not constitutionally sustain the judgment for respondent under the proper rule of law. The case of the individual petitioners requires little discussion. Even assuming that they could constitutionally be found to have authorized the use of their names on the advertisement, there was no evidence whatever that they were aware of any erroneous statements or were in any way reckless in that regard. The judgment against them is thus without constitutional support.

As to the Times, we similarly conclude that the facts do not support a finding of actual malice. . . . [T]here is evidence that the Times published the advertisement without checking its accuracy against the news stories in the Times' own files. The mere presence of the stories in the files does not, of course, establish that the Times "knew" the advertisement was false, since the state of mind required for actual malice would have to be brought home to the persons in the Times' organization having responsibility for the publication of the advertisement. With respect to the failure of those persons to make the check, the record shows that they relied upon their knowledge of the good reputation of many of those whose names were listed as sponsors of the advertisement, and upon the letter from A. Philip Randolph, known to them as a responsible individual, certifying that the use of the names was authorized. There was testimony that the persons handling the advertisement saw nothing in it that would render it unacceptable under the Times' policy of rejecting advertisements containing "attacks of a personal character"; their failure to reject it on this ground was not unreasonable. We think the evidence against the Times supports at most a finding of negligence in failing to discover the misstatements, and is constitutionally insufficient to show the recklessness that is required for a finding of actual malice. . . .

[The Court then considers Alabama's argument that the action was based on a criticism of government but libel of Sullivan personally.] For good reason, "no court of last resort in this country has ever held, or even suggested, that prosecutions for libel on government have any place in the American system of jurisprudence." *City of Chicago v. Tribune Co.*, 307 Ill. 595, 601, 139 N. E. 86, 88 (1923). The present proposition would sidestep this obstacle by transmuting criticism of government, however impersonal it may seem on its face, into personal criticism, and hence potential libel, of the officials of whom the government is composed. There is no legal alchemy by which a State may thus create the cause of action that would otherwise be denied for a publication which, as respondent himself said of the advertisement, "reflects not only on me but on the other Commissioners and the community." Raising as it does the possibility that a good-faith critic of government will be penalized for his criticism, the proposition relied on by the Alabama courts strikes at the very center of the constitutionally protected area of free expression. We hold that such a proposition may not constitutionally be utilized to establish that an otherwise impersonal attack on governmental operations was a libel of an official responsible for those operations. Since it was relied on exclusively here, and there was no other evidence to connect the statements with respondent, the evidence was constitutionally insufficient to support a finding that the statements referred to respondent.

The judgment of the Supreme Court of Alabama is reversed and the case is remanded to that court for further proceedings not inconsistent with this opinion.

Reversed and remanded.

BLACK, J., WITH WHOM DOUGLAS, J. JOINS:

I concur in reversing this half-million-dollar judgment against the New York Times Company and the four individual defendants. In reversing the Court holds that "the Constitution delimits a State's power to award damages for libel in actions brought by public officials against critics of their official conduct." Ante, p. 283. I base my vote to reverse on the belief that the First and Fourteenth Amendments not merely "delimit" a State's power to award damages to "public officials against critics of their official conduct" but completely prohibit a State from exercising such a power. The Court goes on to hold that a State can subject such critics to damages if "actual malice" can be proved against them. "Malice," even as defined by the Court, is an elusive, abstract concept, hard to prove and hard to disprove. The requirement that malice be proved provides at best an evanescent protection for the right critically to discuss public affairs and certainly does not measure up to the sturdy safeguard embodied in the First Amendment. Unlike the Court, therefore, I vote to reverse exclusively on the ground that the Times and the individual defendants had an absolute, unconditional constitutional right to publish in the Times advertisement their criticisms of the Montgomery agencies and officials. I do not base my vote to reverse on any failure to prove that these individual defendants signed the advertisement or that their criticism of the Police Department was aimed at the plaintiff Sullivan, who was then the Montgomery City Commissioner having supervision of the city's police; for present purposes I assume these things were proved. Nor is my reason for reversal the size of the half-million-dollar judgment, large as it is. If Alabama has constitutional power to use its civil libel law to impose damages on the press for criticizing the way public officials perform or fail to perform their duties, I know of no provision in the Federal Constitution which either expressly or impliedly bars the State from fixing the amount of damages. . . .

I regret that the Court has stopped short of this holding indispensable to preserve our free press from destruction.

GOLDBERG, J., WITH WHOM DOUGLAS, J. JOINS, CONCURRING IN THE RESULT:

The Court today announces a constitutional standard which prohibits "a public official from recovering damages for a defamatory falsehood relating to his official conduct unless he proves that the statement was made with 'actual malice'—that is, with knowledge that it was false or with reckless disregard of whether it was false or not." Ante, at 279–280. The Court thus rules that the Constitution gives citizens and newspapers a "conditional privilege" immunizing nonmalicious misstatements of fact regarding the official conduct of a government officer. The impressive array of history[7] and precedent marshaled by the Court, however, confirms my belief that the Constitution affords greater protection than that provided by the Court's standard to citizen and press in exercising the right of public criticism.

---

[7] We fully agree with the Court that the attack upon the validity of the Sedition Act of 1798, 1 Stat. 596, "has carried the day in the court of history," ante, at 276, and that the Act would today be declared unconstitutional. It should be pointed out, however, that the Sedition Act proscribed writings that were "false, scandalous and malicious." For prosecutions under the Sedition Act charging malice, see, e.g., in Wharton, *State Trials of the United States* (1849), "Trial of Matthew Lyon (1798)," p. 333; "Trial of Thomas Cooper (1800)," at 659; "Trial of Anthony Haswell (1800)," at 684; and "Trial of James Thompson Callender (1800)," at 688. [This and note 8, in original.]

In my view, the First and Fourteenth Amendments to the Constitution afford to the citizen and to the press an absolute, unconditional privilege to criticize official conduct despite the harm which may flow from excesses and abuses. The prized American right "to speak one's mind," cf. *Bridges v. California*, 314 U.S. 252, 270, about public officials and affairs needs "breathing space to survive," *N.A.A.C.P. v. Button*, 371 U.S. 415, 433. The right should not depend upon a probing by the jury of the motivation of the citizen or press. The theory of our Constitution is that every citizen may speak his mind and every newspaper express its view on matters of public concern and may not be barred from speaking or publishing because those in control of government think that what is said or written is unwise, unfair, false, or malicious. In a democratic society, one who assumes to act for the citizens in an executive, legislative, or judicial capacity must expect that his official acts will be commented upon and criticized. Such criticism cannot, in my opinion, be muzzled or deterred by the courts at the instance of public officials under the label of libel.

It has been recognized that "prosecutions for libel on government have [no] place in the American system of jurisprudence." *City of Chicago v. Tribune Co.*, 307 Ill. 595, 601, 139 N. E. 86, 88. I fully agree. Government, however, is not an abstraction; it is made up of individuals—of governors responsible to the governed. In a democratic society where men are free by ballots to remove those in power, any statement critical of governmental action is necessarily "of and concerning" the governors and any statement critical of the governors' official conduct is necessarily "of and concerning" the government. If the rule that libel on government has no place in our Constitution is to have real meaning, then libel on the official conduct of the governors likewise can have no place in our Constitution.

We must recognize that we are writing upon a clean slate.[8] As the

---

[8] It was not until *Gitlow v. New York*, 268 U.S. 652 (1925), that it was intimated that the freedom of speech guaranteed by the First Amendment was applicable to the states by reason of the Fourteenth Amendment. Other intimations followed. See *Whitney v. California*, 274 U.S. 357 (1927); *Fiske v. Kansas*, 274 U.S. 380 (1927). In 1931 Chief Justice Hughes speaking for the Court in *Stromberg v. California*, 283 U.S. 359, 368, declared: "It has been determined that the conception of liberty under the due process clause of the Fourteenth Amendment embraces the right of free speech." Thus we deal with a constitutional principle enunciated less than four decades ago and consider for the first

Court notes, although there have been "statements of this Court to the effect that the Constitution does not protect libelous publications . . . none of the cases sustained the use of libel laws to impose sanctions upon expression critical of the official conduct of public officials." Ante, at 268. . . .

This is not to say that the Constitution protects defamatory statements directed against the private conduct of a public official or private citizen. Freedom of press and of speech insures that government will respond to the will of the people and that changes may be obtained by peaceful means. Purely private defamation has little to do with the political ends of a self-governing society. The imposition of liability for private defamation does not abridge the freedom of public speech or any other freedom protected by the First Amendment. . . .

The conclusion that the Constitution affords the citizen and the press an absolute privilege for criticism of official conduct does not leave the public official without defenses against unsubstantiated opinions or deliberate misstatements. "Under our system of government, counterargument and education are the weapons available to expose these matters, not abridgment . . . of free speech. . . ." *Wood v. Georgia*, 370 U.S. 375, 389.

For these reasons, I strongly believe that the Constitution accords citizens and press an unconditional freedom to criticize official conduct. It necessarily follows that in a case such as this, where all agree that the allegedly defamatory statements related to official conduct, the judgments for libel cannot constitutionally be sustained.

■

QUESTIONS AND COMMENTS

1. Note that the underlying premise of this opinion is a commitment to a well-functioning democracy, which requires a "national commitment to the principle that debate on public issues should be uninhibited, robust, and wide-open." Where does the commitment to democracy come from? Is it mentioned in the Constitution?
2. Note the tendency toward absolutist thinking in this opinion. In the

time the application of that principle to issues arising in libel cases brought by state officials.

Griffiths case, the Court was willing to balance the state's interests against the evil of a suspect classification. Why is there no similar process of balancing in this opinion?

3. A distinctive feature of the American attitude toward free speech, one that clearly sets Americans apart from European and Canadian jurisprudence, is the attitude toward hate speech. Punishing Holocaust denial is commonplace in Continental jurisdictions.[9] It is unthinkable in the United States. Instead, Americans have developed the concept of hate crimes, a system for enhancing penalties when the criminal conduct is motivated by bias toward a particular ethnic, racial, or religious group.

4. It would be surprising to find another jurisdiction in the world that less protected public officials against false and defamatory statements. This is an emblem of the American commitment to free speech, which, as footnote 8 indicates, did not begin in earnest until 1925, when the Court interpreted the due process clause of the Fourteenth Amendment to include the First Amendment. Thus we are left with two opinions, *Griffiths* and *Sullivan*, both of which suggest a distinctively American attitude toward both equality and freedom. Is the common theme between them that they are both ultimately about free speech, Griffith's right to speak in court, or the *New York Times*'s right to publish without fear of retaliatory lawsuits? Is this a useful synthesis?

5. Perhaps the common theme in *Griffiths* and *Sullivan* is the union of freedom and equality. We should not forget that the political problem behind the *Sullivan* decision was the campaign for civil rights in the South. Of course, the protection of civil rights was no less of a problem in the North, but beginning in the 1930s the Supreme Court took special aim at the problem of racial justice in the South. The element of regional conflict is evident in this case.

6. The Supreme Court's intervention in this case has clear analogies in the field of international criminal justice. The International Criminal

---

[9] See, e.g., Austrian Law No. 148 (1992); Belgian "La loi anti-négotioniste (1995); French Art. 24b, "La loi Gayssot"; German StGb §§ 130 (1985), 194 (1994); Israeli Prohibition Law No. 1187 (1986); Section 607 of the New Spanish Penal Code (1996); Art. 261 of the Swiss Penal Code (1994).

Court will judge a case only if they decide that the local state where the crime occurred is "unwilling or unable" to do justice in the case. Rome Statute Article 17(1).

7. Note that the Court could have resolved this case very simply by holding that the imposition of punitive damages violated the rights of the *New York Times* to a fair trial under the due process clause of the Fourteenth Amendment. This question came to the court later—in another case originating in Alabama. See Chapter Twenty-Three.

■

Further Reading

Free speech, the obstacles to its protection, and its proper scope are the subject of a vast and contentious literature. A good summary of recent debates is in *Eternally Vigilant: Free Speech in the Modern Era* (Lee C. Bollinger and Geoffrey R. Stone eds.) (Chicago: University of Chicago Press, 2003). On *Sullivan* itself, see Anthony Lewis, *Make No Law: The Sullivan Case and the First Amendment* (New York: Vintage Books, 1992).

ELEVEN

The Jury

The study of comparative law makes us sensitive to features of a foreign system that might seem perfectly normal to a practitioner living within the system. Differences stand out. The native is used to the forest, but the comparativist sees the unusual trees. Three distinctive features of the common law system come to our attention in the case for this chapter: (1) the jury system, (2) the institution of criminal contempt, and (3) the incorporation of the Bill of Rights in the due process clause.

The jury is one of the hallmarks of the American system known to everyone who sees contemporary films or reads John Grisham's novels. Many European young people are so familiar with the American jury that they think their legal system, every legal system, must have the same institution. To be precise, the common law "jury" consists of twelve laypersons (this is the usual number), untrained in the law, who have the power to deliberate on the evidence and decide the liability of the parties in a civil suit or the guilt or innocence of a criminal defendant. In civil cases, juries decide not only the question of liability but also the amount of damages the defendant must pay. Juries in criminal cases do not decide the sentence, with the exception of the power of juries to decide whether the accused deserves the death penalty.[1] The common law jury is not to be confused with bodies of laypeople (assessors) that deliberate together with judges in deciding cases. The latter form of mixed tribunals is common on the European continent.

The jury as we know it exists as well in Belgium for the most serious cases and used to exist in France. The Belgians add the unusual rule that the verdict of the jury of twelve jurors is the final word. There is no appeal. Americans recognize the right of the accused to appeal. In Canada, both the prosecution and the defense may appeal on questions of law, that is, mistaken instructions by the judge to the jury or other errors by the judge, lawyers, or others in conducting the trial.

Some people think that the jury system is an expression of democracy, and some newly democratic states like Spain and Russia are experimenting with the jury. The fact is that the jury is much older than democracy in the West (with the potential exception, of course, of democratic Athens, where the people served on democratic juries).

Indeed, elements of the jury are as old as the common law. Even before the Norman invasion, Laws of King Ethelred II (around the year 1000) required a form of grand jury, in which thirteen men of each locality were to swear, on oath, who they believed had committed crimes. The Normans imported the idea of the inquest, in which witnesses would swear to what they had seen, and the Constitutions of Clarendon of 1164 required both a grand jury (to accuse) and a trial jury (to find guilt or not), although not by those names. A form of civil jury was recognizable by 1179, when Henry II allowed trials to resolve issues of disputed land, to be decided either by combat or by a hearing before twelve knights who lived near the land. The jury was thus an established concept when it was mentioned in the negotiations between the English barons and King John in the famous Magna Carta (1215). This is the origin of the famous phrase "jury of one's peers," which contrary to popular belief does not appear in the U.S. Constitution.

In that same year of 1215, the jury became significantly more important in English law. Until that time the English courts relied on a

---

[1] The law used to permit the judge to ascertain the factors underlying this final decision, but the Supreme Court decided recently that aggravating factors that require the death penalty must be found by the jury. See *Ring v. Arizona*, 536 U.S. 584 (2002).

variety of magical rituals to determine the truth of the allegations (trial by battle, etc.). The Fourth Lateran Council forbade priests' participation in these rituals. An alternative method of determining the facts became necessary. So why not ask the people in the community what they know? The modern jury originated, as it were, as a polling of the people who were likely to know the truth in a local dispute. A few hundred years later, by the seventeenth century, the institution became transformed into a group of laypeople who were supposed to know nothing about the facts of the case.

All of these developments preceded the emergence of democratic institutions in England. There are also two significant differences between the jury system and democratic principles. First, jurors are supposed to judge the case in a neutral and detached way, as judges supposedly do, without bias toward the parties and without being influenced by loyalties toward ethnic, political, or economic groups. Any evidence of bias and extrinsic loyalty provides a sufficient ground to disqualify the juror from being chosen to sit on the jury. Second, common law juries must render their verdict unanimously—at least in criminal cases.[2] There are some deviations from the rule (the required verdict in England and in some U.S. states is 10–2). Still, this requirement differs markedly from the principle of majority rule that governs democratic institutions, as well as voting by judges in resolving the legal issues of the case.

Why should jury verdicts require unanimity or near-unanimity? Unfortunately, no one has offered a convincing reason for this principle. Our best guess is that the principle is based on the idea that the jury is supposed to discover the truth of the matter. Truth is not a function of majority vote. If there is no clear consensus on the matter, the object of belief cannot be considered the truth. There are, of course, many problems with this theory, not the least being that it supposes that each juror has an equal likelihood of discerning what is true or, at least, being persuaded to what is true by a juror who is better at it. Another theory is one of judicial convenience: A requirement of unanimity allows a judge to avoid making compromises with a closely voted verdict, such compromises having been required of the jurors who changed their minds to reach a consensus.

---

[2] Note that Belgian juries can convict on the basis of seven votes to five. This suggests a different philosophical foundation for the institution.

Note that if the criminal jury cannot agree on a verdict, they are called a "hung jury" and the case is dismissed, with the possibility of reprosecuting the defendant.

The specific problem raised in the following case is whether a jury trial should be required in criminal contempt proceedings. "Contempt proceedings" are a peculiar institution of the common law. The original idea was that certain unruly and disobedient behaviors expressed "contempt" for the court. The judge should respond to these signs of contempt in the court by sentencing the suspect immediately, without trial. The use of the contempt power was considered to be an inherent feature of judicial power. It did not have to be granted by statute or any other written source. It simply inhered in the common law conception of a court.

In a case of civil contempt, the judge sentences a contumacious litigant or lawyer to pay a daily or hourly fine or to stay in jail until such time as the person complies with a judicial order. For example, if a defendant has lost a case and been ordered to pay money to the plaintiff but has inexcusably refused to do so, the court may order an additional fine to accrue until the money is paid or, in extreme cases, jail for defendants until they pay. Criminal contempt is imposed retrospectively for "contemptuous behavior" that interferes with the administration of justice, such as when a witness refuses to answer a question (and there is no privilege justifying the refusal) or a lawyer or litigant disrupts the courtroom. In these cases, the judge can order the witness to sit in jail until such time as he or she is willing to answer or punish the litigant or lawyer after the fact. Typically, the judge warns the party, "If you do not stop screaming, I will hold you in contempt." Traditionally, in these cases of criminal contempt, the judge is legislator, judge, and jury, all wrapped into one. A little tyrant, to be precise.

Yet the problem resolved by the institution of criminal contempt is very significant. How do judges maintain order in the court? Continental judges do not have the contempt power. In most countries, the most they can do is to cite a lawyer for disobedience to the bar association or to report criminal conduct to the prosecutor's office. One would think that judges would be thereby precluded from effectively maintaining order, but so far as we know, there is hardly more disorder in European courtrooms than in their American analogues. It is important to remember, however, that Continental judges wield greater power of decision. If lawyers behave obnoxiously and disrespectfully, they are likely to lose on close questions of fact—which are resolved not by an independent jury but by the judge alone. Because the jury makes these findings of fact in the common law system, the judge has less power in deciding the case. Thus the contempt power seems to be necessary.

The existence of the contempt power raises a fundamental question about the nature of courts. Do they have only those powers assigned to them by the legislature or the Constitution? Recall Chief Justice Marshall's argument in *Marbury*. Or do they have inherent powers to take those measures that are necessary to enable them to judge effectively? The contempt power, if it exists, arises from the inherent nature of a court.

The following case challenges the inherent nature of the contempt power and, specifically, the authority of common law trial judges to send people to jail without a trial. The claim is that everyone is entitled not only to a trial but also to a jury trial. The case arises in Illinois, under Illinois law. How does it generate a federal constitutional question? This brings us to the third significant feature of the case, a characteristic more of the U.S. system than of the common law.

Americans have enshrined the jury system in the federal constitution. The Sixth and Seventh Amendments imposed the requirement for criminal and civil trials, but the Bill of Rights, it should be recalled, is applicable only to the federal government. There is nothing in the documents of 1789 and 1791 that explicitly requires jury trials in the states.[3] Yet the Fourteenth Amendment, adopted in 1868, changed the fundamental structure of American law, as it provides: "No State shall . . . deprive any person of life, liberty, or Property, without due Process of law."

The Due Process Clause became the vehicle for extending the Bill of Rights to the states. For example, there is nothing in the First Amendment that prohibits the states from making laws abridging the exercise of free speech. Yet in 1925 the Supreme Court held that any state law abridging freedom of speech or the press violates the due process clause; that is, if the state restricts freedom of speech, it thereby deprives the potential speaker of "liberty without due process of law" [*Gitlow v. New York*, 268 U.S. 652 (1925)]. Thus the Court began a long process of reevaluating

---

[3] The jury system is the only basic right (so far as we know) that is stipulated both in the body of the Constitution and in the Bill of Rights. See Article III, Section 2, Clause 3 ("The Trial of all Crimes, except in Cases of Impeachment, shall be by Jury") and the Sixth and Seventh Amendments. These provisions require jury trials in federal courts.

the laws of the several states to determine whether they conformed with the new federal policy expressed in the Fourteenth Amendment. Of course, no one knew precisely what "due process" required of the states.

A major factor driving the reform was the air of racial oppression in the Southern states. The widespread feeling in the North was that the Southern states were using their police and their criminal trials to suppress African Americans. As the *Mapp* case next illustrates, the Southern states have not been the only focus of the imperative of controlling and disciplining the police. Certainly, antagonism and suspicion toward the South has, since the Civil War, been particularly fierce. Nonetheless, the Supreme Court was reluctant to intervene and reconstruct the states' systems of criminal justice. The turning point was the famous Scottsboro case, in which an Alabama jury convicted eight young black men of raping a white woman. The procedures were so lacking in fundamental fairness that the Supreme Court could not avoid intervening and reversing the conviction as a violation of due process. See *Powell v. Alabama*, 287 U.S. 45 (1932).

The *Powell* or Scottsboro case began a long process of selectively choosing aspects of the Bill of Rights and imposing them on the states as requirements of due process. As we shall develop more in the next chapter, Justice Cardozo coined the most influential working definition of the due process clause: Only those aspects of the Bill of Rights were applicable to the states that were "implicit in the concept of ordered liberty" *Palko v. Connecticut*, 302 U.S. 319 (1937). Cardozo coined this phrase as a conservative move to restrict the extension of the Bill of Rights. The tide of history, however, was against him. The following case illustrates the dominant view that crystallized in the 1960s.

Bloom v. Illinois

Supreme Court of the United States
391 U.S. 194 (1968)

WHITE, J.:

Petitioner was convicted in an Illinois state court of criminal contempt and sentenced to imprisonment for 24 months for willfully petitioning to admit to probate a will falsely prepared and executed after the death of the putative testator. Petitioner made a timely demand for jury trial which was refused. Since in *Duncan v. Louisiana*, ante, p. 145, the Constitution was held to guarantee the right to jury trial in serious criminal cases in state courts, we must now decide whether it also guarantees the right to jury trial for a criminal contempt punished by a two-year prison term.

Whether federal and state courts may try criminal contempt cases without a jury has been a recurring question in this Court. Article III, § 2, of the Constitution provides that "the Trial of all Crimes, except in Cases of Impeachment, shall be by Jury. . . ." The Sixth Amendment states that "in all criminal prosecutions, the accused shall enjoy the right to a speedy and public trial, by an impartial jury. . . ." The Fifth and Fourteenth Amendments forbid both the Federal Government and the States from depriving any person of "life, liberty, or property, without due process of law." Notwithstanding these provisions, until *United States v. Barnett*, 376 U.S. 681, rehearing denied, 377 U.S. 973 (1964), the Court consistently upheld the constitutional power of the state and federal courts to punish any criminal contempt without a jury trial. . . . These cases construed the Due Process Clause and the otherwise inclusive language of Article III and the Sixth Amendment as permitting summary trials in contempt cases because at common law contempt was tried without a jury and because the power of courts to punish for contempt without the intervention of any other agency was considered essential to the proper and effective functioning of the courts and to the administration of justice.

The argument that the power to punish contempt was an inherent power of the courts not subject to regulation by Congress was rejected in *Michaelson v. United States* ex rel. Chicago, St. P., M. & O. R. Co., 266 U.S. 42, 65–67 (1924), which upheld the maximum sentence and jury trial provisions of the Clayton Act.

United States v. Barnett, supra, signaled a possible change of view. The Court of Appeals for the Fifth Circuit certified to this Court the question whether there was a right to jury trial in an impending contempt proceeding. Following prior cases, a five-man majority held that there was no constitutional right to jury trial in all contempt cases. Criminal contempt, intrinsically and aside from the particular penalty imposed, was not deemed a serious offense requiring the protection of the constitutional guarantees of the right to jury trial. However, the

Court put aside as not raised in the certification or firmly settled by prior cases, the issue whether a severe punishment would itself trigger the right to jury trial and indicated, without explication, that some members of the Court were of the view that the Constitution limited the punishment which could be imposed where the contempt was tried without a jury. 376 U.S., at 694–695 and n. 12. Two years later, in *Cheff v. Schnackenberg*, 384 U.S. 373 (1966), which involved a prison term of six months for contempt of a federal court, the Court rejected the claim that the Constitution guaranteed a right to jury trial in all criminal contempt cases. Contempt did not "of itself" warrant treatment as other than a petty offense; the six months' punishment imposed permitted dealing with the case as a prosecution for "a petty offense, which under our decisions does not require a jury trial" [citations omitted]. It was not necessary in *Cheff* to consider whether the constitutional guarantees of the right to jury trial applied to a prosecution for a serious contempt. Now, however, because of our holding in *Duncan v. Louisiana*, supra, that the right to jury trial extends to the States, and because of Bloom's demand for a jury in this case, we must once again confront the broad rule that all criminal contempts can be constitutionally tried without a jury. Barnett presaged a re-examination of this doctrine at some later time; that time has now arrived.

In proceeding with this task, we are acutely aware of the responsibility we assume in entertaining challenges to a constitutional principle which is firmly entrenched and which has behind it weighty and ancient authority. Our deliberations have convinced us, however, that serious contempts are so nearly like other serious crimes that they are subject to the jury trial provisions of the Constitution, now binding on the States, and that the traditional rule is constitutionally infirm insofar as it permits other than petty contempts to be tried without honoring a demand for a jury trial. We accept the judgment of *Barnett* and *Cheff* that criminal contempt is a petty offense unless the punishment makes it a serious one; but, in our view, dispensing with the jury in the trial of contempts subjected to severe punishment represents an unacceptable construction of the Constitution, "an unconstitutional assumption of powers by the [courts] which no lapse of time or respectable array of opinion should make us hesitate to correct." *Black & White Taxicab & Transfer Co. v. Brown & Yellow Taxicab & Transfer Co.*, 276 U.S. 518, 533 (1928) (Holmes, J., dissenting). The rule of our prior cases has strong, though sharply challenged, historical support;[4] but neither this circumstance nor the considerations of necessity and efficiency normally offered in defense of the established rule, justify denying a jury trial in serious criminal contempt cases. The Constitution guarantees the right to jury trial in state court prosecutions for contempt just as it does for other crimes.

II.

Criminal contempt is a crime in the ordinary sense; it is a violation of the law, a public wrong which is punishable by fine or imprisonment or both. In the words of Justice Holmes:

> These contempts are infractions of the law, visited with punishment as such. If such acts are not criminal, we are in error as to the most fundamental characteristic of crimes as that word has been understood in English speech. *Gompers v. United States*, 233 U.S. 604, 610 (1914)

Criminally contemptuous conduct may violate other provisions of the criminal law; but even when this is not the case convictions for criminal contempt are indistinguishable from ordinary criminal convictions, for their impact on the individual defendant is the same. Indeed, the role of criminal contempt and that of many ordinary criminal laws seem identical—protection of the institutions of our government and enforcement of their mandates.

Given that criminal contempt is a crime in every fundamental re-

---

[4] Blackstone's description of the common law practice in contempt cases appears in 4 *Commentaries on the Laws of England* 286–287:

> The process of attachment for these and the like contempts must necessarily be as ancient as the laws themselves; for laws without a competent authority to secure their administration from disobedience and contempt would be vain and nugatory. A power, therefore, in the supreme courts of justice, to suppress such contempts by an immediate attachment of the offender results from the first principles of judicial establishments, and must be an inseparable attendant upon every superior tribunal.
>
> [a long historical survey is omitted]

In any event, the ultimate question is not whether the traditional doctrine is historically correct but whether the rule that criminal contempts are never entitled to a jury trial is a necessary or an acceptable construction of the Constitution. Cf. *Thompson v. Utah*, 170 U.S. 343, 350 (1898). [This and note 5, in original.]

spect, the question is whether it is a crime to which the jury trial provisions of the Constitution apply. We hold that it is, primarily because in terms of those considerations which make the right to jury trial fundamental in criminal cases, there is no substantial difference between serious contempts and other serious crimes. Indeed, in contempt cases an even more compelling argument can be made for providing a right to jury trial as a protection against the arbitrary exercise of official power. Contemptuous conduct, though a public wrong, often strikes at the most vulnerable and human qualities of a judge's temperament. Even when the contempt is not a direct insult to the court or the judge, it frequently represents a rejection of judicial authority, or an interference with the judicial process or with the duties of officers of the court.

The court has long recognized the potential for abuse in exercising the summary power to imprison for contempt—it is an "arbitrary" power which is "liable to abuse." Ex parte Terry, 128 U.S. 289, 313 (1888). "Its exercise is a delicate one and care is needed to avoid arbitrary or oppressive conclusions." Cooke v. United States, 267 U.S. 517, 539 (1925).

These apprehensions about the unbridled power to punish summarily for contempt are reflected in the march of events in both Congress and the courts since our Constitution was adopted. The federal courts were established by the Judiciary Act of 1789; § 17 of the Act provided that those courts "shall have power to . . . punish by fine or imprisonment, at the discretion of said courts, all contempts of authority in any cause or hearing before the same. . . ." 1 Stat. 83. See Anderson v. Dunn, 6 Wheat. 204, 227–228 (1821). This open-ended authority to deal with contempt, limited only as to mode of punishment, proved unsatisfactory to Congress. Abuses under the 1789 Act culminated in the unsuccessful impeachment proceedings against James Peck, a federal district judge who had imprisoned and disbarred one Lawless for publishing a criticism of one of Peck's opinions in a case which was on appeal. The result was drastic curtailment of the contempt power in the Act of 1831, 4 Stat. 487. Ex parte Robinson, 19 Wall. 505, 510–511 (1874); In re Savin, 131 U.S. 267, 275–276 (1889). That Act limited the contempt power to misbehavior in the presence of the court or so near thereto as to obstruct justice; misbehavior of court officers in their official transactions; and disobedience of or resistance to the lawful writ, process, order, or decree of the court. This major revision of the contempt power in the federal sphere, which "narrowly confined" and "substantially curtailed" the authority to punish contempt summarily, *Nye v. United States*, 313 U.S. 33, 47–48 (1941), has continued to the present day as the basis for the general power to punish criminal contempt.

The courts also proved sensitive to the potential for abuse which resides in the summary power to punish contempt. Before the 19th century was out, a distinction had been carefully drawn between contempts occurring within the view of the court, for which a hearing and formal presentation of evidence were dispensed with, and all other contempts where more normal adversary procedures were required. Ex parte Terry, 128 U.S. 289 (1888); In re Savin, 131 U.S. 267 (1889). Later, the Court could say "it is certain that in proceedings for criminal contempt the defendant is presumed to be innocent, he must be proved to be guilty beyond a reasonable doubt, and cannot be compelled to testify against himself." *Gompers v. Bucks Stove & Range Co.*, 221 U.S. 418, 444 (1911). . . .

Judicial concern has not been limited to procedure. . . .*Nye v. United States*, 313 U.S. 33, 47–52 (1941) . . . narrowly limited the conduct proscribed by the 1831 Act to "misbehavior in the vicinity of the court disrupting to quiet and order or actually interrupting the court in the conduct of its business." *Id.*, at 52. Cf. *Toledo Newspaper Co. v. United States*, supra, at 422 (Holmes, J., dissenting). The congressional purpose to fence in the power of the federal courts to punish contempt summarily was further implemented in *Cammer v. United States*, 350 U.S. 399, 407–408 (1956). A lawyer, the Court held, "is not the kind of 'officer' who can be summarily tried for contempt under 18 U. S. C. § 401 (2)." In another development, the First Amendment was invoked to ban punishment for a broad category of arguably contemptuous out-of-court conduct. *Bridges v. California*, 314 U.S. 252 (1941); *Pennekamp v. Florida*, 328 U.S. 331 (1946); *Craig v. Harney*, 331 U.S. 367 (1947). Finally, over the years in the federal system there has been a recurring necessity to set aside punishments for criminal contempt as either unauthorized by statute or too harsh. . . .[5]

---

[5] Most other Western countries seem to be highly restrictive of the latitude given judges to try their own contempts without a jury. See Jann, "Contempt of Court in Western

This course of events demonstrates the unwisdom of vesting the judiciary with completely untrammeled power to punish contempt, and makes clear the need for effective safeguards against that power's abuse. Prosecutions for contempt play a significant role in the proper functioning of our judicial system; but despite the important values which the contempt power protects, courts and legislatures have gradually eroded the power of judges to try contempts of their own authority. In modern times, procedures in criminal contempt cases have come to mirror those used in ordinary criminal cases. Our experience teaches that convictions for criminal contempt, not infrequently resulting in extremely serious penalties . . . , are indistinguishable from those obtained under ordinary criminal laws. If the right to jury trial is a fundamental matter in other criminal cases, which we think it is, it must also be extended to criminal contempt cases.

III.

We cannot say that the need to further respect for judges and courts is entitled to more consideration than the interest of the individual not to be subjected to serious criminal punishment without the benefit of all the procedural protections worked out carefully over the years and deemed fundamental to our system of justice. Genuine respect, which alone can lend true dignity to our judicial establishment, will be engendered, not by the fear of unlimited authority, but by the firm administration of the law through those institutionalized procedures which have been worked out over the centuries.

We place little credence in the notion that the independence of the judiciary hangs on the power to try contempts summarily and are not persuaded that the additional time and expense possibly involved

Germany," 8 *Am. U. L. Rev.* 34 (1959); Bigelow, "Contempt of Court," 1 *Crim. L. Q.* 475 (1959); Pekelis, "Legal Techniques and Political Ideologies: A Comparative Study," 41 *Mich. L. Rev.* 665 (1943). By contrast, there was no right of appeal against a conviction for criminal contempt in England until the Administration of Justice Act, 1960, 8 & 9 Eliz. 2, c. 65. See Harnon, "Civil and Criminal Contempts of Court," 25 *Mod. L. Rev.* 179 (1962). (The traditional claim that contempt of court is specific to the common law is no longer easily maintained. Not only have various non–common law systems adopted a concept of contempt but also there is a growing recognition of the effects of penalties for noncompliance with judicial orders in civilian systems. See, e.g., Ted L. Stein, "Contempt, Crisis, and the Court: The World Court and the Hostage Rescue Attempt," 76 *A.J.I.L.* 499 (1982).)

in submitting serious contempts to juries will seriously handicap the effective functioning of the courts. We do not deny that serious punishment must sometimes be imposed for contempt, but we reject the contention that such punishment must be imposed without the right to jury trial. The goals of dispatch, economy, and efficiency are important, but they are amply served by preserving the power to commit for civil contempt and by recognizing that many contempts are not serious crimes but petty offenses not within the jury trial provisions of the Constitution. When a serious contempt is at issue, considerations of efficiency must give way to the more fundamental interest of ensuring the even-handed exercise of judicial power. In isolated instances recalcitrant or irrational juries may acquit rather than apply the law to the case before them. Our system has wrestled with this problem for hundreds of years, however, and important safeguards have been devised to minimize miscarriages of justice through the malfunctioning of the jury system. Perhaps to some extent we sacrifice efficiency, expedition, and economy, but the choice in favor of jury trial has been made, and retained, in the Constitution. We see no sound reason in logic or policy not to apply it in the area of criminal contempt. . . .

Reversed and remanded.

FORTAS, J., CONCURRING.

HARLAN, J., WHOM STEWART, J. JOINS, DISSENTING:

I dissent for the reasons expressed in my dissenting opinion in *Duncan v. Louisiana*, ante, p. 171, and in my separate opinion in *Cheff v. Schnackenberg*, 384 U.S. 373, 380. See also *United States v. Barnett*, 376 U.S. 681; *Green v. United States*, 356 U.S. 165.

This case completes a remarkable circle. In *Duncan*, supra, the Court imposed on the States a rule of procedure that was neither shown to be fundamental to procedural fairness nor held to be part of the originally understood content of the Fourteenth Amendment. The sole justification was that the rule was found in the Bill of Rights. . . .

QUESTIONS AND COMMENTS

1. On the surface, this case raises a number of important issues about the contempt power and whether the right to a jury trial is included

in the Fourteenth Amendment's due process clause. Behind these questions lies a basic question about the relevance of history to the interpretation of the Constitution. The question is whether when the Constitution and the Bill of Rights came into force in 1789 and 1791, respectively, their purpose was to change all aspects of the pre-existing law or whether their purpose was to incorporate and entrench the practices of the time. The answer is that it had both purposes—even though these two goals are radically inconsistent.

2. The jury trial in criminal cases and in disputes at common law existed in 1791, and therefore the purpose of the Sixth and Seventh Amendments was, at least in part, to entrench and safeguard the practices of the common law. The same could be said of the Fourteenth Amendment. The understanding of "due process" was written against the customs and traditions of the common law. The contempt power constituted part of those "customs and traditions." Does it follow that the contempt power was "grandfathered" into the Constitution?[6]

3. The Constitution is both history and principle. Sometimes the document must be read and interpreted against the backdrop of the practices of the time. This is done in the area of free speech. If certain crimes and other violations involving speech were prohibited in 1791, no claims can be made that the First Amendment suddenly legitimated them. Good examples are copyright violations and criminal conspiracies and, indeed, the libel remedy tested in the *Sullivan* case. The Constitution is also principle, and therefore it can serve to correct and change historical practices. Thus the due process clause served in *Sullivan* as the basis for reforming the traditional law of libel to bring it in line with contemporary notions of fairness. The same phenomenon is evident in the *Bloom* case: The traditional law of contempt is subject to reform in recognition of the current appreciation of jury trials as procedures "implicit in the concept of ordered liberty."[7]

4. Thus there are two great interpretive foundations at war in *Sullivan* and *Bloom*: history and principle. These two approaches to the Con-

---

[6] It is not clear where this expression comes from, but it means basically: The new rule should cover everyone except grandfathers who lived by the old rule. When an exception is "grandfathered" or "grandparented" into the existing body of law, the exception is recognized for no reason except respect for historical practices.

[7] *Palko v. Connecticut*, 302 U.S. 319 (1937) (Cardozo, J.).

stitution clashed in another case of monumental significance: *Ex parte Quirin*, 317 U.S. 1 (1942). The *Quirin* case tested whether eight German saboteurs who landed on the shores of the United States (but were arrested without causing harm) were entitled to a jury trial under the Constitution, the government maintained that they could be tried by military tribunals, and they were so tried, with six suffering immediate execution. The Court found precedents for the similar treatment of spies during the Revolutionary War,[8] and therefore, they concluded, the exception to jury trials was "grandfathered" into the Constitution. See Louis Fisher, *Nazi Saboteurs on Trial: A Military Tribunal and American Law* (Lawrence: University of Kansas Press, 2003). This case took on great political significance in the period after September 11, 2001, when President Bush proclaimed military tribunals based on the *Quirin* model. As of this writing, trials are about to commence at Guantánamo Bay.

5. Is there any systematic way to resolve the conflict between history and principle? Take, for example, the problem of protecting religion under the clause in the First Amendment guaranteeing the "free exercise of religion." One historical interpretation would insist that this clause be limited to the religions that were present on American soil at the time of the founding. A principled approach would seek to define the nature of religion and extend the free exercise of religion to all believers in a supreme power of the universe, whether or not they were strongly represented in 1791. This makes a tremendous difference in considering the rights of Jews, Muslims, and Native Americans, whose religions were already present but not, shall we say, "highly visible" when the framers thought about freedom of religion.

6. The conflict between history and principle should lead us to reexamine the premise of Chapter Five, namely, that the Constitution is a code in the same sense the French and German civil codes are "new beginnings" based on a systematic and interrelated set of legislated

---

[8] The most famous of these was the case of Major John André, a British officer who collaborated with Benedict Arnold. André was summarily hanged after apprehension for spying after crossing enemy lines in civilian clothes. This was the pattern of activity that President Roosevelt and his legal team perceived in the behavior of the eight saboteurs. For an extended analysis of the *Quirin* case and its legal arguments, see George P. Fletcher, *Romantics at War: Glory and Guilt in the Age of Terrorism*, Chapter Five (Princeton, NJ: Princeton University Press, 2002).

provisions. So far as the Constitution's purpose is to entrench con-
temporaneous historical practices, it is not a code in the Continental
sense. But that point, too, requires reassessment; perhaps, as some
scholars have suggested, the civil codes such as the French and
German codes must be read against the ideas and practices that were
current at the time.[9] This would mean that the notion of "code" requires a recognition of historical influence as well. Is there no end to
the questions we can ask?

∎

Further Reading

The best comparative study of the roles of juries is the collection of nationally
focused essays in Neil Vidmar, *World Jury Systems* (Oxford: Oxford University
Press, 2000). The rather controversial history of the jury is explored in John H.
Langbein, *The Origins of Adversary Criminal Trial* (Oxford: Oxford University
Press, 2003). A useful series of debates on current issues regarding the jury, particularly the scope of its use, the role of peremptory challenges, and jury nullification, is in *The Jury System* (Mary E. Williams ed.) (San Diego, CA: Green-
haven Press, 1997). For the specific problems of contempt orders, see Margaret
Meriwether Cordray, "Contempt Sanctions and the Excessive Fines Clause," 76
N.C. L. Rev. 407 (1998). On the forms of interpretation according to principle
or history, see the essays collected in *Law and Interpretation: Essays in Legal Philosophy* (Andrei Marmor and Basil S. Markesinis eds.) (Oxford: Oxford University
Press, 1998).

[9] See, e.g., the debate on the Louisiana civil code, Robert A. Pascal, "Louisiana Civil
Code of 1808: Sources of the Digest of 1808: A Reply to Professor Batiza," 46 *Tul. L.
Rev.* 603 (1972); Radolfo Batiza, "The Louisiana Civil Code of 1808: Its Actual Sources
and Present Relevance," 46 *Tul. L. Rev.* 4 (1971).

TWELVE

Due Process Ascendant

During the drafting and ratification of the Constitution in 1787–88, the great fear was that a central government would be either too weak, like the government under the Articles of Confederation, or too strong and thus potentially tyrannical. Few considered the potential for excessive power in the states themselves. That concern was addressed only in a few clauses, which have been rarely invoked and more rarely applied—especially the Republican Form of Government Clause and the State Bill of Attainder Clause. (See Art. IV § 4; Art. I § 10.) Instead, to the degree that state abuse of powers was considered, it was left to the democratic process and to the state courts' interpretations of state bills of rights.

As we saw in Chapter Six, this all changed with the great upheavals of the Civil War and Reconstruction. With the postwar ratification of the Thirteenth, Fourteenth, and Fifteenth Amendments, the states were now bound by *federal* constitutional strictures to secure certain freedoms to their own citizens, including the right of citizenship itself. The two provisions that would have the most far-ranging effects are both in Section One of the Fourteenth Amendment: "No State shall deny to any person due process of law or equal protection of the laws."

These new limits on state power enshrined phrases with potentially indefinite meanings: What process is "due" and what protection is "equal"? To some extent, a tradition of interpreting "due process" had begun by reading a similar clause in the Fifth Amendment, limiting the central government. This tradition equated "due process" to something like the procedural guarantees of Chapter Thirty-Nine of the Magna Carta in the English common law.[1] Yet it was clear that the drafters of the Fourteenth Amendment intended something more to keep former slave states from mistreating the freed slaves.

Initial interpretations of the Fourteenth Amendment resulted in more opinions about what it did not do than about what it did. The *Slaughterhouse Cases* held that the amendment barred discrimination only against freedmen (emancipated slaves), not against the general population.[2] The *Civil Rights Cases* held the Reconstruction Amendments to a narrow scope of statutes that would eradicate slavery and not broader acts of discrimination against former slaves.[3] There was little in these opinions that guided any understanding of what state action would violate due process of law.

In prior chapters we have mentioned the general assertion of federal authority under the due process clause of the Fourteenth Amendment. Now we document that assertion in greater detail. Much of the case law in the half-century from 1925 to 1975 was about which clauses of the Bill of Rights would be "incorporated" into the Fourteenth Amendment and thus made applicable to the states. A harbinger of this case law development is found as early as 1897, when the court interpreted the due process clause to require a state to give just compensation for the taking of property.[4] In 1925 the Court interpreted due process to include a pro-

---

[1] A translation of Magna Carta is maintained by the British Library at http://www.bl .uk/collections/treasures/magnatranslation.html. The reigning understanding of "the law of the land" in the United States in the nineteenth century was drawn from Sir Edward Coke. See his commentary on Magna Carta Chapter Twenty-Nine (the renumbered Chapter Thirty-Nine), in Steve Sheppard, *The Selected Writings of Sir Edward Coke* 848 (3 vols.) (Indianapolis: Liberty Fund, 2004).

[2] 83 U.S. 36 (1873). In that case, in which the City of New Orleans gave a monopoly over meatpacking to one company to the detriment of the rest, claims were raised under both the privileges and immunities clause and the due process clause. Justice Miller's opinion for the majority was based mainly on a narrow reading of the privileges and immunities clause.

[3] 109 U.S. 3 (1883). This result was reversed in Jones v. Alfred H. Mayer Co., 392 U.S. 409 (1968), in which Congress was held to be empowered by the Thirteenth Amendment to pass any rational statute to abolish the badges and incidents of slavery.

[4] Chicago, Burlington & Quincy Railroad Co. v. Chicago, 166 U.S. 226 (1897). In that

tection for the freedom of speech (*Gitlow v. New York*, 268 U.S. 652 (1925)) and in short order to include the freedoms of press (*Near v. Minnesota*, 283 U.S. 697 (1931)), assembly (*DeJonge v. Oregon*, 299 U.S. 353 (1937)), petition (*Hague v. CIO*, 307 U.S. 496 (1939)), and religion.[5]

The most dramatic expansion of "due process" occurred, however, when the Court was willing to infer general principles underlying the language of the Bill of Rights and therefore conclude in 1965 that the Constitution incorporated a general principle of privacy. The right to privacy includes marital and sexual privacy as expressed in limitations by the state to regulate the use of contraception (*Griswold v. Connecticut*, 381 U.S. 479 (1965)) and abortion (*Roe v. Wade*, 410 U.S. 113 (1973)). The root of the principle of privacy is the Fourth Amendment, which becomes the centerpiece of the case considered in this chapter.

The burning question with regard to the Fourth Amendment is not whether the limitation on government-sponsored searches and seizures applies to the states. That was a relatively easy decision reached in the *Wolf* case in 1949 (*Wolf v. Colorado*, 338 U.S. 25). The bigger problem was whether a certain remedy called the "exclusionary rule" would apply to the states as a requirement of due process.

The exclusionary rule is an American invention that requires the courts to exclude all evidence that is seized in the course of an unconstitutional search of papers, persons, or residential or business premises. Whether the search is unconstitutional depends first on whether it proceeds on the basis of a valid warrant issued by a magistrate or, if there is no warrant, the search is reasonable under all the circumstances. The latter clause is obviously vague and therefore has been the source of an enormous body of case law.

Even before the Court considers whether the search is reasonable, it must decide whether the investigation producing the evidence is really a police "search" in the constitutional sense. (If the search is conducted by private parties, it does not qualify for protection as state action under the due process clause.) On the knotty concept of "governmental searches," there are two important questions to keep in mind:

case, the City of Chicago had condemned, or forced the sale, of property of the railroad, for which the railroad was awarded one dollar.

[5] Cantwell v. Connecticut, 310 U.S. 296 (1940) (free exercise clause); Wolf v. Colorado, 338 U.S. 25 (1949) (establishment clause).

1. Is a physical intrusion necessary for a search? For centuries, the law on this point was governed by the principles of trespass, which requires a physical intrusion. See *Scott v. Shepherd* in Chapter One. Wiretapping and eavesdropping were the main points of contention. Did wiretapping or long-distance eavesdropping constitute searches in the constitutional sense? The general rule was no, but then in 1967 the Court shifted from history to principle as the foundation of its interpretation of the Fourth Amendment and concluded that physical intrusion was an arbitrary requirement, supported only by tradition. In *Katz v. United States*, 389 U.S. 347 (1967), the Court held any violation of the "reasonable expectation of privacy" constituted a search under the Constitution. The specific search in that case was clamping a "bug" to the outside of a phone booth and overhearing the telephone conversation inside the booth. The Court said that Katz, the caller inside the booth, had a reasonable expectation of privacy in his telephone conversations. As a sidelight, note how much the concept of "reasonableness" shapes the Fourth Amendment. If there is no warrant, the search must be reasonable under all the circumstances, and overhearing a conversation constitutes a search only if it violates a "reasonable expectation of privacy." Compare the general discussion of reasonableness in the common law in Chapter Three.

2. Is a physical intrusion by police officers sufficient to constitute a search? In the O. J. Simpson case, Officer Mark Fuhrman and his companions scaled the wall to O. J.'s estate and searched the grounds. They went in because they found blood spots on his car, and they argued that they were trying to protect people inside who might be in danger. The trial judge upheld this argument and concluded that the intrusion was not a "search" and that the evidence seized on the grounds—notably a bloody glove—was therefore admissible. The principle behind this decision is that the Fourth Amendment and the due process clause are designed to protect suspects against searches designed to find evidence of crime. If the search has the purpose of protecting persons in danger rather than collecting evidence of crime, it is not a search under the Constitution. You might be appropriately skeptical of this distinction. If the intrusion is for the purpose of protecting people in danger, why should the police be able to seize evidence that they stumble upon? A similar problem arises in the following case.

The major issue in the *Mapp* case is whether the Due Process Clause should include the exclusionary rule. The federal courts had developed the exclusionary rule in 1914, but no one knew whether this was just a rule of evidence in the federal courts or a constitutional principle. Now the Court had to decide.

■

Mapp v. Ohio

Supreme Court of the United States
367 U.S. 643 (1961).

CLARK, J.:

Appellant stands convicted of knowingly having had in her possession and under her control certain lewd and lascivious books, pictures, and photographs in violation of § 2905.34 of Ohio's Revised Code. As officially stated in the syllabus to its opinion, the Supreme Court of Ohio found that her conviction was valid though "based primarily upon the introduction in evidence of lewd and lascivious books and pictures unlawfully seized during an unlawful search of defendant's home. . . ."

On May 23, 1957, three Cleveland police officers arrived at appellant's residence in that city pursuant to information that "a person [was] hiding out in the home, who was wanted for questioning in connection with a recent bombing, and that there was a large amount of policy paraphernalia being hidden in the home." Miss Mapp and her daughter by a former marriage lived on the top floor of the two-family dwelling. Upon their arrival at that house, the officers knocked on the door and demanded entrance but appellant, after telephoning her attorney, refused to admit them without a search warrant. They advised their headquarters of the situation and undertook a surveillance of the house.

The officers again sought entrance some three hours later when four or more additional officers arrived on the scene. When Miss Mapp did not come to the door immediately, at least one of the several doors to the house was forcibly opened and the policemen gained admittance. Meanwhile Miss Mapp's attorney arrived, but the officers, having secured their own entry, and continuing in their defiance of the law, would permit him neither to see Miss Mapp nor to enter the house. It appears that Miss Mapp was halfway down the stairs from the upper floor to the front door when the officers, in this highhanded manner, broke into the hall. She demanded to see the search warrant. A paper, claimed to be a warrant, was held up by one of the officers. She grabbed the "warrant" and placed it in her bosom. A struggle ensued in which the officers recovered the piece of paper and as a result of which they handcuffed appellant because she had been "belligerent" in resisting their official rescue of the "warrant" from her person. Running rough-shod over appellant, a policeman "grabbed" her, "twisted [her] hand," and she "yelled [and] pleaded with him" because "it was hurting." Appellant, in handcuffs, was then forcibly taken upstairs to her bedroom where the officers searched a dresser, a chest of drawers, a closet and some suitcases. They also looked into a photo album and through personal papers belonging to the appellant. The search spread to the rest of the second floor including the child's bedroom, the living room, the kitchen and a dinette. The basement of the building and a trunk found therein were also searched. The obscene materials for possession of which she was ultimately convicted were discovered in the course of that widespread search.[6]

At the trial no search warrant was produced by the prosecution, nor was the failure to produce one explained or accounted for. At best, "There is, in the record, considerable doubt as to whether there ever was any warrant for the search of defendant's home." 170 Ohio St., at 430, 166 N. E. 2d, at 389. The Ohio Supreme Court believed a "reasonable argument" could be made that the conviction should be reversed "because the 'methods' employed to obtain the [evidence] . . . were such as to 'offend "a sense of justice," ' " but the court [below decided to the contrary].

The State says that even if the search were made without authority, or otherwise unreasonably, it is not prevented from using the uncon-

---

[6] Charging someone with the criminal possession of obscene photos and writings obviously raises problems under the First Amendment. The debate between history and principle, as explained in the preceding chapter, applies here as well. The historical argument is that at the time of the founding, possessing obscene materials was a criminal offense. Therefore, it was not protected as "free speech" under the original understanding of the First Amendment. The argument of principle is that obscenity is an aspect of artistic expression and therefore deserves constitutional protection. See Edward de Grazia, *Girls Lean Back Everywhere: The Law of Obscenity and the Assault on Genius* (New York: Random House, 1992). That issue is not raised in this case, but do you think it might play an implicit role in the decision?

stitutionally seized evidence at trial, citing *Wolf v. Colorado*, 338 U.S. 25 (1949), in which this Court did indeed hold "that in a prosecution in a State court for a State crime the Fourteenth Amendment does not forbid the admission of evidence obtained by an unreasonable search and seizure." At p. 33. On this appeal, of which we have noted probable jurisdiction, 364 U.S. 868, it is urged once again that we review that holding.

Other issues have been raised on this appeal but, in the view we have taken of the case, they need not be decided. Although appellant chose to urge what may have appeared to be the surer ground for favorable disposition and did not insist that *Wolf* be overruled, the amicus curiae, who was also permitted to participate in the oral argument, did urge the Court to overrule *Wolf*.

I.

[I]n the year 1914, in the Weeks case, this Court "for the first time" held that "in a federal prosecution the Fourth Amendment barred the use of evidence secured through an illegal search and seizure." This Court has ever since required of federal law officers a strict adherence to that command which this Court has held to be a clear, specific, and constitutionally required—even if judicially implied—deterrent safeguard without insistence upon which the Fourth Amendment would have been reduced to "a form of words." Holmes, J., *Silverthorne Lumber Co. v. United States*, 251 U.S. 385, 392 (1920). It meant, quite simply, that "conviction by means of unlawful seizures and enforced confessions . . . should find no sanction in the judgments of the courts . . . ," *Weeks v. United States*, supra, at 392, and that such evidence "shall not be used at all." *Silverthorne Lumber Co. v. United States*, supra, at 392.

There are in the cases of this Court some passing references to the Weeks rule as being one of evidence [i.e.. not of constitutional stature]. But the plain and unequivocal language of *Weeks*—and its later paraphrase in *Wolf*—to the effect that the *Weeks* rule is of constitutional origin, remains entirely undisturbed. . . .

II.

In 1949, 35 years after *Weeks* was announced, this Court, in *Wolf v. Colorado*, supra, again for the first time, discussed the effect of the Fourth Amendment upon the States through the operation of the Due

Process Clause of the Fourteenth Amendment. . . . Nevertheless, after declaring that the "security of one's privacy against arbitrary intrusion by the police" is "implicit in 'the concept of ordered liberty' and as such enforceable against the States through the Due Process Clause," cf. *Palko v. Connecticut*, 302 U.S. 319 (1937), and announcing that it "stoutly adhere[d]" to the *Weeks* decision, the Court decided that the *Weeks* exclusionary rule would not then be imposed upon the States as "an essential ingredient of the right." 338 U.S., at 27–29. . . .

III.

Some five years after *Wolf*, in answer to a plea made here Term after Term that we overturn its doctrine on applicability of the *Weeks* exclusionary rule, this Court indicated that such should not be done until the States had "adequate opportunity to adopt or reject the [*Wolf*] rule." And only last Term, after again carefully re-examining the *Wolf* doctrine in *Elkins v. United States*, supra, the Court pointed out that "the controlling principles" as to search and seizure and the problem of admissibility "seemed clear" (at p. 212) until the announcement in *Wolf* "that the Due Process Clause of the Fourteenth Amendment does not itself require state courts to adopt the exclusionary rule" of the Weeks case. . . . Today we once again examine *Wolf*'s constitutional documentation of the right to privacy free from unreasonable state intrusion, and, after its dozen years on our books, are led by it to close the only courtroom door remaining open to evidence secured by official lawlessness in flagrant abuse of that basic right, reserved to all persons as a specific guarantee against that very same unlawful conduct. We hold that all evidence obtained by searches and seizures in violation of the Constitution is, by that same authority, inadmissible in a state court.

IV.

Since the Fourth Amendment's right of privacy has been declared enforceable against the States through the Due Process Clause of the Fourteenth, it is enforceable against them by the same sanction of exclusion as is used against the Federal Government. . . . To hold otherwise is to grant the right but in reality to withhold its privilege and enjoyment. Only last year the Court itself recognized that the purpose of the exclusionary rule "is to deter—to compel respect for the constitutional guaranty in the only effectively available way—by removing the incentive to disregard it." *Elkins v. United States*, supra, at 217.

V.

Moreover, our holding that the exclusionary rule is an essential part of both the Fourth and Fourteenth Amendments is not only the logical dictate of prior cases, but it also makes very good sense. There is no war between the Constitution and common sense. Presently, a federal prosecutor may make no use of evidence illegally seized, but a State's attorney across the street may, although he supposedly is operating under the enforceable prohibitions of the same Amendment. Thus the State, by admitting evidence unlawfully seized, serves to encourage disobedience to the Federal Constitution which it is bound to uphold.
. . . Federal-state cooperation in the solution of crime under constitutional standards will be promoted, if only by recognition of their now mutual obligation to respect the same fundamental criteria in their approaches. . . .

There are those who say, as did Justice (then Judge) Cardozo, that under our constitutional exclusionary doctrine "the criminal is to go free because the constable has blundered." *People v. Defore*, 242 N.Y., at 21, 150 N.E., at 587. In some cases this will undoubtedly be the result. But, as was said in *Elkins*, "there is another consideration—the imperative of judicial integrity." 364 U.S., at 222. The criminal goes free, if he must, but it is the law that sets him free. Nothing can destroy a government more quickly than its failure to observe its own laws, or worse, its disregard of the charter of its own existence. As Justice Brandeis, dissenting, said in *Olmstead v. United States*, 277 U.S. 438, 485 (1928): "Our Government is the potent, the omnipresent teacher. For good or for ill, it teaches the whole people by its example. . . . If the Government becomes a lawbreaker, it breeds contempt for law; it invites every man to become a law unto himself; it invites anarchy." . . .

Having once recognized that the right to privacy embodied in the Fourth Amendment is enforceable against the States, and that the right to be secure against rude invasions of privacy by state officers is, therefore, constitutional in origin, we can no longer permit that right to remain an empty promise. Because it is enforceable in the same manner and to like effect as other basic rights secured by the Due

Process Clause, we can no longer permit it to be revocable at the whim of any police officer who, in the name of law enforcement itself, chooses to suspend its enjoyment. Our decision, founded on reason and truth, gives to the individual no more than that which the Constitution guarantees him, to the police officer no less than that to which honest law enforcement is entitled, and, to the courts, that judicial integrity so necessary in the true administration of justice.

The judgment of the Supreme Court of Ohio is reversed and the cause remanded for further proceedings not inconsistent with this opinion.

Reversed and remanded.

BLACK, J. AND DOUGLAS, J. CONCURRING IN SEPARATE OPINION.

STEWART, J. DID NOT PARTICIPATE IN THE DECISION.

HARLAN, J., WHOM FRANKFURTER, J. AND WHITTAKER, J. JOIN, DISSENTING:

In overruling the *Wolf* case the Court, in my opinion, has forgotten the sense of judicial restraint which, with due regard for stare decisis, is one element that should enter into deciding whether a past decision of this Court should be overruled. Apart from that I also believe that the *Wolf* rule represents sounder Constitutional doctrine than the new rule which now replaces it.

I.

From the Court's statement of the case one would gather that the central, if not controlling, issue on this appeal is whether illegally state-seized evidence is Constitutionally admissible in a state prosecution, an issue which would of course face us with the need for re-examining *Wolf*. However, such is not the situation. For, although that question was indeed raised here and below among appellant's subordinate points, the new and pivotal issue brought to the Court by this appeal is whether § 2905.34 of the Ohio Revised Code making criminal the mere knowing possession or control of obscene material, and under which appellant has been convicted, is consistent with the rights of free thought and expression assured against state action by the Fourteenth Amendment. That was the principal issue which was decided by the

Ohio Supreme Court, which was tendered by appellant's Jurisdictional Statement, and which was briefed[7] and argued[8] in this Court.

In this posture of things, I think it fair to say that five members of this Court have simply "reached out" to overrule *Wolf*. With all respect for the views of the majority, and recognizing that stare decisis carries different weight in Constitutional adjudication than it does in [a] non-constitutional decision, I can perceive no justification for regarding this case as an appropriate occasion for re-examining *Wolf*.

[I]f the Court were bent on reconsidering *Wolf*, I think that there would soon have presented itself an appropriate opportunity in which we could have had the benefit of full briefing and argument. In any event, at the very least, the present case should have been set down for reargument, in view of the inadequate briefing and argument we have received on the *Wolf* point. To all intents and purposes the Court's present action amounts to a summary reversal of *Wolf*, without argument.

I am bound to say that what has been done is not likely to promote respect either for the Court's adjudicatory process or for the stability of its decisions. Having been unable, however, to persuade any of the majority to a different procedural course, I now turn to the merits of the present decision.

---

[7] The appellant's brief did not urge the overruling of *Wolf*. Indeed, it did not even cite the case. The brief of the appellee merely relied on *Wolf* in support of the state's contention that appellant's conviction was not vitiated by the admission in evidence of the fruits of the alleged unlawful search and seizure by the police. The brief of the American and Ohio Civil Liberties Unions, as amici, did in one short concluding paragraph of its argument "request" the Court to reexamine and overrule *Wolf*, but without argumentation. I quote in full this part of their brief:

> This case presents the issue of whether evidence obtained in an illegal search and seizure can constitutionally be used in a State criminal proceeding. We are aware of the view that this Court has taken on this issue in *Wolf v. Colorado*, 338 U.S. 25. It is our purpose by this paragraph to respectfully request that this Court re-examine this issue and conclude that the ordered liberty concept guaranteed to persons by the due process clause of the Fourteenth Amendment necessarily requires that evidence illegally obtained in violation thereof, not be admissible in state criminal proceedings.

[This and note 8, in original.]

[8] Counsel for appellant on oral argument, as in his brief, did not urge that *Wolf* be overruled. Indeed, when pressed by questioning from the bench whether he was not in fact urging the Court to overrule *Wolf*, counsel expressly disavowed any such purpose.

II.

. . . .

I would not impose upon the States this federal exclusionary remedy. The reasons given by the majority for now suddenly turning its back on *Wolf* seem to me notably unconvincing.

The preservation of a proper balance between state and federal responsibility in the administration of criminal justice demands patience on the part of those who might like to see things move faster among the States in this respect. Problems of criminal law enforcement vary widely from State to State. One State, in considering the totality of its legal picture, may conclude that the need for embracing the *Weeks* rule is pressing because other remedies are unavailable or inadequate to secure compliance with the substantive Constitutional principle involved. Another, though equally solicitous of Constitutional rights, may choose to pursue one purpose at a time, allowing all evidence relevant to guilt to be brought into a criminal trial, and dealing with Constitutional infractions by other means. Still another may consider the exclusionary rule too rough-and-ready a remedy, in that it reaches only unconstitutional intrusions which eventuate in criminal prosecution of the victims. Further, a State after experimenting with the *Weeks* rule for a time may, because of unsatisfactory experience with it, decide to revert to a non-exclusionary rule. And so on. From the standpoint of Constitutional permissibility in pointing a State in one direction or another, I do not see at all why "time has set its face against" the considerations which led Justice Cardozo, then chief judge of the New York Court of Appeals, to reject for New York in *People v. Defore*, 242 N.Y. 13, 150 N. E. 585, the *Weeks* exclusionary rule. For us the question remains, as it has always been, one of state power, not one of passing judgment on the wisdom of one state course or another. In my view this Court should continue to forbear from fettering the States with an adamant rule which may embarrass them in coping with their own peculiar problems in criminal law enforcement. . . .

A state conviction comes to us as the complete product of a sovereign judicial system. Typically a case will have been tried in a trial court, tested in some final appellate court, and will go no further. In the comparatively rare instance when a conviction is reviewed by us on due process grounds we deal then with a finished product in the creation of which we are allowed no hand, and our task, far from being one of over-all supervision, is, speaking generally, restricted to a determination of whether the prosecution was Constitutionally fair. The specifics of trial procedure, which in every mature legal system will vary greatly in detail, are within the sole competence of the States. . . .

I regret that I find so unwise in principle and so inexpedient in policy a decision motivated by the high purpose of increasing respect for Constitutional rights. But in the last analysis I think this Court can increase respect for the Constitution only if it rigidly respects the limitations which the Constitution places upon it, and respects as well the principles inherent in its own processes. In the present case I think we exceed both, and that our voice becomes only a voice of power, not of reason.

■

QUESTIONS AND COMMENTS

1. *Mapp* has been the source of great controversy. It not only held state police investigations to national standards but also required the exclusion of evidence from the courtroom in thousands of criminal cases over the decades, evidence that in many cases may have proved a defendant was guilty of a crime.

2. Despite this internal debate, the American exclusionary rule has served as a model to law reform abroad. The typical adaptation, however, requires the court to exercise discretion about whether justice requires the exclusion of the evidence. For example, the Rome Statute establishing the International Criminal Court provides in Article 69(7):

> Evidence obtained by means of a violation of this Statute or internationally recognized human rights shall not be admissible if:

> (A) The violation casts substantial doubt on the reliability of the evidence; or

> (B) The admission of the evidence would be antithetical to and would seriously damage the integrity of the proceedings.

3. The typical adaptation of the exclusionary rule is to leave the exclusion of illegally seized evidence to the discretion of the court.[9] This

---

[9] Canadian Charter of Rights and Freedoms § 24(2) (illegally seized evidence excluded if the "admission of it . . . would bring the administration of justice into disrepute").

element of discretion is implied in Article 69(7)(b): the element "seriously damage the integrity of the proceedings" requires a discretionary judgment. For different views on the concept of discretion, review the analysis in Chapter Three.

4. To what extent do you think the facts in this case contributed to the majority's confidence with the outcome? Miss Mapp was not charged with a violent crime, and the offense of an older woman, a mother, possessing pornography seems quite trivial. The police behaved quite badly, not only lying about the warrant but also making an unnecessarily brutal search without any real justification. They even arrested her for a crime they had not suspected her of committing prior to the search. Do you think the majority could have been as firm in agreeing with Justice Clark if the accused had been a potential murderer and the evidence found had been the murder weapon? What, then, is the role that facts really play in cases such as this? It may well be that the facts are the basis for what is appealed and what is not appealed on various grounds, and that this case came forward on this issue because its facts appeared quite unjust.

5. Following *Mapp*, the Supreme Court under Earl Warren as Chief Justice extended the due process clause to incorporate the right against cruel and unusual punishment (*Robinson v. California*, 370 U.S. 660 (1962)), the right to counsel (*Gideon v. Wainwright*, 372 U.S. 335 (1963)), to be tried before a jury (*Duncan v. Louisiana*, 391 U.S. 145 (1963)), to bar self-incrimination (*Malloy v. Hogan*, 378 U.S. 1 (1964)), to confront the state's witnesses (*Pointer v. Texas*, 380 U.S. 400 (1965)), to have a speedy trial (*Klopfer v. North Carolina*, 386 U.S. 213 (1967)), to compel the testimony of a favorable witness (*Washington v. Texas*, 388 U.S. 14 (1967)), and to avoid double jeopardy (which is the trial of a person already once acquitted of the same crime) (*Benton v. Maryland*, 395 U.S. 784 (1969), overturning the actual holding in *Palko*). In the landmark case of *Miranda v. Arizona*, 384 U.S. 436 (1966), the Court required state police to ensure that suspects are aware of their rights to counsel and against self-incrimination prior to making a statement that might incriminate them, and a statement made without such insurance would be excluded from trial.

6. Then came the reaction. In 1965, the Court addressed the question whether the rule applied retroactively to cases adjudged before the date of the *Mapp* decision (*Linkletter v. Walker*, 381 U.S. 618 (1965)).

How could it not apply retroactively? If two prisoners are in jail side by side, one convicted in 1960 on the basis of evidence seized in violation of the Fourth Amendment and the other convicted by exactly the same kind of evidence seized under similarly illegal circumstances in 1962, should they be treated differently? Would that be compatible with the equal protection of the laws? Yet on the other side of the dispute, the Court must recognize that law enforcement and the courts relied on the Constitution as it was interpreted in 1960. Should their reliance on the "old" Constitution be honored? This is a very difficult issue going to the heart of the problem: What does it mean to interpret the Constitution and particularly the open-ended due process clause? If the Constitution is one and will always be one, then the two prisoners serving time side by side must be treated in the same way. But if the Constitution is an evolving document, a "living" Constitution, then we should not be afraid to recognize change as a fact of constitutional law.

7. The Court found a sensible solution to the problem of "prospective overruling." A new interpretation of the Constitution such as the *Mapp* decision could be applied prospectively only if the decision did not pertain to the fairness of the trial but rather to the dignitary rights of the suspect that were violated independently of the trial and its procedural fairness. For example, the right to counsel was applied retroactively to allow the retrial of defendants convicted before the Court established the right in *Gideon v. Wainwright*. (See *Burgett v. Texas*, 389 U.S. 109 (1967).) The argument is that as to these extrinsic rights, law enforcement and the courts should be allowed to rely on the "old" Constitution. If the issue is the fundamental fairness of the trial, their interest in reliance must defer to the rights of the accused in a fair trial under the due process clause.

The question remains whether violations of the Fourth Amendment put in issue the fairness of the proceedings against the defendant. Article 69(7) of the Rome Statute seems to want to tread the line on the issue. Evidence should be excluded either if it is unreliable (in which case, using it would be unfair to the defendant) or if it puts in issue the integrity of the proceedings (in which case, using the evidence would violate the privacy of the defendant but not increase the likelihood of a false conviction).

If the sole purpose of the exclusionary rule is to protect privacy

in the home—not to ensure defendants of a fair trial—then it would
be acceptable to apply the rule prospectively only. This is the result
reached by the Court in the *Linkletter* case.[10] Prospective overruling
raises serious jurisprudential issues in private law as well. We take
these up in Chapter Twenty-Four.

8. The most serious setback for the *Mapp* rule came in 1984, when the
Court extended the principle of justifiable reliance to protect law enforcement acting in good faith reliance on what turns to be a false
understanding of the law. (See *U.S. v. Leon*, 468 U.S. 897 (1984);
Massachusetts v. Sheppard, 468 U.S. 981 (1984).) The recognition of
the good faith exception converted the exclusionary rule into something like a criminal trial of the police. The police should be punished by exclusion of the evidence only if their violating the law was
culpable. If they acted in good faith, their conduct would not be culpable.

9. Keep in mind that the "trial of the police" under the exclusionary
rule is not a real trial of criminal charges, with the full procedural
protection afforded to suspects under the Constitution. None of the
issues discussed in this presentation of the exclusionary rule goes to
the jury. They are typically resolved by the judge in a pretrial hearing
that, in effect, puts the police on trial. If the police are "acquitted"
and the evidence admitted, then the focus turns to whether the defendant is guilty under the evidence.

10. Despite expectations that *Mapp* might be overruled, the Court affirmed the basic doctrines of *Mapp* and *Miranda* in 1999 (*Dickerson v.
U.S.*, 530 U.S. 428 (2000)). The *Mapp* decision remains an important
fixture in the American legal system. It not only guides courts in
considering unconstitutionally acquired evidence but also guides police in their training and encourages national and state compliance
with the constitutional protections. Perhaps its most enduring role,
however, is its insurance of integrity by the courts, that they do not
become implicated in the willful or intentional violations of constitutional rights by the police.

■

---

[10] See question 6.

Further Reading

For wonderful discussions of two examples of incorporation cases, *Gideon v. Wainwright* and *Near v. Minnesota*, see Anthony Lewis, *Gideon's Trumpet* (New York: Vintage Books, 1989), and Fred W. Friendly, *Minnesota Rag: Corruption, Yellow Journalism, and the Case That Saved Freedom of the Press* (Minneapolis: University of Minnesota Press, 2003).

THIRTEEN

Coordinating the States

The fundamental task of any constitution is to prescribe how government should be "constituted." It must define the authority of each branch of government and delineate the boundaries that separate the different branches. In a federal state, like the United States, the additional burden of the constitution is to provide for sets of complicated relationships: (1) the relationship of the federal to the state governments and (2) the relationships among the states. This basic distinction intersects with another, the distinction between legislative and judicial authority. The result is four very difficult points of conflict, indicated by Table 13.1. Each of these of four points of intersection requires elaboration.

1. *Legislative conflicts between federal and state governments.* This is the familiar problem raised in *McCulloch v. Maryland.* It is resolved by appealing to the constitutionally defined powers of Congress. If Congress has authority to legislate in a particular area, then its authority prevails over the wishes of the states to the contrary. This is a consequence of the supremacy clause in the Constitution, Art. VI, Clause 2, establishing that the Constitution, federal statutes, and treaties of the United States constitute the "supreme law of the land."

2. *Judicial conflicts between federal and state governments.* The Constitution limits the jurisdiction of the federal courts (Art. III, Section 2,

Table 13.1
Federal and State Government Relationships

	Federal/state	State/state
Legislative	1. Limited powers, supremacy clause	3. Due process clause, privileges and immunities clause
Judicial	2. Federal jurisdiction	4. Full faith and credit, due process

Clause 1). This limitation parallels the limitation in Article I of federal legislative authority. There are essentially two categories of federal "judicial power": (1) cases arising under federal law, which includes the U.S. Constitution, all federal statutes, and treaties of the United States, called "federal question" jurisdiction, and (2) suits brought by a citizen of one state against a citizen of another state, provided that the amount in issue is at least $75,000 (28 USC § 1332), called "diversity-of-citizenship jurisdiction."

Sullivan and Mapp illustrate the first category, namely, disputes arising under the Constitution. The applicable law is always the federal law (including the Constitution or a treaty) under which the case arises. The second type of case leaves open the substantive law to be applied in the dispute. And thus we have the problem in the Erie case, which is the subject of the next chapter.

3. Legislative conflicts among the states. The Constitution does not define the authority of state legislatures relative to each other. Yet it is obvious in the structure of federalism that no state legislature can legislate for the entire country. The interesting question is how far a state legislature can go. For example, could the California legislature pass a criminal statute that applied to Californians wherever they went—within the United States or outside? After all, Germany recognizes this "active nationality" principle, which means that German law follows German nationals wherever they go. Or could the United States apply its criminal code to any crime committed against an American anywhere in the world? See United States of America v. Fawaz Yunis, 924 F.2d 1086 (D.C. Cir., 1990), in which criminal jurisdiction was valid over an aircraft hijacking in Lebanon by virtue of two U.S. nationals among the victims. Israel has a comparable application of the "passive nationality" principle.

(This was the basis for the assertion of Israeli jurisdiction against Eichmann for crimes committed against Jews in German concentration camps.) The question has not really come up among the states, largely because state legislatures follow the common law principle of territorial jurisdiction. Even without constitutional guidance, they limit their claims of legislative authority to events that occur on their territory.

4. *Judicial relations among the states.* The problem of coordinating judicial authority is more difficult. From the time of its founding, the United States has been a self-consciously mobile society, with people and goods moving freely among the states. The consequence is a large number of situations in which the citizens of one state have legal disputes with the citizens of other states. To ensure a neutral forum, the Constitution recognizes federal "diversity" jurisdiction in these cases.

But let us suppose the litigants resolve their dispute in state court, say, in Montana. The defendant has property in Louisiana. Can the plaintiff take his judgment, go to Louisiana, and force a sale of the defendant's property in order to enforce the judgment? If the judgment were secured in France, Louisiana might or might not enforce the foreign decree. This would be a matter of "comity" or intercourt courtesy. To create a Union of states, however, it was necessary to secure compliance with judgments secured in "sister states" (as they are called). Thus we find the following provision in Article IV, Section 1, of the Constitution:

> Full Faith and Credit shall be given in each State to the public Acts, Records, and judicial Proceedings of every other State. And the Congress may by general Laws prescribe the Manner in which such Acts, Records and Proceedings shall be proved, and the Effect thereof.

The implication of this "full faith and credit" clause is that judgments secure in one state are automatically enforceable in all states. But what if the state issuing the judgment has no business, no proper basis, for getting involved? If the "full faith and credit" clause applied regardless of the court's claim to legitimate authority, any state could hear disputes from the entire country, resolve them with a particular bias (say, in favor of corporations), and thereby impose its views in the same way that the federal government, within its authority, can impose its views on the states. The plaintiff would always sue in the state that had the law most favorable to its position. Thus there has to be some limit on the authority of state courts relative to each other. This raises a different aspect of the Due Process Clause, an aspect defined by the need to coordinate state judicial power. It is the subject of the following classic case, *Pennoyer v. Neff.*

There are terms of art that you will need to know to follow the reasoning in this opinion:

> *Service of process* means acquiring jurisdiction over the defendant in a lawsuit. If process is not properly served, the Court has no jurisdiction to render a judgment against the defendant. Process can be served by sending a bailiff (an officer) of the court with the proper papers to the residence of the defendant. The bailiff rings the bell and hands the papers to the defendant. This is called "serving process." In this case, the plaintiff tried to secure jurisdiction by
>
> *substituted service of process*, namely, by having notice of the lawsuit published in the local newspaper. This was authorized under state law. The question was whether the state law met constitutional standards.
>
> *Attaching property* is a process similar to serving process on the defendant. The difference is that the papers are not given to the defendant but rather posted on the land or, in the case of movable property, the object is seized and removed.
>
> The *levy of execution* is used to satisfy the debt created by a valid judgment. That is what happened in this case.

Pennoyer v. Neff

Supreme Court of the United States
95 U.S. 714 (1877)

[This action was brought by Neff against Pennoyer for the recovery of a tract of land situated in Multnomah County, Oregon. Pennoyer, in his answer, denied Neff's title and right to possession and set up a title in himself.

By consent of parties, and in pursuance of their written stipulation filed in the case, the cause was tried by the court and a special verdict given, upon which judgment was rendered in favor of Neff; whereupon Pennoyer sued out this writ of error.]

FIELD, J.:

This is an action to recover the possession of a tract of land, of the alleged value of $15,000, situated in the State of Oregon. The plaintiff asserts title to the premises by a patent of the United States issued to him in 1866, under the act of Congress of Sept. 27, 1850, usually known as the Donation Law of Oregon. The defendant claims to have acquired the premises under a sheriff's deed, made upon a sale of the property on execution issued upon a judgment recovered against the plaintiff in one of the circuit courts of the State. The case turns upon the validity of this judgment.

It appears from the record that the judgment was rendered in February, 1866, in favor of J. H. Mitchell, for less than $300, including costs, in an action brought by him upon a demand for services as an attorney; that, at the time the action was commenced and the judgment rendered, the defendant therein, the plaintiff here, was a non-resident of the State; that he was not personally served with process, and did not appear therein; and that the judgment was entered upon his default in not answering the complaint, upon a constructive service of summons by publication.

[In other words, Mitchell sued Neff, a California resident, in Oregon, allegedly because Neff had not paid his legal bill to Mitchell. Neff ignored the attempt to "serve process" on him by publication in a newspaper. The Oregon court rendered a default judgment against the absent defendant. Neff had property in Oregon and therefore Mitchell enforced his judgment by forcing a sale of Neff's property. Pennoyer bought the property. Now Neff tries to get it back from Pennoyer. His argument is that the judgment that led to the sale was invalid because Oregon did not have jurisdiction. If the judgment was invalid, then the sale was invalid, Pennoyer did not become owner, and Neff gets his land back. Neff wins for technical reasons in the courts below, and Pennoyer appeals.]

The Code of Oregon provides for such service when an action is brought against a non-resident and absent defendant, who has property within the State. It also provides, where the action is for the recovery of money or damages, for the attachment of the property of the non-resident. And it also declares that no natural person is subject to the jurisdiction of a court of the State, "unless he appear in the court, or be found within the State, or be a resident thereof, or have property therein; and, in the last case, only to the extent of such property at the time the jurisdiction attached." . . .

The authority of every tribunal is necessarily restricted by the territorial limits of the State in which it is established. Any attempt to exercise authority beyond those limits would be deemed in every other forum, as has been said by this court, an illegitimate assumption of power, and be resisted as mere abuse. . . . In the case against the plaintiff, the property here in controversy sold under the judgment rendered was not attached, nor in any way brought under the jurisdiction of the court. Its first connection with the case was caused by a levy of the execution. It was not, therefore, disposed of pursuant to any adjudication, but only in enforcement of a personal judgment, having no relation to the property, rendered against a non-resident without service of process upon him in the action, or his appearance therein. The court below did not consider that an attachment of the property was essential to its jurisdiction or to the validity of the sale, but held that the judgment was invalid from defects in the affidavit upon which the order of publication was obtained, and in the affidavit by which the publication was proved. . . .

But it was also contended in that court, and is insisted upon here, that the judgment in the State court against the plaintiff was void for want of personal service of process on him, or of his appearance in the action in which it was rendered, and that the premises in controversy could not be subjected to the payment of the demand of a resident creditor except by a proceeding in rem; that is, by a direct proceeding against the property for that purpose. If these positions are sound, the ruling of the Circuit Court as to the invalidity of that judgment must be sustained, notwithstanding our dissent from the reasons upon which it was made. And that they are sound would seem to follow from two well established principles of public law respecting the jurisdiction of an independent State over persons and property. The several States of the Union are not, it is true, in every respect independent, many of the rights and powers which originally belonged to them being now vested in the government created by the Constitution. But, except as restrained and limited by that instrument, they possess and exercise the authority of independent States, and the principles of public law to which we have referred are applicable to them. One of these principles is, that every State possesses exclusive jurisdiction and sovereignty over persons and property within its territory. As a consequence, every State has the power to determine for itself the civil status and capacities of its inhabitants; to prescribe the subjects upon which they may contract, the forms and solemnities with which their contracts shall be executed, the rights and obligations arising from them, and the mode in which their validity shall be determined and their obligations enforced; and also to regulate the manner and conditions upon which property situated within such territory, both personal and real, may be acquired, enjoyed, and transferred. The other principle of public law referred to follows from the one mentioned; that is, that no State can exercise direct jurisdiction and authority over persons or property without its territory. Story, Confl. Laws, c. 2; Wheat. Int. Law, pt. 2, c. 2. The several States are of equal dignity and authority, and the independence of one implies the exclusion of power from all others. And so it is laid down by jurists, as an elementary principle, that the laws of one State have no operation outside of its territory, except so far as is allowed by comity; and that no tribunal established by it can extend its process beyond that territory so as to subject either persons or property to its decisions. "Any exertion of authority of this sort beyond this limit," says Story, "is a mere nullity, and incapable of binding such persons or property in any other tribunals." Story, Confl. Laws, sect. 539.[1]

But as contracts made in one State may be enforceable only in another State, and property may be held by non-residents, the exercise of the jurisdiction which every State is admitted to possess over persons and property within its own territory will often affect persons and property without it. To any influence exerted in this way by a State affecting persons resident or property situated elsewhere, no objection can be justly taken; whilst any direct exertion of authority upon them, in an attempt to give extra-territorial operation to its laws, or to enforce an

---

[1] The way the Court presents the issue, the question is whether the "laws of the state" apply outside its territory. Is this a problem of legislative coordination rather than judicial coordination? Or does the term "laws of the state" refer to the law as interpreted and applied by the courts? For further discussion of the problem, see the *Erie* case in the next chapter.

extra-territorial jurisdiction by its tribunals, would be deemed an encroachment upon the independence of the State in which the persons
are domiciled or the property is situated, and be resisted as usurpation.

Thus the State, through its tribunals, may compel persons domiciled within its limits to execute, in pursuance of their contracts respecting property elsewhere situated, instruments in such form and with
such solemnities as to transfer the title, so far as such formalities can be
complied with; and the exercise of this jurisdiction in no manner interferes with the supreme control over the property by the State within
which it is situated. . . . So the State through its tribunals, may subject
property situated within its limits owned by non-residents to the payment of the demand of its own citizens against them; and the exercise
of this jurisdiction in no respect infringes upon the sovereignty of the
State where the owners are domiciled. Every State owes protection to
its own citizens; and, when non-residents deal with them, it is a legitimate and just exercise of authority to hold and appropriate any property owned by such non-residents to satisfy the claims of its citizens. It
is in virtue of the State's jurisdiction over the property of the non-
resident situated within its limits that its tribunals can inquire into that
non-resident's obligations to its own citizens, and the inquiry can then
be carried only to the extent necessary to control the disposition of the
property. If the non-resident have no property in the State, there is
nothing upon which the tribunals can adjudicate.

These views are not new. . . . [I]n *Boswell's Lessee v. Otis*, 9 How.
336, . . . Justice McLean said:

> Jurisdiction is acquired in one of two modes: first, as against
> the person of the defendant by the service of process; or, sec-
> ondly, by a procedure against the property of the defendant
> within the jurisdiction of the court. In the latter case, the
> defendant is not personally bound by the judgment beyond
> the property in question. And it is immaterial whether the
> proceeding against the property be by an attachment or bill in
> chancery. It must be substantially a proceeding in rem. . . .

If, without personal service, judgments in personam, obtained ex
parte against non-residents and absent parties, upon mere publication
of process, which, in the great majority of cases, would never be seen
by the parties interested, could be upheld and enforced, they would be

the constant instruments of fraud and oppression. Judgments for all sorts of claims upon contracts and for torts, real or pretended, would be thus obtained, under which property would be seized, when the evidence of the transactions upon which they were founded, if they ever had any existence, had perished.

Substituted service by publication, or in any other authorized form, may be sufficient to inform parties of the object of proceedings taken where property is once brought under the control of the court by seizure or some equivalent act. The law assumes that property is always in the possession of its owner, in person or by agent; and it proceeds upon the theory that its seizure will inform him, not only that it is taken into the custody of the court, but that he must look to any proceedings authorized by law upon such seizure for its condemnation and sale. . . . The want of authority of the tribunals of a State to ad-judicate upon the obligations of non-residents, where they have no property within its limits, is not denied by the court below: but the position is assumed, that, where they have property within the State, it is immaterial whether the property is in the first instance brought under the control of the court by attachment or some other equivalent act, and afterwards applied by its judgment to the satisfaction of de-mands against its owner; or such demands be first established in a per-sonal action, and the property of the non-resident be afterwards seized and sold on execution. But the answer to this position has already been given in the statement, that the jurisdiction of the court to inquire into and determine his obligations at all is only incidental to its jurisdiction over the property. Its jurisdiction in that respect cannot be made to depend upon facts to be ascertained after it has tried the cause and rendered the judgment. If the judgment be previously void, it will not become valid by the subsequent discovery of property of the defendant, or by his subsequent acquisition of it. The judgment, if void when rendered, will always remain void: it cannot occupy the doubtful po-sition of being valid if property be found, and void if there be none. Even if the position assumed were confined to cases where the non-resident defendant possessed property in the State at the commence-ment of the action, it would still make the validity of the proceedings and judgment depend upon the question whether, before the levy of the execution, the defendant had or had not disposed of the property.

If before the levy the property should be sold, then, according to this position, the judgment would not be binding. This doctrine would introduce a new element of uncertainty in judicial proceedings. The contrary is the law: the validity of every judgment depends upon the jurisdiction of the court before it is rendered, not upon what may occur subsequently. . . .

The force and effect of judgments rendered against non-residents without personal service of process upon them, or their voluntary appearance, have been the subject of frequent consideration in the courts of the United States and of the several States, as attempts have been made to enforce such judgments in States other than those in which they were rendered, under the provision of the Constitution requiring that "full faith and credit shall be given in each State to the public acts, records, and judicial proceedings of every other State;"[2] and the act of Congress providing for the mode of authenticating such acts, records, and proceedings, and declaring that, when thus authenticated, "they shall have such faith and credit given to them in every court within the United States as they have by law or usage in the courts of the State from which they are or shall be taken." In the earlier cases, it was supposed that the act gave to all judgments the same effect in other States which they had by law in the State where rendered. . . .

This whole subject has been very fully and learnedly considered in the recent case of *Thompson v. Whitman*, 18 Wall. 457, where all the authorities are carefully reviewed and distinguished, and the conclusion above stated is not only reaffirmed, but the doctrine is asserted, that the record of a judgment rendered in another State may be contradicted as to the facts necessary to give the court jurisdiction against its recital of their existence. In all the cases brought in the State and Federal courts, where attempts have been made under the act of Congress to give effect in one State to personal judgments rendered in another State against non-residents, without service upon them, or upon substituted service by publication, or in some other form, it has been held, without an exception, so far as we are aware, that such judgments were without any binding force, except as to property, or interests in property, within the State, to reach and affect which was the object of the action in

---

[2] The reference here is to the U.S. Constitution, Article IV, Section 1.

which the judgment was rendered, and which property was brought under control of the court in connection with the process against the person. . . .

Be that as it may, the courts of the United States are not required to give effect to judgments of this character when any right is claimed under them. Whilst they are not foreign tribunals in their relations to the State courts, are tribunals of a different sovereignty, exercising a distinct and independent jurisdiction, and are bound to give to the judgments of the State courts only the same faith and credit which the courts of another State are bound to give to them.

Since the adoption of the Fourteenth Amendment to the Federal Constitution, the validity of such judgments may be directly questioned, and their enforcement in the State resisted, on the ground that proceedings in a court of justice to determine the personal rights and obligations of parties over whom that court has no jurisdiction do not constitute due process of law. Whatever difficulty may be experienced in giving to those terms a definition which will embrace every permissible exertion of power affecting private rights, and exclude such as is forbidden, there can be no doubt of their meaning when applied to judicial proceedings. . . . It is true that, in a strict sense, a proceeding in rem is one taken directly against property, and has for its object the disposition of the property, without reference to the title of individual claimants; but, in a larger and more general sense, the terms are applied to actions between parties, where the direct object is to reach and dispose of property owned by them, or of some interest therein. Such are cases commenced by attachment against the property of debtors, or instituted to partition real estate, foreclose a mortgage, or enforce a lien. So far as they affect property in the State, they are substantially proceedings in rem in the broader sense which we have mentioned. . . .

It follows from the views expressed that the personal judgment recovered in the State court of Oregon against the plaintiff herein, then a non-resident of the State, was without any validity, and did not authorize a sale of the property in controversy. . . . [Mitchell's judgment against Neff was void and therefore Neff can recover the property from Pennoyer.]

Judgment affirmed.

HUNT, J., DISSENTING:

I am compelled to dissent from the opinion and judgment of the court, and, deeming the question involved to be important, I take leave to record my views upon it.

The judgment of the court below was placed upon the ground that the provisions of the statute were not complied with. This is of comparatively little importance, as it affects the present case only. The judgment of this court is based upon the theory that the legislature had no power to pass the law in question; that the principle of the statute is vicious, and every proceeding under it void. It, therefore, affects all like cases, past and future, and in every State.

The precise case is this: A statute of Oregon authorizes suits to be commenced by the service of a summons. In the case of a non-resident of the State, it authorizes the service of the summons to be made by publication for not less than six weeks, in a newspaper published in the county where the action is commenced. A copy of the summons must also be sent by mail, directed to the defendant at his place of residence, unless it be shown that the residence is not known and cannot be ascertained. It authorizes a judgment and execution to be obtained in such proceeding. Judgment in a suit commenced by one Mitchell in the Circuit Court of Multnomah County, where the summons was thus served, was obtained against Neff, the present plaintiff; and the land in question, situate in Multnomah County, was bought by the defendant Pennoyer, at a sale upon the judgment in such suit. This court now holds, that, by reason of the absence of a personal service of the summons on the defendant, the Circuit Court of Oregon had no jurisdiction, its judgment could not authorize the sale of land in said county, and, as a necessary result, a purchaser of land under it obtained no title; that, as to the former owner, it is a case of depriving a person of his property without due process of law.

In my opinion, this decision is at variance with the long-established practice under the statutes of the States of this Union, is unsound in principle, and, I fear, may be disastrous in its effects. It tends to produce confusion in titles which have been obtained under similar statutes in existence for nearly a century; it invites litigation and strife, and over throws a well-settled rule of property.

The result of the authorities on the subject, and the sound conclusions to be drawn from the principles which should govern the decision, as I shall endeavor to show, are these:

1. A sovereign State must necessarily have such control over the real and personal property actually being within its limits, as that it may subject the same to the payment of debts justly due to its citizens.

2. This result is not altered by the circumstance that the owner of the property is non-resident, and so absent from the State that legal process cannot be served upon him personally.

3. Personal notice of a proceeding by which title to property is passed is not indispensable; it is competent to the State to authorize substituted service by publication or otherwise, as the commencement of a suit against non-residents, the judgment in which will authorize the sale of property in such State.

4. It belongs to the legislative power of the State to determine what shall be the modes and means proper to be adopted to give notice to an absent defendant of the commencement of a suit; and if they are such as are reasonably likely to communicate to him information of the proceeding against him, and are in good faith designed to give him such information, and an opportunity to defend is provided for him in the event of his appearance in the suit, it is not competent to the judiciary to declare that such proceeding is void as not being by due process of law.

5. Whether the property of such non-resident shall be seized upon attachment as the commencement of a suit which shall be carried into judgment and execution, upon which it shall then be sold, or whether it shall be sold upon an execution and judgment without such preliminary seizure, is a matter not of constitutional power, but of municipal regulation only.

To say that a sovereign State has the power to ordain that the property of non-residents within its territory may be subjected to the payment of debts due to its citizens, if the property is levied upon at the commencement of a suit, but that it has not such power if the property is levied upon at the end of the suit, is a refinement and a depreciation of a great general principle that, in my judgment, cannot be sustained. . . .

That a State can subject land within its limits belonging to non-resident owners to debts due to its own citizens as it can legislate upon all other local matters; that it can prescribe the mode and process by which it is to be reached, seems to me very plain.

I am not willing to declare that a sovereign State cannot subject the land within its limits to the payment of debts due to its citizens, or that the power to do so depends upon the fact whether its statute shall authorize the property to be levied upon at the commencement of the suit or at its termination. This is a matter of detail, and I am of opinion, that if reasonable notice be given, with an opportunity to defend when appearance is made, the question of power will be fully satisfied.

QUESTIONS AND COMMENTS

1. This is a classic case, and though it has long been under attack as excessively formalistic and as relic of old-fashioned thinking about sovereignty, it is still good law. Most contemporary discussions of the problem of coordinating state court jurisdiction begin with *International Shoe v. State of Washington*, 326 U.S. 310 (1945). Washington sued to force the International Shoe Corporation to pay contributions to its state unemployment compensation fund. They served process personally on a salesman of the corporation and mailed a notice to its out-of-state office. The Supreme Court upheld the suit and coined an expression that has dominated the discussion of this problem ever since. The new lingo is that the defendant sued must have "minimum contacts" with the forum state. If the defendant is beyond the range of minimum contacts, then the state cannot sue, no matter what form of process it used.

2. Notice that this is not the same problem as that raised in *Pennoyer*. In *International Shoe*, the question was whether the state could collect taxes from a corporation that was present in the state only to extent of having salesmen there. You could express the problem as the distinction between in personam and subject-matter jurisdiction. In *Pennoyer* the problem was whether in personam jurisdiction could be established by mailing the notice. The basis of the lawsuit was recovering a piece of land, a subject matter undoubtedly appropriate for the Oregon Court. The only question is whether the rights of an out-of-state defendant could be adjudicated without personal service of process. In *International Shoe*, the question was whether Washington could force the defendant corporations to pay taxes to the state.

That question goes to the very heart of Washington's power to regulate business within the state. Nonetheless, the Supreme Court aligned the case with the evolving law of in personam jurisdiction and applied the same principles as in other cases posing the problem of due process in suits involving out-of-state defendants.

3. The general problem posed by *Pennoyer* and *International Shoe* is called "long-arm jurisdiction." The state reaches out to grab cases that are not purely local and domestic. The question is whether it can do that. The first place to look in considering a problem of long-arm jurisdiction is the state statute defining the jurisdiction of the local courts. Here is the relevant provision of New York law:

> NEW YORK CIVIL PRACTICE LAW AND RULES § 302:
> Personal jurisdiction by acts of non-domiciliaries
>
> (A) Acts which are the basis of jurisdiction. As to a cause of action arising from any of the acts enumerated in this section, a court may exercise personal jurisdiction over any non-domiciliary, or his executor or administrator, who in person or through an agent:
>
> > 1. transacts any business within the state or contracts anywhere to supply goods or services in the state; or
> >
> > 2. commits a tortious act within the state, except as to a cause of action for defamation of character arising from the act; or
> >
> > 3. commits a tortious act without the state causing injury to person or property within the state, except as to a cause of action for defamation of character arising from the act, if he
> >
> > > (I) regularly does or solicits business, or engages in any other persistent course of conduct, or derives substantial revenue from goods used or consumed or services rendered, in the state, or
> > >
> > > (II) expects or should reasonably expect the act to have consequences in the state and derives substantial revenue from interstate or international commerce; or
> >
> > 4. owns, uses or possesses any real property situated within the state.

What is the problem to which this statute is addressed? Is it the problem posed in *Pennoyer* or in *International Shoe*?

4. One response directly to the rule of *Pennoyer* was to recognize fictitious consent to service of process on a local state official under certain urgent circumstances. One of these pressing cases was that of out-of-state motorists who caused accidents in the state and then went home. To solve this problem, the states passed statutes holding that operating a motor vehicle in the state was treated as consent to having service made on the "registrar" of the state or some other local official. The Supreme Court upheld the principle of fictitious consent as the only pragmatic solution to an obvious problem in the system. See *Hess v. Pawlowski*, 274 U.S. 352 (1927).

5. The outer reaches of "long-arm jurisdiction" were tested in the case of a New York couple who purchased a car in New York and drove it to Oklahoma, where the car caught on fire in a road accident. They sued the New York corporations (both wholesaler and retailer of the car) in Oklahoma under the local long-arm statute, which authorized the local courts to hear any case against any "person causing tortious injury in this state by an act or omission." Although the defendants did no business in Oklahoma and had no "presence" there, the plaintiffs argued that an accident in Oklahoma was a "foreseeable consequence" of the sale of a defective car in New York and therefore the defendant sellers committed a tort in Oklahoma. Relying on both *Pennoyer* and *International Shoe*, the Supreme Court held that the defendants did not have the required "minimum contacts" with the Oklahoma forum. It followed that Oklahoma violated the due process clause by hearing the case. See *World-Wide Volkswagen Corp. v. Woodson*, 444 U.S. 286 (1980).

6. One of the paradoxical features of *Pennoyer* was the all-or-nothing contrast between in rem and in personam jurisdiction. If the plaintiff had attached the land first, then the jurisdiction would have been in rem, and the court could have proceeded, whether the defendant knew about the lawsuit or not. That is, the rules on in personam jurisdiction were very tight, but in rem jurisdiction could give the court almost unlimited authority. Sooner or later, the Court would have to address this radical dichotomy. The issue was posed in *Schaffer v. Heitner*, 433 U.S. 186 (1977), in which the plaintiff attached shares of stock in Delaware and sued the far-flung defendants in a shareholder's derivative suit. The Court had the following reflections on the viability of the *Pennoyer* analysis today:

The Delaware courts rejected appellants' jurisdictional challenge by noting that this suit was brought as a quasi in rem proceeding [same as in rem]. Since quasi in rem jurisdiction is traditionally based on attachment or seizure of property present in the jurisdiction, not on contacts between the defendant and the State, the courts considered appellants' claimed lack of contacts with Delaware to be unimportant. This categorical analysis assumes the continued soundness of the conceptual structure founded on the century-old case of *Pennoyer v. Neff*, 95 U. S. 714 (1878).

Pennoyer was an ejectment action brought in federal court under the diversity jurisdiction. Pennoyer, the defendant in that action, held the land under a deed purchased in a sheriff's sale conducted to realize on a judgment for attorney's fees obtained against Neff in a previous action by one Mitchell. At the time of Mitchell's suit in an Oregon State court, Neff was a nonresident of Oregon. An Oregon statute allowed service by publication on nonresidents who had property in the State, and Mitchell had used that procedure to bring Neff before the court. The United States Circuit Court for the District of Oregon, in which Neff brought his ejectment action, refused to recognize the validity of the judgment against Neff in Mitchell's suit, and accordingly awarded the land to Neff. This Court affirmed.

Justice Field's opinion for the Court focused on the territorial limits of the States' judicial powers. Although recognizing that the States are not truly independent sovereigns, Justice Field found that their jurisdiction was defined by the "principles of public law" that regulate the relationships among independent nations. The first of those principles was "that every State possesses exclusive jurisdiction and sovereignty over persons and property within its territory." The second was "that no State can exercise direct jurisdiction and authority over persons or property without its territory." Id., at 722. Thus, "in virtue of the State's jurisdiction over the property of the non-resident situated within its limits," the state courts "can inquire into that non-resident's obligations to its own citizens . . . to the extent necessary to control the disposition of the property." Id., at 723. The Court recognized that if the conclusions of that inquiry were adverse to the nonresident property owner, his interest in the property would be affected. Ibid. Similarly, if the defendant consented to the jurisdiction of the state courts or was personally served within the State, a judgment could affect his interest in property outside the State. But any attempt "directly" to assert extraterritorial jurisdiction over persons or property would offend sister States and exceed the inherent limits of the State's power. A judgment resulting from such an attempt, Justice Field concluded, was not only unenforceable in other States, but was also void in the rendering State because it had been obtained in violation of the Due Process Clause of the Fourteenth Amendment. Id., at 732–733. See also, e.g., *Freeman v. Alderson*, 119 U.S. 185, 187–188 (1886).

This analysis led to the conclusion that Mitchell's judgment against Neff could not be validly based on the State's power over persons within its borders, because Neff had not been personally served in Oregon, nor had he consensually appeared before the Oregon court. The Court reasoned that even if Neff had received personal notice of the action, service of process outside the State would have been ineffectual since the State's power was limited by its territorial boundaries. Moreover, the Court held, the action could not be sustained on the basis of the State's power over property within its borders because that property had not been brought before the court by attachment or any other procedure prior to judgment. Since the judgment which authorized the sheriff's sale was therefore invalid, the sale transferred no title. Neff regained his land.

From our perspective, the importance of *Pennoyer* is not its result, but the fact that its principles and corollaries derived from them became the basic elements of the constitutional doctrine governing state-court jurisdiction. *See, e.g.,* Hazard, *A General Theory of State-Court Jurisdiction*, 1965 Sup. Ct. Rev. 241 (hereafter Hazard). As we have noted, under *Pennoyer* state authority to adjudicate was based on the jurisdiction's power over either persons or property. This fundamental concept is embodied in the very vocabulary which we use to describe judgments. If a court's jurisdiction is based on its authority over the defendant's person, the action and judgment are denominated "in personam" and can impose a personal obligation on the defendant in favor of the plaintiff. If jurisdiction is based on the court's power over property within its territory, the action is called "in rem" or "quasi in rem." The effect of a judgment in such a case is limited to the property that supports jurisdiction and does not impose a personal liability on the property owner, since he is not before the court. In *Pennoyer's* terms, the owner is affected only "indirectly" by an in rem judgment adverse to his interest in the property subject to the court's disposition.

By concluding that "[t]he authority of every tribunal is necessarily restricted by the territorial limits of the State in which it is established," 95 U.S., at 720, *Pennoyer* sharply limited the availability of in personam jurisdiction over defendants not resident in the forum State. If a nonresident defendant could not be found in a State, he could not be sued there. On the other hand, since the State in which property was located was considered to have exclusive sovereignty over that property, in rem actions could proceed regardless of the owner's location. Indeed, since a State's process could not reach beyond its borders, this Court held after Pennoyer that due process did not require any effort to give a property owner personal notice that his property was involved in an in rem proceeding. See, e.g., *Ballard v. Hunter*, 204 U.S. 241 (1907); *Arndt v. Griggs*, 134 U.S. 316 (1890); *Huling v. Kaw Valley R. Co.*, 130 U.S. 559 (1889).

The *Pennoyer* rules generally favored nonresident defendants by making them harder to sue. This advantage was reduced, however, by the ability of a resident plaintiff to satisfy a claim against a nonresident defendant by bringing into court any property of the defendant located in the plaintiff's State. See, e.g., Zammit, *Quasi-In-Rem Jurisdiction: Outmoded and Unconstitutional?* 49 St. John's L. Rev. 668, 670 (1975). . . .

Pennoyer itself recognized that its rigid categories . . . could not accommodate some necessary litigation. Accordingly, Justice Field's opinion carefully noted that cases involving the personal status of the plaintiff, such as divorce actions, could be adjudicated in the plaintiff's home State even though the defendant could not be served within that State. 95 U.S., at 733–735. Similarly, the opinion approved the practice of considering a foreign corporation doing business in a State to have consented to being sued in that State. Id., at 735–736; see *Lafayette Ins. Co. v. French*, 18 How. 404 (1856). This basis for in personam jurisdiction over foreign corporations was later supplemented by the doctrine that a corporation doing business in a State could be deemed "present" in the State, and so subject to service of process under the rule of Pennoyer. See, e.g., *International Harvester Co. v. Kentucky*, 234 U.S. 579 (1914); *Philadelphia & Reading R. Co. v. McKibbin*, 243 U.S. 264 (1917). See generally Note, *Developments in the Law, State-Court Jurisdiction*, 73 Harv. L. Rev. 909, 919–923 (1960) (hereafter Developments).

The advent of automobiles, with the concomitant increase in the incidence of individuals causing injury in States where they were not subject to in personam actions under *Pennoyer*, required further moderation of the territorial limits on jurisdictional power. This modification, like the accommodation to the realities of interstate corporate activities, was accomplished by use of a legal fiction that left the conceptual structure established in Pennoyer theoretically unaltered. Cf. *Olberding v. Illinois Central R. Co.*, 346 U.S. 338, 340–341 (1953). The fiction used was that the out-of-state motorist, who it was assumed could be excluded altogether from the State's highways, had by using those highways appointed a designated state official as his agent to accept process. See *Hess v. Pawloski*, 274 U.S. 352 (1927). Since the motorist's "agent" could be personally served within the State, the state courts could obtain in personam jurisdiction over the nonresident driver.

The motorists' consent theory was easy to administer since it required only a finding that the out-of-state driver

had used the State's roads. By contrast, both the fictions of
implied consent to service on the part of a foreign corporation and of corporate presence required a finding that the
corporation was "doing business" in the forum State. Defining the criteria for making that finding and deciding
whether they were met absorbed much judicial energy. See,
e.g., *International Shoe Co. v. Washington*, 326 U.S., at 317–
319. While the essentially quantitative tests which emerged
from these cases purported simply to identify circumstances
under which presence or consent could be attributed to the
corporation, it became clear that they were in fact attempting to ascertain "what dealings make it just to subject a foreign corporation to local suit." *Hutchinson v. Chase & Gilbert*,
45 F.2d 139, 141 (CA2 1930) (L. Hand, J.). In *International
Shoe*, we acknowledged that fact.

The question in *International Shoe* was whether the corporation was subject to the judicial and taxing jurisdiction of
Washington. Chief Justice Stone's opinion for the Court began its analysis of that question by noting that the historical
basis of in personam jurisdiction was a court's power over
the defendant's person. That power, however, was no longer
the central concern. . . .

Thus, the inquiry into the State's jurisdiction over a foreign corporation appropriately focused not on whether the
corporation was "present" but on whether "there have been
such contacts of the corporation with the state of the forum
as make it reasonable, in the context of our federal system of
government, to require the corporation to defend the particular suit which is brought there.

Mechanical or quantitative evaluations of the defendant's
activities in the forum could not resolve the question of reasonableness: Whether due process is satisfied must depend
rather upon the quality and nature of the activity in relation
to the fair and orderly administration of the laws which it was
the purpose of the due process clause to insure. That clause
does not contemplate that a state may make binding a judgment in personam against an individual or corporate defendant with which the state has no contacts, ties, or relations.

Thus, the relationship among the defendant, the forum, and the litigation, rather than the mutually exclusive sovereignty of the States on which the rules of *Pennoyer* rest, became the central concern of the inquiry into personal jurisdiction. The immediate effect of this departure from *Pennoyer's* conceptual apparatus was to increase the ability of the state courts to obtain personal jurisdiction over nonresident defendants. . . .

No equally dramatic change has occurred in the law governing jurisdiction in rem. There have, however, been intimations that the collapse of the in personam wing of *Pennoyer* has not left that decision unweakened as a foundation for in rem jurisdiction. Well-reasoned lower court opinions have questioned the proposition that the presence of property in a State gives that State jurisdiction to adjudicate rights to the property regardless of the relationship of the underlying dispute and the property owner to the forum.
. . . The overwhelming majority of commentators have also rejected Pennoyer's premise that a proceeding "against" property is not a proceeding against the owners of that property. Accordingly, they urge that the "traditional notions of fair play and substantial justice" that govern a State's power to adjudicate in personam should also govern its power to adjudicate personal rights to property located in the State. See, e.g., Von Mehren & Trautman, *Jurisdiction to Adjudicate: A Suggested Analysis*, 79 Harv. L. Rev. 1121 (1966) (hereafter Von Mehren & Trautman); Traynor, *Is This Conflict Really Necessary?* 37 Texas L. Rev. 657 (1959) (hereafter Traynor); Ehrenzweig, *The Transient Rule of Personal Jurisdiction: The 'Power' Myth and Forum Conveniens*, 65 Yale L. J. 289 (1956).

Although this Court has not addressed this argument directly, we have held that property cannot be subjected to a court's judgment unless reasonable and appropriate efforts have been made to give the property owners actual notice of the action. . . . This conclusion recognizes, contrary to *Pennoyer*, that an adverse judgment in rem directly affects the property owner by divesting him of his rights in the property before the court. . . .

It is clear, therefore, that the law of state-court jurisdiction no longer stands securely on the foundation established in *Pennoyer*. We think that the time is ripe to consider whether the standard of fairness and substantial justice set forth in *International Shoe* should be held to govern actions in rem as well as in personam.

The case for applying to jurisdiction in rem the same test of "fair play and substantial justice" as governs assertions of jurisdiction in personam is simple and straightforward. It is premised on recognition that "[t]he phrase, 'judicial jurisdiction over a thing,' is a customary elliptical way of referring to jurisdiction over the interests of persons in a thing." *Restatement (Second) of Conflict of Laws* § 56, Introductory Note (1971) (hereafter *Restatement*). This recognition leads to the conclusion that in order to justify an exercise of jurisdiction in rem, the basis for jurisdiction must be sufficient to justify exercising "jurisdiction over the interests of persons in a thing." The standard for determining whether an exercise of jurisdiction over the interests of persons is consistent with the Due Process Clause is the minimum-contacts standard elucidated in *International Shoe*.

This argument, of course, does not ignore the fact that the presence of property in a State may bear on the existence of jurisdiction by providing contacts among the forum State, the defendant, and the litigation. For example, when claims to the property itself are the source of the underlying controversy between the plaintiff and the defendant, it would be unusual for the State where the property is located not to have jurisdiction. In such cases, the defendant's claim to property located in the State would normally indicate that he expected to benefit from the State's protection of his interest. The State's strong interests in assuring the marketability of property within its borders and in providing a procedure for peaceful resolution of disputes about the possession of that property would also support jurisdiction, as would the likelihood that important records and witnesses will be found in the State. The presence of property may also favor jurisdiction in cases, such as suits for injury suffered on the land of an absentee owner, where the defendant's ownership of the property is conceded but the cause of action is otherwise related to rights and duties growing out of that ownership.

It appears, therefore, that jurisdiction over many types of actions which now are or might be brought in rem would not be affected by a holding that any assertion of state-court jurisdiction must satisfy the *International Shoe* standard. . . .

Since acceptance of the *International Shoe* test would most affect this class of cases, we examine the arguments against adopting that standard as they relate to this category of litigation. Before doing so, however, we note that this type of case also presents the clearest illustration of the argument in favor of assessing assertions of jurisdiction by a single standard. . . .

The primary rationale for treating the presence of property as a sufficient basis for jurisdiction to adjudicate claims over which the State would not have jurisdiction if *International Shoe* applied is that a wrongdoer "should not be able to avoid payment of his obligations by the expedient of removing his assets to a place where he is not subject to an in personam suit. *Restatement* § 66, Comment a.

This justification, however, does not explain why jurisdiction should be recognized without regard to whether the property is present in the State because of an effort to avoid the owner's obligations. Nor does it support jurisdiction to adjudicate the underlying claim. At most, it suggests that a State in which property is located should have jurisdiction to attach that property, by use of proper procedures, as security for a judgment being sought in a forum where the litigation can be maintained consistently with *International Shoe*. See, e.g., Von Mehren & Trautman 1178; Hazard 284–285; Moreover, we know of nothing to justify the assumption that a debtor can avoid paying his obligations by removing his property to a State in which his creditor cannot obtain personal jurisdiction over him. The Full Faith and Credit Clause, after all, makes the valid in personam judgment of one State enforceable in all other States.

It might also be suggested that allowing in rem jurisdiction avoids the uncertainty inherent in the *International Shoe* standard and assures a plaintiff of a forum. . . . We believe, however, that the fairness standard of *International Shoe* can be easily applied in the vast majority of cases. Moreover, when the existence of jurisdiction in a particular forum under *International Shoe* is unclear, the cost of simplifying the litigation by avoiding the jurisdictional question may be the sacrifice of "fair play and substantial justice." That cost is too high.

We are left, then, to consider the significance of the long history of jurisdiction based solely on the presence of property in a State. Although the theory that territorial power is both essential to and sufficient for jurisdiction has been undermined, we have never held that the presence of property in a State does not automatically confer jurisdiction over the owner's interest in that property. n38. This history must be considered as supporting the proposition that jurisdiction based solely on the presence of property satisfies the demands of due process, cf. *Ownbey v. Morgan*, 256 U. S. 94, 111 (1921), but it is not decisive. "[T]raditional notions of fair play and substantial justice" can be as readily offended by the perpetuation of ancient forms that are no longer justified as by the adoption of new procedures that are inconsistent with the basic values of our constitutional heritage. Cf. *Sniadach v. Family Finance Corp.*, 395 U.S., at 340; *Wolf v. Colorado*, 338 U.S. 25, 27 (1949). The fiction that an assertion of jurisdiction over property is anything but an assertion of jurisdiction over the owner of the property supports an ancient form without substantial modern justification. Its continued acceptance would serve only to allow state-court jurisdiction that is fundamentally unfair to the defendant.

We therefore conclude that all assertions of state-court jurisdiction must be evaluated according to the standards set forth in International Shoe and its progeny. . . .

7. In very general terms, there has been an obvious shift of emphasis from the time that *Pennoyer* was decided. In 1877 the problem was adjusting the power of one state relative to another. Now it seems that the central question is fairness to the litigants, and particularly to the defendant. The shift has been from political theory to the question of justice in the particular case.

8. All of the questions addressed are of immediate relevance to the current dispute about universal jurisdiction in the criminal law. Criminal law was traditionally tied to the same territorial principle that shapes the analysis of *Pennoyer*. Since the Second World War, however, there has been a strong trend toward recognizing the authority of every state to prosecute the most serious crimes against the values of international community, in particular, genocide, war crimes, and crimes against humanity. See *The Princeton Principles on Universal Jurisdictions* (Princeton, NJ: Princeton University Press, 2001). See also the new German Code of International Criminal Law (*Völkerstrafgesetzbuch*) (2002).

The claims of countries like Belgium and Germany to universal jurisdiction has generated a strong backlash. If Oregon cannot issue a judgment binding the entire country, then why should Belgium or Germany judge crimes as the representative of entire world? In the summer of 2003, Belgium modified its law, and the German courts reached a similar conclusion. In both cases, the retreat from universal jurisdiction has explicitly favored a standard analogous to that implied in *International Shoe*, namely, *Anknüpfungspunkte* in German, or in the idiom of the U.S. Supreme Court, "minimum contacts."

■

FOURTEEN

Multiple Common Laws?

The federal courts have jurisdiction in diversity-of-citizenship cases, but what law should they apply? The case does not arise under the Constitution or under federal statutes. It arises under the common law. Therefore, it seems that a federal court should, like any court, be able to interpret the common law as it sees fit. Yet the first statute on the organization of the federal courts, the Judiciary Act of 1789, established the rule that in "trials at common law" the federal court should apply the "laws" of the several states. Therefore, the federal courts interpreted the Judiciary Act to mean that they should apply the law of state in which they sit. If there was a state statute on the point, the federal court applied the statute, but this left a vast repository of cases to be resolved under the common law. If the state could interpret the common law principles of liability, why should the federal courts not be able to do the same? The Supreme Court recognized in *Swift v. Tyson*, 41 U.S. (16 Pet.) 1 (1842), that indeed federal courts were allowed to develop the common law as they saw fit. But *Swift v. Tyson* was long under attack. The final battle was fought in the following landmark case:

■

Erie Railroad Co. v. Tompkins

Supreme Court of the United States
304 U.S. 64 (1938).

BRANDEIS, J.:

The question for decision is whether the oft-challenged doctrine of *Swift v. Tyson* [citations omitted] shall now be disapproved.

Tompkins, a citizen of Pennsylvania, was injured on a dark night by a passing freight train of the Erie Railroad Company while walking along its right of way at Hughestown in that State. He claimed that the accident occurred through negligence in the operation, or maintenance, of the train; that he was rightfully on the premises as licensee because on a commonly used beaten footpath which ran for a short distance alongside the tracks; and that he was struck by something which looked like a door projecting from one of the moving cars. To enforce that claim he brought an action in the federal court for southern New York, which had jurisdiction because the company is a corporation of that State.[1] It denied liability; and the case was tried by a jury.

The Erie insisted that its duty to Tompkins was no greater than that owed to a trespasser. It contended, among other things, that its duty to Tompkins, and hence its liability, should be determined in accordance with the Pennsylvania law; that under the law of Pennsylvania, as declared by its highest court, persons who use pathways along the railroad right of way—that is a longitudinal pathway as distinguished from a crossing—are to be deemed trespassers; and that the railroad is not liable for injuries to undiscovered trespassers resulting from its negligence, unless it be wanton or wilful. Tompkins denied that any such rule had been established by the decisions of the Pennsylvania courts; and contended that, since there was no statute of the State on the subject, the railroad's duty and liability is to be determined in federal courts as a matter of general law.

The trial judge refused to rule that the applicable law precluded recovery. The jury brought in a verdict of $30,000; and the judgment

---

[1] Note the implicit rule: A corporation is regarded as a citizen of the state in which it is incorporated.

entered thereon was affirmed by the Circuit Court of Appeals, which held, 90 F.2d 603, 604, that it was unnecessary to consider whether the law of Pennsylvania was as contended, because the question was one not of local, but of general, law and that "upon questions of general law the federal courts are free, in the absence of a local statute, to exercise their independent judgment as to what the law is; and it is well settled that the question of the responsibility of a railroad for injuries caused by its servants is one of general law. . . . Where the public has made open and notorious use of a railroad right of way for a long period of time and without objection, the company owes to persons on such permissive pathway a duty of care in the operation of its trains. . . . It is likewise generally recognized law that a jury may find that negligence exists toward a pedestrian using a permissive path on the railroad right of way if he is hit by some object projecting from the side of the train."

The Erie had contended that application of the Pennsylvania rule was required, among other things, by § 34 of the Federal Judiciary Act of September 24, 1789, c. 20, 28 U.S. C. § 725, which provides:

> The laws of the several States, except where the Constitution, treaties, or statutes of the United States otherwise require or provide, shall be regarded as rules of decision in trials at common law, in the courts of the United States, in cases where they apply.

Because of the importance of the question whether the federal court was free to disregard the alleged rule of the Pennsylvania common law, we granted certiorari.

First. *Swift v. Tyson*, 16 Pet. 1, 18, held that federal courts exercising jurisdiction on the ground of diversity of citizenship need not, in matters of general jurisprudence, apply the unwritten law of the State as declared by its highest court; that they are free to exercise an independent judgment as to what the common law of the State [requires]. . . . The Court in applying the rule of § 34 to equity cases, in *Mason v. United States*, 260 U.S. 545, 559, said: "The statute, however, is merely declarative of the rule which would exist in the absence of the statute." The federal courts assumed, in the broad field of "general law," the power to declare rules of decision which Congress was confessedly without power to enact as statutes. Doubt was repeatedly expressed as to the correctness of the construction given § 34[2] and as to the sound-ness of the rule which it introduced. [citations to scholarly authority omitted] But it was the more recent research of a competent scholar, who examined the original document, which established that the con-struction given to it by the Court was erroneous; and that the purpose of the section was merely to make certain that, in all matters except those in which some federal law is controlling, the federal courts exercising jurisdiction in diversity of citizenship cases would apply as their rules of decision the law of the State, unwritten as well as written.[3]

Criticism of the doctrine became widespread after the decision of *Black & White Taxicab Co. v. Brown & Yellow Taxicab Co.*, 276 U.S. 518 [scholarly references omitted]. There, Brown and Yellow, a Kentucky corporation owned by Kentuckians, and the Louisville and Nashville Railroad, also a Kentucky corporation, wished that the former should have the exclusive privilege of soliciting passenger and baggage trans-portation at the Bowling Green, Kentucky, railroad station; and that the Black and White, a competing Kentucky corporation, should be prevented from interfering with that privilege. Knowing that such a contract would be void under the common law of Kentucky, it was arranged that the Brown and Yellow reincorporate under the law of Tennessee, and that the contract with the railroad should be executed there. The suit was then brought by the Tennessee corporation in the federal court for western Kentucky to enjoin competition by the Black and White; an injunction issued by the District Court was sustained by the Court of Appeals; and this Court, citing many decisions in which the doctrine of *Swift v. Tyson* had been applied, affirmed the decree.

Second. Experience in applying the doctrine of *Swift v. Tyson*, had revealed its defects, political and social; and the benefits expected to flow from the rule did not accrue. Persistence of state courts in their own opinions on questions of common law prevented uniformity; [omitted] and the impossibility of discovering a satisfactory line of de-

---

[2] George Wharton Pepper, *The Border Land of Federal and State Decisions* 57 (Philadelphia: T. & J. W. Johnson & Co., 1889); John Chipman Gray, *The Nature and Sources of Law* (New York: Columbia University Press, 1909 ed.) §§ 533–534; Trickett, "Non-Federal Law Administered in Federal Courts," 40 *Am. L. Rev.* 819, 821–824 (1906).

[3] Charles Warren, "New Light on the History of the Federal Judiciary Act of 1789," 37 *Harv. L. Rev.* 49, 51–52, 81–88, 108 (1923). [Notes 2 through 5, in opinion.]

marcation between the province of general law and that of local law developed a new well of uncertainties.[4]

On the other hand, the mischievous results of the doctrine had become apparent. Diversity of citizenship jurisdiction was conferred in order to prevent apprehended discrimination in state courts against those not citizens of the State. *Swift v. Tyson* introduced grave discrimination by non-citizens against citizens. It made rights enjoyed under the unwritten "general law" vary according to whether enforcement was sought in the state or in the federal court; and the privilege of selecting the court in which the right should be determined was conferred upon the non-citizen. Thus, the doctrine rendered impossible equal protection of the law. In attempting to promote uniformity of law throughout the United States, the doctrine had prevented uniformity in the administration of the law of the State.

The discrimination resulting became in practice far-reaching. This resulted in part from the broad province accorded to the so-called "general law" as to which federal courts exercised an independent judgment. In addition to questions of purely commercial law, "general law" was held to include the obligations under contracts entered into and to be performed within the State, [case citations omitted] the extent to which a carrier operating within a State may stipulate for exemption from liability for his own negligence or that of his employee; the liability for torts committed within the State upon persons resident or property located there, even where the question of liability depended upon the scope of a property right conferred by the State; and the right to exemplary or punitive damages. Furthermore, state decisions construing local deeds, mineral conveyances, and even devises of real estate were disregarded. [case citations for all these propositions omitted]

In part the discrimination resulted from the wide range of persons held entitled to avail themselves of the federal rule by resort to the

---

[4] Compare Charles Warren, *The Supreme Court in United States History* 89 (rev. ed.) (Boston: Little, Brown & Co., 1935): "Probably no decision of the Court has ever given rise to more uncertainty as to legal rights; and though doubtless intended to promote uniformity in the operation of business transactions, its chief effect has been to render it difficult for business men to know in advance to what particular topic the Court would apply the doctrine. . . ." The Federal Digest, through the 1937 volume, lists nearly a thousand decisions involving the distinction between questions of general and of local law.

diversity of citizenship jurisdiction. Through this jurisdiction individual citizens willing to remove from their own State and become citizens of another might avail themselves of the federal rule. And, without even change of residence, a corporate citizen of the State could avail itself of the federal rule by re-incorporating under the laws of another State, as was done in the *Taxicab* case.

The injustice and confusion incident to the doctrine of *Swift v. Tyson* have been repeatedly urged as reasons for abolishing or limiting diversity of citizenship jurisdiction. [references to congressional hearings] Other legislative relief has been proposed. If only a question of statutory construction were involved, we should not be prepared to abandon a doctrine so widely applied throughout nearly a century. But the unconstitutionality of the course pursued has now been made clear and compels us to do so.[5]

Third. Except in matters governed by the Federal Constitution or by Acts of Congress, the law to be applied in any case is the law of the State. And whether the law of the State shall be declared by its Legislature in a statute or by its highest court in a decision is not a matter of federal concern. There is no federal general common law. Congress has no power to declare substantive rules of common law applicable in a State whether they be local in their nature or "general," be they commercial law or a part of the law of torts. And no clause in the Constitution purports to confer such a power upon the federal courts. . . .

The fallacy underlying the rule declared in *Swift v. Tyson* is made clear by Justice Holmes. The doctrine rests upon the assumption that there is "a transcendental body of law outside of any particular State but obligatory within it unless and until changed by statute," that fed-

---

[5] The doctrine has not been without defenders. See Eliot, "The Common Law of the Federal Courts," 36 *Am. L. Rev.* 498, 523–525 (1902); A. B. Parker, "The Common Law Jurisdiction of the United States Courts," 17 *Yale L. J.* 1 (1907); Schofield, "*Swift v. Tyson*: Uniformity of Judge-Made State Law in State and Federal Courts," 4 *Ill. L. Rev.* 533 (1910); Brown, "The Jurisdiction of the Federal Courts Based on Diversity of Citizenship," 78 *U. Pa. L. Rev.* 179, 189–191 (1929); J. J. Parker, "The Federal Jurisdiction and Recent Attacks upon It," 18 *A. B. A. J.* 433, 438 (1932); Yntema, "The Jurisdiction of the Federal Courts in Controversies Between Citizens of Different States," 19 *A. B. A. J.* 71, 74–75 (1933); Beutel, "Common Law Judicial Technique and the Law of Negotiable Instruments—Two Unfortunate Decisions," 9 *Tul. L. Rev.* 64 (1934).

eral courts have the power to use their judgment as to what the rules of common law are; and that in the federal courts "the parties are entitled to an independent judgment on matters of general law": "but law in the sense in which courts speak of it today does not exist without some definite authority behind it." The common law so far as it is enforced in a State, whether called common law or not, is not the common law generally but the law of that State existing by the authority of that State without regard to what it may have been in England or anywhere else. . . . "the authority and only authority is the State, and if that be so, the voice adopted by the State as its own [whether it be of its Legislature or of its Supreme Court] should utter the last word." Thus the doctrine of *Swift v. Tyson* is, as Justice Holmes said, "an unconstitutional assumption of powers by courts of the United States which no lapse of time or respectable array of opinion should make us hesitate to correct." In disapproving that doctrine we do not hold unconstitutional § 34 of the Federal Judiciary Act of 1789 or any other Act of Congress. We merely declare that in applying the doctrine this Court and the lower courts have invaded rights which in our opinion are reserved by the Constitution to the several States.

Fourth. The defendant contended that by the common law of Pennsylvania as declared by its highest court in *Falchetti v. Pennsylvania R. Co.*, 307 Pa. 203; 160 A. 859, the only duty owed to the plaintiff was to refrain from wilful or wanton injury. The plaintiff denied that such is the Pennsylvania law. In support of their respective contentions the parties discussed and cited many decisions of the Supreme Court of the State. The Circuit Court of Appeals ruled that the question of liability is one of general law; and on that ground declined to decide the issue of state law. As we hold this was error, the judgment is reversed and the case remanded to it for further proceedings in conformity with our opinion.

Reversed.

BUTLER, J., CONCURRING:

The case presented by the evidence is a simple one. Plaintiff was severely injured in Pennsylvania. While walking on defendant's right of way along a much-used path at the end of the cross ties of its main track, he came into collision with an open door swinging from the side of a car in a train going in the opposite direction. Having been warned by whistle and headlight, he saw the locomotive approaching and had time and space enough to step aside and so avoid danger. To justify his failure to get out of the way, he says that upon many other occasions he had safely walked there while trains passed.

Invoking jurisdiction on the ground of diversity of citizenship, plaintiff, a citizen and resident of Pennsylvania, brought this suit to recover damages against defendant, a New York corporation, in the federal court for the southern district of that State. The issues were whether negligence of defendant was a proximate cause of his injuries and whether negligence of plaintiff contributed. He claimed that, by hauling the car with the open door, defendant violated a duty to him. The defendant insisted that it violated no duty and that plaintiff's injuries were caused by his own negligence. The jury gave him a verdict on which the trial court entered judgment; the circuit court of appeals affirmed. 90 F.2d 603.

Defendant maintained, citing *Falchetti v. Pennsylvania R. Co.*, 307 Pa. 203; 160 A. 859, and *Koontz v. B. & O. R. Co.*, 309 Pa. 122; 163 A. 212, that the only duty owed plaintiff was to refrain from willfully or wantonly injuring him; it argued that the courts of Pennsylvania had so ruled with respect to persons using a customary longitudinal path, as distinguished from one crossing the track. The plaintiff insisted that the Pennsylvania decisions did not establish the rule for which the defendant contended. Upon that issue the circuit court of appeals said (p. 604): "We need not go into this matter since the defendant concedes that the great weight of authority in other states is to the contrary. This concession is fatal to its contention, for upon questions of general law the federal courts are free, in absence of a local statute, to exercise their independent judgment as to what the law is; and it is well settled that the question of the responsibility of a railroad for injuries caused by its servants is one of general law." Upon that basis the court held the evidence sufficient to sustain a finding that plaintiff's injuries were caused by the negligence of defendant. It also held the question of contributory negligence one for the jury.

Defendant's petition for writ of certiorari presented two questions: Whether its duty toward plaintiff should have been determined in accordance with the law as found by the highest court of Pennsylvania, and whether the evidence conclusively showed plaintiff guilty of contributory negligence. Plaintiff contends that, as always heretofore held by this Court, the issues of negligence and contributory negligence are to be determined by general law against which local decisions may not be held conclusive; that defendant relies on a solitary Pennsylvania case of doubtful applicability and that, even if the decisions of the courts of that State were deemed controlling, the same result would have to be reached.

No constitutional question was suggested or argued below or here. And as a general rule, this Court will not consider any question not raised below and presented by the petition. . . . Here it does not decide either of the questions presented but, changing the rule of decision in force since the foundation of the Government, remands the case to be adjudged according to a standard never before deemed permissible.

The opinion just announced states that "the question for decision is whether the oft-challenged doctrine of *Swift v. Tyson* [1842, 16 Pet. 1] shall now be disapproved. . . ." The doctrine of that case has been followed by this Court in an unbroken line of decisions. So far as appears, it was not questioned until more than 50 years later, and then by a single judge. . . . [citing Justice Brewer of the Supreme Court][6]. . . . And since that decision, the division of opinion in this Court has been one of the same character as it was before. In 1910, Justice Holmes, speaking for himself and two other Justices, dissented from the holding that a court of the United States was bound to exercise its own independent judgment in the construction of a conveyance made before the state courts had rendered an authoritative decision as to its meaning and effect. *Kuhn v. Fairmont Coal Co.*, 215 U.S. 349. But that dissent accepted (p. 371) as "settled" the doctrine of *Swift v. Tyson*, and insisted (p. 372) merely that the case under consideration was by nature and necessity peculiarly local.

Thereafter, as before, the doctrine was constantly applied. In *Black & White Taxicab Co. v. Brown & Yellow Taxicab Co.*, 276 U.S. 518, three judges dissented. The writer of the dissent, Justice Holmes, said, however (p. 535): "I should leave *Swift v. Tyson* undisturbed, as I indicated in *Kuhn v. Fairmont Coal Co.*, but I would not allow it to spread the assumed dominion into new fields." . . .

While amendments to § 34 have from time to time been suggested, the section stands as originally enacted. Evidently Congress has intended

---

[6] Compare this generalization with the reliance of the majority on scholarly opinion.

throughout the years that the rule of decision as construed should continue to govern federal courts in trials at common law. The opinion just announced suggests that Warren's research has established that from the beginning this Court has erroneously construed § 34. But that author's "New Light on the History of the Federal Judiciary Act of 1789" does not purport to be authoritative and was intended to be no more than suggestive. The weight to be given to his discovery has never been discussed at this bar. Nor does the opinion indicate the ground disclosed by the research. In his dissenting opinion in the *Taxicab* case, Justice Holmes referred to Warren's work but failed to persuade the Court that "laws" as used in § 34 included varying and possibly ill-considered rulings by the courts of a State on questions of common law. See, e.g., *Swift v. Tyson*, supra, 16–17. It well may be that, if the Court should now call for argument of counsel on the basis of Warren's research, it would adhere to the construction it has always put upon § 34. Indeed, the opinion in this case so indicates. . . .

So far as appears, no litigant has ever challenged the power of Congress to establish the rule as construed. It has so long endured that its destruction now without appropriate deliberation cannot be justified. There is nothing in the opinion to suggest that consideration of any constitutional question is necessary to a decision of the case. By way of reasoning, it contains nothing that requires the conclusion reached. Admittedly, there is no authority to support that conclusion. Against the protest of those joining in this opinion, the Court declines to assign the case for reargument. It may not justly be assumed that the labor and argument of counsel for the parties would not disclose the right conclusion and aid the Court in the statement of reasons to support it. Indeed, it would have been appropriate to give Congress opportunity to be heard before divesting it of power to prescribe rules of decision to be followed in the courts of the United States. [See *Myers v. United States*, 272 U.S. 52, 176.]

The Court's opinion in its first sentence defines the question to be whether the doctrine of *Swift v. Tyson* shall now be disapproved; it recites (p. 72) that Congress is without power to prescribe rules of decision that have been followed by federal courts as a result of the construction of § 34 in *Swift v. Tyson* and since; after discussion, it declares (pp. 77–78) that "the unconstitutionality of the course pursued [meaning the rule of decision resulting from that construction] compels" abandonment of the doctrine so long applied; and then near the end of the last page the Court states that it does not hold § 34 unconstitutional, but merely that, in applying the doctrine of *Swift v. Tyson* construing it, this Court and the lower courts have invaded rights which are reserved by the Constitution to the several States. But, plainly through the form of words employed, the substance of the decision appears; it strikes down as unconstitutional § 34 as construed by our decisions; it divests the Congress of power to prescribe rules to be followed by federal courts when deciding questions of general law. In that broad field it compels this and the lower federal courts to follow decisions of the courts of a particular State.

I am of the opinion that the constitutional validity of the rule need not be considered, because under the law, as found by the courts of Pennsylvania and generally throughout the country, it is plain that the evidence required a finding that plaintiff was guilty of negligence that contributed to cause his injuries and that the judgment below should be reversed upon that ground.

McReynolds, J. concurs.

Reed, J:

I concur in the conclusion reached in this case, in the disapproval of the doctrine of *Swift v. Tyson*, and in the reasoning of the majority opinion except in so far as it relies upon the unconstitutionality of the "course pursued" by the federal courts.

The "doctrine of *Swift v. Tyson*," as I understand it, is that the words "the laws," as used in § 34, line one, of the Federal Judiciary Act of September 24, 1789, do not include in their meaning "the decisions of the local tribunals." Justice Story, in deciding that point, said (16 Pet. 19):

> Undoubtedly, the decisions of the local tribunals upon such subjects are entitled to, and will receive, the most deliberate attention and respect of this Court; but they cannot furnish positive rules, or conclusive authority, by which our own judgments are to be bound up and governed.

To decide the case now before us and to "disapprove" the doctrine of *Swift v. Tyson* requires only that we say that the words "the laws" include in their meaning the decisions of the local tribunals. As the majority opinion shows, by its reference to Warren's researches and the first quotation from Justice Holmes, that this Court is now of the view that "laws" includes "decisions," it is unnecessary to go further and declare that the "course pursued" was "unconstitutional," instead of merely erroneous. . . .

In this Court, stare decisis, in statutory construction, is a useful rule, not an inexorable command. . . . It seems preferable to overturn an established construction of an Act of Congress, rather than, in the circumstances of this case, to interpret the Constitution.

∎

QUESTIONS AND COMMENTS

1. Who more prepared the way for this decision, the scholars or the courts? We have deliberately left in many of the citations to the scholarly authority in order to focus on this question. Note the role played by Harvard law professor Charles Warren. Justice Louis Brandeis, the author of this opinion, and Charles Warren were good friends and together authored a highly influential article that is credited with generating the protection of privacy in American law. See Brandeis and Warren, "The Right to Privacy," 4 *Harv. L. Rev.* 193 (1890).

2. What are the jurisprudential implications of holding that there is no "federal general common law" or that "law in the sense in which courts speak of it today does not exist without some definite authority behind it"? This line of reasoning rejects the idea of the common law as a body of principles based on reason. Now, the law of the state has to be understood as deriving from "some definite authority." Legal positivism consists in the view that all law is enacted by some "definite authority." See H. L. A. Hart, *The Concept of Law* (Oxford: Oxford University Press, 1960). Thus, jurisprudentially, *Erie* stands for a view of the common law as positive law. As the universal common law envisioned by Blackstone became the national law of particular countries, now it breaks down even more: It becomes the law of particular states.

3. What are the "policy" arguments that support this critical reorientation of the federal courts?

4. Note that the federal courts employ their own rules of procedure, namely, the Federal Rules of Civil Procedure. Thus implicit in *Erie* is the rule employed in the conflicts of law, that a forum is always entitled to apply its own law of procedure. It applies the law of another jurisdiction, the state in which it sits, only with regard to the issues of substantive law. The distinction between procedure and substance, therefore, is critical to the administration of the *Erie* doctrine.

5. But how should we decide what is procedure and what is substance? How do we classify rules on the burden of persuasion, rules of evidence, and the statute of limitations? The rule eventually emerged that all rules that "substantially affect the outcome of the case" are substantive. See *Guaranty Trust v. York*, 326 U.S. 99 (1945). This was a rather expansive definition of substantive law. Because the burden of persuasion and the statute of limitations definitely affect the outcome of the trial, they are considered substantive, which means that on these issues the federal courts must apply the rules of the state in which they sit. Even though the Federal Rules of Civil Procedure affect the outcome of the case, they are considered procedural.

6. Note that the state court would apply the law of another jurisdiction under principles of the conflicts of laws. If New York would apply California law in a case in which one of the parties was a California resident and the accident giving rise to the suit occurred in California, then a federal court would do the same.

7. Recall the problems of constitutional interpretation in Chapter Six. Is *Erie* mandated by the structure of Article III? By the case and controversy clause? By the Tenth Amendment? For a classic argument that *Erie*'s constitutional premises were weak, see Alfred Hill, "The Erie Doctrine and the Constitution," 53 *Nw. U. L. Rev.* 427, 439–449 (1958).

■

III

The Theory of the Common Law

Liberalism and Its Alternatives

The next series of chapters—Fifteen to Twenty-Six—address the nature of the foundational principles of the common law. Although
our purpose is to communicate the basics of American private law, the
best way to grasp these fundamentals is to approach them as aspects of
political philosophy. What kind of legal culture is the common law? Is
there a single legal culture? Or is the common law constantly torn by
conflicting assumptions about the possibility of individual autonomy in
the face of the demands of the state? We shall consider four basic theories of political organization, defined as follows:

   1. *Liberalism:* The classical liberal ideal holds that individuals are
free to engage in private transactions as they see fit. The state cannot
control their decisions on the grounds that they are immoral or inefficient or contrary to the public good. The idea of private law—as it is
found in the great private codes of the Continent—expresses a liberal
principle. The German Civil Code (BGB) and the *Code civil* are liberal
documents. Their rules address the private choices of individuals as expressed in legal transactions generating obligations, family relations, and
transfers of property. The state should not influence the shape of these
transactions except, in principle, to enforce the private choices of the
parties. This liberal ideal was important in the development of both the
common law and the civilian tradition. The common law argument of
liberty underlay John Locke's great *Second Treatise of Civil Government* in
1690. The great monument of Continental liberal legal theory is Immanuel Kant's *Philosophy of Right* (1797). Nineteenth-century commentators on French and German private law (even before enactment of
the BGB) developed the basic ideas of private transactions expressing
the autonomy or will of the parties.

   The central ideas in liberal legal thought are private rights (that individuals may assert against other private parties as well as against the
government) and the importance of individual freedom. Kant defined
the concept of Right (Law) as that set of rules that enables the fullest
expression of freedom compatible with an equal freedom in others.

   2. *Feudalism:* Feudalism is historically the most significant alternative to liberalism. Feudalism restricts human freedom by tying individuals to their duties of loyalty and fealty to their feudal lords. In feudal
systems, individuals are born into their stations in life, and they bear
obligations based on their status. The history of the transition from feudal to liberal legal culture is, as the historian Sir Henry Maine empha-

sized, the transition from status to contract. For Karl Marx, the history of economic relations moved ineluctably from feudalism to capitalism (liberalism), and then—not so necessarily, it turns out—to socialism.

3. *Paternalism:* The state, presenting the dominant opinions of society, often thinks that it knows better than private individuals what is good for them. Thus the state requires drivers and passengers to wear seat belts, motorcyclists to wear helmets, and individuals to pay premiums for medical insurance and retirement programs. These are all paternalistic programs that violate strict liberal principles based on freedom and personal choice.

4. *Efficiency and Public Welfare:* The major challenge to liberal principles of individual freedom and personal rights lies in claims of the public good. Many people think that it is appropriate to override claims of individual freedom if the public good is thereby served. Thus taxes are imposed to serve the public, restrictions are placed on the use of property to promote the welfare of all, and private rights are sometimes overridden to further the economy as a whole. This is the conflict between efficiency and liberalism.

There is, admittedly, some ambiguity about the difference between liberalism and libertarianism. For example, many people might think that promoting the public good, even at the cost of individual rights, is also a liberal idea. Jeremy Bentham is considered a liberal writer even though he favored applying the principles of utilitarianism (promoting the greater good) in reforming the law as laid down by Blackstone. Likewise, there are some ambiguities about the distinction between liberalism and paternalism, illuminated in the works of John Stuart Mill, particularly in the degree to which the law subtly coerces or uses educational techniques to influence behavior. For the time being, we should not let these ambiguities bother us. We shall treat liberalism as the theory that stresses, above all, individual rights and freedom to make those transactions that one wants to make. For these purposes, utilitarian arguments represent an alternative to liberalism.

There is one more distinction that we should clarify at the outset. Aristotle distinguished in the *Nicomachean Ethics* between distributive and corrective justice. Distributive justice addresses the distribution of the basic goods of society. Aristotle coined the famous maxim "To each according to his due." Marx reformulated the proper principle of distribution as "From each according to his ability, to each according to his need." John Rawls's influential book, *A Theory of Justice* (1971), argues that the principle of equality in distribution should be the basic norm: All departures from equal distribution must be justified. These are all claims of distributive justice.

These distributive claims should be distinguished clearly from arguments of corrective justice, which address the correction of individual instances of wrongdoing. By enforcing contracts, prohibiting encroachment on property, and requiring the payment of compensation for harm done, the law enforces principles of corrective justice. The basic idea of corrective justice is that a wrong has occurred to somebody and that the law should correct this wrong and return the parties to the status quo ante. Liberal legal theory is committed to the idea that private law should enforce the principle of corrective justice and only the principle of corrective justice. The corollary is that distributive justice should not play a part in the private law of property, contracts, and torts.

We will test these claims in the chapters that follow. Our central concern is the extent to which the common law and the legal cultures of Continental Europe embody liberal theory or one of its alternatives.

FIFTEEN

Feudalism in Land Law

Lawyers in the civil law tradition are rarely aware of the great influence of the French Revolution on the structure of their legal ideas. In the field of real property, at least, the revolution changed everything. It converted the feudal order into a liberal system of ownership in which a single owner could own and alienate (sell, give away, transfer by will) his or her entire interest in a piece of land. The liberal idea is that a piece of land should be owned in exactly the same way that a chattel (a piece of movable property) can be owned. If you transfer ownership in a car or horse, why should you not be able to transfer title to a piece of land? The whole idea of the feudal system was that land was different; land provided the basis of the interlocking set of obligations that constituted the basic structure of society. To understand how this system worked, we turn back to the early common law in England, to the beginning of the feudal system.

We are about to discuss the common law as it evolved between 1066 and the end of the thirteenth century. This span of a little more than 200 years was critical for defining the law of real property in the common law tradition. With only a few changes, the system defined then still prevails in the United States and the rest of the common law world.

Imagine the situation after King William and his Norman-French forces cross the Channel and conquer England in 1066—William controls the land, but he needs a political system in order to rule effectively. He is not going to surrender power to the people, and therefore he must build a political system not from the ground up but from the top down. The way to do this is to follow the Norman legal tradition of granting parcels of land to certain powerful figures in return for their undertaking obligations of loyalty, support, and service to the king. These obligations to the king were known as *homage* and *fealty*. The person who owed these to a *lord* was called a *vassal* or *tenant*. The tenants-in-chief held their grants directly from the king; these earls and barons were vassals to the king, their lord. In addition to duties of loyalty and defense, the practical content of the noble vassal's duty—in most cases—was to supply a certain number of fighting men for the king's army and similar services. So far, the arrangement sounds like a simple market transaction, but there was a catch. The king could not risk losing control over the land entirely, and therefore he held the ultimate interest in the land. The idea of ownership was divided, with the right to possess the land in the vassal but subject to certain rights in the lord, including the right to take back the land if the tenant failed to maintain the tenant's duties to the lord. This was the beginning of many devices that the English tradition utilized to fracture the idea of ownership and to prevent the localization of title in a single person.

The System of Estates

The law of real property in the common law today retains the arcane terminology of the feudal past. Here are some basic concepts to enable you to begin to find your way in this ancient system.

> *Grantor.* The person who holds an interest in property and then transfers it to someone else. The grantor can transfer only as much of an interest as the grantor holds. So, if the grantor holds a lease as the tenant and has the right to assign the lease, the grantor can transfer only the lease, and not the whole ownership of the property. (We commonly think of the grantor as including all of the grantor's successors in interest, including those who will succeed the grantor's interests at death.)

Grantee: The person who receives the transfer of an interest in property from someone else. Once a person has received an interest in property, the person may then grant it on to others; thus, every grantee can become a grantor.

Estate: The "status" in the property. There was no real notion of "ownership" yet, but what we consider ownership interests in the land was divided into "estates." Some of these estates were possessory, and others were in the nature of future interests.

Fee: The person who had a right to possess the land had a fee. There are different kinds of fee: fee simple, fee tail, and so on. We take up these distinctions presently.

Fee Simple: The most comprehensive estate the law allows. It is alienable, in that it can be given or sold to another during the life of the grantor, and it is heritable, in that it will descend at the owner's death either to the "heirs" designated by law, or later, to "devisees" named in a testament written before death. A fee simple may either be *absolute*, which is unconditional, or it can be conditional or determinable upon later events.

Future Interest: Estates that were not possessory were in the nature of future interests, which means that the person holding the estate acquires in the present the right to possess sometime in the future. These future interests were of two kinds—reversions and remainders.

Reversion: The most common form of future estate kept by the grantor, keeping some interest that limits the scope of the fee given to the grantee. Whenever a grant of less than all of the interests in a fee is made, the common law implies a reversion to the grantor.

Remainder: The remainder is like a reversion, except that it is given to a grantee, a third party who was not (or need not have been) the prior holder of the fee.

There are other present interests and other future interests, which we will describe, but these are enough for our present purposes. The idea is that the grantor has the power to divide the rights to possess into interests in the present and in the future and may give either a present or a future interest to a grantee.

When the king granted the land to a vassal, the king retained a form of interest in the land. If for some reason the vassal or his successors did not perform his obligations under the grant, the land could be forfeit to the king. The conditions under which the land would be forfeit, or revert to the lord, were the *conditions subsequent*. For instance, imagine Blackacre[1] was given to Baron A, provided Baron A supplied a troop of fifty men at arms on horse every year. The land became security for the performance of personal military obligations. These personal obligations constituted the relationship of *tenure*. The system of estates was coupled with a system of tenure. The relationship was neither purely in rem nor purely in personam. Nor was it exclusively private or public. Feudalism stands for an alternative way of thinking about all these later, liberal categories.

The next level in the structure of feudalism was the delegation by the vassal of certain of the vassal's lands and duties to provide services to the king. In other words, the earl or baron who was tenant-in-chief could, usually with the king's permission, grant the land to another person and transfer the obligations, in whole or in part, to the third person. This was called the process of *subinfeudation*. The vassal would become a *mesne lord*, or intermediate lord over another vassal or vassals who owed duties to him. To these lower vassals, who were called *villeins* if they had no control over what work they did for their lord, the lord of the mesne lord was the overlord, and lower vassals rarely had any direct obligations to him, although they might provide services for the overlord as part of their lord's obligations to him. So if Baron A held Blackacre subject to homage and to military service to the king, he might grant Smith a part of Blackacre called Oldcottage, in return for Smith giving homage to Baron A and serving as a man at arms on horse (or sending one) when Baron A calls him yearly. Smith receives Oldcottage, and a part of Baron A's obligation to the king will be satisfied as a result. Smith might then have the rights to labor from villeins who were born into families that by custom worked the land of Oldcottage and cared for its lord's horse, in return for rights to grow their food and live in actual cottages on the land attached to Oldcottage. Baron A would have rights of reversion over Oldcottage if Smith fails to meet his obligations, including providing a

---

[1] For centuries, property students in the common law have been taught about land using hypothetical parcels, especially "Blackacre." The name does not imply merely an acre; a single estate, whether called an acre or a cottage or anything else, could comprise thousands of acres and several towns. Other parcels might be called "Whiteacre" or "Greenacre," but they are all quite imaginary.

man at arms on horse. This process could be carried on with as much complexity by the mesne lords as the overlords would allow, according to the conditions by which they had granted the mesne lord the land, each act of subinfeudation creating a smaller interest that would be given to another in return for personal duties of service. (Subinfeuding, as such, was prohibited in England in 1290, but it is still part of the law of Scotland.)

Note that the basic distinction between the fee and the reversionary future interests was a matter of time. The time limit of the fee could be the life of the fee holder. This was called, naturally enough, a *life estate*.[2] At the end of the grantee's life, the land returned to the grantor in fee. A "life estate *pur autrie vie*" was the right to use for the duration of another person's life (note the charming intrusion of Law French—a creole dialect of French that evolved from the language of William the Conqueror and has persisted to this day in the language of the law). Moreover, one grantor who owned a fee could give a life estate to one grantee and at the same time give away the future interest to another grantee. Thus a lawyer could draft a grant deed (the instrument that transferred an interest in land) to read:

From O to A for life, and then to B.

Thus O could grant to A a life estate and to B a remainder. By doing this, the grantor did not keep a reversionary interest at all but gave it away to B, who is called the *remainderman*. If the draftsman had simply written:

From O to A for life,

O would have retained the reversionary interest. In either case, A would surrender the property at death, and the successor to A's interests would not inherit the property. During A's life, A would have the right to use the land and even to transfer it to others for as long as A lived, subject to occasional limitations. The law would only imply an obligation on A, the life tenant, not to waste the land, in other words, not to diminish the

---

[2] As a matter of medieval history, there were very few life estates for one life. Most estates were assigned to "A and his heirs," not yet to mean then that A had a fee simple (see previous definition), but that there was an expectation of a succession of life estates, each life tenant owing homage and service to his lord.

ultimate value of the land, to the detriment of O (or the remainderman, if there is one).

The fee could be granted with other limits. The estate need not be ended only by death (whether by the death of the life tenant or by the death of the person whose life was the *autre vie*, or other life). The estate could also be given until some event occurs, or until some event fails to occur, at which time the estate could be designed to end. These estates are called *conditional fees*. Like life estates, conditional fees must be followed by future interests, and there is a different name for the future interest that can be retained by grantors from that of the future interest that could be given to subsequent grantees. If the grantor gives the future interest to another grantee, then the grant is a fee simple subject to an executory limitation. This is written,

From O to A, until event X occurs, and then to B.

Then, whenever event X happens, B takes the land. X might occur while A is alive, or it might occur long after A dies or has sold off the fee and someone else holds it. But when X happens, the land becomes B's. For example, "Grantor gives Blackacre to Alpha Church for as long as the land is used to support a church, after which it becomes Beta Church's or its successor in interest," gives a fee simple subject to an executory limitation in Alpha Church and an executory interest in Beta Church. If Alpha Church later sells Blackacre to Gamma Church, which still uses it to support a church, there is no change. But if Gamma Church then dissolves, and the land is sold to a business, the executory interest becomes possessory, and Beta Church may demand or sue to possess Blackacre. The business would have a claim only against the person it bought from.

There is another choice the grantor can make, however. The grantor can keep the future interest and then make different types of fee dependent on the nature of the condition. If the condition is described as one that will continue for as long as the estate, and when it ends the estate ends, the conditional fee is called a *fee simple determinable*. If the condition is described as one that has not occurred, but if it ever does occur, the estate will be terminated, the conditional fee is called a *fee simple subject to a condition subsequent*. The difference between them is how they relate to their future interests. The fee simple determinable is automatically destroyed when the condition ends, and the holder of the future interest, called a *possibility of reverter*, is considered then to have an immediate right to possess the land. The fee simple subject to a condition subsequent is forfeit when the condition occurs, but the holder of its future interest, called the *right of entry*, must prove that the condition has occurred. The differences between these estates in modern procedure have diminished considerably, although they are still treated differently in certain circumstances.

One way to see the powerful tools of these estates is to realize that the common law allows grantors to create future interests and reserve for themselves the present possessory interests. The grantor can reserve a life estate and give the remainder to someone else. This type of transaction is a substitute for a will. The grantor can reserve a conditional fee and give an executory interest to someone else, so that the property is limited by the condition if it is sold or transferred at the grantor's death.

Last, the fee could be granted for a term of years, which is a grant for any length of time that is specified at the outset of the grant, or for successive terms of time, such as from month to month or from year to year. The grantor would keep a reversionary interest, which would become possessory when the time lapsed for a term of years, or if the grantor or the grantee decided not to renew for a successive term. This is called a *leasehold*.

Most Americans are familiar with this transaction. The lease is the form by which we rent apartments and other property. The leasehold in the common law is considered a property transaction, even though it arises in most instances from a contract, and the terms of the contract are "incorporated into" the lease. In a lease, the landlord retains the fee but not a possessory interest, and the leasehold is given to the tenant. The tenant cannot sell the property or give it away, although, unless the contract limits the tenant's property right, the tenant can give away all or part of the leasehold through assignment (in which the new tenant replaces the old tenant) or sublease (in which the new tenant is actually a tenant of the old tenant, who like the feudal mesne lord remains the tenant of the landlord). Besides complying with whatever covenants the tenant has to the landlord, such as a covenant to pay rent, the tenant has the additional covenant implied by law not to waste (use the land to the owner's permanent detriment).

These property aspects of the lease are quite different from the civilian approach. Because of the indivisibility of ownership in the post–Napoleonic civil law, the civilian rental arrangement is considered solely a matter of contract. The property interest in the civil law is closest to the fee simple absolute.

In the modern common law, the fee simple absolute is the basic unit of ownership. It allows the owner, while alive, to grant the property to anyone and to leave it by testament to devisees at death, or to leave it by operation of law to the heirs established by law at death. It is not subject to anyone else's future interests, because none currently exist. The very power of this unlimited fee in the common law, though, is that the landholder is allowed to exercise residual feudal powers and carve it up. This power is the root of the complexity of future interests. A holder of land in fee simple absolute may give any number of limited fees and future interests, making them like nested Russian dolls, granting one interest to A, then to B, then to C, and so on, while keeping the future interests created by the limited fees given to A, B, and C.

Now you will notice a problem immediately. The danger of the feudal system was that the process of feudal limitation could go on forever. There were very few simple fees. Most of them were subject to feudal obligations, and so when they were transferred (usually with the lord's consent), they bound the new tenant to the old feudal obligations. When the lands were subject to subinfeudation, a transfer of one estate could involve the transfer of many lesser obligations. Further, so long as there are outstanding future interests (reversions, possibilities of reverter, remainders, executory interests, and the like), there is a problem with transferring interests to which they are related. What happens to the future interests when the land is transferred? Are they cut off? It would not make sense to allow the grantor to cut off preexisting future interests that limit his own grant. It would be like saying that a tenant who has rented a house could sell the house and cut out the landlord. Thus, the common law usually follows the maxim that no person may transfer a greater interest in property than they hold. As with many doctrines, however, this maxim is subject to exceptions.

A somewhat complicated example of this problem arose in recognizing and protecting the kind of estate that was called a *fee tail*. A fee tail was created when O granted land to A "and to the heirs of his body." The phrase "heirs of the body" here gives these heirs nothing at the time of the grant but is the code language to limit A's interest and to signal that O (or O's estate) will receive back the land if there is a failure of issue. A failure of issue occurs if A dies without children, or if their children die without children, or their children's children, and so forth. So A acquired a fee tail, and O retained a reversion. The potentially surviving children acquired nothing at the time of the grant. When A dies, the children receive the fee tail. This ties up the property in the same family for as long as the family continues.

The judges of the common law, however, began to allow a present owner in fee tail to disentail, or cut off, the potential rights of the children and of the grantors. In the thirteenth century, the courts allowed special judicial proceedings by which the owner could grant the property to a third party in fee simple, thus cutting off the interests of the heirs in the fee tail.

The judicial impulse to convert fees tail into fees simple reflected an early appreciation for what we would later know as the liberal value of free alienation or transfer of land. The more land is free to come into the hands of the people willing to give the most for it, the better the conditions for capitalist development. Liberal thinking correlates here with an earlier instinct favoring capitalist development.

But the feudal interests would fight back. The first major statute of the common law was enacted by Parliament in 1285. Called *de Donis Conditionalibus*, it sought to curtail the courts' efforts by securing the fee tail against efforts by the holder of the fee simple to sell the land and cut off the reversioner's rights. This strengthened the feudal system against those who advocated the liberal principle of "free alienation" of land (being able to sell the entire fee, the entire ownership in the land).

This excess of entailment—and other feudal limits on alienation of the land—remained a matter of concern, though, and was limited in the second major statute of the common law enacted by Parliament in 1290, called *Quia Emptores*. The statute created the possibility of substituting a new feeholder for the old, ending the practice of mesne conveyances and nearly all subinfeudation in England. Substitution created the possibility of a grant to a person of one's choice, or of sale in the modern sense of the word. This was a major step toward the liberal conception of property. *Quia Emptores* was a radical step toward rendering feudal obligations less personal and more commercial.

If we ask the question, then, how did the feudal system come about, the answer is not what one would expect. The feudal system in land evolved as a matter of practice or customary law, and Parliament had to step in a few times to correct the deficiencies of the customary practices.

After the thirteenth century, other statutes would be necessary to correct the deficiencies of the system. For example, the common law recognized only three ways of transferring a fee simple in land: (1) by conveyance (sale under *Quia Emptores*), (2) according to the terms of feudal grant (i.e., holding a future interest that becomes a fee simple), or (3) inheritance. A fee simple subject to the law of inheritance was called a fee simple absolute. It was absolute in the sense that there was no future interest that could prevent the conveyance of the full interest in ownership. This interest is still commonly written as an interest given to the freeholder and his (or later her) heirs. (Notice that this is not the same as "heirs of the body," which signals a fee tail.) To grant Blackacre "to Sally and her heirs" means to give it to her in fee simple absolute.

In the early sixteenth century, the common law still lacked a voluntary system for disposition of property at death. Lands held in tail or subject to a use (an early form of trust, discussed more in the next chapter) would be transferred according to the entailment of terms of the use, but otherwise property was distributed according to a formula of heirs, who were designated and given their shares by law, at the time of death. Only with the passage of the Statute of Wills (1540) could property be transferred by written instrument, or "testament," that would become valid at death.

Further steps toward allowing landholders to transfer, or alienate, the lands in a free market were faster in coming in the early modern era, although some were in fact revivals of medieval law, limiting the strength of some statutes such as the Statute *de Donis Conditionalibus*. Many of these important steps were taken in cases in which courts not only limited the ability of grantors to create additional limitations on their grants but also interpreted the allowable limitations narrowly. The early steps in this process led to the rule in *Shelley's Case* in 1579, which held that if a conveyance was to A for life, with a remainder in A's heirs, A does not have a life estate but a fee simple. This reduced grants of a life estate followed by a remainder in the grantee's heirs to a fee simple. This reform alone, however, did not end the possibility of the first variation we mentioned on the Russian doll problem, in which a particularly controlling grantor could make a succession of limited grants that could go on nearly indefinitely. Imagine a grant of Blackacre from O to A for life, then to B for life, then to the children of A for their lives, then to C's children or grandchildren then alive for their lives, then to D's heirs. All of the grants to children and grandchildren of various people are contingent upon who will be around to possess Blackacre when the time comes. It could take a century to determine who will control Blackacre from that one grant, and each person who does will take it subject to all those feudal obligations to children yet unborn, who might or might not be well suited to manage them.

The solution evolved in a variety of limits on long-running grants and tails, culminating in the *Duke of Norfolk's Case* in 1682 with what is still called the Rule Against Perpetuities. (It is sometimes called the Doctrine of Remoteness.) This rule prevents a grantor from giving grants to people who might or might not possess them, if these people will not be identified for at least one generation in the future. The language used today for the Rule is often that of Harvard Professor John Chipman Gray, who described it as a rule according to which a contingent remainder or executory interest must vest (or be certain that the grantee will—not might—possess the land one day) within twenty-one years of a life in being. A life in being, sometimes called a *measuring life*, is someone who is alive at the time of the grant and who must logically be alive in time for the next grantee to take its interest.[3] The law is used to determine whether an interest violated the rule by declaring invalid any interest that *might* violate the rule in the future. Modern jurisdictions have allowed time to pass to see if events actually lead the rule to be violated during the lives of the people who were lives in being, plus twenty-one years. Some jurisdictions don't wait that long but just wait for a set period of time, such as ninety years. The rule is illustrated in the following case.

■

Dewire v. Haveles

Supreme Judicial Court of Massachusetts
404 Mass. 274, 534 N.E.2d 782 (1989).

WILKINS, J.:

[A probate of a will, an action in which the will is carried out subject to judicial oversight, led to a motion by the high court in Massachusetts

---

[3] The best discussion of measuring lives is also one of the clearest expositions of the rule itself. See Jesse Dukeminier, "Perpetuities: The Measuring Lives," 85 *Colum. L. Rev.* 1648 (1985).

to review the legal questions arising from "an artlessly drafted will that, among its many inadequacies, includes a blatant violation of the rule against perpetuities." The grant of an interest "twenty-one years after the death of the last surviving child" of the grantor's son, Thomas, Jr., gave a contingent remainder to a group that could not be identified until twenty-one years after the death of someone who might not have been born at the time of the will, because it was quite possible for Thomas, Jr., to have another child after his father's death.]

Thomas A. Dewire died in January, 1941, survived by his widow, his son Thomas, Jr., and three grandchildren (Thomas, III, Paula, and Deborah, all children of Thomas, Jr.). His will placed substantially all his estate in a residuary trust. The income of the trust was payable to his widow for life and, on her death, the income was payable to his son Thomas, Jr., the widow of Thomas, Jr., and Thomas, Jr.'s children.[4] After the testator's death, Thomas, Jr., had three more children by a second wife. Thomas, Jr., died on May 28, 1978, a widower, survived by all six of his children. Thomas, III, who had served as trustee since 1978, died on March 19, 1987, leaving a widow and one child, Jennifer. . . .

In his will, the testator stated: "It is my will, except as hereinabove provided, that my grandchildren, under guidance and discretion of my Trustee, shall share equally in the net income of my said estate." At another point, he referred to the trust income being "divided equally

---

[4] The language of the will directing this distribution appears in article third of the will and reads as follows:

> Third: To my wife, Mabel G. Dewire, I give, devise and bequeath all the rest, residue and remainder of all the estate of which I shall die seized, for and during the term of her natural life, and upon her decease to my son, Thomas A. Dewire, Jr., and his heirs and assigns, but in trust nevertheless upon the following trusts and for the following purposes:
>
>> A. To hold, direct, manage and conserve the trust estate, so given, for the benefit of himself, his wife and children in the manner following, that is to say:
>>
>>> To expend out of the net income so much as may be necessary for the proper care, maintenance of himself and wife conformable to their station in life, and for the care maintenance and education of his children born to him in his lifetime, in such manner as in his judgment and discretion shall seem proper, and his judgment and discretion shall be final.

[This and notes 5–11, in the original.]

amongst my grandchildren." The rule against perpetuities violation occurred because the will provided for the trust's termination "twenty-
one years after the death of the last surviving child of my said son,
Thomas A. Dewire, Jr., when the property of the trust shall be equally
divided amongst the lineal descendants of my grandchildren."[5] . . .

[W]e discuss the rule against perpetuities problem.[6] The prospect
that interests under this will may vest beyond the permissible limit of
the rule against perpetuities is not only theoretically possible, it is ac-
tuarially likely. The interests of the grandchildren in the trust income
vested at their father's death (if not sooner) and, because he was a life
in being at the testator's death, those interests vested within the period
of the rule. The gift over at the end of the class gift of income to the
grandchildren, however, might not vest seasonably because another
grandchild could have been born after the testator's death and could be
the surviving grandchild. In this case, in fact, the three youngest grandchildren were born after the death of the testator but they are measuring
lives for the term of the class gift. The parties agree that the purported
gift of the remainder to the lineal descendants of the testator's grandchildren "twenty-one years after the death of the last surviving" grandchild violates the rule against perpetuities in its traditional form and
would be void. . . . There is no need at this time to decide the question
of the proper distribution of trust income or assets at the death of the
last grandchild. The question will be acute at the death of the last
grandchild, when the class gift of income from the trust will terminate.[7]

---

[5] As we shall explain, the possibility that Thomas, Jr., would have a child born after the
testator's death was sufficient to cause the violation of the rule against perpetuities. The
fact that Thomas, Jr., had children born after the testator's death makes a violation of
the rule an actual fact.

[6] In its classic formulation, the rule against perpetuities declares that: "No interest is good
unless it must vest, if at all, not later than twenty-one years after some life in being at
the creation of the interest." J. C. Gray, *The Rule Against Perpetuities* (4th ed.) § 201, at
191 (Boston: Little, Brown & Co., 1942). See *Eastman Marble Co. v. Vermont Marble
Co.*, 236 Mass. 138, 152 (1920).

[7] The common law rule against perpetuities has been modified by statute. See G. L. c.
184A, § 1 (1986 ed.), applicable to wills of persons dying after January 1, 1955 (St.
1954, c. 641, § 2) and thus not directly applicable in this case. The second look, or
wait-and-see, principle of G. L. c. 184A, § 1, has been applied as a matter of decisional
law to an instrument to which § 1 did not apply. See *Warner v. Whitman*, 353 Mass.
468, 472 (1968). If a wait-and-see approach is applicable here, and if the last surviving
grandchild were to be one of the grandchildren alive at the death of the testator, there

The rule against perpetuities problem need not be resolved at this time. It has some bearing, however, on what should be done during the term of the class gift with the one-sixth share of the trust income that is in dispute. We reject the argument that, because of the violation of the rule against perpetuities, the income interests should be treated as being more than life interests. There is no authority for such a proposition.[8] Although the gift over violates the rule against perpetuities in its traditional form and in time may prove to violate it in actual fact, the language providing for such a distribution may properly be considered in determining a testator's intention with respect to other aspects of his will.[9] For the purposes of distribution of assets, a will is to be construed as if a provision violating the rule against perpetuities is not contained in it . . . , but we have never said that the language of a void clause cannot be used to determine the testator's intention as to dispositions that do not violate the rule. . . .

The testator provided that the trust should terminate twenty-one years after the death of his last grandchild. It is unlikely that the testator intended that trust income should be accumulated for twenty-one years, and we would tend to avoid such a construction. . . . Certainly, we should not presume that he intended an intestacy as to that twenty-one year period.[10] He must have expected that someone would receive distributions of income during those years. . . . The only logical recipients of that income would be the issue (by right of representation) of deceased grandchildren, the same group of people who would take the trust assets on termination of the trust (assuming no violation of the rule against perpetuities).[11] If these people were intended to receive

would be no violation of the rule against perpetuities. We might even decide that there was no violation of the rule if all the grandchildren were to die within twenty-one years of the death of the last grandchild who was living at the testator's death. See *Restatement (Second) of Property*, Donative Transfers § 1.4 (1983).

[8] We also reject the contention that the trust beneficiaries can properly compel termination of the trust and a distribution of the trust assets at this time. They are not all now ascertained or ascertainable, and there is no reason to invalidate the class gift of income. See *Allen v. First Nat'l Bank & Trust Co.*, 319 Mass. 693, 697 (1946).

[9] See J. C. Gray, *The Rule Against Perpetuities* (4th ed.) §§ 629–631, at 599–600 (Boston: Little, Brown & Co., 1942) ("a provision void for remoteness is still to be resorted to for construing the rest of the will").

[10] See *Anderson v. Harris*, 320 Mass. 101, 104–105 (1946).

[11] "[T]he property of the trust shall be equally divided amongst the lineal descendants of my grandchildren." "Equally," referring to a multigenerational class, normally means *per*

income during the last twenty-one years of the trust as well as the trust assets on its termination, it is logical that they should also receive income during the term of the class gift if their ancestor (one of the grandchildren) should die. Such a pattern treats each grandchild and his issue equally throughout the intended term of the trust. Where, among other things, every other provision in the will concerning the distribution of trust income and principal (after the death of the testator and his wife) points to equal treatment of the testator's issue per stirpes, there is a sufficient contrary intent shown to overcome the rule of construction that the class gift of income to grandchildren is given to them as joint tenants with the right of survivorship. . . .

Judgment shall be entered declaring that . . . no declaration shall be made at this time concerning the disposition of trust income or principal on the death of the last grandchild of Thomas A. Dewire. . . . So ordered.

■

QUESTIONS AND COMMENTS

1. If the interest given was good, or legally valid and enforceable, then the trust would continue to exist until the surviving grandchildren could be identified, twenty-one years after the death of Thomas's last surviving child. If that interest failed, then what would happen? The court suggests that the will would be read as if the clause violating the rule never existed. So what then? More than likely, the trust would be dissolved and the assets given away to all of the identified beneficiaries at the death of Thomas's last surviving child. Does this accord with Mr. Dewire's intent? How far should the law allow Mr. Dewire's intent to govern property he once owned? The purpose of the rule is to balance the interests of current owners of property, who desire to control that property into the future, with the interests of others after their death, who would desire to control it also. Does the rule make sense? Should the interests of current owners be given such weight so long after death? (See question three.)

2. The Court noted that it need not resolve the rule against perpetuities

---

stirpes. *New England Trust Co. v. McAleer*, 344 Mass. 107, 112 (1962). *Dexter v. Inches*, 147 Mass. 324, 326 (1888). In such a case, the *stirpes* are normally placed at one generation before the takers. See *Bradlee v. Converse*, 318 Mass. 117, 120 (1945).

violation, even though one was likely. Massachusetts follows the wait-and-see approach, as do the majority of states.

3. Trusts are discussed further in the next chapter. What problems of the trustee will be considerably greater because of the contingent nature of the beneficiaries to whom he might make payments or to whom he will pay the trust at dissolution? He may not know who the beneficiaries are, or will be, for several generations.

4. Because many states want to let rich people create dynastic fortunes, some states have recently done away with the rule as a limit on grants of a benefit in trust. (See Verner F. Chaffin, "Georgia's Proposed Dynasty Trust: Giving the Dead Too Much Control," 35 *Ga. L. Rev.* 1 (2000).) Few of these modifications to the law of trusts affect the grant of the land outright, but to return again to the issue in question one, what is the best balance between the interests of the grantor at death who desires to control property later, and the people who are alive later?

■

This is but an introduction to a very complicated body of law. It is sufficient to get the basic terminology. Test your wits by working through the categories in Table 15.1.

Remember that contingent remainders, executory interests, and option contracts to acquire land are all subject to the rule against perpetuities, which voids grants that tie up lands too long in successive grantees. Ask, "Must the interest necessarily vest or fail within twenty-one years of a life in being?" In other words, ask, "Does the grantor give anything to someone who is not yet born, and we won't know if they might take the grant for twenty-one years?" In general, a grant that does not go to someone specific within three generations of the making of the grant will violate this rule.

Don't despair! These materials are designed to give you a taste of the arcane terminology and interrelated concepts that led Dick the Butcher, one of Shakespeare's characters in *Henry VI,* scene ii, to say:

"[T]he first thing we do, let's kill all the lawyers."

Some critics say that this was an indirect tribute to lawyers. Shakespeare portrayed Dick the Butcher as a rebel who sought to overthrow the Crown and establish a dictatorship. Lawyers were seen as the guardians

Table 15.1

All You Need to Know about Estates in Land

Present possessory interest	Language of creation	Limits of present interest	Future interest
Fee simple absolute	"To A and his heirs . . ."	None	None (Note: heirs are given nothing here)
Fee tail	"To A and the heirs of his body . . ."	Failure of issue	Reversion (grantor or his heirs) Remainder (in third-party grantee)
Leasehold (term of years)	"Until day X" *or* "For X time . . ."	End of term, at a time certain	Reversion (landlord)
Leasehold (periodic)	Month to month or year to year, etc.	Failure of non-renewal	Reversion (landlord)
Leasehold (at will)	"For as long as you want . . ." or "For as long as I can stand you . . ." etc.	Either party terminates lease	Reversion (landlord)
Leasehold (by sufferance)	[Tenancy expired]	Ejectment or tenant quits	Reversion (landlord)
Life estate	"For [your] life . . ." or "Until [your] death . . ."	Your death	Reversion (grantor or his heirs) Remainder (in third-party grantee) (Remainders can be vested or contingent)
Life estate (*pur autrie vie*)	"Until his death . . ." "Until their deaths . . ." "Until my death. . . ."	Death of third party Death of third parties Death of grantor	Reversion (grantor or his heirs) Remainder (in third-party grantee) (Remainders can be vested or contingent) *(continued)*

Table 15.1 (*continued*)

Present possessory interest	Language of creation	Limits of present interest	Future interest
Fee simple subject to a condition subsequent	"But if X oc-curs . . ." or "Pro-vided X never oc-curs . . ." etc.	Beginning of specified condi-tion	Right of entry (or right of reentry or power of termina-tion) (grantor) [requires court action to enforce]
Fee simple deter-minable	"For so long as land is used for X . . ." or "As long as X con-tinues . . ."	End of specified condition	Possibility of reverter (grantor) [automatic; requires no court action]
Fee simple subject to an executory limitation	"But if X should occur then Y shall have it . . ." or "To Y if A [or Y or Z] shall X . . ."	Occurrence of X	Executory interest (grantee) Shifting (if it divests a grantee) Springing (if it divests the grantor)

of stability and established rights. See also Act IV, scene vii. The law is always on trial because its details can be so taxing.

Here is the key idea of this chapter. Feudalism was the antithesis of liberalism. No one except the king held land free and clear. Everyone stood in a relationship of fealty and loyalty to higher lords. Liberalism requires people to be autonomous in their domain. Eventually, the law of real property enabled people to act freely and autonomously, and the tools for controlling the old feudal estates became tools giving people greater flexibility in their choices. But that is not the way English legal history began. Real property, supported by the lawyers, was the basis for a network of duties that held people to their stations in life.

As Shakespeare was writing, another dispute about the law was brew-ing. Equity and law stood in an uneasy relationship. Sooner or later, something would happen to require a decision whether the common law or equity was the supreme authority "law" of the land. In the last years of Shakespeare's life, under the reign of King James I, the fight came out into the open.

Further Reading

On the development of the law of property, see A. W. B. Simpson, *A History of the Land Law* (2d ed.) (Oxford: Oxford University Press, 1986). On the development of the common law and the nature of property, see J. H. Baker, *An Introduction to English Legal History* (4th ed.) (London: Butterworths, 2002). To study further the modern estates in land, see Robert Laurence and Pamela B. Minzner, *A Student's Guide to Estates in Land and Future Interests: Text, Examples, Problems, and Answers* (New York: Matthew Bender, 1993).

SIXTEEN

The Triumph of Equity

Developed over centuries, in response to specific problems, the common law forms of action are multiple and overlapping. Even a system as seemingly unified as the estates in land is hardly a system of logical unity. The estates in land are complicated and do not resolve all interests in property; other rules—for instance, to govern warranty by the owner in sales or leases—were not resolved by the common law until prompted by modernizing statutes in the twentieth century.

The courts of equity were a distinct legal system that developed out of the office of the king called the chancery. The initial judge of equity was the chancellor. The origins of equity—drawn mainly from Roman law, canon law, and judicial prudence—are still debated, but by the fifteenth century it was a firmly established jurisdiction and body of law that competed with the common law. Its most important differences from the courts of law were three:

1. The purpose of equity was to correct the common law in the way that Aristotle described the idea of *epieikeia*: "[The] law is always a general statement, yet there are cases which it is not possible to cover in a general statement." This purpose of correcting the common law in particular cases

was sometimes expressed as seeking to realize the spirit as opposed to the plain letter of the law.[1]

The major critique of equity was that it was uncertain and therefore contrary to the requirement of law as the fair and precise regulation of private rights. The liberal view of law, as expressed by Immanuel Kant in his *Philosophy of Right* (1797), is that the law must be well defined and equally available to all. The danger of equity is that its decisions would vary as John Selden said, "with the length of the Chancellor's foot."

2. The courts of equity operated by commanding the defendant to engage in a particular action. The common law operated by granting a judgment, usually for an amount of money, called *damages*.

3. Courts of equity operated without juries. The chancellor or the judge in equity decided the case as does a civil law judge, by resort to principles, called "maxims," often enunciated in general principles, with a diminished influence of precedent. Juries were essentially limited to cases that arose under the common law.

Law and equity are unified today in what appears to be a single body of law, but in fact each remedy in the law continues to conform either to the principles of law or to the principles of equity. This has led to some overlap and to choices for lawyers that arise in conditions of overlapping opportunity to resolve disputes. Equity functions by commanding a specific act, such as specific performance of a contract. The command was eventually (and still is) expressed in an *injunction*. This has resulted in overlapping remedies in many cases. Suppose that A brings a lawsuit against B in Oregon on the basis of an incident that occurred in New York. A does this simply because he wants to make it difficult and expensive for B to defend himself in the lawsuit. B can request a dismissal of the action on the grounds of *forum non conveniens*. An alternative remedy for B would be to go to a court in New York and petition for an injunction against A's suing him in Oregon. The injunction would not cancel the Oregon lawsuit, but if A disobeyed the injunction, the New York court could imprison him for contempt of court.[2] The likely reso-

---

[1] On the Aristotelian idea of equity, see the superb essay by Paul Vinogradoff, "Equity," in his *Common-Sense in Law* (New York: Henry Holt and Co., 1946).

[2] On the contempt power, review the discussion in Chapter Eleven.

lution would be that the judge in New York could decide whether to grant the injunction. The case would not go to a jury.

The dramatic problem in the evolution of the law was, Which body of law was superior? Would equity rule, or would the common law remain supreme? The following materials document the resolution of this conflict in the early sixteenth century:

Excerpts from Julius Goebel,

The Development of Legal Institutions (1930):[3]
The Contest with Chancery.

Introduction

None of the common law courts' battles was more bitterly fought, and none was more dramatic than the fight with Chancery after (Sir Edward) Coke was elevated to King's Bench in 1613. To comprehend the real issue at stake we must remember the position of the Chancellor at the opening of the 17th century, and his intimate relation with the King. Remember also that the Chancery does not proceed according to the course of the common law, but its principles of practice and justification are derived from other sources, including ecclesiastical law. Chancery assumes the right and power to open up final judgments of the common law courts. This right Coke denies. The issue is a battle for the principle of *res judicata*.

Spence, EQUITY JURISDICTION.[4]

Volume I, pages 673–676

The most frequent exercise of the jurisdiction of the Court in granting injunctions, was to restrain proceedings at law. It must have been very soon found that without such an interference, it would be impossible for the Court to carry out the jurisdiction it had assumed, of controlling the law on the principles of equity and conscience. Accordingly, from the time of Henry VI (1422–61, 1470–71) downwards, we find nu-

---

[3] Julius Goebel, *Cases and Materials on the Development of Legal Institutions* (New York: Columbia Law School Press, 1931).

[4] George Spence, *The Equitable Jurisdiction of the Court of Chancery* (Philadelphia: Lea and Blanchard, 1846–50).

merous instances of the granting of such injunctions. These injunctions were enforced not only against the parties and their solicitors, but their counsel also, as we learn from the cases of Serjeants Glanvil and Powtrel, and of "Master Robert Snagg." The Chancellors having, as before noticed, persevered in granting injunctions to restrain proceedings at law even after judgment; their right was vehemently opposed in the time of Edward IV (1461–1470, 1471–1483). In one case, 21 Edward IV, Fairfax held that the Court of the King's Bench had the power of granting injunctions to restrain parties from resorting to any means of delaying actions, even before judgment, in cases within the jurisdiction of the Courts of Common Law; but the Court of Chancery, as we learn from subsequent authorities, still continued to restrain proceedings at law by action on the case, where a bill was filed in that court for specific performance. In the 22 Edw. IV., Hussey, C.J. of the King's Bench, and Fairfax, J., in the case then before them, declared, that as for the penalty that could not be recovered, and if the Chancellor shall commit any of the parties, the judges would release them on their being brought up before them by *habeas corpus*: Fairfax, however, said he would go to the Chancellor, and endeavor to persuade him to withdraw the injunction; but the Chancellor appears to have been inflexible, and the exercise of the jurisdiction was continued.

The jealousy of the common law judges against this jurisdiction displayed itself again in the reign of Henry VIII (1509–1547); indeed, Robert Wolsey, when Chancellor, appears to have been rather unscrupulous in granting injunctions. Sir Thomas More endeavored, by a conference with the judges, to allay this jealousy; however it broke forth again in the reign of Elizabeth, and a barrister was indicted in the Court of King's Bench under the statute of praemunire, for exhibiting a bill in Chancery for an injunction after judgment of law in that court.

In the reign of James I (1603–25), there was an open rupture between Lord Ellesmere and Lord Coke as to the right of the Courts of Chancery to grant injunctions after judgment. That sovereign took upon himself to settle the matter. For that purpose he desired the attorney-general, Sir Francis Bacon, and the king's counsel to certify what had been the ancient practice in the time of his predecessors. They accordingly certified, that in the time of Henry VII, Henry VIII, Edward VI, and Mary and Elizabeth, there has been a great many injunctions granted after judgement in actions of different natures, real and personal, in the king's several Courts of the King's Bench, Common Pleas, and the Justices in Eyre. King James (14th July, 1616), on this certificate ordered that thenceforth the ancient practice as so certified should be continued. In 1655, the Lords Commissioners held, that where there was an original equity arising out of the nature of the transaction, which was not properly cognizable at law, that the party was not estopped by the verdict from seeking relief in the Court of Chancery, and the Court has since interfered, even after execution executed. . . .

Though injunctions were granted by the Court of Chancery to restrain proceedings in the Ecclesiastical Court, and in the Exchequer, the Court of Chancery would not permit those courts, or any other court, to restrain any one from proceeding in the Court of Chancery— "No court can hinder the point of equity in this court." So that the King's Bench injunctions and prohibitions, if any such were issued, must have been disregarded.

The struggle between Edward Coke as chief justice of the King's Bench and Lord Ellesmere as chancellor came to a head in the following dispute:

Courtney v. Glanvil

Easter Term, 12 James 1 (1614).
In B R. Cro. Jac. 343.[5]

[Glanvil sold Courtney a topaz misrepresented to be a diamond and other jewels for 360 pounds rather than the 20 pounds they were worth. Courtney gave a bond to secure payment for the full amount with bond by Hampton for the full amount, which Glanvil planned to collect through a fast claim on the bond in court, which was granted. Courtney learned of the plot and went to chancery court himself to

[5] Everyone with a proper education in England is supposed to know that James I began his reign in 1603. "B.R." is *Banco Regis*, or the Court of Kings Bench. "Cro. Jac." is the abbreviation for *George Croke's Reports from the Reign of King James*, where this report appeared on page 343.

set aside the grant of the claim on the bond. After an initial refusal of relief, the chancery court awarded Courtney a rescission of the sale, allowing Glanvil to keep the rock and 100 pounds but ordering Courtney to release Hampton from any claims. Glanvil did not make the release, and the chancery court ordered him imprisoned. Glanvil then sued in the King's Bench, a law court, seeking his release.]

Glanvil was committed to the Fleet (in prison for civil contempt) the last day of Michaelmas term, 11 James 1 (November 29, 1613) for not performing a decree in Chancery; and upon a habeas corpus returned, the case was informed to be thus:[6]

Glanvil sold to Courtney, being a young gentleman, a jewel, which he pretended to be of the value of three hundred and sixty pounds, whereas in truth it was worth but twenty pounds, and three other jewels to the value of one hundred pounds; and for his security he took a bond of six hundred pounds in the name of one Hampton, and procured an action to be brought in the said Hampton's name, and the action to be confessed, and Glanvil paid all the charges of both parties, and the confession was out of Court in the vacation.

Courtney finding this deceit, that the jewel was not worth above twenty pounds, which was delivered to him at the rate of three hundred and sixty pounds, exhibited his bill in Chancery for relief, and afterward brought a writ of error to reverse this judgment; but the judgment was affirmed.

Afterwards, upon a hearing in Chancery, it was decreed, that Glanvil should take again his jewel and one hundred pounds, and that he should procure Hampton to release and acknowledge satisfaction: and for not performing this decree he was imprisoned.

Coke, Chief Justice, said, that this decree and imprisonment, being after a judgment at the common law, was unlawful, and that this Court ought to relieve him; and for proof he cited a judgment in Easter Term, 5 Edw. 4 Roll 35. *Cobb v. Moor*, where Cobb procured an action of debt to be brought against Moor, and the action to be confessed by attorney, and a writ of error to be brought thereupon, and the judgment to be affirmed; and all this was done in the absence of Moor, who, being beyond sea, upon his return exhibited his bill in Chancery, to

---

[6] Habeas corpus is the writ at law that requires the jailor to "produce the body" and justify the confinement.

be relieved concerning this practice, there being no debt due: and it was resolved, that after a judgment at the common law he could not be relieved there, but was inforced to deliver his bill in Parliament. And there was a special Act made for his relief. He also cited another precedent in Michaelmas term, 39 and 40 Eliz. *Sir Moyle Finch v. Throgmorton*. . . . An action was brought, and upon special verdict, the question being upon a lease for years by the Queen, rendering rent, and for non-payment to be void. In 3 Eliz. Sir Moyle Finch purchased the reversion, and entered for non-payment of the rent in 9 Eliz. And because it was resolved to be a limitation, and to be a lease void without office, and that the patentee might avoid this lease, and was judged accordingly, and this judgment affirmed in a writ of error; Throgmorton afterwards exhibited a bill in Chancery, complaining, that at the same time that the default of payment was in 9 Eliz. He did send the rent by his servant, who was robbed thereof; which when he knew, he paid it immediately the day after, and that the Queen accepted thereof; and that he continued the payment until 30 Eliz. When the Queen sold it; and that the Queen sold it as a reversion; and charged with this lease; therefore it was against conscience that the patentee should avoid it. And to this bill Sir Moyle Finch pleaded the proceedings at the common law and demanded judgment, if he might now proceed in a Court of Equity. And all the Judges of England were hereupon assembled, and these matters debated before them; and resolved by them all, that although the said bill comprehended much matter of equity, and there was very good cause he should have been relieved, if he has complained before the judgment obtained at the common law, yet now having suffered a judgment at the common law, although it were by way of defence, he comes too late to be relieved in a Court of Equity; and cannot now examine any pretence of equity after a judgment at the common law.—Wherefore Coke and all the Court held her, that the party ought to be bailed; and then let him to bail unto the next term, and he was then discharged. Vide 22 Edw. 4 pl. 37.

These are the moves in the chess game: (1) Glanvil got a judgment at law requiring Hampton to pay the bond; (2) Courtney got a decree in equity restraining Glanvil from enforcing his judgment; (3) Glanvil refused to obey; (4) Equity ordered the imprisonment of Glanvil for civil contempt—he should be kept in jail until he performed—and (5), on a writ of habeas corpus, Coke orders the release of Glanvil. Now what will happen?

Argument Proving from Antiquity the Dignity, Power, and Jurisdiction of the Court of Chancery

1 Chan. Rep. App. 1-49

A question raised in the Court of King's Bench, Whether after a judgment given at the Common Law, the Chancery could in any case give relief in Equity? Or, Whether it were not debarred thereof by the Statutes of 27 E. e, cap. 1, and of 4 H. 4, cap. 23. . . .

His said majesty being informed of this Difference between his two Courts of Chancery and King's Bench, and being informed that there were many Precedents in the Chancery in the times of King Henry VII (1485–1509). And continually since, whereof a Note was delivered to his said Majesty, That such as complained there to be relived in Equity after Judgments at Common Law, (in Cases where the Judges could not relieve them) directed, That his Attorney General, calling to him the Rest of his Learned Counsel, should peruse the said Precedents, and certify his Majesty the Truth thereof with their Opinions.

Whereupon they returned to his majesty this answer as followeth:

According to your majesty's Commandment we have advisedly considered of the Note delivered unto us of the Precedents of Complainings and Proceedings in Chancery after Judgments at Common Law; and have also seen and perused the Originals, out of which the same Note was abstracted; upon all which we do find and observe the Points following: . . .

The Case

A. hath a Judgment and Execution in the King's Bench or Common Pleas against B. in an action of Debt of 1000 £, and in an *Ejectione Firmae* of the Manor of D. B. complains in the Chancery to be relieved against these Judgments according to Equity and Conscience, allowing the Judgment to be lawful and good by the Rigour and strict Rules of the law, and the Matter in Equity to be such, as the Judges of the

Common law being no Judges in Equity, but bound by their Oaths to do the Law, cannot give any Remedy or Relief for the same, either by Error or Attaint, or by any other Means.

Question

Whether the Chancery may relieve B. in this or such like Cases, or else leave him utterly remediless and undone? And if the Chancery be restrained herein by any Statute of Praemunire, then by what Statute, and by what Words in any Statute is the Chancery so restrained, and Conscience and Equity excluded, banished and damned?

Which Case his majesty referred again to his said Attorney and Learned Counsel, calling to them the Prince's Attorney, who returned this Answer. . . .

Upon which Certificate the King gave his Judgment as followeth.

Forasmuch as Mercy and Justice be the true Supporters of our Royal Throne, and that it properly belongeth unto us in our Princely Office to take Care and provide, that our Subjects have equal and indifferent Justice ministered unto them: And that where their Case deserveth to be relieved in Course of Equity by Suit in our Court of Chancery, they should not be abandoned and exposed to perish under the Rigor and Extremity of our Laws, We in our Princely Judgment having well weighed and with mature Deliberation considered of the several Reports of our learned Counsel, and all the parts of them, do approve, ratify and confirm, as well the Practice of our Court of Chancery expressed in their first certificate as the Opinions for the law upon the Statute mentioned in their later Certificate, the same having Relation unto the case sent unto them by our Chancellor: And do will and command that our Chancellor, or Keeper of the Great Seal for the Time being, shall not hereafter desist to give unto our Subjects, upon their several Complaints now or hereafter to be made, such Relief in Equity (notwithstanding any Proceedings at the Common Law against them) as shall stand with the Merit and Justice of their Cause, and with the former, ancient and continued Practice and Presidency of our Chancery have done: And for that it appertaineth to our Princely Office only to judge over all Judges, and to discern and determine such Differences, as at any time may and shall arise between our several Courts touching their Jurisdictions, and the same to settle and determine, as we in our Princely Wisdom shall find to stand most with our

Honour, and the Example of our Royal Progenitors in the Best Times, and the general Weals and Good of our People, for which we are to answer unto God who hath placed us over them; Our Will and Pleasure is, that our whole Proceedings therein, by the Decrees formerly set down, be inrolled in Chancery, there to remain of Record, for the better extinguishing of the like Differences and Questions that may arise in future Times.

Per ipsum Regem 18 July 14, 1616.

Fran. Bacon,[7] Hen. Yelverton

In the end, then, the king decreed that his chancellor should prevail over Chief Justice Coke and his common law. Coke had succeeded in consolidating the jurisdiction of law into a national system of courts, rather than the many local and ecclesiastical courts that had existed before him, and he had won what would be later seen as a victory over Parliament in 1610 when he established the power of the courts to overrule an act of Parliament on the ground that it violated "common right or reason," which we discussed in Chapter Four. Equity, however, proved a more formidable opponent. Why was that? Because the institutions of equity were tied directly to the king? Or because equity could beat Coke at his own game of linking the common law and reason? Equity appealed to even higher principles of reason and natural justice.

The term *equity* as it is used in Anglo-American law fluctuates among different meanings. One meaning is that we have seen drawn from Aristotle: Equity has the function of correcting hard-and-fast rules by appealing to criteria of natural justice. At the same time, a second meaning of equity locates the concept in a set of English institutions that apply a specific body of law. The courts of equity gradually acquired jurisdiction over certain problems that the law had undervalued. For example, equity supplied relief for fraud and for the reformation of contracts after mistakes had been made in the drafting. In this sense, equity is much more like the civilian concept of "general equity" described by Dean François Gény and followed by French scholars in the interpretation of Article 565 of the *Code civil*, which requires "natural equity."

---

[7] The opinion is reported by the philosopher Francis Bacon, who became chancellor in 1618.

The most significant legal creation of equity was the idea of equitable ownership of land. This implied that one form of title would be protected at law (legal title) and another form of title protected in equity (equitable title). This was a remarkable idea that first led to a surrogate for the nonexisting systems of wills for testamentary succession. The idea began, it seems, with landowners' granting the "use" of the land to another. Then the use could spring from one person to another. These uses were protected in equity as equitable estates. Thus a primitive mechanism was set for transferring property at death. The use would spring from one person to another at death, and this transfer would be protected in equity. These procedures found statutory recognition and regulation in the Statute of Uses (1535). The Statute of Wills followed in 1540.

Once equitable ownership of land and chattels became institutionalized, the road was open for the significant invention of the trust. The trust is a three-party transaction. The person who sets up the trust is called the *trustor* or *settlor*. This person conveys legal ownership in the corpus of the trust (the *res*) to the trustee to hold and manage the assets for the sake of a third person, the beneficiary of the trust. Thus, if a parent wants to take care of his children without his children having control of relevant assets, the parent conveys the assets to a trustee (very often a bank) to hold and manage for the sake of the children, the beneficiaries of the trust. The bank gets legal title. The children receive equitable title. In civil law countries, one can achieve the same functional result by using contractual mechanisms such as the *Treuhand* under German law.[8]

The trust has become an indispensable instrument of American law, largely because it is so useful in avoiding probate. Probate is illustrated in the case on the rule against perpetuities considered in the previous chapter. When someone dies in a common law jurisdiction, the property does not transfer directly to the heirs. It goes into "probate," which means that it comes under the jurisdiction of a special branch of the judiciary called the *probate court*. It comes under the control of either an executor (under a will) or an administrator (when there is no will), who works with the

---

[8] The *Treuhand* in Germany is a creation of the courts and the scholars. Except for some special situations (e.g., wills, corporate law), it has no explicit foundation in the civil code. The general definition of *Treuhand* comes quite close to the American understanding of the trust: One can speak of a *Treuhand* when a person is granted rights, which she can dispose of freely but which she is supposed to exercise not in the interest of herself but of other persons or objective purposes.

probate court to make sure that all taxes and debts are paid before the property passes to the beneficiaries designated under the will or under the law (when there is no will). The trust serves to circumvent the role of probate. If the testator establishes a trust, the property remains in the hands of the trustee to distribute according to the terms of the trust. Typically, when the settlor dies, the trustee transfers the property to the beneficiaries. This avoids the cumbersome process of having the property tied up in probate. For this reason, the law of trusts is often taught together with estate planning in a course called "Trusts and Estates." (Note in this latter sense *estate* does not refer to estates in land but rather to the entire wealth of the decedent at the time of death. This is the object of the "estate tax" recently suspended for ten years under federal legislation.)

The notion of equitable ownership has undergone important evolution, largely due to the law of mortgages. In a mortgage transaction, the mortgagor transfers legal title to a mortgagee, who holds the assets as security for a debt. The mortgagee is either a bank or a mortgage company. The mortgagor retains the beneficial use of the property and therefore is analogous to the beneficiary of a trust. The difference between the trust and the mortgage is that the former establishes legal relations among three parties—the trustor, the trustee, and the beneficiary. The mortgage is a two-party transaction,[9] with the trustor and beneficiary united in a single party.

The mortgage has given rise to an important shift in the meaning of the word *equity*. Suppose that you buy a house worth $500,000. You cannot afford the entire purchase price, and therefore you take out a mortgage for $300,000. You borrow that amount from a bank, and, to secure the debt, you transfer legal title to the bank. You pay off the loan by making a payment on the principal, plus interest, every month. In the case of default, the bank will not claim the entire value of the house but merely the amount necessary to cover the outstanding debt. If, at the time of default, you owe only $250,000, and the value of the house has gone up to $600,000, then you have a residual ownership interest in the

---

[9] This is a slight exaggeration because, in the contemporary law of mortgages, there are many third parties waiting in the wings. These are the investors who buy the mortgage, with the accompanying interest-bearing debt, from the mortgagee. Thus a secondary market—comparable to the securities markets—has developed in mortgages. This has not happened in the field of trusts, where the obligation of the trustee to manage the property is personal and not transferable to third parties.

house. This ownership interest is called the *equity of redemption* because it is analogous to the equitable ownership claimed by the beneficiary of a trust. Thus there has arisen a new way of speaking about ownership in cases where assets are encumbered by debt. If you still owe $250,000 on a house worth $600,000, someone might ask you, "How much equity do you have in your house?" The answer would be $350,000.

This fundamental distinction between debt and equity now provides the foundation for corporate finance. The debt of the corporation is owed to the bondholders. The remaining value of the corporation is the equity, and this is owned collectively by the shareholders. Thus, shares of stock in public corporations are now called *equities*. The word *equity* has come a long way from its origins in the courts of equity. The one-time primitive distinction between legal and equitable ownership is now expressed in the most sophisticated branches of corporate finance.

Equitable Pleading and Maxims

Regardless of whether a plaintiff seeks relief for an equitable cause of action or seeks only an equitable remedy for a breach of a legal duty, the plaintiff must bring the suit, even today, before a court competent to act in equity. In most cases, this is the court of general jurisdiction. Chancery courts still exist in a few states, especially Delaware, which is the home of many of the corporations in the United States and so the source of much U.S. corporate law. In most states and in all federal courts, the courts of general jurisdiction may act according to their equitable powers.

Pleading in equity is now much less specialized than it once was, owing to the adoption of uniform rules of civil procedure. Still, certain pleading matters are special to equity, such as the obligation to plead jurisdiction in equity and the requirement that a plaintiff who seeks pretrial relief of an equitable nature (such as a preliminary injunction) must also seek equitable relief in the end (such as a permanent injunction).

Although precedent plays an important role in equity courts, equitable courts often base their decisions on maxims of equity that acquire their binding force from moral reasoning. There are many maxims, and they must be established either by citation to precedent or to the great books of equity, such as Joseph Story's early-nineteenth-century *Equity*

Jurisprudence. A survey of the most common maxims includes the following:

- Equity Suffers No Right to Be Lost nor Wrong to be Suffered Without a Remedy.
- Equity Follows the Law (which is a restatement of the next maxim).
- Equity is Available When There Is No Adequate Remedy at Law.
- Equity Looks to Substance Rather Than Form.
- Equity Regards as Done That Which Ought to Be Done.
- Equity Acts *in Personam*, Not *in Rem*.
- Equity Delights in Doing Justice and Not Just by Halves.
- Equity Abhors Forfeitures.
- Equality is Equity.
- Equity Aids the Vigilant, Not Those Who Slumber on Their Rights.
- He Who Comes into Equity Must Come with Clean Hands.
- He Who Seeks Equity Must Do Equity.

These maxims—as well as the general idea of "balancing the equities," according to which the chancellor will not make an unjust award of too much to one party at the unfair expense of another—persist as the guiding principles for awarding all equitable relief. As principles, they are still subject, at least in part, to their precedential use, but they are also of independent influence in every equitable decree. These ideas are illustrated in the following case:

Malnar v. Whitfield

Court of Appeals of Oklahoma, Division One
1989 Ok. Civ. App. 28; 774 P.2d 1075 (1989).

MacGUIGAN, J.:

[In 1979, Whitfield, a dentist, began to build an office building. Malnar, another dentist, then bought adjoining land. After Whitfield's building was finished but before Malnar began building his own, Malnar discovered Whitfield's building and driveway were partially on Malnar's land. Failing to settle the matter peaceably, Malnar destroyed part of Whitfield's driveway and blocked the rest. Whitfield sued, seeking damages for the destruction of his drive and an injunction to force Malnar to keep it open. Malnar sought an injunction against Whitfield, to order him to remove the building from Malnar's lands, and for some further damages. The trial court granted Whitfield's injunction, granting him an easement over Malnar's lands but then giving damages to Malnar of $3180 for the value of the easement he had lost. Malnar commenced this appeal, which had already been once to the state supreme court before returning for the final judgment. He also then built an otherwise undescribed "tall structure" to interfere with Whitfield's use of his building, and Whitfield sued again, this time winning damages for indirect contempt of court. Malnar also appealed that issue, which he lost; that discussion is omitted in this excerpt. Note in the opinion, Malnar is called the *appellant*, the one who brings the appeal, or the "adjoining property owner," and Whitfield the *appellee*, the one who defends the lower decision on appeal, or the "property owner."]

Appellant [Malnar] contends that the trial court erred in denying Appellant's request for a mandatory injunction based upon principles of equity.

The Supreme Court in its ruling to remand this case to the trial court in *Malnar v. Whitfield*, 708 P.2d 1093, 1096 (Okl. 1985), stated:

> The other factors which must be considered are the cost of removal, the value of the benefit of removal to be gained by the party requesting the injunction, and the availability of compensation by way of money damages.

Testimony during the course of the trial established that to remove that portion of the encroaching structure and reconstruct that space at another part of the structure would cost between $45,000.00 and $60,000.00. The property was appraised at $140,000.00 at the time of the original trial and, therefore, the cost of removal is a significant part of the value of the building. Testimony reflects that Appellant constructed his building after learning of the encroaching structure, and there is some evidence that Appellant even adjusted his architectural plans to relocate his structure in such a manner as to limit the use of Appellees' structure. There is also testimony that even if the encroaching structure of Appellees was removed, because of the position that Appellant placed his building on the lot, it would be of little or no value to Appellant's structure to remove the Appellees' building. Testimony also reflected that the value of Appellant's lot prior to construction was $35,000.00 and an appraiser determined that the loss in value to Appellant's lot because of the encroaching structure reduced Appellant's fair market value by $3,180.00. Appellant therefore could be compensated by the payment of $3,180.00 whereas it would cost Appellees between $45,000.00 and $60,000.00 to remove their structure. Thus, the trial court determined that granting damages to Appellant was the most equitable method of compensating the parties. The Supreme Court in the original *Malnar v. Whitfield* decision at 1096 stated:

> Once all of those competing equities are laid before the Court, the ultimate determination is largely a matter of an exercise of the discretion of the trial court.[10]
>
> We hold after examining the evidence that the judgment given by the trial court was not against the clear weight of the evidence. . . .
>
> We also affirm the trial court's decision that the mandatory injunction should be denied by reason of Appellant's own conduct as constituting "unclean hands" as the findings of the trial court are not against the clear weight of the evidence.
>
> Appellant asserts that the trial court's denial of the mandatory injunction and the consequent award of monetary damages and easements was an error of law. Appellees contend that the trial court sitting in equity has broad powers to fashion remedies suitable for the particular facts and circumstances of the case. The equitable jurisdiction of a trial court is not dependent upon specific statutory authorization. . . . An equity court is not bound by the rigid rules of common law but may adapt its relief and mold its decisions to satisfy the requirements of the case to protect and conserve the entities of the parties. . . . This was a specific factor recognized by the Supreme Court in the appeal of the original case and remand of this matter.[11] The trial court recognized that unless it gave judicial relief to the encroachment of Appellees' structure, Appellee could not have the beneficial enjoyment and use of his build-

---

[10] This sentence is a jurisprudential gem. What does the court mean by discretion in this context? Compare the discussion in Chapter Three.

[11] *Malnar v. Whitfield*, 708 P.2d at 1096.

ing. The evidence further reflected that Appellant had acted oppressively and maliciously to Appellees. Consequently, as a court of equity the trial court fashioned a remedy to meet the extremely unique facts and circumstances of this case. Appellant contends that *Fairlawn Cemetery Association v. First Presbyterian Church*, prohibits the trial court from granting easements and damages. However, we find the pronouncement in *Fairlawn* distinguishable from the present case as *Fairlawn* did not state that a court cannot award easements and damages. In *Fairlawn*, defendant's encroachment transpired long after the plaintiff constructed a fence and, furthermore, the encroachment created an immediate threat to plaintiff's property. We find that the principal [maxims] of equity [are] that one who seeks equity must do equity and come into court with clean hands. In the present case the record reflects that Appellant acted in an oppressive and malicious manner. The trial court was therefore correct to grant to Appellees a limited use to maintain their present utilization of their building.

Therefore, . . . the trial court's refusal to grant a mandatory injunction; its decision to compensate Appellant by suitable monetary damages and its granting to Appellees the right of continued use and enjoyment of their property was correct.

. . . .

Affirmed.

QUESTIONS AND COMMENTS

1. It is important to distinguish at least three different ways in which the notion of equity is employed in contemporary legal opinions:

   A. Sometimes *equity* refers to the law associated historically with the courts of equity. Remember, the primary features of these courts are that

      (1) they had no juries,

      (2) their remedies were always *in personam*, namely, an injunction compelling the defendant to act in a particular way, and

      (3) the approach toward the law is flexible and suited to solving the problem before the court.

Which aspects of this opinion reflect these historical practices?

B. Sometimes *equity* invokes a general principle of fairness. This appears to be what the court had in mind when they referred to
the "competing equities" of the case. Recall that in Romance
languages, the cognate term for *equitable* is as close as one can get
in these languages to the notion of fairness and fair play. Thus in
French the notion of a fair trial is typically translated as *procés
équitable*.

C. Sometimes the notion of "equitable jurisdiction" implies broad
judicial power to fashion new and novel remedies, such as granting an easement (usufruct or, in French, *usufruit*) to one side in
this case and damages to the other.

2. The term *équité* is used twice in the French Civil Code. There are
some similarities with the Anglo-American idea of equity, particularly
as used in the instant case. In the first application, § 565, the code
refers to the problem of determining the ownership of two things
that have become merged. The resolution of the case should be totally "subordinated to the principles of natural equity," and the judge
should decide each unforeseen case on the basis of its unique circumstances. This bears a strong resemblance to the problem of adjusting
the rights between the two warring neighbors in this case. In the
second provision, Article 1135 of the *Code civil* guides the process of
contract interpretation by specifying that contracts are binding according the demands of "*équité*, law, and custom." This sounds like
equity. The Dalloz commentary says explicitly that this form of equity is not a source of law. (See Dalloz, *Code civil*, 99th ed. 2000, Art.
1135, n 1.)

3. Note that calling this case an exercise of equitable jurisdiction implies
that the parties had no right to a jury trial. (See the Seventh Amendment to the Constitution, which guarantees jury trials only in "suits
at common law.") Nonetheless, the court could devise a remedy that
included some elements that originated in the common law rather
than in equity. For example, the notion of an easement was part of
the common law of estates, and damages were the characteristic remedy available at law.

4. How predictable was this case? Recall that John Selden (1584–1654),

an English jurist and scholar and cosponsor of the 1628 Petition of Right, argued that the awards of equity lacked the predictability of law in *Table Talks: Being the Discourses of John Selden, Esq. . . . Relating Especially to Religion and State* (1689), which also contains his most famous remark on equity: " 'Tis all one as if they should make the Standard for the measure, we call a Foot, a Chancellor's Foot; what an uncertain measure would this be! One Chancellor has a long Foot, another a short Foot, a Third an indifferent foot. 'Tis the same thing in the Chancellor's Conscience." Do you agree? Is the predictability of equity enhanced by its usual failure to employ a jury as the finder of fact?

5. One of the most important arenas in which equity functions in the United States is as the source of remedies against the government. Sovereign immunity generally prevents actions against the federal and state governments for damages, except in certain limited tort claims allowed by statute, such as for recoveries for injuries sustained in an automobile accident caused by a government car. (See the Federal Torts Claims Act, 28 U.S.C. § 2401.) But in a whole range of disputes from school integration to the management of state prisons, the courts have invoked the injunction as the best tool for granting constitutional relief. These actions, tried without juries, are subject to the maxims of equity as well as to constitutional principles.

6. You should think of these two chapters as an introduction to the vocabulary and the grammar of a complex body of law. All of these features of the law of property, whether arising from statutes, from the common law benches, or from equity, represent the distinctive and unifying structure of the common law. As we have seen, this structure continues to provide the deciding factor in many current legal disputes, but it can be best understood as an artifact from the peculiar history of the Anglo-American common law.

■

Further Reading

An argument for a comparative understanding of equity, as well as a fuller description of the maxims of equity, is in Steve Sheppard, "Equity and the Law," in *Encyclopedia of Life Support Systems (EOLSS)* (Aaron Swabach ed.), developed under the auspices of UNESCO (Oxford: EOLSS Publishers, 2003). (See also http://www.eolss.net.) An excellent discussion of equity as the basis of constitutional remedies and constitutional law generally is Peter Charles Hoffer, *The Law's Conscience: Equitable Constitutionalism in America* (Chapel Hill: University of North Carolina Press, 1990). Two works by Ralph Newman consider the comparative aspect of equity: *Equity and Law: A Comparative Study* (New York: Oceana Publications, 1961) and *Equity in the World's Legal Systems: A Comparative Study* (Brussels: Établissements Émile Bruylant, 1973); the latter includes the wonderful essay by Peter Stein, "Equitable Principles in Roman Law," which may also be found in Peter Stein, *The Character and Influence of the Roman Civil Law: Historical Essays* (London: Hambledon Press, 1988). The greatest work on equity in U.S. history remains, however, Joseph Story's *Commentary on Equity Jurisprudence* (Boston: Little, Brown and Company, 1846).

SEVENTEEN

Contemporary Property

It is difficult for an outsider to grasp the importance of private property in American legal and political culture. Private property was at the core of the founders' vision of a new society; it was critical in the Civil War, when a plantation-based, slave-owning South sought to defend its way of life; and it remains a foundation of the American understanding of what makes democracy work. The centrality of private property in the Constitutional structure became evident when the framers redrafted the famous line in the Declaration of Independence that all men "are endowed with certain unalienable rights, among them life, liberty, and the pursuit of happiness." In the prior draft, the right to pursue happiness had been a right of property. The final language of the latter phrase impressed the drafters of the postwar Japanese Constitution so much that they included it as a way of expressing the new orientation toward individualism in Japanese culture.[1] But it apparently struck the drafters of the American

---

[1] Japanese Const. (1946), Art. 13 [Individual Rights]:

    1. All of the people shall be respected as individuals.

    2. Their right to life, liberty, and the pursuit of happiness shall, to the extent that it does not interfere with the public welfare, be the supreme consideration in legislation and in other governmental affairs.

Constitution as too vague, for when the Bill of Rights was adopted in 1791, the critical trilogy of American law became "life, liberty, and property." The right to private property took the place of the "pursuit of happiness" in the American commitment to basic human rights.

To quote the relevant portions of the Fifth Amendment: "No person . . . shall be deprived of life, liberty, or property, without due process of law; nor shall private property be taken for public use, without just compensation." The same principle is made applicable to the states in the Fourteenth Amendment: "[N]or shall any State deprive any person of life, liberty, or Property, without due Process of law." Both in the Fifth and the Fourteenth Amendments, the right to private property is placed on a plane equal to life and liberty.

This is an extraordinary statement of American values, particularly in comparison to the values expressed in the postwar constitutions and international treaties protecting human rights. The body of the European Convention of Human Rights (1949) fails to mention private property,[2] although the Universal Declaration of Human Rights (1948) does recognize, in Article 17, that everyone has the right to own property and no one may be arbitrarily deprived of property rights. The Canadian Charter of Rights and Freedoms shows great concern about the rights of criminal defendants and the rights of Francophones to speak their language but says nothing about private property. This casual attitude toward private property is a rather puzzling state of affairs.

The German Basic Law of 1949 includes a reference to the protection of private property in Article 14(1) but then immediately qualifies this protection in Article 14(2): "Property entails obligations. Its enjoyment should simultaneously serve the common good." No one senses about life, liberty, human dignity, equality, or other basic rights that they "entail obligations." The German phrase *Eigentum verpflichtet* ("property entails obligations") is the modern equivalent of the erstwhile apology for nobility: *noblesse oblige* ("Noble status entails obligations").

It is not surprising that the former Communist states express a strong guarantee of private property. The Russian Constitution of 1993, Article 35, declares unequivocally: "The right of private property shall be protected by law." The articles then, in conformity with the American Fifth

---

[2] The Protocol of the European Convention (1952) Article 1 does refer to the right of every person to "peaceful enjoyment of his possessions."

Amendment, protect property owners against the state's taking property without just compensation. One thing that is intriguing about all these provisions, however, is that they do not distinguish between real property and chattels, immovables and movables.

The striking feature of the American commitment to private property is that it did not arise as a reaction to communal ownership or to some other perceived abuse in prerevolutionary society. The commitment to the importance of private property expresses a certain conception of how democracy could take hold and flourish. Private property provides a basis for individuals to act independently of the state. If they are secure in their homes and their income from their lands, they can challenge the government and hold it properly accountable.

In the American view, then, private property in land is part of an ensemble of rights that serve to strengthen the democratic independence of citizens. Many libertarians argue that the Second Amendment—the alleged right to bear arms—also supports the power of the citizenry to resist a potentially dictatorial government.[3] Protecting the free exercise of religion also promotes an alternative to the secular sovereign—by according special exemptions from the law to religious belief and thereby recognizing that citizens think of themselves as subservient to a divine lawgiver.

Under this distinctively American view, the process of promoting freedom and democracy requires opposition to the state. Private property in land represents an opposition to the state because the ownership of land means that private individuals occupy space in much the same way a sovereign claims to rule a specific national territory.[4] For these purposes, the critical feature of property is that it is property in land. Communist societies permitted the private ownership of cars and other movables. In feudal England, peasants owned their livestock and their personal effects. When we speak of the political significance of private property, we

---

[3] For a nuanced analysis of the Second Amendment and its history, see Richard Uviller and William Merkel, *The Militia and the Right to Arms, or, How the Second Amendment Fell Silent* (Durham, NC: Duke University Press, 2003).

[4] The same symbolic imitation of the state occurs when individuals bear arms (the state no longer has a monopoly) and when individuals are allowed exemptions from the law on the grounds of their religious beliefs—say, a right to slaughter animals in violation of the rules designed to avoid cruelty to animals (deference to an alternative lawgiver).

really mean private property land. Only the ownership of land threatens the dominance of the state.

The alternative view is that one need not oppose the state in order to promote freedom and democracy. The state can be a partner in these ventures, and indeed many Continental Europeans think of the state in this way. We need not decide who is right in this debate about the importance of private property in land in supporting the movement toward democracy, and of course there is no reason to assume that democracy in the United States today is stronger than in Canada, Continental Europe, or several countries in Asia. We should acknowledge merely that Americans have nourished a strong faith in private property in land as the foundation of individual freedom.

The remarkable feature of this faith is that it turned feudalism on its head. The law of real property began in England as a system for maintaining the authority and power of the king and nobility. In the New World, the ownership of land became a symbol of democratic independence from the state. All the old forms of feudalism were retained, but the function and meaning of real property was transformed.

In the United States, the primary threat to private property is not the federal government but state and local governments. There are basically three different ways that a state government can undermine the right to the private ownership of land.

1. It can impose taxes. As we know from *McCulloch* in Chapter Seven, the power to tax is the power to destroy. But no American property holder has ever successfully objected to taxes imposed on real property, provided that the levying of the taxes does not violate equal protection of the law under the Fourteenth Amendment.

2. It can take the property under the power of eminent domain. To do this, it must be able to justify the taking under the Fifth Amendment as serving a "public use," and it must provide "just compensation."

3. It can deprive the owner of a portion of the use and value of the property by imposing regulations on the use of land. Every zoning regulation has this effect on the use of privately owned land, as do many laws protecting the environment. The problem is when the regulation is so intrusive that it constitutes a "taking" under the principles of the Fifth Amendment. This kind of taking is called "inverse condemnation" or an "inverse taking." When and if an inverse taking requires compensation is

one of the most hotly contested issues in American law. The problem is addressed in the following case:

Connecticut v. Heller

Supreme Court of Connecticut
123 Conn. 492 (1937).

BROWN, J.:

[Heller owned thirty-eight acres, including his house and a pond, from which a brook flowed 4,200 feet into a reservoir, part of the water system of the Bridgeport Hydraulic Company, which supplies water to Bridgeport, Connecticut, and other towns. On July 11, 1936, Heller walked out of his family house and swam in the pond on his land. He was arrested, charged with violating section 2542 of the Connecticut General Statutes: "Any person who shall bathe in any reservoir from which the inhabitants of any town, city or borough are supplied with water, or in any lake, pond or stream tributary to such reservoir," may be fined, imprisoned, or both. He was convicted and appealed.]

The fundamental question determinative of the appeal is whether § 2542 as applied to the defendant in forbidding his bathing pursuant to his property right in a brook flowing through his own land, is a valid exercise of the State's police power, or is unconstitutional as depriving him of property rights without compensation. It is unquestioned that the defendant as riparian owner had a right which included ordinary and reasonable bathing privileges in this brook by himself, his family, and inmates and guests of his household. . . . It is further undisputed that § 2542 can only be sustained as an exercise of the State's police power. Furthermore, it is not disputed that the object of the statute in question is to protect the health of citizens using water distributed through these reservoirs, and that thus its purpose affords a proper basis for the exercise of the police power inherent in the Legislature. . . . The issue for determination, therefore, is reduced to the sole question of whether or not this exercise of the police power for the purpose indicated, is so unreasonable as to violate the provisions of Section 11 of Article First of the Constitution of the State of Connecticut or Section 1 of Article XIV of the Amendments to the Constitution of the United States.

The foundation of the police power of a State is the overruling necessity of the public welfare. Thus it has been referred to as that inherent and plenary power which enables the State "to make and enforce rules and regulations concerning and to prevent and prohibit all things hurtful to the comfort and welfare of society. It has been aptly termed 'The Law of Overruling Necessity,' and compared with the right of self-protection of the individual, it is involved in the very right and idea of government itself, and based on the two maxims that, 'The Public Welfare is the Highest Law,' and that 'One must so use his own right as not to injure that of another.' " Accordingly all property of every person is owned subject to this power resting in the State. It is an incident of title. "The power to legislate for the safety, health or welfare of its people, is inherent in the State by virtue of its sovereignty. All property is held subject to this power. And all property, too, is held upon the implied promise of its owner or user that it shall not be used against the public welfare."

It is pursuant to these principles that the State may regulate one's use of his property. "In short, it [the police power] may regulate any business or the use of any property in the interest of the public health, safety or welfare, provided this be done reasonably. To that extent the public interest is supreme and the private interest must yield. Eminent domain takes property because it is useful to the public. The police power regulates the use of property or impairs the rights in property, because the free exercise of these rights is detrimental to public interest" (Freund, *Police Power* §511 [other citations omitted]). "The use of property may be regulated as the public welfare demands. . . . Beyond this, private property cannot be interfered with under the police power, but resort must be had to the power of eminent domain and compensation made" (1 Lewis, *Eminent Domain* (3rd ed.) p. 492 §249). "The protection of the public safety, health or morals, by the exercise of the police power, is not within the inhibitions of the Constitution. And since all property is held subject to such regulation, there is no obligation upon the State to indemnify the owner of property for the damage done him by the legitimate exercise of the police power. Property so damaged is not taken: its use is regulated in order to promote the public welfare" (*Connecticut v. Samford*, 95 Conn. 26, 30).

But there are definite limits upon the application of the foregoing principles. "The power of regulation by government is not unlimited; it cannot, as we have stated, be imposed unless it bears rational relation to the subjects which fall fairly within the police power and unless the means used are not within constitutional inhibitions. The means used will fall within these inhibitions whenever they are destructive, confiscatory, or so unreasonable as to be arbitrary" (*Euclid v. Ambler Realty Co.* 272 U.S. 365). "A large discretion is necessarily vested in the Legislature to determine not only what the interests of public health, security and morals require, but what measures are necessary for the protection of such interests . . ." (*Young v. Lemieux*, 79 Conn. 434). Furthermore, " 'incidental damage to property resulting from governmental activities, or laws passed in the promotion of the public welfare, is not considered a taking of the property for which compensation must be made' " (*State v. Hillman*, 110 Conn. 92, 104).

The foregoing principles are established by abundant authority. The difficulty arises in their application, to determine where the proper exercise of the police power ends and that of the other governmental power of eminent domain begins, that is, how far the State can properly go to deprive an owner of valuable rights under the former without compensation, as distinguished from necessary resort to the latter with compensation. The right of the State in the exercise of its police power to limit the use of property even when prejudicial to the pecuniary interests of the owner, has been made increasingly clear by our more recent decisions. Whether a statute enacted pursuant to the police power is a means reasonable in quality and extent, and in time, place and circumstance, presents a question to be determined by the court. It is the court's duty in such case, in the exercise of great care and caution, to make every presumption and intendment in favor of the validity of the statute, and to sustain it unless its invalidity is beyond a reasonable doubt. It is in the light of the principles above stated, that we must determine whether the provisions of § 2542 are so unreasonable as to constitute an unconstitutional invasion of the defendant's rights.

The defendant claims the statute is invalid in that its unlimited scope constitutes an unreasonable exercise of the police power, it being contended that it goes far beyond what is necessary to accomplish the legislative purpose and so does not bear a reasonable relation thereto.

... [T]he tendency of such pollution to produce public injury, even though no actual injury occurs, affords ground sufficient to sustain the Legislature's act. Upon the record before us we cannot hold that bathing in a tributary of a reservoir might not have such a tendency to endanger the health of users of the water that the Legislature might not reasonably prohibit it. It is our conclusion that the statute by its terms is not of such broad scope that it fails to bear a rational relation to the protection of the public health, thus constituting an unreasonable exercise of the police power. . . .

The further and basic contention is, that since this statute entirely deprives the defendant of his valuable property right of bathing in this stream, it goes beyond regulation within the police power, and constitutes a taking, warranted only under eminent domain proceedings with proper compensation. The principles above recited make clear that this conclusion does not necessarily follow. Of the legion of decisions illustrative of this, we refer to but two cases very closely analogous to the present. In the former, a statute for the protection of Boston Harbor, forbidding any person to take stones, gravel, or sand from the shore, was sustained as against one taking where he owned the fee, as was the statute in the latter forbidding any person to fish with a line in a stream or lake, even as against an owner fishing upon his own land. Thus a law which in fact in certain respects deprives the owner of a use of his property involving its physical consumption, if to protect a common right of all citizens, is valid within the police power. . . . "Regulations may result to some extent, practically in the taking of property, or the restricting of its uses, and yet not be deemed confiscatory or unreasonable."

There is no distinction in principle between the legal restriction in the present case which without compensation deprives the owner of his right to bathe in the stream crossing his property, and that in *State v. Hillman, supra,* prohibiting the use of property for business purposes; or that in *Windsor v. Whitney, supra,* depriving him of the right to build on the entire area of his lot; or that in *Ingham v. Brooks,* 95 Conn. 317, denying an owner the right to move a building from one place to another, which was held within the police power although the ordinance in question was void by reason of the arbitrary and unfettered discretion in the town officials thereunder; or that in *Application of St. Bernard Cemetery Asso.,* 58 Conn. 91, denying an owner the right to use its property for cemetery purposes unless the court determined such use would not be detrimental to public health; or those in a number of cases that have come before us involving various zoning ordinances. The restriction imposed by § 2542 was not a taking contravening any constitutional provision, but rather a regulation within the State's police power.

Two decisions, where the precise question here presented on substantially the same factual situation was determined, have reached diametrically opposite conclusions. In the earlier case of *People v. Hulbert*, 131 Mich. 156, decided in 1902, where the defendant, a riparian owner on a pond or lake from which a city took its water supply, was convicted of bathing therein, under a statute which made it a criminal offense to pollute such waters, the court held in a very brief statement citing no authorities that as such owner the defendant had a right to a reasonable use of the waters of the lake including the right to bathe and swim therein, and that he could not be deprived of this right by the police power of the State. The later case of *State v. Morse*, decided in 1911, on a similar state of facts, criticized the earlier case and arrived at the opposite conclusion. In the case of *Battle Creek v. Goguac Resort Asso., Ltd.*, 181 Mich. 241, decided in 1914, in an opinion concurred in by three of the judges of the equally divided court, some question is intimated as to the soundness of the court's decision in the *Hulbert* case.

In the *Morse* case the court pointed out that since the defendant's right to bathe conflicted with the public's rights concerning its health, safety, and welfare, the former must yield and the latter prevail, and that the enforcement and protection of these paramount rights is the proper function of the police power. It went on to conclude that within the principles definitive of the police power and those applicable to the interpretation of enactments pursuant thereto, which we have already mentioned, the action of the state board of health in question was a valid exercise of the police power. We reach a similar conclusion in the case before us. What the court says in the *Morse* case well states the effect of the statute here: "Such use in such circumstances may be prohibited in a valid exercise of the police power. The owner's rights are not then 'taken' in a constitutional sense; or, if this statement savors too much of refinement of reasoning, as some suggest, the 'taking' is not such as the Constitution prohibits. The beneficial use of the property is curtailed in some measure but all the other incidents of ownership are left unimpaired. The fact that this is a property right does not determine the question." The regulation imposed by § 2542 is neither destructive, confiscatory nor arbitrary, but is on the contrary upon all the facts in the case, reasonable in time, place, and circumstance, and therefore a reasonable exercise of the police power. . . .

There is no error. In this opinion the other judges concurred.

∎

QUESTIONS AND COMMENTS

1. Note the options available to a court hearing a challenge to an inverse taking. The question could be posed whether the inverse taking is a public use under the Fifth Amendment. If not, it violates the Fifth Amendment. Or the question could be whether the taking is invalid because, although the government takes the land for a public use, it does not provide just compensation. If there is no just compensation, the taking violates the Fifth Amendment. Notice that in this case the court takes a third route: It denies that there is any taking at all. But are not the arguments it uses the same as the court would make to conclude that the taking was a "public use"? After all, what it means is that the regulation is a "reasonable exercise of the police power."

2. The word *police* should not confuse you. In this context, the word means that the state should pursue the common good. This use of the word is related to the word *policy*, as explained in Chapter Three. Note that the states have a general police power, but the federal government, as a government of limited powers, does not.

3. The defendant Heller gets hit twice. First, he loses the right to use his land the way he wants to, and then he suffers a criminal conviction because he thinks that his rights are absolute. Do you have any trouble with this?

∎

Limiting Other People's Use of Land

The common law also gives landholders two quite powerful tools—trespass and nuisance—for regulating their neighbors' conduct that affects their land. Trespass is an action brought by a landholder for another person's entry on the land without a license to do so. A landholder's right to exclude is not absolute, and certain state officers, such as sheriffs, fire-fighters, police, and the like, cannot be trespassers when carrying out their duties. Neither can a holder of an easement be a trespasser, so long as the easement holder is using the easement within its scope. (Recall the recognition of the easement in the *Malnar* case in the previous chapter.) Another exception is recognized for emergency situations, as we will see in *Vincent v. Lake Erie Transportation Co.*, a famous torts case discussed in Chapter Twenty-Two. Otherwise, a possessor of land sues for damages for past trespasses or for an injunction against current and future trespasses. The trespass need not occur in person but by animal or chattel, so that the neighbor's dog in the garden is a trespass by the neighbor, as is the bullet from the neighbor's rifle, fired across the property at a target on the other side.

Nuisance is an action for the use of another's land in a manner that harms one's own. It does not require a physical presence on the land that is harmed. If the owner of Blackacre runs a rock festival in the back fields so that the noise makes the owner of Whiteacre unable to enjoy that property, the owner of Whiteacre has an action in nuisance against the owner of Blackacre, even if there is no trespass on Whiteacre. The difficulty would be proving damages, but this can often be established if one can prove that the resale value of one's property is diminished or if the cost of buying an easement to allow the nuisance would have been significant.

Serious problems arise when an industrial enterprise burdens land belonging to another but does so in a manner that benefits the public as a whole. The problem then is whether the affected party can force the enterprise to shut down, thus injuring the public. This is the problem faced in the following case:

■

Boomer v. Atlantic Cement Co.

Court of Appeals of New York
26 N.Y.2d 219; 257 N.E.2d 870 (1970)

BERGAN, J.:

Defendant operates a large cement plant near Albany. These are actions for injunction and damages by neighboring land owners alleging injury to property from dirt, smoke and vibration emanating from the plant. A nuisance has been found after trial, temporary damages have been allowed; but an injunction has been denied.

The public concern with air pollution arising from many sources in industry and in transportation is currently accorded ever wider recognition accompanied by a growing sense of responsibility in State and Federal Governments to control it. Cement plants are obvious sources of air pollution in the neighborhoods where they operate.

But there is now before the court private litigation in which individual property owners have sought specific relief from a single plant operation. The threshold question raised by the division of view on this appeal is whether the court should resolve the litigation between the parties now before it as equitably as seems possible; or whether, seeking promotion of the general public welfare, it should channel private litigation into broad public objectives.

A court performs its essential function when it decides the rights of parties before it. Its decision of private controversies may sometimes greatly affect public issues. Large questions of law are often resolved by the manner in which private litigation is decided. But this is normally an incident to the court's main function to settle controversy. It is a rare exercise of judicial power to use a decision in private litigation as a purposeful mechanism to achieve direct public objectives greatly beyond the rights and interests before the court.

Effective control of air pollution is a problem presently far from solution even with the full public and financial powers of government. In large measure adequate technical procedures are yet to be developed and some that appear possible may be economically impracticable.

It seems apparent that the amelioration of air pollution will depend on technical research in great depth; on a carefully balanced consideration of the economic impact of close regulation; and of the actual effect on public health. It is likely to require massive public expenditure and to demand more than any local community can accomplish and to depend on regional and interstate controls.

A court should not try to do this on its own as a by-product of private litigation and it seems manifest that the judicial establishment is neither equipped in the limited nature of any judgment it can pronounce nor prepared to lay down and implement an effective policy for the elimination of air pollution. This is an area beyond the circumference of one private lawsuit. It is a direct responsibility for government and should not thus be undertaken as an incident to solving a dispute between property owners and a single cement plant—one of many—in the Hudson River valley.

The cement making operations of defendant have been found by the court at Special Term to have damaged the nearby properties of plaintiffs in these two actions. That court, as it has been noted, accordingly found defendant maintained a nuisance and this has been affirmed at the Appellate Division. The total damage to plaintiffs' properties is, however, relatively small in comparison with the value of defendant's operation and with the consequences of the injunction which plaintiffs seek.

The ground for the denial of injunction, notwithstanding the finding both that there is a nuisance and that plaintiffs have been damaged substantially, is the large disparity in economic consequences of the nuisance and of the injunction. This theory cannot, however, be sustained without overruling a doctrine which has been consistently reaffirmed in several leading cases in this court and which has never been disavowed here, namely that where a nuisance has been found and where there has been any substantial damage shown by the party complaining an injunction will be granted.

The rule in New York has been that such a nuisance will be enjoined although marked disparity be shown in economic consequence between the effect of the injunction and the effect of the nuisance.

The problem of disparity in economic consequence was sharply in focus in *Whalen v. Union Bag & Paper Co.* A pulp mill entailing an investment of more than a million dollars polluted a stream in which plaintiff, who owned a farm, was "a lower riparian owner." The economic loss to plaintiff from this pollution was small. This court, reversing the Appellate Division, reinstated the injunction. . . . "Although the damage to the plaintiff may be slight as compared with the defendant's expense of abating the condition, that is not a good reason for refusing an injunction." . . . The rule laid down in that case, then, is that whenever the damage resulting from a nuisance is found not "unsubstantial," viz., $100 a year, injunction would follow. This states a rule that had been followed in this court with marked consistency.

There are cases where injunction has been denied. *McCann v. Chasm Power Co.* is one of them. There, however, the damage shown by plaintiffs was not only unsubstantial, it was non-existent. . . . Thus if, within *Whalen v. Union Bag & Paper Co.* (supra) which authoritatively states the rule in New York, the damage to plaintiffs in these present cases from defendant's cement plant is "not unsubstantial," an injunction should follow.

[Returning to this case] although the court at Special Term and the Appellate Division held that injunction should be denied, it was found that plaintiffs had been damaged in various specific amounts up to the time of the trial and damages to the respective plaintiffs were awarded for those amounts. The effect of this was, injunction having been denied, plaintiffs could maintain successive actions at law for damages thereafter as further damage was incurred.

The court at Special Term also found the amount of permanent damage attributable to each plaintiff, for the guidance of the parties in the event both sides stipulated to the payment and acceptance of such permanent damage as a settlement of all the controversies among the parties. The total of permanent damages to all plaintiffs thus found was $185,000. This basis of adjustment has not resulted in any stipulation by the parties.

This result at Special Term and at the Appellate Division is a departure from a rule that has become settled; but to follow the rule literally in these cases would be to close down the plant at once. This court is fully agreed to avoid that immediately drastic remedy; the difference in view is how best to avoid it.

One alternative is to grant the injunction but postpone its effect to a specified future date to give opportunity for technical advances to permit defendant to eliminate the nuisance; another is to grant the injunction conditioned on the payment of permanent damages to plaintiffs which would compensate them for the total economic loss to their property present and future caused by defendant's operations. For reasons which will be developed the court chooses the latter alternative.

If the injunction were to be granted unless within a short period— e.g., 18 months—the nuisance be abated by improved methods, there would be no assurance that any significant technical improvement would occur.

The parties could settle this private litigation at any time if defendant paid enough money and the imminent threat of closing the plant would build up the pressure on defendant. If there were no improved techniques found, there would inevitably be applications to the court at Special Term for extensions of time to perform on showing of good faith efforts to find such techniques.

Moreover, techniques to eliminate dust and other annoying by-products of cement making are unlikely to be developed by any research the defendant can undertake within any short period, but will depend on the total resources of the cement industry Nationwide and throughout the world. The problem is universal wherever cement is made.

For obvious reasons the rate of the research is beyond control of defendant. If at the end of 18 months the whole industry has not found a technical solution a court would be hard put to close down this one cement plant if due regard be given to equitable principles.

On the other hand, to grant the injunction unless defendant pays plaintiffs such permanent damages as may be fixed by the court seems to do justice between the contending parties. All of the attributions of economic loss to the properties on which plaintiffs' complaints are based will have been redressed.

The nuisance complained of by these plaintiffs may have other public or private consequences, but these particular parties are the only ones who have sought remedies and the judgment proposed will fully redress them. The limitation of relief granted is a limitation only within the four corners of these actions and does not foreclose public health or other public agencies from seeking proper relief in a proper court.

It seems reasonable to think that the risk of being required to pay permanent damages to injured property owners by cement plant owners would itself be a reasonable effective spur to research for improved techniques to minimize nuisance.

The power of the court to condition on equitable grounds the continuance of an injunction on the payment of permanent damages seems undoubted.

The damage base here suggested is consistent with the general rule in those nuisance cases where damages are allowed. "Where a nuisance is of such a permanent and unabatable character that a single recovery can be had, including the whole damage past and future resulting therefrom, there can be but one recovery." It has been said that permanent damages are allowed where the loss recoverable would obviously be small as compared with the cost of removal of the nuisance. . . .

The judgment, by allowance of permanent damages imposing a servitude on land, which is the basis of the actions, would preclude future recovery by plaintiffs or their grantees.

This should be placed beyond debate by a provision of the judgment that the payment by defendant and the acceptance by plaintiffs of permanent damages found by the court shall be in compensation for a servitude on the land. . . .

JASEN, J.

. . . It has long been the rule in this State, as the majority acknowledges, that a nuisance which results in substantial continuing damage to neighbors must be enjoined. To now change the rule to permit the cement company to continue polluting the air indefinitely upon the payment of permanent damages is, in my opinion, compounding the magnitude of a very serious problem in our State and Nation today. . . .

I see grave dangers in overruling our long-established rule of granting an injunction where a nuisance results in substantial continuing damage. In permitting the injunction to become inoperative upon the payment of permanent damages, the majority is, in effect, licensing a continuing wrong. It is the same as saying to the cement company, you may continue to do harm to your neighbors so long as you pay a fee for it. Furthermore, once such permanent damages are assessed and paid, the incentive to alleviate the wrong would be eliminated, thereby continuing air pollution of an area without abatement.

It is true that some courts have sanctioned the remedy here proposed by the majority in a number of cases, but none of the authorities relied upon by the majority are analogous to the situation before us. In those cases, the courts, in denying an injunction and awarding money damages, grounded their decision on a showing that the use to which the property was intended to be put was primarily for the public benefit. Here, on the other hand, it is clearly established that the cement company is creating a continuing air pollution nuisance primarily for its own private interest with no public benefit. . . .

I would enjoin the defendant cement company from continuing the discharge of dust particles upon its neighbors' properties unless, within 18 months, the cement company abated this nuisance.

It is not my intention to cause the removal of the cement plant from the Albany area, but to recognize the urgency of the problem stemming from this stationary source of air pollution, and to allow the company a specified period of time to develop a means to alleviate this nuisance.

I am aware that the trial court found that the most modern dust control devices available have been installed in defendant's plant, but, I submit, this does not mean that better and more effective dust control devices could not be developed within the time allowed to abate the pollution.

Moreover, I believe it is incumbent upon the defendant to develop such devices, since the cement company, at the time the plant commenced production (1962), was well aware of the plaintiffs' presence in the area, as well as the probable consequences of its contemplated operation. Yet, it still chose to build and operate the plant at this site.

In a day when there is a growing concern for clean air, highly developed industry should not expect acquiescence by the courts, but should, instead, plan its operations to eliminate contamination of our air and damage to its neighbors.

QUESTIONS AND COMMENTS

1. Think about this combination of remedies compared with other cases read in this course. How does the denial of the injunction plus damages compare with the result in *Malnar*? Suppose that Atlantic Cement was the government and it told Boomer that he must suffer air pollution on his land. Would that constitute a taking? Is this case, in effect, a judgment legitimating a private taking? Some states give private companies, especially utility companies, the power of eminent domain. Does Atlantic Cement have the right to take private property for a public use? Is it all right so far as they pay "just compensation"?

2. How does the interference with Boomer's property rights differ from restricting Heller in the use of his property? Why does Boomer get compensation while Heller goes to jail (perhaps)?

3. Suppose the government imposes a quarantine to prevent the spread of SARS. Are the people deprived of their freedom entitled to com-

pensation? The answer everywhere, we believe, would be no. But why not? Is not a quarantine a taking of liberty for public purposes?

■

Further Reading

The nature of modern property rights is explored in two books, building from the Lockean tradition: Jeremy Waldron, *The Right to Private Property* (Oxford: Oxford University Press, 1991), and James Penner, *The Idea of Property in Law* (Oxford: Oxford University Press, 2000). The classic argument against property rights remains Pierre-Joseph Proudhon, *What Is Property?* (Cambridge: Cambridge University Press, 1994). The economic analysis of property law is considered in Chapter Twenty-Three.

EIGHTEEN

The Frontiers of Property

The concept of property is central to American legal thinking. This follows from several legal propositions that attach more significant legal consequences to property than to contract rights. One of the primary propositions is the constitutional principle that neither the states nor the federal government may deprive one of property without due process of law. As a result of this idea, there is an enormous push to regard various government benefits as property rights. Social security, welfare payments, unemployment insurance, Medicaid—they could all be treated as vested property rights rather than as mere statutory entitlements. Calling them "property" raises procedural barriers to the government's denial of payment in particular cases: The officials must meet the standards of "due process"; they cannot simply decide that A deserves benefits and B does not. In an influential article written in the liberal spirit of the 1960s, Charles Reich introduced the term "the new property" to refer to these governmental entitlements.[1]

Property also serves as the basis for taking jurisdiction over a dispute *in rem* or, over the property. Under *Pennoyer* (Chapter Thirteen), a plaintiff

[1] Charles Reich, "The New Property," 73 *Yale L.J.* 733 (1964).

could get jurisdiction over any defendant simply by attaching the defendant's property within the jurisdiction. Thus, if a leasehold is a property interest according to the common law, then attaching the leasehold generates jurisdiction over the lessor wherever he or she happens to be. This rule was applied to shares of stock in *Schaffer*—also in Chapter Thirteen—but then the Supreme Court ruled that the same principles of fairness should apply to both *in rem* and *in personam* jurisdiction.

Property, tort, and contract are all associated with different writs at common law. The writ of trover presupposed a conversion of property. An allegation of conversion would justify not the return of the thing but damages for the loss. Significantly, there was no requirement to prove fault. The conversion—taking control and depriving the owner of his property—was sufficient to justify a duty to pay damages. To recall the terminology used in the 1927 German abortion case discussed in Chapter Two, the ground for liability was not a culpable but a *wrongful* conversion. Indeed, the law of conversion under German law provided a compelling illustration for German private lawyers of the nineteenth century of the difference between wrongdoing and culpability. The important point about conversion is that you interfere, without justification, with the rights of the owner. That in itself requires you to pay compensation.

The distinction between property and contract also plays a major role in criminal law. Breach of contract is never a crime. If there are exceptions, they are rare and would be associated with other wrongs, such as fraud. But taking and carrying away movable property is the core of the crime of theft. Unlawfully keeping possession of a thing entrusted to you is embezzlement.[2]

These ancient ideas come into play in the field of medical malpractice in the next case. If a person has a property right in his or her bodily parts, he or she abandons and forfeits that right in a medical operation only if informed of the full consequences of the operation. In this case, then, the plaintiff Moore would have a right to the profits gained by developing a patented cell line based on his spleen. In the *Moore* case, the problem is

---

[2] Unfortunately, in this book we cannot much devote much space to the fascinating twists and turns in the history of theft and embezzlement. The interested reader should refer to George P. Fletcher, *Rethinking Criminal Law*, Chapters One and Two (Oxford: Oxford University Press, 1978).

whether this conception of property in bodily parts is too rough and unwieldy to handle the complexities of the case. There are various questions you should think about as you read the opinion:

A. Was the plaintiff Moore wronged? How? Can we answer that question without knowing exactly how to characterize the legal problem?
B. If Moore *was* wronged, what is the best way—in law—to describe the wrong? Is it a problem of property or of tort? And what is the difference?
C. What is the appropriate remedy?

Moore v. The Regents of the University of California

Supreme Court of California
51 Cal. 3d 120; 793 P.2d 479 (1990)

PANELLI, J.:

I. Introduction

We granted review in this case to determine whether plaintiff has stated a cause of action against his physician and other defendants for using his cells in potentially lucrative medical research without his permission. . . . We hold that the complaint states a cause of action for breach of the physician's disclosure obligations, but not for conversion.

II. Facts

The plaintiff is John Moore (Moore), who underwent treatment for hairy-cell leukemia at the Medical Center of the University of California at Los Angeles (UCLA Medical Center). . . . Moore first visited UCLA Medical Center on October 5, 1976, shortly after he learned that he had hairy-cell leukemia. After hospitalizing Moore and "withdr[awing] extensive amounts of blood, bone marrow aspirate, and other bodily substances," [Dr.] Golde confirmed that diagnosis. At this time all defendants, including Golde, were aware that "certain blood products and blood components were of great value in a number of commercial and scientific efforts" and that access to a patient whose blood contained these substances would provide "competitive, commercial, and scientific advantages."

On October 8, 1976, Golde recommended that Moore's spleen be removed. . . . Moore signed a written consent form authorizing the splenectomy.

Before the operation, Golde and Quan "formed the intent and made arrangements to obtain portions of [Moore's] spleen following its removal" and to take them to a separate research unit. Golde gave written instructions to this effect on October 18 and 19, 1976. These research activities "were not intended to have . . . any relation to [Moore's] medical . . . care." . . .

Moore returned to the UCLA Medical Center several times between November 1976 and September 1983. He did so at Golde's direction and based upon representations "that such visits were necessary and required for his health and well-being, and based upon the trust inherent in and by virtue of the physician-patient relationship. . . ." On each of these visits Golde withdrew additional samples of "blood, blood serum, skin, bone marrow aspirate, and sperm." . . .

Sometime before August 1979, Golde established a cell line from Moore's T-lymphocytes [a type of white blood cell that produces proteins regulating the immune system]. On January 30, 1981, the Regents applied for a patent on the cell line, listing Golde and Quan as inventors. "[B]y virtue of an established policy . . . , [the] Regents, Golde, and Quan would share in any royalties or profits . . . arising out of [the] patent." The patent issued on March 20, 1984, naming Golde and Quan as the inventors of the cell line and the Regents as the assignee of the patent. . . .

With the Regents' assistance, Golde negotiated agreements for commercial development of the cell line and products to be derived from it. Under an agreement with Genetics Institute, Golde "became a paid consultant" and "acquired the rights to 75,000 shares of common stock." Genetics Institute also agreed to pay Golde and the Regents "at least $330,000 over three years, including a pro-rata share of [Golde's] salary and fringe benefits, in exchange for . . . exclusive access to the materials and research performed" on the cell line and products derived from it. On June 4, 1982, Sandoz "was added to the agreement," and compensation payable to Golde and the Regents was increased by $110,000. "[T]hroughout this period, . . . Quan spent as much as 70 [percent] of her time working for [the] Regents on research" related to the cell line.

Based upon these allegations, Moore attempted to state 13 causes of action. Each defendant demurred to each purported cause of action. The superior court, however, expressly considered the validity of only the first cause of action, conversion. Reasoning that the remaining causes of action incorporated the earlier, defective allegations, the superior court sustained a general demurrer to the entire complaint with leave to amend. . . .

With one justice dissenting, the Court of Appeal reversed, holding that the complaint did state a cause of action for conversion. The Court of Appeal agreed with the superior court that the allegations against Genetics Institute and Sandoz were insufficient, but directed the superior court to give Moore leave to amend. The Court of Appeal also directed the superior court to decide "the remaining causes of action, which [had] never been expressly ruled upon."

III. Discussion

A. Breach of Fiduciary Duty and Lack of Informed Consent

Moore repeatedly alleges that Golde failed to disclose the extent of his research and economic interests in Moore's cells before obtaining consent to the medical procedures by which the cells were extracted. These allegations, in our view, state a cause of action against Golde for invading a legally protected interest of his patient. This cause of action can properly be characterized either as the breach of a fiduciary duty to disclose facts material to the patient's consent or, alternatively, as the performance of medical procedures without first having obtained the patient's informed consent.

B. Conversion

Moore also attempts to characterize the invasion of his rights as a conversion—a tort that protects against interference with possessory and ownership interests in personal property. He theorizes that he continued to own his cells following their removal from his body, at least for the purpose of directing their use, and that he never consented to their use in potentially lucrative medical research. Thus, to complete Moore's argument, defendants' unauthorized use of his cells constitutes a conversion. As a result of the alleged conversion, Moore claims a proprietary interest in each of the products that any of the defendants might ever create from his cells or the patented cell line.

No court, however, has ever in a reported decision imposed conversion liability for the use of human cells in medical research. While
that fact does not end our inquiry, it raises a flag of caution. In effect,
what Moore is asking us to do is to impose a tort duty on scientists to
investigate the consensual pedigree of each human cell sample used in
research. To impose such a duty, which would affect medical research
of importance to all of society, implicates policy concerns far removed
from the traditional, two-party ownership disputes in which the law of
conversion arose. Invoking a tort theory originally used to determine
whether the loser or the finder of a horse had the better title, Moore
claims ownership of the results of socially important medical research,
including the genetic code for chemicals that regulate the functions of
every human being's immune system.

. . . [W]e first consider whether the tort of conversion clearly gives
Moore a cause of action under existing law. We do not believe it does.
Because of the novelty of Moore's claim to own the biological materials
at issue, to apply the theory of conversion in this context would frankly
have to be recognized as an extension of the theory. Therefore, we
consider next whether it is advisable to extend the tort to this context.

I. MOORE'S CLAIM UNDER EXISTING LAW

> To establish a conversion, plaintiff must establish an actual in-
> terference with his ownership or right of possession. . . .
> Where plaintiff neither has title to the property alleged to have
> been converted, nor possession thereof, he cannot maintain an
> action for conversion . . .

Since Moore clearly did not expect to retain possession of his cells
following their removal, to sue for their conversion he must have retained an ownership interest in them. But there are several reasons to
doubt that he did retain any such interest. First, no reported judicial
decision supports Moore's claim, either directly or by close analogy.
Second, California statutory law drastically limits any continuing interest of a patient in excised cells. Third, the subject matters of the Regents' patent—the patented cell line and the products derived from it—
cannot be Moore's property.

Neither the Court of Appeal's opinion, the parties' briefs, nor our
research discloses a case holding that a person retains a sufficient interest
in excised cells to support a cause of action for conversion. We do not

find this surprising, since the laws governing such things as human tissues, transplantable organs, blood, fetuses, pituitary glands, corneal tissue, and dead bodies deal with human biological materials as objects sui generis, regulating their disposition to achieve policy goals rather than abandoning them to the general law of personal property. It is these specialized statutes, not the law of conversion, to which courts ordinarily should and do look for guidance on the disposition of human biological materials.

Lacking direct authority for importing the law of conversion into this context, Moore relies, as did the Court of Appeal, primarily on decisions addressing privacy rights. One line of cases involves unwanted publicity.[3] These opinions hold that every person has a proprietary interest in his own likeness and that unauthorized, business use of a likeness is redressible as a tort. But in neither opinion did the authoring court expressly base its holding on property law. Each court stated, following Prosser,[4] that it was "pointless" to debate the proper characterization of the proprietary interest in a likeness. For purposes of determining whether the tort of conversion lies, however, the characterization of the right in question is far from pointless. Only property can be converted.

Not only are the wrongful-publicity cases irrelevant to the issue of conversion but the analogy to them seriously misconceives the nature of the genetic materials and research involved in this case. Moore, adopting the analogy originally advanced by the Court of Appeal, argues that "[i]f the courts have found a sufficient proprietary interest in one's persona, how could one not have a right in one's own genetic material, something far more profoundly the essence of one's human uniqueness than a name or a face?" However, as the defendants' patent makes clear—and the complaint, too, if read with an understanding of the scientific terms which it has borrowed from the patent—the goal and result of defendants' efforts has been to manufacture lymphokines (a gene produces lymphokines by attracting protein molecules). Lym-

---

[3] *Lugosi v. Universal Pictures* (1979) 25 Cal.3d 813 (160 Cal.Rptr. 323, 603 P.2d 425, 10 A.L.R.4th 1150); *Motschenbacher v. R. J. Reynolds Tobacco Company* (9th Cir. 1974) 498 F.2d 821. [This and notes 4 and 5, in the opinion.]

[4] Prosser, William Lloyd and W. Page Keeton, *The Law of Torts* (5th ed.) (St. Paul, MN: West Publishing Co., 1984).

phokines, unlike a name or a face, have the same molecular structure in every human being and the same, important functions in every human being's immune system. Moreover, the particular genetic material which is responsible for the natural production of lymphokines, and which defendants use to manufacture lymphokines in the laboratory, is also the same in every person; it is no more unique to Moore than the number of vertebrae in the spine or the chemical formula of hemoglobin.

Another privacy case offered by analogy to support Moore's claim establishes only that patients have a right to refuse medical treatment.[5] In this context the court in Bouvia wrote that " '[e]very human being of adult years and sound mind has a right to determine what shall be done with his own body. . . . ' " Relying on this language to support the proposition that a patient has a continuing right to control the use of excised cells, the Court of Appeal in this case concluded that "[a] patient must have the ultimate power to control what becomes of his or her tissues. To hold otherwise would open the door to a massive invasion of human privacy and dignity in the name of medical progress." Yet one may earnestly wish to protect privacy and dignity without accepting the extremely problematic conclusion that interference with those interests amounts to a conversion of personal property. Nor is it necessary to force the round pegs of "privacy" and "dignity" into the square hole of "property" in order to protect the patient, since the fiduciary-duty and informed-consent theories protect these interests directly by requiring full disclosure.

The next consideration that makes Moore's claim of ownership problematic is California statutory law, which drastically limits a patient's control over excised cells. Pursuant to Health and Safety Code section 7054.4, "[n]otwithstanding any other provision of law, recognizable anatomical parts, human tissues, anatomical human remains, or infectious waste following conclusion of scientific use shall be disposed of by interment, incineration, or any other method determined by the state department [of health services] to protect the public health and safety." Clearly the Legislature did not specifically intend this statute to resolve the question of whether a patient is entitled to compensation for the nonconsensual use of excised cells. A primary object of the

[5] *Bouvia v. Superior Court* (1986) 179 Cal.App.3d 1127 (225 Cal.Rptr. 297).

statute is to ensure the safe handling of potentially hazardous biological waste materials. Yet one cannot escape the conclusion that the statute's practical effect is to limit, drastically, a patient's control over excised cells. By restricting how excised cells may be used and requiring their eventual destruction, the statute eliminates so many of the rights ordinarily attached to property that one cannot simply assume that what is left amounts to "property" or "ownership" for purposes of conversion law.

It may be that some limited right to control the use of excised cells does survive the operation of this statute. There is, for example, no need to read the statute to permit "scientific use" contrary to the patient's expressed wish. A fully informed patient may always withhold consent to treatment by a physician whose research plans the patient does not approve. That right, however, as already discussed, is protected by the fiduciary-duty and informed-consent theories.

Finally, the subject matter of the Regents' patent—the patented cell line and the products derived from it—cannot be Moore's property. This is because the patented cell line is both factually and legally distinct from the cells taken from Moore's body. Federal law permits the patenting of organisms that represent the product of "human ingenuity," but not naturally occurring organisms. Human cell lines are patentable because "[l]ong-term adaptation and growth of human tissues and cells in culture is difficult—often considered an art . . . ," and the probability of success is low. It is this inventive effort that patent law rewards, not the discovery of naturally occurring raw materials. Thus, Moore's allegations that he owns the cell line and the products derived from it are inconsistent with the patent, which constitutes an authoritative determination that the cell line is the product of invention. Since such allegations are nothing more than arguments or conclusions of law, they of course do not bind us.

2. SHOULD CONVERSION LIABILITY BE EXTENDED?

There are three reasons why it is inappropriate to impose liability for conversion based upon the allegations of Moore's complaint. First, a fair balancing of the relevant policy considerations counsels against extending the tort. Second, problems in this area are better suited to legislative resolution. Third, the tort of conversion is not necessary to protect patients' rights. For these reasons, we conclude that the use of excised human cells in medical research does not amount to a conversion.

Of the relevant policy considerations, two are of overriding importance. The first is protection of a competent patient's right to make autonomous medical decisions. That right, as already discussed, is grounded in well-recognized and long-standing principles of fiduciary duty and informed consent. This policy weighs in favor of providing a remedy to patients when physicians act with undisclosed motives that may affect their professional judgment. The second important policy consideration is that we not threaten with disabling civil liability innocent parties who are engaged in socially useful activities, such as researchers who have no reason to believe that their use of a particular cell sample is, or may be, against a donor's wishes.

To reach an appropriate balance of these policy considerations is extremely important. . . .

Indeed, so significant is the potential obstacle to research stemming from uncertainty about legal title to biological materials that the Office of Technology Assessment reached this striking conclusion: "[R]egardless of the merit of claims by the different interested parties, resolving the current uncertainty may be more important to the future of biotechnology than resolving it in any particular way."

We need not, however, make an arbitrary choice between liability and nonliability. Instead, an examination of the relevant policy considerations suggests an appropriate balance: Liability based upon existing disclosure obligations, rather than an unprecedented extension of the conversion theory, protects patients' rights of privacy and autonomy without unnecessarily hindering research.

To be sure, the threat of liability for conversion might help to enforce patients' rights indirectly. This is because physicians might be able to avoid liability by obtaining patients' consent, in the broadest possible terms, to any conceivable subsequent research use of excised cells. Unfortunately, to extend the conversion theory would utterly sacrifice the other goal of protecting innocent parties. Since conversion is a strict liability tort,[6] it would impose liability on all those into whose

---

[6] That is, there is no need to prove culpability by the defendant.

hands the cells come, whether or not the particular defendant participated in, or knew of, the inadequate disclosures that violated the patient's right to make an informed decision. In contrast to the conversion theory, the fiduciary-duty and informed-consent theories protect the patient directly, without punishing innocent parties or creating disincentives to the conduct of socially beneficial research.

Research on human cells plays a critical role in medical research. . . .

The extension of conversion law into this area will hinder research by restricting access to the necessary raw materials. Thousands of human cell lines already exist in tissue repositories, such as the American Type Culture Collection and those operated by the National Institutes of Health and the American Cancer Society. These repositories respond to tens of thousands of requests for samples annually. Since the patent office requires the holders of patents on cell lines to make samples available to anyone, many patent holders place their cell lines in repositories to avoid the administrative burden of responding to requests. At present, human cell lines are routinely copied and distributed to other researchers for experimental purposes, usually free of charge. This exchange of scientific materials, which still is relatively free and efficient, will surely be compromised if each cell sample becomes the potential subject matter of a lawsuit.

To expand liability by extending conversion law into this area would have a broad impact. . . . In deciding whether to create new tort duties we have in the past considered the impact that expanded liability would have on activities that are important to society, such as research. For example, in *Brown v. Superior Court*, the fear that strict product liability would frustrate pharmaceutical research led us to hold that a drug manufacturer's liability should not be measured by those standards.

Indeed, this is a far more compelling case for limiting the expansion of tort liability than *Brown*. In *Brown*, eliminating strict liability made it more difficult for plaintiffs to recover actual damages for serious physical injuries resulting from their mothers' prenatal use of the drug diethylstilbestrol (DES).[7] In this case, by comparison, limiting the expansion of liability under a conversion theory will only make it more difficult

---

[7] *Brown v. Superior Court*, supra, 44 Cal.3d at pp. 1054–1055. [In the original.]

for Moore to recover a highly theoretical windfall. Any injury to his right to make an informed decision remains actionable through the fiduciary-duty and informed-consent theories.

If the scientific users of human cells are to be held liable for failing to investigate the consensual pedigree of their raw materials, we believe the Legislature should make that decision. . . .

Finally, there is no pressing need to impose a judicially created rule of strict liability, since enforcement of physicians' disclosure obligations will protect patients against the very type of harm with which Moore was threatened. So long as a physician discloses research and economic interests that may affect his judgment, the patient is protected from conflicts of interest. . . .

For these reasons, we hold that the allegations of Moore's third amended complaint state a cause of action for breach of fiduciary duty or lack of informed consent, but not conversion.

ARABIAN, J., CONCURRING.

I join in the views cogently expounded by the majority. I write separately to give voice to a concern that I believe informs much of that opinion but finds little or no expression therein. I speak of the moral issue. . . .

The ramifications of recognizing and enforcing a property interest in body tissues are not known, but are greatly feared—the effect on human dignity of a marketplace in human body parts, the impact on research and development of competitive bidding for such materials, and the exposure of researchers to potentially limitless and uncharted tort liability.

Whether, as plaintiff urges, his cells should be treated as property susceptible to conversion is not, in my view, ours to decide. The question implicates choices which not only reflect, but which ultimately define our essence. A mark of wisdom for us as expositors of the law is the recognition that we cannot cure every ill, mediate every dispute, resolve every conundrum. Sometimes, as Justice Brandeis said, "the most important thing we do, is not doing."

Where then shall a complete resolution be found? Clearly the Legislature, as the majority opinion suggests, is the proper deliberative forum. . . .

MOSK, J., DISSENTING:

Contrary to the principal holding of the Court of Appeal, the majority conclude that the complaint does not—in fact cannot—state a cause of action for conversion. I disagree with this conclusion for all the reasons stated by the Court of Appeal, and for additional reasons that I shall explain. . . .

The majority's first reason is that "no reported judicial decision supports Moore's claim, either directly or by close analogy." Neither, however, is there any reported decision rejecting such a claim.[8] The issue is as new as its source—the recent explosive growth in the commercialization of biotechnology.

The majority . . . conclude(s) in effect that in the present case we should also "look for guidance" to the Legislature rather than to the law of conversion. Surely this argument is out of place in an opinion of the highest court of this state. As the majority acknowledge, the law of conversion is a creature of the common law. . . . In short, as the United States Supreme Court has aptly said, "This flexibility and capacity for growth and adaptation is the peculiar boast and excellence of the common law. . . . Although the Legislature may of course speak to the subject, in the common law system the primary instruments of this evolution are the courts, adjudicating on a regular basis the rich variety of individual cases brought before them" (*Rodriguez v. Bethlehem Steel Corp.*, 12 Cal. 3d 382 (1974)).

Especially is this true in the field of torts. I need not review the many instances in which this court has broken fresh ground by announcing new rules of tort law: time and again when a new rule was needed we did not stay our hand merely because the matter was one of first impression. . . . ". . . The response of the courts can be either to adhere rigidly to prior doctrine, denying recovery to those injured by such products, or to fashion remedies to meet these changing needs" (*Sindell v. Abbott Laboratories*, 26 Cal. 3d 588, 610 (1980)). We took the latter course.

The majority's second reason for doubting that Moore retained an ownership interest in his cells after their excision is that "California

---

[8] Who should have the burden of proof on this issue? Moore or the defendants?

statutory law . . . drastically limits a patient's control over excised cells." . . .

The concepts of property and ownership in our law are extremely broad. A leading decision of this court approved the following definition: " 'The term "property" is sufficiently comprehensive to include every species of estate, real and personal, and everything which one person can own and transfer to another. It extends to every species of right and interest capable of being enjoyed as such upon which it is practicable to place a money value.' "

Being broad, the concept of property is also abstract: rather than referring directly to a material object such as a parcel of land or the tractor that cultivates it, the concept of property is often said to refer to a "bundle of rights" that may be exercised with respect to that object—principally the rights to possess the property, to use the property, to exclude others from the property, and to dispose of the property by sale or by gift. . . .

In each of the foregoing instances, the limitation or prohibition diminishes the bundle of rights that would otherwise attach to the property, yet what remains is still deemed in law to be a protectible property interest. "Since property or title is a complex bundle of rights, duties, powers and immunities, the pruning away of some or a great many of these elements does not entirely destroy the title. . . ." The same rule applies to Moore's interest in his own body tissue: even if we assume that section 7054.4 limited the use and disposition of his excised tissue in the manner claimed by the majority, Moore nevertheless retained valuable rights in that tissue. Above all, at the time of its excision he at least had the right to do with his own tissue whatever the defendants did with it: i.e., he could have contracted with researchers and pharmaceutical companies to develop and exploit the vast commercial potential of his tissue and its products. . . .

In the absence of such authority—or of legislation to the same effect—the right falls within the traditionally broad concept of property in our law.

The majority's third and last reason for their conclusion that Moore has no cause of action for conversion under existing law is that "the subject matter of the Regents' patent—the patented cell line and the products derived from it—cannot be Moore's property." The majority then offer a dual explanation: "This is because the patented cell line is both factually and legally distinct from the cells taken from Moore's body." . . .

[T]he majority conclude that the patent somehow cut off all Moore's rights—past, present, and future—to share in the proceeds of defendants' commercial exploitation of the cell line derived from his own body tissue. The majority cite no authority for this unfair result, and I cannot believe it is compelled by the general law of patents: a patent is not a license to defraud. . . .

Having concluded—mistakenly, in my view—that Moore has no cause of action for conversion under existing law, the majority next consider whether to "extend" the conversion cause of action to this context.

The majority focus . . . on . . . their concern "that we not threaten with disabling civil liability innocent parties who are engaged in socially useful activities, such as researchers who have no reason to believe that their use of a particular cell sample is, or may be, against a donor's wishes." As will appear, in my view this concern is both overstated and outweighed by contrary considerations. . . .

To begin with, if the relevant exchange of scientific materials was ever "free and efficient," it is much less so today. . . .

An even greater force for restricting the free exchange of new cell lines and their products has been the rise of the biotechnology industry and the increasing involvement of academic researchers in that industry. When scientists became entrepreneurs and negotiated with biotechnological and pharmaceutical companies to develop and exploit the commercial potential of their discoveries—as did defendants in the case at bar—layers of contractual restrictions were added to the protections of the patent law. . . .

Secondly, to the extent that cell cultures and cell lines may still be "freely exchanged," e.g., for purely research purposes, it does not follow that the researcher who obtains such material must necessarily remain ignorant of any limitations on its use: by means of appropriate recordkeeping, the researcher can be assured that the source of the material has consented to his proposed use of it, and hence that such use is not a conversion. . . .

A second policy consideration adds notions of equity to those of ethics. Our society values fundamental fairness in dealings between its members, and condemns the unjust enrichment of any member at the expense of another. This is particularly true when, as here, the parties are not in equal bargaining positions. We are repeatedly told that the commercial products of the biotechnological revolution "hold the promise of tremendous profit." In the case at bar, for example, the complaint alleges that the market for the kinds of proteins produced by the Mo cell line was predicted to exceed $3 billion by 1990. . . .

Yet defendants deny that Moore is entitled to any share whatever in the proceeds of this cell line. This is both inequitable and immoral. As Dr. Thomas H. Murray, a respected professor of ethics and public policy, testified before Congress, "the person [who furnishes the tissue] should be justly compensated. . . . If biotechnologists fail to make provision for a just sharing of profits with the person whose gift made it possible, the public's sense of justice will be offended and no one will be the winner."

There will be such equitable sharing if the courts recognize that the patient has a legally protected property interest in his own body and its products: "property rights in one's own tissue would provide a morally acceptable result by giving effect to notions of fairness and preventing unjust enrichment. . . . Societal notions of equity and fairness demand recognition of property rights. . . .

In short, as the Court of Appeal succinctly put it, "If this science has become science for profit, then we fail to see any justification for excluding the patient from participation in those profits." . . .

The majority's final reason for refusing to recognize a conversion cause of action on these facts is that "there is no pressing need" to do so because the complaint also states another cause of action that is assertedly adequate to the task; that cause of action is "the breach of a fiduciary duty to disclose facts material to the patient's consent or, alternatively, . . . the performance of medical procedures without first having obtained the patient's informed consent." . . .

The remedy is largely illusory. "[A]n action based on the physician's failure to disclose material information sounds in negligence. As a practical matter, however, it may be difficult to recover on this kind of negligence theory because the patient must prove a causal connection between his or her injury and the physician's failure to inform." . . . ". . . Such a causal connection arises only if it is established that had revelation been made consent to treatment would not have been given" (*Cobbs v. Grant*, 8 Cal. 3d 229, 245 (1972)).

[I]t is not even enough for the plaintiff to prove that he personally would have refused consent to the proposed treatment if he had been fully informed; he must also prove that in the same circumstances no reasonably prudent person would have given such consent. The purpose of this "objective" standard is evident: "Since at the time of trial the uncommunicated hazard has materialized, it would be surprising if the patient-plaintiff did not claim that had he been informed of the dangers he would have declined treatment. . . .

The second reason why the nondisclosure cause of action is inadequate for the task that the majority assign to it is that it fails to solve half the problem before us: it gives the patient only the right to refuse consent, i.e., the right to prohibit the commercialization of his tissue; it does not give him the right to grant consent to that commercialization on the condition that he share in its proceeds. . . .

Third, the nondisclosure cause of action fails to reach a major class of potential defendants: all those who are outside the strict physician-patient relationship with the plaintiff. . . .

I would affirm the decision of the Court of Appeal to direct the trial court to overrule the demurrers to the cause of action for conversion.

∎

QUESTIONS AND COMMENTS

1. Who do you think has the better argument, Justice Arabian or Justice Panelli? In part, your decision might turn on your view of the relationship between doctors and patients or on your belief of the best outcome for Moore or the best outcome for the doctors. In part, it might turn on Justice Panelli's concern for the proper deference of the court to the lack of precedent or legislative delegation of the power to award Moore relief, or it might turn on Justice Arabian's acceptance, with the court of appeals, that the model we have of the noble scientist laboring among patients solely for public health is less likely today than a model of an entrepreneur using the patient for a profit. We can consider each in turn.

2. Many students reading this case feel great sympathy for Moore. At least, he seems to have been misled, if for no other reason than when he was told to travel to the hospital for his own good, he really was going for his doctor's benefit. The cause of action that was allowed,

however, was based on exactly this problem, leaving open the problem of the lost cells and their potential profit. This story upsets our view of the doctor as fiduciary, someone in whom a patient must trust to act always for the patient's benefit. Is this ideal of the fiduciary naive? Should doctors try to heal the patient or advance medicine for the public? What is their obligation, and to whom is it owed, particularly when they are increasingly reimbursed not from patient pockets but from insurance pools? The doctor-patient relationship has been increasingly institutionalized, thanks to the growth of intermediate organizations like managed-care groups. The legal allowance for the resulting diminution of the personal relation between doctor and patient has been made, partly, by legislatures. It has been more the result of little or no legal development other than private contracts between employers who pay insurance premiums and the insurers. What, then, is the status of the contract between doctor and patient? What should it be? Who should determine its content? Is Judge Panelli correct that this is a policy matter and so for legislatures to decide?

3. In the final analysis, the problem in this case is how best to capture our intuition that Moore suffered a wrong. If the patented cell line turned out to be worthless, would he still have a claim for damages based on the breach of a fiduciary duty? It seems implausible to think there would be anything for him to complain about. Is the essential wrong, then, the failure to share in the proceeds from the economic exploitation of the cell line? That sounds more like a theory of property—property yields a return, and when you lose the property, you lose the economic return. In effect, Moore is arguing that his being deprived of economic participation is a wrong. For that claim to make sense, he must have had a property interest in the cell line.

4. One of the primary reasons why the common law historically has forbidden a property interest in body parts was to prevent the desecration of corpses for money. This rule, of course, evolved in an age when the single cell had no value, the cornea or another organ could hardly be transplanted, and blood transfusions were unimaginable. Today, body part sales are a reality but not for the initial donor. They are, in various indirect manners, sold between companies, institutions, and states, provoking a variety of concerns both for the availability of

parts and the fairness of the payment structure.[9] Does it make sense, then, for property not to be recognized in the body? On the other hand, what would property in the body mean for taxes? For the rights of creditors? Of heirs?[10] Even so, medical advances are now rarely possible without extremely expensive investments in laboratories and information bases, and without significant cash flows, new developments come more slowly.

5. We probably accept without much analysis the notion that Moore's cells were in some sense "his" before they became, in some sense, Golde's and UCLA's. To an extent, this sort of genetic lottery, for good or ill, distributes not only cells but also intellect, talent, beauty, and medical limitations to each of us, and they are ours. Perhaps this makes sense, but John Rawls argued that the genetic lottery was arbitrary "from a moral point of view." He meant from a "liberal" point of view. Accordingly, if Moore's cells turned out to be valuable, that is not to Moore's credit. Why should he deserve an economic benefit when it was just chance that he had cells that enable the defendants to develop a profitable cell line?[11]

■

Further Reading

The changes wrought by technology will bring more—not less—challenge to our notion of property. These books address just a few current issues: E. Richard Gold, *Body Parts: Property Rights & the Ownership of Human Biological Materials* (Washington, DC: Georgetown University Press, 1998); Lawrence Lessig, *The Future of Ideas: The Fate of the Commons in a Connected World* (New York: Vintage Books, 2002); David R. Koepsell, *The Ontology of Cyberspace: Philosophy, Law, and the Future of Intellectual Property* (Chicago: Open Court Publishing Company, 2003); Ingrid Wickelgren, *The Gene Masters: How a New Breed of Scientific Entrepreneurs Raced for the Biggest Prize in Biology* (New York: Times Books, 2002); Steven M. H. Wallman et al., *Unseen Wealth* (Washington: Brookings Inst., 2001).

[9] See E. Richard Gold, *Body Parts: Property Rights & the Ownership of Human Biological Materials* (Washington, DC: Georgetown University Press, 1998).

[10] See A. Michele Dickerson, "From Jeans to Genes: The Evolving Nature of Property of the Estate," 15 *Bank. Dev. J.* 285 (1999).

[11] See John Rawls, *A Theory of Justice* 85–87 (Cambridge, MA: Belknap Press of Harvard University, 1971).

NINETEEN

Contract as Law

As the term is understood in both the French and the common law traditions, "contracts" represents the highest achievement of the liberal theory of law. Independent parties come together and make a deal. They act voluntarily and choose their obligations. No one is bound by something not agreed to. Yet, once two or more parties do make an agreement, subject to only a few limits, the law will enforce it between them. At this theoretical level, each person has an equal power to create the rules the law will enforce between them, without regard to whether they were born rich or poor, or one race, gender, religion, or class or another. As claimed by Sir Henry Maine, "the movement of the progressive societies has hitherto been a movement from Status to Contract."[1]

A valid contract is effectively a law created by the parties to the contract. This relationship of the free will of a party to the creation of laws binding the party is surely the reason why the contract is a dominant metaphor in explaining the relationships between governments and their subjects or citizens in liberal society. There are limits to this metaphor, well known to philosophers, and there are limits also to the freedom of

---

[1] Sir Henry Sumner Maine, *Ancient Law* 99 (London: J. M. Dent & Sons, Ltd., 1917) (1861).

contract, particularly when the parties do not have similar capacities of understanding, negotiation, or bargaining power, but also when the promises the contract would enforce are illegal or so immoral that to enforce them would violate public policies enshrined in law.

This idea that contracts are a private source of law has many implications, not only in that the parties alone (within limits) determine their legal obligations but also in the manner in which the law interprets the language according to which those obligations were created. In their written form, contracts are subject to interpretation not unlike statutes.

The great liberal principle of binding voluntary agreement finds its expression in the *Code civil*, which holds in § 1134: *Les conventions légalement formées tiennent lieu de loi à ceux qui les ont faites* ("Contracts, properly made, take the place of the law between the contracting parties"). This is probably the boldest statement of party autonomy to be found in any modern legal system. The parties actually write their own law. Immediately following § 1134, however, is § 1135, already discussed, which invokes the principle of *équité* as a guide to the interpretation of contracts. A similar provision is found in the German Civil Code (BGB) § 157, which brings to bear the famous German equivalent of equity (*Treu und Glauben*) to the interpretation of contracts.

The rules of contract formation in the major legal systems of the world are much the same, with all systems requiring an offer and an acceptance. The offeror says, "I will sell you my book for fifty dollars." The offeree, the person to whom the offer is made, says "Deal!" and thereby accepts the offer.

All the details of offer and acceptance are spelled out in the *Restatement of Contracts*, a summary of the basic common law doctrine prepared by the American Law Institute. The German code never actually defines the conditions for making a contract of obligation. This is left to the textbook writers, who elaborate on the assumption behind the code that a contract consists of two overlapping declarations of will, one by the offeror and the other by the accepting party. By contrast, the *Code civil* Art. 1108 explicitly requires *consentement* ("consent") as a condition for a valid contract.

The difference among the three leading systems of law—German, French, and common law—is expressed in the third factor for making a valid contract. Contract is not simply a set of promises. We could have a tennis date, but that would not be a legal contract. Something more is required. Table 19.1 presents a breakdown on the three possibilities.

German law defines a contract as a two-way commitment to be bound. In theory, these commitments cover any case in which the parties intend to be legally bound. It would not cover a date to meet for dinner because in that case the parties would not intend to be legally bound. But it would cover, in principle, an agreement to make a gift or to leave money to someone in one's will.

As Germans define the concept of "contract," it includes a transfer of property, as well a promise to do so in the future. For example, if one of us hands you a book and says, "It's yours," that is a contract of transfer. Both sides mean to be bound by the transfer. This is a striking feature of German legal theory, which distinguishes it from French and common law thinking. Neither French law nor American law would call the transfer of the book a contract. The only contract in these systems is an "executory" contract to sell the book in the future. The rest of our discussion concentrates on these mutual promises to do something in the future.

Germans solve the third factor by building it into the required promises. The third factor added by French law is the element of *cause*, which refers generally to the motivation for entering into the contract. The cause must be legitimate. Beyond this requirement, just about any cause will do.

The distinguishing feature of the common law of contracts is its third factor, called "consideration." Understanding consideration and how it works is probably the greatest challenge for the beginning law student. It is worth taking some time to appreciate how this factor affects the way common lawyers think about contracts.

The basic idea of consideration is that the law should protect only

Table 19.1

Factors in Valid Contracts

System	Requisite third factor (after offer and acceptance)
German law	Third factor built into the promises
French law	Cause
American law, common law	Consideration

bargains that benefit both sides. The implication is that a promise to make a gift should not be enforced (though an actual gift is valid). No one can bind himself by a unilateral act. Thus traditionally, at common law, an offer could not be binding unless the offeree paid something to make it binding and thus converted the offer into an option contract. Consideration is the *quid pro quo*—something given in exchange for the promise.

The *Restatement of Contracts, Second* (1981) defines consideration in § 71:

(1) To constitute consideration, a performance or a return promise must be bargained for.

(2) A performance or return promise is bargained for if it is sought by the promisor in exchange for his promise and is given by the promisee in exchange for that promise.

(3) The performance may consist of
   (A) an act other than a promise, or
   (B) a forbearance, or
   (C) the creation, modification, or destruction of a legal relation.

(4) The performance of a return promise may be given to the promisor or to some other person. It may be given by the promisee or by some other person.

Let us see how this complicated definition comes to bear in a concrete case:

E. J. Baehr and Another v. Penn-O-Tex Oil Corp.

Supreme Court of Minnesota
258 Minn. 533, 104 N.W.2d 661 (1960).

[Baehr leased some gasoline stations to Kemp; under the lease, Kemp collected monthly rents from each station operator and then paid monthly rents to Baehr. At the same time, Kemp borrowed money from Penn-O-Tex. In 1955, Kemp fell behind in his payments to Penn-O-Tex and assigned all of his rights to rents over to Penn-O-Tex, including his right to rents from the operators of the gas stations actually owned by Baehr. Penn-O-Tex sent an agent to Kemp's office to collect the moneys paid there. Baehr sought to collect his now-unpaid rents from Penn-O-Tex. Penn-O-Tex's agent stated several times to Baehr that Penn-O-Tex would pay the rents and repeated the statement after Baehr threatened to sue. Penn-O-Tex never did so. In 1956, Baehr terminated his leases to Kemp for nonpayment of rents and then sued Penn-O-Tex for the unpaid rents, claiming that a person in possession of leased property was presumed to have been assigned the lease and that Penn-O-Tex had "contracted to pay the rent during this period."

The trial court ruled as a matter of law that Penn-O-Tex had not taken possession of the gas stations and had not taken an assignment of the leases. The jury heard evidence on the contract issue and gave a verdict for Baehr, but the trial judge granted Penn-O-Tex's motion for judgment notwithstanding the verdict. Baehr appealed, seeking to enforce the promise made by defendant's agents.]

LOEVINGER, J.:

. . . .

The issue whether there was a contract by defendant to pay plaintiff is . . . doubtful. Unfortunately, contract, like most of the basic terms constituting the intellectual tools of law, is conventionally defined in a circular fashion. By the most common definition, a contract is a promise or set of promises for the breach of which the law gives a remedy or the performance of which the law recognizes as a duty. This amounts to saying that a contract is a legally enforceable promise. But a promise is legally enforceable only if it is a contract. Thus nothing less than the whole body of applicable precedents suffices to define the term "contract."

Although the definition of contract does not help much in determining what expressions shall be held to impose legal obligations, it does direct attention to a promise as the starting point of inquiry. Both in popular and legal usage, a promise is an assurance, in whatever form of expression given, that a thing will or will not be done.[2] While we must take care to distinguish between statements meant to express merely present intention and those meant to give an assurance as to a

---

[2] *Webster's New International Dictionary* (2d ed.) 1980 (Springfield, MA: G. & C. Merriam & Co., 1947); Oliver Wendell Holmes Jr., *The Common Law* 299 (1881, reprinted in Mineola, NY: Dover Publications, 1991).

future event, this involves no more than the common difficulty of seeking precise meaning in the usually imprecise, and often careless, expressions of ordinary colloquy.

If we accept plaintiff's version of the statements made by defendant's agent, as we are required to do by the verdict,[3] there was an unequivocal assurance given that the rents would be paid. This cannot be anything but a promise.

However, the fact that a promise was given does not necessarily mean that a contract was made. It is clear that not every promise is legally enforceable. Much of the vast body of law in the field of contracts is concerned with determining which promises should be legally enforced. On the one hand, in a civilized community men must be able to assume that those with whom they deal will carry out their undertakings according to reasonable expectations. On the other hand, it is neither practical nor reasonable to expect full performance of every assurance given, whether it be thoughtless, casual and gratuitous, or deliberately and seriously made.

The test that has been developed by the common law for determining the enforceability of promises is the doctrine of consideration. This is a crude and not altogether successful attempt to generalize the conditions under which promises will be legally enforced. Consideration requires that a contractual promise be the product of a bargain. However, in this usage, "bargain" does not mean an exchange of things of equivalent, or any, value. It means a negotiation resulting in the voluntary assumption of an obligation by one party upon condition of an act or forbearance by the other. Consideration thus insures that the promise enforced as a contract is not accidental, casual, or gratuitous, but has been uttered intentionally as the result of some deliberation, manifested by reciprocal bargaining or negotiation. In this view, the requirement of consideration is no mere technicality, historical anachronism, or arbitrary formality. It is an attempt to be as reasonable as we can in deciding which promises constitute contracts. Although the doctrine has been criticized, no satisfactory substitute has been suggested. It is noteworthy that the civil law has a corresponding doctrine of

---

[3] Because the trial court granted a judgment for the defendant notwithstanding the verdict (still abbreviated JNOV from the Latin term *non obstante veredicto*), all of the contested facts are read on appeal in the favor of the plaintiff.

"causa" which, to the eye of a common-law lawyer, is not much different than consideration.

Consideration, as essential evidence of the parties' intent to create a legal obligation, must be something adopted and regarded by the parties as such. Thus, the same thing may be consideration or not, as it is dealt with by the parties. In substance, a contractual promise must be of the logical form: "If . . . (consideration is given) . . . then I promise that. . . ." Of course, the substance may be expressed in any form of words, but essentially this is the logical structure of those promises enforced by the law as contracts.

7. Applying these principles to the present case, it appears that although defendant's agent made a promise to plaintiff, it was not in such circumstances that a contract was created. Plaintiff correctly states that an agreement of forbearance to sue may be sufficient consideration for a contract. Plaintiff further contends that his failure to institute suit immediately upon learning of Kemp's assignment to defendant permits an inference of an agreement to forbear from suit in consideration for defendant's assurance of payment of rents to plaintiff. This court has held that circumstantial evidence may support the inference of such an agreement to forbear. However, such an inference must rest upon something more than the mere failure to institute immediate suit. The difficulty with plaintiff's case is that there is no more than this.

Plaintiff's conversation with defendant's agent was about the middle of February 1956 while plaintiff was in Florida. Plaintiff returned to Minneapolis, which was his residence as well as the jurisdiction where defendant was found, about the latter part of April or the first of May 1956. Soon after this he consulted a lawyer, and suit was started "as rapidly as the lawyer could get moving." There is nothing in the evidence to suggest that plaintiff deferred initiating legal action any longer than suited his own personal convenience. There is nothing in the evidence to suggest that defendant sought any forbearance by plaintiff or thought that it was securing such action; nor is there any evidence that plaintiff's delay from the middle of February until April or May in undertaking legal action was related to defendant's promises. There is no evidence that either of the parties took defendant's assurances seriously or acted upon them in any way. There was, therefore, no consideration, and the promises did not amount to a contract. Since the district court was correct in ordering judgment entered for the defendant, notwithstanding the verdict, on this ground, it is unnecessary to consider other points relating to enforceability of the alleged contract.

Affirmed.

∎

QUESTIONS AND COMMENTS

1. The court's comments about the "civil law" are not well informed. It seems to be clear that the agents' promise to pay over the rents collected to Baehr would have been enforceable under German law. Would it have been supported by *cause* in French law? Yes, it seems so. The idea behind *cause* seems to be that the contract is supported by a serious motivation. As provided in the Civil code of Québec § 1410: *La cause du contrat est la raison qui détermine chacune des parties à le conclure* ("The *cause* is the reason that determines why the parties enter the agreement"). The motivation might consist in an *intention libérale* to make a gift or a will.[4] If an intention to make a gift is sufficiently motivated by *cause*, then one would think that the promise to pay the rents in recognition of a prior debt would also be sufficient. Compare the Civil code of Québec § 1381, which recognizes that some contracts might be made exclusively for the benefit of another (*le contract à titre gratuit*).

2. What is the implication of the doctrine of consideration for making the offer irrevocable? Suppose A offers B his car for $10,000 and says that B can have until Tuesday to decide. Is this binding? Suppose that A gets a higher offer for the car on Monday; would he breach any obligations to B by selling to someone else? The answer of the common law has been no. Can you apply the doctrine of consideration and explain why?

3. Is it possible that the doctrine of consideration provides a bulwark against the temptation to use threats and blackmail in commercial transactions? One of the firm rules is that the performance of a preexisting duty does not constitute consideration. Suppose that professor S comes to class twenty minutes late every day. Fed up with the

---

[4] See Jean Carbonnier, 4 *Droit Civil* 128 (22d ed) (Paris: Presse Universitaires de France, 2000).

behavior, the students get together and promise S a thousand dollars if he begins and ends the lecture on time. S complies, but the students do not pay. They are not contractually bound because the professor has a preexisting duty to show up on time. He does not provide any consideration for the students' promise. Look at the definition in § 71 the *Restatement of Contract, Second* to see how this follows. Would it be socially desirable to encourage people to hold back on their duties in order to extort greater payments for their services?

4. The basic principle of the common law has undergone a great transformation as a result of a proposal made in § 90 of the *Restatement, Second* of Contracts. This is the language of the provision:

> § 90 (1) A promise, which the promisor should reasonably expect to induce reliance or forbearance on the part of the promisee or a third person and which does induce such action or forbearance is binding if injustice can be avoided only by enforcement of the promise. The remedy granted for breach may be limited as justice requires.

The basic elements of this new version of contract are (1) a promise, (2) detrimental reliance, (3) damages, and (4) avoidance of injustice. The hypothetical cases covered by this provision are all the gift promises that are rendered unenforceable by the doctrine of consideration. Your uncle promises to pay for your education in American law at Columbia University. You incur great expense to get settled and start school and then he says, "Sorry, I cannot do it." Under § 90, the student who relied to her detriment on this promise can collect damages, as justice requires.

Notice there are no requirements of form. The uncle's promise does not have to be in writing. Suppose this case came up under German law. The matter is not so simple because under the German as well as many other civil law systems, a contract to make a gift must be in writing and be endorsed by a notary. (See BGB § 781; *Code civil* Art. 931.) Is it possible that with regard to the student whose uncle leaves her in the lurch, American law under § 90 of the Restatement II would be conducive to reaching the just result? The reasoning of the German code appears to be that if the state requires a certain form for gift contracts, then you must satisfy the requirements of form. If you do not, you lose.

■

The following case illustrates the relationship between consideration and the principle underlying Section 90:

Feinberg v. The Pfeiffer Company

Court of Appeals of Missouri, St. Louis District
322 S.W.2d 163; 1959 Mo. App. LEXIS 568

DOERNER, C.

This is a suit brought in the Circuit Court of the City of St. Louis by plaintiff, a former employee of the defendant corporation, on an alleged contract whereby defendant agreed to pay plaintiff the sum of $200 per month for life upon her retirement. A jury being waived, the case was tried by the court alone. Judgment below was for plaintiff for $5100, the amount of the pension claimed to be due as of the date of the trial, together with interest thereon, and defendant duly appealed.

The parties are in substantial agreement on the essential facts. Plaintiff began working for the defendant, a manufacturer of pharmaceuticals, in 1910, when she was but 17 years of age. By 1947 she had attained the position of bookkeeper, office manager, and assistant treasurer of the defendant, and owned 70 shares of its stock out of a total of 6503 shares issued and outstanding. . . .

On December 27, 1947, the annual meeting of the defendant's Board of Directors was held at the Company's offices in St. Louis, presided over by Max Lippman, its then president and largest individual stockholder. . . . At that meeting the Board of Directors adopted the following resolution, which, because it is the crux of the case, we quote in full:

"The Chairman thereupon pointed out that the Assistant Treasurer, Mrs. Anna Sacks Feinberg, has given the corporation many years of long and faithful service. Not only has she served the corporation devotedly, but with exceptional ability and skill. The President pointed out that although all of the officers and directors sincerely hoped and desired that Mrs. Feinberg would continue in her present position for as long as she felt able, nevertheless, in view of the length of service which she has contributed provision should be made to afford her retirement privileges and benefits which should become a firm obligation of the corporation to be available to her whenever she should see fit to retire from active duty, however many years in the future such retirement may become effective. It was, accordingly, proposed that Mrs. Feinberg's salary which is presently $350.00 per month, be increased to $400.00 per month, and that Mrs. Feinberg would be given the privilege of retiring from active duty at any time she may elect to see fit so to do upon a retirement pay of $200.00 per month for life, with the distinct understanding that the retirement plan is merely being adopted at the present time in order to afford Mrs. Feinberg security for the future and in the hope that her active services will continue with the corporation for many years to come. After due discussion and consideration, and upon motion duly made and seconded, it was—

> RESOLVED, that the salary of Anna Sacks Feinberg be increased from $350.00 to $400.00 per month and that she be afforded the privilege of retiring from active duty in the corporation at any time she may elect to see fit so to do upon retirement pay of $200.00 per month, for the remainder of her life.

At the request of Mr. Lippman his sons-in-law, Messrs. Harris and Flammer, called upon the plaintiff at her apartment on the same day to advise her of the passage of the resolution. Plaintiff testified on cross-examination that she had no prior information that such a pension plan was contemplated, that it came as a surprise to her, and that she would have continued in her employment whether or not such a resolution had been adopted. It is clear from the evidence that there was no contract, oral or written, as to plaintiff's length of employment, and that she was free to quit, and the defendant to discharge her, at any time.

Plaintiff did continue to work for the defendant through June 30, 1949, on which date she retired. In accordance with the foregoing resolution, the defendant began paying her the sum of $200 on the first of each month. Mr. Lippman died on November 18, 1949, and was succeeded as president of the company by his widow. Because of an illness, she retired from that office and was succeeded in October, 1953, by her son-in-law, Sidney M. Harris. Mr. Harris testified that while Mrs. Lippman had been president she signed the monthly pension check paid plaintiff, but fussed about doing so, and considered the payments as gifts. After his election, he stated, a new accounting firm employed by the defendant questioned the validity of the payments to plaintiff on several occasions, and in the Spring of 1956, upon its recommendation, he consulted the Company's then attorney, Mr. Ralph Kalish. Harris testified that both Ernst and Ernst, the accounting firm, and Kalish told him there was no need of giving plaintiff the money. He also stated that he had concurred in the view that the payments to plaintiff were mere gratuities rather than amounts due under a contractual obligation, and that following his discussion with the Company's attorney plaintiff was sent a check for $100 on April 1, 1956. Plaintiff declined to accept the reduced amount, and this action followed. Additional facts will be referred to later in this opinion. . . .

Appellant's next complaint is that there was insufficient evidence to support the court's findings that plaintiff would not have quit defendant's employ had she not known and relied upon the promise of defendant to pay her $200 a month for life, and the finding that, from her voluntary retirement until April 1, 1956, plaintiff relied upon the continued receipt of the pension installments. The trial court so found, and, in our opinion, justifiably so. Plaintiff testified, and was corroborated by Harris, defendant's witness, that knowledge of the passage of the resolution was communicated to her on December 27, 1947, the very day it was adopted. She was told at that time by Harris and Flammer, she stated, that she could take the pension as of that day, if she wished. She testified further that she continued to work for another year and a half, through June 30, 1949; that at that time her health was good and she could have continued to work, but that after working for almost forty years she thought she would take a rest. Her testimony continued:

Q. Now, what was the reason—I'm sorry. Did you then quit the employment of the company after you—after this year and a half?
A. Yes.
Q. What was the reason that you left?
A. Well, I thought almost forty years, it was a long time and I thought I would take a little rest.
Q. Yes.

A. And with the pension and what earnings my husband had, we figured we could get along.

Q. Did you rely upon this pension?

A. We certainly did.

Q. Being paid?

A. Very much so. We relied upon it because I was positive that I was going to get it as long as I lived.

Q. Would you have left the employment of the company at that time had it not been for this pension?

A. No.

MR. ALLEN: Just a minute, I object to that as calling for a conclusion and conjecture on the part of this witness.

THE COURT: It will be overruled.

Q. (Mr. Agatstein continuing): Go ahead, now. The question is whether you would have quit the employment of the company at that time had you not relied upon this pension plan?

A. No, I wouldn't.

Q. You would not have. Did you ever seek employment while this pension was being paid to you—

A. (interrupting): No.

Q. Wait a minute, at any time prior—at any other place?

A. No, sir.

Q. Were you able to hold any other employment during that time?

A. Yes, I think so.

Q. Was your health good?

A. My health was good.

It is obvious from the foregoing that there was ample evidence to support the findings of fact made by the court below.

We come, then, to the basic issue in the case . . . "whether plaintiff has proved that she has a right to recover from defendant based upon a legally binding contractual obligation to pay her $200 per month for life."

It is defendant's contention, in essence, that the resolution adopted by its Board of Directors was a mere promise to make a gift, and that no contract resulted either thereby, or when plaintiff retired, because there was no consideration given or paid by the plaintiff. It urges that a promise to make a gift is not binding unless supported by a legal consideration; that the only apparent consideration for the adoption of the foregoing resolution was the "many years of long and faithful service" expressed therein; and that past services are not a valid consideration for a promise. Defendant argues further that there is nothing in the resolution which made its effectiveness conditional upon plaintiff's continued employment, that she was not under contract to work for any length of time but was free to quit whenever she wished, and that she had no contractual right to her position and could have been discharged at any time.

Plaintiff concedes that a promise based upon past services would be without consideration, but contends that there were two other elements which supplied the required element: First, the continuation by plaintiff in the employ of the defendant for the period from December 27, 1947, the date when the resolution was adopted, until the date of her retirement on June 30, 1949. And, second, her change of position, i.e., her retirement, and the abandonment by her of her opportunity to continue in gainful employment, made in reliance on defendant's promise to pay her $200 per month for life.

We must agree with the defendant that the evidence does not support the first of these contentions. There is no language in the resolution predicating plaintiff's right to a pension upon her continued employment. She was not required to work for the defendant for any period of time as a condition to gaining such retirement benefits. She was told that she could quit the day upon which the resolution was adopted, as she herself testified, and it is clear from her own testimony that she made no promise or agreement to continue in the employ of the defendant in return for its promise to pay her a pension. Hence there was lacking that mutuality of obligation which is essential to the validity of a contract. . . .

But as to the second of these contentions we must agree with plaintiff. By the terms of the resolution defendant promised to pay plaintiff the sum of $200 a month upon her retirement. Consideration for a promise has been defined in the Restatement of the Law of Contracts, Section 75, as:

(1) Consideration for a promise is
   (A) an act other than a promise, or
   (B) a forbearance, or

(c) the creation, modification or destruction of a legal relation, or

(d) a return promise, bargained for and given in exchange for the promise.

As the parties agree, the consideration sufficient to support a contract may be either a benefit to the promisor or a loss or detriment to the promisee. . . . Section 90 of the Restatement of the Law of Contracts states that: "A promise which the promisor should reasonably expect to induce action or forbearance of a definite and substantial character on the part of the promisee and which does induce such action or forbearance is binding if injustice can be avoided only by enforcement of the promise." This doctrine has been described as that of "promissory estoppel," as distinguished from that of equitable estoppel or estoppel in pais, the reason for the differentiation being stated as follows:

> It is generally true that one who has led another to act in reasonable reliance on his representations of fact cannot afterwards in litigation between the two deny the truth of the representations, and some courts have sought to apply this principle to the formation of contracts, where, relying on a gratuitous promise, the promisee has suffered detriment. It is to be noticed, however, that such a case does not come within the ordinary definition of estoppel. If there is any representation of an existing fact, it is only that the promisor at the time of making the promise intends to fulfill it. As to such intention there is usually no misrepresentation and if there is, it is not that which has injured the promisee. In other words, he relies on a promise and not on a misstatement of fact; and the term "promissory" estoppel or something equivalent should be used to make the distinction. Williston on Contracts, Rev. Ed., Sec. 139, Vol. 1

In speaking of this doctrine, Judge Learned Hand said in *Porter v. Commissioner of Internal Revenue*, 60 F.2d 673, 675, that " 'promissory estoppel' is now a recognized species of consideration."

As pointed out by our Supreme Court *In re Jamison's Estate, Mo.*, 202 S.W.2d 879, 886, it is stated in the Missouri Annotations to the Restatement under Section 90 that:

There is a variance between the doctrine underlying this section and the theoretical justifications that have been advanced for the Missouri decisions.

That variance, as the authors of the Annotations point out, is that:

This § 90, when applied with § 85, means that the promise described is a contract without any consideration. In Missouri the same practical result is reached without in theory abandoning the doctrine of consideration. . . . In Missouri three theories have been advanced as ground for the decisions (1) *Theory of act for promise.* The induced 'action or forbearance' is the consideration for the promise. (2) *Theory of promissory estoppel.* The induced 'action or forbearance' works an estoppel against the promisor. (3) *Theory of bilateral contract.* When the induced 'action or forbearance' is begun, a promise to complete is implied, and we have an enforceable bilateral contract, the implied promise to complete being the consideration for the original promise.

Was there such an act on the part of plaintiff, in reliance upon the promise contained in the resolution, as will estop the defendant, and therefore create an enforceable contract under the doctrine of promissory estoppel? We think there was. One of the illustrations cited under Section 90 of the Restatement is: "2. A promises B to pay him an annuity during B's life. B thereupon resigns a profitable employment, as A expected that he might. B receives the annuity for some years, in the meantime becoming disqualified from again obtaining good employment. A's promise is binding." This illustration is objected to by defendant as not being applicable to the case at hand. The reason advanced by it is that in the illustration B became "disqualified" from obtaining other employment *before* A discontinued the payments, whereas in this case the plaintiff did not discover that she had cancer and thereby became unemployable until *after* the defendant had discontinued the payments of $200 per month. We think the distinction is immaterial. The only reason for the reference in the illustration to the disqualification of A is in connection with that part of Section 90 regarding the prevention of injustice. The injustice would occur regardless of when the disability occurred. Would defendant contend that the contract would be enforceable if the plaintiff's illness had been discovered on March 31, 1956, the day before it discontinued the payment of the $200 a month, but not if it occurred on April 2nd, the day after? Furthermore, there are more ways to become disqualified for work, or unemployable, than as the result of illness. At the time she retired plaintiff was 57 years of age. At the time the payments were discontinued she was over 63 years of age. It is a matter of common knowledge that it is virtually impossible for a woman of that age to find satisfactory employment, much less a position comparable to that which plaintiff enjoyed at the time of her retirement. . . .

The fact of the matter is that plaintiff's subsequent illness was not the "action or forbearance" which was induced by the promise contained in the resolution. As the trial court correctly decided, such action on plaintiff's part was her retirement from a lucrative position in reliance upon defendant's promise to pay her an annuity or pension. . . .

The Commissioner therefore recommends, for the reasons stated, that the judgment be affirmed.

QUESTIONS AND COMMENTS

1. To what body of law does Section 90 belong? Is it part of contract law? The court goes to great pains to argue that justifiable reliance under Section 90 is a form of consideration. They want to think of this case as a type of contract. In contrast, see Grant Gilmore, *The Death of Contract* (2nd ed) (Columbus: Ohio State University Press, 1995), who relates what he takes to be the inside story of the Restatement deliberations on the definition of consideration and the drafting of Section 90. Contracts are dead, according to Gilmore, because they are becoming subsumed under the general principle of tort liability for causing harm to others.

Further Reading

The best introduction to the law of contracts is E. Allen Farnsworth, *Contracts* (New York: Aspen Press, 1999). The origins of contract are treated in A.W.B. Simpson, *The History of the Law of Contracts* (Oxford: Oxford University Press, 1991). A pioneering work in comparative contracts is *Formation of Contracts: A Study of the Common Core of Legal Systems* (Rudolf Schlesinger ed.) (New York: Oceana, 1968).

TWENTY

Contract as Justice

Culpa in Contrahendo

For the time being at least, contracts are alive and well. They testify to an important liberal principle, namely, that people can come together as strangers and voluntarily commit themselves to an agreement that takes the place of the law between them. The final contract, whether it is written or spoken, is not the only manner in which the law acknowledges voluntary actions that give rise to commitments a stranger may enforce. In the common law, such commitments may arise through conduct on which another person has a right to rely, or act in detrimental reliance. This right of reliance may occur as a result not just of the making of a contract but also of the negotiation and conduct prior to a contract. In the process of negotiating a contract, the negotiators establish a relationship, and they come to expect certain behavior of their negotiating partners. This relationship is particularly important in the civil law, and we will illustrate the common law aspect of it through its civilian counterpart.

The nineteenth-century German legal philosopher Rudolf von Jhering and his followers have referred to this relationship as one of reciprocal trust (*Vertrauensverhältnis*). Trust breeds duties. And if you negligently breach the trust of another, you should pay compensation. They captured this idea in the doctrine of *culpa in contrahendo*.

With the emphasis on trust and reciprocity, the contract is converted from a competitive institution determining who gets the best deal into a potentially cooperative enterprise. The idea behind Jhering's emphasis on the contracting relationship is that duties arise, and they are not necessarily duties of performance. They might be duties of concern, of reciprocal attention to the interests of the other, and to the success of the venture as a whole. In the common law world, these precontractual duties would be hard to ground because there would be no consideration to support them. They are, by definition, precontractual.[1]

The importance of *culpa in contrahendo* is the shift in political theory it represents. Contracts cease being the instrument of the liberal individualist and become the expression of a communal philosophy of reciprocal caring.

The difficulty with this high-flying language is that it lacks clear paradigms of application. What are the cases that really concern Jhering and his followers? The commentators often mention rather trivial cases of people being injured when they enter a store for the purpose of doing business. These "slip-and-fall" cases are well known in the common law of torts, and they offer little theoretical interest. The potential patron is called a "business invitee" in the store, and the owner and possessor of the property owes the invitee duties of care under the general principles of tort law.

The more interesting cases would be those of bad faith or malicious conduct in the course of contract negotiations. Suppose a law firm in Hong Kong is courting you for a job. The partner plans to fly in from Hong Kong to take you to dinner and convince you to join his firm. Before the partner leaves for the airport, you accept a competing offer from a midtown New York firm. You have the partner's cell phone number, but you do not bother to call. The partner arrives in New York and is furious that you did not let him know sooner. Does he have a right to recover at least his airfare and compensation for the loss of his time?

If there is any case that should be covered by *culpa in contrahendo*, this

---

[1] See Rudolf von Jhering, "Culpa in contrahendo oder Schadensersatz bei nichtigen oder nicht zur Perfektion gelangen Verträgen," 4 *Jherings Jahrbücher für die Dogmatik des Bürgerlichen Rechts* 1–112 (1861).

should be it, but it is difficult to know whether it is in fact covered by Jhering's doctrine. It is relatively sure, however, that there would be no recovery under the common law of contracts. There is no promise, no consideration, and no basis for contractual liability.

Significantly, the BGB did not initially endorse Jhering's theory. Nonetheless, the doctrine, developed in an article in 1861, remained binding in German customary law. (The Germans never claimed that their code was exhaustive of all the relevant doctrines of private law.) Sometimes it is treated as an aspect of the general provision in the BGB requiring that all contracts be performed in good faith (*Treu und Glauben*), § 242. Others treated *culpa in contrahendo* as an aspect of the principle of fault or as a principle lying at the foundation of liability. Common lawyers would probably think of this doctrine as something like a tort of "abuse of trust" committed in the course of negotiations. However it is grounded, Jhering's general principle of precontractual liability became part of German law. Yet apart from the negligent injuries to invitees— those that would be treated as torts under the common law—it is difficult to assess how far the doctrine extends in practice.

The BGB formally absorbed the principle of *culpa in contrahendo* in 2001 as part of a general reform of the code. By examining two of these amendments, we can get a better picture of what *culpa in contrahendo* should imply in practice.

BGB § 241 defines the basic commitments that arise in a relationship of obligation. The old definition was simply that in a relationship of obligation each side has the right to demand a performance from the other side. The 2001 amendment expands the conception of obligatory relationship to include a relationship in which, according to its terms, each side is bound to pay attention (*Rücksicht*) to the rights, goods, and legal interests of the other. This is § 241(2).

To explain how these new kinds of relationships could arise, BGB § 311 was also amended. The basic rule of this provision is that obligatory relationships arise only through contract. An amendment of (1) added the phrase "unless the law otherwise provides" to the exclusivity of contract, and then (2) explains what this means:

§ 311(2): A relationship of obligation in the sense of § 241(2) might arise

A. from taking up contract negotiations

B. from initiating a contractual relationship [thus the relevance of § 241(2)]

C. from similar commercial contacts.

The implication is that the mere process of beginning negotiations could entail a relationship in which each side is "bound to pay attention to the rights, goods, and legal interests of the other." Contracts as the bastion of self-seeking individuals is thus transformed into an arena of solidarity and mutual respect. One wonders whether a single institution can both be the crown jewel of liberal individualism and represent a commitment to reciprocal caring.

In a classic article highlighting the conflicting ambitions of contract, Duncan Kennedy elicited this contradiction between individualism and altruism even in the common law theory of contracts.[2] This is a seminal article in the Critical Legal Studies movement. The "critical" dimension of the article lies in the emphasis on the irresolvable contradiction between individualism (liberalism) and altruism (communitarianism) in contract theory.

The amendment of the BGB brings Jhering's thesis within the statutory law, but it hardly clarifies the reach of the principle. All we can say, in theory, is that German law has led the way to establishing the principle of reciprocal caring in contract negotiations and, further, that faultfully injuring another in negotiations should be a basis for liability. The element of fault, or *culpa*, is critical to Jhering's doctrine. The faultful breach of trust is the foundation of the duty to compensate for harm done.

One of the challenges of comparative law is coping with nominal differences of legal doctrine. How do we know when the verbal differences point to an operative difference in the lives of people affected by the law? In the following case, the court claims that Puerto Rican law recognizes *culpa in contrahendo* in § 1802 of its civil code. In its text, though, the provision merely recognizes the general tort of negligently causing harm to another.

---

[2] See Duncan Kennedy, "Form and Substance in Private Law Adjudication," 89 *Harv. L. Rev.* 1685 (1976).

Shelley v. Trafalgar House Public Ltd. Co.

United States District Court for the District of Puerto Rico
977 F. Supp. 95 (1997).

DOMINGUEZ, J.:

. . . [In 1988, Shelley was planning a marina village in Fajardo, when Trafalgar House Public expressed interest in the project. The parties negotiated until October 24, 1989, when they entered a nonbinding "Joint Venture in Puerto Rico," which planned development, construction, and equity participation. Shelley made investments and forwent other development opportunities during the negotiations, but in the end, Trafalgar House rejected the joint venture.]

In the March 11, 1996, Opinion and Order,[3] the Court determined that although there was a contractual choice of law clause in favor of New York law, Puerto Rico law was applicable to the culpa in contrahendo tort claim. The mere determination that there is no contract does not absolve the withdrawing party from all liability. Although there is the dissolution of contractual liability, in a civil code system there is the possibility of extra contractual liability. Puerto Rico recognizes the duty to continue negotiations in good faith. The unjust withdrawal of said negotiations is recognized as the tort doctrine of culpa in contrahendo.[4] "Preliminary negotiations . . . generate a social relationship that imposes on the parties a duty to act in good faith."

. . . Parties have a right to withdraw from negotiations, but the civil code system recognizes that the exercise of said right "is not devoid of liability when it is carried out in an abusive manner." The court provided further guidance by enumerating six factors that should be considered in determining the existence of culpa in contrahendo . . . : (1) the development of the negotiations; (2) the commencement of the negotiations; (3) the direction of the negotiations; (4) the conduct of the parties throughout this time; (5) the stage at which the negotiations

---

[3] *Trafalgar House,* 918 F. Supp. at 522.
[4] See Civil Code Art. 1802, P.R. Laws Ann. tit. 31 § 5141 (1990) ("[a] person who by an act or omission causes damage to another through fault or negligence shall be obliged to repair the damage so done").

ended; and (6) the reasonable expectations of the parties in the con-
summation of the contract.

IV. Damages

The following damages are the subject of the motion to dismiss: Loss
of revenues and operating loss at the marina, $12,233,000; Loss of pro-
ceeds from sale of 60% of the project to Trafalgar House, $14,040,000;
Lost profits from the Shelleys' share of the project, $40,000,000. De-
fendants urge that the aforementioned damages be quashed. . . .

As conceded by Defendants, Plaintiffs are entitled to out-of-pocket
expenses. In fact, Defendants argue that Plaintiffs are entitled to reliance
damages. Reliance damages are defined as those remedies necessary to
place the injured party, who in relying on negotiations to consummate
a contract changed his position, in the same position as he was prior
to relying on said negotiations. But reliance damages are more than
merely out-of-pocket expenses. Reliance damages also include damages
for lost opportunities, specifically in the context of culpa in contrahendo. . . .

The civil code treatise writers provide a further independent basis
for awarding lost opportunity costs. Nevertheless, there are treatise writers who believe that culpa in contrahendo should not include compensation for foregone opportunities. This Court, faced with two opposing views, must decide which path to follow. The Court finds the
reasoning of the former treatise writers more compatible with the interpretation of article 1802. In Puerto Rico, under article 1802, the
doctrine of extra contractual liability is very broad. In 1994, the Puerto
Rico supreme court defined the scope of this liability. " 'Injury is any
material or moral loss suffered by a person, either in its natural rights
or in its property or patrimony, brought about by violation of a legal
provision and which is chargeable on another party.' " As a result, the
damages for lost opportunities shall be authorized if they are not spec-
ulative in nature.

Plaintiffs argue that they are entitled to expectation damages otherwise known as benefit-of-the-bargain damages. The Court refuses to
extend the doctrine of culpa in contrahendo to those reaches. A final
agreement was never reached; Plaintiffs are then not to receive the
benefit of the bargain. . . .

In sum, under culpa in contrahendo, the lost profits included within subparagraph e must be dismissed because they fall outside the scope of reliance damages and all expectation damages are clearly unwarranted under the culpa in contrahendo theory. . . .

QUESTIONS AND COMMENTS

1. One of the interesting side issues in the *Trafalgar House* litigation was whether the plaintiff had a right to a jury trial to determine whether the defendant was liable for *culpa in contrahendo*. The Seventh Amendment to the U.S. Constitution, guaranteeing a jury trial in all "suits at common law" over a certain amount, applies in Puerto Rico. The problem was whether *culpa in contrahendo* should be classified as "legal" or "equitable." If the latter, the plaintiff would not have a right to a jury trial. There was an argument for saying that it was equitable because the closest doctrine in Anglo-American law is "promissory estoppel," which prevents the defendant from denying the existence of a contract under certain circumstances. Promissory estoppel is treated as a principle in equity. Yet, because the court considered the doctrine as arising under a code provision on tort law, it held that the action was in tort and that the plaintiff Shelley was entitled to a jury trial. Though we do not know the final outcome of this dispute, one could imagine that the jury trial was helpful to the local investors.

2. Without going into the facts in greater detail, there is no way of knowing whether in this case the plaintiff had a sound legal claim based on *culpa in contrahendo*. Therefore, it is difficult to find guidance in this case on the question whether the law student who lets the partner fly in from Hong Kong is liable in *culpa in contrahendo*. Is the student negligent, malicious, an intentional wrongdoer, or just careless and selfish?

Communal Judgments of Fairness

The common law of contract was wary of judging the adequacy of consideration, that is, of deciding whether the bargain was fair. The liberal view is that everyone is responsible for the choices he or she makes. The state should not interfere and judge whether the price is just. Of course, if there is coercion, the giving of consent is undermined. All codes contain a principle that, in cases of duress, the nominal giving of consent is not binding.[5] The principle is fundamental in the common law as well.

But what if there are no threats? What if the parties appear to consent but the terms are very onerous? This is the problem posed in the following case. The seller, Walker-Thomas Furniture Company, wrote conditions into the installment contract that appear to be unfair. If the buyer buys several items from the seller, the debt on all items must be paid in full before the buyer acquires full title to any single item. It goes without saying that the typical buyer would not understand this condition written into the standard printed sales agreement (note the legalese in which the condition is expressed). What do the courts do then? The liberal theory says: Enforce the contract. The alternative is a form of paternalism: The courts will undertake to protect the weak, the needy, and the ill informed.

The legal basis for the community's paternalistic intervention remains in doubt. The French have an explicit provision on unfair bargains with regard to the sale of land. (See § 1674: "If the seller of land is deprived of seven-twelfths of the value of the land, he or she has the right to demand the rescission of the sale. . . .") This provision seems to have different roots from our present concern with installment contracts made according to standardized forms. The French law seems to reveal a class bias. The families that owned land for many generations should not lose their wealth simply because one reckless offspring sells the land for too low a price. With regard to ordinary contracts, particularly for the sale of goods, the French code (Art. 1118) is explicit that this principle (called *lésion*) does not apply.

There are two traditional techniques for asserting judicial power in order to protect people like Ora Williams in the following case. One technique is to expand the idea of duress or undue influence to include these cases of imposing conditions on consumers of inferior bargaining power. The alternative to invoking the idea of "good morals and public order" is to read into the law certain conditions of fairness as a condition of valid contracts. For example, the German provision on "good morals," BGB § 138(II), includes a clause referring to "the exploitation of a condition of distress, inexperience, poverty, or weakness" to generate a con-

---

[5] See *Code civil* § 1109 (no consent if extorted by violence); BGB § 123 (1) (expressions of the will voidable if given under threats).

tractual advantage disproportionate to the consideration given. Contracts that are immoral in this way are considered null and void.

The Uniform Commercial Code (UCC) offers the most influential response to this problem in the common law world. Recognizing the need for paternalistic intervention, the UCC established the new legal ground of "unconscionability" as a ground for attacking the validity of a contract. The following case illustrates the way the new provision works. Note that the provision actually applied is not the UCC, which is merely a model code for the states to consider, but the UCC as adopted in the District of Columbia:

Williams v. Walker-Thomas Furniture Co.

United States Court of Appeals for the District of Columbia
121 U.S. App. D.C. 315; 350 F.2d 445 (1965)

SKELLY WRIGHT, J.:

Appellee, Walker-Thomas Furniture Company, operates a retail furniture store in the District of Columbia. During the period from 1957 to 1962 each appellant in these cases purchased a number of household items from Walker-Thomas, for which payment was to be made in installments. The terms of each purchase were contained in a printed form contract which set forth the value of the purchased item and purported to lease the item to appellant for a stipulated monthly rent payment. The contract then provided, in substance, that title would remain in Walker-Thomas until the total of all the monthly payments made equaled the stated value of the item, at which time appellants could take title. In the event of a default in the payment of any monthly installment, Walker-Thomas could repossess the item.

The contract further provided that "the amount of each periodical installment payment to be made by [purchaser] to the Company under this present lease shall be inclusive of and not in addition to the amount of each installment payment to be made by [purchaser] under such prior leases, bills or accounts; and all payments now and hereafter made by [purchaser] shall be credited pro rata on all outstanding leases, bills and accounts due the Company by [purchaser] at the time each such payment is made." The effect of this rather obscure provision was to keep a balance due on every item purchased until the balance due on all items, whenever purchased, was liquidated. As a result, the debt incurred at the time of purchase of each item was secured by the right to repossess all the items previously purchased by the same purchaser, and each new item purchased automatically became subject to a security interest arising out of the previous dealings.

On May 12, 1962, appellant Thorne purchased an item described as a Daveno, three tables, and two lamps, having total stated value of $391.10. Shortly thereafter, he defaulted on his monthly payments and appellee sought to replevy all the items purchased since the first transaction in 1958. Similarly, on April 17, 1962, appellant Williams bought a stereo set of stated value of $514.95. She too defaulted shortly thereafter, and appellee sought to replevy all the items purchased since December, 1957. The Court of General Sessions granted judgment for appellee. The District of Columbia Court of Appeals affirmed, and we granted appellants' motion for leave to appeal to this court. [At the time of this purchase her account showed a balance of $164 still owing from her prior purchases. The total of all the purchases made over the years in question came to $1,800. The total payments amounted to $1,400.] . . .

Appellants' principal contention, rejected by both the trial and the appellate courts below, is that these contracts, or at least some of them, are unconscionable and, hence, not enforceable. In other jurisdictions, it has been held as a matter of common law that unconscionable contracts are not enforceable. While no decision of this court so holding has been found, the notion that an unconscionable bargain should not be given full enforcement is by no means novel. In *Scott v. United States*, 79 U.S. (12 Wall.) 443, 445, 20 L. Ed. 438 (1870), the Supreme Court stated:

> If a contract be unreasonable and unconscionable, but not void for fraud, a court of law will give to the party who sues for its breach damages, not according to its letter, but only such as he is equitably entitled to.

Since we have never adopted or rejected such a rule, the question here presented is actually one of first impression.

Congress has recently enacted the Uniform Commercial Code, which specifically provides that the court may refuse to enforce a contract which it finds to be unconscionable at the time it was made. 28 D.C.CODE § 2-302 (Supp. IV 1965). The enactment of this section, which occurred subsequent to the contracts here in suit, does not mean that the common law of the District of Columbia was otherwise at the time of enactment, nor does it preclude the court from adopting a similar rule in the exercise of its powers to develop the common law for the District of Columbia. In fact, in view of the absence of prior authority on the point, we consider the congressional adoption of § 2-302 persuasive authority for following the rationale of the cases from which the section is explicitly derived. Accordingly, we hold that where the element of unconscionability is present at the time a contract is made, the contract should not be enforced.

Unconscionability has generally been recognized to include an absence of meaningful choice on the part of one of the parties together with contract terms which are unreasonably favorable to the other party. Whether a meaningful choice is present in a particular case can only be determined by consideration of all the circumstances surrounding the transaction. In many cases the meaningfulness of the choice is negated by a gross inequality of bargaining power. The manner in which the contract was entered is also relevant to this consideration. Did each party to the contract, considering his obvious education or lack of it, have a reasonable opportunity to understand the terms of the contract, or were the important terms hidden in a maze of fine print and minimized by deceptive sales practices? Ordinarily, one who signs an agreement without full knowledge of its terms might be held to assume the risk that he has entered a one-sided bargain. But when a party of little bargaining power, and hence little real choice, signs a commercially unreasonable contract with little or no knowledge of its terms, it is hardly likely that his consent, or even an objective manifestation of his consent, was ever given to all the terms. In such a case the usual rule that the terms of the agreement are not to be questioned should be abandoned and the court should consider whether the terms of the contract are so unfair that enforcement should be withheld.[6]

In determining reasonableness or fairness, the primary concern

---

[6] See the general discussion of "Boiler-Plate Agreements" in Karl Llewellyn, *The Common Law Tradition: Deciding Appeals* 362–371 (Boston: Little, Brown, 1960). As an expert in the law of sales, he became the leading architect of the Uniform Commercial Code.

must be with the terms of the contract considered in light of the circumstances existing when the contract was made. The test is not simple, nor can it be mechanically applied. The terms are to be considered "in the light of the general commercial background and the commercial needs of the particular trade or case." Corbin suggests the test as being whether the terms are "so extreme as to appear unconscionable according to the mores and business practices of the time and place." [Corbin's *Treatise on Contracts* is one of the two leading treatises on the subject in English. The other is Williston, which is older and more traditional in its orientation.] We think this formulation correctly states the test to be applied in those cases where no meaningful choice was exercised upon entering the contract.

Because the trial court and the appellate court did not feel that enforcement could be refused, no findings were made on the possible unconscionability of the contracts in these cases. Since the record is not sufficient for our deciding the issue as a matter of law, the cases must be remanded to the trial court for further proceedings.

So ordered.

DANAHER, J., DISSENTING:

The District of Columbia Court of Appeals obviously was as unhappy about the situation here presented as any of us can possibly be. Its opinion in the Williams case, quoted in the majority text, concludes: "We think Congress should consider corrective legislation to protect the public from such exploitive contracts as were utilized in the case at bar."

My view is thus summed up by an able court which made no finding that there had actually been sharp practice. Rather the appellant seems to have known precisely where she stood.

There are many aspects of public policy here involved. What is a luxury to some may seem an outright necessity to others. Is public oversight to be required of the expenditures of relief funds? A washing machine, e.g., in the hands of a relief client might become a fruitful source of income. Many relief clients may well need credit, and certain business establishments will take long chances on the sale of items, expecting their pricing policies will afford a degree of protection commensurate with the risk. Perhaps a remedy when necessary will be found within the provisions of the "Loan Shark" law, D.C.CODE §§ 26-601 et seq. (1961).

I mention such matters only to emphasize the desirability of a cautious approach to any such problem, particularly since the law for so long has allowed parties such great latitude in making their own contracts. I dare say there must annually be thousands upon thousands of installment credit transactions in this jurisdiction, and one can only speculate as to the effect the decision in these cases will have.

I join the District of Columbia Court of Appeals in its disposition of the issues.

■

QUESTIONS AND COMMENTS

1. To anticipate the economic analysis of legal relations, discussed in detail in Chapter Twenty-Three, think about the impact of this decision on future credit transactions among furniture stores and poor buyers. Will the buyers be able to obtain credit so easily? Will the prices go up to compensate the sellers for the loss sustained in this case? If the market always adjusts prices in recognition of the relative advantage of buyer and seller, is there a good reason for courts to intervene in the market in order to improve the condition of buyers like Ms. Williams?

2. What is the political philosophy reflected in the Williams case? Is it liberalism or paternalism? Is the state intervening here because it cannot trust buyers to know what they are getting into? Or is this a case of protecting one person from harm inflicted by another, namely, from a buyer suffering "exploitation" by a seller?

■

Further Reading

An important perspective on the limits of the enforceability of contracts is presented in E. Allan Farnsworth, *Changing Your Mind: The Law of Regretted Decisions* (New Haven, CT: Yale University Press, 1998).

TWENTY-ONE

Contractual Harm

Breach of Contract and Harm

If all people were honest and performed their contracts in good faith, we would hardly need laws, courts, and coercive means of enforcement. The courts become relevant only because contractual relationships occasionally break down. There are more differences among legal systems than one might imagine in the theory and regulation of "breakdown."

The German system is most unusual for attempting to regulate the field of a breakdown without relying on a concept of breach.[1] The pillars of the German system are "impossibility" and "delay" in enforcement. The primary remedy under § 249 BGB is performance of the original obligation, an obligation that the obligee can convert under certain circumstances in monetary damages. By contrast, the common law states that someone who has breached once is likely to breach again. There is no point to asking for the originally promised performance; it's better to seek monetary compensation for the loss represented by the nonperformance. The standard common law remedy in contracts as well as torts is damages—money to make good the loss. Only if the performance has a

[1] The French system relied on the concept of breach from the beginning. See *Code civil* § 1147.

unique object—for example, a promise to convey a specific painting or piece of land—can one think about injunction in equity to compel the performance. The drafters of the BGB were so keen about developing their symmetrical system of obligations in book two of the code that they overlooked certain practical problems, such as the problem of negligently breaching subsidiary duties of care in contracts that have business purposes. Shortly after the BGB came into force, scholars noticed that their system was insufficient, that certain problems required a supplementary concept of breach. Thus they—and subsequently the court—fashioned an extrastatutory remedy called "affirmative breach of contract." Admittedly, as in the case of *culpa in contrahendo*, many of these problems are instances of causing harm in the course of contractual relationships and could be handled under the law of torts.

German scholars have internal reasons for pushing the contract remedy as far as it would go in place of the tort remedy. German tort law has no strict rule of the type known in the common law, holding the employer vicariously liable for the torts of their employees. There is always a question whether the employer was at fault in selecting and supervising the employees. (See BGB § 831: An employer is not liable for unlawful tortious conduct of employee if there was no fault in the selection or supervision of the employee.)

The biggest single doctrinal difference between the civil law and the common law of contracts is that the former system requires intentional or negligent fault as a condition of liability for breach. Though there are some exceptions (such as the law of express warranties), contract resembles tort liability, with fault at the center of both. Common lawyers claim not to be interested in fault in contract breach, but this seems not to be true in many critical areas, such as the law of mistake.

Consider the problem of the passerby who enters into an auction and, without knowing it, gives the signal for a bid by standing up and folding her arms. Is she bound by the bid she thereby signaled? Every observer took her to be bidding. Therefore, the meaning of her actions—not to herself, but to others—was to make a bid on the item then being auctioned. Those who say that she is not bound follow the subjective theory of contracts; according to this view, all that matters is what she intends by her words or actions. Those inclined to say that she is bound follow the objective theory, which holds that she is bound by the way reasonable people interpret what she has done.

Every legal system adopts some version of the objective theory of contracts, and therefore there might be some circumstances in which someone does not wish to be bound but uses language in a way that induces others reasonably to rely on a certain meaning. Is this the case with our passerby who inadvertently makes a bid at the auction? The sensible approach to this problem in all legal systems is to inquire who was at fault for the misunderstanding. In this case, the passerby was not at fault because there was no obvious way for her to know that standing up and folding her arms would be understood in that context as a bid. But there might be some cases in which individuals were liable for using trade language they did not completely understand. (For example, a client gets confused about the meaning of the words and gives a broker a "limit" order when the intent is to make a "stop" order to sell shares of stock. The client is bound by what he or she says.)

To be clear about the impact of the mistake, the general approach to contract law is that the passerby makes a reasonable mistake; she is not at fault for inducing others to think that she had made a bid, and she has not made a contract. She is not liable even if others have relied on the apparent contract.

According to some German sources, the faultless, misunderstood passerby would not have made an offer at all; according to other sources, she would be bound by the apparent offer but could void the subsequent contract on the basis of mistake, subject to liability for reliance damages. BGB §§ 119, 122.

Issues of mistake readily blend into the topic of contractual interpretation. Ask yourself whether the following influential case is one about mistake or interpretation? Is it too late to void the contract and part company?

Jacob & Youngs, Inc. v. Kent

New York Court of Appeals
230 N.Y. 239, 129 N.E. 889, 23 A.L.R. 1429 (1921)

CARDOZO, J.:

[The plaintiff builder is seeking the defendant houseowner to pay the last construction bill, which the houseowner is trying to avoid by claiming that the builder installed pipes other than those required in their construction contract. The contract required Reading pipe, but the builder mistakenly installed Cohoes pipe. To fix the mistake would cost the builder more than the amount owed it, but the difference in the value of the pipe was negligible.]

The plaintiff built a country residence for the defendant at a cost of upwards of $77,000, and now sues to recover a balance of $3,483.46, remaining unpaid. The work of construction ceased in June, 1914, and the defendant then began to occupy the dwelling. There was no complaint of defective performance until March, 1915. One of the specifications for the plumbing work provides that "all wrought iron pipe must be well galvanized, lap welded pipe of the grade known as 'standard pipe' of Reading manufacture." The defendant learned in March, 1915, that some of the pipe, instead of being made in Reading, was the product of other factories. The plaintiff was accordingly directed by the architect to do the work anew. The plumbing was then encased within the walls except in a few places where it had to be exposed. Obedience to the order meant more than the substitution of other pipe. It meant the demolition at great expense of substantial parts of the completed structure. The plaintiff left the work untouched, and asked for a certificate that the final payment was due. Refusal of the certificate was followed by this suit.

The evidence sustains a finding that the omission of the prescribed brand of pipe was neither fraudulent nor willful. It was the result of the oversight and inattention of the plaintiff's subcontractor. Reading pipe is distinguished from Cohoes pipe and other brands only by the name of the manufacturer stamped upon it at intervals of between six and seven feet. Even the defendant's architect, though he inspected the pipe upon arrival, failed to notice the discrepancy. The plaintiff tried to show that the brands installed, though made by other manufacturers, were the same in quality, in appearance, in market value and in cost as the brand stated in the contract—that they were, indeed, the same thing, though manufactured in another place. The evidence was excluded, and a verdict directed for the defendant. The Appellate Division reversed, and granted a new trial.

We think the evidence, if admitted, would have supplied some basis for the inference that the defect was insignificant in its relation to the project. The courts never say that one who makes a contract fills the measure of his duty by less than full performance. They do say, however, that an omission, both trivial and innocent, will sometimes be atoned for by allowance of the resulting damage, and will not always be the breach of a condition to be followed by a forfeiture. The distinction is akin to that between dependent and independent promises, or between promises and conditions. Some promises are so plainly independent that they can never by fair construction be conditions of one another. Others are so plainly dependent that they must always be conditions. Others, though dependent and thus conditions when there is departure in point of substance, will be viewed as independent and collateral when the departure is insignificant. Considerations partly of justice and partly of presumable intention are to tell us whether this or that promise shall be placed in one class or in another. The simple and the uniform will call for different remedies from the multifarious and the intricate. The margin of departure within the range of normal expectation upon a sale of common chattels will vary from the margin to be expected upon a contract for the construction of a mansion or a "skyscraper." There will be harshness sometimes and oppression in the implication of a condition when the thing upon which labor has been expended is incapable of surrender because united to the land, and equity and reason in the implication of a like condition when the subject-matter, if defective, is in shape to be returned. From the conclusion that promises may not be treated as dependent to the extent of their uttermost minutiae without a sacrifice of justice, the progress is a short one to the conclusion that they may not be so treated without a perversion of intention. Intention not otherwise revealed may be presumed to hold in contemplation the reasonable and probable. If something else is in view, it must not be left to implication. There will be no assumption of a purpose to visit venial faults with oppressive retribution.

Those who think more of symmetry and logic in the development of legal rules than of practical adaptation to the attainment of a just result will be troubled by a classification where the lines of division are so wavering and blurred. Something, doubtless, may be said on the score of consistency and certainty in favor of a stricter standard. The courts have balanced such considerations against those of equity and fairness, and found the latter to be the weightier. The decisions in this state commit us to the liberal view,[2] which is making its way, nowadays, in jurisdictions slow to welcome it. Where the line is to be drawn between the important and the trivial cannot be settled by a formula. "In the nature of the case precise boundaries are impossible." The same omission may take on one aspect or another according to its setting. Substitution of equivalents may not have the same significance in fields of art on the one side and in those of mere utility on the other. Nowhere will change be tolerated, however, if it is so dominant or pervasive as in any real or substantial measure to frustrate the purpose of the contract. There is no general license to install whatever, in the builder's judgment, may be regarded as "just as good." The question is one of degree, to be answered, if there is doubt, by the triers of the facts, and, if the inferences are certain, by the judges of the law. [I.e., not by the jury!] We must weigh the purpose to be served, the desire to be gratified, the excuse for deviation from the letter, the cruelty of enforced adherence. Then only can we tell whether literal fulfilment is to be implied by law as a condition. This is not to say that the parties are not free by apt and certain words to effectuate a purpose that performance of every term shall be a condition of recovery. That question is not here. This is merely to say that the law will be slow to impute the purpose, in the silence of the parties, where the significance of the default is grievously out of proportion to the oppression of the forfeiture. The willful transgressor must accept the penalty of his transgression. For him there is no occasion to mitigate the rigor of implied conditions. The transgressor whose default is unintentional and trivial may hope for mercy if he will offer atonement for his wrong.

In the circumstances of this case, we think the measure of the allowance is not the cost of replacement, which would be great, but the difference in value, which would be either nominal or nothing. . . . It is true that in most cases the cost of replacement is the measure. The owner is entitled to the money which will permit him to complete, unless the cost of completion is grossly and unfairly out of proportion to the good to be attained. When that is true, the measure is the difference in value. . . . The rule that gives a remedy in cases of sub-

---

[2] What do the words *equity* and *liberal* mean in this context? It is safe to assume that the meaning differs from the usual sense in which we used those terms.

stantial performance with compensation for defects of trivial or inap-
preciable importance, has been developed by the courts as an instrument of justice. The measure of the allowance must be shaped to the
same end.

The order should be affirmed, and judgment absolute directed in
favor of the plaintiff upon the stipulation, with costs in all courts.

McLAUGHLIN J., DISSENTING.

I dissent. The plaintiff did not perform its contract. Its failure to do so
was either intentional or due to gross neglect which, under the uncon-
tradicted facts, amounted to the same thing, nor did it make any proof
of the cost of compliance, where compliance was possible.

Under its contract it obligated itself to use in the plumbing only
pipe (between 2,000 and 2,500 feet) made by the Reading Manufacturing Company. The first pipe delivered was about 1,000 feet and the
plaintiff's superintendent then called the attention of the foreman of
the subcontractor, who was doing the plumbing, to the fact that the
specifications annexed to the contract required all pipe used in the
plumbing to be of the Reading Manufacturing Company. They then
examined it for the purpose of ascertaining whether this delivery was
of that manufacture and found it was. Thereafter, as pipe was required
in the progress of the work, the foreman of the subcontractor would
leave word at its shop that he wanted a specified number of feet of
pipe, without in any way indicating of what manufacture. Pipe would
thereafter be delivered and installed in the building, without any examination whatever. Indeed, no examination, so far as appears, was
made by the plaintiff, the subcontractor, defendant's architect, or any
one else, of any of the pipe except the first delivery, until after the
building had been completed. Plaintiff's architect then refused to give
the certificate of completion, upon which the final payment depended,
because all of the pipe used in the plumbing was not of the kind called
for by the contract. After such refusal, the subcontractor removed the
covering or insulation from about 900 feet of pipe which was exposed
in the basement, cellar and attic, and all but 70 feet was found to have
been manufactured, not by the Reading Company, but by other manufacturers, some by the Cohoes Rolling Mill Company, some by the
National Steel Works, some by the South Chester Tubing Company,
and some which bore no manufacturer's mark at all. The balance of

the pipe had been so installed in the building that an inspection of it could not be had without demolishing, in part at least, the building itself.

I am of the opinion the trial court was right in directing a verdict for the defendant. The plaintiff agreed that all the pipe used should be of the Reading Manufacturing Company. . . . Defendant contracted for pipe made by the Reading Manufacturing Company. What his reason was for requiring this kind of pipe is of no importance. He wanted that and was entitled to it. It may have been a mere whim on his part, but even so, he had a right to this kind of pipe, regardless of whether some other kind, according to the opinion of the contractor or experts, would have been "just as good, better, or done just as well." He agreed to pay only upon condition that the pipe installed were made by that company and he ought not to be compelled to pay unless that condition be performed. The rule, therefore, of substantial performance, with damages for unsubstantial omissions, has no application. . . .

For the foregoing reasons I think the judgment of the Appellate Division should be reversed and the judgment of the Trial Term affirmed.

Hiscock, C.J., Hogan and Crane, JJ., concur with Cardozo, J.; Pound and Andrews, JJ., concur with McLaughlin, J.

QUESTIONS AND COMMENTS

1. Two different visions of contract collide in this case, one favored by Cardozo and the other by the dissent. The dissent emphasizes at the end of the opinion that the defendant wanted Reading pipe and he did not get it. This meant that the plaintiff breached and that the plaintiff either replaced the pipe or paid damages to the defendant. In any event, since the plaintiff had not performed properly, the defendant did not have to pay the final installment on the contract. This is the strict liberal view of contract. The parties make a deal, and each can rely on each word in the agreement.

2. By contrast with this view, Cardozo applies the rule that if the plaintiff has substantially performed his obligations, the defendant becomes liable for the reciprocal performance, subject to collecting damages from the plaintiff for that portion that was not performed. That means that the defendant was liable for the final payment minus any

loss that occurred to him because he got one brand of pipe rather than another.

3. Note that the underlying disagreement between the majority and the dissent turns on how faultful the plaintiff's substituting one brand of pipe for another seems to have been. According to Cardozo, it was "neither fraudulent nor willful." In the view of the dissent, the switch in the pipes was "either intentional or due to gross neglect." This difference in the evaluations of the builder's behavior shapes the rest of the analysis. If he was not at fault, he should not be penalized by the trivial difference between the two different kinds of pipe. If he really was intentionally in breach, then the defendant had a stronger case. The radical disagreement about the facts and their valuation occurred because the case never went to a jury. The trial court found for the defendant, and the appellate division affirmed. Here the Supreme Court directed a verdict for the plaintiff.

4. What is this case about? Is it a problem of contractual interpretation, whether the defendant really thought that Reading pipe was the essence of the contract? If so, why should it not have been turned over to a jury in the way interpretation issues are usually handled? Or is the case, as Cardozo suggests, about the law of contracts, about what a claimant can legitimately demand of someone who complies substantially, but not fully, with his contractual obligations? The most important question about imperfect performance is dealt with in the common law by the doctrine of "material breach." For more details on the factors determining whether a breach is material, see the *Restatement, Second, of Contracts*, § 241.

5. The German analysis of this case would rely on the concept of "abuse of rights." The defendant would have a right to demand replacement of the pipes, but he would abuse that right by exercising it under these circumstances. Does that make more sense than Cardozo's reliance on substantial performance?

■

German law is more explicit about the importance of fault in analyzing cases of mistake. In the following excerpt, the authors advocate applying the theory of the BGB to a famous common law case of misunderstanding on both sides. Under the common law approach, the mutual mistake precluded the conclusion of a contract; neither side was liable to the other for anything. But the result would be different under American law, the authors claim, if one party was at fault and the other innocent. Even if there is no contract under German law, the courts would apply the doctrine of *culpa in contrahendo*, which also considers the relative fault of the parties:

From Friedrich Kessler and Edith Fine

"Culpa in Contrahendo, Bargaining in Good Faith, and Freedom of Contract: A Comparative Study"
77 *Harvard Law Review* 401 (1964)

The difficulties encountered by rigidly applying an objective theory stand out vividly in cases, such as the celebrated *Raffles v. Wichelhaus* (England 1864), involving latent ambiguity, frequently called "mutual misunderstanding" or "mutual mistake." This case dealt with the sale of a cargo of cotton "to arrive ex 'Peerless' from Bombay." Unfortunately, there were two ships with the same name but with different sailing dates. The seller meant a Peerless which arrived in December, the buyer a Peerless which arrived in October, and refused the December shipment. In the suit by the seller against the buyer for nonacceptance the court gave judgment for the buyer. Under our law the decision makes good sense since there was no meeting of minds (no consensus ad idem—about the object of the contract) and due to the ambiguity of the phrase, the objective theory could not be invoked. Of course, this is only true if we assume that neither party was nor should have been aware of the ambiguity or that both were equally negligent.

The solution denying contractual liability in the absence of culpa in contrahendo would be acceptable to a German lawyer. If both parties were negligent the loss would be divided in accordance with the comparative negligence of the parties. If one of the parties knew or should have known that there were two vessels with different sailing dates, then under the American law there would be a contract for the goods from the steamer which the innocent party had in mind. German law, by contrast, would deny that a contract had come into existence. But following culpa in contrahendo rules, liability would be imposed on the "negligent" party to the extent of the reliance interest of the other party. To sum up, under the German solution of latent ambiguity, the nonassenting party is not liable at all if he was not negligent or if there were no reliance damages; under the American solution, the party who knew or had reason to know the meaning placed on the contract by the other party is bound in accordance with the objective theory of contracts. But notions of good faith and culpa in contrahendo often furnish the justification for applying the objective theory. Cases denying the existence of a contract or recovery typically stress either that both parties acted in good faith or that the losing party was lacking in good faith or was guilty of negligent use of language.

■

The common law recognizes reliance damages as the proper measure in § 90 cases, where recovery is based on justifiable reliance. But what about other cases of breach? Should the plaintiff's condition be measured against what would have been the case, had the contract been performed?

This problem is addressed in the following classic case in which the jury found that the defendant physician had promised to provide the patient plaintiff with a hand as good as new, "100% perfect"—but that is not the way things turned out. The question was the proper extent of damages.

■

Hawkins v. McGee

Supreme Court of New Hampshire
84 N.H. 114; 146 A. 641 (1929) (citations omitted)

BRANCH, J.:

"By 'damages' as that term is used in the law of contracts, is intended compensation for a breach, measured in the terms of the contract." The purpose of the law is to "put the plaintiff in as good a position as he would have been in had the defendant kept his contract." The measure of recovery "is based upon what the defendant should have given the plaintiff, not what the plaintiff has given the defendant or otherwise expended." "The only losses that can be said fairly to come within the terms of a contract are such as the parties must have had in mind when the contract was made, or such as they either knew or ought to have known would probably result from a failure to comply with its terms." . . .

The present case is closely analogous to one in which a machine is built for a certain purpose and warranted to do certain work. In such cases, the usual rule of damages for breach of warranty in the sale of chattels is applied and it is held that the measure of damages is the difference between the value of the machine if it had corresponded with the warranty and its actual value, together with such incidental losses as the parties knew or ought to have known would probably result from a failure to comply with its terms. . . . The rule thus applied is well settled in this state. "As a general rule, the measure of the vendee's damages is the difference between the value of the goods as they would have been if the warranty as to quality had been true, and the actual value at the time of the sale, including gains prevented and losses sustained, and such other damages as could be reasonably anticipated by the parties as likely to be caused by the vendor's failure to keep his agreement, and could not by reasonable care on the part of the vendee have been avoided." . . . We, therefore, conclude that the true measure of the plaintiff's damage in the present case is the difference between the value to him of a perfect hand or a good hand, such as the jury found the defendant promised him, and the value of his hand in its present condition, including any incidental consequences fairly within the contemplation of the parties when they made their contract. Damages not thus limited, although naturally resulting, are not to be given.

The extent of the plaintiff's suffering does not measure this difference in value. The pain necessarily incident to a serious surgical operation was a part of the contribution which the plaintiff was willing to make to his joint undertaking with the defendant to produce a good hand. It was a legal detriment suffered by him which constituted a part of the consideration given by him for the contract. It represented a part of the price which he was willing to pay for a good hand, but it furnished no test of the value of a good hand or the difference between the value of the hand which the defendant promised and the one which resulted from the operation.

It was also erroneous and misleading to submit to the jury as a separate element of damage any change for the worse in the condition of the plaintiff's hand resulting from the operation, although this error

438   THE THEORY OF THE COMMON LAW

was probably more prejudicial to the plaintiff than to the defendant. Any such ill effect of the operation would be included under the true rule of damages set forth above, but damages might properly be assessed for the defendant's failure to improve the condition of the hand even if there were no evidence that its condition was made worse as a result of the operation. . . .

New trial.

∎

QUESTIONS AND COMMENTS

1. How should the value of a perfect hand be measured, compared with the plaintiff's injured hand? In workers' compensation statutes, an injured hand has a fixed amount. That is, for injuries on the job, we let the legislature decide the value. But what should the theoretical guide be? Some guides have horrific aspects. How would a slave market compare the value of a slave with a perfect hand against the value of one with a hand like this plaintiff's? How can we imagine a jury determining what value Hawkins would have realized with a whole and perfect hand? Can a judge do it better?

2. Why did the court not follow the "substantial performance" rule in this case? After all, the defendant physician might have made Hawkins's hand "substantially" perfect. Is that not all that can be reasonably expected?

3. In the end, there are only two theories of damages that cut across all three fields of private law (property, tort, and contracts). The more basic theory is called the *negative interest*, and the alternative (naturally) is called the *positive interest*. The way things are before the legal incident is the bench line 0. If the legal incident sets you back behind the bench line-100, then you suffer a negative loss of 100, and you are entitled to compensation of 100 units to bring you to the bench line. This is expressed by saying that you are entitled to be made whole, to be brought to the condition you would have been in, had the incident never occurred. Of course, the assumption is that money provides a surrogate for other kind of losses—for having someone encroach on your driveway or for their not supplying the kind of pipe you had your heart set on. Under Section 90, the negative interest is based on reliance. In torts, as we shall see, it is based on physical damage. But this should not blind us to the similarity in

the philosophy of damages—to restore the situation to the status quo ante, the situation that would have existed had the damage-causing incident not occurred.

4. The alternative theory of damages, the positive interest, is based on a possibility of moving forward from the bench line, say 100 units. Suppose Bob has a summer cottage that Bob could rent out for 100 units every summer. One summer Bob decides to leave it vacant, and an interloper squats in Bob's house without his knowledge. The interloper leaves the place spic and span, but Bob later discovers that he was there. Is Bob entitled to the rental value of the premises for the summer? Yes. Bob is not hurt by the interloper's living there. There is no negative loss, but there is a deprivation of an opportunity that Bob could have realized had he chosen to, and as owner he is entitled to make that choice. This is the positive interest that accrues to Bob by virtue of his ownership of the cottage.

These same principles underlie the *Hawkins* case. A contract generates a positive interest, in this case, an expectation of a perfect hand. If we treat the contracting party as the bearer of that legitimate expectation, then the possibility of improving his or her situation is comparable to that of a house owner who could rent out the house. Whether either realizes that opportunity should be that party's choice, just as it is the choice of the cottage owner to rent out the cottage for 100 units. The doctor's breach is like the interloper's squatting. Both deprive someone of a positive interest, a claim based on law to improve their situation if they so choose. Both are entitled, therefore, to compensation in place of the positive interest.

■

Further Reading

For the canonical view of remedies for breach of contracts, see E. Allan Farnsworth, *Contracts* (New York: Aspen Law & Business, 1999). For a more detailed consideration of the damages problem in *Hawkins*, see Robert Cooter and Melvin Aron Eisenberg, "Damages for Breach of Contract," 73 *Cal. L. Rev.* 1432 (1985). The origin of the notion that contract damages should be based on the reliance of the injured party is in the famous and still quite relevant exposition by Lon L. Fuller and William Purdue, "The Reliance Interest in Contract Damages" (pts. 1 & 2), 46 *Yale L.J.* 52, 373 (1936–37).

TWENTY-TWO

Foundations of Tort Law

The fundamental notion of a private action for a wrong done by one person to another in the absence of a contract between them is called a tort in the common law. Regardless of the name used, the tort systems of the West follow the same basic structure: They all recognize intentional torts, negligent torts, and cases of high-risk activity that generate strict liability. In French law, the three categories of torts are grounded in a few basic provisions. Sections 1382 and 1383 require compensation for harm caused intentionally or negligently. Section 1384 imposes liability for high-risk activities under the rubric: damage caused by *des choses que l'on a sous sa garde* ("the things under one's control"). The German code is slightly better developed. The categories of damage are enumerated in BGB § 823: "life, body, health, freedom, property or other right of another." Any intentional or negligent violation of one of these interests generates liability if the violation is "unlawful." The French code does not expressly recognize that the invasion of a protected interest might be justified and therefore lawful. (Recall our discussion of this question in Chapter Two.)

In addition, German law recognizes a general principle of liability based on dangerous things (*Gefährdungshaftung*), even though the principle is not expressed in the BGB itself. The main difference between French and German law is that in the former, the category of strict liability lends itself to limitless expansion. By contrast, the German principle of strict liability is, for now, limited to cases stipulated in the statutory law.

The common law of torts recognizes a series of *intentional torts* (battery, assault, false imprisonment, invasion of privacy, intentional infliction of emotional distress) and a general principle of liability for causing harm negligently. The latter is simply called the *tort of negligence*. Both of these former categories are called *liability based on fault*. Fault stands in constant tension with the common law categories of strict liability—of liability without fault. More about that in a minute, but first we should clarify the concept of negligence.

Every legal system uses a different definition of this basic concept. French law and all systems that have followed the *Code civil* rely upon the hypothetical standard behavior of *un bon père de famille*. This rather amusing male-chauvinist standard relies upon the "good father of the family" as the appropriate guide to behavior—the French analogue to the "reasonable person" in the common law tradition. The more appropriate reference is to "the reasonable person under the circumstances." German law, in BGB § 276, defines *negligence* as failing in "the degree of care appropriate in the particular transaction." (This standard has its own amusing aspect because it relies on the word *Verkehr* to refer to "transaction." Ask German students what they first think of when they hear the word.)

For the last half-century or so, American scholars have interpreted the standard of the reasonable person in utilitarian or economic terms. The reasonable person weighs the prospective costs and benefits of a course of action and decides accordingly. Conduct is reasonable when its benefits outweigh its costs and unreasonable when its costs prevail over the benefits. Both costs and benefits are calculated on the basis of two factors: (1) the ultimate result, whether good (G) on one side or bad (B) on the other, and (2) the probability, P(G) or P(B), that this result will occur. The comparison, therefore, is between P(G) x G and P(B) x B. This is called the *Learned Hand formula* because Judge Learned Hand was apparently the first judge to use it (admittedly with a different notation) in an opinion explaining negligence.[1]

---

[1] *United States v. Carroll Towing Co.*, 159 F.2d 169 (2d Cir. 1947). Judge Hand wrote that a company should be liable for not taking a precaution against a risk if the burden the precaution entails (B) is less that the loss that might occur (L) multiplied by the probability the precaution will prevent the loss (P). For a criticism of the Hand formula from a Kantian perspective, see Richard W. Wright, "The Standards of Care in Neg-

An example illustrates the way the Learned Hand formula works. Suppose safety regulators are trying to decide whether all automobiles should have air bags installed in the passenger seats. The benefit is calculated by the probability of saving lives, as multiplied by the value of each life saved. The cost is based on undesired side effects, such as the bags expanding when they are not supposed to and, even worse, their suffocating small children sitting in the front seat. These costs are also calculated on the basis of assessed probability and the dollar signs placed on the negative outcomes if they should occur. Unfortunately, there is no way of making this calculation of benefits and costs without assessing the dollar value of human lives. Judges and juries must do the same thing.

From a strictly economic point of view, the expense of installing the air bags is not part of the cost-benefit judgment. The consumers will pay this cost in the form of higher prices. If there is a net safety benefit in the air bags, consumers will be forced either to pay for it or to reevaluate alternative means of transportation. (For the way in which these costs are passed on to the public, see the discussion of externalities in the next chapter.) The way the courts administer the Learned Hand test, however, they might consider the monetary cost of taking safety measures in order to decide whether not doing so is reasonable under the circumstances. In the end, the economic analysis of these issues is largely an economic exercise. Juries are always instructed to decide what a reasonable person would have done under the circumstances.

The common law jury is a critical part of the concept of negligence and in large part explains its popularity. All cases of alleged negligence go to the jury for resolution if "reasonable people might disagree about the issue." If there is a plausible case of negligence, therefore, laypeople will decide both the question of liability and the extent of damages. For most of the twentieth century, juries sympathized with injured parties—particularly when the defendant was a railroad, car manufacturer, or other business corporation. Also, the range of damages included not only medical expenses and lost income but also, most important, pain and suffering and, in many cases, punitive damages. (The last is taken up in Chapter Twenty-Six.) It has never been permissible to inform the jury whether the defendant carries insurance to cover the costs of a tort judgment, but

ligence Law" in *Philosophical Foundations of Tort Law* 249 (David G. Owen ed.) (Oxford: Oxford University Press, 1995).

many scholars in the generation after the Second World War thought that the tort system should impose liability against enterprises in order to ensure the compensation of victims. In a country without obligatory medical insurance, this was a critical factor in the expansion of tort liability. It is worth noting that most common law countries have abolished the jury in torts cases, but the United States is committed to the common law jury under the Seventh Amendment to the Constitution.

The third major prong of liability—strict liability—has many sources in the common law. First, tort liability on the writ of trespass originally had nothing to do with the fault or intention of the defendant—recall the case of *Scott v. Shepherd* in Chapter One. Liability is based on directly causing injury. A voluntary act is required, but fault—in the sense of intention or negligence—is not. Second, specific cases like the *Vincent* case here recognize strict liability, and third, both the First and Second Restatement of Torts took the initiative to formulate a general standard of strict liability. This was originally called "abnormally dangerous activity," and now it is called "ultra-hazardous activity." The basic idea is that when an activity like blasting in the city streets invariably causes harm, the entrepreneur should be held responsible.

To avoid misunderstanding, note that the leading legal systems of the West have carved out products liability from the basic tort system and subjected this area to a special set of regulations. The key concept is a "defect" that causes harm. Though the language of negligence and strict liability is used, it is clear that the terms mean something different in this context. Products liability is effectively its own branch of law, based partly on contractual warranty and partly on tort principles of negligence and strict liability. The same special identity of the field obviously exists in the European Union, which has issued a special directive in an effort to unify this body of law.

Although the manufacture and distribution of consumer products crosses the boundaries of states and countries (see Chapter Twenty-Six for a good example of the problems raised by mass distribution), most torts are purely local affairs. The following case is a good example. *Vincent* has become the darling of the scholars because it raises basic philosophical problems about the foundations of liability. The debate in the literature rages on two fronts:

1. What is the fundamental political or moral principle that underlies the tort system? Is it corrective justice, distributive justice, or economic

efficiency (namely, the welfare of the entire society)? (For clarification of these concepts, refer back to the Prologue to Part Three, immediately before Chapter Fifteen.) This is a three-sided conflict, and it will take some time to sort out all the issues.

2. When should the doctrine of negligence apply? When should strict liability apply? Suppose that behavior is not negligent; it is reasonable under the circumstances. Is there nonetheless a good reason for holding the defendant liable? That is the problem posed in the following classic dispute, the *Vincent* case. It was reasonable for the defendant to keep his ship moored in a storm. Should he nonetheless pay for the damage to plaintiff's dock? If so, liability is imposed for liability without fault, that is, for reasonable, nonnegligent behavior. However we resolve that question, we shall eventually have to address the relationship between this doctrinal problem and the philosophical problem about the foundations of liability. We will return to this problem after reading and analyzing the following case.

Vincent v. Lake Erie Transportation Company

Supreme Court of Minnesota
109 Minn. 456; 124 N.W. 221 (1910)

O'BRIEN, J.:

The steamship *Reynolds*, owned by the defendant, was for the purpose of discharging her cargo on November 27, 1905, moored to plaintiffs' dock in Duluth. While the unloading of the boat was taking place a storm from the northeast developed, which at about ten o'clock p.m., when the unloading was completed, had so grown in violence that the wind was then moving at fifty miles per hour and continued to increase during the night. There is some evidence that one, and perhaps two, boats were able to enter the harbor that night, but it is plain that navigation was practically suspended from the hour mentioned until the morning of the twenty ninth, when the storm abated, and during that time no master would have been justified in attempting to navigate his vessel, if he could avoid doing so. After the discharge of the cargo the *Reynolds* signaled for a tug to tow her from the dock, but none could be obtained because of the severity of the storm. If the lines

holding the ship to the dock had been cast off, she would doubtless
have drifted away; but, instead, the lines were kept fast, and as soon as
one parted or chafed it was replaced, sometimes with a larger one. The
vessel lay upon the outside of the dock, her bow to the east, the wind
and waves striking her starboard quarter with such force that she was
constantly being lifted and thrown against the dock, resulting in its
damage, as found by the jury, to the amount of $500.[2]

We are satisfied that the character of the storm was such that it
would have been highly imprudent for the master of the *Reynolds* to
have attempted to leave the dock or to have permitted his vessel to
drift away from it. One witness testified upon the trial that the vessel
could have been warped into a slip, and that, if the attempt to bring
the ship into the slip had failed, the worst that could have happened
would be that the vessel would have been blown ashore upon a soft
and muddy bank. The witness was not present in Duluth at the time
of the storm, and, while he may have been right in his conclusions,
those in charge of the dock and the vessel at the time of the storm
were not required to use the highest human intelligence, nor were they
required to resort to every possible experiment which could be suggested for the preservation of their property. Nothing more was demanded of them than ordinary prudence and care, and the record in
this case fully sustains the contention of the appellant that, in holding
the vessel fast to the dock, those in charge of her exercised good judgment and prudent seamanship.

It is claimed by the respondent that it was negligence to moor the
boat at an exposed part of the wharf, and to continue in that position
after it became apparent that the storm was to be more than usually
severe. We do not agree with this position. The part of the wharf where
the vessel was moored appears to have been commonly used for that
purpose. It was situated within the harbor at Duluth, and must, we
think, be considered a proper and safe place, and would undoubtedly
have been such during what would be considered a very severe storm.
The storm which made it unsafe was one which surpassed in violence
any which might have reasonably been anticipated.

The appellant contends by ample assignments of error that, because
its conduct during the storm was rendered necessary by prudence and

[2] Why this amount? P. claimed $1,200. Did the jury split the difference?

good seamanship under conditions over which it had no control, it cannot be held liable for any injury resulting to the property of others, and claims that the jury should have been so instructed. An analysis of the charge given by the trial court is not necessary, as in our opinion the only question for the jury was the amount of damages which the plaintiffs were entitled to recover, and no complaint is made upon that score.

The situation was one in which the ordinary rules regulating property rights were suspended by forces beyond human control, and if, without the direct intervention of some act by the one sought to be held liable, the property of another was injured, such injury must be attributed to the act of God, and not to the wrongful act of the person sought to be charged. If during the storm the *Reynolds* had entered the harbor, and while there had become disabled and been thrown against the plaintiffs' dock, the plaintiffs could not have recovered. Again, if while attempting to hold fast to the dock the lines had parted, without any negligence, and the vessel carried against some other boat or dock in the harbor, there would be no liability upon her owner. But here those in charge of the vessel deliberately and by their direct efforts held her in such a position that the damage to the dock resulted, and, having thus preserved the ship at the expense of the dock, it seems to us that her owners are responsible to the dock owners to the extent of the injury inflicted.

In *Depue v. Flatau*, 100 Minn. 299, this court held that where the plaintiff, while lawfully in the defendants' house, became so ill that he was incapable of traveling with safety, the defendants were responsible to him in damages for compelling him to leave the premises. If, however, the owner of the premises had furnished the traveler with proper accommodations and medical attendance, would he have been able to defeat an action brought against him for their reasonable worth?

In *Ploof v. Putnam* (Vt.) 71 Atl. 188, the supreme court of Vermont held that where, under stress of weather, a vessel was without permission moored to a private dock at an island in Lake Champlain owned by the defendant, the plaintiff was not guilty of trespass, and that the defendant was responsible in damages because his representative upon the island unmoored the vessel, permitting it to drift upon the shore, with resultant injuries to it. If, in that case, the vessel had been permitted to remain, and the dock had suffered an injury, we believe the shipowner would have been held liable for the injury done.

Theologians hold that a starving man may, without moral guilt, take what is necessary to sustain life; but it could hardly be said that the obligation would not be upon such person to pay the value of the property so taken when he became able to do so. And so public necessity, in times of war or peace, may require the taking of private property for public purposes; but under our system of jurisprudence compensation must be made.

Let us imagine in this case that for the better mooring of the vessel those in charge of her had appropriated a valuable cable lying upon the dock. No matter how justifiable such appropriation might have been, it would not be claimed that, because of the overwhelming necessity of the situation, the owner of the cable could not recover its value.

This is not a case where life or property was menaced by any object or thing belonging to the plaintiffs, the destruction of which became necessary to prevent the threatened disaster. Nor is it a case where, because of the act of God, or unavoidable accident, the infliction of the injury was beyond the control of the defendant, but is one where the defendant prudently and advisedly availed itself of the plaintiffs' property for the purpose of preserving its own more valuable property, and the plaintiffs are entitled to compensation for the injury done.

Order affirmed.

LEWIS, J.:

I dissent. It was assumed on the trial before the lower court that appellant's liability depended on whether the master of the ship might, in the exercise of reasonable care, have sought a place of safety before the storm made it impossible to leave the dock. The majority opinion assumes that the evidence is conclusive that appellant moored its boat at respondents' dock pursuant to contract, and that the vessel was lawfully in position at the time the additional cables were fastened to the dock, and the reasoning of the opinion is that, because appellant made use of the stronger cables to hold the boat in position, it became liable under the rule that it had voluntarily made use of the property of another for the purpose of saving its own.

In my judgment, if the boat was lawfully in position at the time the storm broke, and the master could not, in the exercise of due care, have left that position without subjecting his vessel to the hazards of the storm, then the damage to the dock, caused by the pounding of the boat, was the result of an inevitable accident. If the master was in the exercise of due care, he was not at fault. The reasoning of the opinion admits that if the ropes, or cables, first attached to the dock had not parted, or if, in the first instance, the master had used the stronger cables, there would be no liability. If the master could not, in the exercise of reasonable care, have anticipated the severity of the storm and sought a place of safety before it became impossible, why should he be required to anticipate the severity of the storm, and, in the first instance, use the stronger cables?

I am of the opinion that one who constructs a dock to the navigable line of waters, and enters into contractual relations with the owner of a vessel to moor the same, takes the risk of damage to his dock by a boat caught there by a storm, which event could not have been avoided in the exercise of due care, and further, that the legal status of the parties in such a case is not changed by renewal of cables to keep the boat from being cast adrift at the mercy of the tempest.

Jaggard, J.: I concur with Lewis, J.

QUESTIONS AND COMMENTS

1. The dissent thinks that the negligence principle provides a ground for exempting the defendant from liability. If the ship's captain acted reasonably—that is, nonnegligently—under the circumstances of the storm, there should be no liability. The majority develops an argument for liability despite the reasonableness of the defendant's behavior. What precisely is the argument? Does it really depend on whether the defendant replaced the cables?

2. Note that the majority has no real authority for its position. The *Ploof* case raises a different issue. What would have happened if the dock owner had come out and unmoored the *Reynolds* to protect his dock, and as a result the ship was damaged? *Ploof* holds that the property owner must tolerate the intrusion when the circumstances make it necessary. The German code is in accord. (See BGB § 904, sentence 1: "The owner of a thing is not entitled to prevent intrusions

of others, if the intrusion is necessary to avoid an imminent risk and the threatened risk is disproportionately great relative to the harm the owner must endure.")

How does the majority in *Vincent* reason from the dock owner's duty to tolerate the intrusion to the shipowner's duty to make compensation for the resulting damage? Some writers think that the case is grounded in principles of unjust enrichment, namely, that the defendant has received a benefit without legal warrant. (See BGB § 812.) The court suggests this theory in the sentence: "[H]aving thus preserved the ship at the expense of the dock . . . her owners are responsible to the dock owners to the extent of the injury inflicted." But was not the defendant entitled to do this? Was there anything unjust or improper about his receiving that benefit?

German theory has an elegant expression to cover the case. The defendant's claim is called *ein Aufopferungsanspruch* ("a claim based on sacrifice"). Precisely because the dock owner must sacrifice his property rights and tolerate the intrusion, he or she is entitled to compensation for damage. From this point of view, the purpose of the shipowner is irrelevant. (See BGB § 904, sentence 2: "The owner who must tolerate an intrusion can demand compensation for the damage he suffers.")

3. *Depue* is not really an authority either. In that case, the plaintiff rendered a positive service to the defendant by providing him with room and board. The defendant accepted. This is more in the nature of an implicit contract. In *Vincent*, the defendant takes a risk by keeping his ship moored. It is hard to think of the case as implied contract to pay for the damages that everyone would have preferred to avoid.

4. The principle of *Vincent* is subject to great debate. England and Canada appear to have reached the opposite result, and many important scholars like Ernest Weinrib and Yitzhak Englard think the case is wrongly decided. What do you think?

5. It is important to distinguish among the different kinds of arguments that might be made for either the principle of negligence or strict liability. For either result, the argument might be based on corrective justice or on the principle of efficiency. Here is a quick sketch of the positions that can be taken:

     A. Corrective Justice

        1. *For Negligence*: He did everything right and had no control over the situation. It is like an act of God—not his responsibility.

        2. *For Strict Liability*: It is unfair to expect the dock owner to tolerate the intrusion and not to be paid for damages resulting.

     B. Efficiency

        1. *For Negligence*: It is socially desirable to encourage people to act reasonably, to make decisions that favor the greater interest (benefits over costs).

        2. *For Strict Liability*: Causing damage to docks is an externality of owning and operating ships. To make the market work properly, the costs of causing the damage should be charged to shipowners. They will raise their rates for commercial shipping, and the costs will be passed on to the consumers of this service.

6. Note that the arguments of corrective justice emphasize the behavior of the parties in the past. The arguments of efficiency focus on the consequences of the decision for the future welfare of society. This difference between retrospective and prospective decision making has generated a profound debate in the literature about the proper foundations of tort liability. The liberal view holds that torts should be based on corrective justice. The purpose of the law should be to protect the rights of the parties involved. The challenge comes from utilitarianism, which holds that rights are less important than the welfare of society.

7. Within the position favoring justice (or fairness) over efficiency, there is an important division between two theories of justice: corrective and distributive. The former focuses exclusively on transactions between individuals. The latter takes into consideration the status of the parties. For example, the claim that enterprises should be held to a different standard from private individuals is an argument of status and therefore of distributive justice. The claim could be founded on the assumptions that corporations have more money ("deep pockets"), that they are more likely to have insurance, or that by raising prices they can more easily pass on the costs to others. It may be that

the special treatment of products liability (consumer vs. manufacturer) reflects considerations of status and distributive justice. By and large, however, the law formally ignores the status and wealth of the parties. An exception is BGB § 829, which provides that where the defendant is excused on grounds of insanity, the court may impose liability if the defendant has much more money than the plaintiff. The common law courts might reach the same result, but they would do so without explicitly invoking the idea of preferring the poor over the rich.

8. The most controversial argument made in the field of law and economics addresses the internalizing of externalities. We take a detour to consider one of the great debates in law and economics of the last forty years. In the following survey of law and economics, the central place is occupied by the Coase theorem, based on the famous article by Ronald Coase, "The Problem of Social Cost," 3 *J. Law & Econ.* 1 (1960). This article, for which Coase won the Nobel Prize in Economics in 1991, is the most frequently cited article in the academic legal literature of the United States. Understanding American tort law today means understanding the Coase theorem.

■

Further Reading

For some of the books and articles in the debate between corrective and efficient views of justice, see Jules Coleman, *Risks and Wrongs* (Cambridge: Cambridge University Press, 1992); Ernest Weinrib, *The Idea of Private Law* (Cambridge, MA: Harvard University Press, 1995); Richard Epstein, "A Theory of Strict Liability," 2 *J. Leg. Stud.* 151 (1973); and George P. Fletcher, "Fairness and Utility in Tort Theory," 85 *Harv. L. Rev.* 537 (1972).

TWENTY-THREE

Economic Efficiency

Traditional ideas of justice and morality in the law now face a radical challenge from economists and economically trained lawyers. Every good law school faculty now includes at least one scholar trained in a field called "law & economics" (L&E, for short).[1] A novel form of interdisciplinary research has become a movement. In some areas, such as antitrust and unfair competition law, economic understanding is indispensable. But the devotees of L&E make their most challenging contributions in other fields of law where economics has had, until recently, no apparent bearing. The battleground for this new way of thinking about law has been torts or accident law.

The insight that initiated this challenge was Yale law professor Guido Calabresi's reconceptualization of the field of accident law and its goals. He began by noting that both accidents and accident prevention generate costs that can be measured in a single common denomination of dollars

---

This chapter is excerpted from George P. Fletcher, *Basic Concepts of Legal Thought* (New York: Oxford University Press, 1996).

[1] For general treatment of the field, see Richard Posner, *Economic Analysis of the Law* (3d ed) (Boston: Little, Brown, 1986).

and cents.[2] Accidents cost money, as reflected in the dollar sign that juries place on the victims' physical and emotional harm, medical bills, lost wages, and pain and suffering. Accident prevention also costs money—the funds expended, for example, on making cars, airplanes, and microwave ovens safer. These, plus the costs of administering the legal system, constitute the total costs of accidents. The aim of tort law, Calabresi inferred, should be to minimize the sum of these costs. As expressed in economic language, the goal of tort law should be to bring about an optimum number of accidents. This optimum is reached at the equilibrium point where the marginal cost of one more accident exactly equals the marginal cost of preventing that accident. An optimum number of accidents is also considered the efficient solution to the accident problem.

These terms *optimum* and *efficient* are now common parlance in American law. The courts have yet to go over to the new language, but there are many teachers of law who think that efficiency is the *summum bonum*, the supreme good, of legal arrangements. Though they are loath to identify their theories as "normative" as opposed to "positive" and scientific, the advocates of efficiency espouse a new morality for the lawyer—at least, a new mode of expressing the principles of utilitarian morality.

The quest for efficiency has led to efforts to restructure, or at least reinterpret, the traditional criteria for making one person pay for harm caused to another. Submerged in this search for efficiency is the recognition that economics itself contains diverse schools of thought. There is far more conflict and contradiction in economic theory than the advocates of L&E are willing to concede. Explicating this conflict of ideas is the task of this chapter.

Voluntary Markets and Pareto Efficiency

Efficiency—like so many of the terms we have considered in this book—signifies different things to different people. One influential notion of efficiency derives from the ideal of trading in a frictionless market. Let us

---

[2] See Guido Calabresi, *The Cost of Accidents: A Legal and Economic Analysis* (New Haven, CT: Yale University Press, 1970).

take a closer look at the meaning of allocating goods and services efficiently.

Imagine that the goods of society are distributed to the members of society in a more or less equal way. Yet the goods are different. Some people have television sets, others have shoes, others have sugar, and still others, tobacco. As life begins in this imaginary society, the players realize that they have different goods. The one with shoes realizes that he would like a TV set, and the possessor of the TVs senses immediately that she would like some shoes. The two of them consider a trade and begin negotiating. Eventually they agree on a "price" for the TV set in the currency of shoes, say, five pairs of shoes for one nineteen-inch color set. The two parties exchange the goods. The exchange is based on consent, freely given, informed by knowledge of all the available alternatives.

Now what do we want to say about the effects of this exchange on the welfare of these parties? Have they merely exchanged an "equal" amount of goods, leaving them in exactly the same situation they were in before the exchange? Or are they, as a result of the trade, better off, happier in some sense? Recall Aristotle's view that the exchange is a form of commutative justice: The traded goods are equal in value, and therefore no one is better or worse off as a result of the exchange. Modern economic theory departs radically from this premise of equality in the exchange. The guiding assumption today is that both sides benefit from the exchange. If they would not benefit, economists now say, they would have no incentive for making the trade. The party who gets the shoes values five pairs of shoes more than she values a television set. The party who gets the TV set prefers it to five pairs of shoes. Both parties, therefore, are better off. Their "utilities," viewed subjectively, are enhanced.

The trade makes the world better off, insofar as it makes at least one of the parties better off and it makes no one worse off. This is the definition of a *Pareto–superior move*, a trade that benefits at least one side and harms no one. Our trade of a TV set for shoes was a Pareto–superior move for both sides. Note that in the economic view of the world, if parties have the same stack of goods in front of them, trade occurs only because the trading partners have different sets of preferences. They are individuals, with different tastes and desires. If everyone were alike, if we all valued shoes and TV sets in exactly the same way, there would no incentive for trade. There would be no point to trading goods if we did not gain something. The economist begins by noting that trade does in fact take place in the real world. His theory of Pareto–superior moves explains what we observe in the marketplace.

Now note what happens when the possessor of tobacco wants to trade his stock for a TV set. He goes to a TV owner and offers her an amount of tobacco. She responds that she despises tobacco and that, in fact, you would have to pay her to take it. What should the tobacco holder do? He has two ways of obtaining a TV set: He can search around for other parties who are willing to trade something for tobacco (shoes will work, or possibly sugar) that he can use to entice the TV holder into selling a TV set, or he can wait until someone who likes tobacco comes into possession of a TV set. The world would be much simpler for the tobacco holder if everyone used an intermediate, common commodity that everyone liked. That common denominator is money. If they had a common currency—say, dollars—everyone would trade first for dollars and then use the dollars to buy what they really wanted.

The assumptions that underlie this simple version of a market are very important. First, everyone participates with an initial set of property rights. They could not trade if they were uncertain about what they owned. Second, each of them is an idiosyncratic individual, each having different tastes and preferences. And third, each is capable of consenting to voluntary transfers that will transplant their property rights to others. The first and third assumptions illustrate how the market and the legal system interact. Without a legal regime specifying who owns what and a system for transferring rights, the market could not operate. Without these basic rights firmly secured, there can be no market. This principle is becoming clear to Eastern Europeans who are struggling to make the transition from a Communist order in which the state owned almost everything to a market economy based on private ownership.

Sooner or later the market transactions in our imaginary society of shoes and TV sets will come to an end. When they do—that is, when there is no longer the possibility of making a Pareto–superior move—the resulting equilibrium is called a Pareto–optimal state. This is the optimal point beyond which trading cannot improve the welfare of these two participants. Trading ceases until either new goods are brought into the game or the preferences of one of the parties suddenly change and thus create the possibility of a new Pareto–superior transaction.

This model of economic relations carries with it certain points of avowed ignorance. As a matter of principle, economists claim that there is nothing to know economically about the relative merits of different Pareto–optimal states. The Pareto–optimal state might be a roughly equal distribution, or it might be a situation in which one player possesses all the goods; in neither case would a move be possible that would not leave someone worse off. All of these Pareto–optimal states are equally efficient in the sense that no readjustment of the goods can bring about a better state of affairs. Optimality or efficiency in this economic sense has nothing to do with the justice or desirability of the distribution.

Another point of avowed ignorance is the quantitative extent of the gain that occurs from each trade. We know that when the shoe holder and the TV possessor trade, both make themselves better off, but we do not know how much better off each becomes. Nor can we say whether one gains more than the other. The reason for this limitation is that utility in economics is entirely subjective. It depends on how much individuals are actually willing to pay for the goods they want. The precise way of stating this assumption is: *no interpersonal comparison of utilities*. The most we can do is derive a map of utilities for each person, and that map is based on the choices he or she actually makes.

As it stands, this pure version of the market could not possibly be of relevance to the law. Its underlying principle is the sovereignty and autonomy of every player in the market. The market is voluntary; its supreme principle is consent. But the law is coercive. The market depends on decentralized, uncoordinated decisions, but the law stands for centralized decision making. To achieve relevance to lawyers and policy makers, the system of Pareto efficiency had to undergo a transformation that would enable it to appeal to partisans of coercive intervention. How this transformation occurred is the tale we now tell.

Kaldor/Hicks and Collective Efficiency

The beginnings of the transformation took hold in the late 1930s, when a British economist, Nicholas Kaldor, turned his mind to a problem that national legislatures have often confronted.[3] May they make a legislative

---

[3] Nicholas Kaldor, "Welfare Propositions of Economics and Interpersonal Comparisons of Utility," 49 *Economics Journal* 549 (1939).

change that will benefit the economy as a whole even if the change implies that a certain group in the society will lose? The specific problem was the nineteenth–century debate in Britain about the Corn Laws, the protective tariffs that shielded British farmers from foreign competition. A similar debate occurred recently in the United States about our joining the North American Free Trade Association (NAFTA). Participating in the tariff reduction program of NAFTA might be good for the country as a whole, but certain producers would lose out to cheaper Mexican imports.

Kaldor argued that abolishing the Corn Laws was a Pareto–superior move in the modified sense that the gains to the country as a whole from free trade were likely to be sufficiently great to outweigh the loss to some corn farmers. Kaldor believed that the winners could have purchased the right to remove the tariffs from the farmers and still have gains left over. That they could have purchased the right (but did not) meant that the move was Pareto–superior in a modified sense. Another economist, J. R. Hicks, quickly extended the argument to all market impediments.[4]

There is nothing surprising about the aim of these arguments. Free market economics imply general social benefits from free trade. Economists in this tradition are naturally opposed to tariffs and other impediments to competition. They understandably favored the repeal of the Corn Laws and other protective tariffs. An economist truly committed to free trade would think of the gains from tariffs as illegitimate, reaped by the grain farmers at the expense of the rest of society. Ending this illegitimate state of affairs is hardly a basis for thinking (even hypothetically) about compensation. There would be no more reason for Kaldor and Hicks to favor compensation for the farmers who would lose under the repeal of the Corn Laws than it would have been appropriate for abolitionists to pay compensation to the slaveholders who lost their human property under Abraham Lincoln's Emancipation Proclamation. Yet for some reason, it seemed important to Kaldor and Hicks to reconcile the abolition of a tariff with the principles of Pareto efficiency. This effort led them to inquire whether the society as a whole stood to gain enough from the increase in free trade to pay off (hypothetically) the farmers who benefited from the tariffs.

[4] Cecil R. Hicks, "The Foundations of Welfare Economics," 49 *Economics Journal* 696 (1939).

It is sometimes said that hard cases make bad law, and this is an instance in which an easy economic problem (abolishing restraints on free trade) generated a dubious moral principle. Kaldor and Hick's ruminations about the Corn Laws transformed the Pareto principle of efficiency into an instrument for legislation and judicial policy making. *The Kaldor/Hicks test*, as it is now formulated, holds that any reallocation of property rights is acceptable so long as it generates more gain to the winners than loss to the losers. This means that, in principle, the winners could compensate the losers and still have a gain left over. The emphasis here is on "could compensate"; they need not actually make the transfer for the change to be Pareto superior under the Kaldor/Hicks test.

To see how the Kaldor/Hicks test works in practice, let us return to our example of trading shoes for a television set. Suppose that the parties could not communicate with each other but that some third party (call it the state) knew that party A wanted a TV set and that she was willing to pay five pairs of shoes as compensation. The third party also knew that B was willing to accept five pairs of shoes for a TV set. This means that under the Kaldor/Hicks test, the state would be engaging in a Pareto–superior move by taking the TV set from B and giving it to A. A could compensate B for the set, and under ideal economic conditions, she would simply have bought the set from B. But in our imaginary situation, the parties are unable to trade, and therefore the state must do it for them.

Now you might wonder why the state should not at the same time take five pairs of shoes from A and give them to B. Perhaps it should. But the fact is that under the Kaldor/Hicks test, as interpreted by the school of L&E, A need not compensate B for the TV set. Herein lies the trick. In the original example of voluntary trading, the two transactions were conceptually linked—a TV set for shoes, and shoes for the TV set. The only basis we have for saying that the trade made the parties better off is that they actually made the trade. Yet under the Kaldor/Hicks test of hypothetical trading, the single transaction splits into two. Moving the TV set from one party to the other is one move toward efficiency in the Kaldor/Hicks sense, and moving the shoes in the opposite direction is another move toward efficiency.

Of course, you might be puzzled by all this. It seems very unfair to take the TV set from B and give it to A free of charge. If you confronted an advocate of the Kaldor/Hicks test with this problem, the conversation might go like this:

Skeptic: How can you do that? Take from one person and give to another? Do you think you're Robin Hood?

Advocate: I'm merely reallocating goods so that people who enjoy them more get to use them. You admit if A had to compensate B, she would go ahead and buy the set, and B would take the five pair of shoes for the TV set. Does not this show that A would enjoy that particular TV set more than B does?

Skeptic: Yes, it is clear that A and B would trade if they could. But without the actual trade, how do you know that A would actually pay five pairs of shoes for the set? Also, isn't it unfair for B not to get paid for the TV set?

Advocate: I'm stipulating that A would pay five pairs of shoes for the TV. After all, it's my example. As far as fairness goes, that is a problem of distribution, not of efficiency.

Skeptic: But in real life, you cannot stipulate how much A would be willing to pay. If you ask A how much she would pay (when she does not have to pay), she will, of course, exaggerate her willingness to pay. The only way you can know how much A would pay would be, as a good economist, to watch what she does, not what she says.

Advocate: How about looking at what some other person would pay for a TV set in a situation in which trading was possible?

Skeptic: You cannot do that. After all, the assumption of your "science" is that everyone has a distinct and different set of preferences. There are no other traders just like A and B.

Admittedly, this argument leaves out of consideration the possibility of measuring preferences across a large group of people by observing how they behave in the markets where there is choice between two versions of a single commodity. For example, if smokers were willing, on average, to pay 10 percent more to dine in restaurants where smoking is permitted, then we would have a rough idea how much particular smokers are willing to pay to light up after a meal.

Still, the point holds that the advocates of the Kaldor/Hicks test have manipulated the idea of Pareto superiority to make it suitable for the law. Kaldor originally advocated eliminating a restraint on free competition on the ground that it would benefit the society as a whole more than it would harm one segment of the society. The current advocates of Kaldor's revision of Pareto's principle now seek to reallocate property rights when it is more efficient to do so. There is method in this manipulation. The Kaldor/Hicks test converts a principle of voluntary market transactions into a standard for judicial intervention. Using the Kaldor/Hicks test, courts can redefine property rights "from time to time as the relative values of different uses of land change."[5]

As a result of the Kaldor/Hicks revision, the concept of efficiency takes on a new meaning. Efficiency is no longer synonymous with the workings of a perfect market. It becomes equivalent to a utilitarian standard justifying intervention in the market and in property rights when the benefits outweigh the burdens of intervention. Suppose, for example, that a railroad emits sparks and thereby destroys the property of a farmer with land abutting the railroad right of way. It appears that the railroad's sparks are encroaching upon the farmer's land and that therefore the farmer should be compensated for the resulting damage. But the Kaldor/Hicks test suggests a different answer. The relevant question becomes whether the railroad gains more from emitting sparks than the value of the loss to the farmer. As we will discuss later, the market could decide the question if the market is able to function properly between the parties. If the market does not work, then the Kaldor/Hicks test would require a court to assess which of the parties would make more valuable use of the land. That question turns out to be equivalent to determining which of the parties would pay more for the right to use the strip of (the farmer's) land potentially affected by the railroad's sparks.

As applied in cases of this sort, the Kaldor/Hicks test merely restates the utilitarian principle that, in a dispute about property rights, the courts should make the decision that would promote the interests of society as a whole. Awarding the disputed land to the railroad or the farmer serves the interests of society if the use of the land goes to the party who makes better use of it—with "better use" being measured by the economic rewards of railroading or farming. The only difference between the utilitarian and the advocate of the Kaldor/Hicks test is that the former relies upon the standard of happiness and the latter relies on a standard implicit in a hypothetical willingness to pay for the disputed resource.

American law professors have been receptive to economic analysis of

[5] Richard Posner, *Economic Analysis of the Law* (3d ed) (Boston: Little, Brown, 1986) at 47.

the Kaldor/Hicks variety because the culture of American law has long had strong ties to utilitarian thought. The devotee of L&E writes in a long line of theorists who think that all legal institutions should serve the interests of society—or at least of American society. Yet we have traced a remarkable transformation. The discussion begins with Pareto's principles of efficiency, grounded in the values of secure property rights, individual choice, and the necessity of voluntary transactions. In light of Kaldor's modest amendment, later generalized to cover all property rights, we end up with a theory of legal intervention that permits the periodic redefinition of property rights for the sake of a collective vision of efficiency. A theory of individual supremacy ends up as a philosophy of group supremacy. This is a remarkable metamorphosis. Any theory that can successfully obfuscate the difference between individual sovereignty in the market and the dominance of group interests in coercive decision making will surely gain a large number of followers.

Pigovian Efficiency

The preceding tale of transformation is not nearly as dramatic as another story that began to unfold at the University of Chicago in the early 1960s. Since the late nineteenth century, the courts have occasionally relied on free–market principles as a justification for liability in cases like that of the railroad sparks. These are cases of "externalities," typified by pollution and other burdens on society that the entrepreneur imposes on others. The basic claim has been that the law should serve to perfect the market by making each enterprise pay the full costs of production. Firms have to pay for the costs of capital and labor, but they do not have to pay for the social costs, such as sparks, air pollution, and noise, of the factories and machines they operate. According to the economic argument for liability, the free market cannot work properly unless these externalities are charged to the producers who generate them. Internalizing the social costs by forcing the entrepreneur to pay for them leads to an efficient allocation of resources. The injuring firm's liability costs are subsequently passed on to consumers in the form of higher prices. Consumers make the ultimate decision of allocative efficiency by purchasing those commodities that, in view of their costs of production and their harmful effects on others, best satisfy their preferences.

To see how this works in practice, think about the way that the flying of supersonic airplanes used to inflict noise on the surrounding area as an externality. If the airline was not liable for the harm caused by its sonic booms, the price of a ticket would have been lower and consumers would have purchased "too much" supersonic travel. If the price of a ticket reflected the harm inflicted on people in the flight path (i.e., the externality is internalized), the price would have correctly reflected its social desirability. Consumer sovereignty would then have yielded the most efficient satisfaction of everyone's preferences—and the victims would have been no worse off, for they would have been compensated for suffering the noise. (The assumption, of course, is that some sum of money can make up for the disturbance of the ear–splitting noise.) Calabresi developed the same argument for the externality represented by automobile accidents.[6] The harm that cars do to pedestrians and bicyclists is a social cost of producing and driving cars. By holding manufacturers (and drivers?) liable for accidents, the law could internalize the social costs of accidents in the price of cars. Consumers would then decide whether a vehicle as risky as the automobile is worth the cost. If manufacturers are not liable for accidents, the price of cars is lower, and consumers invest more in cars than in safer modes of transport. The policy of nonliability functions, in effect, as a subsidy to automobile manufacturers and distorts the free–market system as a mechanism for the efficient allocation of resources.

The distortion of the market results from subsidizing some producers at the expense of others. Any form of subsidy, whether it be for wages, machines, or the social consequences of production, has the effect of supporting weaker producers. The contrary principle is "Each industry must pay its own way." Lord Bramwell developed an argument of this sort in imposing liability against a railroad for emitting sparks and destroying an abutting farmer's crops. There was no doubt in his mind that the sparks were an externality of railroading, not of farming.[7] There was no reason for the farmer to subsidize the railroad by bearing the loss himself. For those who believe in market efficiency, subsidies are an evil. The function of the law should be to eliminate the natural subsidy that occurs

---

[6] See Guido Calabresi, "The Decision for Accidents: An Approach to Nonfault Allocation of Costs," 78 *Harv. L. Rev.* 713 (1965).

[7] *Vaughan v. Taff Vale Railway*, 157 *English Reports* 1351 (Exch. Ch. 1860).

when industries cause harmful side effects and they are not legally liable; the function of liability is to ensure that each industry pays its way.

This principle, now associated with the writing of English economist Arthur C. Pigou in the early twentieth century,[8] has had a great impact on the law. It is the reigning view of externalities in the courts. It is an eminently sensible way of thinking about applying economic principles in legal analysis. The influential doctrine of "enterprise liability" also seems to be based on the idea that each enterprise in society should bear the cost in human suffering it inflicts on the unwary. Because of the Pigovian principle and its related doctrines in the law, we have witnessed an enormous expansion of products liability (i.e., when products cause injuries to consumers) over the last three or four decades. The expansion has been so great that many politicians now claim that American business is now less competitive with foreign producers who are not subject to the same demanding rules of products liability. Until the 1960s, this was the only theory in town. It seemed obvious that the way to internalize the social costs of industrial enterprises was to make them pay for the harm they caused.

Note the way in which the latter argument of efficiency differs from the Kaldor/Hicks standard of efficiency. The Pigovian claim is simply "Let the market work." Incorporate the social costs into the price, and let the consumers decide what they want and how much they are willing to pay for it. There is no need in this market–based method to make a centralized cost-benefit judgment, no call for a common denominator for expressing the value of competing interests. The process of internalizing the social costs of production need not assume what the economists call the "interpersonal comparison of utilities," a process implicit in reducing the competing interests to a common standard of measurement. The market works on the assumption of consumer sovereignty—each consumer is considered to be unique. Though we can rank her utilities and preferences, we cannot compare them quantitatively or qualitatively with the utilities (or preferences, pleasures, or pains) of anybody else. The great appeal of the Pigovian theory is that it demands fewer assumptions. All we need to assume is that consumers will make consistent decisions about what they want. Or so it seems.

---

[8] The first edition of *The Economics of Welfare* was published in 1920.

The Coasian Reaction

Nothing makes academic waves more than a refutation of received wisdom. In the early 1960s, when the Pigovian theory was dogma in the analysis of tort liability, Ronald Coase, an economist then at the University of Virginia, burst on the scene with his article "The Problem of Social Cost."[9] In 1963 Aaron Director, one of the early leaders in the nascent field of L&E, walked into class at the University of Chicago Law School and made a prescient announcement: This article will change the way lawyers think about law. He was right, at least about the way academic lawyers think about externalities.

Coase's basic claim is that what Pigou said "ain't necessarily so." Imposing liability against polluters and other injuring firms is not the only way to achieve efficiency in the allocation of resources. Coase has two basic strategies for countering Pigou. Both strategies depend on shifting the focus of economic analysis from decisions by consumers to potential decisions by victims. The first strategy is worked out in speculations about potential "bribes"[10] by victims to prevent impending harm. Suppose that, unlike the example of supersonic air travel, there are no impediments to the victims bargaining with enterprises that injure them. To take Coase's example, a rancher must decide whether to let the nth (say, the third) steer graze on his property. If so, the steer will roam and cause harm to the neighboring farmer. Does economic efficiency require the rancher to pay for the harm? Pigou would say yes, in order to avoid the victims' (the farmer and his customers) "subsidizing"[11] the cost of beef by absorbing the damage done by the third steer. The gist of Coase's response is that the only relevant economic question is whether the rancher grazes the third steer or not, and that, he showed, was a function not of the liability rule but exclusively of the relative value of the steer to the rancher and the damage to the farmer's crops.

There are only four relevant cases. In cases I and II, the steer can generate $300 in revenue for the rancher, and the crop damage is $200. In cases III and IV, the figures are reversed: $200 for the rancher and $300 damage to the farmer.

---

[9] 3 *Journal of Law and Economics* 1 (1960).

[10] Economists often use terms like *bribe* in unusual ways.

[11] The comment in note 10 *supra* applies as well to the use of *subsidy* in economic jargon.

Case I: *Premises*: $300 gain for rancher; $200 loss for farmer. According to the law, the rancher is liable for the damage by the steer.

Consequence: Rancher grazes the steer and pays farmer $200 in damage costs. He retains $100 of the gain.

Case II: *Premises*: $300 gain for rancher; $200 loss for farmer. According to the law, rancher is not liable for the damage.

Consequence: Rancher will obviously graze the steer because he nets the full $300.

Case III: *Premises*: $200 gain for rancher; $300 loss for farmer. According to the law, rancher is liable for damage.

Consequence: Rancher will not graze the steer because his loss in liability costs to the farmer ($300) would be greater than the potential gain ($200) from the steer.

Case IV: *Premises*: $200 gain for rancher; $300 loss for farmer. According to the law, rancher is not liable for damage.

Consequence: Even though rancher is not liable for the damage, negotiations between rancher and farmer will result in the steer's not grazing. It will be worth it to farmer to offer rancher more than $200 but less than $300 (the loss that would occur from grazing) to induce rancher not to graze the steer, and it will be in rancher's interest to accept some sum greater than $200 from farmer in place of the $200 he could earn from grazing the steer.

This is all there is to the Coase theorem. In Cases I and II, the steer grazes; in Cases III and IV, it does not. This is a consequence not of liability but of the economic productivity of the rancher and the farmer. If it is worth it to the rancher and farmer to have the steer graze, it will graze; if not, it will not graze. It goes without saying that the same method applies to any conflict over whether a single resource, such as land or air, should be used in one way or another. You could play out the same argument in a dispute about smoking in restaurants or industrial pollution. The only assumptions necessary are that parties seek gain, that they are able to bargain with each other, and that they have full information about alternatives in the market. The only move in this demonstration that might puzzle the noneconomist is the resolution of case IV: Farmer will bribe rancher not to graze the steer if the numbers so dictate. The rancher will accept the bribe and hold back the steer. It seems unfair that a potential victim should have to pay "protection money" to someone who might injure him. It is indeed unfair, but the premise of the economic argument is that fairness is irrelevant. It is efficient for the potential victim to pay not to be injured, and efficiency is the only value considered.

Though this brief demonstration is sufficient to prove Coase's theorem, his classic article is devoted largely to a second attack on Pigou. It seems very important to Coase to undermine the judgments that courts routinely make about who causes what. The point of this attack is clear. Pigovian analysis presupposes that we can determine which enterprises cause which injuries, that we can carry out the task that Calabresi dubbed "cost accounting." If there is no way to know whether the cause of sonic booms is flying supersonic planes or the failure of affected people to use thicker glass in their windows, then there is no way of applying the Pigovian principle to concrete cases. A little skepticism enables us to perceive victims as causal factors in their own suffering. After all, if the farmer insisted on planting next to the railroad, then of course the crops would be destroyed by spark–induced fires. If pedestrians walk near the highway, then they participate in bringing on accidents with cars. If it takes two to tango, then, according to Coase, it takes two to create pollution, an accident, or, indeed, any externality. The victim is as much of a cause as the industrial enterprise.

Though this causal nihilism is not a necessary part of the economic proof of Coase's theorem, it is a part of the general attack on the Pigovian tradition. The function of this attack, it seems, is to undermine confidence in making judgments about whether manufacturing automobiles causes accidents or, indeed, whether factories' emission of smoke causes air pollution. Despite the vigor of Coase's critique, however, the Pigovian principle has had far more influence in the development of the law than has the Coase theorem. First, the Pigovian principle applies in nonideal as well as ideal bargaining conditions between injurer and noninjurer. The Coase theorem does not apply in the case of supersonic travel because the costs of bargaining (organizing and communicating with the affected class) are insuperable. Coase has created an elegant theory limited to ideal conditions. He attempts to adjust his model to reality by noting that the costs of bargaining (transactions costs) will enter into the analysis of negotiating parties on whether to make a deal. For example, the farmer in Case IV will not bribe the rancher if the transactions costs are more than $100, for in that case he cannot gain anything by paying the rancher his minimum of $200. (The fee to the rancher plus the transactions costs will be greater than the damage that the steer would do.)

The Pigovian theorem will continue to reign in the courts so long as the bench is staffed by lawyers rather than economists. In addition to its readier applicability, the Pigovian theorem dovetails well with the commonsense judgment that he who causes harm without justification ought to pay for it. "Making industry pay its way" appears to be a principle of fairness as well as efficiency. Coase will never succeed in the courts, because his view of efficiency is incompatible with elementary principles of fairness: It boggles the noneconomic mind to expect the farmer to pay the rancher to keep his steer from grazing.

The remarkable feature of Coase's theorem is that it has any influence at all. His theorem that the rule of liability does not matter under ideal conditions runs parallel to the model of voluntary bargaining under Pareto's principles. As the latter could not have impact without undergoing a transformation, so Coase's theorem could not guide legal thought unless it became a rationale for coercive legal intervention. A theory about the irrelevance of law might be exciting in the ideal world of economic models, but it is surely of little utility in the real world of legal conflict. The great mystery, therefore, is how the Coase theorem underwent a metamorphosis from a critique of Pigou's theory into a tool for analyzing liability in real cases of economic conflict.

Coase himself had virtually nothing to do with this transformation. The critical work came from those, like Richard Posner and the legions of L&E supporters, who saw in Coase an implicit endorsement of the market for solving legal problems. The steps in this reasoning can be broken down into these:

1. Under ideal conditions, the market will produce efficient results.
2. Efficiency is good.
3. Where the market does not operate perfectly (e.g., the problem of supersonic air travel), the courts should intervene.
4. What should the courts do? They should allocate liability in an effort to generate the result that a free market would generate if it could operate.
5. Why should courts do this? Because efficiency is good. (See step two.)

There we have it. A plausible defense for converting the Coase theorem into a standard for resolving concrete disputes: Mimic the market by assigning rights and liabilities. This particular manipulation of economic ideas should not come as a surprise. It replicates the intellectual history that led from Pareto's principles of bargaining under ideal conditions to coercive intervention under the Kaldor/Hicks test.

It is worth pinpointing the fallacy in the argument that courts should mimic the market. We must distinguish between two senses or conceptions of efficiency that have run through this chapter. One form of efficiency is built into a model of trading under ideal circumstances. If trading continues to the point that no further trade is possible without making someone worse off, then the resulting state of affairs is Pareto–optimal and, by definition, efficient. All that efficiency means in this context (as well as in step two) is that people get what they want. It is tautologically true that under ideal circumstances, the market will produce efficient results; it will give people what they want. This is an example of what Rawls calls "pure procedural justice."[12] If the game is played according to the rules, the outcome will, as a matter of logical necessity, be right.

A totally distinct form of efficiency derives from making cost-benefit judgments about whether the benefits to passengers of flying the SST outweigh its costs to people in the flight path. Flying a supersonic airplane is efficient in this sense if its benefits outweigh its costs. There is no market mechanism, no ideal game, for determining the balance of the competing goods and bads of supersonic flight. Ideal markets cannot be inefficient, but whoever makes a centralized judgment of efficiency in this situation might make a mistake and opt for an inefficient outcome. Ideal markets cannot be wrong, but centralized decisions can be, and they often are. In Rawls's terms, this is an instance not of pure but of imperfect procedural justice. I want to distinguish between these two conceptions of efficiency by calling the first *M-efficiency* (M for market) and the second *C-efficiency* (C for centralized). The first depends on the hidden hand of a decentralized market; the second, on the heavy hand of a single decision maker (or committee) that makes an assessment of competing costs and benefits.

If efficiency is good, it is good in these two different senses. M-efficiency is good because people get what they want; C-efficiency is

12 John Rawls, *A Theory of Justice* 85–87 (Cambridge, MA: Belknap Press of Harvard University, 1971).

good because it generates a net surplus of benefit over cost. The former is a libertarian value; the latter, good because it is better for society, collectively, to have more rather than less. The fallacy in the demonstration is the shift between these two meanings of efficiency. Step 2 is based on M-efficiency; step 4 on C-efficiency. The effort to mimic the market turns out to consist in centralized cost-benefit decisions. The pretense of mimicking the market, therefore, converts a libertarian value into a utilitarian standard for maximizing the welfare of the group.

Methods and Insights

The concept of efficiency suffers internal contradictions, but these contradictions may be no worse than those that infect the legal culture as a whole. Despite their obfuscation of the political and moral issues at stake, economists have brought great insights to the law and have stimulated debate about the foundations of liability. I group their contribution under the heading of "morality in the law," for their propositions are a form of moral argument. Either they argue in the libertarian tradition that individual autonomy and consent are supreme values, or they replicate, in a quite different language, the interventionist arguments of utilitarians.

The major difference between the economic and the philosophical style of argument lies less in substance and more in method. The philosophical style of this book expresses a primary commitment to clarity and conceptual analysis. Understanding differences and distinctions is a prime goal. In contrast, the methods of economists are functional rather than analytic. Their style of argument trades on perceiving similarities rather than differences. A typical economic argument is that a tax exemption is functionally equivalent to a grant–in–aid from the government. The similarity consists in the economic consequences of, say, a $1,000 tax exemption and a $1,000 grant-in-aid. The notion of "subsidy" is used rather freely in a similar way to describe any reduction of liability that runs counter to an assumed base line. Supporters of Pigovian theory would say that not requiring industry to pay for externalities is, in effect, to subsidize industry. Because they regard the assignment of externalities as a more fluid issue, supporters of the Coase theorem deny the charge of subsidization.

Calabresi is adept at spotting functional similarities. He claims that both contract rights against specific people and rights to use things should be called property rights.[13] Lawyers have spent centuries trying to clarify the distinction between rights *in personam* (against particular people) and rights *in rem* (against the entire world), but this distinction gets lost in a single stroke of the economist's pen. Calabresi also claims that the term *liability* should cover the case of a plaintiff who is denied recovery. We ordinarily say in this case that there is no liability, but Calabresi and many people influenced by him would say that the plaintiff is "liable" for his own injuries.[14] The result of this careless speech is to camouflage the difference between getting stuck with a loss and being able to shift the loss to someone else.

Economic theorists of law are lumpers rather than splitters. They see similarities but downplay conceptual differences. They blur the meaning of causation, of property, and of liability. Other concepts fall as well to the impulse to see functional similarities. The distinction between corrective and distributive justice gets erased in the economist's division of the world into questions of efficiency and questions of distribution. The latter category includes both corrective and distributive justice.

The consequences of economic analysis of the law reminds us of the way legal realists systematically misused the language of discretion in order to make a valuable point about judicial creativity. The realists, too, were lumpers rather than splitters. They grouped together decisions by administrative agencies, decisions by police on the beat, verdicts by juries, and judicial decisions under the law. All of these turned out to be discretionary. Arguments of lumping generate a temporary sense of understanding: "Ah," says the student, "now I see a functional relationship I did not see before." The price of this understanding is a widespread debasing of the language. Without precise language, careful thought and argument come to an end.

Economic analysis of the law displays virtues as well as vices. The tension between these views and those who believe strongly that accident law should be about justice rather than efficiency has enormously enriched legal debate. Yet the most serious ramification of the L&E move-

---

[13] Guido Calabresi and A. Douglas Malamed, "Proper Rules, Liability Rules, and Inalienability: One View of the Cathedral," 85 *Harv. L. Rev.* 1089 (1972).

[14] See Jules Coleman, *Risks and Wrongs* 230–232 (Cambridge: Cambridge University Press, 1992).

ment has been the pretense that L&E is simply an extension of the neutral, nonpolitical science called "positive economics." In this chapter, we have attempted to show that though the argument begins in the methods of descriptive economics, it ends up by taking a stand on controversial moral and political principles of individual rights and group interests.

The supposed neutrality of L&E correlates in time with the emergence in the late 1970s of a large school of avowedly political scholars who campaigned under the banner of "Critical Legal Studies" (CLS).[15] It's hard to know whether L&E itself triggered the CLS reaction, but the pretense of an apolitical science in law might well have had (and properly should have had) this effect. The central thrust of CLS is that political commitments play a greater role in the life of the law than ordinarily assumed. In recent years, the CLS movement itself has fragmented into diverse political camps, some arguing as feminists for women's interests, others stressing the significance of race and gender in thinking about legal issues.

The political reaction against the pseudoscience of economic analysis coincides with a renewed debate about the possibility of impartial thinking in morality and public affairs. The universal and impartial ambitions of Bentham and Kant have given way to a renewed appreciation for local and partial commitments. These, of course, are the commitments that drive political action. They support the aims of previously disempowered groups—such as gays and lesbians, ethnic minorities, and women—to assert themselves as "communities" with rights of their own. The new challenge for American law is to fathom the relationship between individuals and the groups from which they derive their identity.

Further Reading

A fuller exposition of these ideas is in George P. Fletcher, *Basic Concepts of Legal Thought* (New York: Oxford University Press, 1996). The works cited in the notes to this chapter are also of particular significance as the foundation of many of these concepts.

---

[15] See generally, Roberto M. Unger, *Critical Studies Movement* (Cambridge, MA: Harvard University Press, 1986); Mark Kelman, *A Guide to Critical Legal Studies* (Cambridge, MA: Harvard University Press, 1987).

TWENTY-FOUR

From Contributory
to Comparative Fault

A ll of private law and criminal law reduce to two basic models of human interaction. One model is illustrated by the plaintiff sitting in his living room when an airplane crashes into his house, causing injury to him and damage to the house. Call this the model of aggression. The alternative is typified by the automobile accident in the case selected for this chapter, *Li v. Yellow Cab*. Two cars collide on the highway. Neither is the apparent aggressor. They are interacting parties. And the question is, When both parties contribute to the accident, how do you decide which should pay for it?

Part of the law is based on the model of aggression and part on the model of interaction. Think back to *Scott v. Shepherd* and the writ of trespass. The basic idea was that the defendant committed aggression against the innocent plaintiff who was minding his own business. Direct causation is part of the idea of aggression. If the causation is indirect, in the proverbial example when D throws a log into the road and P trips over it, then the model of interaction becomes relevant. After all, the log throwing is only part of the cause. With proper care, the plaintiff can avoid tripping over the log, and therefore he, too, contributes to the accident. Thus we can understand the original distinction between trespass and trespass on the case. The former was about aggression, and the latter, interactions producing harm.

Criminal law is about aggression. The victim raped in Central Park at night might have been able to avoid the accident by not running at night, but she obviously has the right to run any time she wants to and therefore she cannot be blamed for contributing to the crime. This is true about all crimes. Criminologists might investigate the behavior of victims as factors generating crime, but the approach of the law, quite rightly, is to treat the criminal as the aggressor solely responsible for the harm. The same is true about intentional torts—battery, assault, violations of privacy, and the like. Strict liability in tort is based on the same image of aggression against a passive victim, such as the plane crashing into the plaintiff's house.

Contract law, as applied in a case like *Hawkins v. McGee* (Chapter Twenty-One), looks like aggression. The doctor deprives the innocent patient of his legitimate expectation of a perfect hand. Perhaps some contracts are properly understood on this model, but in the sale of goods the model clearly seems to be interactional. The proof of this is the duty of the victim to minimize damages. If the seller breaches his duty to deliver the goods, the buyer must go out into the open market and buy the goods at the best available price. If there would be no loss—that is, if the price has not gone up—the buyer cannot recover more than nominal damages for the breach (see *Restatement of Contracts, Second*, Section 346).

The thrust of Coase's influence in law and economics has been to deny the relevance of aggression and to insist that the model of interaction applies in all cases. Their mantra is that it "takes two to tort." If the victim's nose is in the way of the defendant's fist, then both contribute to the punch in the nose. As pointed out in the last chapter, Coase did not need to make these arguments to sustain his economic analysis of externalities, but it was important to him and his followers to undermine the model of aggression as a basis for liability. The advocates of corrective justice as an alternative to economic efficiency typically fall back on the model of aggression. This is most obviously true in Richard Epstein's early work.[1]

In the history of tort law, the model of interaction gradually tri-

---

[1] See Richard Epstein, "A Theory of Strict Liability," 2 *J. Leg. Stud.* 151 (1973).

umphed over the paradigm of aggression. In other words, the principle of negligence implicit in trespass on the case triumphed over the model of aggression implicit in the writ of trespass. The turning point in American law was a modest little dispute in 1850 in Massachusetts about using a stick to break up a dogfight. The defendant swung the stick back and hit the plaintiff in the eye. The plaintiff sought to recover in trespass, but the defendant wanted to assert the relevance of the plaintiff's negligence and thus prevailed in his argument that the proper standard was not strict liability based on aggression but negligence or the failure to exercise due care in swinging the stick. Thus the model of interaction prevailed (though not in so many words).[2] When we reason in the model of interaction, the negligence of both defendant and plaintiff becomes relevant.

But these rules are of very recent vintage, not only in the common law but also in France and Germany. The relevance of the plaintiff's negligence is not mentioned in the 1804 *Code civil*. The common law recognized it in 1809. The great debate that emerged was whether the proper standard should be an all-or-nothing or relative standard. The former principle holds that if the plaintiff is contributorily negligent, she is the final cause of the accident (an aggressor against herself, as it were), and therefore there should be no recovery. The relative standard, comparative negligence, starts on the assumption that both negligent parties contributed to the accident and that the damages should be judged accordingly. The conflict between these two approaches came to a head when the California Supreme Court turned to the interpretation of a provision in the 1872 California Civil Code, which reads as follows:

> § 1714 Everyone is responsible, not only for the result of his willful acts, but also for an injury occasioned to another by his want of ordinary care or skill in the management of his property or person, *except so far as the latter* has, willfully or by want of ordinary care, brought the injury upon himself. The extent of liability in such cases is defined by the Title on Compensatory Relief. [Italics added]

If you had just read this provision, what would you say is the law of California—contributory or comparative negligence, the all-or-nothing rule or apportionment of liability according to relative fault? Let us see

---

[2] See *Brown v. Kendall*, 60 Mass. 292 (1850).

how the California Supreme Court approached this problem of interpretation.

■

Nga Li v. Yellow Cab Company of California

Supreme Court of California

13 Cal. 3d 804; 532 P.2d 1226 (1975)

SULLIVAN, J.:

In this case we address the grave and recurrent question whether we should judicially declare no longer applicable in California courts the doctrine of contributory negligence, which bars all recovery when the plaintiff's negligent conduct has contributed as a legal cause in any degree to the harm suffered by him, and hold that it must give way to a system of comparative negligence, which assesses liability in direct proportion to fault. As we explain in detail *infra*, we conclude that we should. In the course of reaching our ultimate decision we conclude that: (1) The doctrine of comparative negligence is preferable to the "all-or-nothing" doctrine of contributory negligence from the point of view of logic, practical experience, and fundamental justice; (2) judicial action in this area is not precluded by the presence of section 1714 of the Civil Code, which has been said to "codify" the "all-or-nothing" rule and to render it immune from attack in the courts except on constitutional grounds; (3) given the possibility of judicial action, certain practical difficulties attendant upon the adoption of comparative negligence should not dissuade us from charting a new course—leaving the resolution of some of these problems to future judicial or legislative action; (4) the doctrine of comparative negligence should be applied in this state in its so-called "pure" form under which the assessment of liability in proportion to fault proceeds in spite of the fact that the plaintiff is equally at fault as or more at fault than the defendant; and finally (5) this new rule should be given a limited retrospective application.

The accident here in question occurred near the intersection of Alvarado Street and Third Street in Los Angeles. . . . The court, sitting without a jury, found as facts that defendant Phillips was traveling at approximately 30 miles per hour when he entered the intersection, that such speed was unsafe at that time and place, and that the traffic light controlling southbound traffic at the intersection was yellow when defendant Phillips drove into the intersection. It also found, however, that plaintiff's left turn across the southbound lanes of Alvarado "was made at a time when a vehicle was approaching from the opposite direction so close as to constitute an immediate hazard." The dispositive conclusion of law was as follows: "That the driving of Nga Li was negligent, that such negligence was a proximate cause of the collision, and that she is barred from recovery by reason of such contributory negligence." Judgment for defendants was entered accordingly.

I.

"Contributory negligence is conduct on the part of the plaintiff which falls below the standard to which he should conform for his own protection, and which is a legally contributing cause cooperating with the negligence of the defendant in bringing about the plaintiff's harm." (Rest. 2d Torts, § 463.) Thus the American Law Institute, in its second restatement of the law, describes the kind of conduct on the part of one seeking recovery for damage caused by negligence which renders him subject to the doctrine of contributory negligence. What the effect of such conduct will be is left to a further section, which states the doctrine in its clearest essence: "Except where the defendant has the last clear chance, the plaintiff's contributory negligence *bars recovery* against a defendant whose negligent conduct would otherwise make him liable to the plaintiff for the harm sustained by him." (Rest. 2d Torts, § 467.)

This rule, rooted in the long-standing principle that one should not recover from another for damages brought upon oneself . . . has been the law of this state from its beginning. . . . Although criticized almost from the outset for the harshness of its operation, it has weathered numerous attacks, in both the legislative and the judicial arenas, seeking its amelioration or repudiation. We have undertaken a thorough reexamination of the matter, giving particular attention to the common law and statutory sources of the subject doctrine in this state. As we have indicated, this reexamination leads us to the conclusion that the "all-or-nothing" rule of contributory negligence can be and ought to be superseded by a rule which assesses liability in proportion to fault.

It is unnecessary for us to catalogue the enormous amount of critical comment that has been directed over the years against the "all-or-nothing" approach of the doctrine of contributory negligence. The essence of that criticism has been constant and clear: the doctrine is inequitable in its operation because it fails to distribute responsibility in proportion to fault. Against this have been raised several arguments in justification, but none have proved even remotely adequate to the task. The basic objection to the doctrine—grounded in the primal concept that in a system in which liability is based on fault, the extent of fault should govern the extent of liability—remains irresistible to reason and all intelligent notions of fairness.

Furthermore, practical experience with the application by juries of the doctrine of contributory negligence has added its weight to analyses of its inherent shortcomings: "Every trial lawyer is well aware that juries often do in fact allow recovery in cases of contributory negligence, and that the compromise in the jury room does result in some diminution of the damages because of the plaintiff's fault. But the process is at best a haphazard and most unsatisfactory one."[3] . . .

It is in view of these theoretical and practical considerations that to this date 25 states have abrogated the "all-or-nothing" rule of contributory negligence and have enacted in its place general apportionment statutes calculated in one manner or another to assess liability in proportion to fault. . . .

II.

It is urged that any change in the law of contributory negligence must be made by the Legislature, not by this court. Although the doctrine of contributory negligence is of judicial origin—its genesis being traditionally attributed to the opinion of Lord Ellenborough in *Butterfield v. Forrester* (K.B. 1809) 103 Eng. Rep. 926—the enactment of section 1714 of the Civil Code in 1872 codified the doctrine as it stood at that date and, the argument continues, rendered it invulnerable to attack in the courts except on constitutional grounds. Subsequent cases of this court, it is pointed out, have unanimously affirmed that—barring the appearance of some constitutional infirmity—the "all-or-nothing" rule

---

[3] Justice Sullivan is citing William L. Prosser, the leading authority on torts.

is the law of this state and shall remain so until the Legislature directs otherwise. The fundamental constitutional doctrine of separation of powers, the argument concludes, requires judicial abstention. . . .

We have concluded that the foregoing argument, in spite of its superficial appeal, is fundamentally misguided. As we proceed to point out and elaborate below, it was not the intention of the Legislature in enacting section 1714 of the Civil Code, as well as other sections of that code declarative of the common law, to insulate the matters therein expressed from further judicial development; rather it was the intention of the Legislature to announce and formulate existing common law principles and definitions for purposes of orderly and concise presentation and with a distinct view toward continuing judicial evolution.

Before turning our attention to section 1714 itself we make some observations concerning the 1872 Civil Code as a whole. Professor Arvo Van Alstyne, in an excellent and instructive article entitled "The California Civil Code" which appears as the introductory commentary to West's *Annotated Civil Code* (1954), has carefully and authoritatively traced the history and examined the development of this, the first code of substantive law to be adopted in this state. Based upon the ill-fated draft Civil Code prepared under the direction and through the effort of David Dudley Field for adoption in the state of New York, the California code found acceptance for reasons largely related to the temperament and needs of an emerging frontier society. "In the young and growing commonwealth of California, the basically practical views of Field commanded wider acceptance than the more theoretic and philosophic arguments of the jurists of the historic school. In 1872, the advantages of codification of the unwritten law, as well as of a systematic revision of statute law, loomed large, since that law, drawing heavily upon the judicial traditions of the older states of the Union, was still in a formative stage. The possibility of widely dispersed popular knowledge of basic legal concepts comported well with the individualistic attitudes of the early West." (Van Alstyne, *supra*, p. 6.)

[W]e turn to a specific consideration of section 1714. . . . The present-day reader of the foregoing language is immediately struck by the fact that it seems to provide in specific terms for a rule of comparative rather than contributory negligence—i.e., for a rule whereby plaintiff's recovery is to be diminished to the extent that his own actions have been responsible for his injuries. The use of the compound conjunction "except so far as"—rather than some other conjunction setting up a wholly disqualifying condition—clearly seems to indicate an intention on the part of the Legislature to adopt a system other than one wherein contributory fault on the part of the plaintiff would operate to bar recovery. Thus it could be argued—as indeed it has been argued with great vigor by plaintiff and the amici curiae who support her position—that no change in the law is necessary in this case at all. Rather, it is asserted, all that is here required is a recognition by this court that section 1714 announced a rule of comparative negligence in this state in 1872 and a determination to brush aside all of the misguided decisions which have concluded otherwise up to the present day. (See also Bodwell, "It's Been Comparative Negligence For Seventy-Nine Years" (1952) 27 *L.A. Bar Bull.* 247.)

Our consideration of this arresting contention—and indeed of the whole question of the true meaning and intent of section 1714—cannot proceed without reference to the Code Commissioners' Note which appeared immediately following section 1714 in the 1872 code. That note provided in full as follows: "Code La., § 2295; Code Napoleon, § 1383; *Austin vs. Hudson River R.R. Co.,* 25 N.Y., p. 334; *Jones vs. Bird,* 5 B. & Ald., p. 837; *Dodd vs. Holmes,* 1 Ad. & El., p. 493. *This section modifies the law heretofore existing.*—See 20 N.Y., p. 67; 10 M. & W., p. 546; 5 C. B. (N. S.), p. 573. This class of obligations imposed by law seems to be laid down in the case of *Baxter vs. Roberts,* July Term, 1872, Sup. Ct. Cal. Roberts employed Baxter to perform a service which he (Roberts) knew to be perilous, without giving Baxter any notice of its perilous character; Baxter was injured. Held: that Roberts was responsible in damages for the injury which Baxter sustained. (See facts of case.)" (1 Annot. Civ. Code (Haymond & Burch 1874 ed.) p. 519; italics added.)

Each of the parties and amici in this case has applied himself to the task of legal cryptography which the interpretation of this note involves. The variety of answers which has resulted is not surprising. We first address ourselves to the interpretation advanced by plaintiff and the amici curiae in support of her contention set forth above, that section 1714 in fact announced a rule of comparative rather than contributory negligence.

The portion of the note which is relevant to our inquiry extends from its beginning up to the series of three cases cited following the italicized sentence: "This section modifies the law heretofore existing." Plaintiff and her allies point out that the first authorities cited are two statutes from civil law jurisdictions, Louisiana and France; then comes the italicized sentence; finally there are cited three cases which state the common law of contributory negligence modified by the doctrine of last clear chance. The proper interpretation, they urge, is this: Civil law jurisdictions, they assert, uniformly apportion damages according to fault. The citation to statutes of such jurisdictions, followed by a sentence indicating that a change is intended, followed in turn by the citation of cases expressing the common law doctrine—these taken together, it is urged, support the clear language of section 1714 by indicating the rejection of the common law "all-or-nothing" rule and the adoption in its place of civil law principles of apportionment.

This argument fails to withstand close scrutiny. The civil law statutes cited in the note, like the common law cases cited immediately following them, deal not with "defenses" to negligence but with the basic concept of negligence itself. In fact the Code Commissioners' Note to the parallel section of the Field draft cites the very same statutes and the very same cases in direct support of its statement of the basic rule. Moreover, in 1872, when section 1714 was enacted and the Code Commissioners' Note was written, neither France nor Louisiana applied concepts of comparative negligence. The notion of "faute commune" did not become firmly rooted in French law until 1879 and was not codified until 1915. (See Turk, "Comparative Negligence on the March" (1950) 28 *Chi.-Kent L. Rev.* 189, 239–240.) Louisiana, in spite of an 1825 statute which appeared to establish comparative negligence, firmly adhered to the "all-or-nothing" common law rule in 1872 and has done so ever since. (Turk, *supra*, at pp. 318–326.) In fact, in 1872 there was no American jurisdiction applying concepts of true comparative negligence for general purposes, and the only European jurisdictions doing so were Austria and Portugal. (Turk, *supra*, at p. 241.) Among those jurisdictions applying such concepts in the limited area in which they have traditionally been applied, to wit, admiralty, was California itself: in section 973 of the very Civil Code which we are now considering (now Harb. & Nav. Code, § 292) apportionment was provided for when the negligence of the plaintiff was slight. Yet the Code Commissioners' Note did not advert to this section.

In view of all of the foregoing we think that it would indeed be surprising if the 1872 Legislature, intending to accomplish the marked departure from common law which the adoption of comparative negligence would represent, should have chosen to do so in language which differed only slightly from that used in the Field draft to describe the common law rule. . . . It would be even more surprising if the Code Commissioners, in stating the substance of the intended change, should fail to mention the law of any jurisdiction, American or foreign, which then espoused the new doctrine in any form, and should choose to cite in their note the very statutes and decisions which the New York Code Commissioners had cited in support of their statement of the common law rule. It is in our view manifest that neither the Legislature nor the Code Commissioners harbored any such intention— and that the use of the words "except so far as" in section 1714 manifests an intention other than that of declaring comparative negligence the law of California in 1872.

That intention, we have concluded, was simply to insure that the rule of contributory negligence, as applied in this state, would not be the harsh rule then applied in New York but would be mitigated by the doctrine of last clear chance. The New York rule, which did not incorporate the latter doctrine, had been given judicial expression several years before in the case of *Johnson v. The Hudson River Railroad Company* (1859) 20 N.Y. 65. It is apparent from the Code Commissioners' Note that this rule was considered too harsh for adoption in California, and that the Legislature therefore determined to adopt a provision which would not have the effect of barring a negligent plaintiff from recovery without regard to the quantity or quality of his negligence. . . .

We think that the foregoing establishes conclusively that the intention of the Legislature in enacting section 1714 of the Civil Code was to state the basic rule of negligence together with the defense of contributory negligence modified by the emerging doctrine of last clear chance. It remains to determine whether by so doing the Legislature intended to restrict the courts from further development of these concepts according to evolving standards of duty, causation, and liability.

This question must be answered in the negative. As we have explained above, the peculiar nature of the 1872 Civil Code as an avowed continuation of the common law has rendered it particularly flexible and adaptable in its response to changing circumstances and conditions.

To reiterate the words of Professor Van Alstyne, "[the code's] incompleteness, both in scope and detail have provided ample room for judicial development of important new systems of rules, frequently built upon Code foundations." By the same token we do not believe that the general language of section 1714 dealing with defensive considerations should be construed so as to stifle the orderly evolution of such considerations in light of emerging techniques and concepts. On the contrary we conclude that the rule of liberal construction made applicable to the code by its own terms (Civ. Code, § 4), together with the code's peculiar character as a continuation of the common law (see Civ. Code, § 5) permit if not require that section 1714 be interpreted so as to give dynamic expression to the fundamental precepts which it summarizes.

The aforementioned precepts are basically two. The first is that one whose negligence has caused damage to another should be liable therefor. The second is that one whose negligence has contributed to his own injury should not be permitted to cast the burden of liability upon another. The problem facing the Legislature in 1872 was how to accommodate these twin precepts in a manner consonant with the then progress of the common law and yet allow for the incorporation of future developments. The manner chosen sought to insure that the harsh accommodation wrought by the New York rule—i.e., barring recovery to one guilty of any negligence—would not take root in this state. Rather the Legislature wished to encourage a more humane rule—one holding out the hope of recovery to the negligent plaintiff in some circumstances.

The resources of the common law at that time (in 1872) did not include techniques for the apportionment of damages strictly according to fault—a fact which this court had lamented three years earlier. They did, however, include the nascent doctrine of last clear chance which, while it too was burdened by an "all-or-nothing" approach, at least to some extent avoided the often unconscionable results which could and did occur under the old rule precluding recovery when any negligence on the part of the plaintiff contributed in any degree to the harm suffered by him. Accordingly the Legislature sought to include the concept of last clear chance in its formulation of a rule of responsibility. We are convinced, however, as we have indicated, that in so doing the Legislature in no way intended to thwart future judicial progress toward the humane goal which it had embraced. Therefore, and for all of the foregoing reasons, we hold that section 1714 of the Civil Code was not intended to and does not preclude present judicial action in furtherance of the purposes underlying it.

III.

. . . .

It remains to identify the precise form of comparative negligence which we now adopt for application in this state. Although there are many variants, only the two basic forms need be considered here. The first of these, the so-called "pure" form of comparative negligence, apportions liability in direct proportion to fault in all cases. . . . The second basic form of comparative negligence, of which there are several variants, applies apportionment based on fault up to the point at which the plaintiff's negligence is equal to or greater than that of the defendant—when that point is reached, plaintiff is barred from recovery. Nineteen states have adopted this form or one of its variants by statute. The principal argument advanced in its favor is moral in nature: that it is not morally right to permit one more at fault in an accident to recover from one less at fault. Other arguments assert the probability of increased insurance, administrative, and judicial costs if a "pure" rather than a "50 percent" system is adopted, but this has been seriously questioned. We have concluded that the "pure" form of comparative negligence is that which should be adopted in this state. . . .

For all of the foregoing reasons we conclude that the "all-or-nothing" rule of contributory negligence as it presently exists in this state should be and is herewith superseded by a system of "pure" comparative negligence, the fundamental purpose of which shall be to assign responsibility and liability for damage in direct proportion to the amount of negligence of each of the parties. Therefore, in all actions for negligence resulting in injury to person or property, the contributory negligence of the person injured in person or property shall not bar recovery, but the damages awarded shall be diminished in proportion to the amount of negligence attributable to the person recovering. The doctrine of last clear chance is abolished, and the defense of assumption of risk is also abolished to the extent that it is merely a variant of the former doctrine of contributory negligence; both of these are to be subsumed under the general process of assessing liability in proportion to negligence. Pending future judicial or legislative developments, the trial courts of this state are to use broad discretion in seeking to assure that the principle stated is applied in the interest of justice and in furtherance of the purposes and objectives set forth in this opinion.

It remains for us to determine the extent to which the rule here announced shall have application to cases other than those which are commenced in the future. It is the rule in this state that determinations of this nature turn upon considerations of fairness and public policy. . . . Upon mature reflection, in view of the very substantial number of cases involving the matter here at issue which are now pending in the trial and appellate courts of this state, and with particular attention to considerations of reliance applicable to individual cases according to the stage of litigation which they have reached, we have concluded that a rule of limited retroactivity should obtain here. Accordingly we hold that the present opinion shall be applicable to all cases in which trial has not begun before the date this decision becomes final in this court, but that it shall not be applicable to any case in which trial began before that date (other than the instant case)—except that if any judgment be reversed on appeal for other reasons, this opinion shall be applicable to any retrial.

The judgment is reversed.

MOSK, J., DISSENTING (IN PART) AND CONCURRING (IN PART):

[Concerned solely about the issue of prospective overruling and agrees with the majority's principle of applying the new rule to these parties and all future cases.]

CLARK, J.:

I dissent. For over a century this court has consistently and unanimously held that Civil Code section 1714 codifies the defense of contributory negligence. Suddenly—after 103 years—the court declares section 1714 shall provide for comparative negligence instead. In my view, this action constitutes a gross departure from established judicial rules and role.

First, the majority's decision deviates from settled rules of statutory construction. A cardinal rule of construction is to effect the intent of the Legislature. The majority concedes "the intention of the Legislature in enacting section 1714 of the Civil Code was to state the basic rule of negligence together with the defense of contributory negligence modified by the emerging doctrine of last clear chance." Yet the majority refuses to honor this acknowledged intention—violating established principle.

The majority decision also departs significantly from the recognized limitation upon judicial action—encroaching on the powers constitutionally entrusted to the Legislature. The power to enact and amend our statutes is vested exclusively in the Legislature. . . .

I dispute the need for judicial—instead of legislative—action in this area. The majority is clearly correct in its observation that our society has changed significantly during the 103-year existence of section 1714. But this social change has been neither recent nor traumatic, and the criticisms leveled by the majority at the present operation of contributory negligence are not new. I cannot conclude our society's evolution has now rendered the normal legislative process inadequate.

Further, the Legislature is the branch best able to effect transition from contributory to comparative or some other doctrine of negligence. Numerous and differing negligence systems have been urged over the years, yet there remains widespread disagreement among both the commentators and the states as to which one is best. (See Schwartz, *Comparative Negligence* (1974) Appendix A, pp. 367–369 and § 21.3, fn. 40, pp. 341–342, and authorities cited therein.) This court is not an investigatory body, and we lack the means of fairly appraising the merits of these competing systems. Constrained by settled rules of judicial review, we must consider only matters within the record or susceptible to judicial notice. That this court is inadequate to the task of carefully selecting the best replacement system is reflected in the majority's summary manner of eliminating from consideration all but two of the many competing proposals—including models adopted by some of our sister states.

By abolishing this century-old doctrine today, the majority seriously erodes our constitutional function. We are again guilty of judicial chauvinism.

■

QUESTIONS AND COMMENTS

1. The history of contributory and comparative negligence reveals a striking diversity of positions. At the beginning of the nineteenth

century, the *Code civil* totally ignored the issue of plaintiff's fault. A few years later, the common law courts devised the doctrine of contributory negligence on the basis of causation. If the plaintiff is negligent (riding her bike with her eyes closed) and this brings on the accident, it cannot be said that the defendant's negligence caused the accident. Had the plaintiff kept her eyes open, she could have avoided the accident. (Causation also explains the doctrine of "last clear chance." If the defendant could have avoided the accident despite his own negligence and the plaintiff's riding with her eyes shut, the defendant has the last clear chance and remains fully liable for the ensuing harm.) Thereafter, at the end of the century, the German BGB (§ 254) clearly accepted the general principle of comparative fault, both for torts and contracts. Finally, the French accepted the principle of comparative fault, and the Americans eventually fell into line. All of this happened, it appears, with little cross-fertilization from one legal system to another. Nonetheless, this particular opinion reveals a striking awareness of the comparative legal developments.

2. The Field Code, upon which § 1714 is based, was designed to bring to bear civilian influence to overcome certain aspects of the common law. The problem is that "civilian" in this context means French and not German. The *Code civil*, as noted, lagged in its development of tort law.

3. Is the real issue comparative blameworthiness or comparative causation? Do we really care how much at fault each side is in creating a high risk of an accident, or are we rather interested in the degree to which each negligent side contributes to the occurrence of the accident? [Note that BGB § 254 (1) provides: "If the fault of the injured party contributes to the harm suffered, then the content and degree of the duty to pay compensation depends on the circumstances; in particular, on the extent to which the harm was caused by one party or the other."] The emphasis is clearly on the relative causal contribution. This seems to us correct, but the common law systematically avoids the idea of causation as a matter of degree. Causation is either present or not present, but the fault, the courts believe, comes in degrees.

4. Would a civilian court care so much about the original intent of the

legislature? Why should common lawyers interpret statutes and codes in this way?

■

Further Reading

The story of the move from contributory to comparative fault is told in G. Edward White, *Tort Law in America: An Intellectual History* (expanded ed.) (New York: Oxford University Press, 2003).

TWENTY–FIVE

Disputed Boundaries: Punitive Damages

The codification movement in Continental Europe, particularly in Germany, proceeded on the basis of sharp distinctions among particular bodies of private law. The BGB has one book devoted to the law of obligations and another to "things," or the law of property, both movable and immovable. Within the law of obligations, there is a sharp distinction among particular kinds of contracts, on the one hand, and unjust enrichment and torts on the other. Each particular body of law within the law of obligations has its own rules, which are subject to the general principles laid down first in the general part governing the entire law of obligations and second in the general part governing the entire civil code. The civilian trained in this tradition has clear categories in his or her mind. Fact patterns must be classified one way or the other.

Some of the civilian categories, however, manipulate the boundaries to achieve certain ends. For example, the German lawyers invented "affirmative breach of contract" as a doctrine supplementary to the code in order to augment the category of contract and diminish the scope of tort; the reason was that the rules of employer liability are more favorable in contract than in tort. Despite this pushing and pulling on the boundaries, the categories enjoy internal integrity and doctrinal consistency.

Nothing quite like this conceptual clarification has ever occurred in the common law. Products liability is both tort and contract. The law of nuisance (see *Boomer*, Chapter Seventeen) lies in a zone where property and tort overlap. The writ of trespass, with which we began this book, has features of both tort and criminal law. The basic idea behind trespass *vi et armis* ("by force and violence") is that it had qualities of both tort and criminal law. This intersecting identity of tort accounts for one of the most puzzling features of the common law of torts—namely, punitive damages. The very existence of this institution must boggle the minds of the civilian lawyers. Tort is supposed to be about compensation for injury, not punishment. Criminal law is for punishment. Well, think again. We are in the common law, where history counts for more than principle. What better way to end our survey of constitutional and private law in the United States than to see the way these historical encrustations trouble the conscience of the Supreme Court?

BMW of North American, Inc., v. Ira Gore, Jr.

Supreme Court of the United States
517 U.S. 559; 116 S. Ct. 1589 (1996) (some citations omitted)

STEVENS, J.:

. . . The Due Process Clause of the Fourteenth Amendment prohibits a State from imposing a " 'grossly excessive' " punishment on a tortfeasor. The wrongdoing involved in this case was the decision by a national distributor of automobiles not to advise its dealers, and hence their customers, of predelivery damage to new cars when the cost of repair amounted to less than 3 percent of the car's suggested retail price. The question presented is whether a $2 million punitive damages award to the purchaser of one of these cars exceeds the constitutional limit.

I.

In January 1990, Dr. Ira Gore, Jr. (respondent), purchased a black BMW sports sedan for $40,750.88 from an authorized BMW dealer in Birmingham, Alabama. After driving the car for approximately nine months, and without noticing any flaws in its appearance, Dr. Gore took the car to "Slick Finish," an independent detailer, to make it look " 'snazzier than it normally would appear.' " (646 So. 2d 619, 621 (Ala.

1994).) Mr. Slick, the proprietor, detected evidence that the car had been repainted. Convinced that he had been cheated, Dr. Gore brought suit against petitioner BMW of North America (BMW), the American distributor of BMW automobiles. Dr. Gore alleged, inter alia, that the failure to disclose that the car had been repainted constituted suppression of a material fact. The complaint prayed for $500,000 in compensatory and punitive damages, and costs.

At trial, BMW acknowledged that it had adopted a nationwide policy in 1983 concerning cars that were damaged in the course of manufacture or transportation. If the cost of repairing the damage exceeded 3 percent of the car's suggested retail price, the car was placed in company service for a period of time and then sold as used. If the repair cost did not exceed 3 percent of the suggested retail price, however, the car was sold as new without advising the dealer that any repairs had been made. Because the $601.37 cost of repainting Dr. Gore's car was only about 1.5 percent of its suggested retail price, BMW did not disclose the damage or repair to the Birmingham dealer.

Dr. Gore asserted that his repainted car was worth less than a car that had not been refinished. To prove his actual damages of $4,000, he relied on the testimony of a former BMW dealer, who estimated that the value of a repainted BMW was approximately 10 percent less than the value of a new car that had not been damaged and repaired. To support his claim for punitive damages, Dr. Gore introduced evidence that since 1983 BMW had sold 983 refinished cars as new, including 14 in Alabama, without disclosing that the cars had been repainted before sale at a cost of more than $300 per vehicle. Using the actual damage estimate of $4,000 per vehicle, Dr. Gore argued that a punitive award of $4 million would provide an appropriate penalty for selling approximately 1,000 cars for more than they were worth.

In defense of its disclosure policy, BMW argued that it was under no obligation to disclose repairs of minor damage to new cars and that Dr. Gore's car was as good as a car with the original factory finish. It disputed Dr. Gore's assertion that the value of the car was impaired by the repainting and argued that this good-faith belief made a punitive award inappropriate. BMW also maintained that transactions in jurisdictions other than Alabama had no relevance to Dr. Gore's claim.

The jury returned a verdict finding BMW liable for compensatory damages of $4,000. In addition, the jury assessed $4 million in punitive damages, based on a determination that the nondisclosure policy constituted "gross, oppressive or malicious" fraud. (See Ala. Code §§ 6-11-20, 6-11-21 (1993).) [The Alabama Supreme Court held that the trial court did not have jurisdiction over the German manufacturer and therefore reversed the judgment against that defendant. On the question of long-arm jurisdiction, see Chapter Thirteen.]

The Alabama Supreme Court did, however, rule in BMW's favor on one critical point: The court found that the jury improperly computed the amount of punitive damages by multiplying Dr. Gore's compensatory damages by the number of similar sales in other jurisdictions. Having found the verdict tainted, the court held that "a constitutionally reasonable punitive damages award in this case is $2,000,000," (*id.*, at 629), and therefore ordered a remittitur in that amount.[1] The court's discussion of the amount of its remitted award expressly disclaimed any reliance on "acts that occurred in other jurisdictions"; instead, the court explained that it had used a "comparative analysis" that considered Alabama cases, "along with cases from other jurisdictions, involving the sale of an automobile where the seller misrepresented the condition of the vehicle and the jury awarded punitive damages to the purchaser."

Because we believed that a review of this case would help to illuminate "the character of the standard that will identify unconstitutionally excessive awards" of punitive damages . . . we granted certiorari.[2]

II.

Punitive damages may properly be imposed to further a State's legitimate interests in punishing unlawful conduct and deterring its repetition. . . . In our federal system, States necessarily have considerable flexibility in determining the level of punitive damages that they will allow in different classes of cases and in any particular case. . . .

No one doubts that a State may protect its citizens by prohibiting deceptive trade practices and by requiring automobile distributors to disclose presale repairs that affect the value of a new car. But the States need not, and in fact do not, provide such protection in a uniform manner.

[1] A remittitur is the reduction of a damage award by a judge.
[2] This means the court accepted the petition to hear the case.

That diversity demonstrates that reasonable people may disagree about the value of a full disclosure requirement. Some legislatures may conclude that affirmative disclosure requirements are unnecessary because the self-interest of those involved in the automobile trade in developing and maintaining the goodwill of their customers will motivate them to make voluntary disclosures or to refrain from selling cars that do not comply with self-imposed standards. Those legislatures that do adopt affirmative disclosure obligations may take into account the cost of government regulation, choosing to draw a line exempting minor repairs from such a requirement. In formulating a disclosure standard, States may also consider other goals, such as providing a "safe harbor" for automobile manufacturers, distributors, and dealers against lawsuits over minor repairs.

We may assume, arguendo, that it would be wise for every State to adopt Dr. Gore's preferred rule, requiring full disclosure of every presale repair to a car, no matter how trivial and regardless of its actual impact on the value of the car. But while we do not doubt that Congress has ample authority to enact such a policy for the entire Nation, it is clear that no single State could do so, or even impose its own policy choice on neighboring States.

We think it follows from these principles of state sovereignty and comity that a State may not impose economic sanctions on violators of its laws with the intent of changing the tortfeasors' lawful conduct in other States. . . . When the scope of the interest in punishment and deterrence that an Alabama court may appropriately consider is properly limited, it is apparent—for reasons that we shall now address—that this award is grossly excessive.

III.

Elementary notions of fairness enshrined in our constitutional jurisprudence dictate that a person receive fair notice not only of the conduct that will subject him to punishment, but also of the severity of the penalty that a State may impose. Three guideposts, each of which indicates that BMW did not receive adequate notice of the magnitude of the sanction that Alabama might impose for adhering to the nondisclosure policy adopted in 1983, lead us to the conclusion that the $2 million award against BMW is grossly excessive: the degree of reprehensibility of the nondisclosure; the disparity between the harm or potential harm suffered by Dr. Gore and his punitive damages award; and the difference between this remedy and the civil penalties authorized or imposed in comparable cases. We discuss these considerations in turn.

Perhaps the most important indicium of the reasonableness of a punitive damages award is the degree of reprehensibility of the defendant's conduct. As the Court stated nearly 150 years ago, exemplary damages imposed on a defendant should reflect "the enormity of his offense." . . . In this case, none of the aggravating factors associated with particularly reprehensible conduct is present. The harm BMW inflicted on Dr. Gore was purely economic in nature. The presale refinishing of the car had no effect on its performance or safety features, or even its appearance for at least nine months after his purchase. BMW's conduct evinced no indifference to or reckless disregard for the health and safety of others. To be sure, infliction of economic injury, especially when done intentionally through affirmative acts of misconduct (*id.*, at 453), or when the target is financially vulnerable, can warrant a substantial penalty. But this observation does not convert all acts that cause economic harm into torts that are sufficiently reprehensible to justify a significant sanction in addition to compensatory damages.

Dr. Gore contends that BMW's conduct was particularly reprehensible because nondisclosure of the repairs to his car formed part of a nationwide pattern of tortious conduct. . . . Because this case exhibits none of the circumstances ordinarily associated with egregiously improper conduct, we are persuaded that BMW's conduct was not sufficiently reprehensible to warrant imposition of a $2 million exemplary damages award.

The second and perhaps most commonly cited indicium of an unreasonable or excessive punitive damages award is its ratio to the actual harm inflicted on the plaintiff. The principle that exemplary damages must bear a "reasonable relationship" to compensatory damages has a long pedigree. Scholars have identified a number of early English statutes authorizing the award of multiple damages for particular wrongs. Some 65 different enactments during the period between 1275 and 1753 provided for double, treble, or quadruple damages. Our decisions in *Haslip*[3]

---

[3] *Pacific Mut. Life Ins. Co. v. Haslip*, 499 U.S. 1, 23, 113 L. Ed. 2d 1, 111 S. Ct. 1032 (1991).

and *TXO*[4] endorsed the proposition that a comparison between the compensatory award and the punitive award is significant.

In *Haslip* we concluded that even though a punitive damages award of "more than 4 times the amount of compensatory damages" might be "close to the line," it did not "cross the line into the area of constitutional impropriety." *TXO*, following dicta in *Haslip*, refined this analysis by confirming that the proper inquiry is " 'whether there is a reasonable relationship between the punitive damages award and the harm likely to result from the defendant's conduct as well as the harm that actually has occurred.' " Thus, in upholding the $10 million award in *TXO*, we relied on the difference between that figure and the harm to the victim that would have ensued if the tortious plan had succeeded. That difference suggested that the relevant ratio was not more than 10 to 1.

The $2 million in punitive damages awarded to Dr. Gore by the Alabama Supreme Court is 500 times the amount of his actual harm as determined by the jury. Moreover, there is no suggestion that Dr. Gore or any other BMW purchaser was threatened with any additional potential harm by BMW's nondisclosure policy. The disparity in this case is thus dramatically greater than those considered in *Haslip* and *TXO*. . . .

Of course, we have consistently rejected the notion that the constitutional line is marked by a simple mathematical formula, even one that compares actual and potential damages to the punitive award. Indeed, low awards of compensatory damages may properly support a higher ratio than high compensatory awards, if, for example, a particularly egregious act has resulted in only a small amount of economic damages. A higher ratio may also be justified in cases in which the injury is hard to detect or the monetary value of noneconomic harm might have been difficult to determine. . . .

Comparing the punitive damages award and the civil or criminal penalties that could be imposed for comparable misconduct provides a third indicium of excessiveness. . . . The sanction imposed in this case cannot be justified on the ground that it was necessary to deter future misconduct without considering whether less drastic remedies could be

---

[4] *TXO Production Corp. v. Alliance Resources Corp.*, 509 U.S. 443, 454, 125 L. Ed. 2d 366 (1993).

expected to achieve that goal. The fact that a multimillion dollar penalty prompted a change in policy sheds no light on the question whether a lesser deterrent would have adequately protected the interests of Alabama consumers. In the absence of a history of noncompliance with known statutory requirements, there is no basis for assuming that a more modest sanction would not have been sufficient to motivate full compliance with the disclosure requirement imposed by the Alabama Supreme Court in this case. . . .

We cannot, however, accept the conclusion of the Alabama Supreme Court that BMW's conduct was sufficiently egregious to justify a punitive sanction that is tantamount to a severe criminal penalty. The fact that BMW is a large corporation rather than an impecunious individual does not diminish its entitlement to fair notice of the demands that the several States impose on the conduct of its business. Indeed, its status as an active participant in the national economy implicates the federal interest in preventing individual States from imposing undue burdens on interstate commerce. While each State has ample power to protect its own consumers, none may use the punitive damages deterrent as a means of imposing its regulatory policies on the entire Nation.

The judgment is reversed, and the case is remanded for further proceedings not inconsistent with this opinion.

It is so ordered.

BREYER, J. WITH WHOM O'CONNOR, J. AND SOUTER, J. JOIN, CONCURRING.

[another explanation of why the damage award violates due process]

SCALIA, J. WITH WHOM THOMAS, J. JOINS, DISSENTING.

Today we see the latest manifestation of this Court's recent and increasingly insistent "concern about punitive damages that 'run wild.' " *Haslip.* Since the Constitution does not make that concern any of our business, the Court's activities in this area are an unjustified incursion into the province of state governments.

In earlier cases that were the prelude to this decision, I set forth my view that a state trial procedure that commits the decision whether to impose punitive damages, and the amount, to the discretion of the jury, subject to some judicial review for "reasonableness," furnishes a defendant with all the process that is "due." . . . I do not regard the

Fourteenth Amendment's Due Process Clause as a secret repository of substantive guarantees against "unfairness"—neither the unfairness of an excessive civil compensatory award, nor the unfairness of an "unreasonable" punitive award. What the Fourteenth Amendment's procedural guarantee assures is an opportunity to contest the reasonableness of a damages judgment in state court; but there is no federal guarantee a damages award actually be reasonable. . . .

This view, which adheres to the text of the Due Process Clause, has not prevailed in our punitive damages cases. . . . When, however, a constitutional doctrine adopted by the Court is not only mistaken but also insusceptible of principled application, I do not feel bound to give it stare decisis effect—indeed, I do not feel justified in doing so. . . . Our punitive damages jurisprudence compels such a response. The Constitution provides no warrant for federalizing yet another aspect of our Nation's legal culture (no matter how much in need of correction it may be), and the application of the Court's new rule of constitutional law is constrained by no principle other than the Justices' subjective assessment of the "reasonableness" of the award in relation to the conduct for which it was assessed.

Because today's judgment represents the first instance of this Court's invalidation of a state-court punitive assessment as simply unreasonably large, I think it a proper occasion to discuss these points at some length.

The most significant aspects of today's decision—the identification of a "substantive due process" right against a "grossly excessive" award, and the concomitant assumption of ultimate authority to decide anew a matter of "reasonableness" resolved in lower court proceedings—are of course not new. *Haslip* and *TXO* revived the notion, moribund since its appearance in the first years of this century, that the measure of civil punishment poses a question of constitutional dimension to be answered by this Court. Neither of those cases, however, nor any of the precedents upon which they relied, actually took the step of declaring a punitive award unconstitutional simply because it was "too big."

At the time of adoption of the Fourteenth Amendment, it was well understood that punitive damages represent the assessment by the jury, as the voice of the community, of the measure of punishment the defendant deserved. . . . Today's decision, though dressed up as a legal opinion, is really no more than a disagreement with the community's sense of indignation or outrage expressed in the punitive award of the Alabama jury, as reduced by the State Supreme Court. It reflects not merely, as the concurrence candidly acknowledges, "a judgment about a matter of degree," (*ante*, at 596); but a judgment about the appropriate degree of indignation or outrage, which is hardly an analytical determination.

There is no precedential warrant for giving our judgment priority over the judgment of state courts and juries on this matter. . . . The only case relied upon in which the Court actually invalidated a civil sanction does not even support constitutional review for excessiveness, since it really concerned the validity, as a matter of procedural due process, of state legislation that imposed a significant penalty on a common carrier which lacked the means of determining the legality of its actions before the penalty was imposed. (See *Southwestern Telegraph & Telephone Co. v. Danaher*, 238 U.S. 482, 489-491 (1915).) The amount of the penalty was not a subject of independent scrutiny. As for the remaining cases, while the opinions do consider arguments that statutory penalties can, by reason of their excessiveness, violate due process, not a single one of these judgments invalidates a damages award. . . .

More importantly, this latter group of cases—which again are the sole precedential foundation put forward for the rule of constitutional law espoused by today's Court—simply fabricated the "substantive due process" right at issue. . . . [T]he only authority for the Court's position is simply not authoritative. These cases fall far short of what is needed to supplant this country's longstanding practice regarding exemplary awards, see, e. g., *Haslip*, 499 U.S. at 15-18; *id.*, at 25-28 (Scalia, J., concurring in judgment).

One might understand the Court's eagerness to enter this field, rather than leave it with the state legislatures, if it had something useful to say. In fact, however, its opinion provides virtually no guidance to legislatures, and to state and federal courts, as to what a "constitutionally proper" level of punitive damages might be.

We are instructed at the outset of Part II of the Court's opinion . . . that "the federal excessiveness inquiry . . . begins with an identification of the state interests that a punitive award is designed to serve." On first reading this, one is faced with the prospect that federal punitive damages law (the new field created by today's decision) will be beset by the sort of "interest analysis" that has laid waste the formerly comprehensible field of conflict of laws. [This is a reference to the revolutionary theories of Brainerd Currie in the 1960s, which established the "active nationality" principle in interstate conflict of laws; namely, a state should apply its own law whenever one of its citizens is involved in the litigation. The theory was that the state should apply its law whenever it has interest to do so; its interests are defined by the welfare of its citizens.] The thought that each assessment of punitive damages, as to each offense, must be examined to determine the precise "state interests" pursued, is most unsettling. Moreover, if those "interests" are the most fundamental determinant of an award, one would think that due process would require the assessing jury to be instructed about them.

These significant issues pronounced upon by the Court are not remotely presented for resolution in the present case. There is no basis for believing that Alabama has sought to control conduct elsewhere. The statutes at issue merely permit civil juries to treat conduct such as petitioner's as fraud, and authorize an award of appropriate punitive damages in the event the fraud is found to be "gross, oppressive, or malicious," Ala. Code § 6-11-20(b)(1) (1993). To be sure, respondent did invite the jury to consider out-of-state conduct in its calculation of damages, but any increase in the jury's initial award based on that consideration is not a component of the remitted judgment before us. As the Court several times recognizes, in computing the amount of the remitted award the Alabama Supreme Court—whether it was constitutionally required to or not—"expressly disclaimed any reliance on acts that occurred in other jurisdictions." . . . Thus, the only question presented by this case is whether that award, limited to petitioner's Alabama conduct and viewed in light of the factors identified as properly informing the inquiry, is excessive. The Court's sweeping (and largely unsupported) statements regarding the relationship of punitive awards to lawful or unlawful out-of-state conduct are the purest dicta. . . .

In Part III of its opinion, the Court identifies "three guideposts" that lead it to the conclusion that the award in this case is excessive: degree of reprehensibility, ratio between punitive award and plaintiff's actual harm, and legislative sanctions provided for comparable misconduct. The legal significance of these "guideposts" is nowhere explored, but their necessary effect is to establish federal standards governing the hitherto exclusively state law of damages. . . . Of course it will not be easy for the States to comply with this new federal law of damages, no matter how willing they are to do so. In truth, the "guideposts" mark a road to nowhere; they provide no real guidance at all. . . .

These crisscrossing platitudes yield no real answers in no real cases. And it must be noted that the Court nowhere says that these three "guideposts" are the only guideposts; indeed, it makes very clear that they are not—explaining away the earlier opinions that do not really follow these "guideposts" on the basis of additional factors, thereby "reiterating our rejection of a categorical approach." In other words, even these utter platitudes, if they should ever happen to produce an answer, may be overridden by other unnamed considerations. The Court has constructed a framework that does not genuinely constrain, that does not inform state legislatures and lower courts—that does nothing at all except confer an artificial air of doctrinal analysis upon its essentially ad hoc determination that this particular award of punitive damages was not "fair."

. . . .

For the foregoing reasons, I respectfully dissent.

GINSBERG, J. WITH WHOM REHNQUIST, C.J. JOINS, DISSENTING.

The Court finds Alabama's $2 million award not simply excessive, but grossly so, and therefore unconstitutional. The decision leads us further into territory traditionally within the States' domain, and commits the Court, now and again, to correct "misapplication of a properly stated rule of law." But cf. this Court's Rule 10 ("A petition for a writ of certiorari is rarely granted when the asserted error consists of erroneous factual findings or the misapplication of a properly stated rule of law."). The Court is not well equipped for this mission. Tellingly, the Court repeats that it brings to the task no "mathematical formula," no "cat-egorical approach," no "bright line." It has only a vague concept of substantive due process, a "raised eyebrow" test as its ultimate guide.

In contrast to habeas corpus review under 28 U.S.C. § 2254, the Court will work at this business alone. It will not be aided by the federal district courts and courts of appeals. It will be the only federal court policing the area. The Court's readiness to superintend state-court punitive damages awards is all the more puzzling in view of the Court's longstanding reluctance to countenance review, even by courts of appeals, of the size of verdicts returned by juries in federal district court proceedings. . . . And the reexamination prominent in state courts and in legislative arenas serves to underscore why the Court's enterprise is undue.

For the reasons stated, I dissent from this Court's disturbance of the judgment the Alabama Supreme Court has made.

QUESTIONS AND COMMENTS

1. Think about how the result in this case would have influenced the outcome of the *Sullivan* case, discussed in Chapter Ten. The jury in that case, also in Alabama, had awarded Sullivan damages in the amount of $500,000. There was no proof of any actual damage to Sullivan at all, and the verdict included an undifferentiated portion of punitive damages. The lawyers for the *New York Times* did not challenge the constitutionality of the damage award because, in 1964, they did not think they had a chance on that issue. Today, after the *BMW* decision, the controversy would be framed differently. It is possible the Court would have reversed on the issue of damages and not have introduced the partial exemption for public figures in the law of libel.

2. *Plus ça change, c'est plus la même chose.* As Oregon could not bind the entire United States in *Pennoyer* (see Chapter Thirteen), now an Alabama jury may not calculate damages on the basis of BMW's impact on customers all over country. Is this the beginning of the end for punitive damages in the United States? Or could it have the opposite effect by placing greater emphasis on the internal motivations of the company subject to potential liability? To assess the tactical consequences of the decision, you need to pay attention to the particularities of American civil procedure, in particular, the possibility of extensive discovery as a litigation cost imposed on the defendant. These and other tactical issues are addressed in the next chapter.

3. In *State Farm Mutual Automobile Ins. Co. v. Campbell*, 123 S. Ct. 1513 (2003), the Court clarified the position it took in the *BMW* case. First, they emphasized more clearly that a state does not have legitimate interest in regulating bad acts that occur outside of its jurisdiction. Second, and more important, the Court suggested that awards

greater than a single-digit ratio (i.e., a maximum of nine-to-one) of punitive to compensatory damages would almost always violate due process. See Catherine M. Sharkey, "Punitive Damages as Societal Damages," 113 *Yale L.J.* 347 (2003).

4. Here we offer an apology for punitive damages—not necessarily in this case but in general. As we move toward criminal law, we should keep in mind a procedural oddity of the United States and a few other common law jurisdictions. If a jury acquits in a criminal case, the prosecution cannot appeal—even for egregious legal mistakes benefiting the defense. There are two remedies for mistakes by state court juries that favor the defense. One is to bring a federal civil rights action for a criminal deprivation of the victim's constitutional rights, and the other is a tort suit for compensatory and punitive damages. In many high-profile cases, juries acquit, and the most effective remedy for the victims is an action of punitive damages. We will return to this theme when we take up the subject of criminal law.

■

Further Reading

An empirical study of the use of punitive damages, and the difference between that use and myths about it, is in Theodore Eisenberg, John Goerdt, Brian Ostrom, David Rottman, and Martin T. Wells, "The Predictability of Punitive Damages," 26 *J. Legal Stud.* 623 (1997). A fascinating study exploring the mechanisms of award is in *Punitive Damages: How Juries Decide* (Cass R. Sunstein ed.) (Chicago: University of Chicago Press, 2002).

TWENTY-SIX

The American Civil Trial in Outline

The American adversary system of civil procedure is probably better known than any other to both lawyers and nonlawyers across the globe. Depicted in movies and books distributed to audiences worldwide, the drama of attorney confrontation over the evidence is ubiquitous. As lawyers from states with civilian and other systems know, the common law trial is an unusual process, which not only gives the judge little or no role in gathering or sifting the evidence but also leaves the verdict entirely to lay jurors, even in complicated commercial lawsuits.[1] Indeed, given the central role of the jury trial as the model for all common law litigation—even litigation before a judge alone—it is not unfair to say that the trial as common lawyers think of it has no counterpart in civilian procedure at all.[2]

The process of litigation between private parties in the United States is lengthy and expensive. The more complicated the facts of the dispute, the more people involved in it, or the longer the course of dealings

---

[1] For more on the differences, see John H. Langbein, "The German Advantage in Civil Procedure," 52 *U. Chi. L. Rev.* 823 (1985).

[2] See, on this point, John Henry Merryman and David S. Clark, *Comparative Law: Western European and Latin American Legal Systems, Cases and Materials* 652 (Indianapolis: Bobbs-Merrill, 1978).

between the parties prior to the dispute, the lengthier and more expensive the litigation is. The greatest source of this delay and cost is rarely the trial itself but rather the preliminary stages, during which parties are identified, evidence is gathered, and legal claims are refined. As a result of such a pretrial effort, however, the parties are often able to reach a settlement of their claims prior to trial, and the vast majority of civil suits, even though they have been filed in courts and pursued over several years, end in a settlement negotiated between the parties rather than a judgment decreed by the jury or the judge.[3]

Pretrial settlements, however, depend on the parties being in greater fear of the decree that they might receive from the court than from the compromise they will have to reach, and this balance is not always predictable. So even if a case never reaches the courtroom, it is usually treated as if it will, and the entire process is carried out, all according to the law governing civil litigation.

Civil litigation is regulated by constitutional provisions, statutes, national and local court rules, and judicial decisions, but the bulk of this regulation comes from court rules. The rules of civil procedure govern most questions, although matters of evidence are subject to the rules of evidence. Most states have adopted these rules, modeling them after the federal rules. Both types of rules are—like all codes in the United States— subject to considerable bodies of interpretative judicial precedent. The conduct of the lawyers in carrying out these rules is also subject to regulation by the courts and the bar, according not only to the rules of procedure but also to professional standards of conduct, which are considered in more detail in Chapter Twenty-Nine.

The preparation and conduct of a civil trial are thus highly regulated and follow a general pattern, which for our purposes may be seen generally in these steps:

I. Initial Investigation
II. Drafting and Service of Pleadings
III. Preliminary Motions
IV. Discovery

---

[3] In 2001, only 1.9 percent of all federal civil cases reached trial. Indeed, of 248,377 civil cases disposed of, only 3,112 went to a jury, and 1,654 went to a judge alone for trial. See Federal Judicial Caseload Statistics, March 31, 2002, Table C-4 (http://www .uscourts.gov/caseload2002/tables/c04mar02.pdf).

v. Summary Motions

vi. Pretrial Conference

vii. Jury Selection

viii. Trial

ix. Jury Instruction

x. Verdict and Judgment

xi. Post-trial Motions

xii. Appeal

xiii. Execution

xiv. Settlements and Alternative Dispute Resolution

I. Initial Investigation

Although formal civil litigation begins with the service of a pleading by the plaintiff upon the defendant, in a manner of speaking the litigation begins much earlier—when the person, which may be a government or corporation, an individual, or a group, first discusses its problems with its lawyers. At that time, the lawyers must listen to the problems described and begin a process of determining whether there is a legal remedy against another party that will alleviate their client's problem. This process then involves careful examination of both the facts and the law involved in the client's problem.

The factual research involves the lawyers' making a good faith effort not only to determine whether the story told them by their client is true but also to uncover any other relevant facts that they should have been told by their client or should have known, as a matter of common knowledge, if it would affect the legal interests of their clients or their opponents. This investigation often involves discussions with the potential opponent or the opponent's lawyers.

The legal research includes researching and considering not only what doctrines of law might have been violated by the other party but also what remedies might be available against that party for those violations. The lawyer must research many questions to answer the fundamental query of what remedy can be had. What are the available jurisdictions and choices of venue, and which is the most appropriate court to hear the client's claims? Is the action timely, neither too late under the statutes of limitations (or moot under the prudential rules) nor too soon to be ripe? Are there problems of immunity, such as a government might have, or capacity, such as a deceased person or a child might lack?

The defenses and counterclaims the other party might have must also be considered and researched. Was there a justification or excuse for the opponent's conduct? Did the client do anything that has given rise to liability toward the defendant? Will the client be in a better position by bringing an action or by staying out of court?

The same form of investigation is required whether the lawyer is learning of the problem from a client who seeks to bring suit (or whom the lawyer advises to bring suit) or from a party who has been served as a defendant in a suit. These inquiries must be made before either filing the complaint or filing the answer.

The question often researched before any other, particularly for new clients, is whether the lawyer is professionally capable of representing the matter. The lawyer's duty of loyalty to all clients forbids representation of one client against another, unless all of the parties involved have been told of the conflict of representation and have waived any interest. Even so, some conflicts will be thought by most lawyers to be too important to be waivable. Besides direct conflicts of interest between clients opposed in the same matter, the lawyer may be barred in other cases, such as those in which the attorney has an economic interest adverse to the clients or cases in which the lawyer would be expected to represent clients with conflicting interests in different cases.

A further arena of professional concern is one not subject to research but still one of perennial inquiry. The lawyer should have no reason to believe that the client's claims or defenses are fraudulent or untruthful or that the client intends to commit or incite perjury. In such cases, the lawyer cannot represent the claims in court.

Lawyers too often neglect these investigations, making them liable under Rule 11 of the federal rules and most state rules to sanctions, which can include not only dismissal of the case but also monetary penalties.[4] For a variety of political, institutional, and cultural reasons, judges have been reluctant to impose penalties under Rule 11, and they have been particularly reluctant to impose penalties on defendants who present a frivolous defense in their answer. Still, the rules are there, and in time they may be more fairly enforced. Some states have gone further and

---

[4] Rule 11 is reprinted and discussed in Chapter Nine.

made statutory causes of action for frivolous litigation or abuse of legal process, in which case the jury may award damages against a party who brings an unjustifiable suit or defense.

II. Drafting and Service of Pleadings

As we saw in Chapter One, the old common law system of writs depended upon the form of the initial pleadings filed in the court. In the writ system, a plaintiff was required to choose a form of writ that was both recognized by the law and sufficiently fit the facts for the court to find that the plaintiff was entitled to the relief required by that writ from the defendant. The modern rules of pleading are much more flexible, but they still reflect something of the old pleadings tradition.

In most civil actions, the initial pleading is the *complaint*.[5] The plaintiff must state why the court has jurisdiction over its claim, allege sufficient facts to put the defendant on notice of the allegations of fact and claims of law and equity that are being brought, and ask for the relief the plaintiff seeks (see Fed. R. Civ. Pro. 8). In federal courts, a complaint arising on a question of federal law is subject to the "well-pleaded complaint" rule, according to which the reliance of the claim on the federal Constitution or a U.S. statute or doctrine must be clearly apparent in the text, or "on the face" of the complaint.

The complaint must then be filed in the court and also served upon the defendant (or defendants), which is done usually by a person handing the complaint to the defendant, with a summons to appear before the court in which the complaint was filed. The complaint and summons may be handed to an appropriate agent or employee of that person. (Service on a corporation is usually made by service on an agent.) In some circumstances, it can be mailed, which is usually done by certified post, so that a record of the received mail is returned to the plaintiff. In all cases, the plaintiff's lawyer must see that a record of the service is filed in the court.

---

[5] There are certain noncriminal actions in America that begin with other pleadings, such as actions in admiralty that begin with a *libel*, actions in equity pleading in some states, or other unusual actions that begin with a *motion*, but the vast majority of civil litigation commences with the complaint.

The defendant has a short time, usually twenty days, to file an *answer*, in which the defendant admits or denies the allegations of the plaintiff's complaint, and (if the defendant does not want to give the relief sought by the plaintiff) to deny that the plaintiff is entitled to any relief. Instead of filing an answer, the defendant could *move to dismiss* the complaint. If the motion fails, the defendant then must file its answer. Often, at the same time the defendant files its answer, it also files *affirmative defenses*, which are defenses that are beyond the scope of merely denying the allegations or claims of the plaintiff. The defendant may also file *counterclaims*, which are claims the defendant might have put into its own complaint, had the plaintiff not been the first to file.

Some counterclaims must be brought at this time or are waived forever. These are compulsory counterclaims, which meet five criteria: (1) the counterclaim must exist when the suit was filed, (2) it has to arise out of the transaction or occurrence that is the subject matter of the plaintiff's claim against the defendant, (3) it can be adjudicated without the presence of third parties beyond the court's jurisdiction, (4) it was not already pending in court in another case, and (5) the plaintiff's suit did not commence by asserting jurisdiction over property alone but over the person of the defendant (see Fed. R. Civ. Pro. 13). All other counterclaims are permissive and may be brought by the defendant then or later.

The plaintiff must then file an answer to the counterclaims. As with all pleadings and motions, a copy of the answer must be given to all of the parties in the case, as well as filed with the court (or if a motion is made aloud, it must be on the record made by the court that is to be filed). Also, as with the answer by the defendant, a failure by the plaintiff to file the answer may result in a default judgment.

If any party fails to file an answer to a complaint or to counterclaims, the party that filed them may move the court for a *default judgment*, winning them outright, unless the nonfiling party can show a good reason for not filing an answer or for delay in filing an answer, in which case the nonfiling party will move to set aside the default judgment and move forward in the case. If an allegation is not denied in an answer, the court in most circumstances may consider that allegation to be true.

One aspect of this phase of the trial, the pleading in of third parties, might occur earlier or later. The rules distinguish the plaintiffs and defendants from several forms of third parties. These distinctions can be a bit confusing, particularly when there are multiple plaintiffs or multiple defendants. In practice, there is ordinarily only one difference between a third party (usually brought in through service by a defendant) and the initial defendant, who is brought in through service by the plaintiff. All other differences turn on who seeks the remedy from the third party.

A defendant might bring in, or *implead*, a third party to indemnify the defendant if the defendant loses. Or a defendant might implead a third party that might also be liable for the same conduct for which the defendant has been sued, so that the third party will be held jointly liable and reduce the defendant's liability. A plaintiff may bring in third parties to share in liability or to indemnify it against a counterclaim. Third-party complaints served later than ten days after filing an answer require the permission of the court. A third party who enters a case voluntarily and not by the claim of a plaintiff or a defendant is an *intervenor*.

Parties may also bring *interpleader actions*, which are a cross between a regular suit and a third-party action, according to which the plaintiff admits it owes money to one of several defendants, deposits the money with the court, and forces the defendants to sort out who has the best claim to it (see Fed Rules Civ Pro. 22). Furthermore, a plaintiff may *cross-claim* against other plaintiffs, and a defendant may cross-claim against other defendants.

As to multiple parties, there are several manners in which multiple plaintiffs may sue. The most important common form is when different plaintiffs join in a single suit, either through subscribing to a single complaint or by filing motions to join a variety of individual actions against a common defendant. Quite famously, a large group of plaintiffs may be represented by a single plaintiff or small group of plaintiffs in a *class action*. To be certified, a class must meet four prerequisites: (1) It is so numerous that joinder of all members as individual litigants is impracticable, (2) there are questions of law or fact in common among every member of the class, (3) the claims or defenses of the representative parties are typical of the claims or defenses of every member of the class, (4) and the representative parties will fairly and adequately protect the interests of the class. If these prerequisites are met, the court may certify the class to be represented if any of three justifications are met: A requirement of separate actions by each class member might lead to some members' cases being affected by others or to varying or unfair results in different trials, the defense has more or less acted toward them like a class, or a class action would be more fair or efficient (see Fed. R. Civ. Pro. 23).

Not all states allow class actions, although all allow actions by multiple named plaintiffs. There are other methods of bringing actions on behalf of larger groups of unidentified plaintiffs, particularly the *common fund* cause in equity, but such actions are rare.

III. Preliminary Motions

Often, after the complaint is filed, each side (but most often the defense) is likely to make a series of motions, seeking to dismiss the case or at least limit the scope of the suit. These motions may take several forms and may be designed to accomplish many ends beyond those that appear on their face. Unfortunately, many lawyers file them merely to generate additional hours to bill their client or to increase the costs for their opponents. But when these motions are used well, they are useful not only for limiting the liability the client might face but also for narrowing the issues in the case and making the work in the next stage, discovery, more manageable.

One of the earliest motions in a case is for a *scheduling order*. This may be made by the court *sua sponte*, or on its own motion, in the absence of a motion by one of the parties. In federal courts, it is to be entered within ninety days of the filing of the answer. The scheduling order sets the limits for the time during which parties may join other parties and amend the pleadings, file motions, and complete discovery, and it often sets the date for a pretrial conference. This order may be amended from time to time, but it sets the pace for the proceedings until the pretrial conference, which is usually set about one month before the trial date.

The most important form of preliminary motion is the motion to dismiss, which may be based on procedural or substantive grounds. On procedural grounds, the defendant may move to dismiss the case because the court lacks jurisdiction over the subject matter of the plaintiff's complaint or lacks jurisdiction over the person of the defendant (even if there is jurisdiction over the claim), because the court is not the proper venue and another court is, because the service of process on the defendant was ineffective or insufficient, or because a necessary party was not joined in the suit (see Fed. R. Civ. Pro. 12). Or the defendant may move to dismiss or to stay proceedings because it is not the appropriate party, the real party in interest, or because one of the parties lacks the capacity to be in court and must be represented by a guardian or next friend (see Fed. R. Civ. Pro. 17). The defendant makes such motions, the plaintiff may file objections to the motions, and either or both sides may file written briefs summarizing the law—the case precedents, rules, and statutes—supporting their views. The court may hear oral argument, or it may not. It then rules, and usually a dismissal under these grounds does not bar the plaintiff from going back to the drawing board and filing a new complaint, although it might well be in a different court.

Defenses raised at this time include lack of personal jurisdiction and lack of valid process (see Fed. R. Civ. Pro.12(b)(2) and (4)). To assert these defenses, the defendant is allowed to make a *special appearance*, or appear only for the purpose of arguing that the court lacks the jurisdiction necessary to force the defendant to appear. A failure to raise the issue in an answer or responsive pleading or by motion will mean that these defenses are waived.

There are several distinct bases on which lack of personal jurisdiction may be argued, but each manifests the propositions that the court's jurisdiction over the defendant and over the cause of action must be proved by the plaintiff. Moreover, the plaintiff must prove, first, that the court has been granted jurisdiction over the defendant by an appropriate statute or, in rare instances, by the judicial precedents appropriate for that court or by the inherent powers of the court and, second, that any grant of jurisdiction that does apply does not violate the constitutional limits of procedural due process of law.

Determining whether valid process has been made is not always a straightforward inquiry of whether the rules were observed for service by the appropriate personnel in the appropriate manner. To be valid, the service must be made within the limits of the statute governing service, which usually has a geographic limitation. For state statutes, service on nonresidents is a traditional difficulty, turning on interpretations of the state "long-arm" statute, which usually allows service within a zone of one hundred miles around the courthouse, regardless of state lines, on anyone who committed a tort in the state, entered a contract to be performed there, or is registered for service of process through an agent there. Applications of the service statute then raise the underlying question of jurisdiction—have the laws of the state asserted jurisdiction over the defendant for claims such as this? If the laws have not, service is ineffective, but there would also be no personal jurisdiction in the court. These are not perfectly coordinate, in that a defendant might have waived the limit on jurisdiction in certain matters but still not have waived the limits on service.

A defendant in state court may still move to dismiss the complaint, even if the jurisdictional statute is applied to allow service (see Fed. R. Civ. Pro. 12(b)(2)). The statute cannot exceed the federal constitutional limits of due process, in which a foreign defendant must have sufficient "minimum contacts" with a jurisdiction that enforcing a remedy there would not offend "traditional notions of fair play and substantial justice." See Chapter Thirteen for further elaboration of the constitutional issues.

On substantive grounds, the defendant moves to dismiss the complaint, under the well-known subpart, Rule 12(b)(6), for "failure to state a claim upon which relief can be granted." This is an argument that the terms described in the complaint are just not enough to warrant the relief sought, that even if the plaintiff could prove all it has argued, the plaintiff cannot win what it seeks from the defendant. The parties argue this motion, and the court might grant it either with leave to the plaintiff to amend the complaint or with prejudice, in which case the plaintiff has lost for good. A 12(b)(6) motion is sometimes heard on not just the statements made in the pleadings but with reference to information that is filed or presented from sources besides the complaint and the answer. In these cases, the motion is treated as a *motion for judgment on the pleadings*, which is like a motion for summary judgment.

One other motion sometimes filed at this stage is a *motion for more definite statement*. A party may ask for either a complaint or a counterclaim to be clarified, or written more clearly, if it is "so vague or ambiguous that a party cannot reasonably be required to frame a responsive pleading." The motion must describe not only the defects but also the manner of details desired. A successful motion that is not obeyed can lead to the court's striking the vague pleading from the record.

Another form of preliminary motion is a motion for pretrial remedies, such as an *attachment* or *replevin* order securing or seizing property in dispute or a *preliminary injunction* (PI) enjoining the defendant from conduct the plaintiff seeks to prevent at the close of the case. A *temporary restraining order* (TRO) is an emergency order enjoining the defendant from such conduct, entered so quickly that the defendant is not told of it before the hearing, but these are usually valid for only a few days and will be vacated unless a hearing with notice replaces the TRO with a PI.

IV. Discovery

Often the longest period of trial preparation is the discovery phase. In the common law system, discovery is managed almost entirely by the counsel for the parties. The judge acts only as an arbiter or referee when counsel disagree over some matter, such as the application of a rule to a request for some evidence or a refusal to provide it. The management—and inquiry—by judges in the civilian system at this stage is very rare indeed in the common law.

As in criminal procedure, the basic purpose of discovery is to ensure that both sides have adequate knowledge of the evidence known to the other. When the rules of discovery are followed, both sides are able to prepare their cases with full knowledge of the other's case. There are no surprises. Even more than in a criminal procedure, discovery is likely to be far broader in scope than the limits of admissibility; in other words, each party is entitled to learn more from the other than would be allowed to be presented in court. In part, this difference in scope results from the need to evaluate evidence before determining what is admissible. In part, this difference results directly from differences in the rules, which sometimes reflect policies other than those of acquiring the greatest scope of evidence possible.

Unscrupulous lawyers and clients often seek to hide damaging information, or dump great volumes of distracting evidence, in order to increase the costs and inconvenience to their opponents. The courts, despite Rules 11 and 37, usually do a poor job of monitoring such misbehavior. Lawyers who value their reputations and professional integrity, however, are careful to require their clients to conform to their discovery obligations.

Discovery takes three major forms: written questions, called *interrogatories*; requests for the production of documents and tangible evidence; and depositions, which are the recorded questioning of witnesses by lawyers. Interrogatories are limited to twenty-five questions, unless the court allows more. Depositions may be based on written questions provided in advance or on oral questions alone.

There are less-known forms. *Requests for admissions* seek the opponent to admit to facts or claims that, if denied but later proved, may give rise to sanctions. Medical and psychiatric exams may be ordered for a variety of reasons. Land may be inspected. Third parties may be subpoenaed. But most discovery amounts to volleys of interrogatories and production requests and long hours spent in depositions.

V. Summary Motions

Following discovery, either party often moves for judgment, either as a *judgment on the pleadings*, which is rather more like a motion to dismiss but incorporates some information outside the pleadings (see Fed. R. Civ. Pro. 13), or as a motion for *summary judgment*, which is allowable after discovery if the case can be decided solely on undisputed facts (see Fed. R. Civ. Pro. 56). After such motions, particularly if there are sufficient stipulations of facts between the parties, the court might hear arguments on the law alone, and it can render judgment without a trial. Most such motions are for summary judgment, and it is up to the moving party to prove that there is no dispute over any facts that are germane, or material to the issues between the parties, and to prove that the moving party is entitled to judgment as a matter of law. Summary judgment is to be denied if there is a "genuine issue as to any material fact." Although summary judgment might not be granted to decide a whole case, a party may move for, or a court may grant, partial summary judgment to reduce the number of claims subject to trial.

VI. Pretrial Conference

Although it is a rather informal affair in many state courts, in federal courts the pretrial conference is a formal discussion of the case prior to trial, between all the attorneys and the judge. Prior to the conference, each side prepares draft pretrial orders, placing the arguments, evidence, and results in the light they believe most favors their side of the case. During the conference, motions to exclude certain arguments or evidence are often argued and resolved.

When both sides are well prepared for the conference and both are behaving professionally, considerable amounts of the evidence may be stipulated as appropriate for admission. Even some legal conclusions may be stipulated to be determined according to facts yet to be found. The evidence that will be introduced, including the witnesses, is finalized.

Despite the many television shows, movies, and novels that turn on the last-minute introduction of a surprise witness or of a bit of mysterious evidence, it is very hard to introduce a witness or other evidence that was not produced during discovery and recorded in the pretrial order. The party offering such evidence must show that the delay in production was excusable, and even then the court might not allow it into the record.

VII. Jury Selection

Not all trials are by jury. Many state civil actions are before a judge alone, and by long custom, civil actions in equity rather than law are tried by a judge alone. Certain specialized actions in the federal courts, mainly voting-rights actions, are tried by three-judge courts without a jury. Last, the parties may both agree to have a judge hear the case as trier of fact as well as of law, although the judge might still order trial before a jury. Indeed, most civil trials are before a judge and a jury, and jury selection is the first step of the trial itself. Most civil juries now have six members, although they may be as large as the traditional twelve.

The process of jury selection, or jury *voir dire*, begins with the selection of a *venire*, or jury pool. This is usually a large group of people summoned by the clerk of the court from a list randomly drawn from the rolls of registered voters living in the court's jurisdiction. Thus, federal courts, with jurisdiction over a larger area, usually have a more geographically dispersed venire than do state courts.

Members of the *venire* are then examined. This usually takes the form of a series of questions, asked by the lawyers for both sides, as well as by the judge. Following the answers to these questions, the judge selects jurors from the *venire*. Attorneys for each side may challenge potential jurors prior to selection, either challenging them peremptorily, in which case the challenging attorney need not give a reason (although case law makes clear that these challenges may not be used to eliminate jurors on the basis of race or gender), or for cause, such as appearing to have an interest in the case or lacking capacity to serve.[6]

---

[6] In federal court, 28 U.S.C. § 1870 gives each side three peremptory challenges.

VIII. Trial

After a jury is impaneled, the trial proceeds in four main stages: opening statements, plaintiff's evidence, defense evidence, and closing arguments. Each is usually given a particular number of days, half-days, or hours in the pretrial order.

In the opening statements, each side attempts to explain to the jurors what the case is about. Each side argues its theory of who has sued whom, what the evidence is, and why their side is entitled to win under the appropriate standards of law. The plaintiff goes first, summarizing the evidence that shows the plaintiff is entitled to relief, as well as the reasons that relief is possible under the law. The defendant goes second, arguing not only that the plaintiff cannot prove its case but also that there are facts to support any affirmative defenses or counterclaims that are offered.

The presentation of evidence is managed almost exclusively by counsel. Civilian lawyers will find the degree of attorney control over the case, and of judicial noninterference, to be nearly total. This is not, however, always the case, and particularly when a judge is acting as a trier of fact, as in an equity case, the judge may ask quite a few questions directly of a witness or inspect tangible evidence with personal care. Although such judicial interrogation is possible in a jury trial, it is rare indeed.

Evidence includes the production of documents and tangible evidence, as well as the examination of witnesses. All evidence is subject to the rules of evidence, which determine not only what evidence may be introduced and what not but also how evidence is to be used and what must be proved for a court to treat evidence as authentic. The underlying doctrines of evidence are that all evidence relevant to the matter is presumptively allowed, that evidence that is irrelevant is not allowed, and that all evidence is subject to a controlling question of whether it is prone to help the finder of fact establish the truth of the matter.

The plaintiff may offer witnesses, asking witnesses favorable to its side general questions to tell what they know of the case. The defendant may cross-examine them with more leading questions. (In the defendant's presentation of evidence, or if either calls hostile witnesses, these roles are reversed.) In most situations, the evidence of a witness is entirely oral, and there is no equivalent to the civilian "articles of proof." The exception, however, is a *proffer*, in which the lawyer who seeks to have some testimony or other evidence put in the record over the objection of an opponent may, out of the hearing of the jury, summarize that testimony or evidence to allow the judge to rule on its admissibility.

At the end of the plaintiff's case, the defense often moves to dismiss the case by granting a *directed verdict*. The defense then argues that the plaintiff has not proved the case well enough for there to be any way a reasonable jury could find the defendant liable. If the court grants that motion, the case ends, the defense puts on no evidence, and the jury is dismissed. But it is rare for such motions to be granted, and they are usually denied or held under advisement. The defense then puts on its case, including often recalling many of the same witnesses called by the plaintiff. At the close of the evidence, the defense again moves for a directed verdict, usually with the same results as before.[7]

Each side then presents its closing arguments—the plaintiff, who bears the burden to persuade the jury, usually going last. Following closing arguments, each side customarily moves again for judgment as a matter of law (which is required if the attorney will later move for a judgment notwithstanding the verdict), and these motions are usually denied.

IX. Jury Instruction

One of the most important aspects of the common law trial is the instruction of the jury. Most instructions are provided by the attorneys to the judge, and the attorneys usually draft instructions that place the law or the evidence in the light most favorable to their side. The judge reads through the proposed instructions and may add instructions either drafted in chambers or from pattern books of instructions. Each lawyer may object to particular instructions, usually before they are read to the jury but

---

[7] Although this repeat of a failed motion might seem fruitless, it is required by the structure of Rule 50, which makes it necessary if the defense intends to appeal on the basis of insufficiency of the evidence. Rule 50(a) motions for directed verdict at the close of a plaintiff's evidence are not the same as Rule 50(a) motions for insufficient evidence at the close of trial. Motions at the close of all the evidence are required under Rule 50(3) for appeal on the grounds of insufficient evidence. Professor Carlton Bailey, my colleague in Arkansas, has been kind enough to share his distress at ruling on quite a few disciplinary proceedings of lawyers who failed to make the final motion, thinking they had preserved the issue in the earlier motion but negligently sacrificing the appellate rights of their clients.—SS

always out of the hearing of the jury (see Fed. R. Civ. Pro. 51). The side that loses may not later appeal from a poor instruction if it did not object to it at this time. The result is a list of instructions to the jury that detail their tasks in general and then ask specific questions necessary for them to reach a verdict.

The instructions usually take three forms. First are general instructions, such as the obligation to act unanimously, to elect a foreman, and to base their decision solely on the evidence they heard in the courtroom and not on prior impressions or on extraneous factors such as the race or wealth of the parties. In these instructions, the jury will be usually told about the burden of persuasion, which ordinarily rests with the plaintiff; the plaintiff must prove the case, and if the jurors remain unpersuaded by either argument, they should vote for the defendant. (The defense, however, has the burden of persuasion for its counterclaims, as well as for certain affirmative defenses.[8]) The jurors will also be told of the burden of proof, which in civil cases requires the party with the burden of persuasion to prove its case to a given level of certainty. Usually this level is a "preponderance of the evidence," according to which the evidence must be at least more than halfway persuasive. For intentional torts and other deliberate wrongful acts, such as breach of a fiduciary duty, the plaintiff must prove the case to a higher level of confidence, presenting a case, including the defense's argument, that is clear and convincing. Instructions also detail the elements of the pending claims at law, usually defining the terms necessary to understand the particular claims and defenses. Last are the specific instructions to determine whether the facts as alleged have been proved sufficiently to support the claims or the defenses.

The final determination of the case then rests with the jury. Unlike the civilian system, the jury is left to decide how much credibility to assign to all witnesses and evidence. There are no irrebuttable presumptions in the common law. The jury must decide for itself if the evidence is sufficient to meet the standard of proof for the plaintiff's claims, as well as for the defendant's affirmative defenses or counterclaims.

---

[8] There are occasions when the burden of persuasion may shift from the plaintiff to the defendant, such as when a plaintiff has demonstrated a prima facie case in certain matters, after which the defendant is required to prove a defense. But usually the plaintiff retains the burden to prove the whole case.

X. Verdict and Judgment

In most states and in the federal courts, the jury must reach a verdict that all of the members agree upon. Juries usually are asked to bring in general verdicts, such as whether a defendant is liable to the plaintiff, or how many dollars of harm a plaintiff has suffered that must be compensated by the defendant. A jury may, however, be asked to answer a list of questions in a *special verdict* or in *interrogatories* (see Fed. R. Civ. Pro. 49). The jury may then find a series of facts, allowing the court then to determine whether the jury has found sufficient facts to support its general verdict. If there are inconsistencies, the court may enter the general verdict or send the verdicts back to the jury for further consideration.

If a verdict is entered for the plaintiff, the court usually enters a judgment, decreeing that the defendant must give to the plaintiff the relief sought. When this is an amount of money in damages, the court usually enters the dollar amount, subject to interest until it is paid. When it is an injunction, the court enters an order specifying what the defendant can or cannot do. If the verdict is entered for the defendant, the court enters an order dismissing the case.

In either case, the losing party may be taxed with court costs, which can be considerable and include the cost of court reporters, jurors' expenses, and set fees of the court or its clerk. In certain rare cases, such as civil rights actions subject to 42 U.S.C. § 1988, the court awards attorneys' fees, so that the losing party must pay the winning party's lawyers' fees, subject to court approval.

XI. Post-trial Motions

The end of the trial is hardly the end of the case. Three later phases may well take as much or more time as the preparation and trial itself. The first of these is usually expeditious—the filing and resolution of *post-trial motions*. The other two may be much more difficult—*appeal*, if one is taken, and *execution of judgment*, if there is resistance by the defense.

Post-trial motions are usually made by the losing party. The most powerful is a request for a *judgment notwithstanding the verdict*, or JNOV ("nov" from *non obstante veridicto*), in which the losing side requests the judge to set aside the jury verdict and grant it judgment anyway. The court grants this only if it determines that no reasonable jury could have reached the verdict rendered, and it is rare for such a motion to be granted. Slightly more likely is a motion for a new trial, which is particularly used if there is newly discovered evidence not presented to the jury or if there is evidence of injustice resulting from some error during trial. Motions for new trials must be made within ten days of the entry of judgment.

Other motions request a moderation or suspension of the judgment rather than its reversal. Motions may be brought for up to a year after the judgment for alteration of a judgment if there is a clerical mistake in it, or the whole judgment may be suspended or vacated if there is a substantive mistake (see Fed. R. Civ. Pro. 60). Substantive mistake may arise from actual mistake, inadvertence, surprise, or excusable neglect in developing the moving party's case; if the moving party has found newly discovered evidence that by due diligence the moving party could not have discovered within ten days of the judgment; or if the moving party has discovered fraud, misrepresentation, or other misconduct of an adverse party. The judgment may also be suspended or vacated if it has become technically void; if it has been satisfied, released, or discharged; if a prior judgment upon which it is based has been reversed or otherwise vacated; if it is no longer equitable that the judgment should have prospective application; or for any other reason justifying relief from the operation of the judgment.

Two continuing common law motions in the state courts are motions for *additur* or *remittitur*. A plaintiff may move for reconsideration of a verdict or judgment by the court to increase an award of damages or money in restitution by moving for additur, arguing that the amount awarded either was mistakenly written or calculated or was unjustly low according to the other elements of the evidence or the verdict. Likewise, a defendant may move for reconsideration and remittitur, which is a motion on similar grounds to reduce the amount awarded to the plaintiff. Federal courts allow actions for remittitur but usually grant only a motion for new trial rather than additur (see Fed. R. Civ. Pr. 59 and 60).

XII. Appeal

After the usual post-trial motions, it is quite likely that the losing party will appeal the judgment against it to a higher court, usually an intermediate court of appeals. In the federal system, most appeals are brought first in one of the circuit courts of the U.S. Court of Appeals. Appeals are usually governed by separate rules of procedure, such as the Federal Rules of Appellate Procedure (FRAP), as well as by the local rules of both the trial court and the appellate court.

The appellant takes the appeal, first by paying a fee and filing a *notice of appeal* with the trial court clerk and with opposing counsel within thirty days of the entry of judgment or of the resolution of the last posttrial motion. Other parties wishing to appeal must file their notices in an additional fourteen days. The notice of appeal must specify the party or parties taking the appeal by naming each one or by listing them as "all plaintiffs," "the defendants," or "all defendants except X." The notice must designate the judgment, order, or part of a judgment or order that is being appealed, and it must name the court to which the appeal is taken. The clerk mails the notice to all the lawyers on the record, although most lawyers do so as a courtesy, and they must do so if they seek to stay operation of the judgment during the appeal. Upon filing a notice of appeal, the appellant must pay the district clerk all required fees. The district clerk receives the appellate docket fee on behalf of the court of appeals.

The trial court frequently requires the appellant to file a bond or provide some other security to ensure payment of costs on appeal. The appellant usually moves to stay the operation of the judgment during the appeal, which is in the discretion of the trial court to grant. If it is stayed, many courts require the filing of a bond if the appellant has been ordered to pay damages, the bond securing payment of the damages if the appeal does not succeed.

Once an appeal has been filed, the clerk transmits the record, which includes the original papers and exhibits filed in the trial court, any transcripts of proceedings, and a certified copy of the docket sheet. Preparing the trial transcript is usually quite time-consuming and costly and is paid for by the appellant.

Once the record reaches the appellate court, the case is docketed, and the appellant files a written brief. The brief first states the issues— the particular errors of law or rulings against the great weight of the evidence—on which the appellant desires the appeals court to reverse the trial court. The brief next usually summarizes the facts and procedural history of the case, presents arguments in support of its argument of the issues, and then asks either for the judgment below to be overruled, reversed, and remanded to the trial court for more work or for entry of judgment for the appellant. If the appellee timely filed its own notice of appeal, when it files its reply brief arguing against the appellant's points, it may also raise issues of its own in *cross-appeal*. The appellant then may file a *rebuttal brief* to the reply to its brief, as well as a reply to any arguments made on cross-appeal. The appellee may then file a rebuttal to replies to its cross-appeal, but by this time, few people are paying attention to the parties anymore.

The court then decides whether to hear the lawyers in oral argument on the appeal. This is common in state courts and rare in federal court.

One of the most important procedural requirements on appeal has dramatic substantive effects—the standards of review. Unlike most civilian systems, the appellate court in the common law system does not hear the whole case *de novo*.[9] Only questions of law are subject to such review without regard to the decision made in the trial court. Other questions, such as whether the evidence was sufficient to support a verdict, are likely to be limited by deference to a jury. Still others, such as whether a particular witness was qualified to testify, are limited by deference to the sound discretion of the trial judge. Neither form of deference is unlimited, and the appellate courts reverse if there is "manifest evidence of a clear error."[10]

The decisions of appeals courts are usually handed down by panels of three, sometimes with the concurrence of other members of that court, even though they only read the opinion and did not consider the evidence or argument.

XIII. Execution

In many cases, winning the judgment is not enough. The plaintiff (or the defendant pursuing a counterclaim) who wins relief usually drafts the judgment that the court enters. The losing party, however, quite frequently attempts to delay or avoid doing what the court has ordered.

[9] Peter Gottwald, "Civil Procedure Reform in Germany," 45 *Am. J. Comp. L.* 753, 762 (1997).

[10] See Steven Childress and Martha S. Davis, *Federal Standards of Review* (2d ed) (Salem, NH: Butterworth, 1992).

If the court has entered an injunction and the party enjoined violates the injunction, then the winning party moves the court for a *hearing to show cause*, at which the losing party may be held in contempt of court. Contempt, as we discussed in Chapter Eleven, may include damages, fines, or incarceration.

If the court has entered an order for damages, it is the responsibility of the losing party to pay the damages. If the losing party does not do so in a timely manner, the winning party has to seek formal execution of the order. In federal court, this is done by seeking a *writ of execution* under Rule 69. It may also be done by seeking orders of attachment over accounts or money, replevin over goods, or garnishment of future payments from third parties, such as employers or trust accounts. Certain forms of property, such as a primary residence, cannot be taken, although a lien can be filed against it if ever the property is sold. Certain forms of income, such as payments of death benefits from a life insurance policy, cannot be garnished. The winning party may continue to collect money by these methods until the damages and interest are fully satisfied. Other motions and actions to assist in the collection include the appointment of a receiver, the ordering of an accounting, and the appointment of special masters.

XIV. Settlements and Alternative Dispute Resolution

As noted at the start of this chapter, the parties may settle their disputes prior to the court's judgment. Indeed, they can settle their disputes following the court's judgment with a different outcome, if they decide to do so. The process of negotiating the settlement is usually informal, although the final settlement is usually subject to judicial approval.

The most common form of settlement is through direct negotiation of the parties through their lawyers. An agreement reached in this manner must be agreed to by the parties, and it must be approved by the court. (However, the plaintiff has the absolute right to withdraw the complaint and end a suit any time prior to the defendant filing an answer.)

Two forms of settlement may result from work with a third party— *mediation* and *arbitration*. Mediation is the use of a neutral third party to assist in negotiation. Arbitration is the use of a third party by agreement to decide disputes between the plaintiff and defendant, in lieu of hearing the dispute in courts. Only if there is a valid contract between the parties by which they each agree to mediation or arbitration can one side compel the other to engage in it, although a court may order either one if it believes either method might more efficiently and speedily resolve the dispute. Indeed, judges often act as mediators and arbitrators and chair settlement conferences prior to the trial or prior to the judgment.

One tool that is available in the federal courts and most state courts to encourage settlement is the *offer of judgment* (see Fed. R. Civ. Pro. 68). Ten days or more prior to trial, a defendant may offer an amount of money or property to settle the claims against it. If the plaintiff accepts within ten days, the clerk enters judgment and ends the case. But if the plaintiff rejects the offer or ignores it, and then the plaintiff does not win a more favorable judgment, the plaintiff must pay the costs the defendant incurred in the case after the making of the offer.

Further Reading

Numerous books detail the modern American civil trial. Two that are often used for instruction in U.S. law schools are Gerald M. Stern, *The Buffalo Creek Disaster: How the Survivors of One of the Worst Disasters in Coal-Mining History Brought Suit Against the Coal Company—And Won* (New York: Random House, 1977), and Jonathan Harr, *A Civil Action* (New York: Vantage Books, 1996). Harr's book has also been made into a movie of the same name, but a more valuable resource is Lewis A. Grossman, Robert G. Vaughn, and Jonathan Harr, *A Documentary Companion to a Civil Action* (New York: Foundation Press, 1999).

There are many guides to U.S. civil procedure, the industry standard being the hornbook by Jack H. Friedenthal, Mary Kay Kane, and Arthur Miller, *Civil Procedure* (3d ed) (St. Paul: West Wadsworth, 1999). On the law of evidence, see Jack B. Weinstein and Margaret A. Berger, *Weinstein's Evidence Manual, Student Edition* (6th ed) (Newark: Matthew Bender, 2003). As to trial practice itself, again there are many books. Two books popular with practitioners are Richard C. Waites, *Courtroom Psychology and Trial Advocacy* (New York: ALM, 2002), and the now-classic Francis L. Wellman, *The Art of Cross-Examination* (4th ed) (New York: Touchstone, 1997).

A growing body of commentary has arisen in comparative civil procedure, driven in part by the negotiations over international standards for private law, for the recognition of foreign judgments, and for transnational practice. A good story arising from work of the United Nations Commission on International Trade

Law (UNCITRAL) and the Roman International Institute for the Unification of Private Law (UNIDROIT) is told by Allen Farnsworth in E. Allen Farnsworth, "A Common Lawyer's View of His Civilian Colleagues," 57 *La. L. Rev.* 227 (1996), although the resulting instruments have been collected and analyzed in numerous works. For the negotiations concerning the still-ongoing development of conventions to enforce foreign judgments, see Ronald A. Brand, "Enforcement of Judgments in the United States and Europe," 13 *J.L. & Com.* 193 (1994). For current drafts and reports of the Hague Conference on Private International Law, Future Hague Convention on International Jurisdiction and Foreign Judgments in Civil and Commercial Matters, see http://www.hcch.net/e/workprog/jdgm.html. For a discussion of the American Law Institute's standards on transnational practice, see Geoffrey C. Hazard, Jr., "Preliminary Draft of the ALI Transnational Rules of Civil Procedure," 33 *Tex. Int'l L.J.* 489 (1998).

IV

Criminal Law

The Adversary System
and Its Alternatives

Criminal law is the most parochial of fields. There are some common crimes punished in all civilized nations—homicide, theft, rape, and others that are called *malum in se* ("wrong in itself")—but much of criminal law depends on local legislation, as well it should. The underlying liberal mandate of criminal law is the principle *nulla poena sine lege*. That is, no punishment for an action is permissible unless the action was clearly prohibited by law prior to the action. This principle of *nulla poena* is indirectly recognized in the constitutional prohibition against ex post facto laws, as discussed in Chapter Four. The *nulla poena* principle is also found in the German Basic Law, the Canadian Charter of Rights and Freedoms, and in many international treaties. In every state of the United States, there are literally thousands of statutory crimes, based on both state and federal law.

Yet criminal law is the most international of fields. There is no international court for legal disputes between individuals (the International Court of Justice is for states as litigants), but since July 2002 we have had an International Criminal Court (ICC) in The Hague. The United States is not yet a party to the ICC, but we are parties to the Hague Conventions and to the International Torture Convention. Since 1996, Americans have committed to punish grave breaches of the Geneva Conventions under federal law (see 18 U.S.C. § 2441, now called "war crimes").

Although there has been some question of U.S. commitment to compliance with international law during the military and police actions beginning in 2001, such questions must be seen in the longer light of history.

American judges and prosecutors were active in the creation and management of the International Military Tribunals in Nuremberg and Tokyo, and Americans today participate in the international criminal tribunals sponsored by the United Nations Security Council to punish war crimes and genocide in the former Yugoslavia and in Rwanda. International criminal law is very much a part of the law of the United States.

Though we cannot exhaust these very rich fields in two chapters, we must try to present criminal law in a way that it is not yet taught in American law schools—namely, as a subject that is both local and international. We try to do this by focusing on some very practical questions that arise out of a single case: *People v. Bernhard Goetz*, tried in New York in 1987.

This is the way the Court of Appeals in New York, the highest court in the state, described the disputed facts:

> The precise circumstances of the incident giving rise to the charges against defendant are disputed, and ultimately it will be for a trial jury to determine what occurred. We feel it necessary, however, to provide some factual background to properly frame the legal issues before us. Accordingly, we have summarized the facts as they appear from the evidence before the Grand Jury. We stress, however, that we do not purport to reach any conclusions or holding as to exactly what transpired or whether defendant is blameworthy. The credibility of witnesses and the reasonableness of defendant's conduct are to be resolved by the trial jury.
>
> On Saturday afternoon, December 22, 1984, Troy Canty, Darryl Cabey, James Ramseur, and Barry Allen boarded an IRT express subway train in The Bronx and headed south toward lower Manhattan. The four youths rode together in the rear portion of the seventh car of the train. Two of the four, Ramseur and Cabey, had screwdrivers inside their coats, which they said were to be used to break into the coin boxes of video machines.
>
> Defendant Bernhard Goetz boarded this subway train at 14th Street in Manhattan and sat down on a bench towards the rear section of the same car occupied by the four youths. Goetz was carrying an unlicensed .38 caliber pistol loaded with five rounds of ammunition in a waistband holster. The train left the 14th Street station and headed towards Chambers Street.
>
> It appears from the evidence before the Grand Jury that Canty approached Goetz, possibly with Allen beside him, and stated "give me five dollars." Neither Canty nor any of the other youths displayed a weapon. Goetz responded by standing up, pulling out his handgun and firing four shots in rapid succession. The first shot hit Canty in the chest; the second struck Allen in the back; the third went through Ramseur's arm and into his left side; the fourth was fired at Cabey, who apparently was then standing in the corner of the car, but missed, deflecting instead

off of a wall of the conductor's cab. After Goetz briefly surveyed the scene around him, he fired another shot at Cabey, who then was sitting on the end bench of the car. The bullet entered the rear of Cabey's side and severed his spinal cord.

All but two of the other passengers fled the car when, or immediately after, the shots were fired. The conductor, who had been in the next car, heard the shots and instructed the motorman to radio for emergency assistance. The conductor then went into the car where the shooting occurred and saw Goetz sitting on a bench, the injured youths lying on the floor or slumped against a seat, and two women who had apparently taken cover, also lying on the floor. Goetz told the conductor that the four youths had tried to rob him.

While the conductor was aiding the youths, Goetz headed towards the front of the car. The train had stopped just before the Chambers Street station and Goetz went between two of the cars, jumped onto the tracks and fled. Police and ambulance crews arrived at the scene shortly thereafter. Ramseur and Canty, initially listed in critical condition, have fully recovered. Cabey remains paralyzed, and has suffered some degree of brain damage.

On December 31, 1984, Goetz surrendered to police in Concord, New Hampshire, identifying himself as the gunman being sought for the subway shootings in New York nine days earlier. Later that day, after receiving *Miranda* warnings, he made two lengthy statements, both of which were tape recorded with his permission. In the statements, which are substantially similar, Goetz admitted that he had been illegally carrying a handgun in New York City for three years. He stated that he had first purchased a gun in 1981 after he had been injured in a mugging. Goetz also revealed that twice between 1981 and 1984 he had successfully warded off assailants simply by displaying the pistol.

According to Goetz's statement, the first contact he had with the four youths came when Canty, sitting or lying on the bench across from him, asked "how are you," to which he replied "fine." Shortly thereafter, Canty, followed by one of the other youths, walked over to the defendant and stood to his left, while the other two youths remained to his right, in the corner of the subway car. Canty then said "give me five dollars." Goetz stated that he knew from the smile on Canty's face that they wanted to "play with me." Although he was certain that none of the youths had a gun, he had a fear, based on prior experiences, of being "maimed."

Goetz then established "a pattern of fire," deciding specifically to fire from left to right. His stated intention at that point was to "murder [the four youths], to hurt them, to make them suffer as much as possible." When Canty again requested money, Goetz stood up, drew his weapon, and began firing, aiming for the center of the body of each of the four. Goetz recalled that the first two he shot "tried to run through the crowd [but] they had nowhere to run." Goetz then turned to his right to "go after the other two." One of these two "tried to run through the wall of the train, but . . . he had nowhere to go." The other youth (Cabey) "tried pretending that he wasn't with [the others]" by standing still, holding on to one of the subway hand straps, and not looking at Goetz. Goetz nonetheless fired his fourth shot at him. He then ran back to the first two youths to make sure they had been "taken care of." Seeing that they had both been shot, he spun back to check on the latter two. Goetz noticed that the youth who had been standing still was now sitting on a bench and seemed unhurt. As Goetz told the police, "I said '[you] seem to be all right, here's another,' " and he then fired the shot which severed Cabey's spinal cord. Goetz added that "if I was a little more under self-control . . . I would have put the barrel against his forehead and fired." He also admitted that "if I had had more [bullets], I would have shot them again, and again, and again."

Against the background of these facts, what do you do? What crimes do you charge against Goetz? How do you defend Goetz against these charges? The possibilities of a successful prosecution and defense depend not only on the evidence in the case but also on the prosecutorial institutions and the substantive law applicable in the particular state or country.

As a way of illuminating some important differences among systems of criminal law, our approach will be to ask, if you were Bernhard Goetz, where would you prefer to be tried? In a New York court? Or in a court in Frankfurt or Paris? Asking this question will enable us to elicit some critical differences between the two modes of trials. We will try to more than merely scratch the surface in this engaging field of comparative criminal law.[1]

[1] For background reading, you should consult George P. Fletcher, *Rethinking Criminal Law* (Oxford: Oxford University Press, 1978), and George P. Fletcher, *Basic Concepts of Criminal Law* (Oxford: Oxford University Press, 1996).

TWENTY-SEVEN

Where Would You Rather Be Tried?

Despite the tendency toward global thinking in criminal law, each country retains its distinctive approach to criminal procedure. The differences in procedural systems probably run deeper than in substantive law. To compare these systems, we should first be clear about the terminology we use. The most common terms for describing systems of criminal procedure are *adversarial, inquisitorial,* and *accusatorial.* These systems are defined according to the way in which the three different functions of the trial are allocated. These functions are (1) gathering evidence and presenting it at trial, (2) charging the accused with a crime, and (3) judging guilt or innocence.

The inquisitorial system is the easiest to define because it unites all three of these functions in the person of the judge. A single official gathers the evidence, charges the accused, and decides guilt or innocence. The obvious objection is that each of these functions breeds a certain bias against the accused, and the combination of all three in one person can easily lead to a triple bias in favor of conviction. If the judge has gathered the evidence, charged the defendant, and then conducted the trial, it would take a superhuman effort for the judge to reverse such efforts in all these dimensions and find the defendant not guilty. Therefore, all legal systems of the world have sought to distance themselves from the inquisitorial methods used in medieval Europe and by the Star Chamber in England. It is incorrect to describe European systems of procedure today as inquisitorial. Never make that mistake (though some American law professors still do).

The adversarial system that prevails in the common law world today is based on a radical division of the four functions of investigation, accusation, factual determination, and punishment. The police and the lawyers (including the prosecution) investigate, the grand jury charges on the basis of a prosecutorial recommendation, and after presentation of the evidence by the lawyers, the petit jury decides guilt or innocence. The role of the judge in this system seems to be left out until the assessment of punishment. If all three functions are allocated to other players, what is the judge supposed to do? In fact, under the jury system, the trial judge acquires new and important managerial functions. We will return to these functions later.

The accusatorial system is a compromise between the outdated inquisitorial system and the common law adversarial system. The prosecution—not the judge—charges the crime, and the lawyers have responsibility for presenting the evidence at trial. Yet the judge does retain the power of deciding guilt (sometimes with the assistance of lay assessors), and the judge also bears the ultimate responsibility for the investigation and presentation of all the relevant evidence. Thus the system requires some—but not total—distribution of power among the three "branches" of the trial authority.

These three components of the trial resemble political systems, each associated with a certain tradition of authority. The inquisitorial system reflects the mentality of monarchical power; concentrating all the power in the judge is like thinking of the king as font of all political power. The adversarial system resembles the structure of the tripartite system of government conceived by Montesquieu and incorporated in the U.S. Constitution. The division of legislative, executive, and judicial power provides a model for understanding how functions and authority are distributed among judge, jury, and lawyers at the trial. As we shall see, there are functions like "checks and balances" in the jury trial, as there are in the relations among the three branches of government. A judge can intervene against both lawyers and juries to make sure they do their jobs properly. And lawyers can control judges by filing objections with the intention to appeal. Juries can check the power of both lawyers and judges by engaging in their imaginative reconstruction of both the law and the facts. The jury trial turns out to be a delicate dance of conflicting authority.

The accusatorial trial resembles constitutional democracy in modern European systems. The judge still retains power but within a system of controls and rules that constrain what he or she is capable of doing. The days of the judge as monarch or dictator are over.

Before returning to the story of Bernhard Goetz, we should note one important feature of American criminal justice that is easily ignored. Mirjan Damaška stresses this point in his thoughtful account of the differences between common law and civilian procedures.[1] Damaška focuses on structures of authority and review. The Continental model is always hierarchical—prosecutors function within a nationwide system with internal appeals to control local decision making. American prosecutors operate on a local basis. The New York county district attorney responsible for the *Goetz* case was not subservient to any higher figure—not at the state level, not at the national level. This kind of local autonomy would be unthinkable in a Continental legal system.

One warning about the American prosecutorial system: Although the prosecutor is understood as a party trying to prove the guilt of the defendant, the modern prosecutor is understood as having an absolute duty to act neutrally in the name of justice. The prosecutor must disclose exculpatory material to the defense. Although he or she may try to convict, every modern prosecutor is more than a litigant. They will all say that their primary duty is to serve justice. In this respect, we do not think there is much difference between the attitudes of Continental and American prosecutors. Both wear two hats: They represent justice, and they seek to persuade the judge or jury that the defendant is guilty.

The role of defense counsel is significantly different. The defense counsel represents the legal system (recall the debate about the nature of lawyers and their responsibilities in Chapter Nine), but the primary and unequivocal duty of the defense lawyer is to further the interests of the client. Any defense lawyer who thinks about the social good as more important than the interests of the client betrays the ethics of the adversary system.

---

[1] Mirjan R. Damaška, *The Faces of Justice and State Authority* (New Haven, CT: Yale University Press, 1986).

Now let us turn to the question whether, if you were Bernhard Goetz, you would rather be tried in Germany or in New York.[2] This requires us to pay more attention to what in fact happened in the *Goetz* case. Goetz fled from the subway car and drove to New Hampshire. Eventually stricken by guilt, he walked into a police station in Concord and confessed. Thus began a series of developments that tell us a great deal about American procedure.

Extradition

The first problem was that Goetz was in New Hampshire. His trial would have to be in New York, where the crime occurred. But the New York police could not simply come and get him. They have no power of arrest outside New York. Therefore, they had to institute extradition proceedings, exactly as are required in international cases. There would have been no problem securing the extradition, but in the end Goetz agreed to return voluntarily to New York.

Interrogation

When Goetz was in custody in New Hampshire, both New Hampshire and New York police began their interrogations regarding the shootings in the subway car, some eight days earlier. As soon as the interrogations commenced, Goetz was clothed in a set of constitutional rights that have become foundations of American criminal justice and that Americans have gradually exported abroad. Under the *Miranda* rule (1966), he was entitled to the assistance of a lawyer and to remain silent, whether he had a lawyer or not. If he could not afford a lawyer, one would be appointed for him.

If these rules are violated, the exclusionary rule precludes the use at trial of any evidence gathered as a result of the violative conduct. (See Chapter Twelve for analysis of the exclusionary rule in the context of the Fourth Amendment.) The same principle applies to the use of a confession

---

[2] This discussion is drawn from George P. Fletcher, *A Crime of Self-Defense: Bernhard Goetz and the Law on Trial* (New York: Free Press, 1988). This book is available in translation in Spanish, Italian, German, and Japanese.

secured in violation of the *Miranda* rule. Because the question of whether an interrogation is properly conducted has such great legal significance, the police have begun, in high-profile cases, to record the confession on audio and videotape. Goetz spent two hours talking to the New Hampshire police, and that confession was recorded on an audiotape. When the New York police arrived, they begin to videotape the proceedings. At one point, Goetz said that he did not want to talk to the New Yorkers, but they persisted and engaged him for two hours of emotional and revealing conversation, all of which is readily seen on videotape.

Even though the police violated the *Miranda* rule, the tape was subsequently shown at trial. How is this possible? The use of the tape reveals a critical feature of the adversarial system. Very few rules favoring the defense apply unless the defense makes a motion. The defense had its reasons for wanting the confession to be shown, but to understand why, we need to explore the substantive issues in the case. That is the focus of the next chapter.

Under the adversarial system, the court is not a paternalistic watchdog of the defendant's rights. The defense must assert those rights if it decides that doing so is in its interest. How about the prosecution? Does it have the right to exclude evidence seized in violation of the Fourth Amendment? It would be odd, would it not, if the prosecution could claim that evidence should be excluded because the police—their agents!—seized it in violation of the Constitution. The more general point about constitutional rights is that only the defendant has rights. The prosecution cannot invoke the Constitution on behalf of the state or the victim.

Arraignment and Bail

After Goetz was taken back to New York and spent a few nights in Riker's Island, a tough prison and detention center in New York City, he appeared on January 7, 1985, before a New York magistrate for the purpose of considering his release pending trial. In the federal courts, a bail hearing is scheduled after the initial appearance, although in state courts, it is sometimes combined with the initial appearance or arraignment. Magistrates and judges may order a person awaiting trial or sentencing to be released on the defendant's own recognizance (i.e., promise to appear at trial), released subject to bail or the sureties of another person, or detained until the trial or sentence hearing.[3] In some state jurisdictions, the authority to determine the amount of bail rests with the police, usually with a watch commander or supervisor, in accord with a county bail schedule posted under judges as a matter of local rules.

Release pending trial may be ordered in many ways. The best known is the requirement of bail. A defendant can post bail in several ways, including the deposit with the clerk of the court of cash or checks for the full amount of the bail, which will be returned, less a service charge, either at the defendant's appearance for trial or (more often) at the conclusion of the case. Bail may also be posted through the conditional assignment to the court of property worth the dollar value of bail required. Frequently, defendants secure the services of a bail bondsman, who posts the required bail in return for a 10 percent fee, as well as collateral for the whole value of the bail. The bondsman keeps the 10 percent regardless of the defendant's later appearance.

The Eighth Amendment forbids excessive bail, and the judge is bound to grant bail unless the defendant is reasonably likely to present a danger of flight or of tampering with the evidence. Whether the judge may consider the risk of recidivism (*Weiderholungsgefahr*) is highly controversial because the hypothesis that the suspect will repeat the crime obviously violates the presumption of innocence. How can a suspect who has not been convicted of the first crime be suspected of "repeating" it? The presumptive right to be released prior to trial—even if secured by the payment of bail—is fundamental to the American conception of a fair trial. The notion of preventive detention on the basis of suspected danger to the community has always been hostile to the American ethics of crime and punishment. Yet the Bail Reform Act of 1984 authorized the federal courts to consider danger to the community as a factor bearing on bail decisions.[4]

Bail is a mixed blessing. It costs the defendant money. If you are not rich enough to put up the entire amount, you have to forfeit at least the 10 percent fee to the bail bondsman. Whether your pretrial rights in another jurisdiction would be superior to those under the American bail system would depend on the disposition of judges to forgo the option of preventive detention, a matter on which it is difficult to generalize.

---

[3] See 18 U.S.C. § 3142 and Fed. R. Crim. Pro. 46.
[4] See *United States v. Salerno*, 481 U.S. 739 (1987).

Grand Jury Indictment

Keep in mind that as of January 7, 1984, Goetz had not been charged with anything. Whether he would be charged would depend on the decision of the New York grand jury, a lay body selected from the voting rolls that determines whether to issue indictments to try felony suspects. Without a grand jury indictment in New York, no felony can be subject to trial and conviction. But no state requires grand juries in all cases. The Fifth Amendment requires grand juries for federal prosecutions, but this is one of the few provisions of the Bill of Rights that the Supreme Court has declined to incorporate in the due process clause of the Fourteenth Amendment.

The New York grand jury has twenty-three members. They sit without the trial judge present. The only official in the room is the prosecutor. Defense counsel and the defendant are both absent. (Hard to believe, but that is the way it works.) The only safeguard of the defendant's rights is that every word is transcribed by a court reporter.

Once the grand jury is summoned, impaneled, and sworn by the court, it is largely independent of court control. The prosecutor proposes the indictment and then offers evidence and calls witnesses to support the charges. The task of the grand jury is to assess whether the indictment is supported by "probable cause." This is a vague standard, equivalent to the level of evidence required to avoid a dismissal of the indictment at trial.

The grand jury returns an indictment if at least twelve jurors concur that probable cause exists to believe a crime has been committed by the accused. In the federal system, if they do not concur in the complaint or the information, the foreperson must report their failure to concur to the magistrate in open court.

The distinction between accusation and judging guilt or innocence is fundamental to all modern systems of criminal procedure. But there is nothing quite like a grand jury on the Continent. In some countries, typified by Germany, the prosecution takes charge of the decision as to whether there is sufficient evidence to indict. The trial court then passes on the sufficiency of the indictment. In other countries, typified by France, a magistrate—*le juge d'instruction*—takes charge of the investigation and reaches a decision about whether there is sufficient evidence to indict. Germany once had a comparable judicial officer (*der Untersuchungs-richter*) but abolished the institution in the postwar period.

In the past, there was some confusion about the standard that the investigating magistrate should use in issuing an indictment. When the standard of proof was sufficient to convict, some Continental scholars were skeptical about whether it was appropriate to talk about a presumption of innocence in criminal cases. The argument was the following: If the investigating magistrate is convinced that the defendant is guilty, how can you presume that he or she is innocent?[5] This argument was eventually overcome, largely by scaling down the standard of proof required for indictment. If all that is required to bring the defendant to trial is "probable cause" or "reasonable grounds" to believe in guilt, then the presumption of innocence seems more plausible. Today the presumption is taken for granted in all Western legal systems and in the ICC.[6]

Not One, but Two Grand Juries

The most striking feature of the pretrial phase of the *Goetz* case is that the first grand jury that heard his case in January 1985 decided not to indict him on any charges except minor gun possession. None of the four victims testified about their intentions because they were afraid that they might be indicted for attempted robbery. Goetz immediately became a media celebrity. He was the "subway avenger," who was now vindicated in the courts. He urged the distribution of handguns to people so they could protect themselves.

District Attorney Morgenthau came under criticism for having failed to grant immunity, at least to the three victims who had sufficiently recovered from their wounds to appear before a grand jury. Someone who receives "transaction immunity" cannot be prosecuted for anything said in the course of the particular transaction—in this case, testifying before the grand jury. Transaction immunity nullifies the privilege against self-incrimination. That is, when someone receives immunity, he or she must testify. With the fear of prosecution absent, there is no excuse for withholding testimony. The failure to talk, then, constitutes contempt of court.

---

[5] The debate was acute in the former Soviet Union, but there have been analogous issues in other Continental jurisdictions. See George P. Fletcher, "The Ongoing Soviet Debate About the Presumption of Innocence," 3(1) *Criminal Justice Ethics* 69 (1984).

[6] Rome Statute, Article 66.

The option of granting immunity to potential witnesses reveals a critical feature of the American system of justice. Continental Europeans should immediately perceive this institution as an aspect of the "expediency principle" or *Oppotunitätprinzip,* as opposed to the principle of legality, or *Legalitätsprinzip.* It is expedient to forgo prosecution of some in order to convict others, but that tactic is anathema to the devotees of legality, who hold that every offender must be prosecuted and punished, so far as the evidence permits. Germany is committed to the legality principle and therefore would be taken aback by the technique of making one or more perpetrators of a crime into "witnesses for the crown" [*Kronzeugen*]. Yet the vast majority of countries today have overcome these moral compunctions and are willing to think tactically about making sacrifices to gain advantages elsewhere in their prosecutorial strategy. The result in the American system of justice is that the best defense against a criminal charge is to be able to "flip" and offer testimony incriminating a higher-up in a criminal organization.

At the end of January 1985, the public mood began to shift against Goetz. District Attorney Morgenthau had leaked a police report to the press that disclosed for the first time that Goetz had said to Cabey, "You seem to be all right, here's another." The time was ripe for an effort to convene a second grand jury, which the DA can do, with permission of the supervising trial court, provided there is new evidence. The new evidence this time would be the testimony of Troy Canty and James Ramseur, because Morgenthau had granted them immunity from all charges that might arise from their testimony. If they testified that they were about to mug Goetz, they would not be subject to punishment, but if they lied and said the opposite, they could be prosecuted for perjury.

When the second grand jury convened, a new prosecutor was in charge. Susan Braver had represented the state in the first grand jury, but she bore responsibility for the failure to secure an indictment on the violent crimes. Morgenthau wanted to win, so he put in one of his ace lawyers, Gregory Waples, to take her place in the second grand jury.

The decision of the second grand jury would prove to be more favorable to the prosecution, but only in part because Canty and Ramseur testified that they had no hostile intentions toward Goetz. A much bigger incident centered on the way Waples explained self-defense to the jury.

A major dispute had been brewing in the New York appellate courts between the so-called subjective and objective standards of self-defense.

The subjective standard holds that anyone who sincerely believes that an attack is imminent may invoke defensive force to avert the attack. In the context of the *Goetz* case, this means that if he believed that he was to be attacked, he could permissibly shoot the attackers to guard his safety. It should be added, of course, that shooting to wound would have had to be the minimal force that he could have been fairly expected to use under the circumstances.

The objective standard adds to these requirements the element of conformity to a community standard defined by the reasonable person under the circumstances. The New York statute required the defender to "reasonably believe that such other person is committing or attempting to commit a . . . robbery."[7] That the word *reasonably* is used in the statute seems to point to the standard of the reasonable person under the circumstances. Nonetheless, the appellate courts had interpreted the statute to impose a subjective standard. Yet the Court of Appeals—the highest court in the state—had not ruled on the question.

Gregory Waples had the responsibility of explaining the law of self-defense to the second jury. At first, he chose not to advise the jurors that the subjective standard had prevailed in the appellate courts. His tactic was to adhere strictly to the language of the statute, but then one of the jurors asked him how they were to evaluate self-defense if they thought that Goetz overreacted. In other words, if they thought that Goetz had not conformed to the standard of a reasonable person under the circumstances, they should reject the claim of self-defense and find that Goetz had committed attempted murder against each of the four victims.

How should Waples have responded to this question? He was duty-bound to explain the law of New York. But what was the law of New York? Should Waples have been guided by the decisions of the appellate division, even if he thought the decisions were an incorrect interpretation of the New York statute? At stake in this dispute are two different views of the law—a topic we first considered in Chapter Two. Here are the conflicting interpretations:

A. Law as fact: The appellate court had ruled on the interpretation of the statute. That was the law.

---

[7] New York Penal Law § 35.15 (2)(b).

B. Law as principle: The statutes of New York should be understood in their "best light,"[8] which means the way an enlightened court would interpret the provision, and which the New York courts might well adopt in this case, particularly on appeal.

There is no way of knowing Waples's motivation at the critical moment of decision, but he acted as though he were advising the jury to interpret the law as it should be properly understood, regardless of what the appellate division had ruled. Influenced in part by this instruction, the grand jury indicted Goetz on nine counts of unjustified violent aggression against the victims. The presiding judge in the case, Stephen Crane, read the minutes of the grand jury, discovered the way in which Waples had explained self-defense, and informed the defense accordingly.

The defense—led by Barry Slotnick, a superb trial lawyer—then faced a tactical decision. Should they go to trial under the law as interpreted by the appellate division? If they did, they could prevent the prosecution from appealing the issue to the Court of Appeals, and when they went to trial, Crane would apply the subjective standard mandated by the appellate division. Or should the defense move to dismiss the indictment, thereby giving the prosecution an opportunity to appeal, all the way to the Court of Appeals if necessary? Getting the indictment dismissed would lead to a short-term gain, but the long-term cost might be a decision by the Court of Appeals mandating the use of the objective standard.

Before examining how the defense resolved this quandary, we should consider some of the other factors bearing on whether, as a defendant like Goetz, you would prefer to be charged and tried in a common law or civil law system. Two other major factors bear on the tactical situation of the defense. One is the jury system and its implications. The other is the relationship between the trial and the pretrial investigation.

The *Goetz* defense was obligated to ask for a jury. They could have waived the jury for the sake of a trial by a single judge. The lay jury is per se no better or worse for criminal defendants than standing before a single professional judge, a triad of judges, or a mixed panel of professional

---

[8] This is the view of statutory interpretation advocated in Ronald Dworkin, *Law's Empire* 337–338 (Cambridge, MA: Harvard University Press, 1986).

judges and lay assessors. But in cases like the Goetz shooting, the defense might have hoped that a jury sympathetic to the "subway vigilante" might nullify the law.

If a popular defendant is tried on a charge that is at odds with community mores, the jury has the ultimate, unreviewable power of nullification, to find the defendant not guilty despite certain evidence that the defendant violated the law. When Dr. Jack Kevorkian was prosecuted for homicide after he invented a suicide machine and made it available to two women who wanted to commit suicide, the jury acquitted him despite the evidence of guilt. Indeed, in the preindictment proceedings, Kevorkian carried himself as though he had already been acquitted, so confident was he that his message of voluntary exit had struck a chord in public sentiment. Repeated efforts to convict him failed because of jury nullification. Only after he allowed a television program to show a tape of a patient committing suicide with his machine was he finally convicted and sentenced to prison.[9] To take another example, a physician named Henry Morgentaler who performed an abortion was tried three times for one act and acquitted three times by Canadian juries.[10] This would not have been possible in the United States, because if the jury *once* finds the defendant not guilty, the prosecution is over. The defense might have hoped that a jury might rule this way in the *Goetz* case.

Yet the fantasies of lawyers that they can make a few clever moves and induce the jury to nullify the law are grossly exaggerated. According to the best available evidence, juries assiduously seek to apply the judge's instructions on the law. It is true that even most law students do not understand the arcane and convoluted instructions that one finds in the desk books of trial judges, but juries nonetheless make an effort to do their job. It made a difference, therefore, whether the instructions would adopt the subjective or the objective standard on self-defense.

The racial factor in the *Goetz* case is more difficult to assess. The once rampant antiblack sentiments that induced the U.S. Supreme Court, beginning in the 1930s, to intervene in state criminal justice, seem to many people to have subsided. Yet unspoken assumptions about propensities of young black men for violent behavior still inform the thinking

---

[9] See Dirk Johnson, "Kevorkian Sentenced to 10 to 25 Years in Prison," *New York Times*, April 14, 1999, at A1.
[10] See *Regina v. Morgentaler*, [1988] 1 S.C.R. 30.

of laypeople, both black and white. The problem is whether professional judges, also exposed to the same stereotypical thinking, master their biases more effectively. In the *Goetz* case, the jury—whether black or white—would probably be affected by the then-widespread New York fear of violence by black youths who look like street toughs, the profile represented by the four youths who approached Goetz on the subway.

More important than the jury trial per se are the implications of the jury for the rest of the trial. These include the following.

The Separation of Conviction and Sentencing

A little-appreciated feature of the jury, as we know it in Anglo-American legal systems, is that it leads to the separation of fact-finding on guilt and innocence from the sentencing phase of the trial. Juries could conceivably determine sentences in the number of years to be served, as civil juries assign a dollar sign to the defendant's liability. Yet if the jury were to issue a composite verdict as it does in civil cases—for example, guilty of an assault worth five years—there would be a greater danger that juries would reach compromised verdicts. Now the compromises are limited to convicting on some counts and acquitting on others. Significantly, the jury is not informed about the gravity of the charges and how serious it would be to convict of one rather than another.

Civilian trials combine the inquiry into guilt with sentencing. In Germany, at least, a single judgment is announced at the end. Even in cases where the defendant claims insanity and the plea is rejected by the court, the single judgment imposes a sentence on the defendant; if the defendant committed the act but is found insane, the judgment imposes a mode of administrative detention on the defendant on the assumption that he or she is dangerous to the public.

The common law practice has significant advantages for the defense because many facts relevant for sentencing—notably, the fact of prior convictions—are considered irrelevant at the stage of finding guilt for the commission of the crime. The interweaving of the two questions—responsibility for the crime and society's response to the crime—leads to one of the most disquieting features of the civilian trial. As the trial begins, the civilian judges interrogate the defendant about his person: name, residence, occupation, marital status, and—believe it or not—prior criminal record. This is obviously incriminating material that could prejudice the entire trial.

The assumption underlying civilian criminal trials is that professional judges can handle this kind of provocative material without losing their impartiality. Civilian systems would not even consider prohibiting their judges, as Americans do their jurors, from watching television or reading the newspaper during a highly publicized political trial. It is not surprising that they believe, contrary to every instinct of human nature, that judges can inquire about a defendant's criminal record and then proceed as though the defendant were presumed innocent until proven guilty. German reformers tried for years to separate the sentencing from the guilt-finding phase of the trial by introducing the *Schuldinterlokut*, a stage akin to a verdict of guilty, but these efforts seem now to have been abandoned.

Rules of Evidence

The great advantage of the jury system is that we build a recognition of human fallibility into the process. As civilians enthrone their judges on a pedestal of superhuman neutrality, common law lawyers start on the assumption that jurors are imperfect, corruptible, and weak. This seemingly condescending attitude toward the jury accounts for the restrictive rules of evidence. In principle, hearsay, prior convictions, and inflammatory evidence are inadmissible. The *Goetz* jury was not allowed to hear, for example, that prior to the shooting, Goetz was heard to say at a meeting of his neighborhood association, "The only way to clean up [14th Street] is to get rid of the spics and niggers." Had they heard this statement, the jury would likely have had a different take on the racial dimension in the case.

Of course, this highly complex body of law generates a battleground for lawyers to show their wits. A good trial lawyer shows his or her skill in debating the subtleties of hearsay and its exceptions: spontaneous utterances, states of mind, business records, and prior convictions bearing solely on credibility. Although these finely honed rules may restrict the jury's access to material that would be beneficial to the defense (for example, the criminal records of the four youths in *Goetz*), the exclusion of evidence generally helps the defense. The prosecution has a smaller domain of evidence to work with in mustering the innuendo of guilt; in principle, all the evidence that is introduced comes under cross-examination. These factors work to the benefit of the defendant.

It would be an exaggeration to say that civilians have no rules of evidence. Using presumptions would violate the Continental principle of "free evaluation of the evidence" and judgment based on the judge's "personal conviction" (*intime conviction*), but the Germans do have well-developed exclusionary rules (*Beweisverbote*) that in some respects go further than our own. There is even a preference for direct and immediate evidence—as opposed to what we call hearsay. Yet the scope of these debates is far more limited. The assumption behind the free admissibility of evidence is that judges can properly assess the relevance of evidence that strikes us as too unreliable, too tangential, or too inflammatory to be considered at all.

It is worth noting that during the sentencing phase, American judges put aside the normal rules of evidentiary filtering. They play the role of superhuman civilian judges, capable of gauging the proper weight of provocative testimony, including statements by the victims and emotional letters from the community, about what should be done with the convicted offender. Perhaps the separation of sentencing from the guilt phase in the United States is designed precisely to free the sentencing determination from the evidentiary constraints associated with the jury trial. The nominal justification for the separation is that sentencing has many social purposes other than retributive justice, and presumably judges are in a better position to strike the proper balance among conflicting goals.

The Asymmetrical Rules of Appeal

This feature of the common law trial has a paradoxical twist. If the jury cannot be trusted with all the evidence, if it cannot be trusted with sentencing decisions, one would expect appellate courts to exercise close supervision over the jury's finding of fact. The opposite is true. The jury exercises considerable autonomy over findings of guilt. It is difficult, if not virtually impossible, to secure a reversal solely on the grounds that the evidence does not support the verdict. And regarding a finding of not guilty, the jury's autonomy is absolute—there is no appeal, no recourse against the jury's acquitting the defendant. The principle of asymmetrical appeal (appeal permitted from a verdict of guilty but not from a verdict of not guilty) stands in sharp contrast to civilian modes of appellate review, where the first appeal typically gives both the prosecution and the defense the opportunity to retry questions of fact. Even if there is an acquittal after this initial round, access to the higher appellate courts is open to both sides. Common law deference to the power of the jury to acquit is thought necessary to guarantee the jury's independence; civilians see no reason to defer in the same way to their trial courts.

Aggressive Lawyering

Beyond these first three implications of the jury system, we would single out a fourth structural feature of the common law jury trial as generating the most significant advantage for the defense. The division of function between judge and jury liberates common law defense lawyers to be far more aggressive and zealous in their defense than one can expect from civilian defense lawyers. The reason is simple. Civilian lawyers must constantly ingratiate themselves with the judge; in the end, the judge renders the low-visibility judgments of fact on which the trial ultimately turns. Alienating the judge by arguing too vigorously means losing the trial. Common law defense lawyers can go much further in their arguments on points of law with the judge. These arguments take place outside the hearing range of the jury, and therefore no matter how obnoxious the lawyers become, they do not risk losing votes on the jury.

Neither the Judge nor the Jury Learns of the Pretrial Dossier

The common law trial begins totally anew, unaffected by the evidence collected prior to trial. In contrast, the civilian pretrial investigator turns over the entire file—the dossier—to the judge for examination prior to trial. Therefore, it is difficult for civilian judges, who know already the police story of how guilty the suspect is, to pretend that the entire process of proving guilt beyond a reasonable doubt starts again from scratch. The purpose of the civilian trial is to test whether the dossier contains a proper case. The only evidence that the judge may properly consider on the question of guilt must be heard in open court. The judge must write an opinion defending the court's conclusion on guilt or innocence, and this opinion may not be based on the evidence contained in the dossier, which was never subjected to public examination. In the sense that it tests the conclusions reached in the preliminary investigation, the civilian trial comes closer to being an appeal from the pretrial phase than an entirely fresh and independent hearing. The proper image for a civilian trial is that of a book that grows and grows—from arrest, to preliminary investigation, to trial, to appeal and trial de novo, to appeal on questions of law. The process does not peak in a moment of truth at trial but rather continually gathers material and weight as it proceeds.

The corresponding image for the common law trial is a series of independent and closed books, each written at a different stage of the proceeding. When the pretrial investigation is over, that book is disclosed to the defense under the process of discovery, but then it is closed and the prosecutor must present evidence at trial to the ears of a judge and jury who know nothing about the case.

There is little doubt that the use of the dossier at trial severely undercuts the interests of the defendant. The defendant loses an opportunity for a totally fresh look at the evidence, uncompromised by the prestige of the prosecutor's pretrial findings. The presumption of innocence means more if the trial begins without any credit given to the pretrial findings of guilt. With the advent of discovery in common law jurisdictions— when the prosecution must lay all its cards on the table before trial— there is very little to be said for the Continental practice of transferring the dossier to the judge prior to trial.

On balance, there is little doubt that common law procedures greatly favor the interests of the accused. This is true, even without considering the panoply of rights offered by current interpretations of the Fourth, Fifth, and Sixth Amendments. If procedure were everything, there is little doubt that a well-advised criminal defendant would choose to stand trial in the United States rather than in a civilian jurisdiction. In the *Goetz* case, in particular, the accused would have little to gain if he could have chosen a court in France or Germany instead of the trial court in downtown Manhattan.

Further Reading

There are many, many books chronicling criminal trials. The chronicles of several highly publicized trials, with an emphasis on the role of the victim, are in George P. Fletcher, *With Justice for Some: Rights of Victims in Criminal Trials* (Reading, MA: Addison-Wesley, 1995). A recent book, with an emphasis on the lawyering in an Oregon state murder trial, is Gerry Spence, *The Smoking Gun: Day by Day through a Shocking Murder Trial* (New York: Scribner, 2003). For a view of the other desk, see Gary Delsohn, *The Prosecutors: A Year in the Life of a District Attorney's Office* (New York: E. P. Dutton, 2003).

TWENTY-EIGHT

The Fate of Bernhard Goetz

We left the *Goetz* defense with a hard decision to make. Should they go for the short-term benefit of moving to dismiss the indictment, or should they stick with the indictment as is and avoid the risk of a long-term disaster—namely, a decision on appeal that the binding law in New York was really the objective standard after all?

From the prosecution's point of view, Waples's instruction to the grand jury was the setting of a very clever trap. The only way he could prior to trial get an appellate ruling that the objective standard should apply at trial was to induce a dismissal of the indictment in which the central issue in the dismissal was the objective standard versus the subjective standard. The prosecution could then go to an appellate court and ask for a change in the law.

Whether Waples laid this trap intentionally or inadvertently, the defense counsel Slotnick took the bait. He moved to dismiss the indictment. Crane dismissed the indictment on January 16, 1986. According to Crane—now an appellate judge in New York—an appeal was likely, and he was pleased that the subjective standard mandated by the appellate division was now going to be clarified by the higher courts.

Not surprisingly, the appellate division in Manhattan affirmed Crane's decision to dismiss the indictment.[1] After all, the law as they saw it required a subjective interpretation of the phrase "reasonably believes" in the statute. The only hope for the prosecution was to take the case all the way to Albany for a ruling by the Court of Appeals. This is what happened. Let us see how they decided.

■

The People of the State of New York v. Bernhard Goetz

Court of Appeals of New York
68 N.Y.2d 96; 497 N.E.2d 41; 506 N.Y.S.2d 18

Appeal, by permission of a Justice of the Appellate Division of the Supreme Court in the First Judicial Department, from an order of that court, entered April 17, 1986, which affirmed so much of an order of the Supreme Court at Criminal Term . . . entered in New York County, as granted a motion by defendant to the extent of dismissing the counts of a consolidated indictment charging defendant with attempted murder (four charges), assault in the first degree (four charges) and criminal possession of a weapon in the second degree (one charge), with leave to resubmit these charges to another Grand Jury.

WACHTLER, CJ:

A Grand Jury has indicted defendant on attempted murder, assault, and other charges for having shot and wounded four youths on a New York City subway train after one or two of the youths approached him and asked for $5. The lower courts, concluding that the prosecutor's charge to the Grand Jury on the defense of justification was erroneous, have dismissed the attempted murder, assault and weapons possession charges. We now reverse and reinstate all counts of the indictment.

I.

[the facts are given above]

II.

After waiving extradition, Goetz was brought back to New York and arraigned on a felony complaint charging him with attempted murder and

---

[1] *People v. Goetz*, 116 AD2d 316 (April 17, 1986).

criminal possession of a weapon. The matter was presented to a Grand Jury in January 1985, with the prosecutor seeking an indictment for attempted murder, assault, reckless endangerment, and criminal possession of a weapon. Neither the defendant nor any of the wounded youths testified before his Grand Jury. On January 25, 1985, the Grand Jury indicted defendant on one count of criminal possession of a weapon in the third degree (Penal Law § 265.02), for possessing the gun used in the subway shootings, and two counts of criminal possession of a weapon in the fourth degree (Penal Law § 265.01), for possessing two other guns in his apartment building. It dismissed, however, the attempted murder and other charges stemming from the shootings themselves.

Several weeks after the Grand Jury's action, the People, asserting that they had newly available evidence, moved for an order authorizing them to resubmit the dismissed charges to a second Grand Jury (see, CPL 190.75 [3]). Supreme Court, Criminal Term, after conducting an in camera inquiry, granted the motion. Presentation of the case to the second Grand Jury began on March 14, 1985. Two of the four youths, Canty and Ramseur, testified. Among the other witnesses were four passengers from the seventh car of the subway who had seen some portions of the incident. Goetz again chose not to testify, though the tapes of his two statements were played for the grand jurors, as had been done with the first Grand Jury.

On March 27, 1985, the second Grand Jury filed a 10-count indictment, containing four charges of attempted murder (Penal Law §§ 110.00, 125.25 [1]), four charges of assault in the first degree (Penal Law § 120.10 [1]), one charge of reckless endangerment in the first degree (Penal Law § 120.25), and one charge of criminal possession of a weapon in the second degree (Penal Law § 265.03 [possession of loaded firearm with intent to use it unlawfully against another]). Goetz was arraigned on this indictment on March 28, 1985, and it was consolidated with the earlier three-count indictment.

On October 14, 1985, Goetz moved to dismiss the charges contained in the second indictment alleging, among other things, that the evidence before the second Grand Jury was not legally sufficient to establish the offenses charged (see, CPL 210.20 [1] [b]), and that the prosecutor's instructions to that Grand Jury on the defense of justification were erroneous and prejudicial to the defendant so as to render its proceedings defective (see, CPL 210.20 [1] [c]; 210.35 [5]). . . .

In an order dated January 21, 1986, Criminal Term granted Goetz's motion to the extent that it dismissed all counts of the second indictment, other than the reckless endangerment charge, with leave to resubmit these charges to a third Grand Jury. The court, after inspection of the Grand Jury minutes, first rejected Goetz's contention that there was not legally sufficient evidence to support the charges. It held, however, that the prosecutor, in a supplemental charge elaborating upon the justification defense, had erroneously introduced an objective element into this defense by instructing the grand jurors to consider whether Goetz's conduct was that of a "reasonable man in [Goetz's] situation." The court, citing prior decisions from both the First and Second Departments (see, e.g., *People v Santiago*, 110 AD2d 569 [1st Dept]; *People v Wagman*, 99 AD2d 519 [2d Dept]), concluded that the statutory test for whether the use of deadly force is justified to protect a person should be wholly subjective, focusing entirely on the defendant's state of mind when he used such force. It concluded that dismissal was required for this error because the justification issue was at the heart of the case. . . .

On appeal by the People, a divided Appellate Division affirmed Criminal Term's dismissal of the charges. The plurality opinion by Justice Kassal, concurred in by Justice Carro, agreed with Criminal Term's reasoning on the justification issue,[2] stating that the grand jurors should have been instructed to consider only the defendant's subjective beliefs as to the need to use deadly force. Justice Kupferman concurred in the result reached by the plurality on the ground that the prosecutor's charge did not adequately apprise the grand jurors of the need to consider Goetz's own background and learning. . . .

Justice Asch, in a dissenting opinion in which Justice Wallach concurred, disagreed with both bases for dismissal relied upon by Criminal Term. On the justification question, he opined that the statute requires consideration of both the defendant's subjective beliefs and whether a reasonable person in defendant's situation would have had such beliefs.

---

[2] Due to a linguistic confusion, New York lawyers refer to claims of self-defense as the issue of "justification." The concept of justification is broader. Review the recognition of necessity as a justification in Chapter Two. Necessity is also recognized under New York law, NYPL § 35.05.

Accordingly, he found no error in the prosecutor's introduction of an objective element into the justification defense. . . . In a separate dissenting opinion, Justice Wallach stressed that the plurality's adoption of a purely subjective test effectively eliminated any reasonableness requirement contained in the statute.

Justice Asch granted the People leave to appeal to this court. We agree with the dissenters that . . . the prosecutor's charge to the Grand Jury on justification . . . [did not require] dismissal of any of the charges in the second indictment.

III.

Penal Law article 35 recognizes the defense of justification, which "permits the use of force under certain circumstances." . . . One such set of circumstances pertains to the use of force in defense of a person, encompassing both self-defense and defense of a third person . . . Penal Law § 35.15 (1) sets forth the general principles governing all such uses of force: "[a] person may . . . use physical force upon another person when and to the extent he *reasonably believes* such to be necessary to defend himself or a third person from what he *reasonably believes* to be the use or imminent use of unlawful physical force by such other person." [emphasis by court]

Section 35.15 (2) sets forth further limitations on these general principles with respect to the use of "deadly physical force": "A person may not use deadly physical force upon another person under circumstances specified in subdivision one unless (a) He *reasonably believes* that such other person is using or about to use deadly physical force . . . or (b) He *reasonably believes* that such other person is committing or attempting to commit a kidnapping, forcible rape, forcible sodomy or robbery." [emphasis by court]

Thus, consistent with most justification provisions, Penal Law § 35.15 permits the use of deadly physical force only where requirements as to triggering conditions and the necessity of a particular response are met (see, Robinson, Criminal Law Defenses § 121 [a], at 2). As to the triggering conditions, the statute requires that the actor "reasonably believes" that another person either is using or about to use deadly physical force or is committing or attempting to commit one of certain enumerated felonies, including robbery. As to the need for the use of deadly physical force as a response, the statute requires that the actor "reasonably believes" that such force is necessary to avert the perceived threat.

Because the evidence before the second Grand Jury included statements by Goetz that he acted to protect himself from being maimed or to avert a robbery, the prosecutor correctly chose to charge the justification defense in section 35.15 to the Grand Jury. . . . The prosecutor properly instructed the grand jurors to consider whether the use of deadly physical force was justified to prevent either serious physical injury or a robbery, and, in doing so, to separately analyze the defense with respect to each of the charges. He elaborated upon the prerequisites for the use of deadly physical force essentially by reading or paraphrasing the language in Penal Law § 35.15. The defense does not contend that he committed any error in this portion of the charge.

When the prosecutor had completed his charge, one of the grand jurors asked for clarification of the term "reasonably believes." The prosecutor responded by instructing the grand jurors that they were to consider the circumstances of the incident and determine "whether the defendant's conduct was that of a reasonable man in the defendant's situation." It is this response by the prosecutor—and specifically his use of "a reasonable man"—which is the basis for the dismissal of the charges by the lower courts. As expressed repeatedly in the Appellate Division's plurality opinion, because section 35.15 uses the term "*he* reasonably believes," the appropriate test, according to that court, is whether a defendant's beliefs and reactions were "reasonable *to him.*" Under that reading of the statute, a jury which believed a defendant's testimony that he felt that his own actions were warranted and were reasonable would have to acquit him, regardless of what anyone else in defendant's situation might have concluded. Such an interpretation defies the ordinary meaning and significance of the term "reasonably" in a statute, and misconstrues the clear intent of the Legislature, in enacting section 35.15, to retain an objective element as part of any provision authorizing the use of deadly physical force.

Penal statutes in New York have long codified the right recognized at common law to use deadly physical force, under appropriate circumstances, in self-defense. . . . These provisions have never required that an actor's belief as to the intention of another person to inflict serious injury be correct in order for the use of deadly force to be justified, but they have uniformly required that the belief comport with an objective notion of reasonableness. The 1829 statute, using language which was followed almost in its entirety until the 1965 recodification of the Penal Law, provided that the use of deadly force was justified in self-defense or in the defense of specified third persons "when there shall be a reasonable ground to apprehend a design to commit a felony, or to do some great personal injury, and there shall be imminent danger of such design being accomplished."

In *Shorter v People* (2 NY 193), we emphasized that deadly force could be justified under the statute even if the actor's beliefs as to the intentions of another turned out to be wrong, but noted there had to be a reasonable basis, viewed objectively, for the beliefs. We explicitly rejected the position that the defendant's own belief that the use of deadly force was necessary sufficed to justify such force regardless of the reasonableness of the beliefs (id., at pp 200–201).

In 1881, New York reexamined the many criminal provisions set forth in the revised statutes and enacted, for the first time, a separate Penal Code. . . . The provision in the 1881 Penal Code for the use of deadly force in self-defense or to defend a third person was virtually a reenactment of the language in the 1829 statutes, and the "reasonable ground" requirement was maintained.

The 1909 Penal Law replaced the 1881 Penal Code. The language of section 205 of the 1881 code pertaining to the use of deadly force in self-defense or in defense of a third person was reenacted, verbatim, as part of section 1055 of the new Penal Law. Several cases from this court interpreting the 1909 provision demonstrate unmistakably that an objective element of reasonableness was a vital part of any claim of self-defense. In *People v Lumsden* (201 NY 264, 268), we approved a charge to the jury which instructed it to consider whether the circumstances facing defendant were such "as would lead a reasonable man to believe that [an assailant] is about to kill or to do great bodily injury" (see also, *People v Ligouri*, 284 NY 309, 316, 317). We emphatically rejected the position that any belief by an actor as to the intention of another to cause severe injury was a sufficient basis for his use of deadly force, and stated specifically that a belief based upon "mere fear or fancy or remote hearsay information or a delusion pure and simple" would not satisfy the requirements of the statute (201 NY, at p 269). In *People v Tomlins* (213 NY 240, 244), we set forth the governing test as being whether "the situation justified the defendant as a reasonable man in believing that he was about to be murderously attacked."

Accordingly, the Law Revision Commission, in a 1937 Report to the Legislature on the Law of Homicide in New York, summarized the self-defense statute as requiring a "reasonable belief in the imminence of danger," and stated that the standard to be followed by a jury in determining whether a belief was reasonable "is that of a man of ordinary courage in the circumstances surrounding the defendant at the time of the killing" (Communication Relating to Homicide at 814). The Report added that New York did not follow the view, adopted in a few States, that "the jury is required to adopt the subjective view and judge from the standpoint of the very defendant concerned" (id., at 814).

In 1961 the Legislature established a Commission to undertake a complete revision of the Penal Law and the Criminal Code. The impetus for the decision to update the Penal Law came in part from the drafting of the Model Penal Code by the American Law Institute, as well as from the fact that the existing law was poorly organized and in many aspects antiquated. . . . Following the submission by the Commission of several reports and proposals, the Legislature approved the present Penal Law in 1965 (L 1965, ch 1030), and it became effective on September 1, 1967. The drafting of the general provisions of the new Penal Law (see, Penal Law part I), including the article on justification (id., art 35), was particularly influenced by the Model Penal Code (see, Denzer, *Drafting a New York Penal Law for New York*, 18 Buff L Rev 251, 252; Wechsler, *Codification of Criminal Law in the United States: The Model Penal Code*, 68 Colum L Rev 1425, 1428). While using the Model Penal Code provisions on justification as general guidelines, however, the drafters of the new Penal Law did not simply adopt them verbatim.

The provisions of the Model Penal Code with respect to the use of deadly force in self-defense reflect the position of its drafters that any culpability which arises from a mistaken belief in the need to use such force should be no greater than the culpability such a mistake would give rise to if it were made with respect to an element of a crime (see, ALI, *Model Penal Code and Commentaries, part I*, at 32, 34 [hereafter cited as *MPC Commentaries*]; Robinson, *Criminal Law Defenses, op. cit.*, at 410). Accordingly, under *Model Penal Code* § 3.04 (2) (b), a defendant

charged with murder (or attempted murder) need only show that he
"*[believed]* that [the use of deadly force] was necessary to protect himself
against death, serious bodily injury, kidnapping or [forcible] sexual intercourse" to prevail on a self-defense claim (emphasis added). If the
defendant's belief was wrong, and was recklessly, or negligently formed,
however, he may be convicted of the type of homicide charge requiring
only a reckless or negligent, as the case may be, criminal intent (see,
Model Penal Code § 3.09 [2]; *MPC Commentaries, op. cit.*, part I, at 32,
150).

The drafters of the Model Penal Code recognized that the wholly
subjective test set forth in section 3.04 differed from the existing law
in most States by its omission of any requirement of reasonableness (see,
MPC Commentaries, op. cit., part I, at 35; LaFave & Scott, *Criminal Law*
§ 53, at 393–394). The drafters were also keenly aware that requiring
that the actor have a "reasonable belief" rather than just a "belief"
would alter the wholly subjective test (*MPC Commentaries, op. cit.*, part
I, at 35–36). This basic distinction was recognized years earlier by the
New York Law Revision Commission and continues to be noted by
the commentators (*Communication Relating to Homicide, op. cit.*, at 814;
Robinson, *Criminal Law Defenses, op. cit.*; Note, *"Justification: The Impact
of the Model Penal Code on Statutory Reform,"* 75 Colum L Rev 914,
918–920).

New York did not follow the Model Penal Code's equation of a
mistake as to the need to use deadly force with a mistake negating an
element of a crime, choosing instead to use a single statutory section
which would provide either a complete defense or no defense at all to
a defendant charged with any crime involving the use of deadly force.
The drafters of the new Penal Law adopted in large part the structure
and content of *Model Penal Code* § 3.04, but, crucially, inserted the word
"reasonably" before "believes."

The plurality below agreed with defendant's argument that the
change in the statutory language from "reasonable ground," used prior
to 1965, to "he reasonably believes" in *Penal Law* § 35.15 evinced a
legislative intent to conform to the subjective standard contained in
Model Penal Code § 3.04. This argument, however, ignores the plain
significance of the insertion of "reasonably." Had the drafters of section
35.15 wanted to adopt a subjective standard, they could have simply
used the language of section 3.04. "Believes" by itself requires an honest

or genuine belief by a defendant as to the need to use deadly force (see, e.g., Robinson, *Criminal Law Defenses, op. cit.* § 184 (b), at 399–400). Interpreting the statute to require only that the defendant's belief was "reasonable to *him,*" as done by the plurality below, would hardly be different from requiring only a genuine belief; in either case, the defendant's own perceptions could completely exonerate him from any criminal liability.

We cannot lightly impute to the Legislature an intent to fundamentally alter the principles of justification to allow the perpetrator of a serious crime to go free simply because that person believed his actions were reasonable and necessary to prevent some perceived harm. To completely exonerate such an individual, no matter how aberrational or bizarre his thought patterns, would allow citizens to set their own standards for the permissible use of force. It would also allow a legally competent defendant suffering from delusions to kill or perform acts of violence with impunity, contrary to fundamental principles of justice and criminal law.

We can only conclude that the Legislature retained a reasonableness requirement to avoid giving a license for such actions. The plurality's interpretation, as the dissenters below recognized, excises the impact of the word "reasonably." . . .

The change from "reasonable ground" to "reasonably believes" is better explained by the fact that the drafters of section 35.15 were proposing a single section which, for the first time, would govern both the use of ordinary force and deadly force in self-defense or defense of another. Under the 1909 Penal Law and its predecessors, the use of ordinary force was governed by separate sections which, at least by their literal terms, required that the defendant was *in fact* responding to an unlawful assault, and not just that he had a reasonable ground for believing that such an assault was occurring (see, *1909 Penal Law* §§ 42, 246 [3]; *People v Young,* 11 NY2d 274; 7 Zett, *New York Criminal Practice* para. 65.3). Following the example of the Model Penal Code, the drafters of section 35.15 eliminated this sharp dichotomy between the use of ordinary force and deadly force in defense of a person. Not surprisingly then, the integrated section reflects the wording of *Model Penal Code* § 3.04, with the addition of "reasonably" to incorporate the long-standing requirement of "reasonable ground" for the use of deadly force and apply it to the use of ordinary force as well (see, Zett, *New*

York Criminal Practice, § 65.3 [1], [2]; Note, *"Proposed Penal Law of New York,"* 64 Colum L Rev 1469, 1500).

The conclusion that section 35.15 retains an objective element to justify the use of deadly force is buttressed by the statements of its drafters. The executive director and counsel to the Commission which revised the Penal Law have stated that the provisions of the statute with respect to the use of deadly physical force largely conformed with the prior law, with the only changes they noted not being relevant here (Denzer & McQuillan, *Practice Commentary, McKinney's Cons Laws of NY, Book 39, Penal Law* § 35.15, p 63 [1967]). Nowhere in the legislative history is there any indication that "reasonably believes" was designed to change the law on the use of deadly force or establish a subjective standard. To the contrary, the Commission, in the staff comment governing arrests by police officers, specifically equated "[he] reasonably believes" with having a reasonable ground for believing (*Penal Law* § 35.30; *Fourth Interim Report of the Temporary State Commission on Revision of the Penal Law and Criminal Code* at 17–18, 1965 NY Legis Doc No. 25).

Statutes or rules of law requiring a person to act "reasonably" or to have a "reasonable belief" uniformly prescribe conduct meeting an objective standard measured with reference to how "a reasonable person" could have acted (see, e.g., *People v Cantor,* 36 NY2d 106; *Donovan v Kaszycki & Sons Contrs.,* 599 F Supp 860, 871; Fletcher, *The Right and the Reasonable,* 98 Harv L Rev 949; 57). In *People v Cantor (supra),* we had before us a provision of the Criminal Procedure Law authorizing a police officer to stop a person "when *he reasonably suspects* that such person is committing, has committed or is about to commit [a crime]" (CPL 140.50 [1]; emphasis added). We held that this section authorized "stops" only when the police officer had "the quantum of knowledge sufficient to induce an ordinarily prudent and cautious man under the circumstances to believe criminal activity is at hand" (*People v Cantor,* 36 NY2d, at pp 112–113, *supra*).

In *People v Collice* (41 NY2d 906), we rejected the position that section 35.15 contains a wholly subjective standard. The defendant in *Collice* asserted, on appeal, that the trial court had erred in refusing to charge the justification defense. We upheld the trial court's action because we concluded that, even if the defendant had actually believed that he was threatened with the imminent use of deadly physical force, the evidence clearly indicated that "his reactions were not those of a reasonable man acting in self-defense" (id., at p 907). Numerous decisions from other States interpreting "reasonably believes" in justification statutes enacted subsequent to the drafting of the Model Penal Code are consistent with *Collice*, as they hold that such language refers to what a reasonable person could have believed under the same circumstances (see, e.g., *State v Kelly*, 97 NJ 178, 478 A2d 364, 373–374; *Weston v State*, 682 P2d 1119, 1121 [Alaska]).

The defense contends that our memorandum in *Collice* is inconsistent with our prior opinion in *People v Miller* (39 NY2d 543). In *Miller*, we held that a defendant charged with homicide could introduce, in support of a claim of self-defense, evidence of prior acts of violence committed by the deceased of which the defendant had knowledge. The defense, as well as the plurality below, place great emphasis on the statement in *Miller* that "the crucial fact at issue [is] the state of mind of the defendant" (id., at p 551). This language, however, in no way indicates that a wholly subjective test is appropriate. To begin, it is undisputed that section 35.15 does contain a subjective element, namely that the defendant believed that deadly force was necessary to avert the imminent use of deadly force or the commission of certain felonies. Evidence that the defendant knew of prior acts of violence by the deceased could help establish his requisite beliefs. Moreover, such knowledge would also be relevant on the issue of reasonableness, as the jury must consider the circumstances a defendant found himself in, which would include any relevant knowledge of the nature of persons confronting him (see, e.g., *People v Taylor*, 177 NY 237, 245; *Communication Relating to Homicide, op. cit.*, at 816). Finally, in *Miller*, we specifically recognized that there had to be "reasonable grounds" for the defendant's belief. . . .

Goetz also argues that the introduction of an objective element will preclude a jury from considering factors such as the prior experiences of a given actor and thus, require it to make a determination of "reasonableness" without regard to the actual circumstances of a particular incident. This argument, however, falsely presupposes that an objective standard means that the background and other relevant characteristics of a particular actor must be ignored. To the contrary, we have frequently noted that a determination of reasonableness must be based on the "circumstances" facing a defendant or his "situation" (see, e.g., *People v Ligouri*, 284 NY 309, 316, *supra; People v Lumsden*, 201 NY 264, 268, *supra*). Such terms encompass more than the physical movements of the potential assailant. As just discussed, these terms include any relevant knowledge the defendant had about that person. They also necessarily bring in the physical attributes of all persons involved, including the defendant. Furthermore, the defendant's circumstances encompass any prior experiences he had which could provide a reasonable basis for a belief that another person's intentions were to injure or rob him or that the use of deadly force was necessary under the circumstances.

Accordingly, a jury should be instructed to consider this type of evidence in weighing the defendant's actions. The jury must first determine whether the defendant had the requisite beliefs under section 35.15, that is, whether he believed deadly force was necessary to avert the imminent use of deadly force or the commission of one of the felonies enumerated therein. If the People do not prove beyond a reasonable doubt that he did not have such beliefs, then the jury must also consider whether these beliefs were reasonable. The jury would have to determine, in light of all the "circumstances," as explicated above, if a reasonable person could have had these beliefs.

The prosecutor's instruction to the second Grand Jury that it had to determine whether, under the circumstances, Goetz's conduct was that of a reasonable man in his situation was thus essentially an accurate charge. It is true that the prosecutor did not elaborate on the meaning of "circumstances" or "situation" and inform the grand jurors that they could consider, for example, the prior experiences Goetz related in his statement to the police. We have held, however, that a Grand Jury need not be instructed on the law with the same degree of precision as the petit jury. . . . This lesser standard is premised upon the different functions of the Grand Jury and the petit jury: the former determines whether sufficient evidence exists to accuse a person of a crime and thereby subject him to criminal prosecution; the latter ultimately determines the guilt or innocence of the accused, and may convict only where the People have proven his guilt beyond a reasonable doubt (see, *People v Calbud, Inc.*, 49 NY2d, at p 394, *supra*). In *People v Calbud, Inc.* (*supra*, at pp 394–395), we stated that the prosecutor simply had to "[provide] the Grand Jury with enough information to enable it intelligently to decide whether a crime has been committed and to determine whether there exists legally sufficient evidence to establish the material elements of the crime." Of course, as noted above, where the evidence suggests that a complete defense such as justification may be present, the prosecutor must charge the grand jurors on that defense, providing enough information to enable them to determine whether the defense, in light of the evidence, should preclude the criminal prosecution. The prosecutor more than adequately fulfilled this obligation here. His instructions were not as complete as the court's charge on justification should be, but they sufficiently apprised the Grand Jury of the existence and requirements of that defense to allow it to intelligently decide that there is sufficient evidence tending to disprove justification and necessitating a trial. The Grand Jury has indicted Goetz. It will now be for the petit jury to decide whether the prosecutor can prove beyond a reasonable doubt that Goetz's reactions were unreasonable and therefore excessive.

Accordingly, the order of the Appellate Division should be reversed, and the dismissed counts of the indictment reinstated.

∎

Waples won! The case would go forward under the objective standard as clarified by the Court of Appeals. The appellate division's interpretation of the law was wrong, and a good lawyer would know that the words "reasonably believes" imply the standard of a reasonable person under the circumstances.

It is important to understand the differing structures of the Model Penal Code and the New York Penal Law. The MPC has two applicable provisions, and the NYPL only one. The MPC § 3.04(1) initially inquires whether the "actor believes that such force is immediately necessary." If the actor does so believe, as Goetz apparently did, then the inquiry shifts to § 3.09(2), which holds that the first section is not applicable if the "actor's belief is reckless or negligent" and if the actor is charged with "an offense for which recklessness or negligence, as the case may be, suffices to establish culpability." The analysis of Goetz's liability is very complicated and need not detain us here.[3] The analysis under the MPC

---

[3] Those interested in the finer points of the problem may consult Fletcher, *A Crime of Self-Defense*.

was obviously too complicated for the New York legislators as well. They read the relationship of two provisions as applying the rule of negligence to modify the subjective standard in § 3.04. The equivalent in a single provision would require the addition of the word *reasonably* in the single New York provision. This is, at least, a plausible reconstruction of what happened in the legislature (no one knows for sure).

The German law on this point would have been a mixed blessing for Goetz, had he been tried in Frankfurt instead of Manhattan. The German provision on self-defense, StGB § 32, reads: "A defensive use of force is legitimate when necessary to avert an imminent unlawful attack to oneself or others." The advantage for Goetz in this provision is that the use of deadly force would be permissible, if necessary, to avert a mugging or even a minor assault.[4] If the perceived threat had merely been of theft without force, rather than robbery, Goetz would have had no right to use deadly force under New York law but would not have lost his right to use all necessary force under German law.

Another advantage of German law for Goetz would have been a special provision covering instances of exercising self-defense in cases of "confusion, fear or fright." StGB § 33 provides that if someone exceeds the bounds of self-defense under these circumstances, the use of force is not punishable. The ordinary case of self-defense is justifiable conduct; the excessive use of force under trying circumstances is excusable. This is a common rule in Continental criminal codes but unknown in the common law. It would not be so hard for Goetz to avail himself of this special provision.

On the issue that went to the Court of Appeals, however, Goetz would have done better in Germany than in New York. Although the German code is silent on this point, the theoretical literature has come to the conclusion that the subjective standard should be applied, that Goetz did not attack the youths "intentionally" if he believed sincerely (reasonably or not) that he had to defend himself. Here German law dovetails with the complicated rule of the MPC, which means that if Goetz negligently or unreasonably assumed that he was about to be at-

---

[4] The only limitation on necessary force would occur in a case of "abuse of rights," a judge-made doctrine in private law applied. The private law application is mentioned in Chapter Twenty-One.

tacked, he could have been liable for negligent battery at most. Negligent battery is an offense in Germany but not in common law jurisdictions.

To summarize the comparative analysis, Goetz does better under the procedural protections of American law than under German law, but the opposite is true of the substantive law. The advantages of the common law procedures are offset by the disadvantages of the substantive law of self-defense. This is not so surprising. Legal systems tend toward an equilibrium of advantage for prosecution and defense. If a system tends to be very favorable in one, you should expect some compensation in another.

■

QUESTIONS AND COMMENTS

1. One prime mode of compensation in the American system—and one that is proving to be of increasing influence in the rest of the world— is plea-bargaining. The state promises an elaborate criminal trial, with rights and privileges fit for a nobleman. It turns out that, in many cases, only a nobleman can afford it. Legal aid does provide counsel free of charge to the indigent. But the cost of first-class representation is prohibitive for everyone but the rich. As to medical expenses, most people are insured, but not so as to catastrophic legal expenses. Also, the state makes it attractive for defendants to plead guilty. By threatening draconian punishments, including the death penalty, the state generates an image of leniency in cases of voluntary guilty pleas. At least 90 percent of criminal cases in the United States are disposed of in this way.

As viewers of the TV series *Law & Order* know well, the prosecutor and the defense can make a deal at any time from the beginning of the investigation until the sentence. The decision to accept the plea does not, however, rest with either the defendant or the prosecutor, but with the court in which it is entered. After the court hears the plea, it decides whether to enter a judgment of conviction upon it and then to enter a sentence of punishment. The court will reject a plea that is not intelligently and voluntarily made, that does not appear to be grounded in fact, or that results in a sentence the court considers to be unfounded in the law or otherwise manifestly unjust.

A conviction based on a plea is as binding on the defendant as a conviction based on a trial verdict of guilt. The sentence and the effect of the conviction on later trials for other offenses are the same. Primarily for this reason (but also for reasons of fairness and contract), in most instances the government, and not just an individual prosecutor, is bound to perform the agreement after the defendant confesses guilt, unless the defendant withdraws. It is unprofessional conduct for a prosecutor to withdraw from a plea bargain without cause to do so from the defendant,[5] but oddly the defendant has no legal means to enforce the agreement.[6]

The interesting question is why plea-bargaining did not become a factor in the *Goetz* case. Any theories?

2. The *Goetz* case belongs to a special category of crimes that is becoming more and more common in courts around the world. They are crimes committed by people who are morally committed to their actions. The category includes not only famous Americans such as Timothy McVeigh and the Unabomber Ted Kaczynski but also all the international terrorists who have moved front and center in our consciousness since September 11, 2001. Criminals of this category feel no remorse and could escape liability by pleading insanity. But when Goetz's first lawyer, Frank Brenner, urged him to rely on the insanity defense, Goetz fired him. He wanted to be tried on the issue of "right" and "wrong." Does this moral disposition explain why Goetz would refuse to engage in plea-bargaining?

3. The trial of Bernhard Goetz did not begin until April 27, 1987, two and a half years after the shooting. The trial itself contained many instructive lessons about law and the moral principles underlying the law. We pose some of these questions here. You should attempt to come to your own answers about these questions. The way they were resolved in the trial is a matter of historical record that might or might not have been right. If you are interested in what actually happened, you can refer to George P. Fletcher, *A Crime of Self-Defense: Bernhard Goetz and the Law on Trial* (New York: Free Press, 1988), but try to formulate your own views first:

---

[5] See *American Bar Association Standards for Criminal Justice* (1980), Standard 3–4.2.

[6] See *Santobello v. New York*, 404 U.S. 257 (1971); Annotation, Right of Prosecutor to Withdraw from Plea Bargain Prior to Entry of Plea, 16 A.L.R. 4th 1089 (1981, Supp. 2003).

A. During the trial, would it have been right to refer to the four youths as "victims"?

> FOR: Of course, they are victims—they suffered from the shooting.
>
> AGAINST: The word *victims* implies that they were unjustly injured. That was the issue in the trial.

B. Goetz was to be judged according to the standard of the reasonable person under the circumstances. Would you allow into evidence surveys about how people would act in Goetz's situation or about whether they agree or disagree with his actions?

> FOR: Of course, how else can you know what a reasonable person would do?
>
> AGAINST: The standard is a moral one, and popular opinion cannot control morality.

C. Goetz was mugged in 1981 by three black kids on the subway. It became clear in the course of the trial that this experience weighed heavily on his frame of mind when he was first confronted by the four young African Americans in 1984. On the question of reasonable conduct under the circumstances, would you allow into evidence testimony about the race of the 1981 muggers?

> FOR: Of course, the incident influenced his judgment, and race was part of it.
>
> AGAINST: It is not reasonable to act on the basis of racial stereotypes.

D. Goetz was charged with four counts of attempted murder and four counts of battery. All of these required proof of an intent to harm the victims. How would you explain this required intention to the jury? (1) As having "the conscious aim or object" of shooting the four youths? (2) Or as desiring to harm the four youths?

> FOR (1): This is the standard instruction used in New York. It defines intention as a nonmoral state of mind.
>
> FOR (2): Emphasizing "desire to harm" adds a moral element that might confuse the jury.

4. The last issue turned out to be most significant in the jury's delibera-

tions. Judge Crane used the phrase "conscious aim or object" as the definition. The jury did not understand. They tried to work out their own intuitions about the required intention. Finally, juror D. Wirth Jackson, a seventy-four-year-old retired engineer, asked, "Where have they proved the intent to murder?" This question became the focal point of subsequent negotiations by the jury. In the end, their reasoning was that if Goetz had the intent to defend himself, he did not have the intent to murder. Perhaps he had the intent to kill but not the intent to murder. Do you see the difference? In a case of self-defense, a killing is not murder; it is justifiable homicide. Therefore, if the intention is to avoid an attack, it is not an intention to murder (nor does it reflect a "desire to harm"). On the basis of this reasoning, the jury acquitted Goetz of all charges to which self-defense was a defense. They found him guilty only of the illegal possession of a gun.

5. Do you see the irony of this result? In the end, which standard of self-defense controlled the thinking of the jury? The subjective or the objective?

6. If Goetz had been tried in Germany, he would probably have been found guilty of the same offense and not more. How then do we answer the question, Where would it have been better to be tried?

■

Further Reading

On criminal procedure generally, see Wayne R. Lafave, Jerold H. Israel, and Nancy J. King, *Hornbook on Criminal Procedure* (3d ed) (St. Paul, MN: West, 2000). On the law of evidence, see Jack B. Weinstein, John H. Mansfield, Norman Abrams, and Margaret A. Berger, *Evidence* (New York: Foundation Press, 2003). The federal sentencing guidelines are described and criticized in Kate Stith and Jose A. Cabranes, *Fear of Judging: Sentencing Guidelines in the Federal Courts* (Chicago: University of Chicago Press, 1998). For the background of criminal procedure, see John H. Langbein, *The Origins of Adversary Criminal Trial* (Oxford: Oxford University Press, 2003).

TWENTY-NINE

Self-Defense: Domestic and International

As self-defense was the central issue in the *Goetz* case, it is also the anchor that orients the law of war. Military aggression is prohibited under international law, but the use of military force in self-defense is permissible under the United Nations Charter Article 51. At some point, prohibited military aggression becomes justifiable self-defense. The activity might look exactly the same, with battles on the ground and in the air, but the legal valence is just the opposite. The problem for lawyers is fathoming the point of transformation when aggression becomes self-defense. The classification might be controversial. Consider the Israeli defense against Egypt in 1967; some people claim that the Six Day War was a war of aggression. Or judge the American invasion of Iraq in 2003. For many, this was a war of aggression; for others, it was a justifiable form of self-defense against a dangerous regime.

The challenge for us is to understand the relationship between the domestic and international laws of self-defense. There is no better way to conclude this book than to ponder this set of issues as a way of bridging the gap between domestic and international law. This is part of the study of American law "in a global context."

Our point of departure is that the contours of self-defense in these two areas of conflict—individual conflict in domestic law and collective conflict in international law—are essentially the same. The challenge for the student is to question this assumption and to think about how international conflict might be different.

The positive, or written, law varies from place to place largely in the detail with which self-defense is described. The German statute, § 32, sums it up in a few words: "A defensive use of force is legitimate when necessary to avert an imminent unlawful attack to oneself or others." That is, in principle, an attack against any interest—life, limb, property, or freedom of movement—will suffice.

The New York statute formulates a general rule for all cases:

NYPL §35.15(1) A person may, subject to the provisions of subdivision two, use physical force upon another person when and to the extent he reasonably believes such to be necessary to defend himself or a third person from what he reasonably believes to be the use or imminent use of unlawful physical force by such other person, unless:

(A) The latter's conduct was provoked by the actor himself with intent to cause physical injury to another person; or

(B) The actor was the initial aggressor; except that in such case his use of physical force is nevertheless justifiable if he has withdrawn from the encounter and effectively communicated such withdrawal to such other person but the latter persists in continuing the incident by the use or threatened imminent use of unlawful physical force; or

(C) The physical force involved is the product of a combat by agreement not specifically authorized by law.

The standard then modifies this rule for cases of deadly force:

NYPL § 35.15(2) A person may not use deadly physical force upon another person . . . unless:

(A) He reasonably believes that such other person is using or about to use deadly physical force. Even in such case, however, the actor may not use deadly physical force if he knows that he can with complete safety as to himself and others avoid the necessity of so doing by retreating; except that he is under no duty to retreat if he is:

(i) in his dwelling and not the initial aggressor; or

(ii) a police officer or peace officer or a person assisting a police officer or a peace officer at the latter's direction, acting pursuant to section 35.30; or

(B) He reasonably believes that such other person is committing or attempting to commit a kidnapping, forcible rape, forcible criminal sexual act or robbery; or

(C) He reasonably believes that such other person is committing or attempting to commit a burglary, and the circumstances are such that the use of deadly physical force is authorized by subdivision three of section 35.20.

The Rome Statute, establishing the International Criminal Court as of July 1, 2002, is our guide to international criminal law. The statute provides:

Art. 31(1). In addition to other grounds for excluding criminal responsibility provided for in this Statute, a person shall not be criminally responsible if, at the time of that person's conduct:

(c) The person acts reasonably to defend himself or herself or another person or, in the case of war crimes, property which is essential for the survival of the person or another person or property which is essential for accomplishing a military mission, against an imminent and unlawful use of force in a manner proportionate to the degree of danger to the person or the other person or property protected. The fact that the person was involved in a defensive operation conducted by forces shall not in itself constitute a ground for excluding criminal responsibility under this subparagraph. . . .

■

QUESTIONS AND COMMENTS

1. Note that the German provision covers all interests of third parties. By contrast, the Rome Statute distinguishes clearly between two kinds of threats. With regard to the threats to persons, the ordinary rules of reasonableness and proportionality apply. In the case of threats to property, the right to use force depends on whether the property is essential to some other purposes. The acceptable purposes mentioned are (1) the survival of a human being, such as the food or wa-

ter supply and (2) accomplishing a military mission. On the face of things, at least, the Rome Statute provides less protection for property than does the German Code, which at least nominally treats property on a par with all other interests.

2. The reluctance to protect property interests under the law of self-defense becomes evident upon inspection of the New York Penal Law. The privilege to use deadly force (a special category not recognized in the other statutes) applies only to repel certain crimes. If you go down the list, all of the targeted crimes are crimes against the person—or at least partially against the person, as in the case of robbery, defined as theft by force or threat of force. The only possible exception is burglary, which is defined at common law as breaking and entering a dwelling house at night, intending to commit a felony. Even in burglary, there is an indirect threat to personal interests, because the occupant might be in the dwelling at the time of the break-in.

3. In the following material, we analyze the general contours of self-defense under four headings: imminence, necessity, proportionality, and intention. To prepare for this analysis, ask yourself the question, What is the distinction between normal force and deadly force about? This distinction is commonly drawn in American statutes but nowhere else. What are the key words or phrases in the Rome Statute that address the same issue? Is the issue mentioned in the German provision?

■

The Four Dimensions of Self-Defense

The struggle between passion and reason in the law of self-defense is played out against a background of shared abstract assumptions about the contours of the defense. There is no statute or authoritative legal source expressing this consensus, but lawyers all over the world would readily concur that the basic structural elements of a valid claim of self-defense are imminence, necessity, proportionality, and intentionality.

Imminence

The requirement of imminence means that the time for defense is now! The defender cannot wait any longer. This requirement distinguishes self-defense from the illegal use of force in two temporally related ways: A preemptive strike against a feared aggressor is illegal force used too soon, and retaliation against a successful aggressor is illegal force used too late. Legitimate self-defense must be neither too soon nor too late. The requirement of imminence is expressed in all three statutory provisions used as our representative models.

But there are some dissenters. The Model Penal Code rejected the standard of imminence in favor of the looser criterion of "practical necessity on the present occasion."[1] The impulse behind this change was to make self-defense more readily available in case of slow-fuse attacks where there was no way out, such as being trapped in the desert with the threat of poisoning all the available water. The drafters of the code did not anticipate that their loosening the bonds of self-defense would turn out to be very practical in battered-wife cases, particularly when a husband threatens to kill his wife and then goes to sleep. This recurrent problem of killing a potential aggressor in his sleep generated considerable controversy in the 1980s and 1990s, when feminist legal scholars attacked the "imminence" standard as unfair to women, who allegedly have fewer options than do men in resisting violent attack.[2]

The same kinds of considerations have entered the debate about when it is permissible to attack a country in order to prevent the development and possible use of weapons of mass destruction. As is well known, this is one of the arguments that the United States offered for its invasion of Iraq in the spring of 2003. The American position was not a direct extension of the battered women's defense, which arguably would have applied on behalf of small countries like Iraq and North Korea, who have good grounds to fear aggression by the superpowers. Rather, the argument was that the risk of weapons of mass destruction (WMDs) in the hands of "rogue" states justified the preemptive use of force.[3]

---

[1] MPC § 2.04.

[2] See Cathryn Jo Rosen, "The Excuse of Self-Defense: Correcting a Historical Accident on Behalf of Battered Women Who Kill," 6 Am. U.L. Rev. 11 (1986); Richard Rosen, "On Self-Defense, Imminence, and Women Who Kill Their Batterers," 71 N.C. L. Rev. 371 (1993); Elizabeth M. Schneider, "Equal Rights to Trial for Women: Sex Bias in the Law of Self-Defense," 15 Harv. C.R.-C.L.L. Rev. 623 (1980).

[3] The foundation for the U.S. policy on preemptive military operations is in The National Security Strategy of the United States of America, issued on April 29, 2002, available online at http://www.whitehouse.gov/nsc/nss.html. One of the many announcements of the requirement of Iraq to disclose its efforts related to WMD or face military consequences

The debate about these issues was confused by dissonance in the use of the phrase "preemptive self-defense." The divergence is noted in the two sets of conceptual distinctions for discussing these issues presented in Table 29.1.

So far as we have noted in the literature and the cases, the domestic law of self-defense is based on the basic system of distinctions. As this chart suggests, there is no difference in the case of resisting actual aggression. This is the core case that arises, as the UN Charter Article 51 says, when "an armed attack occurs." The problem of description is more acute in Case 2. The basic system would treat cases of apparent imminence as actual attacks subject to self-defense; the alternative system requires that the defense be described as "preemptive," thus calling into question but necessarily excluding the legitimate use of force.

A good case for pondering the difference between these two ways of classifying apparent threats is Israel's attack against Egypt in June 1967, initiating the spectacular Israeli victory in the Six Day War. Egypt closed the Straits of Tiran to Israeli shipping, amassed its troops on Israel's border,

Table 29.1

Describing the Use of Force

	The basic system	The alternative mode
1. Actual shooting	Actual self-defense	Actual self-defense
2. Pointing a gun, threatening to shoot—imminent threat	Actual self-defense	Preemptive use of force
3. Acquiring weapons with aggressive intentions	Preemptive war	Preventive war

was made by President Bush shortly before the invasion. George Bush, Radio Address by the President to the Nation, December 7, 2002 (http://www.whitehouse.gov/news/releases/2002/12/20021207.html). The history of Iraq's WMD and the response of the United States can be traced online at http://en.wikipedia.org/wiki/Iraq_and_weapons_of_mass_destruction.

The history of American decisions leading to the invasion of Iraq is still being written. It appears, a year after the invasion, that the original justification that Iraq possessed weapons of mass destruction that it was willing to use against the United States and its allies was indeed unfounded. Thus, our assessment of that justification according to the evidence prior to the invasion has become all the more critical.

and secured command control over the armies of Jordan and Iraq. In the two weeks preceding the Israeli response on June 5, Nasser had repeatedly made bellicose threats, including the total destruction of Israel. The question is whether Egypt's threat was sufficiently imminent to justify Israel's response under international law. Perhaps Egypt was merely bluffing; perhaps its leaders did not know whether they intended to attack or not. There is no doubt, however, that Egypt was attempting to intimidate Israel by behaving as though it were about to attack. Israel took the Egyptians at face value: It responded to what appeared to be an attack in the offing. Could Israel have waited longer? Of course it could have. But the requirement of imminence does not require that guns actually fire, that bombs be in the air. And if anything short of letting the missiles fly can constitute an imminent attack, then that requirement was fulfilled in the June 1967 conflict between Egypt and Israel.

In his influential nonlegal approach to just war, Michael Walzer argues that cases of this sort are instances, at best, of preemptive self-defense.[4] Apparently anything short of physically pushing back an aggressor constitutes preemptive self-defense. It is not clear how widespread this alternative system is, but it is a dangerous and counterproductive way to draw the legal contours of permissible force. This loose way of using the term *preemptive* inevitably waters down the standard of imminence, and that, in our view, opens the door to abuse.

Consider the case of the Israeli strike against the Osirak nuclear reactor in 1981, when the supposition, based on military intelligence, was that the Iraqis would use the reactor for military purposes. Even if it is true that the Iraqis intended to manufacture a nuclear bomb, that activity hardly constitutes an attack against Israel. Israel has its own nuclear weapons, and its government would hotly contest the inference that this fact alone establishes its intention to bomb Arab territory.

Under both conceptual systems, the basic and the alternative, the attack on the Osirak reactor would be described as preemptive. The real problem, however, is whether a possible Iraqi attack was imminent and therefore the response justified. It might have been reasonable to fear the military potential of the Iraqi reactor in the long run, but there was no overt manifestation of an immediate intention to attack.

---

[4] Michael Walzer, *Just and Unjust Wars: A Moral Argument with Historical Illustrations* 47, 80 (3d ed) (New York: Basic Books, 2000).

Preemptive strikes are always based on assumptions, more or less rational, that the enemy is likely to engage in hostile behavior. Israel could well argue that it did not wish to take the chance that Iraq would use nuclear weapons against the Jewish state, as well as against Iran and other opponents of the Baghdad regime. Be that as it may, imminence as the required condition for war requires a manifest sign of present intention to attack, and the acquisition of the reactors did not pose an imminent risk. The Israeli response, of course, would be that they did not want to run the risk that a "rogue state" would have nuclear weapons at its disposal. The risks were arguably too great. Perhaps. But switching to risk analysis takes us away from the requirement of imminence and to the independent factors of necessity and proportionality.

If the Israeli attack on the Osirak reactor was not justified as a response to an imminent risk, then the U.S. invasion of Iraq in 2003 was hardly more defensible. At least in the Osirak case, Israel knew that Iraq had a reactor. In 2003, the United States knew nothing except that sometime in the past Iraq had made an effort to acquire nuclear weapons.

Under the standard mode of analysis, the American as well as the Israeli attacks on Iraq were preemptive strikes and therefore illegitimate. Under the alternative scheme, the analyst would label them preemptive, but that would not resolve the question of legitimacy because some preemptive strikes are justified. In the alternative scheme, everything turns on the line drawn between preemptive and preventive wars. The former are dubious; the latter clearly illegitimate. The problem is that there seems to be no coherent principle to distinguish between the two categories.

In the end, we have to concede that the concept of imminence is contestable. There are two distinct approaches. One stresses the necessity of an observable sign of a present intention to attack; the other emphasizes the risk that justifies the use of force to minimize the overall danger to the world. If you choose the former, how do you apply the test? Was there an imminent attack when the Soviet Union stationed nuclear-tipped missiles in Cuba capable of hitting targets in the United States? Was there an imminent attack when Canty asked Goetz for five dollars and did so in a particular tone of voice and with his body language? The request for five dollars could be understood as panhandling, as harassment, as intimidation ("Hand it over or else!"), or as a prelude to a violent assault, whatever Goetz did. If Canty was merely begging, with no threat implicit in his request, there was no imminent attack. If the request was a veiled threat of violence, the circumstances are much closer to an imminent attack.

If you apply the cost-benefit approach—the risk of the rogue state's acquiring WMDs is so great that violence is justified to counter the risk— then you have a standard that anyone can apply in a self-interested manner. A coalition of Islamic states fearful of American intervention might justify bombing American bases on the same perception of risks and benefits.

The imminence test requires that states use force neither too soon nor too late. Though the premature responses have often been the subject of international and domestic controversy, the problem of response after the fact is no less troubling. The use of force is often a passionate retaliation for past wrongs suffered by a victim—either a person or a nation. Retaliatory acts seek to even the score to inflict harm because harm has been suffered in the past. For example, it is difficult to classify responses of the Israeli army to suicide bombing—whether the air strikes are purely defensive in nature or whether they have a motive to even the score as well. Suicide bombings by Palestinians appear to be acts of revenge and are often so justified by spokespersons for Hamas who link them to prior Israeli attacks, but there are some, to be sure, who claim that Palestinians are defending their lands against Israeli encroachment. When it becomes difficult to distinguish between preventive and retaliatory attacks, it becomes natural to speak of a "circle of violence."

Borderline situations lying between defense and retaliation are commonplace in cases arising from wife battering and domestic violence. The injured wife waits for the first possibility of striking against a distracted or unarmed husband. He may even be asleep when the wife finally reacts. Of course, she can argue that the standard of "practical necessity" as an alternative to the imminence test might justify the killing as defensive. But the punitive element—"the guy is getting what he deserves"—is hard to avoid.

Goetz's response to the four young men was retaliatory insofar as he perceived them as "four young muggers" rather than as individuals; he was striking back for having been mugged by the "same type of guys" in 1981 and for suffering lasting injuries to his knee and chest.

Retaliation is the standard case of "taking the law into one's own hands." There is no way, under the law, to justify killing a wife-batterer or rapist as retaliation, however much sympathy there may be for a wife wreaking vengeance. Private citizens cannot function as judge and jury toward each other; that is not what judges or juries are. Private citizens have no authority under the law to pass judgment and to punish each other for past wrongs. The same is true of countries, though they often think that it is their function to enforce international law by engaging in reprisals against other countries perceived to have violated the law.

Those who defend the use of violence rarely admit that their purpose is retaliation for a past wrong. The argument typically is that the actor feared a recurrence of the past violence; thus the focus shifts from past to future violence, from retaliation to an argument of defending against an imminent attack. This is the standard maneuver in battered-wife cases. In view of her prior abuse, the wife arguably has reason to fear renewed violence. Killing the husband while he is asleep then comes into focus as an arguably legitimate defensive response rather than an illegitimate act of vengeance for past wrongs.

An ambiguity similar to the tension between retaliation and defense runs through the entire field of international criminal law and punishment for war crimes, genocide, and crimes against humanity. When lawyers seek punishment of the German general staff in Nuremberg, Eichmann in Jerusalem, or Milosevic in The Hague, they rarely admit that the purpose is retribution pure and simple. There is always an attempt to dress up criminal punishment as a means of social defense, as a general deterrence against crimes in the future. This move, often fictitious, plays on our general sentiment that it is all right to use force to defend ourselves and our societies, but it is dubious—if not dead wrong—to use it simply to punish wrongdoers.

Necessity

Force is never justified unless it is necessary. The German Penal Code is explicit on this requirement. The New York Penal Code requires that the actor "reasonably believes" the use of force "to be necessary to defend himself or a third person." Interestingly, the Rome Statute says nothing about necessity in defending persons, but as to property the statute is demanding: The use must be "essential," either for human survival or for the success of a military mission. (For our purposes, *essential* and *necessary* are treated as synonyms.)

The requirement of necessity implies that the means chosen must be the least costly available. There can be no reasonable alternative that is less costly. In the *Goetz* case, was there an effective response less drastic than firing the gun at the four feared assailants? Would it have been enough merely to show the gun in its holster? Or to draw and point the weapon without firing? Goetz had twice scared off muggers on the street merely by drawing the gun. This suggests that perhaps shooting to kill was not the least costly choice among the reasonable alternatives in the situation.

There are many arguments in Goetz's favor. The jolting floor of the accelerating train made Goetz's footing uncertain. During his initial exchange with Canty, he rose to his feet and was standing in close quarters with his feared assailants. Showing the gun in the holster or drawing it would have risked one of the four young men's taking the gun away and shooting him. Gauging necessity under the circumstances turns, in the end, on an elusive prediction of what would have happened if Goetz had tried this or that maneuver, short of shooting. In the end, the telling consideration is Justice Holmes's wise aphorism, "Detached reflection cannot be demanded in the presence of an uplifted knife."[5]

In the international context, it would be difficult to argue self-defense if diplomatic means were available to solve the conflict. If Israeli delegates could have sat down with their Egyptian counterparts to negotiate a satisfactory end to the conflict, the resort to arms would not have been justifiable. In this context, the United Nations Charter Article 51 includes an important qualification on the right of states to resort to defensive force. The "inherent" right of self-defense applies only "until the Security Council has taken measures necessary to maintain international peace and security." The analogy in the domestic scene would be that if a cowboy is engaged in a shootout with bandits and the sheriff's men arrive on the scene, the cowboy would have to holster his gun and let the state's officials take care of the situation.

Proportionality

The third element, proportionality, adds a problem beyond the necessity of the defensive response. To understand the distinction between proportionality and necessity, think about the case of an orchard owner

---

[5] *Brown v. United States*, 256 U.S. 335, 343 (1921) (Holmes, J.).

shooting an escaping apple thief. If we consider preventing the escape as an aspect of preventing the crime, then of course it might be *necessary* to shoot. But shooting to kill, or even to wound, would not be *proportional* to the harm threatened. The disproportion between life and limb, on the one hand, and apples on the other is too obvious to require discussion. No legal regime that imposes a rule of proportionality would treat the shooting of the apple thief as justifiable.

Proportionality in self-defense requires a balancing of competing interests, the interests of the defender and those of the aggressor. Women may kill to prevent rape; as the innocent party, the woman's interests weigh more heavily than those of the aggressor. She may kill to ward off a threat to her sexual autonomy, but she has no license to take life to avoid being kissed or touched. If the only way she can avoid unwanted contact is to kill, that response seems clearly excessive relative to the interests at stake. Even if our thumb is on the scale in favor of the defender, there comes a point at which the aggressor's basic humanity will outweigh the interests of an innocent victim, thumb and all. There is obviously no way to determine the breaking point, even theoretically. At a certain point, our sensibilities are triggered, our compassion for the human being behind the mask of the evil aggressor is engaged, and we have to say, "Stop! That's enough."

The rule of proportionality makes sense, but not all legal regimes require it. The German provision does not explicitly require this balancing of the competing interests, and the limitation of proportionality was resisted for decades. The traditional view was that the party in the right should never yield an inch to the party in the wrong. Finally, in the postwar period the German courts imposed the rule of "abuse of rights" to limit the expansive rule of self-defense in Article 32 of the Penal Code.

The New York Penal Law has a rough principle of proportionality implicitly built into its distinction between the two levels of defensive response—between the use of "physical force" and the use of "deadly physical force." The former is permissible to prevent the "imminent use of physical force" against oneself or against a third person; the more serious response, the use of deadly force, is permissible in specified cases where the threatened force is more serious. Of the cases enumerated in the provision on self-defense, the threats relevant to the justification of Goetz's conduct are (1) the threat to "use deadly physical force" and (2) the attempt to commit a robbery.

The rule of proportionality is of dubious relevance in international armed conflict. Suppose that the Soviet Union had invaded Alaska and declared itself content with occupying this—and only this—part of the United States. Americans could accept this state of affairs, or they could respond with sufficient force to expel the Russians from Alaska. Suppose the force that was necessary to accomplish this objective included the nuclear bombing of Russian cities. If the only choice is surrender or nuclear war, very few people would have moral qualms about employing all the force necessary, even if the implication was that the costs to the Russians would far exceed the gains to Americans. Similar arguments were made about the necessity of bombing Hiroshima and Nagasaki to avoid a costlier American land invasion and conquest of Japan. This is the logic of "total war."

Yet there is a conundrum here that we have to address sooner or later. The puzzle is that the Rome Statute obviously has a principle of proportionality built into it. The distinction between protecting persons and protecting property speaks precisely to that issue. The strict rules of the defense of property also testify to the same concern. What are these rules doing here when, if the argument of the preceding paragraph is correct, proportionality has no role in defining the contours of military defense against aggression?

The way out of this quandary is to recognize two distinct dimensions of the law of war—the problem of justifying war as a collective activity and the problem of justifying individual actions in war. The first is governed by a body of rules called *jus ad bellum*, which prescribes when states rightfully go to war. The second is subject to the set of norms called *jus in bello*, which prescribes the proper use of violence in warfare. Today there is only one rule—or possibly two rules—governing *jus ad bellum*. The primary rule is that states have a right to go to war under the United Nations Charter only if they are acting in self-defense against aggression by another state. The subsidiary rule is that states may also engage in armed conflict if they are executing a Security Council resolution "to maintain peace and stability." In light of the primacy of self-defense in *jus ad bellum*, there is a natural tendency to think of the Rome Statute provision on self-defense as governing the question of when states have the right to go to war. The temptation to read the statute this way is supported by the inclusion of "aggression" among the crimes punished in the International Criminal Court. Self-defense is the primary defense against the charge of aggression.

But in fact all of the rules in Article 31 of the Rome Statute are drafted with individual responsibility in mind. The first two of the four subparts in the article address insanity and intoxication, arguments that are clearly not available to states that seek to explain or excuse their aggression against other states.[6] The third part, laying down rules of self-defense, also addresses individual conduct—namely, the kind of conduct that in the absence of self-defense would constitute a war crime or crime against humanity.

Intention

The preceding three characteristics of self-defense—imminence, necessity, and proportionality—speak to the objective characteristics of the attack and the defense in response. To establish that these requirements are satisfied, we need not ask any questions about what Goetz himself knew and thought as he shot the four youths. But suppose that while being attacked without knowing it, he started shooting with the aim of inflicting harm on the four black youths. In this hypothetical situation, could he invoke self-defense on the ground that his act did, in fact, frustrate the attack? It would be a de facto act of self-defense, even though Goetz had his own reasons for shooting.

The consensus among Western legal systems is that in order to invoke a sound claim of self-defense, the defender must know about the attack and act with the intention of repelling it. Why should Goetz receive the benefit of a justification if he acted maliciously, without fear of attack? Surprisingly, some leading scholars think that in a case of criminal homicide, the accused should be able to invoke self-defense even if he does not know about the attack.[7]

Their argument is that if you cannot be guilty of homicide by killing someone who is already dead (no matter what your intent), you should not be guilty of homicide by killing an aggressor (no matter what your

---

[6] Rome Statute Article 31(1)(a) and (b).

[7] See Glanville Williams, *Textbook of Criminal Law* 504 (2d ed) (London: Stevens, 1983); Paul H. Robinson, *Criminal Law Defenses* 12–29 (St. Paul: West, 1984).

intent). No harm, no crime. And there is arguably no harm in killing an aggressor.

The better rule is that self-defense is a privilege that can be properly exercised only by people who know the relevant facts. The German courts accept this rule even though the code is silent on this point. The New York Penal Code explicitly requires that the actor "reasonably believes" that the circumstances warrant defensive action. The implications in the *Goetz* case were far-reaching. Ramseur and Cabey were carrying screwdrivers in their coat pockets. Some circles even reported that the screwdrivers were sharpened. The reports confirmed what many people wanted to believe: that these four kids were about to mug Goetz and that therefore his response was justified as self-defense. Yet there was no evidence that Goetz knew of the screwdrivers. Not one of the four victims pulled a screwdriver from his pocket, either before or during the shooting. If Goetz did not know of the screwdrivers, however, they had no bearing on his claim of justification. They had no more legal relevance than a secret, undisclosed plan to kill Goetz because he was white.

The same rule should apply in the international context. Yet the Rome Statute says nothing about a required defensive intention or awareness of danger. In the debate leading up to the American invasion of Iraq in 2003, many people argued that the invasion would be justified if they later discovered weapons of mass destruction in Iraq.[8] But this was the wrong question. The right question is not justification by hindsight but justification *ex ante*, before the action. What did the Americans know on the eve of the invasion? Did they have reasonable grounds to believe in an Iraqi threat? Whether they subsequently discovered weapons should not be regarded as decisive. The real question was whether they had credible evidence to believe they would find something that was then kept secret from the United Nations inspectors. President Bush might have believed that he would find something, but as in the *Goetz* case, the problem was whether his belief was reasonable on the basis of the evidence then known to him.

The requirements of imminence, necessity, and intentionality are found in diverse legal systems, as well as in the international law of armed conflict. Proportionality is a more contested requirement, obvious in some

---

[8] See Anne-Marie Slaughter, "Good Reasons for Going Around the U.N.," *New York Times*, March 18, 2003, A-33.

contexts and less so in others. Yet these basic structural elements account only for the surface language of the law. Beneath the surface surge conflicting moral and ideological forces that drive the interpretation of the law in particular directions. We may all be united in the terms with which we discuss self-defense, but we are divided in our loyalties to unarticulated theories that account for our willingness now to stretch the law broadly, now to interpret it narrowly.

Four Models of Self-Defense

At least four models of self-defense run through the debates that inform litigation on claims of self-defense around the world. The foundational concepts of imminence, necessity, and proportionality take on differing connotations, depending on the theory in which they are anchored. By articulating these conflicting value systems, we can begin to examine the larger issues at stake in every dispute about self-defense—whether claimed in a graffiti-ridden New York subway or on the border between France and Germany.

Self-Defense as Punishment

Our commitment to justice and to the symbolic expiation of evil pulls us in the direction of thinking of self-defense as a form of just punishment. The individual acts in place of the state in inflicting on wrongdoers their just deserts. If Troy Canty, Barry Allen, James Ramseur, and Darrell Cabey were in fact muggers, then this rough principle of justice holds that "they got what they deserved." These are the exact words of a black witness, Andrea Reid. Present with her baby in the subway car at the time of shooting, she was also afraid of the four "punks who were bothering the white man." Barry Slotnick referred to her words "they got what they deserved" dozens of times in the course of the trial. Sometimes he paraphrased the comment in a more respectable legal idiom: "They got what the law allowed."

Goetz became a folk hero because, as many people saw it, he brought the arrogant predators to their knees. Yet even under a punitive theory of giving criminals what they deserve, there remain questions of fact. Did these kids have records long enough to support the judgment that they were criminals and predators? Or is the public perception of Canty, Cabey, Ramseur, and Allen as criminal types largely a function of their race and youth? When our passions seek gratification, when our lust to avenge evil gains the upper hand, we don't always ponder the facts and weigh the gradations of evil, or their fitting punishment.

That people should be rewarded and punished on the basis of their character and their lifelong behavior expresses a principle of justice, but it is a principle better suited for infallible divine punishment than the imperfect institutions of the law. In fairy tales, the witch may receive her comeuppance at the end. But surely it is not the business of human in-stitutions—not to mention a lone rider on the subway—to determine who is a witch, or a wicked person, or a habitual criminal.

The law wisely limits itself to the question of whether a particular act constitutes a crime and merits punishment or whether, in the context of self-defense, a particular aggressive attack properly triggers a defensive response. The general character of suspects is important neither for human punishment nor for the assessment of whether defensive force was per-missible in a particular situation. Some people who passionately sided with Goetz's victims may think that when Goetz's lawyer Slotnick was jumped and assaulted a few weeks after the trial was over, he, too, got what he deserved. They are entitled to their opinion. But their passion for justice on the streets should not be heard in court. Nor should Slotnick's repeated reiteration of Andrea Reid's words "they got what they deserved" have been heard as a persuasive argument about the proper scope of self-defense.

In the international arena, the urge to punish often overwhelms the proper analysis of self-defense. This certainly appeared true in the Amer-ican invasion of Iraq in 2003, when American policymakers tried to stretch self-defense to fit the facts but also spoke passionately about the great evil represented by Saddam Hussein. Crimes against the Kurds and other political opponents were recited in detail. Whether the purpose of "regime change" was punitive or philanthropic was not so clear, but these motives readily become intertwined with the analysis of self-defense against the prospect of WMDs.[9]

---

[9] The shift in American justification for the war from justification through self-defense to justification through humanitarian intervention has become more pronounced in retrospect. But the doctrine of humanitarian intervention is not yet fully recognized in

Self-Defense as Excuse

An alternative approach to self-defense shifts our focus away from our anger toward the aggressor and our passion to punish and directs our attention instead to the personal plight of the defender. In the closing portions of his summation to the jury, Barry Slotnick played on this theme. He stressed Goetz's fear, his back to the steel wall of the subway car, with no choice but to strike back.

The theme of fear invokes the primordial form of self-defense in English law. From roughly the thirteenth to the sixteenth century, the plea of self-defense, called *se defendendo*, came into consideration whenever a fight broke out and one party retreated as far as he could go before resorting to defensive force. His back had to be literally against the wall.

If he then killed the aggressor, *se defendendo* had the effect of saving the defendant from execution, but it left intact the other stigmatizing effects of the criminal law. The defendant forfeited his goods as expiation of his having taken human life. The murder weapon was also forfeited to the crown as a *deodand*, a tainted object. Killing *se defendendo* was called *excusable homicide*, for though the wrong of homicide had occurred, the circumstances generated a personal excuse that saved the manslayer from execution. The defense of *se defendendo* springs more from compassion for the predicament of the trapped defender than from a commitment to justice. If we would all act the same way if caught in the same circumstances, we can hardly condemn and execute the manslayer who had no choice.

Although the theory of excuses plays a large role in domestic criminal law, it has lesser sway in international criminal law. The reason is that all actions between states are assumed to be voluntary. States do not go

international law, even by the United States. When committed outside of the apparatus of the United Nations Security Council, the dominant view was, prior to 2003, that such intervention is contrary to the United Nations Charter. See Sean D. Murphy, *Humanitarian Intervention: The United Nations in an Evolving World Order* (Philadelphia: University of Pennsylvania Press, 1996). Although one might say that this principle has been breached so often that there is no longer a norm of international law, it remains far from clear whether such interventions are justified by international law. See George R. Lucas and Anthony C. Zinni, *Perspectives on Humanitarian Military Intervention* (Washington, DC: Institute of Governmental Studies Press, 2001); and Michael J. Glennon, *Limits of Law, Prerogatives of Power: Interventionism after Kosovo* (New York: Palgrave-Macmillan, 2001).

insane; they cannot excuse aggression because their people are hungry, because their leader makes a mistake about their legal obligations, or because they feel in danger of attack. This might well be the most significant feature distinguishing individual behavior in domestic law from collective action in the international sphere. For self-defense to apply internationally, the foundation of the claim must be a theory not of excuse but of justification.

Self-Defense as the Justified Vindication of Autonomy

English lawyers of the fifteenth and sixteenth centuries paid close attention to the jurisprudence of the Bible; in Exodus 22 we read that there is no bloodguilt, no taint, in killing a thief who seeks at night to break into one's home. It was odd, then, that the common law recognized no similar justification that would totally exempt a manslayer from liability. Accused killers had to rely on a claim of excuse that left them subject to the forfeiture of their goods.

Eventually Parliament filled this gap in the common law. A statute enacted in 1532 licenses the killing, without any taint whatsoever, of robbers and other assailants on the public highway. This statutory defense came to be called *justifiable*—as opposed to excusable—*homicide*. The defense is not based on compassion for someone with his back to the wall, but rather it expresses a right to hold one's ground against wrongful aggressors. The claim is not "I could not do otherwise" but rather "Don't tread on me!" As the leading scholar of the seventeenth century, Sir Edward Coke, said of this defense, "no man shall ever give way to a thief, etc. neither shall he forfeit anything."[10] The consequence of justifiable homicide, as the 1532 statute prescribes, is total acquittal. There was no forfeiture of goods.

This version of justifiable self–defense is appropriately called "individualist," for it is guided by the imperative to vindicate individual autonomy. Its philosophical champions were John Locke and Immanuel Kant. Kant conceived of an unqualified right of self–defense as the foundation of a liberal legal system in which each citizen recognized and willed maximum freedom for himself as well as for his fellow citizens. That the legal system should be organized on the basis of maximum freedom was,

---

[10] Sir Edward Coke, 3 *The Third Institute* 55 (1644).

for Kant, the implication of pure reason in human affairs. Relying implicitly on this tradition, Slotnick invoked the individualist theory in his opening statement:

> [N]o one can ever take away your inalienable right to protect your property or your life or your family. No one can walk up to me and say, "give me that watch," "give me your ring," "give me five dollars." And if they do, heaven help them if I'm armed, because I know what the law allows.

This way of thinking about autonomy draws sustenance from an analogy between persons and states. The individual is an island self-reflexively sovereign, as nations are sovereign over their territory. Indeed, the individual right of self-defense makes sense as an extension of the idea that nations can use force to maintain dominance over their own people and their own territory. Because self-defense is so strongly connected with what it means to be a person or a nation, we speak readily of self-defense as a natural right or, with the United Nations Charter, as an "inherent right." In this context, the principles of domestic and international law are so tightly interwoven that we have trouble deciding which came first.

Self-Defense as a Maximization of Interests

The "individualist" stands in contrast to the "social" variation of justifiable self-defense. The difference between the two is expressed in a very loose—as opposed to very strict—approach to proportionality. The extreme version of the individualist defense rejects proportionality altogether. Any encroachment on an individual's rights represents an intolerable violation of personal autonomy. The affected individual can do everything in his power and deploy all necessary means to end the encroachment and vindicate his autonomy.

The individualist theory has always expressed itself most strongly in the protection of one's home. Any intrusion against one's "castle," against one's refuge from the heartless world, seems intolerable. The individualist theory would vindicate the use of all necessary means to defend one's home against an attempted intrusion. Perhaps, as Kant would say, our moral concern for the welfare of others would lead us not to exercise our right of defense,[11] but liberal writings leave no doubt that freedom entails the option to resist all forms of encroachment.

The social variation of the same defense rejects absolutes like the imperative to secure one's rights, one's autonomy, or one's private physical space. The individualist treats every person as an island, entitled to full sovereignty in his own domain. This way of thinking views human beings as though they were states—thus ignoring our interdependence, both in shaping our sense of self and in cooperating in society for mutual advantage. The alternative social view regards the aggressor as another member of the same society of interdependent selves. He has interests that we cannot ignore, even if he acts wrongfully in aggressing against someone else. These interests are expressed in the obligation of the defender to consider the aggressor not merely as an intrusive force but as a fellow human being as well. In the end, the defender's interests may be worth more, but those of the aggressor are not totally discounted.

Recognizing the humanity of the aggressor implies that in some situations the defender must absorb an encroachment on his autonomy rather than inflict an excessive cost on the aggressor. If the only way to prevent an intrusion and nonviolent theft in one's home is to kill the aggressor, the defender may voluntarily have to forgo the defense and risk losing his property. He must suffer a minor invasion and hope that the police will recover his goods; the alternative of killing the aggressor is too costly and too callous a disregard of the human interests of the aggressor.

Yet self-defense is not punishment. The purpose of a defensive act is not to inflict harm according to the desert of the aggressor. Its purpose is to repel the attack. And if there is a principle of proportionality that restricts self-defense, it cannot be the same principle of justice that governs sentencing after trial and conviction. As the example of repelling rape by deadly force demonstrates, the right to subject an aggressor to a risk of death attaches even when capital punishment would be unacceptable.

In the 1950s and the 1960s, a strong defense of the social theory emerged from the general and seemingly uncontroversial view that the purpose of the criminal law was to further the public good. After all, who could be against the public good? The consequence of this view in the

---

[11] See Immanuel Kant, *The Metaphysics of Morals* 60 (1797) (Mary Gregor trans.) (Cambridge: Cambridge University Press, 1991) (referring to "ethics" as the only reason for not killing "a wrongful assailant on my life").

thinking of criminal law reformers was that the purpose of punishment became primarily to encourage people to act in a socially desirable way, and the determination of socially desirable conduct turned largely on the assessment of the costs and benefits of acting in particular ways.

The consequence of thinking about self-defense as a measure furthering the public welfare led courts and legislatures, for a time, to eschew all absolutist thinking about the right of people to defend their autonomy against aggressive attacks. In cases of burglary, for example, the lawmakers demanded that for a homeowner to use deadly force against an intruder, he must fear violence to himself or the other occupants; the fear of theft would not be sufficient to justify fighting off the burglar with force endangering his life.

An illustrative case is the decision of the California Supreme Court in *People v. Ceballos*,[12] which held that injuring a burglar with a spring gun (an automatic weapon triggered by entry) could not be justified. Because no one was home at the time of the intrusion, the burglary did not subject an occupant to the risk of violence, and therefore the only interest at stake on the side of the homeowner was his property. Defending property alone did not justify the use of deadly force against the burglar.

The social theory of self-defense says, in short, that burglars and muggers also have rights, and the rights of the victims must therefore be restricted when their exercise inflicts an excessive cost on those who attack them. It would be fair to say that if the public at large supported this philosophy a generation ago, their feelings about crime and the rights of criminals have shifted dramatically since then.

The international law of armed conflict has not arrived at the stage where states have no right to use force merely to defend their property. No one questioned the right of the United Kingdom to defend their Falkland Islands against Argentine aggression, regardless of the number of their citizens who actually lived there. The same principle would hold with regard to totally unoccupied territorial possessions.

Yet the principles underlying the social conception of self-defense have also penetrated the international law of war, most notably in the evolution of the field know as international humanitarian law. This is the label given to the body of law that has evolved on the basis of the Geneva

---

[12] 116 Cal. Rptr. 233, 526 P2d 241, 12 C.3d 470 (1974).

Conventions of 1949, which laid down the rules of war and generated protection for prisoners of war and civilians not engaged in combat. These are the rules constituting the field of *jus in bello*—defining how wars are properly fought. The basic moral point underlying international humanitarian law is that enemy soldiers are also human beings; when they are sick or taken prisoner, they regain the protection owed to all members of the human species. If civilians never don a uniform or carry a rifle, they are entitled to same basic rights that they always enjoyed. That their nation goes to war does not forfeit their inherent right to be treated as human beings.

As recognizing the humanity of aggressors imposes restrictions on the exercise of defensive force, so does this same moral insight impose restrictions on the way wars are fought. We must never forget that war, aggression, and self-defense represent conflicts among human beings who—from a moral point of view—are created equal. As Lincoln recalled that "all men are created equal" in the midst of the American Civil War, we should never forget that our enemy is essentially "like us."

In the aftermath of September 11, 2001, we encounter a new urgency in working out the proper principles of self-defense to apply in cases of armed conflict with potential terrorists. The lessons we draw from domestic self-defense and from international humanitarian law can aid us in this intellectual and moral quest for the right rules in an era of new dangers. Those who study law as presented here "in a global context" will be the best suited to contribute to the collective ambitions of humankind to live under the rule of law.

Further Reading

On the problem of self-defense, generally see George P. Fletcher, *Basic Concepts of Criminal Law* (Oxford: Oxford University Press, 1998); for a consideration of self-defense as a matter of international law, see Ian Brownlie's new classic book, *International Law and the Use of Force by the States* (Oxford: Oxford University Press, 1982). In a more contemporary context, see George P. Fletcher, *Romantics at War: Glory and Guilt in the Age of Terrorism* (Princeton, NJ: Princeton University Press, 2002), and Steve Sheppard, "Passion and Nation: War, Crime, and Guilt in the Individual and the Collective," 78 *Notre Dame L. Rev.* 761 (2003).

Summary

The Right and the Reasonable

S tudying law in a global perspective has subversive implications. If you are American, you realize that other cultures have other sources of law that are as important to their citizens and lawyers as the U.S. Constitution is to Americans. If you come from abroad and if you are accustomed to thinking history began with the enactment of your civil code in 1804 or 1900, suddenly you find yourself with a new set of historical dates providing points of reference. You have unwittingly absorbed a different history—one that stresses 1776, 1787, 1861, 1868, and 1954 instead of the dates that stand out in your home country's liturgy of legal turning points. In effect, you have experienced a forced adaptation to a new legal culture—something like a required conversion to a new religion. Your sense of what constitutes a sound legal source now includes the ancient common law, the American Constitution, the Uniform Commercial Code, the Model Penal Code, and a new set of concepts such as estates in land, equity, consideration, conversion, and efficiency. Perhaps you now take cases more seriously as a source of law, at least such doctrinal cases as *Marbury*, *McCulloch*, *Erie*, and *Brown*.

In this summary, we plan to retrace our progress from the first chapter to the end and to assess the basic ideas from a different point of view. We are going to explore the general relationship between the Right[1] and the reasonable as it plays out in the subjects covered in the preceding twenty-nine chapters. We need first to clarify the concepts of the Right and the reasonable and then proceed to show how these two ideas have provided the grid on which many of the distinct topics have developed.

The word *Right* is simply a translation of *derecho, droit, Recht, prava, jog, jus*—the notion of law as a higher, unwritten standard of principle. The Right stands for good law, sound law. It is a univocal standard. In any single legal culture, there is only one standard of Right (even if there are debates as to its ultimate content), and indeed that standard is taken to be synonymous with that legal system. Thus we speak of French Right (*Le droit français*) and German Right (*deutsches Recht*).[2]

The Reasonable stands for the possibility of many right answers. Not every answer is right, but a range of answers is acceptable. In the universe of possible answers, there is a subset called "reasonable." The others are unreasonable or, at least, not sufficiently reasonable. The notion of the reasonable as an acceptable range of possibilities between two unreasonable extremes has its roots in the common law jury trial. The judge assigns a case to the jury when reasonable persons might disagree about the facts. If reasonable persons would not disagree in a private law dispute, then the judge directs a verdict, either for the plaintiff or the defendant. In a criminal case, the judge cannot direct a verdict for the prosecution (that would violate the defendant's right to a jury trial) but dismisses the charges if reasonable persons would not disagree that they are unfounded. To be precise, we should refer to this interpretation of reasonableness as the procedural version. As we note later, there is also a substantive interpretation of reasonableness.

The Right assumes a single standard, a single truth. Within the particular legal culture at least, it is the only "right" understanding of justice. By contrast, the reasonable is a recognition of diversity; it's an argument for tolerance; it is an appeal to deference. A legal system that incorporates the reasonable reflects a recognition that there are many acceptable ap-

---

[1] Because the word *right* is not usually used this way, we capitalize the word to highlight its meaning here as "law."

[2] These two concepts of law in European legal cultures are discussed earlier in Chapter Three.

proaches within the framework of what John Rawls would call fair systems of cooperation.[3]

In the past, one of us has argued that the Right is characteristic of Continental legal cultures, and the reasonable, of the modern common law systems.[4] Though this may be a bit of an oversimplification, the tolerance for diverse answers appears to be stronger in the common law tradition, at least in the last two hundred years, than it is in the Continental culture of Right. Yet the situation is changing. The term *reasonable* appears ubiquitously in the Rome Statute establishing the International Criminal Court and in many other international legal documents, particularly those bearing on international trade. *Reasonable* is becoming a fundamental term in international legal discourse, and it carries with it the baggage that we will try to explicate here.

There is one paradox of reasonableness that we should note at the outset. The law of reason leads to a single right answer. As scholars, Edward Coke and William Blackstone appealed to the law of reason as the way of establishing the Right. In contrast, the "reasonable" suggests that different interpreters of the law of reason might legitimately come to different and incompatible conclusions.[5] Blackstone believed in reason, but he was hardly an advocate of the reasonable. With this ambiguity in mind, let us begin to review the cases and debates we have encountered in this journey through the high points of American law.

In the first case considered in this book, *Scott v. Shepherd*, Blackstone as judge argues for a certain conception of trespass in order to defend clear boundaries among the traditional common law causes of action. He seeks to uphold the principle that in trespass one can be liable only for direct—and not for indirect—injuries. Trespass-on-the-case would be available for indirect injuries. He defends this distinction as a dictate of

---

[3] For the implications of reasonableness in Rawls's influential system, see John Rawls, *Political Liberalism* 48–53 (New York: Columbia University Press, 1993) (distinguishing between the reasonable and the rational).

[4] See George P. Fletcher, "The Right and the Reasonable," 98 *Harv. L. Rev.* 949 (1985).

[5] Indeed, the attempt to reduce this degree of freedom in decisions subject to reasonableness has led to some pressure to change its operation as a standard of law. See Steve Sheppard, "The Metamorphoses of Reasonable Doubt: How Changes in the Burden of Proof May Weaken the Presumption of Innocence," 78 *Notre Dame L. Rev.* 1165 (2003).

reason. In this particular case, he does not see the injury as direct because two people picked up the squib and threw it further. Therefore, he insisted on dismissing the writ. The other judges in the case are willing to blur the boundaries between trespass and trespass-on-the-case and to apply more flexible standards that favored liability.

So far as the early common law developed under the influence of Coke and Blackstone, we would have to say that it was a system committed to the Right—to a single right answer, to one law of reason.

In the 1927 abortion case, Chapter Two, we encounter an elaboration on the concept of Right, but in a very peculiar way. The German Supreme Court addresses the meaning of Right but at the same time recognizes that the notion of the Right includes within it the balancing of interests, so that it is permissible to solve the abortion problem by balancing the interests of the mother and the fetus and concluding that the interests of the mother are more important.

In this innovative decision, the German high court concluded that balancing competing interests is inherent in the concept of Right. These are the roots of the view that there are different conceptions of the Right—one based upon reason, the other based upon the balancing of interests. The former follows the teachings of Immanuel Kant; the latter adopts the strategy of Jeremy Bentham.

Public Law

When we turn to the American constitutional experience, we encounter a fluctuation between these two theories. If we start with the Declaration of Independence in 1776, we note that the leaders willing to rebel against England committed themselves to unalienable rights, to the principle that all men are created equal, and to the idea of a social contract. These were people who believed in the Right, in one single answer. This was a concept of Right that they were willing to die for. They were willing to pledge their "sacred honor" for this one single right answer.

But when the Constitution is drafted eleven years later, we encounter a different conception of the legal order. The new conception recognizes the necessity of mutual forbearance, tolerance, and diversity. It is the only way to create a union between slaveholding states and abolitionist states. The necessity of forming a union and recognizing that people have to live together despite different visions of the Right generates a different conception of what a constitution is. It is not committed to a single right answer; it is dedicated to the idea of a union of mutually tolerant, independent forces.

This way of thinking about union was an application in the American context of the general theory of international law developed in the post–Westphalian period in Europe, based on total recognition of diversity, autonomy, and mutual forbearance. The decision not to judge internal affairs in other states required a policy of abstention and tolerance toward what a government is doing to its own citizens and whether it conforms to the Right or not.

The Bill of Rights uses the language of individual rights and sometimes, arguably, of collective rights. Thus the controversial Second Amendment concludes: "The right of the people to keep and bear arms shall not be infringed." Some read these words as pertaining to individual rights to bear weapons, and others claim that they refer to the right of the people collectively to form a "well-regulated militia." The same concept of right (or Right) appears in the first phrase of the Fourth Amendment: "The right of the people to be secure . . . against unreasonable searches and seizure shall not be violated." Here the implication seems to be that the people as a whole possess a right against the kinds of abuse associated with the Writs of Assistance and the British use of general searches during the colonial period.

When we come to two of the landmark cases on judicial review, *Marbury v. Madison*, Chapter Six, and *McCulloch v. Maryland*, Chapter Seven, we suddenly witness a reversion to the principle that there has to be one right answer—one view of the Constitution, one conception of the supreme law of the United States—and that it must prevail over Congress and over the states. After all, what did the state of Maryland claim in the *McCulloch* case? They said, in effect, "We just want to impose a reasonable tax on this bank." And the response of Chief Justice Marshall amounted to the message, "No, we can't trust you to be reasonable. We can't trust you to go only part way—we have to establish that there is one Constitution, and that single Constitution prevails against Congress and against even the slightest assertion of a taxing power by the states."

The advent of the Civil War can be looked upon as the apotheosis of conflicting visions of the Right. One vision upheld the sanctity of the Union—or as others put it, the necessity of emancipating the slaves as a requirement of Right. Both sides could appeal to the Declaration of Independence, and as Abraham Lincoln said in 1864 in his Second Inaugural Address, "both sides prayed to the same God and read the same Bible." They could both claim that they were the heirs to the most authentic part of the American tradition.

The fact that people again were willing to die for their singular visions of the Right—that they had the one, true vision of the Right and that together they were willing to sacrifice 620,000 lives to enshrine it—generated a sharp reaction. In the post–Civil War period, that response gave birth to a new sense of the importance of reasonable accommodation. The great champion of reasonableness was Oliver Wendell Holmes Jr.—whose book *The Common Law*, published in 1881, proclaims the importance of reasonableness in every area of law. The standard for private law, Holmes argued, should not be the judgments of the moral or right-thinking person, but the actions of a reasonable person under the circumstances.

Holmes's goal was to distance the law from moral thinking, which he identified with the commitment to the single right answer. He sought a *modus vivendi*, a way of living together under the rule of law without asserting a morally correct, univocal approach to every problem. Thus the rule of law becomes an arena of diversity and tolerance. This is possible because, according to Holmes, the rule of law emphasizes objective criteria instead of subjective attitudes such as malice and hostile intentions. Chief among the objective criteria are the criteria of reasonableness, for as Holmes emphasizes, the correct approach to legal problems is not the moral answer but the standard set by the average person of the community—the reasonable person. Thus he thought it was possible to define law in a way that was free from the subjectivity of moral arguments, free from the commitment to a single right answer. The shift from morality to reasonableness was intended to signal a way that Northerners and Southerners could once again live together under the same legal system.

As a result of the new commitment to reasonableness, the Supreme Court of the 1870s and 1880s was extremely reluctant to interpret its new constitutional provisions—the Thirteenth, Fourteenth, and Fifteenth Amendments—in a way that would intrude upon the independent autonomy of the states. This explains the civil rights cases in 1883, which in effect limited the impact of the three Reconstruction amendments on the internal affairs of the states and severely limited the influence of the

Fourteenth Amendment's equal protection clause and the Thirteenth Amendment's effort to eliminate not only the formal institution of slavery but also the social residue of involuntary servitude.

The reasonable gives way to the Right, and then the Right yields to the reasonable. This is the way of a sensitive legal culture. The principles of tolerance and mutual accommodation lead to the commitment to a single right Constitution, but the unitary interpretation of the Constitution must surrender, in the aftermath of the Civil War, to a renewed appreciation of states' rights.

It turns out that these two ideas—the reasonable and the Right—are in constant tension. The more you favor reasonableness—or the reasonable—the more you create a situation of potential injustice; in a world of total tolerance, some will be able to commit evil and get away with it. Yet the more you gravitate to the principle of Right, the more you create a situation in which people are willing to go to war over their conflicting ideals.

In the post–Civil War period, when the principle of reasonableness was ascendant, there was also widespread and systematic abuse of emancipated slaves. There was a new evil that had to be addressed. Tolerance came to know its limits.

The boundaries of tolerance that we encountered in the late nineteenth century are the same as those we witness in international affairs today. We may begin with the Westphalian principle of mutual tolerance and forbearance between states, but then we have a problem—what are we going to do about apartheid? What are we going to do about ethnic cleansing in Bosnia? What are we going to do about the evils that occur internal to the lives of the particular states? The more we tolerate diversity and forbearance among states, the greater the risk that some states will abuse their citizens, that apartheid will remain entrenched, and that ethnic cleansing will occur without intervention from the international community. That was the same problem that existed in the United States in the late nineteenth century.

Eventually, the Supreme Court and Congress started intervening. We note that the first case of intervention in criminal justice under the Fourteenth Amendment's due process clause was the 1932 decision in *Powell v. Alabama*, discussed in Chapter Eleven. The seemingly false rape conviction of the black "Scottsboro boys" exceeded the bounds of tolerance. The Court intervened in much the same way the International Criminal

Court feels compelled today to intervene in states that are "unwilling or unable" to do justice within their borders. (But there is this difference: The U.S. Supreme Court began to intervene to protect the rights of the accused; the ICC is authorized to intervene to ensure that justice is done by way of convicting the guilty.) The newly emergent principle of due process established a benchmark of unreasonable state behavior. There was a point of injustice beyond which the states could no longer claim autonomy.

Within the emergent principles of the Fourteenth Amendment, there was a tension building between the newly established imperative of equality under the law and the tradition of protecting freedom dating back to the Constitution of 1789. The commitment to equality is in fact as old as that to freedom and individual rights, both anchored in the Declaration of Independence, but the Bill of Rights chose freedom and rights as the values to be laid at the cornerstone of the new republic. Lincoln rediscovered the principle "all men are created equal" in the Gettysburg Address (1863), and it became anchored in black-letter law in 1868 in the Fourteenth Amendment. The new commitment to equality retreated to the shadows, however, as the end of the nineteenth century witnessed a burst of capitalist individualism. Issues of social justice became less important than building the economy of the United States. Not until the Second World War, when blacks and whites again went to war together, did social justice come front and center as a political issue. In 1954, the Supreme Court finally formulated a principle of constitutional Right in the field of racial justice: By a remarkable unanimous vote, they held that segregation in the schools was inherently unequal and therefore unacceptable under the Fourteenth Amendment.[6] Within a year, however, the same court stepped back from its new standard of Right and decided that progress toward the new ideal need not be immediate. It could proceed at a reasonable pace, advancing "with all deliberate speed."[7] Ten years later, about 2 percent of the nation's schools had blacks and whites sitting together in class.

The dialectic of freedom and equality resembles the give-and-take we have noticed in the tension between the Right and the reasonable. The more one side advances, the stronger its opposite becomes. When

[6] *Brown v. Board of Education*, 347 U.S. 483 (1954).
[7] *Brown v. Board of Education* (II), 349 U.S. 294 (1955).

the Right becomes too strong—if the Court unanimously demands integration as the Right—then the forces of reasonable accommodation assert themselves to modify the dogmatism of the Right. The same is true of freedom and equality. The Constitution of 1789 enshrined freedom and individual rights. In the antebellum period, the reverence for freedom and property went so far as to buttress the argument that free persons were entitled to own slaves.[8] After the Civil War, equality became ascendant. At a certain point, there would have to be a reaction in favor of freedom. American jurisprudence seized upon freedom of speech as the vehicle for preserving as much freedom as possible in the face of egalitarian demands.

Beginning with cases decided after the First World War,[9] freedom of speech and of the press gradually became the anchor for the American conception of freedom. Today the United States protects speech more than does any other Western democracy. This commitment stands in clear contradiction with the equally strong commitment to equality. Some instances of speech—particularly hate speech and the elimination of restrictions on campaign contributions—generate inequalities. But at the same time, valuing free speech might be seen as a confirmation of the democratic process, which affirms the equality of all citizens in their right to vote. The claim for democracy is that the untrammeled right to criticize governmental officials is necessary to a well-functioning system of elections.

Thus the notion of free speech leads us to the supremacy of democracy, which in turn brings us back to the problem of the single right answer. The idea of popular government, with law made by the majority, conflicts with the institution of judicial review and its processes of invalidating the decision of the electorate as a violation of either due process or equal protection of the laws. This is the so-called counter-majoritarian difficulty—the problem of reconciling the judicial enforcement of basic values with popular sovereignty.[10]

Free speech, as recognized in *New York Times v. Sullivan*, Chapter Ten, presents itself as the leading light of American constitutional liberties.

---

[8] *Dred Scott v. Sanford*, 60 U.S. 393 (1857).

[9] *Abrams v. United States*, 250 U.S. 624, 630 (1919) (Holmes, J. dissenting).

[10] Professor Alexander Bickel was well known for drawing attention to this problem in constitutional jurisprudence. See Alexander Bickel, *The Least Dangerous Branch: The Supreme Court at the Bar of Politics* (2d ed) (New Haven, CT: Yale University Press, 1986) (particularly his discussion of Lincoln's rejection of popular sovereignty at p. 67).

Its value radiates either by virtue of its contribution to democratic processes or as the recognition of freedom of expression as an end in itself. In the *Sullivan* case, the Court places a special emphasis on the protection of public officials, an orientation justified by the role of free speech in promoting democratic debate. Later, the case law expanded the range of persons protected from libel suits to include all public figures and celebrities, whether or not they were engaged in politics. The only limitation is actual malice, which is interpreted in Holmesian tradition not as a morally negative posture of ill will or hatred but simply as "reckless disregard of the facts."

In the *Bloom* case, in Chapter Eleven, we note that one of the most fundamental principles to be recognized under the due process clause is the jury trial. What did the jury represent in the minds of judges who concluded that the traditional exemption from jury trials for contempt proceedings should no longer prevail under the Constitution? What, after all, is the function of the common law jury? On the one hand, the institution of jury trials is the province of reasonableness; judges send cases to the jury only if they believe that reasonable people could disagree about the outcome.

At the same time, the right to a jury trial is recognized as fundamental under the due process clause. This right is so basic that, even when the courts were skeptical about the reach of the Fourteenth Amendment, they intervened in state criminal cases to nullify laws that prevented African Americans from serving on juries. This is the message of the *Strauder* case, in Chapter Nine.

Thus we see our two themes intersecting. The jury is the great symbol of reasonable judgment and simultaneously an issue about which there is a single right answer. The Fourteenth Amendment principle of due process requires all states to use jury trials in all cases except petty offenses (punished by less than six months of imprisonment). The reach of this principle is contested today because the president's executive order of November 13, 2001, mandates summary trials without juries for suspected terrorists. That there is controversy about this matter reveals that the great constitutional principles studied in this course are far from settled. They are constantly subject to challenge and redefinition.

The coordination of the state power, coming at the end of our constitutional materials, also fits into the theme of the Right versus the reasonable. The problem in *Pennoyer v. Neff*, in Chapter Thirteen, and in the succeeding cases, is determining the duties of mutual respect incumbent on each state in the Union. How should we determine the potential reach of each state's power? Originally, the Supreme Court relied upon the territorial principle to find an accommodation—this is the same principle as traditionally applied in international criminal law, namely, the territorial principle—and then gradually, in the last fifty years, has moved beyond the territorial principle to start including the extra-territorial application of state law.

The familiar standard of "minimal contacts" recognized in the *International Shoe* case now finds resonance in the disputed arena of universal criminal jurisdiction. Belgium and Germany have recently modified their statutes permitting the application of their laws of war crimes and related offenses, wherever and by whomever committed, by requiring *some* contact with the prosecuting state. This is the European version of the "minimal contacts" theory developed in the American law of state court jurisdiction.

The idea behind the *Pennoyer* case and requirement of minimal contacts is that no single state can dictate the right answer for all others—neither in the American Union nor in the international system. In *Pennoyer*, Oregon could not rule for the entire country. Nor can Germany or Belgium make a decision in a criminal case binding on the whole world.

A similar idea informs the holding in *Gore v. BMW*, in Chapter Twenty-Five, that the Alabama jury could not constitutionally calculate punitive damages as though it were disposing of claims that might be made in the entire country. One state cannot represent the whole and do justice, as though its answer should be the single correct answer for everyone. This was a plea for reasonable accommodation, for recognition that other states must have a say as well. The recognition of multiple jurisdictions implies a duty to defer, to recognize limits. Each state must have a sense of restraint; otherwise, the principles of diversity and tolerance cannot work.

In the *Erie* case, in Chapter Fourteen, we encounter a special extension of this basic American preference for reasonableness over the Right. In *Erie*, the Court holds, both as a matter of statutory interpretation and as constitutional analysis, that the rules of decision in diversity-of-citizenship cases must be based on the written and unwritten laws of every state. This means that the federal court will not follow federal common law if there is a state common law on point, as there is in all private law disputes. This decision exemplifies Holmes's philosophy that "the common law is not a brooding omnipresence in the sky."[11] It is not a single theory of Right, in the Blackstonian sense, but a diverse system of individual governments, each adopting its own interpretation of the common law. Each interpretation of the common law is to be recognized as fully valid and binding, governing the decisions in that particular case.

Private Law

When we move from the area of public law to private law, the basic thesis on the conflict between the Right and the reasonable holds, but it requires some modification. There are admittedly some problems in understanding how the feudal theory of property fits into the system. Our approach to the law of real property seems to be based on respect for tradition as a distinct value—neither Right nor reasonable, but anchored in the contingent solutions of questions past.

Yet, in fact, the system of property is transposed in the founding of the American republic. It is not simply a set of categories and conveyancing techniques that we must live with because they have used from "time immemorial." In the American agrarian society of the eighteenth century, real property became the source of the liberal theory of individual autonomy. Property holders acquired the right to vote (at least if they were male citizens). Real property became the mainstay of the democratic commitment at the local level.

In the analysis of private law, the notions of the Right and reasonable are slightly transformed. The Right comes to stand for private right and individual autonomy. Reasonableness becomes the touchstone of the social interest, of balancing social cost and social benefit (very much as the 1927 German abortion case did in calculating the Right under German law). We can see this general theme—of autonomy and private rights in conflict with the public interest—running through all the cases on private law we have examined.

In the first case—the *Heller* case, Chapter Seventeen—the conflict is

---

[11] *Southern Pacific Co. v. Jensen*, 244 U.S. 205, 222 (1917) (Holmes, J. dissenting).

dramatic. Heller had a pond on his land and wanted to go swimming. He was arrested and imprisoned because he violated a state law designed to protect the water supply from contamination—surely a reasonable legislative objective. Heller's argument was basically a claim of private right. He argued, in effect, "This is my land and I should have the right to go swimming in my water." The notion of reasonable regulation of land took precedence over the notion of private right. Heller was denied compensation for the public use of his land and, in addition, he was imprisoned, even though he had a good faith claim of right—namely, that he had a right to swim in a body of water located on his own land.

The conflict between private right and public reasonableness helps us understand the way equity enters the law and supplements the common law of property and private rights. On the one hand, it appears that equity represents a movement away from rigidified categories of law in favor of a single right answer—the answer dictated by reason. If equity were not right, how could it claim to prevail over law, as its institutions ultimately did? This view of equity may be correct in regard to the seventeenth-century attitudes that motivated the conflict between Lords Coke and Ellesmere, depicted in Chapter Sixteen.

In the course of time, however, the concept seems to have evolved to mean something more like "reasonable." Thus in the *Malnar* case, Chapter Sixteen, in which the dentist's building encroaches on the plaintiff's property, the court uses the term *equitable* to refer to the balancing of the competing interests. The question is whether Malnar's interests in the driveway were so important relative to the value of the building that it would be justifiable to tear down the building just to protect his private right. And the answer was, no. The court reasoned that there had to be an equitable solution—and the equitable solution turns out to be the reasonable solution.

The term *equity* becomes a mixed, transitional category, starting with the notion of a commitment to a right answer but coming to be used as meaning something like "reasonable." It is not reasonable to tear down a building just to secure the right to a few inches of private property. Compensation is a viable solution. It is easy to see this if we balance the competing interests.

In the same way, we find that in the *Boomer* case, in Chapter Seventeen, the court is willing to balance the competing interests and decide that the cement factory can continue polluting—but it is going to require compensation as the compromise position. Again, the notion of the public good is in conflict with the notion of private right.

According to Robert Nozick, private rights are established in three distinct ways: acquiring ownership of property, making a contract to transfer property, and being injured by someone else's fault.[12] The public good is expressed in adjusting private rights, as in the *Heller, Malnar,* and *Boomer* cases, and thus recognizing that no one has an absolute claim to the Right. All rights are subject to the principle of reasonableness, to the principle of the common good.

In this scheme of things we can better understand the liberal theory of contract, which corresponds to Nozick's second category. Two people make an agreement, and they become a law unto themselves. Their contract, as the French civil code says, takes the place of the statutory law. It sanctifies the reciprocal transfer of property and services.

The reaction against the liberal theory comes from many different directions. One kind of assault is evident in Cardozo's opinion in *Jacob & Youngs v. Kent,* the famous American case about whether the person contracting for a home can insist on the installation of a specific brand of pipe as stipulated in the contract, even if this performance would lead to inordinate expense for the builder. Cardozo reasons, in effect, "Look, you have a right under the contract to have a certain brand of pipe—but let's be reasonable. The builder installed pipe equivalent in value to the one you specified, and the mistake was hardly willful. Therefore, you cannot expect him to pull out those pipes and replace them exactly as you want." If there was to be an adjustment, it would have to be in monetary terms, based on actual damages. That is reasonableness at work. We need to adjust rights in recognition of their value to the respective parties. But seeking this adjustment implies the abandonment of private right, strictly construed. Contract does not always define the law between the parties, or if it does, then the law must be reasonably interpreted.

In this context of debate about property and contracts, we should have trouble understanding the doctrine of *culpa in contrahendo.* How exactly does it fit? *Culpa in contrahendo* is not exactly a matter of private right, nor is it an idea that serves the public good—unless there's some public good in recognizing that people are somehow reciprocally com-

---

[12] Robert Nozick, *Anarchy, State and Utopia* 149–276 (New York: Basic Books, 1977).

mitted to each other as a result of engaging in negotiations. The notion
that somehow you acquire obligations as a result of being in a negotiating
situation comes from someplace else. It comes from some idea that we
are part of the same community. By virtue of being members of the same
community—even a community created by negotiations—we have obligations toward each other.

Thus we return to the basic values underlying feudalism. In the feudal
structure, your station in life, your position in the feudal chain, defines
your obligations. The same communitarian idea accounts for Lincoln's
view of Southern secession. The Southern states were units within a
nation, a nation that he described in the Gettysburg Address as being
indivisible "under God." Their status precluded their separation. They
were bound to be loyal to the Union. Although this is not a liberal idea,
there are some situations in life where your very status generates duties
of loyalty and subordination.

The liberal view is that you bear duties only as the result of your
personal choices. The social contract is based on choice, at least on a
hypothetical contractual commitment with others to surrender some liberties in return for governmental order and stability. But these obligations
that arise from being in the same community with others come from a
different source. Imposing these obligations is not in the liberal spirit of
contract and private choice. Liability for *culpa in contrahendo* does not
conform to the idea of private right. Nor does it serve the public good.
They are in the nature of individual duties of loyalty based on family and
community. This is the idea that Rudolf von Jhering had when he su-
perimposed the communitarian idea of *culpa in contrahendo* on the liberal
theory of contract.

Against the background of these ideas, how should we resolve the
controversy in the *Moore* case, presented in Chapter Eighteen? How
should we think about Moore's rights after his spleen is removed in a
nominally consensual operation, and then it turns out that the doctors
had failed to disclose relevant information to him and had acquired a
patent with profits in the range of $3 billion?

The *Moore* case engages us in a struggle to find the right categories
to express our intuitions of justice. Should we talk about the public good?
Or should we talk about private rights based upon property in a consensually removed spleen? Should we invoke a fiduciary duty of physician
to patient to reveal research purposes extrinsic to the operation at issue?

In the *Moore* case, we encounter conflicts among all of these ideas. How do we work that out? What is the idea that should prevail? Finding the most appropriate doctrinal structure is hardly easy, but the quest honors us as legal artists, as lawyers who are committed to thinking about fundamental issues in order to solve a problem.

Our inclination in thinking about the *Moore* case is to favor the theory of conversion—the property theory—because it would allow Moore to participate in some approximate way in the benefits of the exploitation. The California Supreme Court rejects this approach, but its authority hardly disposes of the philosophical problem.

To use the property theory here is to build on the distinction made in earlier chapters between the theory of damages in torts and in property. The principle of compensable damage is measured in tort by the personal loss. The measure of damages in property is the lost opportunity to exploit your property. If you're deprived of that opportunity, then you can claim what you would have received, had you exploited your interest in property. These two forms of damage correspond to the reliance interest and the benefit-of-the-bargain damages in contracts.

The wrong of which Moore complains is not a damage to his interests but rather the deprivation of an opportunity to exploit the economic value of his spleen. He is not harmed by the operation—on the contrary. But had he known of the plan to develop and patent the cell line, he would have insisted on a share of the profits. Because the physicians did not reveal their plans, he suffered the loss of that opportunity. The assumption seems to be that the genetic relationship between Moore's body and the cell line gave him a claim, an intuitive moral claim, to participate in the profits of the patented cell line.

In contract law, as we have seen, the theory of damages lends itself to a conflict between the negative (or reliance) interest and the positive (or benefit-of-the-bargain) interest. The negative interest corresponds to damages in tort law, and the positive, to damages in the deprivation of property. The *Hawkins* case, in Chapter Twenty-One, recognizes that the patient who had an operation to "get a perfect hand"—and who, instead, got a badly damaged hand—had a right to the hand that would have existed, had the operation been effectively carried out. That was a property theory based on recognizing the positive interest, or the benefit-of-the-bargain, as a basis of liability. The patient was not harmed relative to the way he was. He was harmed only relative to the way he would have been, had the opportunity promised in the contract been realized.

Before moving on from contracts and back to torts, we must think about the way the requirement of consideration fits into the structure we have proposed. This is not easy because for lawyers in the common law tradition, whether consideration should be required or abandoned is not an open question. It is just assumed, as though there were no other way to think about binding contracts. The way to think about the subject is to recall Holmes's effort to disengage the law of moral thinking and subjective states.

As developed in Holmes's theory of contract, the critical factor in contract formation was not the promise to be bound. This is the way German and French writers of the same period thought about contract, but the emphasis on the will to be bound struck Homes as too moralistic. Therefore, the notion of a binding contract had to be based on something other than the promise to perform. It had to be grounded in something that occurred in public space. That which occurs in the public eye is arguably the reciprocal inducement to enter into the contract. Reciprocal inducement is the essence of consideration. (The truth is that this element of reciprocal inducement also requires an assessment of subjective states and motivation.)

The principle of reciprocal inducement led to the provision in the First Restatement of Contracts in 1932, grounding consideration in a bargained-for performance. If the reciprocal performance is not bargained for, then it cannot be consideration. If there is no consideration, there is no contract.

We know this to be true, but there is an enormous exception, also enacted in the First Statement, called "detrimental reliance" under Section 90. In the *Pfeiffer* case, in Chapter Nineteen, the plaintiff's company promised her a pension of $200 a month when she should retire; when she does retire, there comes a manager who does not know her and claims, "I'm not paying any more—this is a gift, and I can revoke the gift." The court says in effect, "You're right—as a matter of contract theory and consideration—and you're not right, but under Section 90, the plaintiff should nonetheless be protected." You could describe this result as a principle of private right based on justifiable reliance. It is not an argument based on the public good. The plaintiff is wronged as a private person because she is induced to rely on a promise and she suffers a loss. She alone is injured, and she collects under the theory of private right.

In tort law, we encounter the greatest conflict between the general theory of the public good—reasonableness—and the general theory of the private right. The public good is expressed in the economic interpretation of negligence, which begins with the Learned Hand test, based upon the balancing of interests. In this context there arise several contradictions that warrant our attention. One contradiction is between the idea that there is a single right answer and the idea that we balance the benefits and burdens. The Learned Hand formula turns out to be exactly the same as the principle of Right applied by the German court in the 1927 abortion case, in Chapter Two. Theoretically, there is only one correct way to balance the conflicting interests. If you know the costs and the benefits of the conduct, you know whether it is reasonable. This sense of the "reasonable" coincides with the principle of Right.

As applied in *Vincent v. Lake Erie*, in Chapter Twenty-Two, this would mean there is only one correct answer to the question whether it was reasonable or socially useful to keep the ship moored to the dock during the storm. But this idea of a single correct assessment of reasonableness is incompatible with the principles underlying the jury system. Cases go to the jury only if reasonable people can disagree about the result. That means that there are many reasonable answers, many right results—not just one. The economic, interest-balancing interpretation of reasonableness thus stands in contradiction with the institutional function of the jury.

The conflict between a single right answer and many rights is a replay of the basic tension in economic theory between the Benthamite[13] calculus of costs and benefits and the Hayekian[14] school, holding that there are many right answers based upon individual choice in the market. The sense of efficiency that we explored in the chapter on economics corresponds to these schools of thought. Bentham's view of efficiency requires a balancing of costs and benefits; Hayek's view holds that efficiency is determined by voluntary exchange in the market.

However one assesses the reasonableness of the ship owner's behavior

[13] After the English philosopher Jeremy Bentham (1748–1832).
[14] After the Austrian economist Frederick von Hayek (1899–1992).

in the *Vincent* case, the judgment turns out to be based on different grounds. Negligence and the standard of reasonableness give way to another principle—a compromise between property rights and the principle of compensation for injury. The best guide to this compromise is the *Boomer* case, in Chapter Seventeen, which should be understood as a private law version of eminent domain, a recognition that anyone who takes the property of another—or causes damage to it—must pay for it. Unfortunately, if this principle were strictly applied in every case of causing damage, it would totally displace the general rule that those who damage are liable only if they have acted negligently (or unreasonably).

The theory of reasonableness leads us back invariably to the jury system. And in that context we cannot ignore the importance of the criminal law, which we saw illustrated in the *Goetz* case, in Chapter Twenty-Eight. Many people are understandably upset about the outcome in the *Goetz* case. There are disturbing outcomes in most of the high-profile cases of recent years. Think of the acquittal of O. J. Simpson or of the four Los Angeles police officers in the state trial in the Rodney King case. It is hard to recall a major case in recent years that has not, in effect, put the jury system on trial.

But we are inclined to think differently about jury verdicts depending on whether we start from the idea of Right as a single right answer or from the idea of the reasonable as a recognition of many right answers. If you start from the principle of the Right, then you expect justice in every case. The thought of not doing justice becomes intolerable. If you start from the notion of the reasonable, then you can tolerate imperfect justice. We do not always know what justice is. Thus we have the jury to resolve disputes where reasonable people can disagree about the facts and about what justice requires. The jury is the "black box" of American legal culture. The facts are fed into it, and an answer comes out. A system with this kind of uncertainty is possible only in a world where skepticism and tolerance are more important than an absolute faith in finding the right result in every case.

The inconsistencies of the jury system do not disturb us as American lawyers. They are a small price to pay for tolerance and diversity in the legal culture. If we must choose between the distortions of the Right and the distortions of reasonableness, the latter are more appealing. The search for a single right answer may be a healthy heuristic, a sound discipline to force us to take justice seriously, but the compulsion to do Right in every case leads, in private law, to a system of absolute rights that ignores the countervailing values of accommodation. Strict right means that you can always swim on your own land, force others to remove valuable structures that mistakenly encroach an inch onto your property, and demand complete adherence to the letter of every contract. The values of reasonableness go hand in hand with the institution of the jury, which recognizes a range of acceptable right answers and the importance of flexibility and adaptation to the interests of the parties.

There is one further contradiction that arises from thinking about reasonableness as the balancing of interests. If you act upon the public good—if you follow the Benthamite calculus—you run into precisely the problem we encountered in *Pennoyer* and in *Gore v. BMW*, namely, the question whether a single jurisdiction can rule for the entire universe. This overreaching results from the nature of cost-benefit analysis, which must take into consideration the implications of the action for the entire world. Consider the problem in the *Boomer* case. Pollution crosses boundaries. When you make a decision about pollution in New York, you cannot leave out the cost imposed on people and property in Connecticut. The impact on Canada also becomes relevant. If you are going to do an accurate cost-benefit analysis, you must consider the long–range benefits and costs for the whole world.

But if you do that, then you violate the principle that every court in a democratic polity should think first of all about its own people. Every court is a public institution limited by the principle of national sovereignty. Judges are chosen or elected to uphold the constitution of the state and to favor the local law. Their duty, therefore, is to think about the interests of the local population, not those of the entire world.

And here is one additional wrinkle in the dangers of pursuing efficiency to the point of insisting that every citizen act reasonably all the time. At one point in the *Goetz* case, prosecutor Gregory Waples said, "I suggest a solution for the defendant [is] to pack his bags and go somewhere else where his fragile sensibilities will not be so easily assaulted."[15] Shortly thereafter, one of the jurors was overheard saying, "This guy is insulting my intelligence."[16] Waples did not mean to insult anyone's in-

---

[15] George P. Fletcher, *A Crime of Self-Defense: Bernhard Goetz and the Law on Trial* 179 (New York: Free Press, 1988).
[16] Fletcher, *A Crime of Self-Defense* 179.

telligence; he was just applying the principle of efficiency. If Goetz was unhappy, he was, as Guido Calabresi would say, the cheapest cost avoider.[17] He should have gone someplace else. But that juror was reacting to an intuitive understanding that having rights means that you are entitled to act unreasonably. Everyone has the right to walk in Central Park at midnight, even if the risk of mugging surely outweighs the pleasures of the night air. Every citizen in the 1980s had the right to live in New York—and also to complain that the life in the city was intolerable.

In the world today, we face an increasing and intensified debate about these issues. At the same time that we want to live together tolerantly as representatives of different countries and legal cultures, we are also committed to human rights. We believe in accommodation and mutual respect, but we will not tolerate apartheid or ethnic cleansing. In many areas, we believe we know what the Right is and we will insist that the Right prevail. We are drawn, therefore, into the ongoing tension between the values of the reasonable and the imperatives of Right. At the international level, we are still trying to solve the conflict that, as we have seen, runs through the course of American law and all domestic legal systems.

---

[17] Guido Calabresi, *Costs of Accidents: A Legal and Economic Analysis* 138 (New Haven, CT: Yale University Press, 1970).

Appendices

These appendices are designed to give you the basic information and tools of lawyering. They are not exhaustive, but they should spur you to consider not only the information and methods presented but also how you would develop these methods for your own practice of the law.

APPENDIX ONE

How to Read (and Brief) a Case

Beginning with Chapter One, this book requires you to read case opinions. We have raised many questions about the opinions we have given you to read in these chapters, and we hope that both these questions and the opinions themselves have encouraged you to ask many more questions. Each case, each opinion, reflects a nearly unlimited range of inquiry regarding not only how the judge stated the case must be decided as it was but also why the historical development, cultural significance, political environment, or a thousand other influences on the question posed by the dispute of the parties would create the conditions for the judge to believe—or at least, to say—so.

In these chapters, we attempt not only to help you to see this richness of inquiry in each case of American law but also to encourage you to compare this result with alternatives—in particular, the alternative results or methods employed in other major legal systems, such as the family of legal systems we routinely think of as those of civil law. It is, we think, never enough merely to accept the result of a legal decision as a fact, without consideration of how it was derived from the arguments of law and how a better decision might have been made.

This level of historical, comparative, jurisprudential, and linguistic analysis is not always pursued in legal education. American law schools often present cases as the result of a process yielding one result, which is then treated as an immutable rule. Although it is possible to redact a rule or a group of rules from a case and, as we shall see, this can require some art, this redaction should not blind you to the choices that are made in the construction of the arguments the case represents. (See Appendix Two: Common Law Method.) Chapter Two introduced you to a narrower method of case analysis. In that method, the opinion of a judge is examined to determine the *ratio decidendi*, the rationale for the decision, which is the most essential chain of reasoning from premises of law and of fact to the conclusion. The precedent required, so goes the theory, is limited to later situations of similar facts, in which case only the *ratio* is to be applied to those facts to reach whatever result is required.

This division of *ratio* from *dicta* has become widely accepted and influenced the teaching of many law professors employing the case method of instruction, which we introduced you to in the first chapter. This method has been increasingly based on a focused pattern of case analysis, intended to generate a *brief* of each case opinion. This brief is written by the student, who dissects the opinions into categories—facts, issue presented, analysis, judgment, dissents. (Different teachers require additional categories, such as "procedure" or "claim presented" or "rule.") Among some professors, these five categories form the predicate to a rich and wide-ranging discussion of all of those considerations of history, comparative law, jurisprudence, culture, linguistics, and textual analysis that the opinion demands in the context of the course. On the other hand, this does not always happen, and all too many professors use a quiz approach to the dialogue, merely to have students read briefs to the class as the basis for nearly all of their discussion of the case. Students often grow to like the quiz method, which looks superficially like the robust case discussion that develops so many tools of case analysis and criticism.[1] The quiz approach rewards students' prior work through public discussion. It also challenges their skills to very little development during the class, thus diminishing the chance for embarrassment of the student who is asked a difficult question and has no answer to hand. The requirement of disciplined briefing, or any note-taking regimen for that matter, is not in

---

[1] On the development of the quiz method from the case method, see Steve Sheppard, "Casebooks, Commentaries, and Curmudgeons: An Introductory History of Law in the Lecture Hall," 82 *Iowa L. Rev.* 547 (1997).

itself the reason that class discussions may collapse into little more than their review, and many rich discussions can commence with the essentials as the theme from which all the variations will follow.

Regardless of the role case briefing plays in your own experience of legal education, we suspect you will need to know how to do it. What follows are two examples of briefs. The first is for *Scott v. Shepherd*, which we explored more thoroughly in Chapter One. The second is for *Bloom v. Illinois*, which we discussed with an emphasis on its role as a part of the constitutional history of the jury in Chapter Nine.

Compare these briefs to the opinions. Notice how each component is condensed, and notice also the risks of omission that are run by such condensation. These briefs attempt to include the information sufficiently but in a manner that will be accessible later. Try to avoid writing so little that what is needed is omitted, on the one hand, and on the other hand writing so much that you have really only transcribed the original opinion, which may not be an efficient use of your time or helpful when you are later reviewing your work.

Usually facts in a brief are best organized in chronological order, which is rarely the order they are written in the opinions. (Notice that some facts are brought up from the opinions of Nares and Blackstone to fill in the facts as Blackstone wrote them in the report.)

There are many means of organizing the analysis. The two most common approaches are to number the points made in the order the judge wrote them or to gather the various points into clusters by topic or issue.

In any case, beware of artificial limits on length. Try to avoid making briefs fit on one side or sheet of paper, and do not let yourself fall into the habit of reducing complicated facts or issues into one sentence for no reason. Write notes for your later use, making them reasonable, pithy, and clear reductions from the original. Be willing to add your own thoughts and criticisms—but be sure they are so clearly different from the notes of the original that you will not be confused when reviewing them later, when your memory has faded or your method might have evolved to new patterns of note taking.

One last point about starting your own brief: Before writing your case brief, you should read the opinions in the case from start to finish. Not only will you learn the issue and the facts better but also you will begin to see the points of conflict among different approaches to the issues, whether the differences are presented by the litigants or by different judges on the court. If you have difficulty understanding the reasoning or the facts, or even the outcome, you should both reread the case and, preferably, read it in its unedited form in the case reports that are cited for the case. Remember, in this book—as in most casebooks—the cases are edited both to remove extraneous issues from the readings and to make them shorter, and often the opinion is easier to understand in its fuller composition.

Sample Brief One

Scott v. Shepherd, King's Bench (England), 2 Blackstone 892. 96 Eng. Rep. 525 (1773).

Facts

> Oct. 28, 1770, Fair-day at Milbourne Port.
> Shepherd (Δ) threw lit gunpowder squib into the covered market.
> Squib fell on "standing [market stall] of Yates."
> Willis picked up squib & threw it away from Yates's wares.
> Squib falls into standing of Ryal, who also throws it out.
> Squib hits Scott (π) in face, where it (explodes?) putting out his eye
> π struck on face and lost one eye.

Procedural History

> $\pi \rightarrow \Delta$ for trespass and assault, alleging Δ threw squib "at and against"π.
> Δ pled Not Guilty.
> Jury trial at Bridgwater Assizes, Nares, J.
> Jury awards π verdict of £100, contingent on successful appeal to KB.
> Appeal to KB.

Issues Presented

Is throwing a squib into a crowd or at one person actionable if it hits another person not aimed at, causing injury, in either trespass or assault?

Analysis

Nares, J.: Trespass OK.

1. Injury of somebody "natural and probable consequence of the act done" so act was illegal at common law.
2. Throwing of squibs barred by stat. W.3. Since made nuisance.
3. △ liable for consequences of injury "mediate or immediate."
4. *Malus animus* (evil intent) not necessary to trespass after 21 H. 7 28.

De Grey, C.J.: Trespass OK.

1. Trespass v. Action on the Case, line is "very nice and delicate."
2. Trespass = injury accompanied with [resulting from?] force.
3. Action of trespass *vi et armis*[2] lies against the person from whom trespass is received.
4. Agree with Blackstone on principles but not application here.
5. Issue, is injury the "direct and immediate act of the defendant"? Yes.
6. Throwing the squib *unlawful* and *tending* to affright bystanders.
7. Mischief was intended; not particular but indiscriminate and wanton.
8. Thrower is author of whatever mischief therefore follows.
9. Applies criminal law doctrine of author of later mischief *Egreditur personam* (It goes out from him),[3] (9B) BUT criminal cases not rule civil (9C) BUT in trespass there is analogy.
10. "Every one who does an unlawful act is considered as the doer of all that follows . . .
11. if done with a deliberate intent, the consequence may amount to murder;
12. if incautiously, to manslaughter." See Fost. 261.
13. Trespass for man hurt by horse being broken 1 Ventr. 295.
14. *Scienter* (knowledge of result) not required 2 Lev. 172.
15. "All that was done subsequent to the original throwing [was] a

---

[2] "Trespass with force and arms," from the Law French, in which *vi* was pronounced "vay." The form of trespass for damages caused by the defendant by any force or violence against either the plaintiff or the plaintiff's property.

[3] Literally: "It goes out from that person." In other words, that person caused it.

continuation of the first force and first act, which will continue till the squib was spent by bursting . . .

16. any innocent person removing the danger from himself to another is justifiable; the blame lights upon the first thrower."

17. (Contra Blackstone) "The new direction and new force flow out of the first force, and are not a new trespass."

18. Willis and Ryal NOT free agents but compelled by safety and self-preservation.

Gould, J., Trespass OK (described in de Gray)

Judgment

(3 to 1) For π (Scott). Trespass OK.

Rule

$\triangle$ liable to π in trespass for injuries that are "natural and probable result" but not immediate result of $\triangle$'s wrongful actions, regardless of whether $\triangle$ intended or knew that π would be injured.

Dissent

Blackstone, J., Trespass *not* OK.

1. When injury immediate, trespass. When injury consequential, action on the case required.

2. Trespass does not depend on lawful or unlawful nature of act. (*Reynolds v. Clark*)

2A. criticizes report of Raymond, J. in Stra. 635 *contra.*

3. Trespass was against Yates, not Ryal or Scott.

4. Tort complete when squib "lay at rest upon Yates' stall."

5. Yates or bystander had right to remove squib but duty to protect others in doing so.

6. Shepherd "not answerable in an action of trespass and assault for the mischief done by the squib in the (6A) new motion impressed upon it, and the new direction given it, by either Willis or Ryal; (6B) who both were free agents, *and* (6C) acted upon their own judgment."

7. Different from cases of letting loose wild beasts or madmen. (8A) They are only instruments in the hand of the first agent.

8. Different from cases of diverting an enraged ox, ricochet of a stone

or arrow. (9A) because there the original motion, the *vis impressa*,[4] is continued, though diverted. (9B) Instrumentality here at rest until "new impetus and a new direction are given it" (9C) in this case twice.

9. *Contra*—act not complete—squib not at rest—till fizzle or explosion.

> True that squib has potential of fresh mischief, like rock at rest.
> But rock only dangerous if moved, and then action will be
>   against mover.
> Yates could sue Shepherd.
> Counter argument fails for Scott as π.

10. Three actions (at law) for one act would extend liability "in infinitum."

> [Ex: A tosses football into street, 100 people kick it, store window broken. Can store sue A? No, only guy who kicked it into window.]

11. Shepherd has action against Ryal, "immediate actor."

12. Ryal & Willis exceeded self-defense; did not use "sufficient circumspection in removing the danger from themselves." Suggests, they were continuing the sport but "at least unnecessary and incautious."

13. Menaces do not justify a trespass against 3d party.

14. Shepherd not responsible for acts of other men.

15. Lord Raymond (*Reynolds v. Clarke*): "We must keep up the boundaries of actions, otherwise we shall introduce the utmost confusion."

■

---

[4] Literally, "The force that strikes."

Sample Brief Two

∎

Bloom v. Illinois,

U.S. Sp. Ct., 391 U.S. 194 (1968).

Facts

> Bloom made a false Will after another's death.
> Illinois charges him with criminal contempt of court.
> Bloom makes demand for jury trial. Demand refused.
> Judge sentences Bloom to 24 months for contempt.

Procedural History

Petition for habeas corpus. Denied below.

Issues Presented

Does the DPC of the XIV Am. require states to accord 6 Am. right to jury trial to defendant in contempt of court proceeding when △ gets 24 months?

Rules in Issue

> Art III, § 2 "Trial of all Crimes, except in Cases of Impeachment, shall be by Jury. . . ."
> 6 Am. "in all criminal prosecutions, the accused shall enjoy the right to a speedy and public trial, by an impartial jury. . . ."
> DPC 5 Am. Fed. Govt cannot deprive "life, liberty, or property, without due process of law."
> DPC 14 Am. State govt. cannot deprive "life, liberty, or property, without due process of law."
> *Duncan v. Louisiana*, 391 U.S. 145 (1968): states under 6 Am. Rt to Jury Trial in "serious cases."
> *United States v. Barnett*, 376 U.S. 681 (1964), criminal contempt may require a jury trial.

Analysis

WHITE, J.

> 1. Before Barnett, DPC and 6 Am. construed to allow summary trials in contempt cases because (1A) at common law contempt was tried

without a jury and (1B) the power of courts over contempt was necessary to run courts and establish justice.

2. *Michaelson v. U.S.* 266 U.S. 42 (1924), rejected contempt power as inherent in courts and beyond congressional interference.

3. Barnett held jury not required in all contempts, but did not consider severe punishments.

4. *Cheff v. Schnackenberg*, 384 U.S. 373 (1966), 6 mos. in prison for contempt of a federal court was "petty offense." No jury trial required.

5. "Criminal contempt is a petty offense unless the punishment makes it a serious one."

6. Contempt is a crime. See Holmes, *Gompers v. United States*, 233 U.S. 604, 610 (1914).

7. There is no difference between crime of contempt and other crimes.

8. Prosecutions of other crimes are subject to constitutional protection.

9. Constitutional protections apply to contempts.

10. Contempt already limited to prevent abuse by judge.

10A. Judiciary Act of 1789; § 17 gave federal courts broad power to find contempt. Judge James Peck nearly impeached and Act of 1831 limited contempt power to actual interruption of court or its business. See *Nye v. United States*, 313 U.S. 33, 47-52 (1941);

10B. Lawyers not subject to summary trial for contempt. *Cammer v. U.S.*, 350 U.S. 399 (1956).

10C. 1st Am. bars contempt for most out-of-court conduct. *Bridges v. California*, 314 U.S. 252 (1941).

10D. Punishments must be authorized by statute and must not be too harsh.

11. "Our experience" [10A-D] shows contempt "indistinguishable" from other crimes.

12. "If the right to jury trial is a fundamental matter in other criminal cases, which we think it is, it must also be extended to criminal contempt cases."

13. *Contra*—Independent judiciary, respect for judges and courts, need for speed and efficiency require unfettered discretion. Rejected.

14. Fed. R. Crim. Pro. 42(a) allows summary trial for contempt "if the judge certifies that he saw or heard the conduct constituting

the contempt and that it was committed in the actual presence of the court." Fine for petty offense [= penalty of fine or less than a year in jail].

Judgment

Reversed and Remanded

Rule

Sixth Amendment right to jury trials applies to crime of contempt of court in state courts for trials for serious penalties.

Concurring

Fortas: emphasizes the right to jury trial as essential to due process.

Dissent

Harlan with Stewart (dissented in *Duncan* and *Barnett*).
Mere location of rule in Bill of Rights not enough to show rule is fundamental to fairness or in original understanding of the XIV Am.

■

Further Reading

There are many texts written to guide students both in reading a case and in writing briefs. Many of these books promote a terser description of the analysis than we would recommend. The best books on case reading that we know are Karl Llewellyn, *The Bramble Bush: On Our Law and Its Study* (New York: Oceana, 1951), and Eugene Wambaugh, *The Study of Cases* (1892) (Boston: Little, Brown, 1981). Both are somewhat dated, but both reflect a more thorough approach than any we have seen lately.

Common Law Method; or, How to Do Things with Cases

There are many theories of common law method, which are the forms common lawyers employ in argument, whether to make a case as a lawyer or to write an opinion as a judge. Some of these theories have been developed by teachers of the common law, and some developed by its critics, all attempting to show how common law reasoning works. At the heart of them all, however, are the dual recognitions that the common law employs the tools of reason, which are easy to explain, but in a particular manner that is often hard to explain. When Sir Edward Coke described the "artificial reason of the law," he did not mean that the law did not use reason but that it used particular tools of reason according to long-established customs. Thus, even though the tools can be described, only practice in a community of other lawyers can develop the instinct that makes the tools work well.

For our purposes in this summary, we consider common law argument through the use of three tools, each subject to limits by the customs and practices of the community of lawyers practicing the common law. These tools can be described in the ancient logical categories of premises, reasoning, and conclusions.

Premises

Common law argument proceeds from two forms of premise: fact and authority. Very nearly all legal arguments must commence with the establishment of premises of both kinds. The basic structure of legal argument—whether common law, civilian, or any other kind—must support some statement that provides a reason to act according to the law, and this reason must turn on the application of some authority to some facts.

An important qualification to this understanding arises from the many arguments over what the appropriate authority is in a given situation. It hardly matters whether, like some authors, one considers the existence of a legal authority to be a fact or, like other authors, one treats the existence of an authority as an argument from authority. If precedent A supports one rule and precedent B supports a contradictory rule, some authority—such as a rule governing the priority of precedents—will be necessary to select either A or B, and it makes little difference if one describes this analysis as the application of an authoritative premise to a factual premise, or as the application of an authoritative premise to another authoritative premise.

Much of the enterprise of legal argument is concerned with what is authority. Certainly, for the purposes of the simplest arguments of the common law, authority includes precedent, the prior opinions of judges ruling on cases before them. It also includes statutes, which are discussed briefly in Appendix Three. It includes many other sources of law, including constitutional provisions, regulations, opinions of attorneys general, and the writings of scholars. Although their use is more controversial and may not be as persuasive, authority may also include arguments from public policy, economics, and other social sciences, forms of authority famously employed by Louis Brandeis before he became a Supreme Court justice.[1] Of course, none of this can determine what authority is the most persuasive. Such decisions are the result of arguments.

The most common use of legal argument from both factual and au-

---

[1] See Louis D. Brandeis, *Scientific Management and Railroads: Being Part of a Brief Submitted to the Interstate Commerce Commission* (Hive Management History Series, No. 82) (Easton, Penn.: Hive Pub. Co., 1980); Herbert Hovenkamp, "Social Science and Segregation Before Brown," *Duke L.J.* 624 (1985).

thoritative premises can be seen in examples. Imagine the premises for "Sam is speeding."

As a matter of legal argument, this statement is a conclusion. Even if it might appear to be a simple observation, it is necessarily the result of a set of premises properly analyzed to reach this statement.

"Sam is speeding" is based on a premise of fact—Sam's speed—and a premise of authority: The law requires a driver where Sam is driving to drive no more than a certain limit. Without either premise—the speed and the limit—no legal conclusion could be drawn. From these premises, the simple analysis of comparing the fact with the authority allows the conclusion. (Notice that some choices must be made regarding the degree of specificity needed to depict the authority in the manner that will be the most useful. There are many such choices in determining not only what premises to assert but also how to describe them.)

The truth of the conclusion is therefore dependent on both the truth of the premises and the validity of the comparison required by the definition of the law that is required by the authority—in this case, "no more than." If the premises, more fully stated, are "She is driving 40 mph in that zone" and "The legal speed limit in that zone is 50 mph," then the conclusion, "She is speeding," is obviously false. The law invoked by the statement from authority is the legal definition of speeding, and so any analysis comparing the fact with the authority here must be based on that definition. (More about analysis is given later.)

Imagine, then, what premises are required to support these conclusions: "He is his uncle's heir." "You may file your brief any time before Friday." "Robbie is liable for assault." Each conclusion must be premised on both facts and authority.

Analysis

Common law analysis takes several forms, of which we summarize here just two. The first, *deductive*, is familiar to all lawyers, whether common law or civilian. The second, *comparative*, is particularly the means for employing precedent.

Of course, lawyers rarely consider their arguments as logical forms. Far more often they present arguments that reflect one or another of these structures in combination. When they fail to account for some aspect of their argument that would be logically necessary for it to succeed, they open the door for their opponent to point out the error or omission and thus to be more persuasive.

Deduction

Much of legal analysis is logical analysis, or at least it employs logic in very elementary ways. Nearly every legal analysis follows one of the three major deductive forms of logical relationship to move from premises to a conclusion: *syllogism, modus pollens,* and *modus tollens.* These approaches are tools for applying rules to facts. There are many other forms of deductive logical argument, and yet these three are the most routinely used.

SYLLOGISM

The syllogism, the famous Aristotelian argument that a certain relationship between two premises leads to a certain result, is usually illustrated with an example something like this:

All men are bald.	*Major premise*
John is a man.	*Minor premise*
Therefore, John is bald.	*Conclusion*

If both premises are in fact true, and if the relationship of the minor premise is that the object of the minor premise ("a man") is necessarily within the set of objects described in the major premise ("all men"), then the conclusion must also in fact be true. This illustration, however, is a fallacy owing to a faulty premise: Not all men are bald; therefore, it is impossible to tell from the evidence of that premise whether the conclusion is true or false. John might be bald, but one could not prove it this way.

An argument that applies a rule to a given situation follows this form as well.

Driving over 65 mph here is a violation.	*Major premise (authority)*
You were driving over 65 mph here.	*Minor premise (fact)*
Therefore, you committed a violation.	*Conclusion*

Although this argument is rather simplistic, its simplicity makes the conclusion inescapable and clear. Notice, however, that the premises in this example leave considerable room for more work. The premise "Driving over 65 mph here is a violation" is itself a conclusion drawn from another argument. Further, the conclusiveness of the argument depends not only on the accuracy of the premises but also on their completeness. Are these premises really enough to establish a violation? What if a premise is accurate, as far as it goes, but incomplete? What if the statute has an exception, so that all driving over 65 mph is a violation, but some speeding—for instance, by a police officer in pursuit of the suspect of a crime— would not be? The premise is to some degree, then, false; the language of the premise should have been conditional (such as "Driving over 65 mph here is a violation, unless the driving is excepted from the rule"), and so the conclusion must also have been conditional (such as "Therefore, you committed a violation, unless your driving was within the exception of the rule"). Still, such exceptions could be completely irrelevant, as would be the case if you were cited for a speeding violation and were neither a police officer pursuing a suspect nor subject to any other justification or excuse. In that event, the incompleteness of the premise would hardly matter, and the conclusion would remain accurate.

MODUS PONENS

Many legal arguments are based on the satisfaction of a condition. Whether someone owes a particular duty to someone else might depend on whether certain events have occurred, such as entering a contract. The argument that reflects such conditions is the *modus ponens*, the method of proving. It takes this "if-then" structure:

> If P is true, then Q is true.
> P is true.
> Therefore, Q is true.

For example,

> If you drive over 65 mph here, you are speeding.
> You are driving over 65 mph.
> You are speeding.

The truth of the conclusion, once again, depends on the truth of the premises, both in accuracy and in specificity. If either premise is not true— say, there is no rule, or the rule is incompletely stated—and the omission is important to the conduct in the factual premise, then the conclusion is not necessarily proved. Further, the argument is not proved if the factual premise is not true or it assumes too many unproved conditions. (How do we know the speed limit at this place? How do we know the speed? Are we certain that no excuses apply?)

MODUS TOLLENS

Many legal arguments—especially those that deny an argument made already—depend on the failure of a condition. Whether someone owes a particular duty to someone else might depend on whether certain events have occurred (such as entering a contract), and if that had not happened, no such duty would have arisen. The argument that reflects such conditions is the *modus tollens*, the method of elimination. It takes this "if not, then not" structure:

If P is true, then Q is true.   *Or* If P is not true, then Q is not
                                           true.

P is not true.   P is not true.

Therefore, Q is not true.   Therefore, Q is not true.

Therefore,

If you drive over 65 mph here, you are speeding.
You are not driving over 65 mph.
You are not speeding.
Or
If you do not drive over 65 mph here, you not are speeding.
You are not driving over 65 mph.
You are not speeding.

Once again, the truth of the conclusion is dependent on the truth of the premises, in both accuracy and specificity.

Induction, or Comparison

At the heart of many legal arguments is not a deduction but an analogy. The strength of an analogy is the degree to which one case is similar to the case with which it is compared. Precedents are applied to later cases by analogy, largely according to the degrees to which the facts are similar and the issues raised by the parties are similar.

The method of comparison is to examine the components of the things compared, matching the degree of resemblance between the components of one with the components of the other. The components are likely to vary in their significance, and so the more similar relationship arises from higher degrees of similarity among more significant components.

The analogy between a precedent and a current case is one of the enduring questions of the common law. The full analogy requires proof of both similarity of the issues and similarity of the facts.

To what degree is the issue raised before the same as the issue raised later? Measuring this is a matter of the claims based on the facts and of the defenses based on the facts. The law, however, might have been changed since the time of the precedent case, and it is important to ensure that whatever elements of the law that were required then are either still required or not relevant to the later facts.

Assuming identical or sufficiently similar issues, the degree the precedent is similar to the current case turns on the similarity of facts. Some facts are more relevant than others. Facts that are necessary to prove an element are more important than facts that might prove that element. Both types of fact are more relevant than a fact that would merely substantiate a particular fact as true or merely assist in depicting a more complete narrative. Isolating a single fact from a narrative is not always easy, and it must be depicted with an appropriate degree of specificity to be clear in its relevance and in its relationship to an element of the legal issue in dispute.

Once the facts of the precedent and the corresponding facts of the current case are isolated, they can be compared. The degree of similarity or dissimilarity of each comparison is a matter of depiction, but whether the case is precedent cannot be determined according to the outcome reached in the case. Only the degree to which the facts of the old case are comparatively similar to those in the current case can be ascertained. These comparisons are illustrated in the problem at the end of this appendix.

Fallacies

Regardless of the form of argument used, many forms of error are possible. The mistakes most commonly made in logical argument are *fallacies*. In general, these are mistakes based on ambiguity, presumption, and irrelevance. There are many forms of fallacy, and for our purpose here, we list just those that are quite commonly used to attack legal arguments.

AMBIGUITY

Hypostatization is the alternation of abstract for concrete terms. By altering the nature of a general and abstract idea to apply it to a more specific and concrete case, or vice versa, an appearance of authority can be created where one is not proved. "Due process protects all rights necessary to ordered liberty . . . (thus) . . . Due process protects my right to unionize." This would be true only if the equation "rights necessary to ordered liberty" includes "my right to unionize," but that relationship is not proved in the argument.

Composition is a confusion of what is true for one in a group with what is true for all. Consider "John A. is in jail for theft. All of the A. family are thieves." The second sentence cannot be proved from the first.

Division is the confusion of what is true of a group with what is true of only a part. Take "John is a member of political party A, which believes in anarchy. John believes in anarchy." The second sentence cannot be proved from the first.

PRESUMPTION

Presumptions are fallacies because they presume answers that the evidence cannot support, either through ignoring or distorting the facts.

Generalizations arise either from failing to account for exceptional cases or from extrapolating from incomplete data. Three types of generalization are common fallacies in law: the *sweeping generalization*, the *hasty generalization*, and the *slippery slope argument*.

The sweeping generalization ignores an exception to the generality. "No one may enter a private dwelling without the occupant's permission" is fine as far as it goes, but it has nothing to do with whether an exception exists for law enforcement officers executing a lawful search warrant. The hasty generalization generalizes from incomplete data. "Fred robbed a store last year; he must be the person who robbed the store this year" simply cannot be supported.

The slippery slope is a generalization fallacy happily made time and again by lawyers arguing against the application of a rule to a new situation. It is to say that if you allow the rule in circumstances that lead to an outcome you prefer, the rule will be applied in other circumstances as well, leading to outcomes you would not prefer. The later application just does not follow from the first.

Other presumptions include *restatements* and *tautologies*. Restatements are simply reiterations or restatements of the premises as conclusions, as in "It is illegal because it is against the law." Tautologies are circular arguments, in which the conclusion becomes its own premise. "Trespass is wrong because it is breaking the close, and breaking the close is trespass."

IRRELEVANCE

The problem of relevance of facts is of deep concern to the law of evidence. The degree to which a particular fact is relevant is a matter of judicial scrutiny, and arguments are often presented to demonstrate the means by which a fact might be seen as relevant. Most important, those facts are relevant that would be logically necessary to prove or disprove a claim or defense at issue in a case. Facts are also relevant that demonstrate the historical accuracy or inaccuracy of evidence presented to prove a clearly relevant fact. Facts that would help in placing others in a comprehensible context are relevant. Beyond that, the relevance of evidence or facts that might be derived from it becomes more contested.

As to authority, the problem of relevance is quite different. Unlike formal logic, the common law accepts many arguments that are based on irrelevant premises, which, although they are logical fallacies, are not without some influence. Whether an argument is true or not cannot turn on factors that do not affect the truth of the premises or the accuracy of the analysis. Still, these are common influences, particularly to the emotion of the hearer. Two thousand years ago, Cicero in his *On Rhetoric* knew very well that appeals to the emotions could not establish the truth of an argument, but they make a weak argument more persuasive and a strong argument less so.

Likewise, the authority of the source of a particular argument ought to have no bearing on its truth or falsity, which could be independently evaluated. Still, the common law is bound to respect certain arguments arising from great authority, such as a constitutional text, a statute, or a recent opinion. Further, the common law routinely accords greater authority to certain authors of opinions or books than to others, as a matter of custom. Thus, an argument based on an opinion of John Marshall or Oliver Wendell Holmes, Jr., is likely to be given greater consideration than any logical proof could require alone.

Conclusion, or Conclusions

Most rules are more complicated than a speed limit, and quite a few require a host of elements to be satisfied for the rule to apply. In such situations, every single element requires independent analysis. For instance, the trespass rule at issue in *Scott v. Shepherd* in Chapter One required (1) injury to the plaintiff (2) caused (2A) by some forceful conduct (2B) by the defendant. The argument in that case was whether element (2B), the causation requirement, could be met if a third party intervened. Thus the argument in *Scott* could be reduced to a fight over which argument is correct between two arguments over the legal definition of causation in trespass: "causation requires the commission of acts that have injury as a consequence" versus "causation requires the commission of acts that immediately result in injury." To resolve that fight, each side was then required to assert premises and analysis in support of their arguments.

Many times, a critical series of arguments turns on the selection of one authority from among competing authorities. This might be done by resort to a further authority, in which the argument is likely to be deductive but might not be.

For example, if two precedents support contradictory outcomes, a resort to a rule that gives priority to the more recent precedent may be deductively applied to argue for the application of the later precedent. On the other hand, if the rule is that the precedent applies that arose from facts more closely similar to the facts of the case at hand, the two precedents may each be compared to the facts of the current case to argue that one precedent is more similar. What if, in this example, the precedent that is more recent is less similar? Then the argument must include another argument for preferring one rule—for following either the more recent precedent or the more similar one—over the other.

In this way, a single conclusion may be supported by a series of arguments, each argument concluding with a statement that serves as a premise in another argument.

Specific Approaches to the Authority of Precedent

Every judicial opinion presents a complex array of reasons it may or may not serve as a precedent for a later decision. While there are certain questions that must always be asked, others might be significant only in certain situations. We present here a short list of approaches to weigh the authority of a precedent. In reading this overview, beware of falling into the trap of considering precedents as the whole of the law. Although it is a matter of great disagreement among judges and scholars, we subscribe to Sir Edward Coke's reminder that "judgments should be according to laws not precedents."[2] A rule must arise from the law as developed from the whole of its sources, which is unlikely to be a single judicial opinion.

Later Treatment and the Authority of Precedents

If the opinion was not from a court of last resort, such as the U.S. Supreme Court on federal issues, or a state high court, such as the New York Court of Appeals or the California Supreme Court for issues of state law in those states, the most important question is how the opinion fared on direct appeal. It might have not been appealed, in which case this question is moot. If it was, and if the opinion was upheld, then the value of the precedent is greater the more that the reasoning of the upholding opinion endorsed the reasoning employed in the precedent on appeal. If it was, and if the opinion was reversed, the reversal still may not have limited the precedential value of the lower opinion if the reversing opinion reversed on grounds other than those for which the precedent would apply in the later case, and if the reversing opinion either endorsed those grounds or did not reach them. One interesting problem arises when an opinion is reversed on appeal, and then the reversing opinion is itself overturned in a later case. In that instance, the earlier, once-reversed opinion might be quite influential as a precedent.

If the opinion was not overruled, or if it was an opinion that could not be appealed because it was from a high court, the next question is how the opinion has fared in later considerations of the same issue. If the

---

[2] "Proem to the Third Institute," in Sheppard, *Selected Writings of Sir Edward Coke* (Indianapolis, IN: Liberty Fund, 2004) at 950.

opinion has been consistently followed by later courts and none of them criticized it or distinguished it from cases like yours, it is a strong precedent. If the opinion was criticized in opinions that were themselves overturned or criticized, the opinion might be a strong precedent indeed.

If the opinion is simply not discussed in later cases, and the issue within it has been the subject of later opinions that omit discussion of it, the opinion is stronger precedent to the degree that it is consonant with those opinions. It is still an important authority even if it does not agree with them, and the problem of case synthesis now arises.

Significance of the Time and Court of Precedent

Time and jurisdiction provide important qualifications of a precedent, in either synthesizing a rule from precedents or determining the persuasive authority of a single precedent to a later argument. Of the two, jurisdiction is the more susceptible to clear degrees of persuasiveness.

The first question in assessing jurisdictional effects on a precedent is what jurisdiction will hear the new argument. If the argument is a matter of state law that will be presented in the trial court of a given state, then the most influential opinions are those of that state's supreme court, followed by the division of the state court of appeals with jurisdiction over that trial court, followed by that trial court itself.

Opinions from other states vary in their persuasive authority. States that have similar laws in the subject areas of the dispute are more significant as sources of authority than states whose laws in the general area of the dispute have significant differences. For example, imagine two out-of-state cases regarding a dispute over the state tax owed by a trust. The case decided by the court of the state with tax laws and trust laws that are more similar to the state with the new issue would be more persuasive than the opinion that came from the state with the less congruent laws. States whose cases represent a reform in the law that the forum state is likely to adopt are often more persuasive. Some state courts are acknowledged as having special expertise in a given area, such as Delaware on corporations law or New York on the law of investments. In the absence of any other means of discrimination, states nearer the forum state or that will be seen in that state as more similar to the forum state may be given greater weight than others.

Opinions in federal matters are similar. In general, opinions from U.S.

Supreme Court cases are the most persuasive when they are recent and unanimous, and more persuasive when they are decided by a larger majority than by a small one. Plurality opinions, which have less than a majority but the largest number of judges, are less persuasive, but more so than the opinions of the dissenters. All of these gradations alter as time passes, and the question really is how many votes the current court's membership might muster for a given opinion today. Thus, certain dissents become more persuasive in time, as various justices signal—usually in concurrences—that they adopt the reasoning of an older dissenting opinion. Following Supreme Court opinions, the next most persuasive authorities are opinions of the court of appeals with jurisdiction over a given area, and opinions of a majority en banc ("of the whole court") are more persuasive than a majority of a three-judge panel. Then a scale of descending authority could be suggested, beginning with the opinions of the trial court, then the opinions of other federal appellate courts, then the opinions of state courts, and then the opinions of other federal trial courts.

Regardless of these default hierarchies of precedence, opinions that are more clearly "on all fours"—which is to say, opinions that have facts indistinguishably similar to the case under consideration—are more persuasive than those that do not. Further, certain opinions receive persuasive effect beyond their logical significance owing to fame, either of the case or of the judge who authors it. For some judges, an aside made in *Marbury v. Madison* can have greater persuasive force than a clear holding by a modern appellate court. Likewise, an opinion by John Marshall, Joseph Story, Oliver Wendell Holmes, Jr., or other well-known judges will carry an additional cachet. Some recent and contemporary judges, as well, have strong reputations, particularly in certain areas in which they are highly regarded, such as the Fifth Circuit's John Minor Wisdom in admiralty matters, the D.C. Circuit's Patricia Wald in international law, and the Seventh Circuit's Richard Posner in antitrust. Further, professors who enter the bench often develop considerable influence, such as Guido Calabresi, Morris Arnold, and John Noonan.

As to the time between two conflicting opinions from the same court, the most recent opinion is usually said to be the controlling one, or at least the more persuasive. Even so, cases in which a doctrine is developed often have considerable persuasive value, and mere antiquity is never sufficient to disregard authority when it is contrary to a given argument.

So the reasons for a particular opinion having more persuasive authority than another arise from a mass of variables. Each of these variables is controversial, and among all of them there is considerable contradiction. This variability in the persuasive significance of sources is a long-held aspect of the common law. Judges are, in fact, very limited in their discretion to pick and choose precedents, as well as to determine how narrowly to interpret the facts from which any precedent arose. Lawyers, then, must make arguments that persuade the judge to interpret precedent as they would have it, and so the arguments continue.

Rules from Precedents versus Reasons from Case Synthesis

We talk commonly of the "rule in the case," as well as the "common law rule." These are, of course, quite likely to be different from one another—the rule from one case being either the *ratio decidendi* or some other basis for decision that is redacted from it, and the common law rule being one established through a line of cases, although it might have been initially proposed in a single case. Taking seriously the edict of Sir Edward Coke that courts should apply the law and not precedent, one could conclude that both ideas are necessary to one another, that a rule can be found in a case, and this rule is a reason for a future decision to be made similarly. Therefore, a series of cases provides a series of reasons for future decisions, and some coordination is possible among these reasons. This coordination might follow from attempting to synthesize rules from a line of cases. Such a synthesis could proceed through a host of cases, each developing some portion of a more general, or thorough, set of reasons— some cases establishing exceptions, others limitations, others determining particular nuances, and even some wrongly decided cases being reversed, and further establishing the authority of precedents as sources of decision overall.[3]

Case synthesis, then, requires deriving a series of reasons for future decisions from a group of precedents. This is not that easy to do in a coherent fashion, particularly when some precedents reach different re-

---

[3] This is akin to the natural model of precedent, as opposed to the rule or result models, developed by Larry Alexander and Emily Sherwin in their important essay on precedent, *The Rule of Rules: Morality, Rules & The Dilemmas of Law* (Durham, NC: Duke University Press, 2001).

sults. In these cases, you can either demarcate different reasons for factually distinct circumstances, articulate exceptions to reasons other cases establish, or determine that certain precedents have been overruled by later cases and furnish an inadequate authority for reasons for later action. In every instance, the conclusion reached will require careful argument to prove it.

In the following problem, several similar cases may be considered together. Notice that they do not reach perfectly compatible results. Different judges might look to the results of older cases as the reason for a later outcome or look to older cases for reasons about how to use precedent as the basis for later reasons. Try to imagine advising a client like the one depicted at the end of the problem by using the cases described.

Methodology Problem

Three case opinions are summarized here. Each is fictitious, created solely for this exercise, so please do not think these cases represent the law in Arkansas or Missouri.

Abrams v. Brown (Arkansas, 1901)

Brown buys land next to Abrams's farm. Brown opens a massive distillery, which is quite legal, drawing water from the underground springs and, eventually, causing Abrams's spring-fed ponds to run dry, endangering Abrams's cattle. Abrams seeks an injunction and damages against Brown. The court denies both, holding that Brown is entitled to all the resources from the center of the earth to the roof of the sky.

Cather v. Downing (Arkansas, 1955)

Another suit against a distillery, whose use of spring water runs dry the springs in Cather's bathhouse. The suit is brought during prohibition, and the court holds that the use of the water for an illegal distillery is unreasonable. The court granted damages and in *dictum* noted an injunction might lie for such an injury but found here that an injunction was unnecessary, as Cather was in jail and the distillery had been destroyed.

Edwards v. Forest (Missouri, 1991)

Edwards and Forest both hold large tracts of adjoining lands, which have been in their respective families for generations. Edwards's lands include a large rock formation suitable for storing underground natural gas, and he leases the rights to store there to Gasco. Gasco pumped 11 million gallons of water out of the formation, dumping it in a nearby river and causing Forest's wells to run dry. Forest sues Gasco and Edwards. The Missouri court held that Edwards and Gasco were liable for damages, as the water was being unreasonably used, and it granted an injunction to Forest against them.

In re Green (Arkansas, 1950)

The Arkansas Supreme Court was confronted by two of its own precedents (not concerning the issues in these cases), each of which appeared to resolve similar facts but reached different conclusions. The court applied the more recent case, noting, "When all other considerations are equal, the later precedent is the more authoritative exposition of the law."

Henkin v. Issacs (Arkansas 1960)

The Arkansas Supreme Court, again confronted with conflicting precedents (again in a case with facts not relevant here), refused to apply *In re Green* to resolve the conflict, finding that the considerations were not equal, because the facts of the earlier case were clearly more similar to the case "at bar" than the facts of the later case, which could be distinguished.

Your client, Johnson, owns lands in Arkansas that include a small salt dome, suitable for underground storage. Johnson wishes to lease the dome to private waste management companies to store very low-level nuclear waste underground, which would be legal. Your hydrologist assures you that the pumping necessary to clear the water from the dome will probably run neighboring wells dry.

> Question One: Applying only these five cases, will Johnson be liable
> to his neighbors for the loss of their wells if he goes forward?

Question Two: What are Johnson's options?

Question Three: Is there any conduct by Johnson or his lessees that might increase or decrease their liability for running dry the nearby wells?

Question Four: What additional authority would increase your certainty or the persuasiveness of your answers to questions one to three?

Further Reading

Many books explore the structure of legal argument, and indeed there is much still to learn from Cicero's book for lawyers, *On Rhetoric*. The two indispensable books on modern legal argument are Steve Burton, *An Introduction to Law and Legal Reasoning* (New York: Aspen Press, 1995), and Edward H. Levi, *An Introduction to Legal Reasoning* (Chicago: University of Chicago, 1965). For books on the nature of logical argument, see Nicholas Capaldi, *The Art of Deception: An Introduction to Critical Thinking: How to Win an Argument, Defend a Case, Recognize a Fallacy, See Through a Deception* (3d ed) (Buffalo, NY: Prometheus Books, 1987). For the classic argument on the use of precedent as authority, see Karl Llewellyn, *The Case Law System in America* (Paul Gewits ed., Michael Ansaldi trans.) (Chicago: University of Chicago Press, 1989). Laurence Goldstein has edited a wonderful collection of contemporary essays on precedent, *Precedent in Law* (New York: Oxford University Press, 1987).

The Interpretation of Statutes

Legislation is a critical aspect of the common law. With the exception of constitutions and judicial opinions of constitutional interpretation, statutes are the most authoritative sources of law in the common law system. Unfortunately, as we have seen, common law statutes are rarely enacted as a single code. Rather, they are usually drafted as a small number of related statutes, all focused on the cure of a single problem, and these drafts are subject to many revisions, often in last-minute compromises prior to enactment. There is no "general part," and the tools of interpretation must be applied distinctly to every part of the code, often with varying results over time. These tools are sometimes adopted by the legislature as a part of the process of enactment, but more usually they are created and applied in the courts.

Reading a statute is often not easy. Statutes are frequently written in convoluted prose, with many clauses, often broken into sentence fragments. Rather like solving crossword puzzles, nothing is as good as practice in reading American statutes to become competent at the task.

The reason to read a statute is to isolate rules from it: What does the statute require or forbid that is meaningful in a given situation? To derive these rules, the common law employs a variety of distinct methods, the four most important of which are (1) careful reading of the text,

(2) application of statements of policy or purpose, (3) legislative intent, and (4) canons of construction.

Careful Reading of the Text: Plain Meaning

The text is the starting place of every statute. The words are the only tools through which a legislature can act. They are what is negotiated, what is assented to, and what is published. The words are not only the formal expression of the will of the state but also the fundamental exposition that is to be obeyed.

Often, the words and sentences in their context admit to only a single understanding. There is little ambiguity, no mistake, and clear instruction as to what is required by those to whom the statute is addressed, and what is required is both practicable and not unreasonable. In such circumstances, the effort of interpretation is quite minimal.

The words usually have their ordinary meanings—that is, the meanings that someone literate in English would expect them to have, encountering them in a similar context in other places. There are, of course, words that are terms of art that are selected from both the terms of the law and the jargons of certain specialized practices subject to regulation, and these words can be understood only as defined by these subcultures. Some words are given particular meanings within statutes, as placeholders for specific ideas that might or might not correspond with the words' usages in other contexts. These meanings are not difficult to determine, and in sum, they lead to coherent statements of obligation that fit with what the record indicates were the reasons for the legislators to enact the law.

In such cases, the words of the statute are its best guide to application. Further interpretation is likely to lead the interpreter to mistaken results.

Of course, not all legislation is so clear. Sometimes, a statute allows several, truly ambiguous results. For instance, a Washington state statute governing dogs defined a "dangerous dog" and then defined a "potentially dangerous dog." It then created an offense for owners whose dogs injure others. That offense specified: "The owner of any dog that aggressively attacks and causes severe injury or death of any human, whether the dog has previously been declared potentially dangerous or dangerous, shall, upon conviction, be guilty of a class C felony. . . .">[1] A trial court found a dog owner guilty of this felony for an attack by a dog that had never been declared dangerous or potentially dangerous. On appeal, the state supreme court found the clause "whether the dog has previously been declared potentially dangerous or dangerous" had two quite different readings that could fairly be made.

> It can be read to mean "whether or not" the dog has previously been declared potentially dangerous or dangerous, an owner is criminally liable. This is the way in which the trial court construed the statute. The clause can also be read to mean "whether the dog has previously been declared potentially dangerous or whether the dog has been previously declared dangerous," i.e., one or the other. Under this reading, criminal liability would only arise if the dog had previously been classified as either a "potentially dangerous dog" or a "dangerous dog," in accord with the definitions in RCW 16.08.070.[2]

The court went on to interpret the statute according to legislative intent to punish dog bites when the owner is on notice of the danger posed to others by the dog, and it reversed the conviction, much to the disgust of a judge in dissent.[3]

Confronted by such a line in a statute that can reasonably be read in more than one way in its plain meaning, the judges of the court could have made a variety of choices. The most critical is whether the judges are more concerned with reaching a particular result than in employing a method of deriving reasons for the decision from the statute. Assuming the court's rhetoric is honest, it places a higher value on the employment of appropriate methods for deriving reasons than on reaching a given outcome.[4] The court then can derive those reasons from its consideration

---

[1] Rev. Code Wash. (ARCW) § 16.08.100(3) (2003). The words "or not" were added following the mischievous "whether" by an amendment in 2002.

[2] *State v. Bash*, 130 Wn.2d 594, 601 (1996).

[3] *State v. Bash*, at 614 (Dolliver, J.)

[4] Indeed, in most instances when a court finds ambiguity, there is a suspicion that the court worked rather diligently to give weight to a meaning of the statute that is less than obvious.

of the record of the enactment of the statute or derive either a legislative intent according to which the statute can be reformed or a legislative purpose according to which the statute can be interpreted. The court may also look to particular analytical tools announced in earlier cases—the canons of interpretation—according to which statutory language may be interpreted without regard to the history of the statute.

Legislative Intent

To determine legislative intent, the court looks to the record of the enactment of the statute, considering the reports written by legislative committees, statements made by various legislators, and arguments that attended the various political debates that preceded enactment. Such a consideration may yield no information that suggests a particular intention by anyone related to the language in issue, it might yield arguable results that suggest several possible intentions, or it might yield a clear understanding that was generally held by various legislators and not subject to much dispute. The utility and the authority of the intent that can be derived from the record will vary accordingly.

Legislative Purpose

The legislative purpose is the essential goal toward which a statute is enacted. This purpose, or any single purpose, is not always easy to determine after the fact. If, for example, a statute creates a particular crime of cattle rustling, it may not be easy to isolate a more important purpose of protecting cattle from theft than one of punishing those who steal them. Even so, the purpose is often more easily determined than is the legislative intent, and once a purpose is identified, ambiguous terms can be interpreted in a manner that better promotes that purpose. For example, in the dog-bite case, if the purpose is found to be to enact punishments for irresponsible dog owners, the court would be more likely to read the statute to punish the defendant. If the purpose is merely to reduce the number of dog bites, the statute might be read as not intending to punish the defendant.

Canons of Construction

There are many rules of interpretation, as well as other approaches to interpretation that are not easily reduced to rules. Although these canons have been subject to academic criticism as being incoherent, conflicting, or inefficient,[5] courts still apply them, both because of the strength of their precedential use and because of their recurrent logical benefit.

Some of these are substantive, and specific to a particular type of statute or questions regarding a statute:

1. Statutes should be interpreted in accord with the constitution. When two or more interpretations of a statute are possible, the court should choose the interpretation that causes the least conflict between the statute and constitutional requirements.

2. Likewise, ambiguous statutes should, if possible, be interpreted to avoid conflicts with treaties and international law, with the laws of other states, and with prior existing laws.

3. Criminal statutes should be interpreted with lenity. If a statute is ambiguous and would not have given clear notice to a person of what act would be a crime, the statute should be interpreted narrowly so as not to penalize the person who did not have notice.

4. Statutes creating or regularly enforced by an agency should presumptively be interpreted according to the agency's practices and interpretations. (This presumption can, of course, be rebutted.)

5. Statutes should not be interpreted to create impossible or unreasonable requirements on either citizens or officials.

6. Statutes should not be interpreted to create liabilities for the government powers of (or restraints on) officials, unless such liabilities, powers, or restraints are clearly stated.

7. Statutes should not be interpreted to create burdens on groups that have historically been disenfranchised or that have been the victims of harmful discrimination as a matter of law.

Besides these general canons of substantive interpretation, there are canons of linguistic interpretation, which establish patterns derived from their correlation with other legislation, as well as the linguistics, grammar, word

---

[5] See Karl N. Llewellyn, *The Common Law Tradition: Deciding Appeals* 521–535 (Boston: Little, Brown, 1960).

choice, syntax, or textual arrangement of the statutory language. Some of these canons include:

1. Words used in a statute are expected to have the same meaning throughout the statute, as well as the same meaning they have had in previous statutes. (This is known as the doctrine of interpretation *in pari materia*.)

2. The expression of one thing, or the creation of a list that is not explicitly nonexhaustive, excludes all other things, particularly the things not on the list. (This is a variation on the doctrine *expressio unius est exclusio alterius*.)

3. The term *shall* is obligatory, and the term *may* is discretionary.

4. Terms are understood in the context in which they are ordinarily associated. (This is a variation of the doctrine *noscitur a sociis*.)

5. Specific statutes are to be applied in lieu of more general statutes if they conflict, and general terms are defined by more specific terms that are applied in the statutes. (These are both applications of the doctrine *ejusdem generis*.)

6. Each sentence or provision of a statute is to be read as a part of the whole statute.

7. An interpretation that would make a provision of the statute redundant, or duplicative of another provision, is to be avoided.

Further Reading

For an unusually clear exposition of the various tools of legislative interpretation, see Kent Greenawalt, *Legislation: Statutory Interpretation: 20 Questions* (New York: Foundation Press, 1999). Greenawalt presents a cogent argument for and demonstration of the employment of plain meaning, legislative intent, and canons of construction.

For a study of the isolation of legislative intent, see Ronald Benton Brown and Sharon Jacobs Brown, *Statutory Interpretation: The Search for Legislative Intent* (Notre Dame, Ind.: National Institute for Trial Advocacy, 2002). For the manifesto of interpretation by plain meaning, see Antonin Scalia, *A Matter of Interpretation* (Amy Gutmann ed.) (Princeton, NJ: Princeton University Press, 1998). For what is still the best argument for legislative policy, see Henry M. Hart Jr. and Albert M. Sacks's *The Legal Process: Basic Problems in the Making and Application of Law* (William N. Eskridge Jr. and Philip P. Frickey eds.) (New York: Foundation Press, 2001). For a historical development of this debate over the use of legislative intent or plain meaning, see William D. Popkin, *Statutes in Court: The History and Theory of Statutory Interpretation* (Durham, NC: Duke University Press, 1999). For a well-known discussion of the growing influence of the regulatory model in the courts, see Guido Calabresi, *The Common Law in the Age of Statutes* (Cambridge, MA: Harvard University Press, 1985). On the priority of legislation in the common law, see Jeremy Waldron, *The Dignity of Legislation* (Cambridge: Cambridge University Press, 1999).

INDEX

Abbott Laboratories, Sindell v., 388
abolitionists, 169, 175–76, 457
abortion cases
    Canadian case (1988), 542
    German case (1927), 42–53, 55–56, 77,
        79, 377, 594, 602, 608
    Roe v. Wade, 59, 261
Abrams v. United States, 599n9
absolutist thinking, 240
abuse of rights, 66–67, 434, 579
abuse of trust, 415
academic authority. *See* scholarly authority
acceptance, 396–98, *table 19.1*
accessibility, 67
accident law, 452–53, 470
accident prevention, 452–53
accommodation, 597, 610–11
accusation, 532, 537
accusatorial system, 531–33
Ackerman, Bruce, 200, 223
acquittals, 542–43, 545–46, 586
act for promise, 410
"active nationality" principle, 277, 498
act of God, 446–47, 450
Acton, Lord, 34
actual malice, 229, 235–38

Adams, Abigail, 234
Adams, John, 134–35, 215
additur, 519
administrative detention, 543
administrative law, 7, 71–72
admiralty, actions in, 506n5
adversary system, 525–90
    criminal trial procedure in, 531–48
    Goetz, People v., 549–67
    self-defense and, 568–90
advertisements, 226–30, 236–38
affirmative action, 222
affirmative breach of contract, 427, 488
affirmative defenses, 41, 52, 507, 515,
    517
age discrimination, 220–21
aggression
    military, 568, 572–74, 580–81
    model of, 472–74
Agnew, Maryland State Bar Ass'n v., 218
Agnew, Spiro, 218
AIDS, 30
aircraft hijacking, 277
air pollution, 369, 373–74, 461, 466, 604,
    610
Alabama law, 225–42, 248, 489–501, 601

Alabama Supreme Court, 229–30, 237, 491, 494–95, 497–98, 500
Alabama v. See name of opposing party
Alden v. Maine, 198
Alderson, Freeman v., 293
Alexander, Fritz W., II (J.), 562
Alexander, Larry, 638n3
Alfred H. Mayer Co., Jones v., 260n3
alienation, 327–28
aliens, resident, 203–15, 219–22
Allen, Barry, 527, 583
Allen v. First Nat'l Bank & Trust Co., 332n8
Alliance Resources Corp., TXO Production Corp. v., 494, 496
allocation of resources, 461–62, 464
"all-or-nothing" rule of contributory negligence, 475–77, 480, 482–83
alternative Constitution, 172–200
    civil rights cases, 186–99
    Declaration of Independence and, 173–77
    Gettysburg Address and, 178–80
    Reconstruction amendments and, 180–82
    Strauder v. West Virginia, 182–86
alternative dispute resolution, 522–23
alternative lawgiver, 360
altruism, 416
ambiguity, 632
Ambler Realty Co., Euclid v., 364
amendments. *See* U.S. Constitution
American Cancer Society, 386
American Civil Liberties Union, 269n7
American law, ten "simple" facts about, 5–11
American Law Institute, 83n3, 396, 475, 556
American Realist movement, 67n18, 71–72, 470
American Type Culture Collection, 386
amici curiae, 265, 269n7, 479
analogy, 26, 77–80
analysis, 627–34
    deduction, 628–30
        modus ponens, 629–30
        modus tollens, 630
        syllogism, 628–29

induction, 630–34
    fallacies, 631–32
anarchy, 267
ancient forms, 300
Anderson v. Dunn, 252
Anderson v. Harris, 332n10
André, John, 257n8
Andrews, William S. (J.), 433
Andrews v. Law Society, 220
animals
    cruelty to, 360n4
    trespass and, 368
Anknüpfungspunkte, 301
Annotated Civil Code (West), 478
answer, filing of, 505, 507, 509–10
antigiuridicità, 55
antijuridicidad, 55–56
apartheid, 597, 611
"appeal of death," 98
appellate jurisdiction, 6–9, 70. *See also* Court of Appeals
    civil trial and, 516, 518–21
    criminal law and, 540–41, 545–47, 549, 562
        asymmetrical rules of, 545–46
    due process and, 270
    U.S. Supreme Court and, 124, 134, 139–41, 147, 167
Application of St. Bernard Cemetery Ass'n, 365–66
Arabian, Armand (J.), 387, 392
Arabic law, language of, 61, 65
arbitration, 522–23
argument, 9–10
Aristotle, 34, 317, 338–39, 347, 454
Arizona v. See name of opposing party
Armstrong, Scott, 27
Arndt v. Griggs, 294
Arnold, Benedict, 257n8
Arnold, Morris, 637
arraignment, 535–36
Articles of Confederation (U.S.), 129, 155, 173, 259
"articles of proof," 515
Asch, Sidney H. (J.), 552–53
Asian law, 29, 40
assault, 21, 23, 441, 473, 550–51
assessors, 244
assignment, 325

assignments of error, 445
Assizes, 22, 22n7
assumption of risk, 483
Atlantic Cement Co., Boomer v., 368–75, 489, 603, 609–10
attachment, 279, 281, 293, 377, 511, 522
Attorney General (U.S.), 8
attorney's oath, 207, 215, 218
audiotapes, 535, 551
ein Aufopferungsanspruch, 449
Austin v. Hudson River Railroad Co., 479
Australian law, 106
Austrian law, 480
authority, 533
autonomy, individual
   civil law tradition and, 595
   common law and, 316
   contract law and, 396
   economic efficiency and, 455–56, 459, 461, 469
   Right and reasonable, 602
   self-defense as justified vindication of, 586–89
avoidance of injustice, 403

B. & O. Railway Co., Koontz v., 309
Bacon, Francis, Sir, 341, 347
bad faith, 414
Baehr v. Penn-O-Tex Oil Corp., 398–404
bail, 535–36
Bailey, Carlton, 516n7
Bail Reform Act (1984), 536
Bakke, U. of California v., 222
"balancing the equities," 351
balancing theory, 48, 52, 594
Ballard v. Hunter, 294
banks, 150–52, 155–57, 161–62, 166–67, 169
Bantam Books, Inc., v. Sullivan, 230
bar, 130, 503
bargaining, 400, 423, 465–67
Barnett, United States v., 249–50, 255, 624
battered-wife cases, 572, 576–77
battery, 441, 473
battle, trial by, 244–45
Battle Creek v. Goguac Resort Ass'n, 366
Baxter v. Roberts, 479
Belgium law, 244, 245n2, 301, 601
beneficial use, 349

beneficiaries, 348–50
benefit-of-the-bargain damages, 418, 606
Bentham, Jeremy, 317, 471, 594, 608, 610
Benton v. Maryland, 272
Bergan, Francis (J.), 368–73
Berman, Harold, 39n12
Bethlehem Steel Corp., Rodriguez v., 388
Beweisverbote, 545
Beyle, Marie-Henri. *See* Stendhal, Henri
BGB (German Civil Code). *See* German Civil Code (BGB)
biases, 245, 420, 531, 543
Bible, 33, 77, 178, 596
Bible. Exodus, 79–80, 586
Bible. Genesis, 176
Bickel, Alexander, 599n10
bilateral contract, 410
Bill of Rights (U.S.), 127–30. *See also First through Tenth Amendments under* U.S. Constitution
   due process and, 243, 247–48, 255–56, 260–61
   freedom and, 224
   property law and, 359
   Right and reasonable, 595, 598
   slavery and, 170
biotechnology, 378–94
Bird, Jones v., 479
Black, Charles, 199
Black, Hugo L. (J.), 237–38, 268
Black & White Taxicab Co. v. Brown & Yellow Taxicab Co., 250, 305, 307, 310–11
Black Code, 191
black-letter rules, 83, 598
blackmail, 402
Blackstone, William, Sir, 15, 23–26, 35–37, 71, 77–79, 83, 102, 107, 134n6, 138, 145, 185, 251n4, 313, 317, 593–94, 602, 617, 620–21
Bloom v. Illinois, 248–58, 600, 617, 621–24
BMW of North American, Inc. v. Gore, 489–501, 601, 610
Board of Education, Brown v., 201, 598
Board of Trustees of Univ. of Ala. v. Garrett, 199
body parts, property in, 393–94
"Boiler-Plate Agreements," 423n6
bond, 520

bondholders, 350
bondsman, 536
un bon père de famille, 65, 441
Boomer v. Atlantic Cement Co., 368–75,
    489, 603, 609–10
"Boston Massacre," 215
Boswell's Lessee v. Otis, 283
la bouche de la loi, 31, 31n1, 71
Bouie v. City of Columbia, 88, 90–101
bound by law, 72–74, 427–28, 607
Bouvia v. Superior Court, 383
Bowers v. Hardwick, 60, 77n1
Bradlee v. Converse, 332–33n11
Bradley, Joseph P. (J.), 187–92
Bradwell v. State, 204, 219
Bramwell, Lord, 462
Branch, Oliver Winslow (J.), 436–38
Brandeis, Louis D. (J.), 267, 303–8, 313,
    387, 626
Braver, Susan, 539
breach of contract, 377, 402–3, 426–39
    Hawkins v. McGee, 436–39
    Jacob & Youngs, Inc. v. Kent, 428–34
    Kessler and Fine on, 435–36
breach of fiduciary duty, 380, 383–87,
    391, 393, 517, 605
breakdown, 426
Brennan, William J., Jr. (J.), 225–37
Brenner, Frank, 565
*Brentwood Academy v. Tennessee Secondary
    School Athletic Ass'n.*, 198
Brethern: Inside the Supreme Court, The
    (Woodward and Armstrong), 27
Brewer, David J. (J.), 310
Breyer, Stephen (J.), 102, 495
"bribes" by victims, 464–67
Bridges v. California, 239, 253, 623
briefs, writing of, 21, 615–24
British Commonwealth, 107
British law, 132, 457
Brooks, Ingham v., 365
"brother," 26–27
Brown (J.), 362–67
*Brown & Yellow Taxicab Co., Black & White
    Taxicab Co. v.*, 250, 305, 307, 310–
    11
Brown v. Board of Education, 201, 598
Brown v. Superior Court, 386
Brown v. United States, 578n5

Bucks Stove & Range Co., Gompers v., 253
Buder, Douglas v., 92
Bundesverfassungsgericht, 132
"bundle of rights," 389
burden of persuasion, 314, 517
burden of proof, 64n12, 388n8, 517
Burger, Warren E. (C.J.), 77n1, 213–15
Burgett v. Texas, 273
burglary, 570–71, 589
Bush, George W., 76, 197, 257, 572–73n3,
    582
Bush v. Gore, 76
Butler, Pierce (J.), 308–12
Butterfield v. Forrester, 477
Button, N.A.A.C.P. v., 230–32, 239

Cabey, Darryl, 527–29, 539, 582–84
Calabresi, Guido, 452–53, 462, 466, 469–
    70, 611, 637
Calbud, Inc., People v., 561
Calhoun, John C., 234
California Civil Code, 30, 474–75, 477–86
"California Civil Code, The" (Van
    Alstyne), 478
California Criminal Code, 83–84
California Supreme Court, 378–94, 474–
    87, 589, 606
California v. See name of opposing party
Calvin's Case (Coke), 176
Cammer v. United States, 253
Canadian Charter of Rights and Freedoms,
    61, 106, 271n9, 359, 526
Canadian Constitution, 220, 222
Canadian law, 38, 106–7, 241, 244, 449
Canadian Supreme Court, 38
canon law, 18, 27, 36–37, 338
Cantor, People v., 559
Cantwell v. Connecticut, 261n5
Canty, Troy, 527–29, 539, 551, 575, 578,
    583
capacity, 505
capitalism, 317, 327, 598
capital punishment, 108, 244, 564, 588
Cardozo, Benjamin N. (J.), 59, 248,
    256n7, 267, 270, 428–32, 433–34,
    604
Carmell v. Texas, 89
Caroll Towing Co., United States v., 441
Carrillo, People v., 98

Carro, John (J.), 552
case and controversy clause, 124, 133, 139–
40, 146
casebooks, 9
case law
due process and, 260–61
history of civil law and, 34–36, 39, 44,
50
history of common law and, 15–16, 18–
19, 30
jury selection and, 514
libel and, 600
case method, 9, 21, 616
cases. *See also names of cases*
common law method and, 625–41
reading and briefing of, 21, 80–82, 615–
24
reasons from synthesis of, 638–39
*Cases and Materials on the Development of
Legal Institutions* (Goebel), 340–42
Catholic Church, 37–38
Caton, Commonwealth v., 149
causal nihilism, 466
causation, 486
cause, 397, *table 19.1*, 401–2
Ceballos, People v., 589
celebrities, 600
cell research, 378–94, 605–6
centralized efficiency, 468–69
certiorari, writ of, 84n5, 229, 304, 309,
491, 499
Chaffin, Verner F., 334
challenge for cause, 514
Chancellors, 339–42, 346–47, 356
chancery courts, 338, 340–50
argument from antiquity concerning,
341–42, 345–50
Courtney v. Glanvil, 342–45
in Delaware, 350
Goebel on, 340–42
Chase & Gilbert, Hutchinson v., 296
Chasm Power Co., McCann v., 370
chattels, 360, 368, 437
"checks and balances," 532–33
Cheff v. Schnackenberg, 250, 255, 623
*Chicago, Burlington & Quincy Railroad Co.
v. Chicago*, 260–61n4
Chinese law, 4–5, 61, 65
church law. *See* canon law

CIAL@aol.com, 11
CIO, Hague v., 261
"circle of violence," 576
citizenship, 203–15, 220–21
City of Boerne v. Flores, 198
City of Chicago v. Tribune Co., 236, 239
civil contempt, 246, 255
civilian law. *See* civil law tradition
"civil law," 54, 56–57
civil law tradition, 4–5, 7, 10, 29–53. *See
also* French Code civil; German
Civil Code (BGB)
abortion, problematic case of, 42–53
case law and, 35–36, 39, 44
civil trial and, 502
common law and, 15–28
contempt power and, 246–47
contract law and, 400–402, 413–18, 426–
28
countervoices in, 172–73
criminal law and, 533, 537–39, 541, 543–
47, 563
equity and, 339, 347–48
federalism and, 159n7
feudalism in land law and, 319
freedom and, 225, 241
language of, 54–74
lawyers in, 7, 29, 515
leases in, 325
legal culture, three types of, 33–35
legal reasoning in, 79, 83
liberalism and, 316
Right and, 593
scholarly authority and, 36–42
Civil Rights Act (1866), 196–97
Civil Rights Act (1875), 186–87, 196–97
Civil Rights Act (1964), 201
Civil Rights Act (1983), 198
Civil Rights Cases, 90, 186–99, 201, 260,
596
civil rights movement, 241
civil trial, American, 502–24
appeal, 519–21
discovery, 512–13
execution, 521–22
initial investigation, 504–6
jury, 243, 246–47, 506, 514–19, 521
instruction of, 516–17
selection of, 514

civil trial, American (*continued*)
   pleadings, drafting and service of, 506–9
   posttrial motions, 518–19
   preliminary motions, 509–11
   pretrial conference, 513–14
   settlements and alternative dispute
      resolution, 522–23
   summary motions, 513
   trial, 515–16
   verdict and judgment, 518–19
Clark, Reynolds v., 23, 620–21
Clark, Tom C. (J.), 263–68, 272
Clark, William P. (J.), 484–85
Clarke v. Deckebach, 204
class actions, 508–9
class gift, 331–33
Classic, United States v., 198
Clayton Act, 249
"clean hands," 351, 353–54
Clifford, Nathan (J.), 186
closing arguments, 515–16
CLS. *See* Critical Legal Studies movement
Coase, Ronald, 451, 464, 473
Coase theorem, 451
Coasian reaction, 464–69
Cobbs v. Grant, 391
Cobb v. Moor, 343–44
Code Commissioners' Note (Calif.), 479–
   81
codification, 18–19, 30–34, 478. *See also*
   civil law tradition
coercion, 420, 456, 461, 467
Coke, Edward, Sir, 15–18, 35–36, 71, 133,
   146, 176, 260n1, 340–44, 347,
   586, 593–94, 603, 625
Coke on Littleton (Coke), 16–17n3
Coleman, Jules, 451, 470
Coleman v. MacLennan, 235
Cole v. State, 86
colleague, 27
collective efficiency, 456–61
collective rights, 595
Collice, People v., 559–60
Colorado v. See name of opposing party
"color of state law," 198
comity, 278, 282, 492
Commentaries (Blackstone), 26, 251n4
Commissioner of Internal Revenue, Porter v.,
   409

commissioner's oath, 207
common currency, 455
common fund cause in equity, 509
common good, 359, 367, 604. *See also*
   public welfare; social good
common law, 4–6, 54, 56–57
   analogy and, 79
   civil law and, 29–30, 35–38, 52
   criminal law and (*see* criminal law)
   dissenters in, 173
   diversity-of-citizenship jurisdiction and,
      302–14
      Erie Railroad Co. v. Tompkins, 303–14
   due process and, 260
   equality in, 175–76
   freedom and, 225
   history of, 15–28
      Scott v. Shepherd, 21–27
   international law and, 106
   jury and, 243–47, 249, 251n4, 253–
      54n5, 256
   language of, 54–74
   lawyers in, 214–15
   legal reasoning in, 80, 82–90, 94–102,
      347
   as monistic legal system, 34
   Right and reasonable, 593–94, 602
   territorial jurisdiction and, 278
   theory of, 315–24
      American civil trial in outline, 502–24
      contract as justice, 413–25
      contract as law, 395–412, *table 19.1*
      contracts, breach of, 426–39
      economic efficiency, 452–71
      equity, triumph of, 336, 338–57
      feudalism in land law, 319–37, *table*
        15.1
      property, contemporary, 358–75
      property, frontiers of, 376–94
      tort law, foundations of, 440–51
      tort law, from contributory to
        comparative fault, 472–87
      tort law, punitive damages in, 488–
        501
Common Law, The (Holmes), 596
"*le common law*," 56–57
common law method, 625–41
   analysis, 627–34
      deduction, 628–30

induction, 630–34
    conclusion(s), 634
    methodology problem, 639–41
    precedent, 635–39
        later treatment and authority of, 635–36
        natural model of, 638n3
        rules from, 638–39
        significance of time and court of, 636–38
    premises, 626–27
Common Law Tradition, The (Llewellyn), 423n6
Commonwealth v. See name of opposing party
communal judgments of fairness, 419–25
Communism, 359–60, 455
communitarianism, 416, 605
community standard, 64
commutative justice, 454
comparative law, 11, 416, 500, 502n2, 591
    criminal law and, 530–64, 567
comparative negligence, 31–32, 472–87
    Nga Li v. Yellow Cab Co., 475–87
comparison. See induction
compelling state interest, doctrine of, 219
compensation. See also damages
    civil trial and, 518
    contract law and, 438–39
    economic efficiency and, 457–60, 462
    property law and, 361, 363–65, 367, 373–75, 377
    tort law and, 443, 447, 449, 486, 489–90, 493–94, 609
competition, 457, 463, 501
complaints, 21, 505–11, 522, 537
complementarity, 70
compulsory counterclaims, 507
concentration camp victims, 278
Concept of Law, The (Hart), 73n25, 313
conditional fees, 324–25
conditional privilege, 238
conditions subsequent, 322
Confederacy, 178–79, 181–82, 196–97
confessions, 534–35
conflict of laws, 314, 498
conflicts of interest, 505
conflicts of representation, 505
Connecticut Constitution, 362–63
Connecticut law, 203–9, 362–67

Connecticut Practice Book. Rule 8(I), 203–9
Connecticut Supreme Court, 203, 206
Connecticut v. See name of opposing party
consensus, 245
consensus ad idem, 435
consent
    abortion cases and, 47
    contract law and, 396, 420, 423
    economic efficiency and, 455–56, 469
    medical research and, 377, 379–80, 383–87, 390–92
consentement, 396
consideration, doctrine of, 397–98, table 19.1, 400–403, 408–10, 414, 419, 437, 607
conspiracies, criminal, 256
constitutional democracy, 533
constitutional law, 19, 38, 55, 105–314
    alternative Constitution (see alternative Constitution)
    Constitution as code, 111–31
    criminal law and, 535
    diversity-of-citizenship jurisdiction, 302–14
    due process ascendant, 259–75
    equality, 201–23
    federalism, 150–71
    freedom, 224–42
    judicial review, 132–49, 247
    jury, 243–58
    state judicial power, coordination of, 276–301, table 13.1
Constitution Convention (U.S., 1787), 106, 153–54, 160
Constitution for Europe, 167–68, 175, 220–22
Constitutions of Clarendon (1164), 244
consumers, 442, 450–51, 461–64, 495
contemporary property, 358–75
    Heller, Connecticut v., 362–67
    limiting other people's use of land, 367–75
        Boomer v. Atlantic Cement Co., 368–75
contempt, 246–56, 339, 352, 522, 538, 600
Continental Congress (U.S.), 173
Continental law. See civil law tradition
contingent remainders, 334

contraception, 261
contract, 18, 20, 32, 37, 604
  alternative dispute resolution and, 523
  breach of, 377, 402–3, 426–39, 473,
    607
    Hawkins v. McGee, 436–39, 606
    Jacob & Youngs, Inc. v. Kent, 428–34,
      604
    Kessler and Fine on, 435–36
  as justice, 413–25
    communal judgments of fairness, 419–
      25
    culpa in contrahendo, 413–19
    Shelley v. Trafalgar House Public Ltd.,
      417–19
    Williams v. Walker-Thomas Furniture
      Co., 420–25
  as law, 395–412
    Baehr v. Penn-O-Tex Oil Corp., 398–
      404
    Feinberg v. Pfeiffer Co., 404–11
  property law and, 325–26, 355, 377
  tort law and, 427, 447–49, 488–89
le contract à titre gratuit, 402
contract of transfer, 397
contractual warranty, 437, 443
contributory negligence, 31–32, 309–10,
  312, 472–87
  Nga Li v. Yellow Cab Co., 475–87
conventions, 76–77, 79
Converse, Bradlee v., 332–33n11
conversion, 377–78, 380–92, 606
conveyance, 327–28
convicted felons, 222
conviction, 531, 543–44, 564–65
Cooke v. United States, 252
copyright violations, 256
Coquillette, Daniel, 27
Corbin, Arthur L., 424
Corn Laws, 457–58
corporate finance, 350
corporate law, 350
corporations
  civil trial and, 506
  diversity-of-citizenship jurisdiction and,
    303n1, 305, 307, 309
  equity and, 350
  federalism and, 155–57, 161
  tort law and, 450, 495

corrective justice, 317–18, 443, 449–50,
  470, 473
cost accounting, 466
cost-benefit analysis, 68n20, 441–42, 450,
  463, 468–69, 576, 608, 610
counterclaims, 505, 507–8, 511, 515, 517,
  521
countermajoritarian difficulty, 146, 599
countervoices, 172–73, 176, 199
court costs, 518, 520, 523
Courtney v. Glanvil, 342–45
Court of Appeals (D.C.), 421
Court of Appeals (Mo.), 404–11
Court of Appeals (N.Y.), 368–75, 428–34,
  527, 540–41, 550–67
Court of Appeals (U.S.), 38, 249, 304–5,
  308–9, 520
Court of Criminal Appeals (Tenn.), 84,
  86, 88
court of history, 233–34, 238n7
courts of equity, 338–39, 344, 350, 353–55
Cover, Robert, 68n22
Craig v. Harney, 253
Crane, Frederick E. (J.), 433
Crane, Stephen, 541, 549, 567
Crane v. New York, 211
creation texts, 176
credibility, 544
credible evidence, 582
Crime of Self-Defense, A (Fletcher), 565
crimes against humanity, 301, 577, 581
Criminal Code (German), 40–52
criminal conspiracies, 256
criminal contempt, 243, 246–56
criminal law, 7–9, 525–90
  aggression, model of, 473
  common law and, 18–19, 25–26, 34
  contracts and, 377
  due process and, 259–74
  equality and, 202
  freedom and, 234
  jury and, 243, 245–56, 597, 600, 609
  language of, 55, 63
  legal reasoning in, 82–91, 94–102
  self-defense, domestic and international,
    568–90
  self-defense, procedure, 531–48
    aggressive lawyering, 546
    appeal, asymmetrical rules of, 545–46

arraignment and bail, 535–36
conviction and sentencing,
  separation of, 543–44
evidence, rules of, 544–45
extradition, 534
grand jury indictment, 537–43
interrogation, 534–35
pretrial dossier and, 546–47
self-defense, substantive law, 549–67
state judicial power, coordination of,
  277
tort law and, 489, 494–95, 501
universal jurisdiction in, 301
Critical Legal Studies movement, 416, 471
cross-appeal, 520
cross-claim, 508
cross-examination of witnesses, 214, 515,
  545
cruel and unusual punishment, 272
cruelty to animals, 360n4
Cuban missile crisis, 575
culpability, 41, 50, 377, 556, 562
culpa in contrahendo, 413–19, 427, 435–36,
  604–5
"Culpa in Contrahendo, Bargaining in
  Good Faith, and Freedom of
  Contract" (Kessler and Fine), 435–
  36
Currie, Brainerd, 498
customary law, 327

Dalloz edition of French Code civil, 30,
  33, 355
Damaška, Mirjan, 533
damages. *See also* compensation
  civil trial and, 506, 518–20, 522
  contract law and, 403, 418, 426–27,
    433, 435–38, 473
  equity and, 339, 353–56
  property law and, 363–64, 368–74, 377,
    393, 606
  tort law and, 440, 442, 444–50, 476–77,
    482–83, 496–500, 606, 609
damnum absque injuria, 137
Danaher, John A. (J.), 424–25
*Danaher, Southwestern Telegraph & Telephone
  Co. v.*, 497
deadly force, 553–61, 563, 569–71, 579
Death of Contract, The (Gilmore), 411

death penalty, 108, 244, 564, 588
debt, 349–50, 422
decentralization, 7–8, 38, 69, 216
Deckebach, Clarke v., 204
Declaration of Independence (U.S.), 106,
  173–77, 181, 199, 358, 594, 596,
  598
de Donis Conditionalibus (1285), 327–28
deduction, 77–80, 628–30
  modus ponens, 629–30
  modus tollens, 630
  syllogism, 628–29
"deep pockets," 450
defamation, private, 240
defamatory statements, 241
default, 421–22
default judgments, 507
defects, 443
deference, 69–70, 592
Definition of offense, 41, 45, 48, 50
Defore, People v., 267, 270
De Grey (C.J.), 24–26, 79, 81, 619–20
DeJonge v. Oregon, 261
Delaware law, 291–92, 350
democracy
  alternative Constitution and, 179
  common law and, 18, 38–39
  criminal law and, 533
  freedom and, 225, 239–40, 599–600
  jury and, 244–45
  property law and, 358–61, 602
  sovereignty and, 610
  U.S. Constitution and, 106, 108, 259
denials of affirmative dimensions of
  criminal liability, 40
Dennis v. United States, 234
de novo, 521, 547
deontological demands of justice, 58
depositions, 512–13
Depue v. Flatau, 446, 449
derecho, 592
*DeShaney v. Winnebago County Department
  of Social Security*, 197
detrimental reliance, 403, 413, 607
deutsches Recht, 592
*Developments in the Law, State-Court
  Jurisdiction*, 295
devisees, 321, 326
Dewire v. Haveles, 329–36

Dexter v. Inches, 332–33n11
diadic legal systems, 33, 35
Diaz, Mathews v., 221
Dickerson v. United States, 274
dignitary rights, 273
diplomacy, 578
"direct a verdict," 8–9
direct causation, 472
directed verdict, 516n7
Director, Aaron, 464
diritto, 55–57, 59
disclosure, 378, 385–87, 391–92, 488–94, 605
discovery, 500, 509, 512–13, 514, 547
discretion, 70–74
    civil trial and, 520–21
    due process and, 271–72
    equity and, 353
    federalism and, 160
    language of, 470
    property law and, 364–65
    tort law and, 484, 495
discrimination, 181–99, 201–15, 219–22, 260, 306
discussion, 9–10
disentailment, 327
dismiss the complaint, 8–9, 509–11, 513
dissenters, 79, 173, 219, 572
distribution, 459, 470
distributive justice, 317–18, 443, 450–51, 470
district attorneys, 8, 533, 538–39
District of Columbia law, 421
diversity, 592, 595–97, 601, 609
"diversity" jurisdiction, federal, 278
diversity-of-citizenship jurisdiction, 277, 292, 302–14, 601–2
divine right of kings, 176
divorce actions, 295
doctrine, 36–37, 39–40, 52
Doctrine of Remoteness, 329
Dodd v. Holmes, 479
Doerner, Russell (C.), 404–11
dogma, 36–37, 39
domestic violence, 572, 576–77
dominant doctrine, 172
Dominguez, Daniel R. (J.), 417–19
Donation Law of Oregon, 280

Donovan v. Kaszycki & Sons Contrs., 559
double jeopardy, 272, 501
Douglas, William O. (J.), 237–38, 268
Douglas v. Buder, 92
draft, registration for, 219
Dr. Bonham's Case (Coke), 16, 133, 146, 149
Dred Scott v. Sanford, 170, 176–77, 181, 194n11, 211, 224, 599n8
dress codes, 130
Drittwirkung, 197
droit, 55–57, 59, 68, 592
le droit français, 592
"due process," 59–60
due process ascendant, 259–75
    Mapp v. Ohio, 263–74
Due Process Clause (U.S. Constitution), 59–60, 202, 239n8, 241–42, 259–75
    criminal law and, 537
    entitlements and, 376
    jury and, 243, 247–49, 255–56, 597, 600
    legal reasoning and, 91–102
    property law and, 359
    state judicial power, coordination of, 279–301
    tort law and, 489, 495–99
Dukeminier, Jesse, 329
Duke of Norfolk's Case (1681), 329
Duncan v. Louisiana, 249–50, 255, 272, 624
Dunn, Anderson v., 252
duress, 420
duties, 58–59, 413–14
Dworkin, Ronald, 58–59, 72
dynastic fortunes, 334

easements, 352–55, 368
Eastern European law, 29
Eastman Marble Co. v. Vermont Marble Co., 331n6
eavesdropping, 262
ecclesiastical law, 340, 347. *See also* canon law
economic analysis of law, 38, 77, 393–94, 425, 442, 460–61, 463–64, 470–71
economic consequence, 370–72
economic efficiency, 443–44, 452–71

Coasian reaction, 464–69
Kaldor/Hicks and collective efficiency,
   456–61, 463, 468
methods and insights, 469–71
Pigovian efficiency, 461–64, 466–67,
   469
voluntary markets and Pareto
   efficiency, 453–56, 467–68
economic relations, 317
Economics of Welfare, The (Pigou), 463n8
editorial advertisements, 230
Edward IV, King of England, 341
Edward VI, King of England, 341
efficiency, 58–59, 68n20, 317–18, 449–50,
   453–54, 610–11. *See also*
   economic efficiency
egreditur personam, 25, 25n16
Ehrenzweig, Albert A., 297
Eichmann, Adolf, 278, 577
Eigentum verpflichtet, 359
ejectione firmae, 345
ejectment action, 292
Elizabeth I, Queen of England, 341
Elkins v. United States, 266–67
Ellenborough, Lord, 477
Ellesmere, Lord, 341–42, 603
Emancipation Proclamation, 457
embezzlement, 377
eminent domain, 361, 363–65, 374, 609
emotional distress, 441
Englard, Yitzhak, 449
English Civil War, 106
English common law, 15–20, 106, 449
   contempt power and, 253–54n5
   equity, triumph of, 338–47
   feudalism in land law, 319–29, 334–35,
      table 15.1, 336
   jury and, 244–45
   language of, 63
   self-defense and, 585–86
English language, 17, 39
   language of law, common and civil, 54–
      74
entailment, 327–28
enterprise liability, 463
entitlements, 376
enumerated powers, 154–62, 164, 167, 276–
   77, *table 13.1*

environmental laws, 361
epieikeia, 338
Epstein, Richard, 451, 473
equality, 107, 130, 201–23, 594
   about equal protection of laws, 218–23
   alternative Constitution and, 170, 175–
      79, 196
   economic efficiency and, 454
   freedom and, 170, 224–25, 241, 598–99
   Griffiths, In re, 203–16, 218–20
      lawyers, roles and ethics of, 215–18
   international humanitarian law and, 590
equality in distribution, 318
Equal Protection Clause (U.S.
   Constitution), 201–4, 208–11,
   213, 215, 225, 259–60, 361, 596–
   98
equidad, 62
equitable estates, 348
equitable estoppel, 409
equitable juridiction, 17, 336, 338–57
   biotechnology and, 390–91
   chancery courts and, 338, 340–50
      argument from antiquity concerning,
         341–42, 345–50
      Courtney v. Glanvil, 342–45
      Goebel on, 340–42
   culpa in contrahendo and, 419
   pleading and maxims, 350–54
      Malnar v. Whitfield, 351–54, 603
   Right and reasonable, 603
*Equitable Jurisdiction of the Court of Chancery,
   The* (Spence), 340
equitable ownership, 348–50
equitable pleading, 350–54
equitable titles, 348
équité, 62, 355, 396
"equity," 62–63, 304, 347, 349–50, 354–
   55, 431n2, 603
"Equity" (Vinogradoff), 339
equity as principle, 339
Equity Jurisprudence (Story), 350–51
equity of redemption, 349–50
"Erie Doctrine and the Constitution,
   The" (Hill), 314
Erie Railroad Co. v. Tompkins, 19, 277,
   282n1, 303–14, 601–2
Ermessen, 71

Ermessensfreiheit, 72
Ernst and Ernst, 406
error, assignments of, 445
error, writ of, 343–44
"essential." *See* necessity
"establishment" clause, 130
"estates," 321, 349
estates in land, 18, 320–36, *table 15.1*
    Dewire v. Haveles, 329–36
estate tax, 349
estoppel, 409–10, 419
estoppel in pais, 409
Ethelred II, King of England, 244
ethics
    of adversarial system, 533
    of biotechnology, 390–91
    of lawyers, 215–18
    of self-defense, 588n11
ethnic cleansing, 597, 611
ethnic minorities, 471
Euclid v. Ambler Realty Co., 364
European Convention on Human Rights
        (1949), 60, 106, 220–21, 359
European Court of Human Rights, 60,
        81, 106
European law, 241, 244
European Union, 106, 168, 221, 443
evidence, 8–9
    civil trial and, 503, 512–17, 519–21
    criminal law and, 527, 531–32, 534–37,
        539, 542, 544–45, 547, 551–52,
        560–62, 566
    diversity-of-citizenship jurisdiction and,
        314
    due process and, 262–74
    international criminal law and, 582
evidence of law, 35–36
ex ante, 34, 34n6, 582
exceptionalism, 107
excessive bail, 536
exclusionary rule, 261–74, 534, 545
excusable homicide, 585
excuse, 40
    self-defense as, 585–86
execution of judgment, 518
execution of order, 521–22
executors, 348
executory interests, 324–26, 334, *table 15.1*

exemplary damages. *See* punitive damages
Exodus, book of, 79–80, 586
Ex parte. *See name of party*
expectation damages, 418–19
"expediency principle," 539
ex post, 34n6
ex post facto laws, 84–85, 88, 90–97, 100,
        102, 120, 526
express warranties, law of, 427
externalities, 442, 450–51, 461–64, 466,
        469, 473
extradition, 534
extrastatutory necessity, 50–51

factual determination, 532
failure of issue, 326–27
Fairfax (J.), 341
Fairfax, Lord, 150
*Fairlawn Cemetery Association v. First
        Presbyterian Church*, 354
Fairmont Coal Co., Kuhn v., 310
fairness, 60–63, 355
    communal judgments of, 419–25
    economic efficiency and, 459, 466–67
    property law and, 391
    tort law and, 450, 477, 484, 492, 496,
        499
fair play, 61, 63, 511
fair trial, 60–62, 273–74, 536
Falchetti v. Pennsylvania Railway Co., 308–9
Falkland Islands war (1982), 589
fallacies, 631–32
    ambiguity, 632
    irrelevance, 633–34
    presumption, 632–33
false imprisonment, 441
false speech, 235–36, 238, 240
Family Finance Corp., Sniadach v., 300
family law, 37
Family Medical Leave Act, 199
Far Eastern law, 5
Farnsworth, E. Allen, 28, 412, 425, 439,
        524
fascism, 108
fault
    contract law and, 427–28, 434–35
    tort law and, 441, 443–44, 472–87
faute commune, 31, 480

Fawaz Yunis, United States v., 277
FCC. *See* German Federal Constitution
   Court (FCC)
fealty, 320
Federal Criminal Code (U.S.), 33
federalism, 107, 150–71, 276–77, 496–99
Federalist, 165
Federalist Party, 133
Federal Judiciary Act (1789). *See* Judiciary
   Act (1789)
federal law, 5–8. *See also* U.S. Supreme
   Court
   alternative Constitution and, 197
   attorney conduct and, 216
   civil trial and, 502–24
   criminal law and, 526, 535–37
   diversity-of-citizenship jurisdiction and,
      302–14, 601–2
   judicial review and, 133
   jurisdiction of, 124, 276–78, *table 13.1*
   jury and, 247, 249–50, 252–53
   U.S. Constitution and, 130
Federal Rules of Appellate Procedure
   (FRAP), 520
Federal Rules of Civil Procedure (U.S.),
   6, 30, 33, 216, 218, 314, 505
Federal Rules of Criminal Procedure
   (U.S.), 30, 33
fee, 321–25
fee simple, 321, 323n2, 324–28
fee simple absolute, 326, 328, *table 15.1*
fee simple determinable, 324, *table 15.1*
fee simple subject to a condition
   subsequent, 324–25, *table 15.1*
fee tail, 326–28, *table 15.1*
Feinberg, Anna Sacks, 404–5
Feinberg v. Pfeiffer Co., 404–11, 607
felonies, 222, 537, 550, 553–55, 560–61
feminist legal scholars, 471, 572
Ferguson, Plessy v., 201
feudalism, 18, 316–17, 605
   in land law, 18, 319–37, 360–61, 602
      Dewire v. Haveles, 329–36
      estates in land, 320–36, *table 15.1*
fictitious consent, 291, 295–96, 300
fiduciary duty, breach of, 380, 383–87,
   391, 393, 517, 605
Field, David Dudley, 478

Field, Stephen J. (J.), 186, 280–86, 292–93
Field Code of Civil Procedure (N.Y.
   State), 20, 478, 480–81, 486
filing, 505–7, 509
Finch, Moyle, Sir, 344
finder of fact, 515
Fine, Edith, 435–36
First Nat'l Bank & Trust Co., Allen v.,
   332n8
*First Presbyterian Church, Fairlawn Cemetery
   Association v.*, 354
First World War, 599
Fish & Game Comm'n, Takahashi v., 204–5
Fiske v. Kansas, 239n8, 261
Flatau, Depue v., 446, 449
Fletcher, George P., 199, 377n2, 565
"flipping," 539
Flores, City of Boerne v., 198
Florida v. See name of opposing party
forbearance, 398, 401, 409–11, 595, 597
foreign corporations, 295–96
forfeiture of goods, 585–86
formalism, 73n25
forms of action, 20–21
Forrester, Butterfield v., 477
Fortas, Abe (J.), 255, 624
forum non conveniens, 339
Fourth Lateran Council, 245
framers, 89–90, 94–95, 102, 155–56, 184,
   209, 257
franchise, 180–81, 208, 222, 514, 599
Frankfurter, Felix (J.), 268
fraud, 377, 491, 498, 505, 519
free alienation, 327
freedmen, 260
freedom, 59–60, 224–42
   alternative Constitution and, 178–79,
      193–94, 196
   of contract, 395–96
   equality and, 170, 224–25, 241, 598–99
   Kant on, 60, 316, 586–87
   liberalism and, 316–17, 605
   property law and, 360–61, 374–75
freedom of assembly, 261
freedom of petition, 261
freedom of religion, 257, 261
freedom of speech, 107, 130, 225–42, 247,
   256, 261, 264n6, 268, 599–600

freedom of the press, 107, 225–42, 247, 261, 599
"free evaluation of evidence," 545
"free exercise" clause, 130
freeholders, 328
Freeman v. Alderson, 293
free market economics, 328, 457, 461–62, 467
free trade, 457–58
French, Lafayette Insurance Co. v., 295
French Code civil, 17–18, 30–33, 37, 40, 64, 108, 257–58
    contract law and, 396–97, *table 19.1*, 402, 420, 426n1, 604, 607
    equity and, 347, 355
    legal reasoning in, 83
    liberalism and, 316
    tort law and, 30–31, 440–41, 474, 479–80, 485
French law
    criminal law and, 537, 547
    jury and, 244
    language of, 56, 58, 61–62, 64–66, 66–67n17, 71
French Revolution, 319
French Right, 592
frictionless market, 453
frivolous litigation, 216n8, 505–6
Fuhrman, Mark, 262
Fuller, Lon L. 103, 439
Full Faith and Credit Clause, 125, 278, 285–86, 288, 299
future interests, 321, 323–26, 328

Gabor, Zsa Zsa, 54–55n1
Garland, Ex parte, 212
garnishment, 522
Garrett, Board of Trustees of Univ. of Ala. v., 199
gays, 471
Gefährdungshaftung, 440
gender discrimination, 199, 219–22
"general equity," 347
general jurisdiction courts, 350
general law, 304–10, 312–13. *See also* common law
General Theory of State-Court Jurisdiction, A (Hazard), 293

Genesis, book of, 176
Genetics Institute, 379–80
Geneva Conventions (1949), 526, 589–90
genocide, 301, 526, 577
Gény, Dean François, 347
George III, King of England, 174, 176
"Georgia's Proposed Dynasty Trust" (Chaffin), 334
Georgia v. See name of opposing party
German abortion case (1927), 42–53, 55–56, 77, 79, 377, 594, 602, 608
German Basic Law (1949), 73, 129, 132, 219–20, 222, 359, 526
German Civil Code (BGB), 37
    common law and, 41, 47–48, 50, 64
    contract law and, 426–28, 434–35, 607
    legal reasoning in, 83
    liberalism and, 316, 396, 415–16
    tort law and, 31–32, 37, 440–41, 448–49, 451, 486, 488
    U.S. Constitution and, 108, 257–58
German Code of International Criminal Law, 301
German Constitution. *See* German Basic Law (1949)
German Criminal Code, 40–41, 45–52, 66–67, 601
German Federal Constitution Court (FCC), 132–33, 148
German law, 17–19
    civil rights cases and, 197
    common law and, 40–52
    contempt power and, 253–54n5
    contract law and, 397, *table 19.1*, 402–4, 413–16, 420, 434–36
    conversion and, 377
    criminal law and, 537, 539, 543–45, 547, 563–64, 567
    equity and, 348
    language of, 54–56, 58, 62n10, 64–66, 66–67nn17,18, 71–72
    legal reasoning in, 83
    reading cases and, 80
    universal jurisdiction and, 277, 301
German Penal Code, 569, 571, 577, 579, 582
German Right, 592
German Supreme Court, 46–48, 594

Gesetz, 54–56, 73
Gettysburg Address (Lincoln), 178–81, 199, 598, 605
Gideon v. Wainwright, 272–73
gifts, 397–98, 402–4, 406, 408
Gilmore, Grant, 411
Ginossar, Shalev, 65n14
Ginsberg, Ruth Bader, 499–500
Gitlow v. New York, 239n8, 247
Glanvil, Courtney v., 342–45
global context, 4–5, 60, 568, 590–91
God, 175–76, 178–79, 596
    act of, 446–47, 450
Goebel, Julius, 340–42
Goetz, Bernhard, 527–30, 534–44, 550–52, 554, 561, 563–67, 575–76, 578–79, 581–85, 611
Goetz, People v., 527, 533–34, 538, 540–44, 550–67, 578, 582, 609–11
Goguac Resort Ass'n, Battle Creek v., 366
Goldberg, Arthur J. (J.), 238–40
Golde, David W., 378–80, 394
Gompers v. Bucks Stove & Range Co., 253
Gompers v. United States, 251, 623
good faith, 396, 415, 417, 436, 490, 504, 603
good faith exception, 274
Google, 57
Gore, Al, 197
Gore, BMW of North American, Inc. v., 489–501, 601, 610
Gore, Bush v., 76
Gore, Ira, Jr., 489–91, 493–94
governmental searches, 261–62
Graham v. Richardson, 205, 210
"grandfathered," 256–57
grand jury, 182–83, 244, 501, 527, 532, 537–43, 549–54, 561–62
Grant, Cobbs v., 391
Grant, Ulysses S., 177, 182
grant deed, 323
grantees, 321–24, 328–29, 334
grantors, 320–29, 334
grants, 320–29, 334
Gratz v. Bollinger, 222
Gray, John Chipman, 329, 332n9
Great Britain. House of Lords, 80–81
Greenawalt, Kent, 103, 607

Green v. United States, 255
Griffin, Lovell v., 231
Griffiths, Fre Le Poole, 203
Griffiths, In re, 203–16, 218–22, 241
Griggs, Arndt v., 294
Grisham, John, 243
Griswold v. Connecticut, 261
"grossly excessive" punishment, 489, 492, 496, 498–99
group welfare, 469, 471
Grutter v. Bollinger, 222
Guaranty Trust v. York, 314
guardians, 510
guilt, 532, 537–38, 542–47, 561, 565
guilt theory, 52
Gun-Free School Zone Act (1990), 202n1
gun possession, illegal, 527–28, 538, 550–51, 567, 578

habeas corpus, writ of, 177, 341, 343, 345, 499
Hack v. President of Yale College, 198
Hague Conventions, 526
Hague v. CIO, 261
Hamas, 576
Hancock, Stewart F., Jr. (J.), 562
Hand, Learned (J.), 296, 409, 441–42, 608
Hans v. Louisiana, 197
Hardwick, Bowers v., 60, 77n1
Harlan, John Marshall, II (J.), 90–93, 201, 255, 268–71, 624
Harlan, John Marshall (J.), 193–96, 198
Harney, Craig v., 253
Harper, William, 134
Harris, Anderson v., 332n10
Harris, Sidney M., 405–6
Hart, H.L.A., 73n25, 313
Haslip, Pacific Mutual Life Insurance Co. v., 493–94, 496–97
hate crimes, 241
hate speech, 241, 599
Haveles, Dewire v., 329–36
Hawkins v. McGee, 436–39, 473, 606
Hayes, Rutherford B., 197
Hazard, Geoffrey C., 293, 299
health insurance, 442–43
hearing to show cause, 522
hearsay, 544–45

Hebrew language, 64–65
Hefler, State v., 98
Hegel, 54
hegemonic theory, 39
heirs, 321, 326–28
"heirs of the body," 326–28
Heitner, Schaffer v., 291, 377
Hellenistic influence, 64
Heller, Connecticut v., 362–67, 374, 602–3
Henry II, King of England, 244
Henry VI (Shakespeare), 334, 336
Henry VI, King of England, 340
Henry VII, King of England, 22, 36, 341, 345
Henry VIII, King of England, 341
herrschende Lehre, 39, 172
Hess v. Pawloski, 291, 295
Hibbs, Nevada Dep't of Human Resources v., 199
Hicks, J. R., 457–58
high-risk activities, 440
Hill, Albert, 314
Hillman, State v., 364–65
Him v. McCall, 211
Hiroshima bombing, 580
Hiscock, Frank H. (C.J.), 433
historical interpretation, 83
history
    common law and, 17–18
    court of, 233–34, 238n7
    Gettysburg Address and, 179
    in legal reasoning, 88–90, 98
    principle and, 256–58, 262, 264n6, 489
    U.S. Constitution and, 129–30
Hobbes, Thomas, 34
Hogan, John W. (J.), 433
Hogan, Malloy v., 272
holistic legal thought, 66–68
Holmes, Dodd v., 479
Holmes, Oliver Wendell, Jr. (J.), 71, 250–51, 253, 265, 307–8, 310–11, 313, 578, 596, 599n9, 600, 602, 607
Holocaust denial, 241
homage, 320
homicide, 83–91, 94, 98–101, 526, 542, 555, 557, 560, 567, 581, 585–86
l'homme raisonnable, 65
Home Ludens, 63
homosexual sodomy, 60, 77n1, 222–23

Hooe, Robert Townsend, 134
Hopkins, Yick Wo v., 204
hostile witnesses, 515
Hudson River Railroad Co., Austin v., 479
Hudson River Railroad Co., Johnson v., 481
Hughes, Charles E. (C.J.), 239n8
Hulbert, People v., 366
Huling v. Kaw Valley Railway Co., 294
humanitarian intervention, 584–85n9
humanity of aggressors, 588–90
human rights, 18, 59–60, 359, 590, 611
Hungarian language, 54–55n1
"hung jury," 246
Hunt, Ward (J.), 287–89
Hunter, Ballard v., 294
Hunters Lessee, Martin v., 150
Hussein, Saddam, 584
Hussey (J.), 341
Hutchinson v. Chase & Gilbert, 296

ICC. *See* International Criminal Court (ICC)
"I Have a Dream" (King), 199, 225
illegal force, 572
illegitmacy, 202, 211
Illinois Central Railway Co., Olberding v., 295
Illinois law, 247–56
imago dei, 176
Immigration and Naturalization Service, 212
imminence as dimension of self-defense, 571–77
imminent threat, 569–70, 574–77
immunity, 505, 538–39
impeachment, 252
implead, 508
implied consent to service, 295–96
implied contract, 449
in camera inquiry, 551
incarceration, 522
Inches, Dexter v., 332–33n11
incriminating material, 544
indictments, 537–39, 541, 549–53, 562
indirect causation, 472
individual autonomy, 316
individual behavior, 64
individualism. *See* liberalism
individual rights, 59, 64n13, 316–17

economic efficiency and, 455–56, 459, 461

Right and reasonable, 595, 598–99

self-defense and, 587–88

induction, 630–34

  fallacies, 631–32

    ambiguity, 632

    irrelevance, 633–34

    presumption, 632–33

informed consent, 377, 380, 383–87, 390–92

Ingham v. Brooks, 365

"inherent right," 587

inheritance law, 37, 328

initial investigation in civil trial, 504–6

injunctions

  civil trial and, 518, 522

  contract law and, 427

  equity and, 339–42, 350, 352–54, 356

  property law and, 368–74

innocence, 62, 532, 536–38, 543–44, 547, 561

Inns of Court (England), 37

in personam jurisdiction, 289–91, 293–99, 322, 355, 377, 470

inquest, 244

inquisitorial system, 531–32

In re. *See name of party*

in rem jurisdiction, 281, 286, 291–94, 297–300, 322, 376–77, 470

insanity, 40–41, 451, 543, 565, 581

installment contracts, 420–25

Institutes of the Common Law (Coke), 16, 16–17n3

insufficient evidence, motion for, 516n7

insurance, health, 442–43

integrity, insurance of, 274

intention, 52

  contract law and, 430–32, 434

  as dimension of self-defense, 575, 581–83

  in *Goetz, People v.*, 557, 563, 566–67

intentional torts, 440–41, 473, 517

intention libérale, 402

interaction, model of, 472–74

intercourt courtesy, 278

"interest analysis," 497

internalizing of externalities, 451, 461–63

Internal Revenue Code (U.S.), 30, 33

international commerce, 500

International Court of Justice, 526

International Criminal Court (ICC), 61, 70, 106–7, 241–42, 271–72, 526, 538, 570, 580, 593, 597–98

international criminal law, 301, 570, 577, 585–86, 601

International Harvester Co. v. Kentucky, 295

international humanitarian law, 589–90

international law, 526, 568, 570, 577, 584–85n9, 595

international law of armed conflict, 582–83, 589–90

international legal education, 10

International Military Tribunals, 526

international self-defense, 568–90

International Shoe v. State of Washington, 289–91, 296, 298–301, 601

International Torture Convention, 526

international trade, 593

international war crime, 190n9

interpersonal comparison of utilities, 463

interpleader actions, 508

interpretation, 34, 34n7, 35–37, 149, 151, 156, 167, 314

  of contracts, 396, 434

  of Declaration of Independence (U.S.), 175–76

  fear of, 34n7

  history and principle, 256–58, 262, 264n6, 489

  "living" Constitution and, 273

interrogation, 534–35

interrogatories, 512–13, 518

interstate commerce, 495

Interstate Commerce Clause (U.S. Constitution), 202

interstate corporate activities, 295–96

intervenors, 508

intime conviction, 545

intoxication, 581

inverse taking, 361, 366–67

investigation, 532, 541, 546–47

Iraq war (2003), 107, 130, 173, 568, 572, 572–73n3, 575, 582, 584

irrebuttable presumptions, 517

irrelevance, 633–34

irrevocable offers, 402

Islamic law, 4–5

Israel-Arab War (1967), 568, 573–74, 578
Israeli law, 64–65, 277–78
Israeli response to suicide bombings, 576
Israeli strike on Iraqi nuclear reactor
     (1981), 574–75
Is This Conflict Really Necessary? (Traynor),
     297
Italian law, 17, 30, 34, 38, 55

Jackson, D. Wirth, 567
Jacob & Youngs, Inc. v. Kent, 428–34, 604
Jaggard, Edwin A. (J.), 448
James, John, 151
James I, King of England, 336, 341, 345–
     50
James v. United States, 93
Jamison's Estate, Mo., In re, 410
Japanese Constitution, 358
Japanese law, 64n13
Jasen, Matthew J. (J.), 373–74
Jefferson, Thomas, 133–34, 147, 169, 175,
     232, 234
Jensen, Southern Pacific Co. v., 602
Jewish law, 33, 38
Jhering, Rudolf von, 413–16, 605
Jimenez de Asua, Luis, 51
JNOV, 400n3, 516, 518
jog, 55, 592
John, King of England, 244
Johnson, Lyndon, 201
Johnson v. Hudson River Railroad Company,
     481
Johnson v. Zerbst, 215
Johnston, Joseph, 177n4
Jones v. Alfred H. Mayer Co., 260n3
Jones v. Bird, 479
judges, appointment of, 123, 134–49, 167
judging guilt or innocence, 532, 537, 543
judgment
     civil trial and, 511, 513, 516, 518–23
     common law and, 339–45
     criminal law and, 543
     as matter of law, motion for, 516
     notwithstanding verdict, motion for,
          400n3, 516, 518
     on pleadings, motion for, 511, 513
judicial creativity, 470
judicial interrogation, 515
judicial intervention, 458, 460–61, 466–69

judicial restraint, 268, 338, 478, 485
judicial review, 132–49, 478, 481–85, 595,
     599
Judiciary Act (1789), 138–39, 145–47, 252,
     302, 304–5, 308, 310–12
Judiciary Act (1831), 252–53
jurisdiction, 504, 506–7, 509–11, 514
Jurisdiction to Adjudicate (Von Mehren and
     Trautman), 297
jurisgenerative movements, 68n22
"jurispathic" decisions, 68n22
jurisprudence, 34–36
jurisprudence constante, 36
jury, 6–9, 18, 107, 243–58, 272. *See also*
     grand jury
     Bloom v. Illinois, 248–58, 600
     civil trial and, 506, 514–19, 521
     contract law and, 399, 404, 419, 431,
          434, 437–38
     criminal law and, 527, 532–33, 541–46,
          551, 555, 560–61, 566–67, 609
     deference and, 69–70
     equity and, 339, 355–56
     instruction of, 8, 516–17, 542, 549, 551–
          52, 554–55, 561–62, 566
     racial discrimination and, 182–86, 219,
          600
     Right and reasonable, 68, 592, 608–9
     selection of, 245, 514
     tort law and, 442–43, 445–46, 453, 475,
          477, 490–91, 495–98, 500–501
jury pool, 514
jus, 592
jus ad bellum, 580
jus in bello, 580, 590
"just compensation," 361, 374
justice
     common law and, 16, 317–18
     commutative, 454
     contract as, 413–25
     corrective, 317–18, 443, 449–50, 470,
          473
     criminal law and, 533, 545
     distributive, 317–18, 443, 450–51, 470
     economic efficiency and, 454, 456, 468,
          470
     equity and, 347
     language of law and, 58, 61–63
     natural, 347

Rawls on, 62, 318, 468
retributive, 545
Right and reasonable, 592, 609–10
self-defense as punishment and, 583–84
tort law and, 450–51
justifiable homicide, 586
justifiable reliance, principle of, 274, 436, 607
justification, 40–42, 45–47, 49–53, 505, 550–60, 562, 586–87
just war, 574

Kacynski, Ted, 565
Kaldor, Nicholas, 456, 458–59, 461
Kaldor/Hicks test, 456–61, 463, 468
Kalish, Ralph, 406
Kansas Supreme Court, 235
Kansas v. See name of opposing party
Kant, Immanuel, 54, 58, 60, 175, 316, 339, 441n1, 471, 586–87, 594
Kassal, Bentley (J.), 552
Kaszycki & Sons Contrs., Donovan v., 559
Katz v. United States, 262
Kaw Valley Railway Co., Huling v., 294
Kaye, Judith S. (J.), 562
Kelly, State v., 560
Kennedy, Anthony M., 60
Kennedy, Duncan, 416
kenri, 64n13
Kent, Jacob & Youngs, Inc. v., 428–34
Kentucky law, 305
Kentucky v. See name of opposing party
Kessler, Friedrich, 435–36
Kevorkian, Jack, 542
kidnapping, 553, 557, 570
King, Martin Luther, Jr., 199, 225–28
King, Rodney, 609
King's Bench, Court of, 340–43, 345
king's law, 18–19
Klopfer v. North Carolina, 272
Kohn, Rendell-Baker v., 198
Konigsberg v. State Bar of California, 212
Koontz v. B. & O. Railway Co., 309
Kronzeugen, 539
Kuhn v. Fairmont Coal Co., 310
Kupferman, Theodore R. (J.), 552

L&E (law & economics), 451–53, 458, 461, 464, 467, 470–71

Lafayette Insurance Co. v. French, 295
Lake Erie Transportation Co., Vincent v., 20, 368, 444–51, 608–9
"lame-duck," 134
land law, feudalism in, 18, 319–37
Dewire v. Haveles, 329–36
estates in land, 320–36, *table 15.1*
landlords, 325–26
language of law, common and civil, 17, 54–74, 416, 470
"deference," 69–70
"discretion," 70–74
"due process," 59–60
"fairness," 60–63
"law," 54–57
"policy," 58–59
"reasonableness," 63–69
Lanier, United States v., 92
last clear chance, doctrine of, 480–83, 485–86
latent ambiguity, 435–36
Latin American law, 5, 29, 40
"law," 54–57
law & economics (L&E), 451–53, 458, 461, 464, 467, 470–71
Law and Order (television series), 564
law as fact, 540
law as principle, 55–56, 339, 541
Law French, 323
"law of overruling necessity," 363
law of war, 568, 580
Lawrence v. Texas, 60, 81, 223
law schools. *See* legal education
Law Society, Andrews v., 220
lawyers
admission to bar of, 203–15, 217, 220, 222
aggressive, 546
civilian-trained, 7, 29, 515, 546
common law and, 17
criminal law and, 533
deference and, 69–70
professional standards of conduct for, 503, 505–6, 509, 512
roles and ethics of, 7–8, 10, 215–18
Shakespeare on, 334, 336
Learned Hand formula, 441–42
leasehold, 325, *table 15.1*, 377
Lebanon, 277

Lee, Robert E., 177, 181
legal aid, 564
legal culture, 316–18
    Right and reasonable, 592, 597, 609,
        611
    three types of, 33–35
legal education, 3–11, 19–21, 27, 37–38,
        615–17
legal intervention, 458, 460–61, 466–69
Legalitätsprinzip, 539
legality principle, 539
legal ownership, 348, 350
legal philosophy, 58
legal positivism, 73n25, 313
legal reasoning, 75–103
    deduction and analogy, 77–80
    precedent, 90–102
    reading cases, 80–82
    reasoning from statutes, 82–90
legge, 54, 56
legislation, 18, 34–36, 52. See also U.S.
        Congress
    criminal law and, 554, 556–59, 563
    economic efficiency and, 456–58
    judicial review of, 132–49, 247
    legal reasoning and, 81–85, 88, 91, 95,
        102
    medical research and, 387–88, 392–93
    sporting ethic and, 63n11
    state judicial power, coordination of,
        277
    statutes and, 645
    tort law and, 475, 477–85, 492, 497–
        99
    workers' compensation statutes and,
        438
Legrand, Pierre, 57n3
Lemieux, Young v., 364
lenity, rule of, 83
Leon, United States v., 274
lesbians, 471
lésion, 420
Lessig, Lawrence, 394
"letter" of Constitution, 167
Leviathan (Hobbes), 34
levy of execution, 279, 281, 285
Lewis, Charles L. (J.), 447–48
Lewis, Commonwealth v., 98
Lexis-Nexis, 33

liability
    civil trial and, 505, 508–9, 518
    contract law and, 411, 415–18, 427–28,
        435–36, 605–7
    criminal law and, 562–63, 565
    diversity-of-citizenship jurisdiction and,
        302–3, 306, 308
    economic efficiency and, 461–69, 473
    property law and, 377, 384–87, 390
    tort law and, 306, 411, 414–15, 440–43,
        446–51, 474–77, 482–83, 486,
        488, 490, 500
libel, 225–31, 234–40, 256, 500, 599–600
libel (action in admiralty), 506n5
"libel per se", 229, 231
"liberal," 431n2
liberal court, 81
liberalism, 316–17
    contract law and, 396, 413–16, 419–20,
        425, 433, 604–5
    equity and, 339
    feudalism and, 327, 336, 602
    property law and, 394
    self-defense and, 586–88
    tort law and, 450
libertarianism, 317, 360, 469
liberté, egalité, fraternité, 175
liberty. See freedom
liens, 522
life estate, 323–25, 328, table 15.1
life in being, 329
life interests, 332
Ligouri, People v., 555, 561
limitation, feudal, 324, 326–29, table 15.1,
        344
limited fees, 326
Lincoln, Abraham, 177–79, 181–82, 199,
        457, 590, 596, 598, 605
Linkletter v. Walker, 272, 274
Lippman, Max, 404–5
Littleton, Thomas de, 16–17n3
"living" Constitution, 273
Llewellyn, Karl, 67, 67n18, 423n6
LL.M. (master of laws degree), 27
"Loan Shark" law, 425
Lochner v. New York, 71
Locke, John, 175–76, 316, 586
Locke, Rose v., 92
Loevinger, Lee (J.), 399–402

loi, 54, 56–57
London College of Physicians, 133
long-arm jurisdiction, 290–91, 491, 510
Lopez, United States v., 202n1
lost income, 442
lost opportunity costs, 418
Louisiana Civil Code, 258n9, 479–80
Louisiana Purchase, 169–70
Louisiana v. See name of opposing party
Lovell v. Griffin, 231
loyalty, 505, 605
lumpers, 470
Lumsden, People v., 555, 561
Lynce v. Mathis, 93

MacGuigan, Patricia D. (J.), 351–54
MacLennan, Coleman v., 235
Madison, James, 134, 231–33
Madison, Marbury v., 53, 132–49, 150–51,
    160n9, 193n10, 247, 595
Magna Carta, 185n6, 244, 260
Maine, Henry, Sir, 20, 316, 395
Maine v. See name of opposing party
Maitland, Frederic W., 20–21
majority rule, 245, 599
malice, 229, 235–38, 414, 600
Malloy v. Hogan, 272
Malnar v. Whitfield, 351–54, 368, 374, 603
malum in se, 526
malus animus, 22, 22n12
mandamus, writ of, 134–35, 138, 140–41,
    145–48, 167
mandatory injunctions, 352–54
Mapp v. Ohio, 248, 262–74, 277
Marbury, William, 134–35, 137, 145, 148
Marbury v. Madison, 53, 132–49, 150–51,
    160n9, 193n10, 247, 595
market, 453–57, 460–62, 467–69, 608
market efficiency, 468–69
Marks v. United States, 92
Marshall, John (C.J.), 133–49, 151–66,
    168, 195n12, 196, 247, 595
Martin v. Hunters Lessee, 150
Marx, Karl, 317
Mary I, Queen of England, 341
Maryland General Assembly, 151
Maryland law, 150–53, 159–61, 163, 166–
    68
Maryland State Bar Ass'n v. Agnew, 218

Maryland v. See name of opposing party
Mason v. United States, 304
Massachusetts law, 176n2, 329–36, 474
Massachusetts v. See name of opposing party
material breach, 434
Mathews v. Diaz, 221
Mathis, Lynce v., 93
maximization of interests, self-defense as,
    587–90
maxims, 175, 205, 317, 326, 350–54, 363
McAleer, New England Trust Co. v., 332–
    33n11
McCall, Him v., 211
McCann v. Chasm Power Co., 370
McCulloch, James W., 166
McCulloch v. Maryland, 150–70, 195n12,
    196, 234n4, 276, 361, 595
McGee, Hawkins v., 436–39, 473, 606
*McKibbin, Philadelphia & Reading Railway
    Co. v.*, 295
McLaughlin, Chester B. (J.), 432–33
McLaughlin v. Florida, 205
McLean, John (J.), 283
McReynolds, James C. (J.), 312
McVeigh, Timothy, 565
meaningful choice, 423
measuring life, 329
mediation, 522–23
Medicaid, 376
medical exams, 512
medical expenses, 442
medical insurance, 442–43
medical research, 377–90, 605–6
Medicare, 222
meeting of minds, 435
Meiji Restoration, 64n13
mentally ill, protection of, 202
mesne lords, 322–23, 325, 327
Meyer, Bernard S. (J.), 562
Michaelson v. United States, 249, 622
Middle Ages, 18, 20, 37
military draft, registration for, 219
military tribunals, 257, 577
Mill, John Stuart, 235n5, 317
Miller, People v., 560
Miller, Samuel F. (J.), 260n2
Milosevic, Slobodan, 577
minimum contacts, 289, 291, 296, 298,
    301, 511, 601

Minnesota law, 398–404, 444–51

Minnesota Supreme Court, 398–404, 444–51

Minnesota v. See name of opposing party

minorities, 202, 209, 220–21, 471

"minority" rules, 173

Miranda v. Arizona, 272, 274

Miranda warnings, 528, 534–35

Missouri Compromise (1820), 170, 176, 224

Missouri law, 404–11

mistake, law of, 427–28

Mitchell, J. H., 280, 286–87, 292–93

Model Penal Code (U.S.), 30, 32–33, 51–52, 83–84, 556–58, 560, 562–63, 572

modus ponens, 629–30

modus tollens, 630

modus vivendi, 596

monarchical power, 106, 532–33

money, 455

monistic legal systems, 33–35

Montesquieu, 31, 71, 532

Moor, Cobb v., 343–44

Moore, John, 378–84, 387–94, 605–6

Moore v. Regents of the University of California, 377–94, 605–6

moral reasoning, 350, 387, 420–21, 447, 453, 458, 469–71, 483, 565–66, 590, 596, 607

More, Thomas, Sir, 341

Morgan, Ownbey v., 300

Morgentaler, Henry, 542

Morgentaler, Regina v., 542n10

Morgenthau, Robert, 538–39

Morrison, United States v., 202n1

Morse, State v., 366

mortgages, law of, 349

Moses, 33

Mosk, Stanley (J.), 388–92, 484

motions, 506n5, 507–11, 513, 516, 518–19

  for directed verdict, 516

  to dismiss, 507, 509–11, 516, 549, 551–52

  for insufficient evidence, 516n7

  for judgment as matter of law, 516

  for judgment notwithstanding verdict, 400n3, 516, 518

  for judgment on pleadings, 511, 513

  for more definite statement, 511

  for new trial, 519

  motion to dismiss, 513

motivations, 76

motorists' consent theory, 291, 295

mouth of the law, 31, 77

MPC. *See* Model Penal Code (U.S.)

murder, 550–51, 557, 567

Murray, Thomas H., 391

mutual mistake, 435

Myers v. United States, 311

N.A.A.C.P. v. Button, 230–32, 239

NAFTA (North American Free Trade Association), 457

Nagasaki bombing, 580

Napoleon, 37, 169

Nares (J.), 21–22, 25–26, 36, 77, 79, 81, 617, 619

narrow rule of interpretation, 82

Nasser, Gamal Abdel, 574

national bank, 150–52, 155–57, 161–62, 166–67, 169

national crime, 190n9

National Institutes of Health, 386

national law. *See* federal law

national legal education, 10

national origin, 219–21

National Security Strategy of the United States of America, The, 572–73n3

national wrong, 190n9

"natural equity," 347

naturalization, 210–13

natural justice, 347

natural right, 587

Near v. Minnesota, 261

"necessary," 119, 158–59

necessity, 43–47, 52–53, 552n2

  as dimension of self-defense, 575, 577–78

Neff, Pennoyer v., 279–301, 376, 500, 600–601, 610

negative interest theory of damages, 438–39

negligence, 609

  contract law and, 416, 419, 427, 435–36

  criminal law and, 557, 562–64

  economic efficiency and, 68n20

  medical research and, 391

tort law and, 440–46, 448–50, 472–87, 608

negotiations, 396, 413–18, 465–66, 522, 605

Nevada Dep't of Human Resources v. Hibbs, 199

New Birth of Freedom, A (Black), 199

New Deal, 202

New England Trust Co. v. McAleer, 332–33n11

New Hampshire law, 436–39, 534–35

New Hampshire Supreme Court, 436–39

"New Light on the History of the Federal Judiciary Act of 1789" (Warren), 311

New York Civil Code, 30, 478, 481–82

New York law
  civil codes and, 20, 30, 478, 480–81, 486
  contract law and, 428–34
  criminal law and, 527, 534–43, 549–67, 569, 571
  property law and, 368–75
  state judicial power, coordination of, 290–91
  tort law and, 478, 480–82, 486

New York Law Revision Commission, 556–57, 559

New York Penal Law (NYPL), 553–59, 562, 571, 577, 579, 582

New York Times, 130

New York Times Co. v. Sullivan, 225–42, 256, 277, 500, 599–600

New York v. See name of opposing party

next friends, 510

Nga Li v. Yellow Cab Co., 475–87

Nicomachean Ethics (Aristotle), 317

Nobel Prize in Economics, 451

noblesse oblige, 359

noise, 368

noncitizens, protection of, 202–15

nondisclosure policies, 488–94

"nonjusticiable" decisions, 173

non obstante veredicto, 400n3, 518

nonresidents, 279–97, 510

Noonan, John, 637

normalnoe, 61n8

Norman invasion, 244, 319–20

Norman legal tradition, 320

North American Free Trade Association (NAFTA), 457

North Carolina v. See name of opposing party

notaries, 403

notice of appeal, 520

Nozick, Robert, 604

nuclear war, 580

nuclear weapons, 574–75

nuisance, 367–74, 489

nulla poena sine lege, 88, 90, 96, 526

nullification, 542

nullum crimen sine lege, 83

Nye v. United States, 253, 623

oaths, 207–8, 215, 218

obiter dicta, 80–82, 85, 92, 95, 97

objections, 510, 532

objective standard of self-defense, 539–42, 549–63, 567

objective theory of contracts, 428, 435–36

obligations, law of, 415, 427, 488

O'Brien, Thomas Dillon (J.), 444–47

obscenity, 263–64, 268, 272

O'Connor, Sandra Day (J.), 85–87, 93–95, 98–99, 495

offer and acceptance, 396–98, *table 19.1*

offer of judgment, 523

Office of Technology Assessment, 385

"officer of the court," 205–6, 209, 212, 214–15

Ohio Civil Liberties Union, 269n7

Ohio law, 263–74

Ohio Supreme Court, 263–64, 269

Ohio v. See name of opposing party

Oklahoma law, 291, 351–54

Oklahoma Supreme Court, 352–53

Olberding v. Illinois Central Railway Co., 295

Olmstead v. United States, 267

omissions, 197

On Liberty (Mill), 235n5

opening statements, 515

Oppotunitätprinzip, 539

optimality, 453, 455–56, 468

option contracts, 334

oral argument, 510, 520

"ordered liberty," 248

Oregon law, 279–301, 500, 601

Oregon v. See name of opposing party

original jurisdiction, 124, 134, 139–41, 147, 167

orthodoxy, 39

Osirak nuclear reactor, 574–75

Otis, Boswell's Lessee v., 283

Our Secret Constitution (Fletcher), 199

out-of-state motorists, 291, 295

overlapping remedies, 339

overlords, 322–23

Ownbey v. Morgan, 300

Pacific Mutual Life Insurance Co. v. Haslip, 493–94, 496–97

pain and suffering, 442

Palestinian suicide bombings, 576

Palko v. Connecticut, 59n5, 248, 256n7, 266, 272

Panelli, Edward (J.), 378–87, 392–93

Paradigm of offense, 41, 45, 48, 50

Pareto efficiency, 453–61, 467–68

Pareto—optimal states, 455–56, 468

Pareto—superior moves, 454–55, 457–59

Parliament (English), 16–18, 34, 77, 132–33, 146, 327, 344, 347, 586

Parliament (German), 31, 45

passersby, 427–28

"passive nationality" principle, 277–78

patents, 377, 379, 381–82, 384, 386, 389–90, 605–6

paternalism, 317, 420–21, 425, 535

Pawloski, Hess v., 291, 295

Peasant Revolt (England, 1381), 106

Peck, James, 252

Pennekamp v. Florida, 253

Penner, James, 375

Penn-O-Tex Oil Corp., Baehr v., 398–404

Pennoyer v. Neff, 279–301, 376, 500, 600–601, 610

Pennsylvania law, 303–4, 308–10, 312

Pennsylvania Railway Co., Falchetti v., 308–9

Pennsylvania Supreme Court, 308

"people," 153–54, 163–64, 168–69, 179, 195n12

People v. See name of opposing party

Percer v. State, 85–86

peremptory challenge, 514

perjury, 505, 539

permanent damages, 371–73

permanent injunction, 350

permissible force, 574

"Perpetuities: The Measuring Lives" (Dukeminier), 329

personal jurisdiction, 509–10

per stirpes, 332–33n11, 333

persuasion, burden of, 314, 517

persuasive authority, 81

Petition of Right (1628), 356

petit jury. *See* jury

Pfeiffer Co., Feinberg v., 404–11, 607

Philadelphia & Reading Railway Co. v. McKibbin, 295

Philosophy of Right (Kant), 316, 339

physical damages, 438

physician-patient relationship, 379, 392–93

Pigou, Arthur C., 463–64, 466

Pigovian efficiency, 461–64, 466–67, 469

plaintiff's evidence, 515–16

plea-bargaining, 564–65

pleadings, drafting and service of, 506–9. *See also* equitable pleading

Plessy v. Ferguson, 201

Ploof v. Putnam, 446, 448

pluralism, 68–69

Pointer v. Texas, 272

police, "trial" of, 274

police power, 362–67

"policy," 58–59, 72–73, 313, 367

policy theory, 47, 52

political motives, 76, 149, 471

political philosophies, 316–18, 425

"politics," 58

poll tax, 181

pollution, 369, 373–74, 461, 464–66, 604, 610

popular press, 173

pornography, 263–64, 268, 272

Porter v. Commissioner of Internal Revenue, 409

Portuguese law, 480

positive breach of contract, 32

positive economics, 471

positive interest theory of damages, 438–39

positivism, 73n25, 313

Posner, Richard, 38, 72, 467, 637

possessory interests, 324–25

possibilities of reverter, 324, 326

posttrial motions, 518–19
Pound, Cuthbert W. (J.), 433
pouvoir discretionnaire, 71
Powell, Lewis F., Jr. (J.), 203–9
Powell v. Alabama, 212, 248, 597
power corrupts, 34
"practical necessity," 572, 576
praemunire, statute of, 341, 346
pragmatists, 72, 167
pravo, 55–57, 59, 592
precedent, 15, 18–19, 35–36, 67n18, 90–
    102, 635–39
  civil trial and, 503
  equity and, 339–42, 345, 350
  jury and, 257
  in legal reasoning, 80–83, 90–102
  property law and, 392
  tort law and, 496–97
precontractual duties, 414–15
preemptive strikes, 572–75, *table 29.1*
preemptive war, 573, 575, *table 29.1*
preexisting duties, 402–3
prejudice, 544, 551
preliminary injunction (PI), 350, 511
preliminary motions in civil trials, 509–11
premises, 626–27
preponderance of evidence, 517
present interest, 321
President of Yale College, Hack v., 198
presumption, 632–33
presumption of innocence, 62, 536, 538,
    547
pretrial conference, 509, 513–14
pretrial dossier, 546–47
pretrial order, 514–15
pretrial remedies, 511
pretrial settlements, 503
"prevailing theories," 39
preventive detention, 536
preventive war, 573, 575–76, *table 29.1*
prima facie case, 517n8
*Princeton Principles on Universal Jurisdictions,
    The*, 301
principle
  Chancery and, 340
  equity and, 339
  history and, 256–58, 262–63, 264n6,
    489
  policy vs., 58–59, 72–73

Right as, 592
right to privacy as, 261–66, 270–71
tort law and, 443
prior convictions, 543–44
prisoners of war, 590
privacy
  invasion of, 441, 473
  right to, 50, 59–60, 130, 261–74, 313,
    382–83, 385
private law, 316–18, 602–11
private property. *See* property
private rights, 316–17, 602–5, 607–8
private wrong, 190n9
"probable cause," 537–38
probate court, 329, 348–49
"Problem of Social Cost, The" (Coase),
    451, 464
procedure
  civil trial and, 502–24
  common law and, 18–21
  criminal law and, 531–48, 564
  due process as, 59–63, 260
  federal courts and, 314
  reasonableness and, 592
procès équitable, 355
productivity, 465
products liability, 443, 451, 463, 489
professional exemption, 46–47, 49
professional standards of conduct, 503, 505–
    6
professors, 38
proffer, 515
promise, contractual, 398–403, 408–11,
    430
promissory estoppel, 409–10, 419
property, 18, 20, 34, 37, 41–42
  contemporary, 358–75, 603
  economic efficiency and, 455, 458, 460–
    61, 470
  equitable juridiction and, 17, 336, 338–
    57
  feudalism in land law, 18, 319–37, 602
  frontiers of, 376–94, 606
  international criminal law and, 570–71,
    577, 580, 588
  tort law and, 445–49, 488–89, 609
proportionality, 66–67, 570
  as dimension of self-defense, 575, 578–
    81, 587

prosecutorial system, 533
prospective overruling, 273–74
Prosser, William Lloyd, 382, 477n3
Protestant Reformation, 39
Protocol of the European Convention
(1952), 359
Proudhon, Pierre-Joseph, 375
psychiatric exams, 512
public figures, 599–600
publicity, unwanted, 382
public law, 292, 594–602
"public use," 361
public welfare, 363–67, 369, 373–75, 450,
460, 469, 588–89, 602–11. *See also*
social good
Puerto Rican law, 416–19
Puerto Rico Supreme Court, 418
punishment
criminal law and, 532, 539, 564
cruel and unusual, 272
self-defense as, 583–84
tort law and, 489
punitive damages, 442, 488–501
BMW of North American, Inc. v. Gore,
489–501, 601
pur autrie vie, 323–24, *table 15.1*
"pure" comparative negligence, 483
"pure procedural justice," 468
Putnam, Ploof v., 446, 448

Quan, Shirley G., 379
quarantine, 374–75
*Quasi-In-Rem Jurisdiction: Outmoded and
Unconstitutional?* (Zammit), 294
quasi in rem proceeding, 292, 294
Québec Civil Code, 31–32, 66–67n17,
402
Québec law, language of, 65
Quia Emptores (1290), 327–28
quid pro quo, 398
Quirin, Ex parte, 257
quiz method, 616

Rabe v. Washington, 92
racial discrimination, 181–99, 201, 219–22,
260
racial justice, 241, 248, 598
racial minorities, 202, 209, 471

racial sterotypes, 542–43, 566, 584
Raffles v. Wichelhaus, 435
raisonnable, 64–65
Ramirez, Richardson v., 222n10
Ramsay, Dennis, 134
Ramseur, James, 527–28, 539, 551, 582–83
Randolph, A. Philip, 236
rape, 526, 553, 557, 570, 576, 579, 588
ratification clause, 127, 168
ratio decidendi, 80–82, 95, 97, 616, 638
rational-basis test, 211
rationale, 76
Rawls, John, 62, 318, 394, 468, 593
Raymond, Lord, 23–24
razonable, 65
razumnyj, 64
Realists. *See* American Realist movement
reallocation of property rights, 458–60
real property, law of, 360–61. *See also*
property
in English common law, 319–29, 336
reasonableness, 63–69, 130, 262
common law and, 15–17, 593
contract law and, 423, 428
criminal law and, 527, 538, 540, 550,
552–63, 566
international criminal law and, 570, 582
jury and, 8
Right and, 591–611
private law, 602–11
public law, 594–602
state judicial power, coordination of,
296
tort law and, 400, 441–42, 444, 447–48,
492–93, 495–96
reasoning, legal. *See* legal reasoning
rebuttal brief, 520
Recht, 55–57, 59, 68, 592
Rechtslehre (Kant), 54
Rechtsphilosophie (Hegel), 54
rechtspolitisch, 58
Rechtsprechung, 34
Rechtswidrigkeit, 43, 43n20, 55–56
recidivism, 536
reciprocal trust, 413–16, 607
reckless endangerment, 551–52, 562
recognizance, 535
Reconstruction, 197, 199, 259

Reconstruction amendments, 180–99, 259, 596. *See also* Thirteenth, Fourteenth, and Fifteenth Amendments *under* U.S. Constitution

Reed, Stanley (J.), 312–13

Reese, United States v., 194

Regents of the University of California, Moore v., 377–94, 605–6

"regime change," 584

Regina v. Morgentaler, 542n10

Rehnquist, William H. (J.), 209–13, 499

Reid, Andrea, 583–84

release pending trial, 535–36

reliance, 403, 413

reliance damages, 418–19, 435–36, 438, 606

relief, 506–7, 511, 515, 518–19, 521

religion, freedom of, 130, 257, 360

religious legal cultures, 36

religious references, 175–76

remainderman, 323–24

remainders, 321, 323, 325–26, 328, 334, *table 15.1*

remedies
  civil trial and, 504
  contract law and, 403, 418, 426, 431
  equity and, 339, 353–56
  medical research and, 378, 385, 388
  nuisance and, 373–74
  tort law and, 493–94, 501

remittitur, 491, 519

Rendell-Baker v. Kohn, 198

replevin, 422, 511, 522

repossession, 421

reprehensible conduct, 493

representation, conflicts of, 505

Republican Form of Government Clause, 126, 259

republicanism, 107

requests for admissions, 12

resale value, 368

resident aliens, 203–15, 219–22

residuary trusts, 330

res ipsa loquitur, 19

res judicata, 340

responsibility, 41, 474, 482–83, 581

responsive pleading, 510–11

Restatement of Conflict of Laws, Second, 298

Restatement of Contracts, 396, 408–11, 607

Restatement of Contracts, Second, 398, 403, 434, 473

Restatement of Tort, 443

Restatement of Tort, Second, 443, 475

restrained court, 81

retaliation, 572, 576–77

Rethinking Criminal Law (Fletcher), 377n2

retributive justice, 545, 576–77

revenge, 576

reversions, 321–27, *table 15.1*, 344

review, 9, 70, 521, 533

Reynolds v. Clark, 23, 620–21

Richardson, Graham v., 205, 210

Richardson v. Ramirez, 222n10

Right, 57, 59–60, 68–69, 316
  reasonable and, 591–611
    private law, 602–11
    public law, 594–602

right of entry, 325

rights, 58–59, 107, 170, 470

right to bear arms, 360, 595

right to counsel, 272–73

right to privacy, 50, 59–60, 130, 261–74, 313, 382–83, 385

"Right to Privacy, The" (Brandeis and Warren), 313

Ring v. Arizona, 244n1

risk analysis, 575–76

robbery, 553–54, 563, 570–71, 579, 586

Roberts, Baxter v., 479

Robinson, Ex parte, 252

Robinson v. California, 272

Rodney King case, 609

Rodriguez, In re, 222n11

Rodriguez, San Antonio School District v., 224n1

Rodriguez v. Bethlehem Steel Corp., 388

Roe v. Wade, 59, 261

Rogers, Wilbert, 83, 85, 88

Rogers v. Tennessee, 7n, 83–102

rogue states, 572, 575–76

Romance languages, 34, 39, 56, 62, 355

Roman law, 11, 18, 27, 37, 338

Rome Statute
  deference and, 70
  exclusionary rule and, 271, 273

Rome Statute (*continued*)
  fairness and, 61–62
  intention and, 582
  international criminal law and, 570–71
  necessity and, 577
  proportionality and, 580–81
  reasonableness and, 65, 69, 593
Roosevelt, Franklin, 202, 257
Rose v. Locke, 92
Rozsa, Miklós, 54–55n1
Ruane, State v., 86–87
Rücksicht, 415
rule against perpetuities, 329–34, 348
Rule Against Perpetuities, The (Gray), 332n9
rule of law, 34, 60, 69, 106, 108
  discretion and, 72–74
  equality and, 175
  judicial review and, 145, 147, 149
  reasonableness and, 596
  self-defense and, 590
  tort law and, 499
Rules of Professional Responsibility
    (U.S.), 30
Russian Constitution (1993), 359
Russian doll problem, 326, 328
Russian law, 244
  language of, 61, 64

"safe harbor," 492
Salerno, United States v., 536n4
Samford, Connecticut v., 363
San Antonio School District v. Rodriguez,
    224n1
sanctions, 216n8, 505, 512
Sandoz, 379–80
Sanford, Dred Scott v., 170, 176–77, 181,
    194n11, 211, 224, 599n8
Santiago, People v., 552
Santobello v. New York, 565n6
SARS, 374
Savin, In re, 252–53
savir, 64
Scalia, Antonin (J.), 87–89, 94–97, 99–
    102, 149, 495–99
Schaffer v. Heitner, 291, 377
scheduling order, 509
Schnackenberg, Cheff v., 250, 255, 623
Schneider v. State, 231

scholarly authority, 36–42, 52, 313
  alternative Constitution and, 173
  diversity-of-citizenship jurisdiction and,
    310n6
  on due process, 60
school segregation, 598
Schuldinterlokut, 544
scienter, 25, 25n17
Scottish law, 323
Scottsboro case, 248, 597
Scott v. Shepherd, 21–27, 36, 77, 79, 81–82,
    145, 262, 443, 472, 593–94, 617–
    21, 634
Scott v. United States, 422
scrutiny, level of, 219
search, unreasonable, 261–69, 272
secession, 178–79, 605
secondary market, 349n9
Second Inaugural Address (Lincoln), 178,
    596
second look principle. *See* wait-and-see
    principle
Second Treatise of Civil Government (Locke),
    316
Second World War, 598
se defendendo, 585
Sedition Act (1798), 232–34, 238n7
segregation, 598
Selden, John, 339, 355–56
self-defense
  civil law tradition and, 40–41, 46–47,
    53
  in *Goetz, People v.*, 539–42, 549–67
  language of law and, 66–67
self-defense, domestic and international,
    568–90
  dimensions of, 571–83
    imminence, 571–77, *table 29.1*
    intention, 581–83
    necessity, 577–78
    proportionality, 575, 578–81, 587
  models of, 583–90
    as excuse, 585–86
    as justified vindication of autonomy,
      586–87
    as maximization of interests, 587–90
    as punishment, 583–84
self-incrimination, 272, 501, 538

sentencing, 543–45, 565
"separate but equal," 201
separation of powers, 69–70, 478, 532–33
September 11, 2001, terrorist attacks, 257, 565, 590
service of process, 279–81, 283–89, 291–95, 506–11
settlements in civil trial, 503, 522–23
settlors, 348–49
sex discrimination, 199, 202, 204n2, 219–22
sexual orientation, 221
Shakespeare, William, 334, 336
shareholders, 350
Shelley's Case (1579), 328
Shelley v. Trafalgar House Public Ltd., 417–19
Shepherd, Scott v., 21–27, 36, 77, 79, 81–82, 145, 262, 443, 472, 593–94, 617–21, 634
Sheppard, Massachusetts v., 274
Sherwin, Emily, 638n3
Shorter v. People, 555
show-cause proceeding, 522
Silverthorne Lumber Co. v. United States, 265
Simons, Richard D. (J.), 562
Simpson, O. J., 262, 609
Sindell v. Abbott Laboratories, 388
Sir Moyle Finch v. Throgmorton, 344
sister states, 278, 293
sit-in campaigns, 90
Six Day War (1967), 568, 573–74, 578
skepticism, 73n25, 466, 609
Slaughterhouse Cases, 183, 209, 260
slavery, 108–9, 169–70, 175–83, 190–97, 224, 260, 438, 457, 595–97, 599
Slavic languages, 62
Slotnick, Barry, 541, 549, 583–85
slow-fuse attacks, 572
Smith v. California, 230
Sniadach v. Family Finance Corp., 300
social contract, 594
social costs, 461–64, 602
social customs, 38
social good, 59, 71, 317, 359, 367, 469, 533, 602. See also public welfare
socialism, 317
social justice, 196–97, 241, 248, 598

Social security, 376
social theory of self-defense, 587–89
sodomy, 553, 557
sources of law, 33
Souter, David H. (J.), 495
South Carolina law, 88, 90–101
South Carolina Supreme Court, 90–91
Southern Pacific Co. v. Jensen, 602
Southwestern Telegraph & Telephone Co. v. Danaher, 497
sovereign immunity, 356
sovereignty, state
    federalism and, 153, 157, 162, 164, 167, 170, 599
    property law and, 363
    state judicial power, coordination of, 282–83, 288–89, 292, 294
    tort law and, 492
Spanish law, 29–30, 38, 40, 244
    language of, 55, 61–62, 65
special appearance, 510
special verdict, 518
speedy trial, right to, 272
Spence, George, 340
spies, 257
"spirit" of Constitution, 160, 166–67, 193
spirit of the law, 339
splitters, 470
sporting ethic, 63
spravedlivoe, 61n8
ständige Rechtsprechung, 36
Star Chamber (Eng.), 532
stare decisis, 19, 35, 80–82, 268–69, 313, 496
state actor, 197–98
state banks, 161, 166
State Bar of California, Konigsberg v., 212
State Bill of Attainder Clause, 120, 259
state law, 5–8. See also individual state law, e.g., Alabama law
    alternative Constitution and, 173, 178–99
    attorney conduct and, 216
    civil trial and, 503, 505–6, 509–11, 521, 523
    coordination of, 276–301, table 13.1, 601
    criminal law and, 526, 529, 535–37

state law (*continued*)
   diversity-of-citizenship jurisdiction and,
      302–14
   due process and, 247–48, 259–60, 263–
      74
   equality and, 202–15, 219, 221–22
   equity and, 351–54
   federalism and, 150–71
   freedom and, 225–42
   judicial review and, 132–33
   jury and, 247–51, 255
   punitive damages and, 489–501
   U.S. Constitution and, 130
states' rights, 182, 197, 202, 596–97
State v. See name of opposing party
status, 450–51, 605
status quo ante, 318
statute of limitations, 314
Statute of Uses (1535), 348
Statute of Wills (1540), 328, 348
statutes
   codes vs., 32–33
   reasoning from, 82–90, 642–48
      canons of construction, 646–47
      legislative intent, 645
      legislative purpose, 645
      plain meaning, 643–45
   "right" vs., 57
statutes of limitations, 504
statutory entitlements, 376
statutory law, 55–56
statutory law (Calif.), 383–84, 388–89
stay proceedings, 509
Stendhal, Henri, 32, 32n3, 108
Stephen, James Fitzjames, 64
Stevens, John Paul (J.), 89, 102, 489–595
Stevenson, People v., 98
Stewart, Potter (J.), 255, 268, 624
Stone, Harlan Fiske (C.J.), 296
Story, Joseph (J.), 312, 350–51
Strafgasetzbuch (StGB), 53
Strafgesetz, 55
Strafrecht, 55
Strange, John, Sir, 23n13
Strauder v. West Virginia, 182–86, 194, 219,
      600
strict construction, 149, 151, 160n9, 167
strict liability, 440–41, 443, 449–50, 473–74
strict scrutiny, 219

Stromberg v. California, 239n8
Strong, William (J.), 182–86
structured legal theory, 66–68
sua sponte, 509
subinfeudation, 322–23, 326–27
subjective standard of self-defense, 539–42,
      549–63, 567
subjective theory of contracts, 427–28
subject-matter jurisdiction, 289
sublease, 325
subpoenas, 214
subsidies, 462, 464, 469
substantial performance, 431–32, 434, 438
substantive due process, 59, 496–97, 499
substantive law
   civil trial and, 509, 511
   common law and, 19–21
   criminal law and, 529, 531, 549–67
   diversity-of-citizenship jurisdiction and,
      277, 314
   legal reasoning and, 87, 89
   reasonableness and, 592
   tort law and, 478
substantive mistake, 519
substituted service of process, 279, 284,
      287–89, 292
substitution, 327
suffering. *See* pain and suffering
suicide, 542
suicide bombings, 576
Sullivan, Bantam Books, Inc., v., 230
Sullivan, L. B., 225–30, 236–38, 500
Sullivan, New York Times Co. v., 225–42,
      256, 277, 500, 599–600
Sullivan, Raymond L. (J.), 475–84
summary judgment, 511, 513
summary motions, 513
summary power, 249, 252–54
summary reversal, 269
summary trials, 600
summons, 506
summum bonum, 453
Superior Court. See name of opposing party
supremacy clause, 127, 148, 150, 154–55,
      162–66, 276–77, *table 13.1*
suspect classifications, 205, 207, 209–11,
      214, 218–19, 221, 241
Swift v. Tyson, 302–8, 310–12
syllogism, 628–29

Table Talks: Being the Discourses of John Selden, Esq., 356
Taff Vale Railway, Vaughn v., 462n7
Takahashi v. Fish & Game Comm'n, 204–5
taking, 361, 366–67, 374
Talmudic culture, 34
Taney, Roger B. (C.J.), 176–77
tariffs, 457
taxation, right of, 163–66, 169
Taxicab case, 250, 305, 307, 310–11
temporary restraining orders (TRO), 511
tenants, 320, 325–26
tenants-in-chief, 320, 322
Ten Commandments, 79–80
Tennessee law, 84–91, 93–94, 97–102, 305
Tennessee Secondary School Athletic Ass'n, Brentwood Academy v., 198
Tennessee Supreme Court, 84–89, 91, 97–99, 101–2
Tennessee v. See name of opposing party
tenure, 322
territorial jurisdiction, principle of, 278, 281–83, 292–95, 300, 601
terrorists, 257, 565, 590, 600
Terry, Ex parte, 252–53
testamentary succession, 348
testaments, 328
testimony, 516, 538–39, 551
Texas v. See name of opposing party
theft, 377, 526, 589
theology, 37
theory, 35
Theory of Justice, A (Rawls), 62, 318
third parties, 507–8, 512, 522, 569–70
third-party effects, 197
Thomas, Clarence (J.), 102, 495
Thompson v. Utah, 251n4
Thompson v. Whitman, 285
threats, 402, 420
"three-fifths" provision (U.S. Constitution), 108
Throgmorton, Sir Moyle Finch v., 344
Tilden, Samuel, 197
titles, 348
Titone, Vito J. (J.), 562
Toledo Newspaper Co. v. United States, 253
tolerance, 68, 317, 592–93, 595–97, 601, 609, 611
Tomlins, People v., 555

Tompkins, Erie Railroad Co. v., 19, 277, 282n1, 303–14, 601–2
tortious conduct, 290–91, 427, 493–94
tort law
  culpa in contrahendo and, 419
  economic efficiency and, 452–71
  foundations of, 18–20, 440–51
    Vincent v. Lake Erie Transportation Co., 444–51
  French Code civil and, 30–31, 440–41, 474, 479–80, 485
  German Civil Code (BGB) and, 31–32, 37, 427, 440–41, 448–49, 451, 486, 488
  property law and, 356, 378, 380–88
  punitive damages, 488–501
    BMW of North American, Inc. v. Gore, 489–501
  Right and reasonable, 608–9
tort liability, 306, 411, 414–15, 427, 450, 464
"total war," 580
tövény, 54
trading, 453–59, 468
Trafalgar House Public Ltd., Shelley v., 417–19
transaction costs, 466–67
transaction immunity, 538
Transient Rule of Personal Jurisdiction, The (Ehrenzweig), 297
translations, 54–74
Trautman, Donald T., 297, 299
treaties, 130, 359, 526
Treatise on Contracts (Corbin), 424
trespass, writ of
  common law and, 21–26, 593
  diversity-of-citizenship jurisdiction and, 303
  due process and, 262
  legal reasoning and, 77–79
  property law and, 367–68
  tort law and, 443, 446, 472–74, 489
trespass on the case, 473–74, 593
Treuhand, 348
Treu und Glauben, 396, 415
triadic legal systems, 33, 35
trial by battle, 244–45
"trial of the police," 274
tribal law, 4–5

Tribune Co., City of Chicago v., 236, 239
trier of fact, 44, 514–15
tripartite legal structure, 41
trover, 377
trust, 413–16
trustees, 348–49
trustors, 348–49
trusts, 330–34, 348–50
TXO Production Corp. v. Alliance Resources Corp., 494, 496
Tyler, Wat, 106
Tyson, Swift v., 302–8, 310–12

unanimity, requirement of, 245
uncertainty, 385
unconditional privilege, 239
unconscionability, 421–24
"unconstitutional," 134, 138, 166
undue influence, 420
unemployment insurance, 376
Uniform Commercial Code (U.S.), 30, 33, 421–22, 423n6
Union Bag & Paper Co., Whalen v., 370–71
United Nations. Charter, 568, 573, 578, 580, 584–85n9, 587
United Nations. Security Council, 526, 578, 580, 584–85n9
United Nations weapons inspectors, 582
United States v. See name of opposing party
Universal Declaration of Human Rights (1948), 359
universal human equality, 176
universal jurisdiction in criminal law, 301
University of Chicago Law School, 461, 464
University of Virginia, 464
unjust enrichment, 449, 488
unlawfulness, 41, 52, 55–56
unreasonable search, 261–65
unwritten law, 16
U.S. Bill of Rights, 127–30, 170, 224
U.S. Civil War, 109, 177–78, 180, 196–97, 224–25, 248, 259, 595–97, 599
U.S. Congress, 69–70, 130. *See also* legislation
   alternative Constitution and, 177, 180–81, 186, 188–96, 198–99
   contempt power and, 249, 252
   contract law and, 422–24

diversity-of-citizenship jurisdiction and, 304, 307–8, 310–13
due process and, 260n3, 598
enumerated powers of, 157–62, 164, 167, 276–77, *table 13.1*
equality and, 201–2, 211–12, 221
freedom and, 232–34
national bank and, 150–52, 161–62
U.S. Constitution, 90. *See also* constitutional law
   alternative (*see* alternative Constitution)
   as code, 32, 55, 107–9, 111–31, 257–58
   criminal law and, 532
   democracy and, 240
   Gettysburg Address and, 179
   interpretation of (*see* interpretation)
   jury and, 244, 249–52, 255–57
   legal reasoning and, 83
   property law and, 358–59, 363–64
   Right and reasonable, 594–95, 597
   slavery and, 170, 594
U.S. Constitution. First Amendment, 127, 225, 229–35, 237–41, 247, 253, 256–57, 264n6
U.S. Constitution. Second Amendment, 360, 595
U.S. Constitution. Fourth Amendment, 128, 130, 261–62, 265–67, 273, 534–35, 547
U.S. Constitution. Fifth Amendment, 59, 128, 214, 249, 260, 359–61, 366–67, 501, 537, 547
U.S. Constitution. Sixth Amendment, 247, 249, 256, 501, 547
U.S. Constitution. Seventh Amendment, 247, 256, 355, 419, 443
U.S. Constitution. Eighth Amendment, 536
U.S. Constitution. Tenth Amendment, 129, 155, 169, 189, 314
U.S. Constitution. Eleventh Amendment, 198–99, 210
U.S. Constitution. Thirteenth Amendment, 180–81, 186, 190–94, 196–98, 259–60, 596–97
U.S. Constitution. Fourteenth Amendment, 57, 180–98, 229–31, 234–35, 237, 239, 598

Due Process Clause (*see* Due Process Clause (U.S. Constitution))
Equal Protection Clause (*see* Equal Protection Clause (U.S. Constitution))
U.S. Constitution. Fifteenth Amendment, 180–81, 186, 192, 197, 210, 596
U.S. Constitution. Nineteenth Amendment, 181, 210
U.S. Constitution. Twenty-Fourth Amendment, 181, 210
U.S. Constitution. Twenty-Sixth Amendment, 181, 210
U.S. Revolutionary War, 106–7, 257
U.S. Supreme Court, 60, 69–70, 80–81, 129–30. *See also names of cases*
    alternative Constitution and, 173, 176–77, 197–98
    contract law and, 422
    due process and, 247–48, 597–98
    entitlements and, 377
    equality and, 201–2, 218–19, 221–22, 542
    freedom and, 224–25, 241
    judicial review and, 133, 139–41, 145–48, 167
    Right and reasonable, 596, 598–99, 601
    tort law and, 489–501
usufruct, 355
Utah v. See name of opposing party
utilitarianism, 58–59, 71, 317, 441, 450, 453, 460–61, 469
utilities, 454, 456, 463

valid process, 510
Van Alstyne, Arvo, 478, 482
vassals, 320–22
Vaughn v. Taff Vale Railway, 462n7
venire, 514
venue, choices of, 504, 509
verdict, 244–46, 491, 518–19, 521, 543–46, 565
Verkehr, 441
Vermont Marble Co., Eastman Marble Co. v., 331n6
Vermont Supreme Court, 446
Vernunft, 64
vernünftig, 64–65
Vertrauensverhälnis, 413–15

vested property rights, 376
vicarious liability, principle of, 32
victims
    of crime, 473, 566
    economic efficiency and, 464–67
videotapes, 535, 551
vi et armis, 25, 25n15, 489
Vietnam war, 173
villeins, 322
Vincent v. Lake Erie Transportation Co., 20, 368, 444–51, 608–9
Viner, Charles, 37
Vinogradoff, Paul, 339
Virginia, Ex parte, 186
Virginia General Assembly, 232–33
Virginia Resolutions (1798), 232–33
vis impressa, 23, 23n14
voir dire, 514
Völkerstrafgesetzbuch, 301
voluntary guilty pleas, 564
voluntary markets and Pareto efficiency, 453–56, 467–68
Von Mehren, Arthur Taylor, 297, 299
voting rights, 180–81, 208, 222, 514, 599

Wachtler, Sol (C.J.), 550–62
Wade, Roe v., 59, 261
Wagman, People v., 552
Wainwright, Gideon v., 272–73
wait-and-see principle, 329, 331–32n7, 334
Wald, Patricia, 637
Waldron, Jeremy, 146, 175–76, 375, 648
Walker, Linkletter v., 272, 274
Walker-Thomas Furniture Co., Williams v., 420–25
Wallach, Richard W. (J.), 552–53
Walzer, Michael, 574
Waples, Gregory, 539–41, 549, 562, 610
war, law of, 568
war crimes, 61, 301, 526, 570, 577, 581, 601
Warner v. Whitman, 331–32n7
warrant clause, 128, 130, 262
warranty, 437, 443
Warren, Charles, 305, 306n4, 311, 313
Warren, Earl (C.J.), 201, 272
Washington (state) law, 289–91, 296, 298–300
Washington, Rabe v., 92

Washington v. See name of opposing party
Washington v. Texas, 272
wealth, equal distribution of, 224
wealth discrimination, 222
weapons of mass destruction (WMDs),
        572, 574, 576, 582, 584
weapons possession, illegal, 527–28, 538,
        550–51, 567, 578
Wechsler, Herbert, 83n3, 225
Weeks v. United States, 265–66, 270
Weiderholungsgefahr, 536
Weinrib, Ernest, 449, 451
welfare payments, 376
"well-pleaded complaint" rule, 506
Weston v. State, 560
Westphalian principle, 595, 597
West Virginia law, 182–86
West Virginia v. See name of opposing party
Whalen v. Union Bag & Paper Co., 370–71
White, Byron R. (J.), 248–55, 622–23
Whitfield, Malnar v., 351–54, 368, 374, 603
Whitman, Thompson v., 285
Whitman, Warner v., 331–32n7
Whitney, Windsor v., 365
Whitney v. California, 239n8
Whittaker, Charles E. (J.), 268
Wichelhaus, Raffles v., 435
"wilful deprivation," 61n8
Wilkesite riots, 106
Wilkins, Herbert Putnam (J.), 329–33
Willenserklärung, 37, 37n10
William III, King of England, 22, 36
Williams, Ora, 420, 422, 425
Williams v. Walker-Thomas Furniture Co.,
        420–25
William the Conqueror, 319–20, 323
Williston, Samuel, 424
wills, 325, 328–33, 348–49, 397, 402
Windsor v. Whitney, 365
*Winnebago County Department of Social
        Security, DeShaney v.*, 197
wiretapping, 262

Wisdom, John Minor, 637
witnesses, 513–15, 517, 527, 537, 539
"witnesses for the crown," 539
Wolf v. Colorado, 261, 265–66, 268–70, 300
Wolsey, Robert, 341
women, discrimination against. *See* sex
        discrimination
Woodson, World-wide Volkswagen Corp. v.,
        291
Wood v. Georgia, 240
Woodward, Bob, 27
workers' compensation statutes, 438
World War I, 599
World War II, 598
World-wide Volkswagen Corp. v. Woodson,
        291
Wright, J. Skelly (J.), 421–24
writ of error, 343–44
writ of execution, 522
writ of trespass. *See* trespass, writ of
writ of trover, 377
Writs of Assistance, 595
writ system, 20–21, 506
written briefs, 510, 520
written law. *See* statutory law
written opinions, 75–76, 81–82, 625. *See
        also names of cases*
wrongful acts, 446, 517
wrongfulness, 40–53, 55–56, 377
Wythe, George, 148–49

Yale, Hack v., 198
Yellow Cab Co., Nga Li v., 475–87
Yick Wo v. Hopkins, 204
York, Guaranty Trust v., 314
Young, People v., 558
Young v. Lemieux, 364

zakon, 54, 56
Zenger, John Peter, 215
Zerbst, Johnson v., 215
zoning, 361, 366